K

217/99005195/11/1/00

CW00542805

Sot 3/12

CRIMINAL PROCEDURE AND SENTENCING IN THE MAGISTRATES' COURT

Fifth Edition

AUSTRALIA
LBC Information Services
Sydney

CANADA AND USA
Carswell
Toronto

NEW ZEALAND
Brooker's
Auckland

SINGAPORE AND MALAYSIA
Thomson Information (S.E. Asia)
Singapore

CRIMINAL PROCEDURE AND SENTENCING IN THE MAGISTRATES' COURT

Fifth Edition

INIGO BING

Metropolitan Stipendiary Magistrate,
a Recorder

LONDON
SWEET & MAXWELL
1999

First Edition 1990
Second Edition 1992
Third Edition 1994
Fourth Edition 1996
Fifth Edition 1999

Sweet & Maxwell Limited
100 Avenue Road,
London NW3 3PF
(htp://www.smlawpub.co.uk)
Phototypeset by MFK Information Services Ltd,
Hitchin, Herts
Printed and bound in Great Britain by
MPG Books Ltd, Bodmin, Cornwall

A C.I.P. catalogue record for this book is available from the British Library

ISBN 0-421-65700 6

No natural forests were destroyed to make this product. Only farmed timber was used and saplings were re-planted.

©
Inigo Bing
1999

PREFACE

During the currency of this edition, on October 2, 2000, the Human Rights Act 1998 will come into force. It is impossible to predict precisely the effect this legislation will have upon criminal practice but the impact on the work of the magistrates' court is likely to be considerable. For this reason I have attempted to provide the reader with a summary of those features of the European Convention on Human Rights which will mainly impinge upon procedure and sentencing. The Act and the Convention are printed in full in Part III. In addition, I have tried to identify particular features of practice, notably issues surrounding disclosure, the granting of adjournments, bail, binding over orders, contempt and disposals for the mentally ill which are likely to be principally affected by the implementation of the Human Rights Act 1998.

The Human Rights Act 1998 notwithstanding, Parliament's enthusiasm for legislation affecting criminal practice is undiminished. Since the last edition, the Criminal Procedure and Investigations Act 1996, the Crime (Sentences) Act 1997, the Protection from Harassment Act 1997, the Sex Offenders Act 1997, the Magistrates' Courts (Procedure) Act 1998 and the Crime and Disorder Act 1998 have been passed. In doing so the Drug Treatment and Testing Order, the Restraining Order, the Anti-Social Behaviour Order and the Sex Offender Order have been added to the armoury of the sentencer and the practitioner has been required to absorb innumerable changes to procedure and practice.

In case law many aspects of procedure and sentencing have been clarified. The old shibboleth that seriousness in sentencing meant what right thinking members of society thought it meant has finally been laid to rest in *Howells and other appeals*. The confusion over sentencing for "sample charges" has been resolved in *Canavan, Kidd and Shaw*. The way to resolve factual disputes in mitigation is now simply set out in *Tolera*. The hitherto somewhat opaque law on the award of costs has been clarified in *Northallerton Magistrates' Court, ex parte Dove*, and the object and purpose of custody time limits has been underlined in *Manchester Crown Court, ex parte McDonald*. All prosecuting authorities will benefit from *Haringey Justices, ex parte D.P.P.* which lays down the responsibilities involved in calling witnesses. Finally, the penchant of justice to pass sentence in serious cases has now been the subject of comment and guidance in *Warby Magistrates' Court, ex parte D.P.P.*

Despite the enormous changes to criminal practice since this book was first published the aim of the title remains the same: namely to be a practical working guide to the many points of procedure and sentencing which can suddenly crop up as well as to provide sufficient statutory and case law references to enable the reader to understand and follow the ramifications of magistrates' courts practice.

The General Council of the Bar and the Law Society have each given permission to reproduce material in Chapter 11, and the Magistrates' Association have allowed their sentencing guidelines to be printed in Appendix III.

In addition a number of people have helped and assisted with the preparation of this edition. My professional colleagues and my many friends in the Inner London Magistrates' Courts Service have always been willing to comment and advise upon improvements, and I am, as always, grateful to them. I also wish to acknowledge the work on human rights by Geoffrey Robertson Q.C., Ben Emmerson and John Wadham whose individual and collective erudition and experience have assisted me greatly in trying to get to grips with Convention jurisprudence.

Finally, I owe a particular debt of gratitude to my publishers, Sweet and Maxwell Ltd, who have supported and nurtured this title for 10 years and have once again seen an edition go smoothly through the press. As ever I am most grateful to them.

The law is stated as at August 1, 1999.

Inigo Bing
Thames Magistrates' Court
London E3

CONTENTS

PART I: CRIMINAL PROCEDURE

APPENDICES

TABLE OF CASES

TABLE OF EUROPEAN CASES

TABLE OF STATUTES

TABLE OF STATUTORY INSTRUMENTS

TABLE OF INTERNATIONAL TREATIES AND CONVENTIONS

TABLE OF ABBREVIATIONS

BA	1976	— Bail Act 1976
CCA	1981	— Contempt of Court Act 1981
CPIA	1996	— Criminal Procedure and Investigations Act 1996
CJA	1982	— Criminal Justice Act 1982
CJA	1987	— Criminal Justice Act 1987
CJA	1988	— Criminal Justice Act 1988
CJA	1991	— Criminal Justice Act 1991
CJA	1993	— Criminal Justice Act 1993
CJ and POA	1994	— Criminal Justice and Public Order Act 1994
CLA	1977	— Criminal Law Act 1977
CDA	1998	— Crime and Disorder Act 1998
C(S)A	1997	— Crime (Sentences) Act 1997
FSA	1989	— Football Spectators Act 1989
HRA	1998	— Human Rights Act 1998
JPA	1997	— Justices of the Peace Act 1997
LP (E of CP) A	1980	— Licensed Premises (Exclusion of Certain Persons) Act 1980
MCA	1980	— Magistrates' Courts Act 1980
MC(P)A	1998	— Magistrates' Courts (Procedure) Act 1998
MCR	1981	— Magistrates' Courts Rules 1981
MDA	1971	— Misuse of Drugs Act 1971
MHA	1983	— Mental Health Act 1983
PACE	1984	— Police and Criminal Evidence Act 1984
PCCA	1973	— Powers of Criminal Courts Act 1973
POA	1985	— Prosecution of Offences Act 1985
POA	1986	— Public Order Act 1986
RTA	1988	— Road Traffic Act 1988
RTOA	1988	— Road Traffic Offenders Act 1988

Part I

Criminal Procedure

CHAPTER 1

Commencement of Proceedings, Formalities and Disclosure

A. COMMENCEMENT OF PROCEEDINGS

1. Introduction and Definitions

1–01   Criminal proceedings begin in a magistrates' court either because an accused has been charged with an offence or because he has been summoned to appear before the court.

If an accused is charged with an offence this will be because he has been arrested either without a warrant or as a result of a warrant being issued by a justice of the peace. If an accused is summoned before the court this will be because a summons has been issued by the court as a result of the laying of an information.

These terms may be defined as follows:

(i) Charge

1–02   At common law charge means the process whereby the court is informed by the police or other prosecuting authority that an accused is to be brought before the court charged with an offence and the appearance by the accused on that charge (*R. v. Manchester Stipendiary Magistrate, ex p. Hill* [1993] 1 A.C. 329).

Under the Magistrates' Courts Rules 1981 a charge means the description of the offence stated in ordinary language which the accused is alleged to have committed, together with a reference to the Act, regulation or by-law creating the offence (Magistrates' Courts Rules 1981, r. 100).

(ii) Summons

1–03   A summons, like a charge, is simply the description of the offence in ordinary language as defined above.

(iii) Information

1–04 An information is the statement by which a magistrate is informed of an offence (*R. v. Hughes* (1897) 43 J.P. 556) and need not be on oath unless a warrant is sought (Magistrates' Courts Act 1980, s.1(3) and MCR 1981, r. 4).

(iv) Warrant

1–05 A warrant is the authority for the arrest of a person in certain defined circumstances. The circumstances for an adult are generally: (a) that the accused has been summoned but failed to attend and so a warrant for his arrest is issued; (b) that as a result of an information the offence is a serious one and the accused is unlikely to attend as a result of a summons; or (c) that the address of the accused is not sufficiently established for a summons to be served on him. The precise statutory circumstances in which a warrant may be issued are set out in section 1 of the Magistrates' Courts Act 1980.

2. The Procedure for Commencing Proceedings

(i) When an accused is charged with an offence

1–06 When an accused has been charged with an offence this will usually have been by the police at a police station. In these circumstances he must be brought before a magistrates' court in the same petty sessions area as the police station as soon as practicable after being charged and in any event not later than the first sitting of the court after being charged (Police and Criminal Evidence Act 1984, s.46). In practice an accused must be brought before a court within 36 hours. The mandatory duty imposed on the police by the Police and Criminal Evidence Act 1984, s.46, is to produce a person charged before a magistrates' court in the petty sessions area of the police station. However, there is an overriding duty to bring the person before a court as soon as practicable, and there is no statutory requirement on the clerk to arrange sittings every day in the area of each police station. In the course of his administrative duties the clerk should give effect to the wishes of his local justices, particularly when sittings are needed on a Saturday or a Bank Holiday. If the sitting is likely to be of a formal nature, leading to an inevitable further remand, this might weigh in favour of using a large court centre which is sitting anyway rather than arranging a special sitting within the area of the police station (*R. v. Avon Magistrates' Courts Committee, ex p. Broome* [1988] 1 W.L.R. 1246).

These tightly defined time periods will not apply if the accused has been granted bail by the police after being charged. A person charged at a police station may be bailed to appear at a magistrates' court at a time and place specified in the bail notice (PACE 1984, s.47). In practice this will specify a date within a few days or weeks of the charge.

The procedure for commencing proceedings by a charge applies both to indictable and summary offences. In practice the charge sheet which is sent to the court to be read to the accused is the information for the purposes of summary trial. Once the accused is produced before the court in custody or appears on bail after being charged, the court will deal with the case or remand or adjourn the case in accordance with the procedure described elsewhere.

(ii) When an Information is laid before a justice

1–07 A prosecutor or his counsel, solicitor or any other person authorised on his behalf may lay an information before a justice of the peace or a clerk to the justices that a person has, or is suspected of having, committed an offence (MCA 1980, s.1(1), MCR 1981, r. 4).

An information is "laid" when the contents of the information and the fact that the prosecutor wishes to proceed are brought to the attention of the justice or the clerk. This may not necessarily be the same occasion on which the justice or the clerk gives consideration to the information for the purpose of issuing process (*R. v. Leeds Justices, ex p. Hanson* [1981] Q.B. 892).

It has been held that an unincorporated body (*e.g. Thames Valley Police*) may not lay an information. If proceedings are to be commenced by the police the information should be laid by the Chief Constable or some person authorised on his behalf (*Rubin v. D.P.P.* [1990] 2 Q.B. 80). However, such a technical defect in the name of the prosecutor was not held to be fatal in that case and the information could be proceeded upon.

1–08   The purpose of laying an information is to obtain either a summons requiring the person to appear before the court to answer the information, or a warrant for the arrest of the person.

Once an information has been laid a justice of the peace must exercise a judicial discretion in deciding whether or not to issue a summons or a warrant. It used to be the case that this judicial act could be exercised by the clerk to the justices but could not be delegated further. However, new rules now allow the clerk to the justices to authorise a deputy or other appointed clerk to carry out this function on his behalf provided such person has been specifically authorised for such function in writing (Justices' Clerks Rules 1970, r. 3 and r. 4 as inserted by the Magistrates' Clerks (Miscellaneous Amendments) Rules 1993). The judicial act is the consideration of the information and not the subsequent issue of the summons. Therefore it does not matter if a facsimile signature, such as a rubber stamp, of the justice or the clerk appears on the summons (*R. v. Brentford Justices, ex p. Catlin* [1975] Q.B. 455).

In exercising a discretion whether to grant a summons a justice must ascertain:

(i) whether the allegation is of an offence known to the law, and if so whether the essential ingredients of the offence are prima facie present;

(ii) whether the offence is out of time;

(iii) whether the court has jurisdiction; and

(iv) whether the informant has the necessary authority to prosecute.

The consideration of the above matters may take into account all of the relevant circumstances (*R. v. West London Metropolitan Stipendiary Magistrate, ex p. Klahn* [1979] 1 W.L.R. 933). Such circumstances may include the fact that the incident in question has already been investigated by a responsible authority, and a decision had been taken as to the charges to be preferred in respect of it. Justices should be slow to issue a summons to a private prosecutor where the defendant had already been charged at the behest of the Crown (*R. v. Tower Bridge Metropolitan Stipendiary Magistrate, ex p. Chaudhry* [1994] 1 All E.R. 44). The decision to issue a summons, or not, may be taken without the proposed defendant being heard, although there is a discretion as to whether he may be allowed to make representations against the issue of a summons (*R. v. West London Justices, ex p. Klahn* (above)).

A justice must consider whether the allegation is vexatious and whether the offence is known to the law. An example of a refusal of a summons alleging an offence not known to the law occurred when the Chief Metropolitan Stipendiary Magistrate refused a summons for an alleged blasphemous libel which did not apply to the Christian religion (*R. v. Chief Metropolitan Stipendiary Magistrate, ex p. Choudhury* [1991] 1 Q.B. 429).

Delay in the laying of an information, even though strictly within the time limits, is a factor which may be taken into account and a justice or a clerk may legitimately inquire into delay before issuing or refusing to issue a summons (*R. v. Clerk to the Medway Justices, ex p. Department of Health and Social Security* (1986) 150 J.P. 401).

Justices may also consider the previous history of the matter, particularly if there has been a previous summons which was later withdrawn (*R. v. Grays Justices, ex p. Low* [1990] 1 Q.B. 54).

(a) CONSIDERATIONS FOR ISSUING A SUMMONS

1–09 If the offence in the information is a minor one, that is to say neither punishable with imprisonment nor indictable, a magistrate may issue a summons but not a warrant (MCA 1980, s.1(4)).

(b) CONSIDERATIONS FOR ISSUING A WARRANT

1–10 If the person's address is not sufficiently established for a summons to be served on him or the offence is indictable or punishable with imprisonment, a warrant may be issued (MCA 1980, s.1(4)).

A warrant may not be issued unless:

   (i) it is in writing and is substantiated on oath; and

   (ii) the offence is punishable with imprisonment, or the person's address is not sufficiently established for the summons to be served (MCA 1980, s.1(3) and (4)).

If a warrant is issued it may be endorsed for bail. This means that when a person is arrested and taken to the police station he shall be released on bail with or without sureties, to appear at the magistrates' court endorsed on the warrant (MCA 1980, s.117).

The jurisdiction given to a justice of the peace for the purpose of issuing a summons or warrant is wider than the jurisdiction conferred on a court for trying an offence. A summons or a warrant may be issued if the offence was committed within the area, or it is in the interests of justice that the person should be tried jointly with another who is being proceeded against in the area or if the person charged resides, or is believed to reside, within the area (MCA 1980, s.1(2)).

IMPACT OF HUMAN RIGHTS ACT 1998

1–11 If a person has been arrested for an offence prior to being brought before the court then the procedure outlined above must be read in the light of Article 5(2) of the Convention which provides that "[e]veryone who is arrested shall be informed promptly, in a language which he understands, the reasons for his arrest and of any charge against him". This means that the accused must be informed in simple, non-technical language of the allegation against him so that he may challenge it if needs be (*Fox, Campbell and Hartley v. U.K.* (1990) 13 E.H.R.R. 157).

Article 5(2) will apply only to those arrested and charged, not those summonsed to appear before the court, but in the case of proceedings commenced by summons Article 6(3) is relevant. This provides that everyone charged with a criminal offence has the right—"(a) to be informed promptly, in a language which he undertstands and in detail, of the nature and cause of the allegation against him".

The provisions of Article 5(2) and 6(3) will apply with equal force to any accused person who is before the court having been arrested and accordingly it is arguable that an accused is entitled to more information surrounding the allegation once before the court than was provided on the occasion of his arrest. The words *and in detail* appear in Article 6(3) but not in Article 5(2).

If proceedings are commenced by summons Article 6(3) will apply because the word "charge" has an autonomous meaning (see §24–07, below) and may include a procedure whereby a person is notified by a competent authority that he is alleged to have committed an offence (*Fox, Campbell and Hartley v. U.K.*, above). Charge would include the issue of a summons. The lapse of time between the date of the alleged offence and the laying of the information will assume greater importance when the Human Rights Act 1998 is implemented because the accused has a right to be informed *promptly* of the allegation against him (Article 6(3)(a)).

3. The Contents of a Charge or Summons

1–12   A summons or charge is in proper form if it states in ordinary language the elements of the offence, together with the statutory provision, if any, which is alleged to be contravened (MCR 1981, r. 100). The particulars do not have to conform to any special words, providing the accused is given sufficient information, so far as dates and place are concerned, to understand the allegation made against him.

(i) The rule against duplicity

1–13   The rule against duplicity is easy to state in theory, although difficult to apply in practice. The rule means that a summons or charge is bad for duplicity if it reveals more than one offence, and a court may not convict upon it (*Hargreaves v. Alderson* [1964] 2 Q.B. 159); a magistrates' court is prohibited from trying an information that charges more than one offence (MCR 1981, r. 12(1)). The application of this apparantly simple rule in practice has proved troublesome, because the variety of factual situations thrown up in the cases mean that a coherent explanation of the rule is difficult.

On the one hand the Divisional Court has applied a strict interpretation and has held that an information alleging "assault and battery" in a single summons is bad for duplicity, even though for most purposes an assault is synonymous with a battery (*D.P.P. v. Little* [1991] Crim. L.R. 900). On the other hand, in different circumstances the Divisional Court has held that a single charge of theft may properly be preferred on the basis of "general deficiency" even though there is evidence that separate thefts occurred on a number of separate dates, but no evidence of when each individual theft took place (*D.P.P. v. McCabe* (1993) 157 J.P. 443). In that case there was evidence that individual library books had been stolen by the accused from Cardiff City libraries, but no evidence as to which library nor on what date each particular book had been stolen. The Divisional Court held that it was permissible for the prosecution to lay one information charging the accused with stealing 76 library books from South Glamorgan Library between specified dates.

Duplicity is difficult to understand because there are two different circumstances when duplicity may arise: two separate offences may be charged in the same information, or a single information may specify more than one way in which a single offence may be committed. The Divisional Court itself fell into error by misapplying the duplicity rule in *D.P.P. v. Corcoran* [1993] Crim.L.R. 139, and this case was later held to have been wrongly decided (*Shaw v. D.P.P. and other cases* [1993] 1 All E.R. 918.

The rule is best explained if the traditional test propounded by Lord Parker C.J. is applied: does the information charge only one activity, even though the activity may involve one act or more than one act? (*Ware v. Fox; Fox v. Dingley* [1967] 1 W.L.R. 379). In that case it was held that a summons alleging two activities, namely the management of premises used for the purpose of smoking cannabis or for the purpose of dealing in cannabis was bad for duplicity. Therefore, if more than one activity is alleged in a single summons the summons is bad for duplicity.

1–14 This reasoning has proved difficult to apply to recent legislation concerning drinking and driving, in particular the question whether a summons under section 7(6) of the Road Traffic Act 1988 created more than one offence because (a) the penalty may differ depending upon how precisely the offence was committed, and (b) because there may be a request for breath, blood or urine by an officer investigating whether such an offence has been committed. It has now been authoritatively decided by the House of Lords that section 7(6) of the 1988 Act creates only one offence, notwithstanding the fact that a separate penalty for the offence arises upon conviction depending upon whether the accused was driving (or attempting to) or not (*D.P.P. v. Butterworth* [1994] 3 All E.R. 289). For the same reasons it has been held that a summons under section 7(6) is not bad for duplicity if it states a failure to provide "breath/blood/urine" for analysis (*Worsley v. D.P.P.* [1995] Crim.L.R. 572). For a further example of section 7(6) of the Road Traffic Act 1988 being judicially considered in the context of submissions concerning duplicity see *Shaw v. D.P.P. and other cases* [1993] 1 All E.R. 918).

The test propounded by Lord Parker C.J. namely, does the summons charge only one activity, even though the activity may involve more than one act is usually easy to understand. Thus, in a case involving a bus driver charged under the Public Service Vehicle Regulations 1936 the Divisional Court observed that "a bus driver who curses at a passenger with a cigarette in his mouth and refuses to divulge his destination at the same time is not involved in one activity but in three separate activities of cursing, smoking and refusing to divulge" (*Amos v. D.P.P.* [1988] R.T.R. 198). On the other hand if the summons charges just one activity, namely driving without due care and attention in two separately observed incidents, separated by a two-mile distance, the information is not duplicitous even though the one activity involved more than one act (*Horrix v. Malam* (1984) 148 J.P. 30).

(ii) Consequences of a defective information, summons or warrant

(a) GENERAL RULE

1–15 The general rule is that no objection shall be allowed to any defect in the substance or form of any information, complaint, summons or warrant nor may objection be taken if there is a variation between the contents of an information, summons or warrant and the evidence adduced at the hearing (MCA 1980, s.123). If it comes to the notice of the court or the parties that a summons is duplicitous it may be cured by the prosecution electing on which offence to proceed and striking out the offending duplicitous elements (MCR 1981, r. 12(3). An application to cure duplicity may be made at any stage of the proceedings, but if the accused appears to be unfairly prejudiced he must be granted an adjournment (*ibid.*, r. 5).

The wrong description in an information of the person entitled to prosecute is not a defect merely in substance or form within the meaning of section 123 because the accused is entitled to know the identity of his accuser and that person must have authority to lay the information. However, if on the facts of a particular case no one is misled, such an error does not have the effect of rendering the information invalid (*Rubin v. D.P.P.* [1990] 2 Q.B. 80). In that case it was stated that an information laid by "the Thames Valley Police," an unincorporated body, could not cause the accused any injustice because the identity of the actual police officer in whose name the information should have been laid could have been discovered by a simple inquiry.

The purpose of section 123 is that if the variation between the evidence and the information is slight and causes no injustice to the defendant the information remains valid. If, on the other hand, the variation is so substantial that it would be unjust to proceed without amendment, the court may require the prosecution to amend the information (*Garfield v. Maddocks* [1974] Q.B. 7).

In the event of an amendment being allowed the court shall allow an adjournment if the defence are taken by surprise (MCA 1980, s.123(2)).

(b) EXAMPLES OF THE GENERAL RULE

1–16   If the person answering the summons or charge has been incorrectly named, for example with the wrong Christian name, or the wrong street has been inadvertently named, or the date of the offence is incorrect, then such minor variations may be cured by amendments. The basis for the use of this power is that the person intended by the prosecution to be the defendant is the person who actually appears in court, notwithstanding a minor variation in the name or address (*Allan v. Wiseman* [1975] R.T.R. 217).

The test of whether, in the exercise of the court's discretion, an amendment to a defective information should be allowed is whether justice is done between the parties (*R. v. Newcastle-upon-Tyne Justices, ex p. John Bryce (Contractors) Ltd* [1976] 1 W.L.R. 517).

(c) EXCEPTIONS TO THE GENERAL RULE

1–17   If the information is worded in such a way that it discloses no offence known to the law then it is void *ab initio* and cannot be cured by a later amendment (*Garman v. Plaice* [1969] 1 W.L.R. 19).

In addition section 123 may not be used if the wrong person, or the wrong body corporate, is summoned to appear before the court. Thus, if a wholesaler and not the retailer is summoned in respect of offences alleged to be committed by the retailer, section 123 may not be used to substitute the name of the retailer for that of the wholesaler (*R. v. Greater Manchester Justices, ex p. Aldi GMBH and Co. KG* (1995) 159 J.P. 717).

4. Jurisdiction

(i) Territorial Jurisdiction: Indictable and Either Way Offences

GENERAL RULE

1–18 With effect from June 1, 1999 the jurisdiction of magistrates' courts to deal with certain offences of dishonesty and blackmail is governed by the provisions of Part 1 of the Criminal Justice Act 1993 (Criminal Justice Act 1993 (Commencement No. 10) Order 1999). The essential purpose of this legislation is to enable courts in England and Wales to try such offences if any relevant event, which means any act or omission necessary for the commission of the offence or the result of the offence, occurred in England or Wales (CJA 1993, s.2(1), (2) and (3)). The 1993 Act will not apply if such relevant event occurred before June 1, 1999 (*ibid*, s.78(5)).

The offences to which the 1993 Act applies are defined as either a "Group A offence" (CJA 1993, s.1(1)(a)), or a "Group B offence" (*ibid.*, s.1(1)(b)). Group A offences are those contrary to sections 1, 15, 15A, 16, 17, 18, 19, 20(2), 21, 22 and 24A of the Theft Act 1968; offences contrary to section 1 and 2 of the Theft Act 1978; offences contrary to sections 1, 2, 3, 4 and 5 of the Forgery and Counterfeiting Act 1981, and the common law offence of cheating in relation to the public revenue (CJA 1993, s.1(2)(a), (b), (c), (d) and (4), as amended by Theft (Amendment) Act 1996, s.1(1)).

Group B offences are a conspiracy, attempt or incitement to commit a Group A offence, or a conspiracy to defraud (CJA 1993, s.1(3)(a), (b) and (c)).

Offences which are not defined in Part 1 of the 1993 Act (or the above offences where the relevant act occurred before June 1, 1999) remain subject to common law rules governing territorial jurisdiction. In general this means that courts in England and Wales have jurisdiction to try indictable or either way offences if the *last* act or event which is required to be performed to complete the offence occurred in England or Wales (*Tracey v. D.P.P.* [1971] A.C. 537).

APPLICATION OF RULE TO MAGISTRATES' COURTS JURISDICTION

1–19 Indictable offences (which include offences triable either way) may be tried in any magistrates' court, providing the jurisdiction of the criminal law of England and Wales applies to those offences (MCA 1980, s.2(3) and (4)). Thus, the provisions of the 1993 Act and those of common law are applicable by virtue of section 2 of the Magistrates' Courts Act 1980. In the case of substantive offences jurisdiction, in general, arises where the last act or event in relation to the crime in question took place, or was intended to take place, in England or Wales (*McLeod v. Att.-Gen. for New South Wales* [1891] A.C. 455). In a conspiracy case there is jurisdiction even if the conspiracy was entered into abroad and the overt acts in furtherance of the conspiracy occurred abroad providing the conspiracy intended an offence to result in this country (*Somchai Liangsiriprasert v. Government of the United States* [1991] 1 A.C. 225, and *R. v. Sansom; R. v. Williams; R. v. Smith; R. v. Wilkins* [1991] 2 Q.B. 130). In addition there are special rules for murder or manslaughter committed by a British subject abroad (Offences against the Person Act 1861, s.9), and for offences committed aboard a British ship or aircraft.

There is, therefore, a much wider jurisdiction applying to indictable offences than to purely summary offences. A magistrates' court retains its jurisdiction for indictable crimes even if another court had wrongly remanded the accused to that court, because the Magistrates' Courts Act 1980, s.2(3) must be read in conjunction with the Police and Criminal Evidence Act 1984, s.46 (*R. v. Penrith Justices, ex p. Morley* (1991) 155 J.P. 137).

(ii) Age

1–20   Since October 1, 1992 the jurisdiction of the magistrates' court for summary and indictable offences has been reduced to the extent that only offenders of the age of 18 and over will appear in the magistrates' court (CJA 1991, s.68). Offenders under the age of 18 are dealt with in the youth court (*ibid.*, s.70). Schedule 8 of the Criminal Justice Act 1991 amends the Magistrates' Courts Act 1980 to this end, and the Magistrates' Courts Rules 1981 are amended by the Magistrates' Courts (Criminal Justice Act 1991) (Miscellaneous Amendments) Rules 1992.

(iii) Summary offences

1–21   Purely summary offences may only be tried in the county or London commission area within which they were committed (MCA 1980, s.2(1)). There are two minor exceptions to this rule. If justices are already dealing with an accused for one offence they may also try him for offences committed elsewhere. Secondly, if it is expedient in the interests of justice for two persons to be tried jointly in the court, a court not normally having jurisdiction for both may try the case (MCA 1980, s.2(2) and s.1(2)(b)).

1–22   If a magistrates' court is trying an accused for an either way offence the accused may also be tried on the same occasion for any summary offence for which he could be tried in another commission area (MCA 1980, s.2(6)). This provision only applies if the accused is actually being tried in the magistrates' court, rather than being committed for trial in the Crown Court (*R. v. Croydon Magistrates' Court, ex p. Morgan* (1998) 162 J.P. 521).

In addition there is a special jurisdiction conferred on a court in relation to prosecution under Part VI of the Transport Act 1968 (drivers' hours and records offences). In such cases jurisdiction may arise either from the place where the driving occurred, the place where the proposed defendant resides, or the principal place of business of the owner-driver or employer of the driver (Transport Act 1968, s.103(7)).

5. Prosecuting in the Proceedings

(i) The right to prosecute

1–23   Since the Prosecution of Offences Act 1985 came into force the conduct of all cases commenced by the police, other than specified proceedings, is conducted by the Crown Prosecution Service (POA 1985, s.3(2)). Specified proceedings are minor traffic cases, and regulations allow for these to be presented by the police themselves. All other prosecutions instituted by the police must be taken over by the Crown Prosecution Service, with the exception of serious and complex frauds which are prosecuted by the Serious Fraud Office (CJA 1987, s.1). In addition to taking over cases originally investigated and charged by the police, the CPS may discontinue a prosecution at an early stage in the proceedings (POA 1985, s.23). It has been said that this power is a useful and economical way of disposing of a case without a court appearance. A court hearing may still be requested if the accused insists on being cleared in public under the provisions of section 23(7) of the Act, but this cannot be used as a device to require the prosecution to continue to offer evidence in a case which has been dropped (*Cooke v. D.P.P.* (1992) 95 Cr.App.R. 233). In that case it was held that the statutory power to discontinue under section 23 was an additional method of stopping a prosecution to that already possessed by a prosecutor under common law.

An example of a prosecution being dropped under inherent common law powers occurred in *R. v. Grafton* [1993] Q.B. 101. In that case, prosecuting counsel at the Crown Court decided to offer no further evidence mid-way through the Crown's case because the quality of the evidence was such that he no longer had faith in his case. It was held by the Court of Appeal (Criminal Division) that prosecuting counsel was perfectly entitled to take a view and discontinue during a trial, and it is submitted that the same considerations would apply to a summary trial. (For the responsibilities of counsel prosecuting in a criminal trial generally, see §11–21, below.)

THE RIGHTS OF PRIVATE INDIVIDUALS AND OTHER BODIES TO PROSECUTE

1–24 Although the effect of the Prosecution of Offences Act 1985 is to confine almost all prosecutions to the Crown Prosecution Service, the right of a private individual to institute and conduct criminal proceedings is specifically preserved in the Act, subject to the right of the Director of Public Prosecutions to intervene at any stage (POA 1985, s.6(1) and (2)). It has been said that this right exists in order for prosecutions to continue even if there has been inaction on the part of the Crown Prosecution Service (*R. v. Bow Street Stipendiary Magistrate, ex p. South Coast Shipping Co. Ltd and Another* [1993] Q.B. 645). The constitutional importance of the right of a private citizen to bring a prosecution has recently been underlined by the Divisional Court in *Hayter v. L. and Another* [1998] 1 W.L.R. 854.

The right of bodies other than the CPS or the Serious Fraud Office to prosecute is preserved by the wording of the Act, which provides that the CPS shall take over prosecutions instituted by a "police force" (POA 1985, s.3). Accordingly, a local authority, a body constituted for the purpose of public service, or a nationalised industry may continue to prosecute their own cases. Where offences contrary to the customs and excise legislation occur (such as the importation of drugs) it is specifically provided that such cases are prosecuted by officers of HM Customs and Excise (Customs and Excise Management Act 1979, s.145). The right of the Commissioners of Customs and Excise to prosecute such cases is not affected by the fact that the accused may originally have been charged at a police station (*R. v. Stafford Justices, ex p. Customs and Excise Commissioners* [1991] 2 Q.B. 339).

In the case of certain offences the consent of the Attorney-General or the Director of Public Prosecutions is required, and in the case of all prosecutions the Director of Public Prosecutions may intervene and take over the proceedings (POA 1985, s.6(2)).

The Serious Fraud Office has the responsibility of prosecuting serious and complex frauds, and special procedures exist for transferring such cases directly to the Crown Court (see §§6–29 *et seq.*, below).

(ii) Duties of the Crown Prosecution Service

1–25 The duties of the Crown Prosecution Service and the general principles to be applied in determining whether proceedings should be instituted are contained in the Code for Crown Prosecutors (POA 1985, s.10). The Code has been issued in various forms since the Prosecution of Offences Act 1985 was passed and the latest version is printed in full in Appendix II (below).

The duties set out in the Code may not derogate from fundamental professional duties in relation to assisting the court in the administration of justice (*R. v. Highbury Corner Magistrates' Court, ex p. O'Donoghue* (1997) 161 J.P. 217). For fundamental principles of professional duties generally see Chapter 11, below.

If it can be shown that a decision not to prosecute was reached in a way which failed to apply the settled policy of the Code, particularly Code 5 "The Evidential Test" the decision may be reviewed judicially and the Divisional Court has power to remit the case for further consideration by the D.P.P., although such power should be used sparingly (*R. v. D.P.P. and Another, ex p. C.* (1995) 159 J.P. 227). The power to remit for further consideration would also arise if the decision not to prosecute was as a result of some unlawful policy (*R. v. Metropolitan Police Commissioner, ex p. Blackburn* [1968] 2 Q.B. 118), or was perverse (*R. v. Inland Revenue Commissioner, ex p. Mead* [1993] 1 All E.R. 772). A decision to discontinue a prosecution is also reviewable judicially but only in rare circumstances and only in respect of someone who has the *locus standi* to challenge the decision (*R. v. Chief Constable of Kent and Another, ex p. L.* (1991) 93 Cr.App.R. 416).

1–26   If a notice of discontinuance has been served with the usual caveat that the prosecution may be revived if "exceptionally, further significant evidence were to become available" the Divisional Court has refused judicial review of a revival of the prosecution on the decision of the D.P.P. personally, notwithstanding the lack of new evidence (*R. v. D.P.P., ex p. Burke* [1997] C.O.D. 169).

Subject to these exceptions a court has no influence on the decision to pursue a prosecution unless such proceedings are an abuse. (For Abuse of Process see below). This principle may be illustrated in two cases: *R. v. Canterbury and St. Augustine Justices, ex p. Klisiak*; *R. v. Ramsgate Justices, ex p. Warren* [1982] Q.B. 398. In *Klisiak* the accused was charged with criminal damage where the value allowed the accused to elect jury trial, which he did. In *Warren* the accused elected jury trial on a charge of assault occasioning actual bodily harm. In both cases the prosecution preferred new summary only offences and offered no evidence on the indictable charges at the outset of committal proceedings. The Divisional Court (in a judgment of Lord Lane C.J.) held:

(i)   Justices have no power to question the decision of the prosecution to offer no evidence on certain charges at committal stage unless, exceptionally, there has been abuse of process.

(ii) If, on the facts, the prosecution could have charged the new summary offences originally it cannot be unjust or oppressive to do so at a later stage.

(iii) There is no obligation upon the prosecution to charge the gravest possible charge resulting from the facts providing that the offences themselves are not of the gravest, and providing that justices' powers are appropriate. There may be reasons for choosing a lesser charge; for example speed of trial or sufficiency of proof.

(iv) While the prosecution have a right to substitute lesser charges at committal proceedings, it is desirable for the contemplated charges to be preferred at the outset.

(v)   Although the court retains a residual power to declare proceedings an abuse of process the power should be used sparingly and only in the most obvious circumstances which disclose blatant injustice.

The cases of *Klisiak* and *Warren*, (above) were decided before the Crown Prosecution Service became responsible for the conduct of prosecutions in the magistrates' court, but the same principles still apply. Where the police had charged attempted theft from a motor vehicle, and the CPS had substituted a summary only charge of motor vehicle interference in order to deprive the accused from electing jury trial there was no bad faith on the prosecutor's part amounting to an abuse (*R. v. Liverpool Stipendiary Magistrate, ex p. Ellison* [1990] R.T.R. 220).

6. Bringing the Proceedings to the Notice of the Accused

(i) When a person is charged

1–27 If a person is charged at a police station with an offence he must be given written notice of the charge showing the particulars of the offence stated in simple terms and the precise offence in law with which he is charged (PACE 1984, Code of Practice, Annex A, Para. 17). Special provisions exist to protect the interests of an accused who is mentally handicapped, deaf, or ignorant of the English language. The importance of the interpreter's duty to ensure that the accused comprehends the nature of the charge, the proceedings which will ensue, and the defences which are available was underlined by the Court of Appeal in *R. v. Iqbal Begum* (1991) 93 Cr.App.R. 96. In that case it was held that a trial was a nullity where the interpreter was not fluent in the language which the accused was best able to understand.

In addition, when an accused is brought before the court, the charge must be read to him (MCA 1980, s.19). Under common law convention, if the accused is unable to understand English the proceedings must be translated into a language he is able to understand. It is an essential principle of criminal law that an accused should understand the proceedings in court and that a defendant who did not so understand could not be said to have had a fair trial (*Kunnuth v. The State* [1993] 1 W.L.R. 1315). For this reason there is specific statutory authority for the payment of an interpreter for an accused who does not understand English to be paid out of central funds (POA 1985, s.19(3)(b)). It is, therefore, virtually certain that when a person appears before the court charged with an offence he is aware of the nature of the proceedings against him.

IMPACT OF HUMAN RIGHTS ACT 1998

1–28 The fundamental right of an accused person to understand the allegations made against him is central to the concept of justice. Article 6(3)(e) of the Convention guarantees that everyone charged with a criminal offence has the right "to have the free assistance of an interpreter if he cannot understand or speak the language used in court". The word "free" should be given an unqualified meaning and should mean without cost or payment of any sort, whatever the means of the defendant (*Luedicke, Delkasam and Koc v. Germany* (1978) 6 E.H.R.R. 409).

(ii) When a person is summoned

1–29 Service of a summons is effected (a) by delivering it to the person to whom it is directed, or (b) by leaving it for him with some person at his last known or usual place of abode, or (c) sending it by post in a letter addressed to him at his last known or usual place of abode. (MCR 1981, r.99(1). The amendments introduced in 1922 and 1993 considerably simplify the rules as to service. There is no longer any distinction to be made between summary only and indictable or either way offences in order to effect good service nor need the court be satisfied that the summons came to the accused's attention. If the proposed defendant is a corporation service may be effected by delivery or by sending the summons by ordinary post to the registered office of the company in the United Kingdom, or if there is no such office, to a place in the United Kingdom where the company trades or conducts its business (MCR 1981, r.99(3)). In all events, if service is effected by post the summons may be sent by either first or second class post.

A summons requiring a person to attend before a court in the United Kingdom may be issued notwithstanding the fact that the person is abroad (Criminal Justice (International Co-operation) Act 1990, s.2). The arrangements for service must be made through the Central Authority, and where service is to be effected in a non-English speaking country, a translation must accompany the summons.

7. Proceedings in the Absence of the Accused

(i) General Rule

1–30   There is a broad general provision that a magistrates' court may hear a case in the absence of an accused (MCA 1980, s.11). The purpose of this rule is to allow minor cases to be dealt with expeditiously when the accused fails, or refuses, to acknowledge a summons. If, however, the charge is a serious one and the accused is liable to receive a custodial sentence if convicted it is undersirable to proceed in absence because there is an overriding interest of justice that an accused should have an opportunity of defending a serious charge (*R. v. Dewsbury Magistrates' Court, ex p. K., The Times,* March 16, 1994).

1–31   The general rule in section 11 of the Magistrates' Courts Act 1980 is subject to two important provisos. First, if the accused is on bail for an offence (whether granted by the police or by a court) he is under a duty to surrender at the appointed time. If he fails to surrender a warrant may be issued for his arrest (Bail Act 1976, s.7(1)). In these circumstances it is submitted that the court ought not to hear the case in the accused's absence unless there are good reasons, on the particular facts, to do so.

Secondly, if an absent accused is represented by counsel or a solicitor he is deemed not to be absent (MCA 1980, s.122(2)). Representation in these circumstances must be by counsel or a solicitor, and not a friend, relative or representative (unless the accused is a corporation).

(ii) Procedure when the accused is absent and has not entered a guilty plea

1–32   If a summons has been issued and the accused does not appear at the time and place appointed for the trial, the court may *only* proceed in his absence if (a) it is proved that the summons was served on him a reasonable time beforehand, or (b) he has appeared on a previous occasion to answer the information (MCA 1980, s.11).

However, this procedure is subject to the general principles of natural justice that an accused should have a fair trial. Therefore, proceedings in absence (sometimes called the "section 11 procedure") should not take place if there is credible and not fanciful evidence that the accused is ill and unable to attend and would otherwise wish to attend (*R. v. Bolton Justices, ex p. Merna* (1991) 155 J.P. 612).

(a) PROOF OF SERVICE

1–33   Service of a summons is effected (i) by delivering it to the person to whom it is directed, or (ii) by leaving it for him with some person at his last known or usual place of abode, or (iii) by sending it by post in a letter addressed to him at his last known or usual place of abode (MCR 1981, r. 99 as amended). Changes to the rules governing service have been introduced successively in 1992 and 1993 and as a result the task of proving service upon an intended defendant is much easier than it was. These changes are discussed in §1–29, above. If, for any reason the provisions of rule 99 are not satisfied the court may not hear the case in the accused's absence and the proper determination is for the papers to be marked "not served" and for the matter to be adjourned for a further attempt at service to occur.

(b) APPEARANCE ON PREVIOUS OCCASION

1–34 If the accused has appeared on a previous occasion to answer the summons, it follows that he must have had knowledge of the summons, and providing he was given notice of the time and place of the adjourned hearing at that appearance no further service is necessary. The provisions of section 11 of the Magistrates' Courts Act 1980, and the rules accompanying the Act, are mandatory, and if they are not observed the Divisional Court is likely to declare the proceedings a nullity, although the matter could be reopened on application by the prosecution (*R. v. Seisdon Justices, ex p. Dougan* [1982] 1 W.L.R. 1479).

(c) PROCEDURE FOR PROVING A CASE IN THE ACCUSED'S ABSENCE

1–35 If the court is satisfied as to service, or that the accused was given the hearing date on a previous occasion, the court may convict the absent accused only on admissible evidence. In practice this will invariably be sworn evidence on oath, although proof by written statement which complies with section 9 of the Criminal Justice Act 1967 may also be received.

Where such a procedure is followed it will be customary to put before the court the contents, or a summary, of any interview under caution made by the accused. If such an interview amounts to a denial of the offence it is not proper for the court to dismiss the information, because considering the evidence as a whole there appears to be a doubt. The proper procedure is to adjourn the case, and for the accused to be informed that he should attend the new hearing when a proper summary trial may take place (*D.P.P. v. Gokceli* (1989) 153 J.P. 109).

(d) SENTENCING AN ABSENT ACCUSED

1–36 Once the summons is proved the court's powers of sentence are restricted. A court may *not* (i) pass a sentence of imprisonment or order a suspended sentence to be implemented (MCA 1980, s.11(3)), or (ii) pass any sentence which requires the accused's consent, *i.e.* probation or community service order (Powers of the Criminal Courts Act 1973, ss.2, 14 as amended by C(S)A 1997, s.38(2)), or (iii) impose a conditional discharge which requires explanation (PCCA 1973, s.7), or (iv) impose a disqualification *unless* the accused was previously present when the question of sentence was adjourned for inquiries to be made (MCA 1980, s.11(4)).

For these purposes disqualification means any disqualification, although the most common and most serious disqualification is disqualification from driving which may be imposed for a variety of road traffic offences. While the court may technically impose a driving disqualification in the accused's absence if he was previously present, it is considered very unwise practice to do so because the order will be useless unless the accused is aware of it. If the court is considering disqualifying an absent accused from driving the preferable course is to take steps to compel his appearance. (These steps are explained at §1–50, below.)

Where an offender is to be fined in his absence, for example following a written plea of guilty to a traffic summons, and the court has insufficient information about his financial circumstances, the court may make such determination as it thinks fit (CJA 1991, s.18(4)(a)).

(iii) Procedure when the accused fails to respond to the summons

1–37   Until recently it was only possible to prove a case in the defendant's absence if the prosecution witness or witnesses gave evidence on oath or if written statements complying with section 9 of the Criminal Justice Act 1967 had been served in advance of the hearing.

In practice most "proofs in absence" are conducted under the provisions of section 12 of the Magistrates' Courts Act 1980 the all important governing legislative authority for the conduct of many routine traffic cases. As originally drafted section 9 statements were not incorporated into the definition of documents to be served with the summons in section 12 cases. They now have been incorporated by an amendment inserted by the Magistrates' Courts (Procedure) Act 1998 (MCA 1980, s.12(1)(b)(ii), as inserted by MC(P)A 1998, s.1(1)). The effect of this amendment is that for proceedings to which section 12 of the 1980 Act apply the accused may be convicted by proof by written statement on the first occasion which the summons is listed for hearing, even if the accused has not responded to the summons. Plainly this amendment will have a great impact on reducing adjournments.

The 1998 Act allows the prosecutor a discretion as to whether to provide section 9 statements or not, and there are some circumstances, particularly when it may be predicted that the accused will dispute the facts, when it will not be appropriate for the prosecution to rely wholly on written statements for proving a case (*Chapman v. Ingleton* 57 Cr.App.R. 476).

The procedure for such cases is that where the court is satisfied that the summons has been served the court may proceed immediately to proof and the section 9 statement or statements may be read to the court as the evidence comprising the prosecution case. This need not be done by a CPS lawyer because proceedings continue to be specified proceedings for the purpose of the Prosecution of Offences Act 1985. If the court directs a summary of the statement may be read, and the statutory declaration which accompanies each section 9 statement need not be read (MCA 1980, s.12(7A) and (7B)).

(iv) Procedure when an accused wishes to plead guilty in absence

1–38   The court may deal with an absent accused if he (or a solicitor acting on his behalf) informs the clerk of the court that he wishes to plead guilty to any summary only offence which does not carry more than three months' imprisonment, providing certain procedural requirements are complied with (MCA 1980, s.12(4).

This procedure is unaffected by the changes brought about by the 1998 Act summarised above although the accused may inform the clerk that he wishes to plead guilty on the basis of statements served under section 9.

PROCEDURE FOR DEALING WITH AN ABSENT ACCUSED WHO HAS PLEADED GUILTY IN WRITING

1–39   A pre-condition for the hearing of a plea of guilty in writing is that the clerk of the court must be notified by the prosecutor that the following documents accompanied the summons (MCA 1980, s.12(1)(b)). The documents are:

(a) a notice explaining the effect of section 12 generally;

(b) a concise statement of the facts relating to the charges which will be placed before the court if the accused pleads guilty; and

(c) a notice containing any information about the accused (*i.e.* previous convictions) if it is intended to place such information before the court (*ibid*. s.12(3)).

In addition the prosecutor is entitled to claim costs in the statement of facts (*R. v. Coventry City Justices, ex p. D.P.P.* [1991] 1 W.L.R. 1153).

If the clerk of the court is informed in writing by the accused or by a legal representative acting on his behalf that he wishes to plead guilty then, providing it is proved that the documents mentioned above were served on the accused, the court may proceed as if the parties had each appeared and the accused had pleaded guilty in person (MCA 1980, s.12(4) and (5)). If the court does so proceed it shall not permit any statement of facts or information relating to the accused other than that served on the accused to be made or placed before the court (*ibid*., s.12(8)). Before the accused may be convicted in absence the statement of facts must be read out by the clerk of the court and the court must be satisfied that the plea is not equivocal. The court is obliged to hear any mitigation which the accused has sent in writing to the court (*ibid*., s.12(7)). It has been said that it is not sufficient for any mitigating circumstances which accompany a written plea to be handed to the justices without being read in open court (*R. v. Oldham Justices, ex p. Morrissey* [1959] 1 W.L.R. 58).

If the court is satisfied that the plea of guilty is a proper one the court may either sentence the accused in his absence or adjourn sentence for the accused to be present. In practice the accused will be sentenced in his absence if he is to be fined or given an absolute discharge and his driving licence endorsed (providing it has been sent to the court), but any other disposal will require his presence (see §1–36, above).

If the proceedings are adjourned for the hearing of a written plea of guilty in absence on a future occasion there is no obligation for the accused to be served with an adjournment notice if the period of the adjournment is not more than 4 weeks (MCA 1980, s.12(11)).

APPLICATION OF SECTION 12 PROCEDURE WHERE THE ACCUSED APPEARS

1–40   Section 12A of the Magistrates' Courts Act 1980 modifies the above procedure to enable the procedure under section 12 to be followed in two further circumstances:

(a) where the clerk of the court has received written notification from the accused or his legal representative that he wishes to plead guilty without appearing; or

(b) where the clerk of the court has *not* received such notification,

and the accused appears before the court at the time and place appointed for the trial (MCA 1980, s.12A(1) and (2)). In these circumstances section 12A permits the court to proceed, providing the accused consents, as if the accused had sent in a written plea subject to the following modifications:

(a) if the accused who appears has previously sent in a written plea of guilty he must be given an opportunity of making oral submissions in mitigation (MCA 1980, s.12A(4)(a), and

(b) before accepting the plea of guilty the accused must be given an opportunity of making oral submissions in mitigation (*ibid*., s.12A(5)(c)).

This modified procedure will have certain advantages to the prosecution who may not have witnesses at court on the occasion when the accused appears, because an adjournment can be avoided if the documents accompanying the summons comply with the provisions of section 12 and the accused pleads guilty. However, there are also advantages to the defence, because under section 12A the only statement of prosecution facts allowed to be heard is "a concise statement" accompanying the summons (section 12(3)(b)), whereas the accused is permitted to make oral submissions in mitigation. In addition the court would usually be obliged to apply section 48 of the Criminal Justice and Public Order Act 1994 and give the accused credit for a plea entered in circumstances permitted under section 12A.

IMPACT OF HUMAN RIGHTS ACT 1998

1–41   Proceedings in the absence of the accused are not, in themselves, a breach of the Convention. Article 6, the right to a fair trial, does not *require* the presence of the accused in order for the fair trial provisions to be complied with. It has been acknowledged by the European Court that without a procedure enabling trials in absence the process of criminal justice could become paralysed (*Colozza and Rubinat v. Italy* (1985) 7 E.H.R.R. 516). Accordingly, in principle the procedure summarised above would appear to comply with the Convention. On the facts of *Colozza* the Court held that the state had not been sufficiently diligent in seeking to serve notice of the proceedings at an address where the accused would receive it. It was held that the remedy was for the accused to obtain a fresh hearing. The discretion given to justices to re-open proceedings under section 142 of the Magistrates' Courts Act 1980 will assume particular importance when the Human Rights Act 1998 is implemented, and this is discussed further in §§5–81 and 5–82, below.

(v) Proceedings set aside if accused did not know of them

1–42   An accused who has been dealt with in his absence may set aside the conviction if he makes a statutory declaration that he did not know of the summons or the proceedings until a date specified in the declaration (MCA 1980, s.14). In practice, this date will be the date upon which the accused will have received a notice of the court's adjudication. Such an accused must serve the declaration on the clerk to the justices within 21 days of that date, although there is provision for the accused to make application to the court (which may consist of a single justice) after such period to set the conviction aside (MCA 1980, s.14(3)). The effect of such a declaration is to render the proceedings heard in absence as void, and to initiate a new trial of the information before a different bench (MCA 1980, s.14(2) and (4)).

(vi) Miscellaneous procedural steps which may take place in the accused's absence

1–43
(a) *Remand in absence*
   In certain circumstances an accused over 17 who is represented may be remanded in custody in his absence (MCA 1980, s.128). These circumstances are explained fully at §2–12, below.

1–44
(b) *Dismissal of information on the merits*
   If an accused is absent at a summary trial on an occasion when the prosecutor is

also absent the court *may*, if it has not heard evidence on a previous occasion, dismiss the information (MCA 1980, s.16).

1–45

(c) *Plea before venue*

Plea before venue may, in certain circumstances, be dealt with in the accused's absence (MCA 1980, s.17B). These circumstances are fully explained in §4–10, below.

1–46

(d) *Mode of trial and election*

Although the general rule is that mode of trial procedure must take place in the presence of the accused (MCA 1980, s.18(2)), the court *may* deal with mode of trial *and* put the accused to his election in his absence providing (i) the accused is represented by counsel or a solicitor who signifies consent to dealing with the matter in absence, *and* (ii) the court is satisfied there is good reason for proceeding in absence (MCA 1980, s.23). In practice it will be rare for such proceedings to be dealt with in absence because the court is unlikely to be satisfied as to "good reason" unless exceptional circumstances exist.

If there are not good reasons for proceeding in the accused's absence the court may issue a summons requiring the accused's presence (MCA 1980, s.26).

1–47

(d) *Enlargement of bail in absence*

This power arises if the accused is on bail but is absent by reason of accident or illness (MCA 1980, s.129). (The power is explained fully at §2–29, below.)

1–48

(e) *Accused absenting himself through conduct*

If an accused is absent because his behaviour has put him in contempt and he has been ordered to leave by the court, such absence will not invalidate the proceedings (see §10–20, below).

8. Powers to Compel the Accused to Appear

(i) *When the accused fails to appear after being charged*

1–49 The procedure for compelling an absent accused to appear is for the court to issue a warrant for his arrest. Usually an accused will have been granted bail by the police, and if he then fails to surrender to custody the warrant will be issued in accordance with the Bail Act 1976. This is a simple and straightforward procedure in practice and the warrant may either be backed for bail, in which case the accused may be readmitted to bail when arrested, or not backed for bail in which case he must be produced before the court in custody for the question of bail to be considered.

In addition to the power to issue a warrant under the Bail Act 1976, there is a general power under the Magistrates' Courts Act 1980 to issue a warrant when an accused does not appear, described below.

(ii) *When the accused fails to appear after being summoned*

1–50 If an accused either fails to appear in answer to a summons or he has pleaded guilty by letter but the court requires his attendance for the purpose of sentence, steps may be taken to compel his appearance. Such steps will depend upon whether a warrant may lawfully be issued. A warrant for the arrest of an absent accused may only be issued if (a) it is proved to the satisfaction of the court that the summons was served a reasonable time before the hearing date, or (b) the accused has appeared on a previous occasion to answer the information, *and* (c) the offence is punishable with imprisonment, or (d) the court, having convicted the accused in his absence, proposes to impose a disqualification, or (e) having convicted the accused after a written plea of guilty and adjourned it for his attendance, the accused still does not attend and it is undesirable, by reason of the gravity of the offence, further to continue the trial in his absence (MCA 1980, s.13).

In its original form section 13 required every information to be substantiated on oath before a warrant could be issued but this requirement is now abolished (MCA 1980, s.13(1), as amended by MC(P)A 1998, s.3(1)). In addition, a warrant may be issued if the accused has not attained the age of 18 but has been convicted and the court proposes to impose a disqualification on him (*ibid.* s.13(3A)), as inserted by MC(P)A 1998, s.3(2).

Because of the restrictions on the issuing of a warrant described above, the usual procedure is for the court to issue a summons to attend or a summons "to show cause" in the first instance. Only when an absent accused has failed to attend as a result of a summons should the court contemplate issuing a warrant.

9. Time Limits

(i) General rule

1–51   The general rule is that in the case of purely summary offences the court shall not try an information or hear a complaint unless the information was laid or the complaint made within six months from the time when the offence was committed or the matter of complaint arose (MCA 1980, s.127).

It has been said that the purpose of the time limit is to ensure that summary offences are charged and tried as soon as reasonably practicable after their commission (*R. v. Scunthorpe Justices, ex p. McPhee and Gallagher* (1998) 162 J.P. 635).

The statutory limitation placed on the period for laying an information or complaint applies only to summary offences (MCA 1980, s.127(2)). In theory, an indictable offence or an offence triable either way may be tried at any time after the commission of the offence or after an offence came to the notice of the prosecuting authority. In practice, the time limits for these cases come within the subject of abuse of process and this is discussed further at §§1–57 *et seq.* below.

The general rule set out in section 127 of the 1980 Act for summary offences is mandatory. Thus, if an information is laid within time but the summons is not served and then a fresh information (rather than an amended information) is laid out of time and successfully served the proceedings are time barred (*R. v. Network Sites Ltd, ex p. London Borough of Havering* (1997) 161 J.P. 513).

The distinction between the laying of a fresh information and amending an existing information is important. The Divisional Court has held that it is permissible to amend a summons which had been laid within time after the expiry of the time limits (*R. v. Newcastle-Upon-Tyne Justices, ex p. John Bryce (Contractors) Ltd* [1976] 2 All E.R. 611). This rule is sufficiently broad to allow a different offence to be alleged in the amended summons, provided the new offence alleges the same misdoing as the original offence and that it is in the interests of justice for the amendment to be made (*R. v. Scunthorpe Justices, ex p. McPhee and Gallagher*, above). Plainly, each case will depend upon its own facts and the interests of the accused will have to be weighed with those of the prosecution in deciding where the "interests of justice" lie when a new summary offence is laid out of time by the device of amending an original information.

(a) MEANING OF LAYING INFORMATION AND MAKING A COMPLAINT

1–52 An information is laid when it is received at the office of the clerk to the justices. Similarly with a complaint; once a complaint is received at the office of the clerk no more is required of the complainant. The receipt in the office may be by any member of staff expressly or impliedly authorised to receive it. If the information or complaint is made orally it should be addressed to a justice of the peace or the clerk personally (*R. v. Manchester Stipendiary Magistrate, ex p. Hill* [1983] A.C. 328).

(b) COMPUTATION OF TIME

1–53 The date of the commission of the offence is excluded (*Stewart v. Chapman* [1951] 2 K.B. 792). Thereafter, the general rule for periods calculated in months is that the period ends at midnight on the day in the subsequent month that bears the same number as the day of the earlier month or the preceding number if no such number appears in the subsequent month (*Dodds v. Walker* [1981] 1 W.L.R. 1027, HL). Therefore, if a summary offence is committed on March 15, 1997, the six months expires at midnight on September 15, 1997. If the offence occurred on March 31, it would expire on September 30.

In the case of a "continuing offence," an offence taking place continuously or intermittently over a period of time, the period runs from each day on which the offence is committed (*R. v. Chertsey Justices, ex p. Franks* [1961] 2 Q.B. 152). Accordingly, if the prosecution intend to rely on the whole period, the information must be laid within six months of the first offence.

If there is doubt as to whether an information has been laid in time the defendant is entitled to the benefit of it (*Lloyd v. Young* (1963) 107 S.J. 631).

For the purpose of custody time limits under the Prosecution of Offences Act 1985 the period begins at the close of the day during which the defendant was first remanded and expires at the relevant midnight thereafter (*R. v. Governor of Canterbury Prison, ex p. Craig* (1990) 91 Cr.App.R. 7).

(ii) Special time limits for certain offences—Notice of Intended Prosecution

1–54 Special rules apply for certain traffic offences which means that a motorist must be warned at an early stage after an alleged offence that he may be prosecuted. The main offences to which the rules apply are dangerous driving, careless driving (or driving without reasonable consideration), drink-driving offences, leaving a vehicle in a dangerous position, and failing to comply with traffic signs and traffic directions (Road Traffic Offenders Act 1988, s.1).

Subject to the exceptions mentioned below the defendant must either be warned at the time of a possibility of prosecution, or the driver or registered keeper must be sent a notice of intended prosecution within 14 days of the offence, or a summons must be served within 14 days of the offence (Road Traffic Offenders Act 1988, s.1). Service may be effected by personal delivery or by sending the notice by registered post, recorded delivery or first class post (*ibid.*, section 1A, as inserted by CJ and POA 1994, s.168 and Sched. 9, para. 6).

The time limits are complied with if the notice was posted at such a time that it would, in the ordinary course of the post, be received within 14 days of the offence (*ibid.*, s.1).

Failure to comply with a warning at the time or with the serving of a notice within 14 days is fatal to the prosecution and a summons must be dismissed if the provisions of section 1 have not been complied with.

EXCEPTIONS

1–55 There are exceptions to the mandatory requirements imposed by section 1. Broadly, these are:

   (a) Accidents: a warning need not be given nor a notice served if a road accident has occurred. This relieves the police of the duty of warning every party to an accident that he may be prosecuted (RTOA 1988, s.2(1)).

   (b) If a fixed penalty notice has been issued (*ibid.*, s.2(2)).

   (c) If neither the driver's identity nor the identity of the registered keeper can be discovered with reasonable diligence in time for a notice or summons to be served, the time limits do not have to be observed (*ibid.*, s.2(3)).

(iii) Date when proceedings begin

1–56 The date on which proceedings begin is a vexed subject, and there are a variety of statutory and case law definitions. In essence the definitions provide answers to particular questions, and there is no single proposition which embodies the wide range of procedural steps which occur in criminal cases. For example, it is often important to know when the court has "begun to try the case summarily" for the purposes of changing mode of trial. This is dealt with at §4–20, below. Equally, it is frequently necessary to know when proceedings begin for the purposes of calculating custody time limits. This is dealt with in §§2–16 *et seq.*, below. These topics apart, the general rules are as follows:

   (a) Where proceedings are commenced by summons, or where having been commenced by summons a warrant is issued for the arrest of any person, the proceedings are instituted when an information is laid before a justice of the peace (POA 1985, s.15(2)(a) and (b). (For the meaning of laying an information see §1–07, above.)

   (b) Where a person is charged with an offence after being taken into custody, proceedings are instituted when he is informed of the particulars of the charge (*ibid.*, s.15(2)(c) and see *R. v. Brentwood Justices, ex p. Jones* [1979] R.T.R. 155).

The question of whether proceedings begin on the occasion when an accused enters a plea is not capable of an easy answer. It has been held that a summary trial begins on the date on which the court begins to hear evidence in the case, and not on the date on which the accused pleads not guilty; the entering of the plea merely establishes the need for a trial and does not mark the commencement of the trial (*Quazi v. D.P.P.* [1988] Crim. L.R. 529). Similar reasoning has been adopted, in another context, in *R. v. Horseferry Road Magistrates' Court, ex p. K.* [1996] 2 Cr.App.R. 574 (see §4–21, below). On the other hand, for the purposes of calculating the transitional provisions of the Criminal Justice Act 1991 proceedings are deemed to begin in summary only offences when a plea is entered (CJA 1991, Sched. 12, para. 24). Similarly, where a young person (under the age of 18) is before the court and enters a plea, proceedings are then deemed to have begun and the fact that he becomes an adult by the date of trial does not entitle the court to commence mode of trial applications (*R. v. Nottingham Justices, ex p. Taylor* (1991) 93 Cr.App.R. 365). The situation is different if the person was under the age of 18 when charged with the offence at the police station or when the first formal remand took place, but was an adult when mode of trial proceedings were determined. Here the relevant date for calculating the commencement of proceedings is when mode of trial is determined (*R. v. Islington North Juvenile Court, ex p. Daley* [1983] A.C. 347). This principle will apply also to calculating the transitional provisions of the Criminal Justice Act 1991 (CJA 1991, Sched. 12, para. 24).

10. Abuse of Process

1–57   The law on abuse of process has been, and continues to be, in a state of development and expansion. Since 1984 when the doctrine was judicially defined in *R. v. Derby Justices, ex p. Brookes* (1985) 80 Cr.App.R. 164 the nature and extent of abuse applications has grown considerably. The limits on its use urged by Lord Lane C.J. in *Att.-Gen.'s Reference (No. 1 of 1990)* [1992] 1 Q.B. 630 do not seem to have been heeded by practitioners.

The modern definition of an abuse of process has been formulated by the House of Lords as follows: criminal proceedings should be stayed on the grounds of abuse of process if (i) it will be impossible (usually by reason of delay) to give the accused a fair trial or if (ii) it offends the court's sense of justice and propriety to be asked to try the accused in the circumstances of a particular case (*R. v. Horseferry Road Magistrates' Court, ex p. Bennett* (1994) 98 Cr.App. 114).

This definition, provided by Lord Lowry, is so wide that proceedings may be stayed in the circumstances in which the court refuses to countenance behaviour which threatens either basic human rights or the rule of law (*per* Lord Griffiths in *ex p. Bennett*, above). Potentially, the grounds for finding abuse of process are therefore very great but the powers of justices in a magistrates' court to refuse to try a case on such wide grounds are circumscribed. It was said in *ex p. Bennett* that where an issue touching on the responsibility of the High Court to uphold the rule of law, such as the abuse of extradition procedures, was raised, justices should adjourn hearing the merits of the case until the abuse application was heard by the Divisional Court. Such a situation arose in *R. v. Staines Magistrates' Court, ex p. Wesfallen, Same, ex p. Soper, R. v. Swindon Magistrates' Court, ex p. Nangle* [1998] 4 All E.R. 210. There is therefore an important jurisdiction affecting the Divisional Court only but discussion in the following paragraphs is confined to abuse of process in the magistrates' court.

(i) Principle

1–58   An abuse of process may exist:

  (i) where the court concludes the defendant cannot receive a fair trial;

  (ii) where the court concludes that it would be unfair for the defendant to be tried (*R. v. Beckford* [1996] 1 Cr.App.R. 94 (*per* Neill L.J.).

This formulation contains the two main strands which can be detected from the authorities and encompass the many different circumstances in which an abuse application may be based. Such applications are usually based on:

(i) delay; or

(ii) manipulation of the process of the court.

This classification of abuse given in *R. v. Derby Justices, ex p. Brooks* (1985) 80 Cr.App.R. 164 was at one time considered to be exhaustive of the categories of abuse but, as was stated in *R. v. Beckford*, above, in the light of the most recent authorities it only covers part of the ground. There is a developing area of abuse applications which now involve issues of whether there were express or implied undertakings by the Crown not to prosecute. This is discussed fully below at §1–65.

1–59   The interrelationship between abuse of process and the process of a fair trial finds expression in statute. Section 10 of the Criminal Procedure and Investigations Act 1996 provides that a failure by the prosecutor to observe the time limits set out in the Act does not in itself constitute an abuse of process but may only do so if there is such delay by the prosecutor that the accused is denied a fair trial (CP and IA 1996, s.10(2) and (3)).

Although it is clear from the authorities that abuse of process is an expanding doctrine it remains the case that in the magistrates' court the jurisdiction must be "most sparingly exercised" and should be "strictly confined to matters directly affecting the fairness of the trial and the particular accused with whom [the justices] are dealing, such as delay or manipulation of court procedures" (*per* Lord Griffiths in *ex p. Bennet*, above). In addition "the discretion to stay is not a disciplinary jurisdiction and ought not be exercised in order to express the court's disapproval of official conduct" (*per* Lord Lowry in *ex p. Bennet*, above).

A further consequence of the strictly confined jurisdiction of magistrates' courts to stay proceedings on the grounds of abuse is that if justices refuse to grant a stay the Divisional Court will only quash such a decision if the circumstances are exceptional; the threshold for intervention by the Divisional Court in such a case is a high one (*R. v. Liverpool City Justices, and the Crown Prosecution Service* (1998) 162 J.P. 770).

The jurisdiction of justices to hear abuse of process applications applies both to summary trials (*Mills v. Cooper* [1967] 2 Q.B. 459) and to committal proceedings (*R. v. Telford Justices, ex p. Badham* [1991] 2 Q.B. 78).

(ii) Delay

1–60   The essence of an abuse application based on the grounds of delay is that the accused has suffered genuine prejudice and unfairness by reason of the delay rather than whether the delay was actually the fault of the prosecution (*R. v. Bow Street Metropolitan Stipendiary Magistrate, ex p. D.P.P.* (1992) 95 Cr.App.R. 9).

There is no particular category of case where a long delay will amount to an abuse. It has been stressed that each case will depend on its own facts, and that excessive citing of authorities in abuse applications is not helpful (*R. v. Sheffield Stipendiary Magistrate, ex p. Stephens* [1992] Crim.L.R. 873 and *R. v. Newham Justices, ex p. C.* [1993] Crim.L.R. 130). In deciding the question justices should examine all the circumstances of the case, including the length of the delay, the reasons (if any) for it, the nature of the case and the evidence to be relied on, the prejudice or likely prejudice caused, and the conduct of the parties generally.

In the case of indictable offences the court is entitled to consider the whole period involved in the proceedings beginning with the date of the offence or the date of the accused's arrest and ending on the first occasion the accused can raise the issue, normally immediately before the committal (*R. v. Telford Justices, ex p. Badhan* above).

For purely summary offences the relevant period is that between the laying of the information and the first hearing of the summons before the justices (*R. v. Oxford City Justices, ex p. Smith* [1982] R.T.R. 201).

1–61 The essential question is whether the delay, for whatever reason, has caused, or is likely to cause, serious prejudice to the accused. For this reason it is necessary to examine all the circumstances of the case including the accused's own conduct. For example, if, on the facts, it appears that the accused always intended to plead guilty it is unlikely that he would be prejudiced by delay. Similarly if the sole or even a substantial cause of the delay is the conduct of the accused himself, it is unlikely that the continuance of the prosecution would be an abuse (*R. v. West London Stipendiary Magistrate, ex p. Anderson* (1984) 148 J.P. 683).

As the essential question is prejudice, the court is entitled to look at the nature of the evidence which is likely to be called on both sides. If the evidence depends substantially on witnesses' memory of events, and it appears that the accused can no longer call witnesses who could remember the incident accurately, then abuse of process may be found (*R. v. Colwyn Bay Justices, ex p. D.P.P.* (1990) 154 J.P. 989). However, if the case depends largely on documents it is much less likely that delay will prejudice the accused than if the events depended on witnesses' memory (*R. v. Buzalek and Schiffer* [1991] Crim.L.R. 115). In that case the Court of Appeal upheld a Crown Court judge's decision to allow the prosecution in a fraud case to proceed after a six-and-a-half-year delay.

While the reasons for the delay are often relevant it is no longer necessary for the accused to establish that the delay was unjustifiable. Delay in itself may amount to an abuse of process if it gives rise to prejudice and unfairness, and such prejudice and unfairness must be demonstrated to the court on the facts (*R. v. Bow Street Stipendiary Magistrate, ex p. D.P.P.* (1990) 91 Cr.App.R. 283). However, it has been said in a later case that the circumstances in which mere delay will suffice to establish an abuse should be regarded as highly exceptional (*R. v. Bow Street Stipendiary Magistrate, ex p. South Coast Shipping Co. Ltd* [1993] 1 All E.R. 219).

EXAMPLES OF DELAY

1–62 The following examples of the instances where abuse has been found, or refused, are given in order to assist the understanding of the doctrine of abuse of process. However, it has been stressed that justices should apply the principles of abuse to the facts before them, and not seek to reach a principle by comparing the facts of one case with those of another (*R. v. Newham Justices, ex p. C.* [1993] Crim. L.R. 130).

  (i) It was unconscionable to proceed with a rape committal after an eight year delay when relevant forensic evidence had in the meantime been destroyed depriving the defence of an opportunity of examining it (*R. v. Sunderland Magistrates' Court, ex p. Z.* [1989] Crim.L.R. 56).

  (ii) Inordinate delay in the service of a summons due to inefficiency by the police, and not any conduct by the accused, which might seriously prejudice the accused's trial may amount to an abuse (*R. v. Oxford City Justices, ex p. Smith* (1982) 75 Cr.App.R. 200).

  (iii) Delay in serving a summons for 22 months after the laying of the information was an abuse (*R. v. Watford Justices, ex p. Outrim* [1983] R.T.R. 26).

  (iv) It is not an abuse for the CPS to delay issuing a summons for a week so that a juvenile involved in a serious indictable offence should appear in the magistrates' court and not the juvenile court (*R. v. Rotherham Justices, ex p. Brough*

[1991] Crim.L.R. 522). In that case it was said that while the Crown had been wrong, there had been no misconduct and the accused had not been prejudiced because it was highly probable that the juvenile court would have refused jurisdiction in any event.

(v) A delay of 10 months in informing the defence of the identity of the complainant in prosecutions for selling food unfit for human consumption was held to be an abuse (*Daventry District Council v. Olins* (1990) 154 J.P. 478).

(iii) Manipulation of the process of the court

(a) GENERAL CONSIDERATIONS

1–63   The distinction drawn in *R. v. Beckford*, above, between an abuse where the defendant cannot receive a fair trial and one where it would be unfair for the accused to be tried has meant that the category of manipulation of the process now assumes increasing importance. In particular a growing category of abuse cases where an implied promise not to prosecute is argued has developed following the decisions in *R. v. Beckford* and *ex p. Bennett* cited above. This topic is discussed separately in §1–65 below. More generally, an example of the wide application of manipulation of the process of the court may be seen in the case of *R. v. Liverpool Magistrates' Court, ex p. Slade* [1998] 1 Cr.App.R. 147. In that case the prosecution were forced to offer no evidence against an accused charged with an offence of allowing a pit bull terrier to be in a public place unmuzzled because an expert witness failed to attend court. The next day the accused collected his dog from the police station and once again allowed the dog to be unmuzzled. A further information was laid relating to the occasion on which he collected the dog. In that case the Divisional Court, citing *ex p. Bennett*, held that because of the mandatory destruction order which had to follow any conviction under the Dangerous Dogs Act 1991 it was offensive to the court's sense of justice to allow the accused to be tried a second time simply because he was not disabused of his liability of a further prosecution when the dog was collected. The court held that the stipendiary magistrate ought to have stayed the proceedings as an abuse. It was further held that the facts were within the quite exceptional category where justices should find an abuse even though the fairness of the trial was not in question.

Plainly, each case will depend on its own facts and justices should not seek to reach a decision by comparing the facts of one case with another. The essence of abuse in this category is that the prosecution have manipulated or abused the process of the court so as to deprive the defendant of a protection provided by the law or to take advantage of a technicality (*R. v. Derby Justices, ex p. Brooks* (1985) 80 Cr.App.R. 164). A practical example of this principle occurred in *R. v. Forest of Dean Justices, ex p. Farley* [1990] R.T.R. 228. In that case the accused was charged with causing death by reckless driving (triable only on indictment) and driving with excess alcohol (triable only summarily) arising out of the same incident. The prosecution wished to try the accused first in the magistrates' court on the summary offence in order to establish that he was driving with excess alcohol. The burden lay on the accused to negative the assumption that the breath-alcohol analysis at the time of driving was not less than at the time the specimen was provided. The reason for the prosecution's intentions as to the order of trials was that the only evidence of reckless driving was the consumption of alcohol. The Divisional Court held that the reversal of the burden of proof implicit in the Crown's application involved a misuse of those of another, namely manipulating the differing burdens of proof in the two cases to its advantage.

(b) EXAMPLES

1–64

(i) Continual default by the CPS to serve advance information may be an abuse, although mere ineptitude in failing to make disclosure would not be an abuse (*R. v. Willesden Magistrates' Court, ex p. Clemmings* (1988) 152 J.P. 286).

(ii) It has been said, *obiter*, that it would no doubt be an abuse of process for the prosecution to prefer a new charge against an accused already remanded in custody on another charge solely for the purpose of defeating the custody time limits (*R. v. Waltham Forest Justices, ex p. Lee and Lee* [1993] Crim.L.R. 522).

(iv) Implied undertaking not to prosecute

1–65   This is a species of manipulation of the process of the court, but recent cases have tended to show that it is an aspect of abuse which should be treated separately. It is also a topic which demands special consideration for magistrates' court practice because of the provisions of the Prosecutions of Offences Act 1985.

It has been held that the following circumstances amount to an abuse if later the Crown wish to proceed with a prosecution:

(a) where a person has been told he would not be prosecuted for a particular crime, but would instead be called as a prosecution witness in a prosecution against others (*R. v. Croydon Justices, ex p. Dean* (1994) 98 Cr.App.R. 76);

(b) where a defendant has been induced to believe by what prosecuting counsel has said in court that the prosecution would not proceed on a later date (*R. v. Bloomfield* [1997] 1 Cr.App.R. 135);

(c) where a person has been interviewed without caution and was co-operating with the police by making a witness statement and steps were then taken which, on the facts, resulted in manifest prejudice (*R. v. Townsend, Dearsley and Bretscher* [1997] 2 Cr.App.R. 540).

There is a need for caution before applying these principles in the magistrates' court because the concept of discontinuance of proceedings applies in the magistrates' court, but not the Crown Court. Section 23 of the Prosecution of Offences Act 1985 provides that where a prosecution is conducted by the Crown Prosecution Service then at a preliminary stage of a case (whether a summary trial or a committal) the CPS may discontinue the case, but this step "shall not prevent the institution of fresh proceedings in respect of the same offence" (POA 1985, s.23(9)). This express statutory power to enable the prosecution to start again following a discontinuance means that the case of *R. v. Bloomfield* cited above must be read with particular caution when applied to magistrates' court practice.

In addition the principles outlined above will not be applied if to do so would conflict with the constitutional right of a citizen to bring a private prosecution (*Hayter v. L. and Another* [1998] 1 W.L.R. 854). In that case it was held that it was not an abuse for a private citizen to pursue a prosecution against a juvenile in respect of an incident for which the juvenile had previously been cautioned by the police because such a ruling would provide an unjustified constraint on the right to bring a private prosecution.

(v) Procedure on abuse of process

1–66 An application before justices that proceedings should be stayed on the grounds of abuse process should be taken as a preliminary issue before a plea is entered in a summary trial or before justices commence to hear evidence as examining justices in commital proceedings. If an accused has on an earlier occasion pleaded not guilty (simply to preserve his position) it is submitted that this would not prevent an abuse argument being made, although if the accused has pleaded guilty it is difficult to conceive circumstances when it would then be open to justices to entertain an abuse application. It would seem that such plea would not prevent an abuse application being pursued by way of judicial review (*R. v. Schlesinger and others* [1995] Crim.L.R. 137).

The burden of establishing that an abuse exists is upon the accused and he must do so on the balance of probabilities (*R. v. Great Yarmouth Magistrates' Court, ex p. Thomas* [1992] Crim.L.R. 116). This burden may be discharged either by making representations or by calling evidence, and the court has a duty to hear any evidence that the parties may wish to call (*R. v. Clerkenwell Magistrates' Court, ex p. Bell* [1991] Crim.L.R. 468).

If the court decides there has been an abuse of process the court has no jurisdiction to hear the case and the prosecution will thereby fail. If the court is of the view that there has been no abuse then the case will proceed in the normal way.

IMPACT OF HUMAN RIGHTS ACT 1998

1–67 The power to stay proceedings on the grounds of abuse of process is a remedy which may be granted under section 8 of the Act (see §24–15, below) and an accused person may rely on a Convention right or rights in any legal proceedings under section 7 (see §24–15, below). Plainly, the law and practice in relation to abuse of process will be greatly affected following commencement of the Human Rights Act 1998.

B. FORMALITIES

1. Court Shall be Open to the Public

1–68 A magistrates' court is required to sit in public, subject to any enactment to the contrary (MCA 1980, s.121(4)).

This important provision is fundamental to the administration of justice.

As a general rule the English system of administering justice does require that it be done in public. If the way that courts behave cannot be hidden from the public ear and eye this provides a safeguard against judicial arbitrariness or idiosyncrasy and maintains the public confidence in the administration of justice: *Att.-Gen. v. Leveller Magazine Ltd and others* [1979] A.C. 440 at p. 450, *per* Lord Diplock.

Exception to general rule

1–69 A court has an inherent jurisdiction to control the conduct of its proceedings and may depart from the general rule where its application would frustrate or render impracticable the administration of justice, but such a departure is justified only to the extent that it is necessary to serve the ends of justice (*Att.-Gen. v. Leveller Magazine,* above).

(a) THE HEARING OF MITIGATION IN CAMERA

1–70 A court has jurisdiction to sit *in camera* if the administration of justice so requires, but there have to be compelling reasons for the court to adopt such a course, and it is doubtful that such compelling reasons exist if a defendant wishes to advance special reasons for not disqualifying *in camera* (*R. v. Malvern Justices, ex p. Evans* [1988] 2 W.L.R. 218). Equally, there are no compelling reasons for the court sitting *in camera* if the mitigation concerns the offender's role as an informer (*R. v. Reigate Justices, ex p. Argus Newspapers* (1983) 147 J.P. 385). In that case the Divisional Court held that the material supporting the mitigation could have been agreed with the prosecution and handed in to the Bench in written form in those exceptional circumstances.

The procedure for deciding whether the court should sit *in camera* is to clear the court to consider the application, provided the justices are satisfied the application is not frivolous, and then announce the decision in open court. The court will then continue the hearing in public or, if the decision is to the contrary, revert to a private hearing in order to continue the case (*R. v. Ealing Justices, ex p. Weafer* (1982) 74 Cr.App.R. 204). This procedure was approved and applied for an application for committal proceedings to be held *in camera* (*R. v. Tower Bridge Magistrates' Court, ex p. Osborne* (1989) 88 Cr.App.R. 28).

(b) DISORDER

1–71 A court has an inherent jurisdiction to exclude the public if there is tumult or disorder in court or a reasonable apprehension of it (*Scott v. Scott* [1913] A.C. 417).

(c) INSUFFICIENT ROOM FOR THE PUBLIC

1–72 There is no obligation on a court to find room for every member of the public who wishes to attend the proceedings. If a courtroom is simply too small to accommodate large numbers the court must act reasonably in admitting such members of the public as is possible in the circumstances (*R. v. Denbigh Justices, ex p. Williams* (1974) 138 J.P. 145).

(d) STATUTORY EXCEPTIONS

1–73 In proceedings under the Official Secrets Acts 1920 and 1989 the public may be excluded if the evidence would be prejudicial to public safety (Official Secrets Act 1920, s.8(4) and Official Secrets Act 1989, s.11).

In proceedings where a juvenile is giving evidence in relation to an offence involving decency or morality, the public (but not the press) may be excluded (Children and Young Persons Act 1933, s.37).

(e) USE OF SCREENS IN COURT

1–74 Occasionally an application may be made by the prosecution for the witness to be permitted to give evidence from behind a screen to prevent the witness seeing and being seen by the accused. The use of a screen has been approved, providing that justice is done (*per* Lord Lane C.J. in *R. v. X and others* 91 Cr.App.R. 36). In that case the use of a screen was used because young children were witnesses in a case involving sexual misconduct. The use of screens is not confined to cases involving children as witnesses (*R. v. Foster* [1995] Crim.L.R. 333) and every case will depend on its own facts. It is submitted that in the magistrates' court the use of a screen may more readily be allowed in committal proceedings than in summary trials. In a committal justices are not concerned directly with the credibility of a witness (*Brooks v. D.P.P.* [1994] 2 W.L.R. 381) nor on the danger of the accused not receiving a fair trial eventually. In a summary trial, however, justices would be obliged to direct themselves that, by allowing a screen to be used, they were not to read anything adverse to the case of the accused by the fact that a witness gave evidence from behind a screen (*R. v. X and others,* above).

(f) PRIVATE COMMUNICATION BETWEEN THE ADVOCATE AND THE BENCH

1–75   There is a general principle that in certain circumstances the fair and expeditious disposal of a criminal trial at the Crown Court may involve private communication between the lawyer acting for the accused and the Judge (*R. v. Turner* [1970] 2 Q.B. 321). It has been held that such a principle derives from a court's inherent jurisdiction and therefore the principle applies to trials in the magistrates' court (*R. v. Nottingham Magistrates' Court, ex p. Furnell and Another* (1996) 160 J.P. 201). It was stressed in that case that as justices are judges of fact as well as law any private communication between lawyer and the Bench should be used sparingly and with caution. In *ex p. Furnell* the Divisional Court declined to find that private communications were *per se* an irregularity, but it is submitted that the practice should rarely, if ever, occur in magistrates' courts for the following reasons:

(i)   a first principle of criminal law is that justice is done in public and therefore private communications are anomalous;

(ii)   private communications create problems over disclosing confidential discussions and this a fruitful source of misunderstanding;

(iii)   the absence of the defendant in such discussions creates an atmosphere of unfairness (*R. v. Harper-Taylor, R. v. Barker* [1991] R.T.R. 76).

It has been said that these points should be drawn to the attention of courts up and down the country (*R. v. Pitman* [1991] 1 All E.R. 468, *per* Lord Lane C.J.). This observation is of particular importance in magistrates' courts because justices, unlike Judges at the Crown Court, must decide questions of fact. Accordingly, it is submitted, the best practice is for justices to decline to entertain a request for a private discussion during the course of a criminal trial.

2. Proceedings in Court may be Fairly and Accurately Reported

1–76   In criminal cases all evidence communicated to the court is communicated publicly. As respects the publication to a wider public of fair and accurate reports of proceedings that have taken place in the court the principle requires that nothing should be done to discourage this: *Att.-Gen. v. Leveller Magazine Ltd and others* [1979] A.C. 440 at p. 450, *per* Lord Diplock.

Exception to general rule

1–77   There are two powers given to a magistrates' court by the Contempt of Court Act 1981: the power to order publication to be *postponed* and the power to *prohibit* publication.

(a) ORDERING PUBLICATION TO BE POSTPONED

1–78   Where it appears necessary to avoid a substantial risk of prejudice to the administration of justice in the proceedings, or other pending or imminent proceedings, a court may order that the publication of the proceedings be postponed for such a period as the court thinks necessary (CCA 1981, s.4(2)). The purpose of the order is to enable newspaper and other media editors to know whether publication would be a contempt or not. Unless an order under section 4(2) is made the press have a complete protection from being prosecuted for contempt if the report is fair and accurate. In deciding whether to make an order justices should consider whether it is *necessary* in the interests of the administration of justice, giving proper weight to the public interest in having fair and accurate reports of court proceedings (*R. v. Horsham Justices, ex p. Farquharson and Another* [1982] Q.B. 762). If, in committal proceedings, there is no application to lift publicity restrictions it should be rare for any additional order postponing publication until the conclusion of the Crown Court trial to be made (*R. v. Beaconsfield Magistrates' Court, ex p. Westminster Press Ltd* (1994) 158 J.P. 1055).

(b) PROHIBITING PUBLICATION

1–79 Where a court allows a name or other matter to be withheld from the public in proceedings the court may prohibit the publication of that name or matter if it is necessary for the purpose for which it was so withheld (CCA 1981, s.11).

In exercising powers to prohibit publication under section 11 of the Contempt of Court Act 1981 the general principles defined by Lord Diplock in *Att.-Gen. v. Leveller Magazine*, above, must prevail. Section 11 was not enacted for the benefit and comfort of defendants who wished to avoid publicity, and therefore it would usually be wrong to prohibit the publication of a defendant's address (*R. v. Evesham Justices, ex p. McDonagh and Another* [1988] 2 W.L.R. 227). It has also been said: (i) that it would be very rare indeed for an order prohibiting publicity to be made simply because an accused had been acquitted, and (ii) that even if severe economic damage would be done to the accused and his business by charges being publicised before trial, that was not a sufficient reason for departing from the general principles relating to proceedings being properly and fairly reported (*R. v. Dover Justices, ex p. Dover District Council and Wells* [1992] Crim.L.R. 371).

1–80 Different considerations may apply, however, if prohibiting publication is necessary in the interests of personal safety. Therefore, if the identity of a witness is not disclosed in open court (*e.g.* a blackmail victim) the court may prohibit publication of the name because for good reasons it was not disclosed in court (*R. v. Socialist Workers Printers Ltd, ex p. Att.-Gen.* [1975] Q.B. 637). Similarly, the contents of a social inquiry should not be published because the proper administration of justice requires a measure of confidentiality in respect of certain documents (*R. v. Beckett* (1967) 51 Cr.App.R. 180).

The court may also direct that no newspaper report or broadcast shall reveal the name, address, school or any particulars which will lead to the identification of a juvenile concerned in proceedings, whether as witness or defendant (Children and Young Persons Act 1933, s.39, as amended by the Children and Young Persons Act 1963, s.57(4)). It has been said that a section 39 order should be made unless the circumstances are rare and exceptional (*R. v. Leicester Crown Court, ex p. S. (a Minor)* 94 Cr.App.R. 153), but justices must allow those who have a legitimate interest in opposing the making of an order to make representations (*R. v. Central Criminal Court, ex p. Crook and Goodwin* (1995) 159 J.P. 295).

Special rules apply for the publicity which may be given for *committal proceedings* and these are set out in section 8 of the Magistrates' Courts Act 1980. These rules are fully discussed at §6–23, below.

(c) PROHIBITING PUBLICATION UNDER THE SEXUAL OFFENCES (AMENDMENT) ACT 1992

1–81   The Sexual Offences (Amendment) Act 1992, extends the categories of complainants in sexual cases who are entitled to anonymity. Formerly only complainants in rape cases were entitled to protection from publicity under section 4 of the Sexual Offences (Amendment) Act 1976. The offence of rape is now defined to include vaginal or anal intercourse, and may be committed by a man upon another man otherwise than in circumstances of consensual buggery (Sexual Offences Act 1956, s.1(1), as amended by CJ and POA 1994, ss.142 and 143). The anonymity of victims of male rape is made consistent with the anonymity granted to women (CJ and POA 1994, s.168 and Sched. 10, para. 36). As rape is an offence triable only on indictment, the 1976 Act had no relevance to summary trials, although it had application in committal proceedings. The new Act includes many either way offences and therefore must be applied to all proceedings in the magistrates' court.

Section 1 of the Act prohibits the publication or broadcast in England or Wales of any matter which might lead members of the public to identify a person as a complainant, subject to exceptions discussed below, during a complainant's lifetime in the case of any of the following offences: offences contrary to sections 2 to 7, section 9, and sections 10 to 16 of the Sexual Offences Act 1956; an offence contrary to section 128 of the Mental Health Act 1959; an offence contrary to section 1 of the Indecency with Children Act 1960; and an offence contrary to section 54 of the Criminal Law Act 1977, or an attempt or a conspiracy or incitement to commit such offences (Sexual Offences (Amendment) Act 1992 s.2(1).

Although many of these offences are little used, the offences of indecent assault (Sexual Offences Act 1956, s.14) and unlawful sexual intercourse (*ibid.*, s.6) are common crimes and therefore it is important always for the court to have in mind the new law.

Section 3 of the Act gives justices, or a single justice, power to displace the general prohibition under section 1 in certain circumstances. Although much of section 3 uses the word "judge" this means any justice of the peace in respect of all either way offences being tried summarily or where mode of trial has yet to be determined (*ibid.*, s.3(6)(a)).

A justice may lift the reporting restrictions if:

  (a) it should be lifted to encourage witnesses to come forward, and

  (b) the conduct of the accused's trial is likely to be substantially prejudiced unless the restriction is lifted (s.3(1)(a) and (b)).

In addition a justice may lift the prohibition if:

  (a) if it is unreasonable, and

  (b) it is in the public interest to remove or relax the restriction (s.3(2)(a) and (b)).

This means that the court may direct that the prohibition shall not apply in certain respects, which must be specified in the order of the court (s.3(2)), however, such an order must not be given simply because the accused has been found not guilty (s.3(3)).

Section 5 of the Act provides that it is an offence for publishers and editors to contravene the provisions of the Act, and if there is a conviction the court may impose a fine not exceeding the statutory maximum.

IMPACT OF HUMAN RIGHTS ACT 1998

1–82 The concept of a fair and *public* hearing guaranteed under Article 6 of the Convention is central to a civilised system of justice and the provisions of Article 6 provide protection against justice done in secret with no public scrutiny (*Pretto v. Italy* (1983) 6 E.H.R.R. 182). There is little, if any difference between the approach adopted in Strasbourg jurisprudence to that established in English common law on this point. Thus, the European Court has held that there may be legitimate circumstances when the press and public may be excluded from a criminal trial (*Campbell and Fell v. U.K.* (1984) 6 E.H.R.R. 165).

The European Court has also upheld measures to protect witnesses, such as the erection of screens. If the life or liberty of a victim or witness is at stake then the interests of such victim or witness may need to be protected under the guarantees of Article 8 of the Convention (*Doorson v. Netherlands* (1996) 22 E.H.R.R. 330).

3. Classification of Offences

1–83 There are three categories of criminal offences. They are: (i) indictable offences; (ii) summary offences; and (iii) offences triable either way. They are defined as follows:

   (i) "indictable offence" means an offence, which, if committed by an adult, is triable on indictment whether it is exclusively so triable or triable either way;

   (ii) "summary offence" means an offence which, if committed by an adult, is triable only summarily; and

   (iii) "offence triable either way" means an offence which, if committed by an adult, is triable on indictment or summarily (Criminal Law Act 1977, s.64, as amended by the Interpretation Act 1978, Sched. 3).

1–84 Summary offences may be tried only in the magistrates' court, and a summary offence is one mentioned in column 1 of Schedule 1 to the Criminal Law Act 1977 (as amended). If an offence is summary only then certain time limits in which a prosecution must be commenced will apply, and there is a territorial jurisdiction of the court which does not apply in indictable or either way offences (see §§1–21 and 1–22, above). If, however, the accused is charged with aiding, abetting, counselling or procuring another to commit a summary offence the court where the aiding, etc. occurred or where the principal offence occurred both have jurisdiction to try the accused (MCA 1980, s.44). If an accused is charged with inciting another to commit a purely summary offence then the incitement is triable only summarily (MCA 1980, s.45).

1–85 An offence triable either way is an offence defined by section 17 of the Magistrates' Court Act 1980, and set out in Schedule 1 to that Act, or an offence made triable either way by the legislation creating the offence and the provisions of section 32(2) of the Act, or under the schedules of certain legislation, for example, Schedule 6 to the Firearms Act 1968. Offences which are indictable or triable either way are further classified as offences of Class 1, 2, 3, or 4 which is a classification relevant to the status of judge at the Crown Court who may try the offence. The relevance of such classification to the magistrates' court arises on committal when the committing justice must specify the Crown Court where the accused is to be tried (see §6–10, below).

4. Constitution of the Court

1–86   A magistrates' court will consist of either justices of the peace or a stipendiary magistrate. A justice of the peace is a layperson appointed by the Crown and assigned to a petty sessional division within a commission area. Justices sit part-time and are unpaid. Cases heard by justices are decided by a majority of the justices sitting, and therefore whenever possible an uneven number should sit (*Barnsley v. Marsh* [1947] K.B. 672). In practice the invariable rule is that three justices will sit.

A stipendiary magistrate is legally qualified and holds full-time judicial office and sits alone for all criminal cases, although he will have the benefit of advice from the clerk in the same way as lay justices are advised. Most stipendiaries sit in London where they are called Metropolitan Stipendiary Magistrates, and in certain large cities elsewhere where they are called Provincial Stipendiary Magistrates.

The administrative arrangements for magistrates' courts in England and Wales are now governed by Part IV of the Police and Magistrates' Courts Act 1994. This legislation does not impinge directly on daily practice and the Justice of the Peace Act 1997, following consolidation, remains the principal Act of Parliament defining the constitution and jurisdiction of magistrates' courts.

5. Justices not Entitled to Anonymity

1–87   The inherent power of justices to control their own proceedings does not apply to withholding their identity from the public and also the press. Accordingly, the names of the justices, although not their addresses or telephone numbers, must be made known to any bona fide inquirer (*R. v. Felixstowe Justices, ex p. Leigh* [1987] Q.B. 582). In practice, the name of the stipendiary is always made known to advocates and the parties, and upon inquiry the names of the lay justices will be revealed to advocates and the parties.

6. Representation

1–88   Representation in a magistrates' court is by a barrister or a solicitor (MCA 1980, s.122), or by a Crown Prosecutor (POA 1985, s.4). In the case of the prosecution there are two minor exceptions to this rule. First, a police officer may represent the Crown in "specified" proceedings (POA 1985, s.3). Regulations have been made to enable a police officer to present the facts in certain motoring cases under this provision when the facts are not disputed. Secondly, an informant may always present his own case in court without instructing a lawyer (MCR 1981, rr. 13 and 14). This enables not only private citizens to prosecute as complainants, but also allows bodies like the National Television Licence Office to nominate an informant who will take out the summonses and prosecute their cases in court. Where a corporation is the defendant any representative of the company may represent the defendant (MCA 1980, Sched. 3). Also, justices must allow a parent, guardian or other representative to assist a juvenile to conduct his case in the juvenile court (Magistrates' Courts (Children and Young Persons) Rules 1988, rr. 5 and 16), and it is submitted the same rules should apply in the adult court.

An unrepresented accused who is in custody is entitled to be represented by the duty solicitor in respect of an application for bail or on a plea of guilty on his first appearance or if he is in breach of a court order which may lead to further imprisonment (Legal Advice and Assistance (Scope) Regulations 1989, reg. 7).

1–89   A defendant in person who wishes to have the assistance of a friend to present his case does not need the leave of the court to do so because any litigant in the courts has a right to reasonable assistance. This right could be withdrawn if the "assistance" was unreasonable in nature or degree, or was not bona fide, or was for an improper purpose or was provided in a way which was inimical to the proper administration of justice (*R. v. Leicester City Justices, ex p. Barrow* [1991] 3 W.L.R. 368). In that case it was held that justices had been wrong to assume that the leave of the court was needed at the outset to allow a defendant in Community Charge proceedings to be helped by a friend.

1–90 There are rules for the assistance of children and young persons who appear before the magistrates' court. Whenever a child or young person is before the court charged with an offence, or is before the court for an alleged breach of a community sentence, or variation or discharge of a supervision order or attendance centre order the court must allow a parent or guardian to assist in the conduct of the case if the defendant is not legally represented (the Magistrates' Courts (Children and Young Persons) Rules 1992, r. 5(1)). If the parent or guardian cannot be found or reasonably required to attend, a relative or other responsible person may assist in place of the parent (*ibid.*, r. 5(2)).

The mandatory right of a parent or guardian to assist with representation always existed in the juvenile court (now the youth court), but until these new rules it was purely a matter of discretion as to whether a parent would be allowed to assist in the magistrates' court. Although as a matter of practice a parent was rarely denied the opportunity to assist, the new rules make parental assistance a legal right.

C. DISCLOSURE

1–91 The law and practice relating to disclosure is now contained in Part I of the Criminal Procedure and Investigations Act 1996. The Act provides a statutory framework for all aspects of disclosure beginning with the investigation and ending with rulings about disclosure during the course of a criminal trial.

The essential purpose of the 1996 Act was to reduce the burden on the police in retaining and then disclosing large quantities of material which the defence sought in the course of "fishing expeditions". In 1993 the Royal Commission on Criminal Justice (Cm. 2263) had recommended a new system whereby a fairer balance could be struck between the duties of the prosecution and the defence which would involve the defence disclosing its case. The suggestions of the Royal Commission now find their place, in broad terms, in the 1996 Act. Although the Act applies equally to proceeding in the Crown Court and the magistrates' court the disclsoure regime under the Act has had a greater impact in the Crown Court. There are three reasons for this. First, problems of disclosing bulky and voluminous unused material are unlikely to arise frequently in the magistrates' court. Secondly, issues involving the withholding of sensitive material are more likely to occur in the Crown Court; thirdly the disclosure of the defence case is voluntary in summary trials, whereas it is compulsory for trials in the Crown Court.

The framework of the Act is to provide for disclosure in distinct stages:

(i) "primary prosecutions disclosure" to include unused material which might in the prosecutor's opinion undermine the prosecution case, together with schedule of unused material which is not sensitive;

(ii) "defence disclosure" which, if adopted in summary trials, must set out the general nature of the defence case;

(iii) "secondary prosecution disclosure" to include further disclosure of material which might assist the defence case as disclosed, and

(iv) disputes about disclosure, including those concerning sensitive material, to be resolved by the court.

COMMENCEMENT

1–92   Part I of the Act applies in relation to alleged offences into which no investigation has begun before the appointed day (CP and IA 1996, s.1(3)). The appointed day was April 1, 1997. Possible transitional difficulties thrown up by this drafting (which appears elsewhere in the Act also) have now been resolved by the Divisional Court in *R. v. Norfolk Stipendiary Magistrate, ex p. Keable* [1998] Crim.L.R. 510 when it was held that there can only be a criminal investigation into an alleged offence once that offence has been committed. Therefore, if the *offence* is alleged by the prosecution to have taken place after April 1, 1997 the provisions of the Act apply even if there might have been a prior investigation into whether such an offence was suspected of being committed beforehand. The Divisional Court held that to construe Part I of the Act in any other way would lead to uncertainty and confusion and would complicate the task of the prosecutor in a way not intended by Parliament.

1. Primary Prosecution Disclosure

1–93   The prosecutor must—

(a) disclose to the accused any prosecution material which has not previously been disclosed to the accused and which in the prosecutor's opinion might undermine the case for the prosecution against the accused; or

(b) give to the accused a written statement that there is no material of a description mentioned in paragraph (a) (CPIA 1996, s.3(1)(a) and (b)).

This obligation must be complied with in the magistrates' court where—

(a) a person is charged with a summary offence in respect of which the court proceeds to a summary trial and in respect of which he pleads not guilty; and

(b) a person over the age of 18 is charged with an either way offence and the court proceeds to a summary trial in respect of which he pleads not guilty (CPIA 1996, s.1(1)(a) and (b)).

Two points must be noted:

(i) the disclosure obligations of the prosecution only apply if the accused has pleaded not guilty. The defence are not entitled to disclosure under the Act where the accused has pleaded guilty or where the accused has been committed for sentence to the Crown Court following a plea before venue in the magistrates' court. It is only in respect of summary *trials* that the prosecution is obliged to make primary disclosure.

(ii) The disclosure obligations do not apply to the pre-committal stage if the accused is to be committed for trial. Common law rules as to disclosure will apply to this pre-committal stage (CPIA 1996, s.21(3)(b)). This does not mean that full disclosure is required, but only that material which a responsible prosecutor should, in justice and fairness, disclose at an early stage (for example, previous convictions of a complainant which might assist the accused in making an application for bail). No hard and fast rules can be laid down as to what material ought to be disclosed at pre-committal stage: it will often depend upon what the defence wish to reveal about their case at such an early stage (*R. v. Crown Prosecution Service, ex p. Lee*, unreported, Transcript CO/198/99, March 18, 1999).

DUTY TO MAKE DISCLOSURE IS A CONTINUING ONE

1–94 The prosecutor has a statutory duty to keep under review until the conclusion of the trial the material which has been disclosed and to disclose further material which might undermine the case for the prosecution as soon as reasonably practical (CPIA 1996, s.9(1) and (2)).

This continuing obligation follows in statutory form the common law duty of continually keeping disclosure under review laid down by the Court of Appeal in *R. v. Ward* 96 Cr.App.R. 1. It is submitted that this common law duty which springs from elementary principles of fairness ought in principle to apply if an accused has pleaded guilty and in mitigation raised matters which the prosecutor knows can be supported by material not previously disclosed. Strictly, under the Act, such a duty of disclosure would not arise because in summary trials disclosure under the Act arises only following a plea of not guilty.

The continuing duty upon the prosecutor to keep disclosure under review applies equally to secondary disclosure (CPIA 1996, s.9(4) and (5)). For secondary disclosure see §§1–108, *et seq*, below.

(i) Content of Primary Disclosure

1–95 The provision in section 3(1) that the prosecution must disclose material *which has not previously been disclosed* includes an assumption that there will, necessarily, have been material previously disclosed. Such an assumption is correct so far as trial on indictment is concerned because the defence will have the committal papers in the form of written statements. The assumption is not correct so far as summary trials of purely summary offences are concerned because it has been held that in such proceedings the accused does not have a right to see witness statements in advance (*R. v. Kingston-Upon-Hull Justices, ex p. McCann* (1991) 155 J.P. 569). Slightly different considerations apply when an either way offence is being tried summarily because in such a case the accused has a statutory right to see "advance information" (CLA 1977, s.48(1)(a)). Advance information is dealt with separately below (see §1–114, below). Section 3 of the 1996 Act follows the decision in *R. v. Bromley Justices, ex p. Smith, R. v. Wells Street Stipendiary Magistrate, ex p. King* [1995] 1 W.L.R. 994 which held that in principle there should be no difference between summary trials and trials on indictment for the disclosure of *unused* material.

1–96 Primary disclosure by the prosecution is confined to material which, in the prosecutor's opinion might *undermine the case for the prosecution*. This deliberate drafting would appear to place limits on the previous common law test of relevance and materiality laid down in *R. v. Keane* [1994] 1 W.L.R. 764. Despite this stricture it would seem that the duty of the prosecution is to disclose all material which is in the prosecutor's possession unless:

(i) the material does not undermine the prosecution case (CPIA 1996, s.3(1));

   (ii) it is not relevant to any issue raised in the prosecution case or by the material retained (*R. v. Mills, R. v. Poole* [1998] 1 Cr.App.R. 43, HL);

  (iii) the material is not in the public interest to disclose and the court rules accordingly (CPIA 1996, s3(6)) see §1–109, below);

  (iv) the material was intercepted under the Interceptions of Communications Act 1985 (CPIA 1996, s.3(7));

   (v) the material goes only to the credibility or reliability of a defence witness (*R. v. Brown (Winston)* [1998] 1 Cr.App.R. 66, HL);

  (vi) the material is protected material by virtue of the Sexual Offences (Protected Material) Act 1997 when this Act comes into force.

(ii) Examples of disclosure under the Act

1–97   The Code of Practice issued under Part II of the Act provides (in para. 7.3) examples of the sorts of material which should be disclosed. These are:

- records of the first description of a suspect given to the police by a potential witness, whether or not the description differs from that of the alleged offender;

- information provided by an accused person which indicates an explanation for the offence with which he has been charged;

- any material casting doubt on the reliability of a confession;

- any material casting doubt on the reliability of a witness;

- any other material which the investigator believes may fall within the test for primary prosecution disclosure in the Act.

(iii) Examples of disclosure at common law

(a) DISCLOSURE OF PREVIOUS CONVICTIONS OF PROSECUTION WITNESSES

1–98   It is the duty of the prosecution to disclose to the defence any record of criminal convictions recorded against any prosecution witness (*R. v. Collister and Warhurst* 39 Cr.App.R. 100), and this duty includes convictions which are spent (*R. v. Paraskeva* 76 Cr.App.R. 162).

This duty is fundamental to the administration of justice, and is not to be interpreted in a narrow, technical way. Accordingly, if a store detective in a shoplifting case had failed to reveal the true circumstances in which he had previously been dismissed from the police force then that was equivalent to failure by the prosecution to provide the defence with a list of a witness's previous convictions (*R. v. Knightsbridge Crown Court, ex p. Goonatilleke* [1986] 1 Q.B. 1). Similar considerations have been held to apply where a police officer has resigned from the police force (*R. v. McCarthy* 158 J.P. 283). Any failure by the prosecution to comply with this fundamental duty will allow any conviction obtained thereby to be challenged on judicial review (*R. v. Harrow Crown Court, ex p. Dave* [1994] 1 W.L.R. 98).

(b) DISCLOSURE OF STATEMENT OF WITNESS NOT TO BE CALLED

1–99   It is now settled law that the prosecution must disclose to the defence any witness statement which may assist the defence, even if in so doing, a witness called by the defence may be able to tailor his evidence (*R. v. Mills, R. v. Poole* [1998] 1 Cr.App.R. 43). In that case the House of Lords stated that the rule in *R. v. Bryant and Dickson* (1946) 31 Cr.App.R. 146 no longer represented modern practice and should be overruled. The reason given by their Lordships was that the risk that disclosure may assist the defence to tailor its evidence is not a consideration which should outweigh the risk that the operation of the rule may result in injustice. The application of this principle to summary trials may be seen in the case of *R. v. Leyland Justices, ex p. Hawthorn* [1971] 1 Q.B. 283 when it was held that any failure by the prosecution to disclose a witness who might be favourable to the defence amounted to *suppressio veri*.

(c) DISCLOSURE OF PREVIOUS INCONSISTENT STATEMENT

1–100   It is elementary to the concept of fairness that if a witness has made a previous inconsistent statement that this should be disclosed to the defence, and this will apply to a previous written or oral statement. Accordingly if a witness had given a different account in other proceedings, for example an internal inquiry following a complaint, then such account should be disclosed (*R. v. Liverpool Crown Court, ex p. Roberts* [1986] Crim.L.R. 622). Similarly, if a witness had on a previous occasion given an interview about the evidence which could be said to have been a rehearsal for the evidence to be given at trial that should be disclosed (*R. v. Dye, Williamson and Davies* [1992] Crim.L.R. 449). If in the course of a summary trial the prosecutor is aware that his witness has given evidence which is inconsistent with the witness's statement then the statement should be disclosed to the defence (*R. v. Halton Justices, ex p. Hughes* (1991) 155 J.P. 837).

(iv) The schedules

1–101   The duty of the prosecutor to make primary disclosure under section 3 of the Act depends upon a defined structure of responsibility placed upon the investigators of the offence which is laid down in the Code of Practice. The Code provides for the preparation of:

(a) a schedule of unused material, set out in sufficient detail to enable the prosecutor to decide whether it should be inspected before deciding whether it should be disclosed (Code of Practice, paras 6.1—6.9), and

(b) a sensitive schedule, set out in a list to include, *inter alia*, material set out in Code of Practice 6.12.

The defence are not entitled to sight of the sensitive list or its contents unless the court so orders.

The duty of the prosecutor is to inspect copies (or where appropriate the originals) of the material described in the schedule of unused material and then either to disclose it to the defence (CP and IA 1996, s.3(1)(a)), or to give the defence a written statement that there is no such material (*ibid.* s.3(1)(b)).

2. Defence Disclosure

1–102   In cases to which section 1(1) of the Act applies (*i.e.* summary trials of summary offences or of either way offences) *and* where the prosecutor has complied with the duty of primary disclosure or purported to comply with it:

the accused—

(a) may give a defence statement to the prosecutor, and

(b) if he does so, must also give such a statement to the court (CPIA 1996, s.6(1) and (2)).

Thus, the service of a defence statement in the magistrates' court is voluntary and not compulsory. Plainly, it will be a matter for judgment in each case as to whether the defence will wish to serve a defence statement. The advantage of serving one is that it may then trigger secondary prosecution disclosure which is discussed in §§1–108 and 1–109 below. There is no provision for obtaining further disclosure unless a defence statement is served. If a defence statement is volunteered by the defence then the content of the statement and the consequences in terms of adverse inferences will be the same as if the trial were taking place in the Crown Court.

A defence statement is a written statement:

(a) setting out in general terms the nature of the accused's defence;

(b) indicating the matters on which he takes issue with the prosecution; and

(c) setting out, in the case of each such matter, the reason why he takes issue with the prosecution (*ibid.*, s.5(6)).

DISCLOSURE OF ALIBI

1–103 If the defence is one of alibi the defence statement must include, in addition:

(a) the name and address of any proposed alibi witness; or

(b) if the name and address is not known any information which might be of material assistance in finding such witness (*ibid.* s.5(7)).

(i) Time limits

1–104 The defence statement must be given to the court and to the prosecutor within a period of 14 days beginning with the day on which the prosecutor complies or purports to comply with the duty of primary disclosure (CPIA 1996, s.5(9) and the Criminal Procedure and Investigations Act 1996 (Defence Disclosure Time Limits) Regulations 1997, reg. 2). If the Defence Statement is not served within this period an application (or successive applications) may be made to the court for an extension of time, providing the application itself is within the statutory period (*ibid.*, regs 3(2) and 4(3)).

An application for an extension of time shall:

(a) state that the accused believes, on reasonable grounds, that it is not possible for him to give a defence statement under section 5 of the Act during the period referred to in regulation 2;

(b) specify the grounds for so believing; and

(c) specify the number of days by which the accused wishes that period to be extended (*ibid.*, reg. 3(3)).

The court has a complete discretion in ordering further time but *only* if the court is satisfied that the accused cannot reasonably give (or could not have given as the case may be) a defence statement within the time limits permitted or those previously granted (*ibid.*, regs 3(4) and (5) and 4(3)).

PROCEDURE FOR APPLYING FOR AN EXTENSION OF TIME

1–105 The application must be made in writing to the clerk of the court with a copy served on the prosecutor at the same time (Magistrates' Courts (Criminal Procedure and Investigations Act 1996 (Disclosure) Rules 1997, r. 8(2) and (3)). If the prosecutor wishes to oppose an extension of time being granted he should inform the clerk of the court within 14 days of being served with the application (*ibid.*, r. 8(4)). The court must consider the application and any representations from the prosecutor and it may, in its discretion, decide the application without a hearing (*ibid.*, r. 8(5)), but if a hearing is granted the hearing must be *inter partes* and it must be in open court (*ibid.*, r. 8(6) and r. 9(2)).

(ii) Adverse inferences

1–106 If an accused volunteers a defence statement in a summary trial there is a risk of an adverse inference being drawn if the defence statement is inconsistent with the defence advanced at trial or the defence advanced at trial departs from the defence statement. The full circumstances when the court may draw an inference are when the accused:

(a) [*not applicable to summary trials*]

(b) gives a defence statement but does so after the end of the period specified by statute or granted by the court (see §1–104, above);

(c) sets out inconsistent defences in a defence statement;

(d) at his trial puts forward a defence which is different from that set out in the defence statement;

(e) at his trial adduces evidence in support of an alibi without having given particulars of the alibi in a defence statement; or

(f) at his trial calls a witness to give evidence in support of an alibi without having complied with subsection (7)(a) or (b) of section 5 (see §1–103, above) (CPIA 1996, s.11(2)(b) to (f)).

It would appear that Parliament envisaged that the most common circumstance in which these provisions would apply would be the putting forward of a different defence at trial from that disclosed, paragraph (d) above, because in this case the court must have regard—

(a) to the extent of the differences in the defences, and

(b) to whether there is any justification for it

before drawing any adverse inference (*ibid.*, s.11(4(a) and (b)).

1–107 If any of the above provisions apply:

(a) the court or, with the leave of the court, any other party may make such comment as appears appropriate;

(b) the court may draw such inferences as appear proper in deciding whether the accused is guilty of the offence concerned (*ibid.*, s.11(3)),

but an accused may not be convicted solely on such an inference (*ibid.* s.11(5)).

These provisions apply equally to trials in the Crown Court where a defence statement is compulsory and it is submitted that their use in the magistrates' court will be rare. First, it is unlikely that an accused will choose to volunteer a defence statement only to depart from it at trial. More importantly, it will be difficult in practice for justices to apply the provision without causing potential injustice. In summary trials justices are not given any prosecution witness statements in advance and the service on the court of the defence statement without corresponding prosecution statements would be meaningless. Accordingly, it is difficult to envisage circumstances when justices could legitimately make use of these provisions while maintaining fairness at the same time.

3. Secondary Prosecution Disclosure

1–108   If there has been voluntary disclosure of a defence statement the prosecutor must then comply with a duty to provide secondary disclosure. Secondary disclosure is "any prosecution material which has not previously been disclosed to the accused and which might be reasonably expected to assist the accused's defence as disclosed" (CPIA 1996, s.7(2)(a)). The duty is one of scrutiny of the defence *as disclosed* (but not any other defence which might on the facts be available) and then to provide further material which might *reasonably be expected* to assist the presentation of that defence.

The wording of section 7 of the Act is considerably narrower than the common law duty defined in *R. v. Keane* [1994] 1 W.L.R. 764 which had held that the prosecutor should disclose all material which might be relevant or possibly relevant to an issue in the case. This common law duty was a wide one and it is plainly the intention of the Act to limit duty of disclosure to those matters which are actually relevant to the case rather than those which potentially may be relevant.

Order requiring secondary disclosure

1–109   If a defence statement has been served and the accused or his legal representative has reasonable cause to believe that the prosecutor is in possession of material which might assist the defence case and the material has not been disclosed the accused may apply to the court for an order requiring the material to be disclosed (CPIA 1996, s.8(2)(a) and (b)).

The procedure for obtaining such an order is that the accused must make an application in writing to the clerk (with a copy served on the prosecutor at the same time) specifying:

(a) the material to which the application relates;

(b) the fact that the material has not been disclosed;

(c) the reason why that material might assist the defence as disclosed; and

(d) the date on which the copy notice was served on the prosecutor (Magistrates' Courts (Criminal Procedure and Investigations Act 1996) (Disclosure) Rules 1997, r. 7(2)).

The prosecutor must then inform the court within 14 days that he is willing to disclose the material or that he wishes to make representations as to why he is unwilling to make disclosure (*ibid.* r. 7(4)(a)). In the latter case the court must give notice of a hearing date to determine the issue which must be a hearing *inter partes* (*ibid.* r. 7(5)), unless:

(a) the court determines that it may rule on the application without hearing representations; or

(b) the prosecutor applies for the hearing to take place in the absence of the accused or his legal representative (*ibid.*, r. 7(6) and (7)).

A hearing under this rule may be in private (*ibid.*, r. 9(1)).

4. Public Interest Immunity

1–110 The 1996 Act preserves the well-established rule of public policy that the prosecutor is not obliged to disclose material if it is not in the public interest for such material to be disclosed, but whenever an issue of public interest immunity arises the court must determine the matter.

The Act states that "material must not be disclosed . . . to the extent that the court, on application by the prosecutor, concludes that it is not in the public interest to disclose it and orders accordingly" in the following circumstances:

(i) the stage of primary disclosure (CPIA 1996, s.3(6));

(ii) the stage of secondary disclosure (*ibid.*, s.7(5));

(iii) the stage in which the defence apply for an order for disclosure ((*ibid.*, s.8(5); and

(iv) the stage in which the prosecutor exercises a continuing duty to keep disclosure under review (*ibid.*, s.9(8)).

It follows that all the matters discussed in all the preceding paragraphs are subject to the exception known as public interest immunity.

(i) The meaning of public interest immunity

1–111 Public interest immunity is a doctrine which has recently seen a rapid development, although the common law has long recognised that the public interest will preclude certain matters from being disclosed to the defence in the usual way. The most obvious and traditional example is the protection afforded to police informers (see *Marks v. Beyfus* (1890) 25 Q.B.D. 494). Such protection is only an example of a wider doctrine, namely the principle that there are occasions when disclosure would be in breach of some ethical or social value involving the public interest, and that the preservation of the public interest should prevail (*D. v. National Society for the Prevention of Cruelty to Children* [1978] A.C. 171, *per* Lord Edmund-Davies at p. 245). In considering the whole issue of public interest immunity the focus should be on the question whether there is a legal objection to disclosure rooted in the preservation of the public interest as balanced against the interests of the accused (*R. v. Brown* [1994] 1 W.L.R. 1599).

Decisions on applications based on public interest immunity therefore involve an element of balance, although where the interests of justice in favour of disclosure touch on the liberty of the subject (as they do in a criminal case) the weight to be attached to the interests of justice are plainly very great (*R. v. Governor of Pentonville Prison, ex p. Osman (No. 4)* [1991] 1 W.L.R. 281). If the material might prove a defendant's innocence or avoid a miscarriage of justice then the balance comes down resoundingly in favour of disclosure (*R. v. Keane* [1994] 1 W.L.R. 746). Similarly any claim by the prosecution to withhold disclosure based on recognised public interest grounds is always subject to the duty of the court to admit evidence if it is necessary to avoid a miscarriage of justice (*R. v. Brown; R. v. Daley* [1988] Crim.L.R. 239).

These cases show that even where a claim by the Crown to withhold disclosure is justified, the particular circumstances of an individual case may involve injustice if disclosure does not occur. Thus, it does not inevitably follow that the identity of a police informer should never be revealed. If the facts and circumstances of a particular case lead to a conclusion, in the minds of the court, that a miscarriage of justice may occur if an informer's identity is not made known then the court is under a duty to admit the evidence (*R. v. Hallett* [1986] Crim.L.R. 462). Rulings on issues of public interest immunity therefore involve fine judgment, and for this reason it has been suggested that decisions should not be taken at a lower level than the Crown Court (*R. v. Crown Prosecution Service, ex p. Warby* (1994) 158 J.P. 190). This observation cannot apply to summary trials (see below), but if the offence is triable either way and an issue on disclosure is likely to arise the prosecution are entitled to make representations that the case is unsuitable for summary trial (*R. v. Bromley Justices, ex p. Smith and Another, R. v. Wells Street Stipendiary Magistrate, ex p. King* [1995] 1 W.L.R. 994). Such an application would be consistent with the general considerations set out in the National Mode of Trial Guidelines (see Appendix I below). More recently the Divisional Court has stated that justices themselves can properly decide issues of non-disclosure of material and that merely because a case involves a decision about disclosure should not, in itself, be a reason for committing the case to the Crown Court (*R. v. Stipendiary Magistrate for Norfolk, ex p. Taylor* (1997) 161 J.P. 773).

(ii) Procedure for determining P.I.I. applications

APPLICATIONS BY THE PROSECUTOR

1–112   The procedure whereby the prosecutor is entitled to seek an order of the court in relation to the withholding of material follows closely the principles laid down in common law. An application by the prosecutor may fall within one of two categories:

- applications for which the accused is put on notice, or
- applications which are made *ex parte*.

The Magistrates' Courts (Criminal Procedure and Investigations Act 1996) (Disclosure) Rules 1997 provide that in general terms an application by the prosecutor that material should be exempted from disclosure (because it is not in the public interest that it should be disclosed) should be served on the clerk of the court (r. 2(2)), with a copy to the accused (r. 2(3)).

In such circumstances the hearing of the application will be *inter partes* and both the prosecutor and the accused will be entitled to make representations to the court (r. 3(2)(a) and (b)).

Following common law principles the Rules also provide that in sensitive cases the accused shall not be served with a copy of the application:

(i) where the prosecutor has reason to believe that to reveal to the accused the nature of the material to which the application relates would have the effect of disclosing that which the prosecutor contends should not in the public inerest be disclosed ... the prosecutor shall notify the accused *that the application has been made* (r. 2(4)); or

(ii) where the prosecutor has reason to believe that *to reveal to the accused that the application is being made* would have the effect of disclosing that which the prosecutor contends would not be in the public interest to be disclosed (r. 2(5)).

In these circumstances (as with common law principles) the Rules provide that the hearing may be *ex parte* when only the prosecutor may make representations to the court (r. 3(4)(a) and (b)).

There is no reason, in principle, why justices should not determine these applications even if the same bench is to go on and decide the merits of the case (*R. v. Stipendiary Magistrate for Norfolk, ex p. Taylor* (1997) 161 J.P. 161). In that case the Divisional Court stated that the normal practice applicable at the Crown Court whereby the judge at trial should conduct p.i.i. applications should apply to summary proceedings, and only in the exceptional circumstances of highly prejudicial material being revealed should a bench disqualify itself from conducting the trial.

REASONS MUST BE GIVEN FOR NON-DISCLOSURE ORDER

1–113 Justices are obliged to give reasons when making an order relating to public interest immunity (r. 4(2)).

This statutory obligation is innovative in the sense that justices have traditionally never been obliged to give reasons for their decisions and this tradition is for the first time changed by this rule.

5. Advance Information

1–114 There is a duty on the prosecution to provide the accused with details or a summary of the prosecution case if it is requested by the defence in respect of all offences triable either way.

This duty is mandatory and arises under section 48 of the Criminal Law Act 1977 and the Magistrates' Courts (Advance Information) Rules 1985. In so far as the obligation arises under statute the common law duties will be subservient to the duty on the Crown arising from the Act which provides that the accused is entitled to advance information to all, or any prescribed class of, facts and matters of which the prosecutor proposes to adduce evidence (CLA 1977, s.48(1)(a)). This is very limited disclosure compared with the common law obligations, but Advance Information disclosure is only for the purposes of helping the accused and his advisers decide on mode of trial or plea. It is not disclosure for the purposes of any subsequent committal proceedings or summary trial. Advance Information disclosure may therefore be classified as preliminary disclosure only, and at the stage following the service of Advance Information the common law duties of disclosure will arise. If the accused is to be tried summarily then the common law duties will be carried out in the magistrates' court, although if the accused is to be tried on indictment it is appropriate for the duties to be carried out in the Crown Court (*R. v. Crown Prosecution Service, ex p. Warby* (1994) 158 J.P. 190).

1–115 The Magistrates' Court (Advance Information) Rules 1985 provide as follows:

(i) SERVICE OF NOTICE

The prosecution must serve a notice on the accused as soon as practicable after charge or service of a summons explaining his entitlement to advance information (r. 3). Thereafter the accused may request advance information and this must be provided by the prosecution (subject to the exception below) *before* a mode of trial decision is taken and *before* a plea is entered (r. 4).

(ii) CONTENTS OF ADVANCE INFORMATION

The information must be either:

(1) a copy of the written statements and supporting documents on which the prosecution propose to rely; or

(2) a summary of the facts and matters of which the prosecution propose to adduce in evidence (r. 4).

EXCEPTION:

The prosecution need not comply with a duty to disclose its case if it is of the opinion that it might lead to intimidation or the course of justice being interfered with. If the prosecutor wishes to rely on this exception the accused must be informed in writing (r. 5).

(iii) DUTY OF THE COURT IN RELATION TO ADVANCE INFORMATION

(1) The court must satisfy itself that the accused is aware of his entitlement to advance information (r. 6).

(2) If the prosecution has not complied with a request the court must adjourn the case until disclosure is made *unless* the court is satisfied that the conduct of the case for the accused will not be substantially prejudiced by non-compliance with the requirement (r. 7).

(3) If the court does not adjourn the case it must make a record as to why the case for the accused would not be substantially prejudiced by non-disclosure (r. 7).

1–116   The following points should be noted:

(i) Although the rules apply only to offences triable either way prosecutors would be well advised to adopt a policy of informing defendants of their case in summary proceedings unless there were positive reasons for not doing so, for example if a prosecution witness was in fear (*R. v. Kingston-upon-Hull Justices, ex p. McCann* (1991) 155 J.P. 569);

(ii) Justices have no power to direct that Advance Information be served. The proper procedure is to apply rule 7 and to grant an adjournment for the prosecution to comply with rules (*R. v. Dunmow Justices, ex p. Nash* (1993) 157 J.P. 1153). For this reason an information may not be dismissed merely because the prosecution have failed to serve Advance Information (*King v. Kucharz* (1989) 153 J.P. 336).

(iii) Mere failure to serve Advance Information is not an abuse, although continual default in serving Advance Information might become an abuse of process (*R. v. Willesden Magistrates' Court, ex p. Clemmings* (1988) 152 J.P. 286).

IMPACT OF HUMAN RIGHTS ACT 1998

1–117   Implementation of the Human Rights Act 1998 will undoubtedly affect the way in which practictioners will raise points relating to disclosure. The Criminal Procedure and Investigations Act 1996 must be read and given effect in a way which is compatible with Convention rights (HRA 1998, s.3(1) (see generally §24–04, below). In addition the principle of "equality of arms" in criminal proceedings (see §24–18, below) bears directly on the procedure for disclosure laid down in the 1996 Act. Article 6 of the Convention (right to a fair trial) makes no distinction between summary trial or trial on indictment whereas a considerable distinction exists in the 1996 Act. Principally, these are differences in the obligations to make primary disclosure (see §1–95, above) and the circumstances which will trigger secondary disclosure (see §§1–108, above).

It has been held that the failure by the prosecution to serve witness statements in summary only proceedings did not, in itself, breach Article 6 of the Convention (*R. v. Stratford Magistrates' Court, ex p. Imbert, The Times*, February 25, 1999). In that case (in a judgment which was technically *obiter*) the Divisional Court held that the Strasbourg decision in *Foucher v. France* (1997) 25 E.H.R.R. 234 turned on its own special facts relating to the withholding of a court dossier under French criminal procedure and could not be cited as authority for the proposition that the law as stated in *R. v. Kingston Upon Hull Justices, ex p. McCann* (1991) 155 J.P. 569 breached Article 6. The decision in *ex p. Imbert* turned on a particular factual basis, namely the failure by the prosecution at a pre-trial hearing to disclose the witness statements which would later be relied on in the trial of a summary only offence. It was said that this fact did not render the whole of the subsequent proceedings unfair, and that the justices were correct in refusing to stay the proceedings as an abuse.

The decision in *ex p. Imbert* does not therefore close the door on future application relating to Article 6 so far as summary trials, as compared with trials on indictment, are concerned. For example, it may be argued that an accused is at a disadvantage if tried summarily in relation to material disclosed to him by the prosecution. Article 6(3)(b) requires that everyone charged with a criminal offence shall have "adequate ... facilities for the preparation of his defence". The word "defence" in Article 6 would appear to mean answer to the charge in the sense of a defence in a trial, rather than mitigation. The trigger for disclosure in summary trials following a plea of not guilty would not, on its face, appear to conflict with the Convention.

More difficult considerations apply to the word "facilities" because there is plainly a difference in the material revealed to the defence in summary trials, compared to trials on indictment. The European Court has stated that as a general principal Article 6 requires the disclosure by the prosecution of all material evidence for and against the accused (*Edwards v. U.K.* 15 E.H.R.R. 417) but the Court has been reluctant to adjudicate upon the precise systems of disclosure in individual states.

The procedure for determining public interest immunity applications may also become the subject of renewed argument, although there is no decision from the European Court as to whether such *ex parte* hearings in private breach Article 6.

CHAPTER 2

Remand

1. Introduction

2–01   A remand is an adjournment of a case when the court fixes the time and place of the next hearing (MCA 1980, s.10(2)). It is implicit in the nature of a remand that the accused will either be in custody or will be granted bail. Accordingly, the occasions on which remands occur are the occasions when considerations of bail usually arise. Bail is fully discussed in Chapter 3. By its nature a remand is an occasion when an effective trial, committal or sentence does not take place and accordingly a remand is an event which contributes to delay. For some time the government has been concerned about delay within the criminal justice system generally, and the magistrates' court in particular, and a Circular HOC 24/98, was issued reminding practitioners of the PTI (pre-trial issues) time guidelines. These time periods do not have the force of law but legislation was introduced in Part III of the Crime and Disorder Act 1998 to provide statutory obligation to comply with certain time limits. As yet these provisions have not been implemented.

DEFINITION OF A REMAND

2–02   A remand is not the same as an adjournment because in a remand the court must fix the time and place of the next hearing, in an adjournment the time and place is not necessarily fixed (MCA 1980, s.10(1)). It also differs from an adjournment in that a remand applies to all indictable matters which are either tried summarily or where the court is considering the mode of trial (MCA 1980, s.10(3)). However, the word adjournment is commonly applied to the postponement of summary trials whether for purely summary offences or either way offences, and the principles governing the granting of such adjournments is discussed at §§2–31 et seq., below.

At any stage of proceedings for offences triable either way the following "remand" provisions apply. For purely summary offences a more informal adjournment may occur, for example, an adjournment when an accused does not appear to answer a summary information (MCA 1980, s.10(2)). In practice the court often announces an adjournment with the words "adjourned sine die" (without a day) whereas when the court remands an accused the date and time of the next hearing must be announced by the court at the time the remand is made.

2–03   Generally, there are six types of remand available to the court:

(1) pre-trial remands;

(2) remands during a trial;

(3) remands for sentence after conviction;

(4) remands for medical examination;

(5) remands to a police station for inquiries;

(6) remands to customs detention.

The period for which a court may remand in these circumstances will depend upon whether the accused is convicted or unconvicted, whether he is on bail or in custody, and to an extent whether the accused is giving his consent to the remand period.

2. Summary of Remand Periods

2–04   The general rules are as follows:

(i) If an accused is *unconvicted* he may not be remanded in *custody* for more than eight days on his first appearance, and thereafter for no longer than 28 days in *custody* on each subsequent occasion (MCA 1980, ss.128(6) and 128A).

(ii) If an accused is *unconvicted* he may be remanded for any period consistent with the justice of the case if he is on *bail* and the parties consent (MCA 1980, s.128(6)).

(iii) If an accused is *convicted* he may not be remanded for longer than four weeks if he is on bail or three weeks if he is in custody (MCA 1980, s.10(3)).

(iv) If the court at any time considers an accused should be remanded for a *medical examination* he may not be remanded for longer than four weeks if he is on bail or three weeks if he is in custody (MCA 1980, s.30(1)).

(v) If the accused is remanded into police detention the maximum period is three days (MCA 1980, s.128(7), as amended by PACE 1984, s.48).

(vi) If the accused is remanded into customs detention the maximum period is eight days (CJA 1988, s.152).

3. Purpose of Pre-Trial Remands

2–05   These are the most common type of remand because rarely is a case ready to proceed on the very first occasion an accused is brought before the court.

Pre-trial remands are important because usually it is at this stage that the first application for bail is made. The grant or refusal of bail at any early remand hearing affects the whole course of the proceedings. If bail is granted the remand periods and the time between arrest and trial are longer. If bail is refused these periods are shorter and there is greater pressure on the parties to prepare their cases quickly.

The remand powers available to the court at this stage are the same whether the matter is indictable or summary, or whether the mode of trial is determined or not (MCA 1980, ss.5(1), 10(1)). The most common reason for a remand at this early stage in the proceedings is for "advance information" to be disclosed to the defence if the defence request it. The rules as to advance information are fully explained at §§1–114 et seq., above. A court remanding an accused under the powers given in the Magistrates' Courts Act 1980 may properly remand the accused to appear before a court in a different petty sessional division providing it is in the same county (R. v. Avon Magistrates' Courts Committee, ex p. Bath Law Society [1988] Q.B. 409).

Although often pre-trial remands are a formality they serve an important function in the administration of justice. The court is able to keep track of the cases before it, and the remand dates are an opportunity to review the progress of a case. Secondly, the parties may seek directions from the court on remand appearances. For example, the prosecution may be directed to serve statements by a particular date, the defence may be directed to be ready for trial by a particular date. While such directions are not binding upon a different bench of justices (or even the same justices hearing the case again) pre-trial remands are a useful occasion upon which to review the progress of a prosecution. Finally, the remand procedures ensure that the interests of an accused who is in custody are regularly examined.

PROCEDURE IF THE ACCUSED IS TO BE HANDCUFFED

2–06 Occasionally, when an accused is brought to court in custody, a request is made (either by the police or by court security officers) for the accused to be handcuffed. In such cases the following procedure should be followed:

   (i) the prosecution must make representations that there are reasonable grounds for supposing that, unless restrained, the accused may either escape or be violent;

  (ii) justices should rule on that application having regard to those representations and any representations made by the defence;

 (iii) if having ruled that a particular accused may be handcuffed a further application for the removal of the handcuffs must be supported by fresh grounds (R. v. Cambridge Justices and the Chief Constable of Cambridgeshire Constabulary, ex p. Peacock (1997) 161 J.P. 113).

In that case it was stressed that justices have a responsibility to ensure that as far as possible defendants in custody are treated with civility, humanity and respect and that justices themselves, not the police or other bodies, are responsible for regulating how defendants are treated in court.

4. Pre-Trial Remands in Custody

(i) First appearance

2–07 The period for a pre-trial remand in custody on the accused's first appearance shall not exceed eight clear days (MCA 1980, s.128(6)). This means that eight days may intervene between the day the remand is made (say a Monday) and the day of the next remand appearance (the Wednesday of the following week).

(ii) Exceptions

(a) SERVING PRISONERS

2–08 If the accused is already serving a sentence the remand period on his new case may be up to 28 days in custody unless his expected release date will be before that time, in which case the maximum remand period is until his expected date of release (MCA 1980, s.131).

(b) REMAND TO A POLICE STATION FOR INQUIRIES

2–09 If an accused is before the court and the court has power to remand him in custody, he may instead be committed into custody at a police station for a period not exceeding three days providing the purpose is for inquiries to be made into other offences (MCA 1980, s.128(7)). The other offences do not have to be wholly unrelated to those already charged: for example if the accused had been charged with conspiracy to rob, "other offences" could be individual robberies (*R. v. Bailey* [1993] 3 All E.R. 513).

In practice such remand will occur if an accused has been charged with a serious offence and he is willing to admit other offences, and his solicitors are content for him to remain at the police station for those inquiries to be completed. As soon as the need for these further inquiries has ceased the accused must be produced again before the court (*ibid.*, s.128(8). When remanding under these provisions there is no power to remand to another magistrates' court and the accused must be produced again before the court making the remand (*R. v. Penrith Justices, ex p. Morley* (1990) 155 J.P. 137).

(c) REMAND INTO CUSTOMS DETENTION

2–10 If an accused aged 17 or over is charged with possession of a controlled drug or any drug trafficking offence he may be remanded into the custody of a customs officer for a maximum period of eight days (CJA 1988, s.152). Unlike remands into police detention, a remand into customs detention does not have to be for the purpose of inquiries, although the remand power may only be exercised if the court is satisfied that the accused should be refused bail in any event (CJA 1988, s.152(1)(b)).

(iii) Subsequent appearances

2–11 An accused who is already in custody may be remanded for a period of 28 days at a time in custody providing:

(a) he has previously been remanded in custody for the same offence, and

(b) he is before the court (MCA 1980, s.128A(2)(a) and (b).

This provision applies to any accused person irrespective of age (*ibid.*, s.128A(1) as amended by CPIA 1996, s.52(2), and Magistrates' Courts (Remands in Custody) (Amendment) Order 1997)). If, however, the powers are being invoked in respect of a juvenile the magistrates' court should have regard to section 44 of the Children and Young Persons Act 1933 which requires a court to consider the welfare of children and young people who are before the court.

In order for an accused to be remanded under this provision the court must have set a date on which it expects the next stage of the proceedings, other than a remand, to take place and the accused must be given an opportunity to make representations (*ibid.*, s.128A(2)).

In addition the court is obliged, for the purposes of refusing bail, to have regard to the total length of time which the accused would spend in custody if it were to exercise the power (para. 9B of Sched. 1 to the Bail Act 1976). If, having given such consideration to the question, the court decides to exercise the power the accused may be remanded either (a) to the next effective date if that is less than 28 days or, (b) for a period of 28 clear days in custody.

It follows that such a remand cannot be made on an occasion when the accused is absent, having previously consented not to be produced, but the power may be exercised whether or not the accused is represented. If an accused is remanded for 28 days in custody he may nevertheless apply for bail during the period of the remand (MCA 1980, s.128A(3)).

If an accused is aged 17 or over he may be ordered to be brought up to an alternative magistrates' court nearer to the prison where he is held (MCA 1980, s.130). This is called a transfer of remand order. It is a sensible provision, saving the time and expense incurred by bringing an accused long distances, and the alternative magistrates' court has the same powers as the original court for hearing bail applications and dealing with other pre-trial applications. For the committal for trial or summary trial the accused will be brought back to the original court having jurisdiction over the case.

(vi) Remands in Custody in Absence

(a) WHERE THE ACCUSED GIVES HIS CONSENT

2–12 In certain circumstances an accused may be remanded for up to three occasions in custody in his absence, although he must be produced on the fourth occasion. The circumstances are as follows:

    (i)   he must be represented;

    (ii)   he must personally give consent in open court (MCA 1980, s.128(3A)).

This provision applies irrespective of whether the accused is an adult or a juvenile (MCA 1980, s.128(3A), as amended by CPIA 1996, s.52(1)).

The accused is represented for the purposes of this section if he is represented in the proceedings, even if the representative is not present in court (*ibid.*, s.128(1B)).

It is the duty of the court to explain to the accused in ordinary language that he will be produced on the fourth occasion, usually a period of 28 or 32 days, and that he will be produced on every remand hearing should he cease to be legally represented (*ibid.*, s.128(1A)).

The accused may withdraw his consent at any time (*ibid.*, s.128(3A)(d)), in which case he will be produced within the statutory eight day period.

(b) WHERE THE ACCUSED IS NOT PRODUCED

2–13   If an accused has been remanded in custody and has not given his consent to be absent, then if he is not brought before the court he may only be further remanded in custody for the shortest period that it appears to the court to make it possible for him to be produced (MCA 1980, s.128(3D)).

On a strict construction of this subsection such power may only be used once. If, therefore, there has been a short adjournment for an absent accused to be produced and he is not then produced there is no alternative but to release him. "The shortest period" to enable production is likely to be less than the normal seven days, although the precise period will depend on local circumstances and conditions.

There is an exception to this rule if the accused has previously been remanded in custody and is then transferred to a mental hospital by the Secretary of State under section 48 of the Mental Health Act 1983. In these circumstances the accused may be further remanded in his absence providing he has appeared before the court within the previous six months and the time limits imposed under the Magistrates' Courts Act 1980 will not apply (MHA 1983, s.52(3) and (4)).

2–14   If the accused is, in fact, in custody (because of a decision of another court) but has been remanded on bail by the court where the accused is required to attend, there is no unconditional duty upon the prison governor to produce the prisoner in accordance with the remand date (*R. v. Governor of Brixton Prison, ex p. Walsh* [1985] A.C. 154). There is merely a duty upon the governor to consider whether it is desirable in the interests of justice for the prisoner to be produced and not unreasonably to refuse to produce him. In these circumstances the practice is for the court to enlarge the bail of the absent accused and for the prosecution to seek a Home Office Order for his production on the next occasion.

5. Custody Time Limits

(i) Definition

2–15   A custody time limit means a defined limit of time after which an accused who is in custody must be released on bail. Custody time limits were introduced by the Prosecution of Offences Act 1985, s.22 and by a number of regulations made under that Act. Custody time limits apply throughout England and Wales.

Wherever a person is in custody in relation to an indictable or either way offence he may not be held in custody for longer than the following periods:

(i) if the offence is indictable only the accused must not be in custody for longer than 70 days between his first appearance and the commencement of the committal, or the date on which a notice of transfer is given.

(ii) if the offence is either way the accused must not be in custody for longer than 70 days between his first appearance and the commencement of the summary trial or the committal, or the date on which a notice of transfer is given. unless before 56 days the court has determined on summary trial, in which case the period is 56 days (Prosecution of Offences (Custody Time Limits) Regulations 1987, reg. 4).

Custody means custody to which a person is committed in pursuance of section 128 of the Magistrates' Courts Act 1980 (remand) (POA 1985, s.22(11)). Thus, a person who had been remanded pending the taking of a suitable surety is a person in "custody" if a surety is not forthcoming (*Re Ofili* [1995] Crim.L.R. 880).

It follows that custody time limits arise at stages of the criminal process and legal consideration of the due observance of the time limits must be considered at the particular stage under consideration (*R. v. Birmingham Crown Court, ex p. Bell* (1997) 161 J.P. 345).

CALCULATING CUSTODY TIME LIMITS

2–16 For the purpose of calculating a custody time limit the following definitions apply:

(i) the first appearance of the accused in the magistrates' court is the time when he first appears or is brought before the court;

(ii) in a case where an application has been made under section 43B of the 1980 Act (see §3–40, below) it is the time when he appears on that application;

(iii) in a case where the accused appears on a reconsideration application under section 5B of the Bail Act 1976 (see §3–48, below) and the decision which is to be reconsidered is that of a constable it is the time when he appears on that application;

(iv) commencement of a summary trial is the time when the court begins to hear evidence for the prosecution or, if there has been a plea of guilty, the time when the plea is accepted;

(v) commencement of committal proceedings is the time when the court begins to hear evidence from the prosecution (Prosecution of Offences (Custody Time Limits) Regulations 1987, regs. 2(1) and 4, and reg. 2(2) as inserted by the Prosecution of Offences (Custody Time Limits) (Amendment) Regulations 1995).

PURPOSE OF CUSTODY TIME LIMITS

2–17 It has been authoritatively stated (in relation to time limits at the Crown Court) that the overriding purposes of custody time limits are:

(i) to ensure that period for which unconvicted defendants are held in custody awaiting trial are as short as reasonably and practically possible;

(ii) to oblige the prosecution to prepare for trial with all due diligence and expedition; and

(iii) to invest the court with a power and duty to control any extension of the prescribed maximum period (*R. v. Manchester Crown Court, ex p. McDonald* [1999] 1 All E.R. 805, *per* Lord Bingham C.J.). It is submitted that these observations are equally applicable to proceedings in the magistrates' court.

In applying these principles it has been held that it is not a good and sufficient cause to extend the custody time limits simply because there was no courtroom at the Crown Court for the accused's trial (*R. v. Norwich Crown Court, ex p. Stiller and Others* [1992] Crim.L.R. 501).

In calculating the time limit the period begins at the close of the day during which the defendant was first remanded and expires at the relevant midnight thereafter (*R. v. Governor of Canterbury Prison, ex p. Craig* [1991] 2 Q.B. 195).

In certain circumstances these time limits may be extended. These circumstances are explained below.

(ii) Extension of Time Limits

(a) PROCEDURE

2–18 A magistrates' court may, at any time before the expiry of a time limit imposed by the regulations, extend, or further extend, that limit; but the court shall not do so unless it is satisfied:

(a) that the need for the extension is due to—

(i) the illness or absence of the accused, a necessary witness, a judge or a magistrate;

(ii) a postponement which is occasioned by the ordering by the court of separate trials in the case of two or more accused or two or more offences; or

(iii) some other good and sufficient cause; and

(b) that the prosecution has acted with all due diligence and expedition (POA 1985, s.22(3), as amended by CDA 1998, s.43(2)).

These new criteria came into force on June 1, 1999 (Crime and Disorder Act 1998 (Commencement No. 4) Order 1999) and section 22(3)(a)(i) and (ii) add new conditions to the originally drafted ones, which are now "good and sufficient cause" and "due diligence and expedition". This wording is slightly different from the originally drafted section 22(3), but it is submitted that the decisions referred to in this chapter would not have been different had such wording been in the 1985 Act. Authority for this proposition may be found in the judgment of Lord Bingham C.J. in *R. v. Leeds Crown Court, ex p. Bagoutie and another, R. v. Same, ex p. Callaghan, The Times,* May 31, 1999.

The Crown Prosecution Service must make their application to extend the time limits clearly so that the defence have an opportunity to make representations, and the decision upon the application must be announced clearly and unequivocally (*Re Ward, Ward and Bond* [1991] Crim.L.R. 558).

The question of whether the court should hear evidence or rely solely on the representations of the parties will depend on the nature and extent of the controversy in the circumstances of the particular case, but it is always for the court and not just the parties to be satisfied (*R. v. Manchester Crown Court, ex p. Mcdonald, The Times,* [1999] 1 All E.R. 805).

A formal application for an extension must always be applied for in the proper way by the Crown, and the defence cannot agree an extension of time with the prosecution and thereby oust the jurisdiction of the court (*R. v. Sheffield Justices, ex p. Turner* [1991] 2 Q.B. 472).

Although the regulations provide that the prosecution must give two days' written notice of their intention to seek an extension, the regulation is directory and not mandatory (see §2–26, below).

If such an extension is granted by a magistrates' court the defence may appeal the decision to the Crown Court (POA 1985, s.22(7)), and if refused the prosecution may equally challenge the decision before the Crown Court (*ibid.*, s.22(8)).

(b) INTERPRETATION OF PARTICULAR WORDS IN THE ACT AND REGULATIONS

2–19 In construing the words "good and sufficient cause" in POA 1985, s.22(3)(a) the court should first consider the words "good ... cause"; they mean some good reason for postponement carrying with it the need to extend the custody time limit.

Then the court should evaluate the strength of that reason when considering the word "sufficient" (*R. v. Central Criminal Court, ex p. Abu-Wardeh* [1998] 1 W.L.R. 1083). In that case it was held that the original reason for the accused being in custody and being refused bail (for example the protection of the public) cannot in itself be a good reason for extending the time limit. When considering whether to extend custody time limits a court should examine the circumstances rigorously in order to be satisfied that the reason for the extension is a good one and also whether the cause is sufficient for any extension. The court should then go on and consider the length of any extension.

The reasoning in *ex p. Abu-Wardeh* differs from that in other cases which had placed emphasis on the reasonableness of the application. The judgment in *ex p. Abu-Wardeh* underlines the principle that the whole purpose of the regulations is to secure a speedy trial for those in custody. Thus the suggested cause must be a reason for the postponement of the trial rather than simply a reasonable application in the circumstances. This reasoning has since been authoritatively re-stated by the Lord Chief Justice in *R. v. Manchester Crown Court, ex p. McDonald* (see §§2–22—2–26, below). In that case it was said that there were an almost infinite variety of circumstances which could amount to a good and sufficient cause pretexts such as staff shortages, overwork, sickness, absenteeism or matters of that kind could not amount to a good cause. In deciding what is a good cause in a particular case depends on the facts and circumstances in question, having regard to the overriding purposes of the statutory provisions.

2–20 The following contingencies have been held, on the particular facts, to amount to a good and sufficient cause:

(i) an extension for a short period in order for a trial to be accomodated in the court lists (*R. v. Norwich Crown Court, ex p. Cox* (1993) 157 J.P. 593;

(ii) an extension to enable the defence to read committal documents which had been served with due expedition by the prosecution (*McKay White v. D.P.P.* [1989] Crim. L.R. 375).

2–21 The following circumstances have been held not to amount, in themselves, to a good and sufficient cause:

(i) the need to protect the public *per se* and without additional factors relevant to the facts of the case in question (*R. v. Birmingham Crown Court, ex p. Bell* (1997) 161 J.P. 345);

(ii) the need for a trial date to be fixed a very considerable time ahead (*R. v. Maidstone Crown Court, ex p. Schulz and Steinkellner* (1993) 157 J.P. 601).

2–22 The words "due expedition" in the POA 1985, s.22(3)(b) look to the conduct of the prosecution and should pose little difficulty in interpretation. The court must be satisifed that the prosecution had acted with such diligence and expedition as would be shown by a competent prosecutor conscious of his duty to bring the case quickly to trial as reasonably and fairly as possible. In deciding this question the court should bear in mind that the periods specified in the regulations were maximum periods and not targets applicable in all cases. The court should have regard to:

(i) the nature and complexity of the case;

(ii) the extent of preparation necessary;

(iii) the conduct of the defence;

(iv) the extent to which the prosecution was dependent on the co-operation of others outside its control; and

(v) any other matter directly and genuinely bearing on the preparation of the case for trial

in deciding whether the prosecution has acted with due expedition (*R. v. Manchester Crown Court, ex p. McDonald* [1999 1 All E.R. 805).

2–23 The words "the prosecution" in section 22(3) mean those responsible for the conduct of the prosecution before the magistrates' court, whether the police or the Crown Prosecution Service, and collectively they are "the prosecution" for the purposes of the section. The question of whether there is delay or whether, under section 22(3), the prosecution have acted with due expedition is a question of fact in each individual case (*R. v. Birmingham Crown Court, ex p. Ricketts* [1991] R.T.R. 105).

2–24 The words "an offence" in section 22 of the Act, and regulation 4 of the 1987 regulations should be given its ordinary natural meaning: they do not mean a set of facts upon which a charge is based, and for this reason each separate offence laid against an accused attracts its own custody time limit (*R. v. Waltham Forest Justices, ex p. Lee* (1993) 157 J.P. 811, and *R. v. Wolverhampton Justices and Stafford Crown Court, ex p. Uppal* (1995) 159 J.P. 86). Thus, if an accused is charged with several offences on different occasions in the same proceedings separate custody time limits apply to each offence (*R. v. Wirral District Magistrates' Court, ex p. Meikle* (1990) 154 J.P. 1035).

2–25 "Satisfied" in section 22 of the 1985 Act means satisfied on the balance of probabilities, and not beyond reasonable doubt (*R. v. Governor of Canterbury Prison, ex p. Craig*, above).

(c) CONSIDERATIONS FOR GRANTING AN EXTENSION OF THE TIME LIMITS

2–26 In considering whether or not to grant an extension justices should remember that it is for the prosecution to satisfy the court on the balance of probabilities that both statutory conditions in section 22(3) have been met (see §2–18, above). Only if the court is so satisfied is there then the discretion to grant the application. The consideration of any application to extend custody time limits requires careful consideration and rigorous scrutiny (*R. v. Manchester Crown Court, ex p. Mcdonald*, above).

The first question is whether the prosecution have complied with the regulations in giving the requisite notice of their intention to seek an extension. If proper notice has been given then the court is obliged to rule on the application, applying the law summarised above. If the prosecution have not given proper notice then the court is obliged to rule on the preliminary issue of whether it is satisfied on the balance of probabilities that it was not practicable for the prosecution to give the requisite notice, and if so whether, in the court's discretion, the prosecution should be allowed to dispense with the notice (*R. v. Governor of Canterbury Prison, ex p. Craig* [1991] 2 Q.B. 195). This preliminary question must be decided with reference to the whole background to the case, and not simply with reference to the circumstances pertaining at the time of the application. However, even if the court decides that it was practical for notice to have been given, the court may still consider the merits of an application to extend the time limits because regulation 7 is directory and not mandatory (*R. v. Governor of Canterbury Prison*, above).

On the merits of an application the court may consider the nature, extent and complexity of the case generally (*R. v. Norwich Crown Court, ex p. Smith*, June 25, 1991, (unreported)), but the history of the case must be measured against an objective yardstick and the police are not entitled to claim staff shortages as a reason for delay (*R. v. Governor of Winchester Prison ex p. Roddie* [1991] 1 W.L.R. 303). Although the prosecution are not required to act as if the observance of the time limits were their only consideration, the phrase "with all due expedition" connotes that which is appropriate in the circumstances.

CONSIDERATIONS AT PRE-COMMITTAL STAGE

2–27 At pre-committal stage the prosecution must conduct themselves within the framework of the custody time limits. This means that the prosecution should be prepared to achieve, if necessary, a section 6(1) committal within the period; the prosecution may not work to a deadline permitting only a committal under section 6(2) (*R. v. Leeds Crown Court, ex p. Briggs* (1998) 162 J.P. 623). The judgment of the Divisional Court in that case considered that there was no conflict in the dicta of two previous cases on the duty of the prosecution at pre-committal stage. The decision in *R. v. Norwich Crown Court, ex p. Parker and Ward* (1992) 156 J.P. 818 should not be taken to mean that in all cases the prosecution succeed in complying with the time limits simply by preparing themselves for a section 6(2) committal. The decision in *ex p. Parker and Ward* did not conflict with that of *R. v. Central Criminal Court, ex p. Bebbebani* [1994] Crim.L.R. 352 when it was said that when the prosecution case depended substantially on an exhibit or exhibits there was a duty upon the prosecution to serve the evidence, *i.e.* the exhibit evidence, or an intelligible copy, in adequate time for the defence to be able to decide what type of committal is appropriate. In that case the accused was awaiting a committal hearing on a charge of blackmail where part of the evidence consisted of a tape recording of a telephone conversation in a foreign language. Copies of the tape were not made available to the defence by the date fixed for the committal. It was held by the Divisional Court that justices had been correct to refuse an extension of the custody time-limits because a reasonable prosecutor must have appreciated that the defence would need to listen to and evaluate the tape, and as service could have occurred sooner the prosecution had not acted with due expedition.

IMPACT OF HUMAN RIGHTS ACT 1998

2–28 Remands in custody and custody time limits will have to be read in the light of Article 5(3) of the Convention which provides that "everyone … shall be brought promptly before a judge or other officer authorised by law to exercise judicial power and shall be entitled to trial within a reasonable time or release pending trial".

The Divisional Court considered Article 5 of the Convention in *R. v. Manchester Crown Court, ex p. Mcdonald* (see §§2–22—2–26, above). The Court also considered a number of cases decided by the European Court, notably *Wemhoff v. Germany* (1968) 1 E.H.R.R. 55, *Stogmuller v. Austria* (1969) 1 E.H.R.R. 155 and *Zimmerman and Steiner v. Switzerland* (1983) 6 E.H.R.R. 17. The Divisional Court concluded that there did not appear to be anything in English statutory or common law which conflicted with the provisions of Aricle 5, as interpreted by those cases.

6. Pre-Trial Remands on Bail

2–29 The period of such remand on bail may be for any period to which the parties consent (MCA 1980, s.128(6)). The words "on bail" mean bail in fact. If, therefore, an accused has been granted bail by the court but sureties have not entered into recognisances, then the rules as to remands in custody will apply.

Recently, there has been a tendency in practice for the parties to seek longer remand periods than the court regards as just. This is partly due to the provisions of advance information, and partly to the requirements of the Crown Prosecution Service. The court is not bound to agree to the suggested remand date of the parties and the court may require them to be ready sooner if the interests of justice demand an earlier remand date.

If the accused is unable by reason of accident or illness to appear before the court on the remand date then he may be remanded to another date in his absence. However, the court must be satisfied that it is either illness or accident which is preventing the accused answering his bail, and the court will usually require some evidence on the point (MCA 1980, s.129). When exercising remand powers under section 129(1) of the Magistrates' Courts Act 1980 the court must be "satisfied" in the sense of there being solid grounds, on the facts, for forming an opinion that the accused is unable to be brought before the court by reason of illness or accident (*R. v. Liverpool City Justices, ex p. Grogan* (1991) 155 J.P. 450). In that case it was held that the stipendiary magistrate should not have assumed that it was because of widely publicised disturbances at a remand centre that the accused was not produced. The failure of the prison authorities to produce a prisoner is not an "accident" for these purposes. If the accused is on bail with sureties then such sureties may be enlarged in the absence of the sureties also (MCA 1980, s.129(3)).

7. Remand During a Trial

2–30 Once a court has begun to try summarily an indictable offence or is sitting as examining justices the powers of remand are the same as when a court is sitting at the pre-trial stage. This is because the particular remand powers given to a court in sections 5, 10 and 18 of the Magistrates' Courts Act 1980 are all subject to the general remand provisions contained in sections 128 to 131 of the Act. The important aspects of these provisions have been discussed in the preceding paragraphs and it is unnecessary to repeat them.

There are only two outstanding matters not previously discussed:

(i) where the court, containing only one justice and sitting as an examining justice, forms the opinion that the case is more suitable for summary trial, then if the accused is in custody and it is not possible to convene a full bench of justices within the eight-day period the accused may be remanded for longer than eight days (MCA 1980, s.128(6)(c));

(ii) where the court is trying an information and the accused appears but the prosecutor does not,

then if the court decides to remand the case further it shall not remand the accused in custody unless he was originally brought from custody or he cannot be remanded on bail by reason of his failure to find sureties (MCA 1980, s.15).

In practice the exercise of these powers will be rare, as will the exercise of remand powers once a trial has commenced. Usually the parties will have set the trial down for a period of days, if the matter is lengthy, and the court will formally remand from day to day until the hearing is concluded.

8. Granting of Adjournments in Summary Trial

2–31 It frequently happens that one or other of the parties is not ready on the date when a summary trial has been fixed, often because a witness for the prosecution or defence is absent, and justices are called upon to grant or refuse an adjournment. While the consideration of adjournments is pre-eminently a matter of discretion, there has grown up a body of case law which governs the exercise of this discretion. It has been said that justices have a duty to pay attention to the need for expedition in the prosecution of criminal cases (*R. v. Aberdare Justices, ex p. D.P.P.* (1991) 155 J.P. 324), and that applications for adjournments must be subjected to rigorous scrutiny (*R. v. Hereford Magistrates' Court, ex p. Rowlands and Ingram* (1997) 161 J.P. 258). The principles governing adjournments are explained below.

(i) The Statutory Framework

2–32 As the jurisdiction of the magistrates' court is derived entirely from statute, justices are bound to comply with sections 9, 10 and 15 of the Magistrates' Courts Act 1980 when considering adjournments, in particular section 9(2) of the 1980 Act which provides that a court shall dismiss an information only "after hearing the evidence of the parties." If, of course, a bench of two are sitting and are unable to agree whether to convict or acquit there is no alternative but to adjourn so that a new bench can re-try the case (*R. v. Redbridge Justices, ex p. Ram* [1992] 1 Q.B. 384). The statutory framework means that if the prosecution are refused an adjournment the court must nevertheless still invite the prosecutor to present any evidence he wishes (*Harrington v. Roots* (1984) 149 J.P. 211). If the prosecution's application for an adjournment is refused, the proper course is for the chairman to announce that the application for an adjournment is refused, and then to say to the prosecutor "Do you wish to call evidence?" If the prosecutor is unable to call evidence he should offer no evidence, and then the information may properly be dismissed in accordance with section 9(2) of the 1980 Act. Where the accused has been tried upon two informations, which are in the alternative, and he is convicted on one of them, the proper course is for the prosecution to withdraw the remaining charge because justices may not dismiss it in view of section 9(2) (*D.P.P. v. Gane* [1991] Crim.L.R. 711).

Accordingly, if after several abortive hearings justices are of the opinion that it would be unjust for the prosecution to continue, the information may not be dismissed on that ground alone (*R. v. Birmingham Justices, ex p. Lamb* [1983] 1 W.L.R. 339). Justices may not dismiss a case simply because the accused is not produced for his trial because he is in custody for another offence (*R. v. Merthyr Tydfil Justices, ex p. D.P.P.* [1989] Crim.L.R. 148), nor because the bench consider a trial is unnecessary because the accused has already been in custody on remand (*R. v. Watford Justices, ex p. D.P.P.* [1990] R.T.R. 374). Similarly, justices may not dismiss an information on the grounds of "want of prosecution" without going into the history of the case and without hearing evidence simply because the bench is frustrated by numerous previous adjournments (*R. v. Crawley Justices, ex p. D.P.P.* (1991) 155 J.P. 841). On the same principles justices may not dismiss an information simply because they suspect a fair trial might not be possible because a prosecution witness was seen to converse with a defence witness before the commencement of the trial (*R. v. Dorchester Magistrates' Court, ex p. D.P.P.* (1990) 154 J.P. 211).

In all the above examples justices fell into elementary error by failing to observe the statutory framework, and accordingly the purported dismissals were a nullity.

2–33 The Crown Prosecution Service have consistently challenged erroneous dismissals of informations by taking proceedings in the Divisional Court (*R. v. Sutton Justices, ex p. D.P.P.* [1992] 2 All E.R. 130, *R. v. Dudley Justices, ex p. D.P.P.* (1992) 156 J.P.N. 618, *R. v. Hendon Justices, ex p. D.P.P.* (1993) 157 J.P. 181 and *R. v. Parker and the Barnet Magistrates' Court, ex p. D.P.P.* (1994) 158 J.P. 1060). In each of the above cases justices had dismissed informations where the prosecutor, either a solicitor or counsel on behalf of the Crown prosecution Service, was not present in court when the case was ready to be heard.

(i) In *Sutton Justices* the court had been informed that counsel for the prosecution would be 20 to 30 minutes late. When he arrived at 10.40 a.m. he found that the case had been dismissed by justices at 10.30 a.m. for want of prosecution. The Divisional Court held that on the information available the arrival of counsel was reasonably imminent, and therefore the Bench acted peremptorily and wrongly in dismissing the information. Further, it was held that it was a wrong exercise of the discretion to use the power to dismiss an information as a way of disciplining the Crown Prosecution Service. In the judgment of Brooke J., however, considerable sympathy was expressed for Benches who suffer from delay and inefficiency, and specific attention was drawn to the Code of Conduct of the Bar in relation to the late return of briefs which was the cause of counsel's delay in the first place. This aspect of the judgment is discussed further at §11–45, below.

(ii) In *Dudley Justices* the Divisional Court held that the Bench had acted unfairly when, knowing that a case had been wrongly listed and that the arrival of the prosecutor was imminent, it nevertheless went on to dismiss an information.

(iii) In *Hendon Justices* the prosecutor was not present in court when the trial was due to commence due to a listing error. Informations against the accused were dismissed at 11.30 a.m. It was held that that decision was so unreasonable that no reasonable Bench could have come to it. The duty of the court was to hear informations which were properly before it. The prosecution had a right to be heard, and save in exceptional circumstances it should be heard. The Divisional Court went further and granted *mandamus* to the prosecution requiring that the informations be heard in a new trial.

(iv) In *Barnet Magistrates' Court* a summary trial had been listed for 10.00 am but, in error, the Crown Prosecution Service had been told by the court that the case was listed at 2.00 p.m. No prosecution witnesses had appeared by noon when justices refused an adjournment until the aftenoon. The Divisional Court held that the decision was perverse.

(ii) Considerations for the Exercise of Discretion

2–34 Justices must balance the interests of society that the guilty should be convicted with the interests of the accused in having to attend court unnecessarily (*R. v. Aberdare Justices, ex p. D.P.P.* (1991) 155 J.P. 324). In general if, in all the circumstances, there is a risk of unfairness to the accused if an adjournment is refused then it should be granted (*R. v. Kingston-upon-Hull Justices, ex p. McCann* (1991) 155 J.P. 569).

All the circumstances of the case must be considered, in particular:

(a) the practicality of one side or the other putting forward their case adequately if the adjournment were refused;

(b) the passage of time;

(c) whether it was the first application for an adjournment or whether there had been previous adjournments;

(d) whether the party asking for the adjournment was at fault in not being able to proceed (*R. v. Swansea Justices, ex p. D.P.P.* (1990) 154 J.P. 709).

However, every case depends upon its own facts, and the above points should not be regarded as guidelines, but merely issues for consideration.

(a) GENERAL CONSIDERATIONS

2–35 It is not permissible for justices to adjourn a trial from the day on which it was listed to another day simply because on the adjourned date the law would be changed, for example when a new Act of Parliament would be in force (*R. v. Walsall Justices, ex p. W. (a Minor)* [1990] 1 Q.B. 253). In that case the Divisional Court quashed the justices' decision to adjourn a trial for one day by which time section 34 of the Criminal Justice Act 1988, relating to the admissibility of the uncorroborated evidence of children, would have been in force.

If a case is likely to take a number of days, which are spread over such a long period that justice may not be seen to be done, it is not improper to discontinue the hearing, and adjourn the whole case to be heard by a new bench on consecutive days (*R. v. Ripon Liberty Justices, ex p. Bugg* (1991) 155 J.P. 213).

Where on a previous occasion justices have indicated that the case must proceed on the next occasion, this cannot inhibit a further application being made for an adjournment at the next hearing. Such further application must be considered on its merits, having regard to all the relevant circumstances including the justices' earlier indication (*R. v. Aberdare Justices*, above).

While it is frequently frustrating to a bench to grant adjournments when court and bench time is thereby wasted, there is scope now to penalise in costs either the party or the legal representative whose fault the adjournment has been. These powers are discussed fully in Chapter 8, below.

(b) CONSIDERATIONS WHEN THE PROSECUTION ASK FOR AN ADJOURNMENT

2–36 If a prosecution witness is absent without good reason the prosecutor should be given a reasonable period in which to make inquiries. It has been held that justices were wrong to dismiss an information at 10.35 a.m. when police officers could have been at court at 11.00 a.m. for a trial scheduled to last one day (*R. v. Swansea Justices*, above). Similarly, if a police officer is unavoidably required at a Crown Court or other superior court on the day of the trial, justices should look sympathetically at the Crown's application for an adjournment (*R. v. Aberdare Justices*, above). In any event the refusal of a prosecution application should never be on the basis of a desire to punish slackness on the part of the prosecution.

In considering all the circumstances of the case it is submitted that there can be no objection to justices (or their clerk) making general inquiries about the evidence; for example, whether the absent witness is merely corroborative of another witness, or whether parts of his evidence may be agreed, providing these inquiries would not prejudice a fair trial in the event of an adjournment being refused.

(c) CONSIDERATIONS WHEN THE DEFENCE ASK FOR AN ADJOURNMENT

2–37 Different considerations obviously arise when the defence apply for an adjournment because there is no duty of disclosure by the defence of their case. It is, therefore, much more difficult for the bench to assess whether an absent witness is really vital or not to the defence case, particularly as the defence advocate may feel inhibited in revealing what the absent witness is likely to say. For these reasons it has been held that the proper course is for the clerk to inquire as to the prejudice which would be caused to the defence if the adjournment were refused, and to advise the bench accordingly (*R. v. Bracknell Justices, ex p. Hughes* (1990) 154 J.P.N. 46). In that case the Divisional Court held that justices were wrong to refuse a defence application for an adjournment when a defence witness, a barrister who was engaged at the Crown Court, was unable to be present as on the facts he was potentially an independent witness to a public order incident. The decision in *ex p. Hughes* has recently been re-stated on the principle that the accused may not receive a fair trial if an independent witness is unavoidably absent (*R. v. Hereford Magistrates' Court, ex p. Rowlands and Ingram* (1997) 161 J.P. 258).

In general where an accused is unfit to attend his trial, and such unfitness is supported by medical evidence, an adjournment should be granted to enable him to attend (*R. v. Bolton Justices, ex p. Merna* (1991) 155 J.P. 612). In that case justices had become frustrated by repeated adjournments at the defence's request caused by alleged anxiety on the part of the accused, but the Divisional Court held that an adjournment had been wrongly refused on the final trial date because a medical certificate produced by the defence had not been challenged.

Where, however, the reason for a defendant's absence on the day of trial is unmeritorious it may be proper to proceed in his absence under the provisions of section 11 of the Magistrates' Courts Act 1980 (*R. v. Bolton Justices*, above). In addition if an accused is deliberately seeking to postpone a trial without good reason justices should refuse an adjournment (*R. v. Macclesfield Justices, ex p. Jones* [1983] R.T.R. 143).

IMPACT OF HUMAN RIGHTS ACT 1998

2–38 The law and practice in relation to the granting of adjournments will have to be read in the light of Article 6 (3)(b) which provides that everyone shall have adequate time and facilities for the preparation of his defence. Strictly, Article 6 applies only to the process of "determination" but pre-trial procedures, such as adjournments, have been held to come within the provisions of the Article (*Quaranta v. Switzerland* (1991) Series A No. 205). It has been held by the European Court that the very late receipt of instructions by an advocate who is thereby disadvantaged in preparing the defence should lead to the grant of an adjournment (*Goddi v. Italy* (1984) 6 E.H.R.R. 457).

If an advocate is prevented by circumstances such as late instructions or by a late return of a brief from being able properly to represent an accused person, Article 6 (3)(c) may be breached. The words "legal assistance" in this Article means that the accused must have an opportunity to organise his defence in an appropriate manner (*Can v. Austria* (1985) 8 E.H.R.R. 121). In this respect there would seem to be little difference between Strasbourg jurisprudence and English common law on this point.

9. Remand for Sentence after Conviction

2–39 If the court wishes inquiries to be made in order to decide the most suitable method of dealing with a case, the court may adjourn, by way of a remand, the question of sentence (MCA 1980, s.10(3)). In practice this power is used frequently in order to obtain a pre-sentence report. Such remands shall not be for more than three weeks at a time if the accused is remanded in custody or four weeks at a time if he is on bail (MCA 1980, s.10(3)).

Unless the powers given under section 10 of the Magistrates' Courts Act 1980 are used, it is bad practice to postpone sentence generally (*R. v. Easterling* (1946) 175 L.T. 520). The powers available under section 10 must be exercised judicially. For example, it is a wrong use of the powers to adjourn sentence on a young person for no other purpose than to ensure that by the time sentence is passed an accused will have reached the age of 21, thereby giving the court greater sentencing powers (*Arthur v. Stringer* (1987) 84 Cr.App.R. 360).

PROCEDURE WHEN THE COURT ORDERS A PRE-SENTENCE REPORT

2–40 The use of a remand for sentence after conviction is one of the most widely used powers of justices particularly since it became mandatory under the Criminal Justice Act 1991 for a magistrates' court to obtain and consider a pre-sentence report before forming an opinion as to the seriousness of the offence (CJA 1991, s.3(1)).

The pre-sentence report must be served upon the prosecutor (C(S)A 1997, s.50). The reason for this requirement is to enable the prosecution to challenge misleading or inaccurate information which may be placed before the court or to challenge derogatory assertions which may be prohibited under the provisions in sections 58 to 60 of the Criminal Procedure and Investigations Act 1996. (See further in §13–27, below).

It is no longer mandatory for justices to obtain and consider a report before passing a custodial sentence because a custodial sentence may be passed if, in the circumstances of the case, the court is of the opinion that it is unnecessary to obtain a report (CJA 1991, s.3(2), as amended by CJ and POA 1994, s.168 and para. 40 of Sched. 9). The effect of this amendment is to allow the court to pass a custodial sentence without obtaining a report if the court is of the opinion that it is unnecessary to do so. It is submitted that there must be some material before the court, either in the form of the obvious and transparent seriousness of the offence or in the nature of the offender's previous history, which would entitle the court to conclude that it is unnecessary to obtain and consider a report before passing a custodial sentence.

For the above reasons it is submitted that justices will, in most cases, wish to continue to adjourn sentence and order a report from the probation service before forming a final opinion as to the seriousness of the offence and the disposal in terms of sentence.

THE GILLAM PRINCIPLE

2–41 Whenever such an adjournment occurs it is vital that the offender is not given an expectation, by the fact that a pre-sentence report has been ordered, that a non-custodial disposal will eventually take place (*R. v. Gillam* (1980) 2 Cr.App.R. (S.) 267). In that case the Court of Appeal (Criminal Division) quashed a sentence of imprisonment imposed by a Crown Court judge because in ordering a report for an alternative to custody to be explored a legitimate expectation had been raised in the offender's mind that if the report was favourable a non-custodial sentence would follow. This principle, which has become known as "the Gillam principle", has been applied strictly to magistrates' court practice (see *Gutteridge v. D.P.P.* (1987) 9 Cr.App.R. (S.) 279, and *R. v. Inner London Crown Court, ex p. McCann* (1990) 154 J.P. 917). In each case the Divisional Court quashed a custodial sentence because a legitimate expectation of a non-custodial sentence had been given by the stipendiary magistrate when ordering a report before deciding on the sentence to be passed.

2–42 The application of "the Gillam principle" still applies following the statutory framework applicable to the ordering of reports under the Criminal Justice Act 1991 (*R. v. Chamberlain* (1995) 16 Cr.App.R.(S.) 473). In that case a recorder at the Crown Court had adjourned sentence for a pre-sentence report to be prepared, and on the next occasion further adjourned sentence so that a probation order with a specific requirement could be explored. The offender was then sentenced by a circuit judge who imposed a custodial sentence of 18 months' imprisonment. The Court of Appeal (Criminal Division) quashed the sentence and substituted a community penalty holding that nothing had been said by the recorder to displace an expectation by the offender that a non-custodial penalty would be imposed if the offender was suitable for probation with a specific requirement.

This decision is important because two earlier cases, *R. v. Woodin* (1993) 15 Cr.App.R. (S.) 307, and *R. v. Renan* (1994) 15 Cr.App.R. (S.) 722, had suggested that the "Gillam principle" had been watered down following the statutory framework created by the 1991 Act. This would appear not to be so, particularly since the amendments made to the 1991 Act by paragraph 40 of Schedule 9 of the Criminal Justice and Public Order Act 1994 (see §2.40, above). It is submitted that the best practice is for justices to continue to apply "the Gillam principle" and that an offender should invariably be told in clear terms that the fact that sentence is being adjourned for further assessment or investigation does not mean that a particular form of sentence or penalty will necessarily be imposed.

10. Remand for Medical Examination

2–43   The powers available to a court when the court is of the opinion that an inquiry ought to be made into the accused's physical or mental condition are wide. They arise under the provisions of section 30 of the Magistrates' Courts Act 1980, and are discussed fully at §7–14, below dealing with mentally disordered offenders.

CHAPTER 3

Bail

A. THE APPLICATION FOR BAIL

3–01   The law governing the grant of bail in magistrates' courts is to be found in the Bail Act 1976, although this Act has since been considerably amended to take into account changes introduced by later statutes, notably the Magistrates' Courts Act 1980 the Criminal Justice Acts 1988 and 1991, the Criminal Justice and Public Order Act 1994 and the Crime and Disorder Act 1998. The changes wrought in these statutes are such that the purpose and intention of the Bail Act 1976 as originally drafted are almost unrecognisable.

The Bail Act was introduced following a Home Office Working Party on bail procedure in 1974, and the purpose of the Act was to seek to reduce the number of persons remanded in custody to a minimum. This was sought to be done by creating a statutory right to bail for all unconvicted defendants, and to lay down defined exceptions to bail which must be specifically applied if bail is to be refused. This fundamental principle has now been undermined by the Criminal Justice and Public Order Act 1994 which, as amended, introduces a statutory presumption against to the right to bail (see below).

References in this Chapter are to the Bail Act 1976 as amended, unless otherwise stated.

1. Presumptions Against the Grant of Bail

3–02   There is a presumption against the grant of bail to any person to whom section 25 of the Criminal Justice and Public Order Act 1994 as amended by section 56 of the Crime and Disorder Act 1998 applies.

The presumption is that in relation to the circumstances listed below the person shall be granted bail only if the court, or as the case may be, the constable considering the grant of bail is satisfied that there are exceptional circumstances which justify it (CJ and POA 1994, s.25 as substituted by CDA 1998, s.56).

The circumstances are:

   (i) that the person is charged or convicted with one of the following offences (CJ and POA 1994, s.25(1));

   (ii) that the offence or offences consist of or include—

      (a) murder;
      (b) attempted murder;
      (c) manslaughter;
      (d) rape; or
      (e) attempted rape (*ibid.*, s.25(2)), and

   (iii) that the person has been previously convicted of any such offence (or that of culpable homicide in Scotland) in any court in the United Kingdom providing that if the conviction was for manslaughter or culpable homicide the conviction resulted in a sentence of imprisonment or long-term detention (*ibid.*, s.25(3).

This restriction which replaced the absolute prohibition on the grant of bail in serious cases was undoubtedly introduced by Parliament in order to comply with the European Convention on Human Rights and the Human Rights Act 1998. See generally Chapter 24, below.

2. General Right to Bail for Unconvicted Defendants

3–03   Subject to section 25 of the Criminal Justice and Public Order Act 1994 (see above) any person who is accused of an offence and is brought before a magistrates' court shall be granted bail whether or not that person applies for bail (s.4). Furthermore, that bail shall be unconditional unless one or more of the necessary requirements set out at §§3–14 to 3–17—conditional bail—apply.

The provisions of section 4 of the Bail Act 1976 now assume a greater significance following the changes introduced in April 1995 enabling the police to grant conditional bail at a police station. The fact that an accused person may have been refused bail by the police does not detract from his right to bail (subject to section 25) on his first appearance at the magistrates' court. The duty of the court is to consider whether any of the exceptions to the right to apply, and the court should not be influenced by the fact that the accused had previously been refused bail at a police station. The Criminal Justice and Public Order Act 1994 has introduced a procedure of appeal to a magistrates' court if an accused is dissatisfied with any conditions of bail imposed at a police station and these are dealt with below at §3–40. In the light of these changes section 4 has been amended to include an accused person's right to bail at the magistrates' court when applying for a variation of conditions of bail imposed at a police station (s.4(2)(b)).

The general right to bail is subject to the following exceptions:

(i) Exceptions which apply in all cases

3–04   The defendant need not be granted bail if:

(a) he has previously been released on bail in the same proceedings and has been arrested for absconding whilst on bail or breaking his conditions of bail (para. 6 of Part I and para. 5 of Part II, Sched. 1);

(b) the court is satisfied that the defendant should be kept in custody for his own protection or if he is a child or young person for his own welfare (para. 3 of Part I and para. 3 of Part III, Sched. 1);

(c) the defendant is in custody in pursuance of a sentence of a court (para. 4 of Part I and para. 4 of Part II, Sched. 1).

(ii) Exceptions which apply in imprisonable offences only

3–05   If the court is satisfied that there are substantial grounds for believing that the defendant, if released on bail (whether subject to conditions or not) would:

(a) fail to surrender to custody (para. 2(a) of Part I, Sched. 1), or

(b) commit an offence whilst on bail (para. 2(b) of Part I, Sched. 1), or

(c) interfere with witnesses or otherwise obstruct the course of justice (para. 2(c) of Part I, Sched. 1)

bail may be refused.

In addition the defendant need not be granted bail if—

(a) the offence is an indictable offence or an offence triable either way; and

(b) it appears to the court that he was on bail in criminal proceedings on the date of the offence (para. 2A of Part I, Sched. 1).

This amendment, which was inserted by section 26 of the Criminal Justice and Public Order Act 1994, applies if the defendant was in fact arrested for an indictable only or either way offence whilst already on bail, and the court may refuse bail on this ground alone irrespective of whether there is a fear of further offences.

Despite this amendment grounds (a), (b) or (c) above will remain the most common grounds of refusing bail in practice, and are often referred to in court (by reference to Sched. 1) as "2(a), 2(b), 2(c)." Their importance is further underlined when one considers the Conditions of Bail in section 3 of the Act (see §3–14, below). Conditions of bail (other than sureties or the deposit of a security) may only be imposed to *prevent* a defendant (a) failing to surrender, (b) committing a further offence, or (c) interfering with witnesses or otherwise obstructing the course of justice.

(iii) Exceptions Which Apply in Non-Imprisonable Offences Only

3–06   The defendant need not be granted bail if:

(a) he has previously failed to answer bail; *and*

(b) the court believes that if released he would fail to surrender to custody (para. 2 of Part II, Sched. 1).

(iv) General exception if no information

3–07   In *imprisonable* offences the defendant need not be granted bail if the court is satisfied that it has not been practical since the proceedings were instituted to obtain sufficient information to take the bail decision (para. 5 of Part I, Sched. 1).

A remand in custody under para. 5 of Part I, Sched. 1 is not a hearing at which the court decides not to grant bail under Part IIA of Schedule 1 of the Act, discussed at §3–29, below (*R. v. Calder Justices, ex p. Kennedy* (1992) 156 J.P. 716). Accordingly, for the purposes of calculating the number of applications an accused is entitled to make without fresh circumstances arising, a remand under para. 5 must be ignored.

3. No General Right to Bail for Convicted Defendants

3–08   The general right to bail does not apply as respects proceedings on or after a person is convicted of the offence (s.4(2)).

Exception

3–09   A convicted person *does* have a right to bail if he is brought before the court to be dealt with under Part II of Schedule 2 to the Criminal Justice Act 1991 (breach of requirement of a Probation, Community Service or Combination Order (s.4(3)).

A convicted person *does* have a right to bail if his case is adjourned for the purpose of obtaining reports (s.4(4)).

These cases are subject to the same exceptions as stated at §§3–03 to 3–06 above, but *in addition* if the offence is imprisonable the defendant need not be granted bail if it appears to the court that it would be impracticable to complete the inquiries or make the report without keeping the defendant in custody (para. 7 of Part I, Sched. 1).

It follows from this that there is *no right to bail* in the following instances:

— appeal against conviction

— appeal against sentence

— committal for sentence

— appeal by way of judicial review or case stated.

Whether bail is granted in such cases is discretionary but the Act specifically states there is no right to bail for fugitive offenders or those charged with treason (s.4(7)).

4. The Considerations Applying to a Decision on Bail

3–10   In taking the decision to grant unconditional bail or to refuse bail for *imprisonable* offences the court shall have regard to all or any of the following considerations:

(a) the nature and seriousness of the offence or default (and the probable method of dealing with the defendant for it);

(b) the character, antecedents, association and community ties of the defendant;

(c) the defendant's previous record in respect of fulfilling his obligations when granted bail previously;

(d) the strength of the evidence against him of having committed the offence for which he is charged (para. 9 of Part I, Sched. 1).

In addition, if the court is to use its powers under section 128A of the Magistrates' Courts Act 1980 (see §2–11, above) and is considering a remand in custody of more than eight clear days, the court must have regard to the total length of time the accused would spend in custody if it were to exercise that power (para. 9B of Part 1, Sched. 1). Paragraph 9 of Schedule 1 also deals with the procedure so far as certain very serious offences are concerned. This is dealt with at §3–19, below).

3–11   If, having considered these factors, the court is of the opinion that there are no substantial grounds for believing that if released on bail the accused would, either:

(a) fail to surrender; or

(b) commit an offence on bail; or

(c) interfere with witnesses or obstruct the course of justice;

then the court must grant the accused unconditional bail (para. 8 of Part 1, Sched. 1).

5. Circumstances when Conditional Bail may be Imposed

(i) Conditions may only be Imposed if it is Necessary

3–12 Before imposing conditions the court must consider whether it is necessary to do so. Only if it appears to the court that it is necessary to prevent the occurrence of, either:

(a) failure to surrender; or

(b) the commission of an offence on bail; or

(c) an interference with witnesses, or obstructions of justice;

may the court impose any of the above conditions (para. 8(1) of Part I, Sched. 1). If the accused is released on bail on condition that he makes himself available for reports to be prepared under section 3(6)(d) of the Act, no further conditions may be imposed unless it is necessary for the purpose of enabling enquiries or a report to be made (*ibid.*, para. 8(1A)). This rule does not apply, however, if the accused is released on bail in a murder case and medical reports are ordered (see §3–19, below or the accused is mentally disordered and is remanded for reports on bail under section 30(2) of the Magistrates' Courts Act 1980 (see §7–14, below) (*ibid.*, para. 8(3)).

(ii) Definition of Conditional Bail

3–13 The conditions open to the court are defined as follows:

(a) the provision of a surety or sureties (s.3(4));

(b) the deposit of a security (s.3(5) as amended by CDA 1998, s.54(1));

(c) the imposition of other requirements which the court considers necessary to secure that:

— he surrenders to custody,
— he does not commit an offence whilst on bail,
— he does not interfere with witnesses or otherwise obstruct the course of justice, and *if a convicted person*,
— he makes himself available for the preparation of reports,
— he attends an interview with an authorised advocate or authorised litigator (s.3(6) as inserted by CDA 1998, s.54(2)).
— in addition if he is required to reside in a bail hostel or a probation hostel there may be a condition that he complies with the rules of the hostel (s.3(6) and (6ZA)).

3–14 The correct test in considering whether conditions should be imposed under section 3(6) is for the court to ask itself the question: "Is this condition necessary for the prevention of the commission of an offence by the defendant when on bail?" Conditions may be imposed if there is a real, and not a fanciful, risk of an offence being committed. In considering this question justices may apply their local knowledge, and there do not have to be substantial grounds for believing that conditions are necessary (*R. v. Mansfield Justices, ex p. Sharkey* [1985] Q.B. 613).

The general and undefined other requirements give the court wide scope. Commonly-used requirements are the imposition of a curfew where the accused has a record of committing offences at night, or the surrender of the accused's passport to ensure that he does not leave the country during the bail period.

If it is appropriate to impose conditional bail it does not matter whether the offence charged is imprisonable or non-imprisonable. However, if when the conditions are announced the accused states that he will not observe them he may not then and there be remanded in custody. The proper course is to allow the accused an opportunity to comply with the conditions, and if he does not there are ample powers of arrest under section 7 of the Bail Act. (*R. v. Bournemouth Justices, ex p. Cross and Others* (1989) 89 Cr.App.R. 90).

DEPOSIT OF A SECURITY

3–15   Section 54 of the Crime and Disorder Act 1998 has introduced an important change in relation to the powers of the court to require a security as a condition of bail. Originally, the requirement of a security was rare because it was confined to circumstances when there was fear that the accused might leave the United Kingdom. In this latest amendment to the Bail Act 1976 justices enjoy a complete discretion as to requiring a surety or security or a security in addition to a surety, providing the correct test for imposing a condition is applied.

ATTENDING FOR INTERVIEW WITH A SOLICITOR

3–16   This condition of bail was inserted by Parliament in the Crime and Disorder Act 1998 in a direct attempt to reduce delay in the magistrates' courts following a review of delay generally in the criminal justice system conducted by the Home Office. The Circular accompanying the 1998 Act (HO 34/1998) recognised that solicitors could not be expected to report breaches to the court, nor would breaches of this condition necessarily lead to arrests. The purpose is to permit courts to adopt a "robust approach" and order that a defendant seek an interview with a duty solicitor immediately at court if the accused had previously failed to keep an appointment with another solicitor. As such a "robust approach" is suggested only in a Circular it does not have the force of law and only time will tell how efficacious this latest condition of bail will prove to be.

(iii) Considerations if condition is to be a surety

3–17   The court has wide scope for imposing conditions and the most usual condition is the provision of a surety or sureties.

In considering whether any proposed surety is suitable the court may have regard to:

(a) the surety's financial resources;

(b) his character and any previous conviction; and

(c) his proximity whether in point of kinship, place, residence or otherwise to the person for whom he is to be surety (s.8).

It has been said that there is a particular responsibility upon the legal profession to ensure that a surety would, if necessary, be able to meet his financial obligations before he is tendered to the court (*R. v. Birmingham Crown Court, ex p. Rashid Ali and Another* [1999] Crim.L.R. 504).

6. Reasons to be Given in Bail Decisions

(i) Reasons must be given if unconditional bail is not granted

3–18   If bail is refused, or conditions are attached, or conditions are varied, then reasons for the decision must be noted and given in open court to enable the accused to consider an appeal against the refusal of bail (s.5(3) and (4)).

In addition to this general requirement, if an accused is unrepresented he must be told of his right to apply for bail from the High Court or the Crown Court (s.5(6)). Although reasons need not be given if the accused is granted unconditional bail, it is good practice for the court to inform him of his duties whilst on bail and to point out the consequences of failing to surrender.

(ii) Reasons must be given for granting bail in serious cases

3–19   The serious cases to which the following rules apply are:

— murder

— manslaughter

— rape

— attempted murder

— attempted rape.

If the court decides to grant bail to a defendant charged with any of the above offences despite objections to bail based on grounds 2(a), (b) or (c) (see above), the court must state the reasons for its decision and those reasons must be recorded (§9A, Part I, Sched. 1).

7. Special Provisions as to Bail

(i) Defendants charged with murder

3–20   The court is obliged to attach conditions to bail whenever a defendant charged with murder is granted bail, unless, unusually, the court already has satisfactory medical reports. The conditions are: (a) a requirement that the accused shall undergo an examination by two medical practitioners for the purpose of enabling reports to be prepared; and (b) a requirement that he attends for such an examination and complies with any other directions which may be given by the doctors (s.3(6A)).

These conditions are mandatory. If justices commit an accused for trial on a murder charge on bail, but without conditions of bail under s.3(6A) the accused is unlawfully at large and the prosecution may apply to the Crown Court for bail to be revoked (*R. v. Central Criminal Court, ex p. Porter* [1992] Crim.L.R. 121). In practice the grant of bail in murder cases is rare and it has been said that it is often in the accused's own interests that he should be examined by a prison doctor in custody. Justices are entitled to bear this in mind and not to grant bail until such examination has taken place (*R. v. Vernege* [1982] 1 W.L.R. 293).

(ii) The mentally disordered offender

3–21   Special provisions apply to a person to whom an inquiry ought to be made into his physical or mental condition before the method of dealing with him is determined (MCA 1980, s.30). Such defendants, commonly known as mentally disordered, *must* have a condition attached to their bail that they attend a prescribed place for a medical examination. (Bail and remands for mentally disordered offenders are fully discussed in Chap. 7.)

(iii) Children and young persons

3–22 With effect from June 1, 1999, section 23 of the Children and Young Persons Act 1969 is amended by sections 97 and 98 of the Crime and Disorder Act 1998. The effect of the amendment is to allow a court to remand any child or young person (whether male or female) into secure accommodation and 15 and 16-year-old males to a remand centre providing certain criteria are met.

3–23 The general rule is that if a child or young person is refused bail he is remanded to local authority accommodation (CYPA 1969, s.23(1)) but the court may not require the local authority to keep the person in secure place unless certain criteria are met (*ibid.* s.23(4)). The latest statutory amendments provide that a court shall not impose a security requirement except in respect of a child who has attained the age of 12, or a female who is aged 15 or 16 and then only if—

(a) he or she is charged with or has been convicted of a violent or sexual offence, or an offence punishable in the case of an adult with imprisonment for 14 years' or more; or

(b) he or she has a recent history of absconding while remanded in local authority accommodation, and is charged with or has been convicted of an imprisonable offence alleged or found to have been committed while so remanded (CYPA 1969, s.23(5), as amended by CDA 1998, s.97(2)).

3–24 The provisions in respect of males aged 15 or 16 are altered by amendments introduced in section 98 of the Crime and Disorder Act 1998. These allow a court to remand such a young male to a remand centre or secure local authority accommodation, depending upon which statutory criteria are met. If the criteria set out in (a) or (b) above apply then the court must be of the opinion that only remanding him to a remand centre or prison, or to secure local authority accommodation would be adequate to protect the public from serious harm from him (CYPA 1969, s.23(5) as substituted by CDA 1998, s.98(3)). If, by reason of the person's physical or emotional immaturity or propensity to harm himslf, the court is of the opinion that it would be undesirable for him to be remanded to a remand centre or prison, the court may so declare (*ibid.*, s.23(5A)).

PROCEDURAL REQUIREMENTS

3–25 The procedural formalities for remanding children or young persons were laid down in amendments to the 1969 Act by provisions in the Criminal Justice Act 1991, and these are repeated in the latest changes. In essence these provide:

(i) that the child or young person must be legally represented (unless legal aid was refused on grounds of means or that the accused has refused or failed to apply for legal aid);

(ii) that the court must always state in open court its reasons for denying bail and making the order or orders in question;

(iii) that the local authority must have notified the court that secure accommodation is available; and

(iv) that the court has been informed that a remand centre is available for the reception of the young person.

IMPACT OF HUMAN RIGHTS ACT 1998

3–26 Article 5 of the Convention (right to liberty and security) is the Article which guarantees rights prior to trial, and in particular the issue of bail pending trial.

There is a considerable body of Strasbourg case law on the grounds, under Article 5, for which bail may be refused. These are broadly similar, if not identical, to the grounds for refusing bail under the Bail Act 1976, with the additional ground that it has been held that bail may properly be refused in order to preserve public order (*Letellier v. France* (1991) 14 E.H.R.R. 83). This additional ground for refusing bail cannot affect domestic law because existing domestic rights and freedoms survive under the 1998 Act (HRA 1998, s.11(a)). See generally Chapter 24, below.

More difficult questions may arise about the procedural formalities surrounding the grant and refusal of bail. Article 5(3) requires that a person is brought promptly before a judge or other officer authorised to exercise judicial power and shall be entitled to trial within a reasonable time or to release pending trial. Article 5(3) would not appear to require a public hearing (as required under Article 6 for the trial itself) although, in practice, all bail applications in magistrates' courts are heard in public. An appeal against a refusal of bail by justices to a judge of the Crown Court or the High Court is a right set out in Article 5(4) which provides that everyone who is deprived of his liberty shall be entitled to take proceedings by which the lawfulness of the detention may be decided by a court. Although such appeals are invariably heard in private it would not seem that Article 5 is thereby breached, simply because the appellant is not present.

Domestic law has, however, gone further than the bare words of the Convention by providing—

(a) for an appeal by the prosecution against the *grant* of bail (see §§3–43—3–47, below; and

(b) for a reconsideration of a decision taken previously to grant bail (see §§3–48—3–51, below).

In each of these instances bail may be taken away from the accused in a hearing at which the accused may be absent.

While Convention jurisprudence has recognised that certain criminal proceedings may take place in the absence of the accused in order to prevent the system of administering criminal justice becoming paralysed (*Colozza and Rubinet v. Italy* (1985) 7 E.H.R.R. 516) the accused should, in these circumstances, have an opportunity of obtaining a re-hearing. Similarly, it is recognised that an accused who behaves in a disorderly or contemptuous fashion may run the risk of the proceedings continuing without him (*Winterwerp v. Netherlands* (1979) 2 E.H.R.R. 387). In addition, there are procedures in domestic law which permit certain procedural steps to occur in the accused's absence, providing he gives his consent and providing he is represented (see generally §§1–43—1–47). None of the above procedural steps would seem, at first sight, to breach Article 5.

The procedure of appeal against the grant of bail and the reconsideration of bail directly impinge upon Article 5 which guarantees the right to liberty and security. Accordingly, hearings in which the accused may have his rights under Article 5 removed in circumstances when he is absent, without being contemptuous and without having given his consent, raise real questions about the compatibility of such hearings to the Convention.

B. PROCEDURE ON A BAIL APPLICATION

1. Introduction

3–27   The proceedings generally are more informal than most hearings before magistrates and strict rules of evidence are not only unnecessary but inherently inappropriate (*Re Moles* [1981] Crim.L.R. 170).

As the structure of the Bail Act 1976 provides a general right to bail subject to exceptions, the objections to bail are invariably given by the prosecution but this may be done by way of submissions and there is no need for evidence to be called. The applicant's advocate will then make representations.

If, having heard the arguments, the court withholds bail or imposes conditions, or varies the terms by imposing conditions, reasons must be given in open court, and those reasons must be recorded (s.5(3), (4)). In addition the accused must be given a copy of the reasons (s.5(4)). Even if there are no objections to bail by the prosecution the court has a duty nonetheless to consider whether bail should be granted unconditionally, or conditionally, or withheld. This is because section 4 of the Bail Act, which provides for the general right to bail in criminal proceedings, applies when an accused appears or is brought before the court or applies to the court for bail in connection with the proceedings (s.4(2)(a) and (b)).

If the court has heard full argument on an application for bail and either such full argument has not previously been presented, or a full argument has previously been presented under different circumstances and the court has heard new argument and bail is refused, the court must issue a certificate that such full argument was presented (s.6A(b)(i) and (ii)). During any full argument for bail the clerk is obliged to take a note of the argument (MCR 1981, r. 90A).

2. Time for Making a Bail Application

(i) General rule

3–28   Theoretically an application for bail may be made the first time an accused appears in criminal proceedings, and at every appearance thereafter, but the question of whether repeated applications may properly be made is now governed by paragraphs 1–3 of Part IIA of Schedule 1 of the Act. This new provision means that the timetable for bail applications is as follows.

3–29   On his first appearance in court after arrest an accused may support an application for bail with any arguments he wishes, and the court has a duty to consider these arguments in the light of the provisions of the Bail Act. However, whether or not a full application is made on that occasion, the court must consider whether the accused is someone who has a right to bail (s.4(2)(a)). If on that occasion bail is refused then at the first hearing after that at which the court decided not to grant bail, the accused may make a further application based on the same grounds as before, or new grounds. At subsequent hearings the court need not hear arguments which it has heard previously (paragraphs 1–3 of Part IIA of Schedule 1). It has been held that if the accused makes no bail application on his first appearance and agrees to be remanded in custody for three weeks, thereby waiving his right to make a bail application in seven days, a remand in absence does not count as a hearing under Part IIA (*R. v. Dover and East Kent Justices, ex p. Dean* (1992) 156 J.P. 357).

These provisions change slightly, but not fundamentally, the old test in *R. v. Nottingham Justices, ex p. Davies* [1981] Q.B. 38 as to the time for making bail applications. The main change is as follows: if an accused is unrepresented and makes no application on his first appearance, or if his advocate decides not to make a full application on the first hearing, and the court refuses bail, that will count as the first appearance for the purposes of Part IIA of Schedule 1. Accordingly "the first hearing after that at which the court decided not to grant bail" may in practice be the first effective bail application, and if bail is again refused, the next hearing would count as a "subsequent" hearing at which the court would have a discretion to refuse to hear the same arguments again.

3–30 In this respect it may be argued that the new Part IIA to Schedule 1 of the Bail Act restricts the number of times a bail application may be made, although the Act specifically gives the court a discretion in saying "at subsequent hearings the court *need* not hear arguments as to fact or law which it has heard previously." It is submitted that in exercising its discretion the following principles from case law still apply:

(a) The court would be entitled to allow a new application if the accused had previously been represented by a duty solicitor not of his own choice or if previously the full facts were not available to the court (*R. v. Nottingham Justices*, above).

(b) In deciding whether to allow a new application the court must look at the accumulation of facts and circumstances since the first remand in custody and decide whether there are any matters which the court did not consider on an earlier occasion (*R. v. Barking Justices, ex p. Shankshaft* (1983) 147 J.P. 399).

(c) The new circumstances which emerge during the course of remand hearings may result in an accused being deprived of bail and remanded in custody. For example, if evidence of mental instability emerges after an accused has been granted bail giving rise to a fear of further offences being committed on bail the accused may be remanded in custody (*R. v. Tower Bridge Magistrates' Court, ex p. Gilbert* (1988) 152 J.P. 307).

If during such hearings a justice of the peace learns of an accused's previous convictions, that magistrate must not thereafter take part in trying the accused in summary proceedings (MCA 1980, s.42).

(ii) Bail at committal proceedings

3–31 The occasion of the committal for trail is not necessarily a new circumstance entitling the accused to make a new bail application and Part IIA of Schedule 1 of the Bail Act 1976 applies to committal proceedings in exactly the same way as it applies to remand hearings. It has been said that the occasion of the committal may be an occasion when new argument can be advanced on behalf of the accused because the strength of the prosecution case at a committal hearing maybe better known but the committal is not of itself a new circumstance (*R. v. Slough Justices, ex p. Duncan* [1981] Q.B. 451). It is submitted that these propositions must now be read with caution following the substantial and important change to the nature of committal proceedings introduced by the Criminal Procedure and Investigations Act 1996. See generally Chapter 6, below.

The duty of the court in committing the accused for trial on bail must be considered in the light of the *Practice Direction (Crown Court: Plea and Direction Hearings)* [1995] 1 W.L.R. 1318. This provides that where a magistrates' court has been informed by the Crown Court that Plea and Directions Hearings (PDH's) are to be heard that the *Practice Direction* must be observed. A PDH will be held at the Crown Court with the accused being in attendance and should be within six weeks of committal where the accused is on bail and four weeks where he is in custody. The consequence of this practice is that the accused should be committed for trial to a specific date, namely the date on which the PDH is to be held. The obligation on an accused on bail is thus to appear at the Crown Court on a certain date for pre-trial directions to take place, and the duty thereafter of granting bail to ensure that the accused attends his trial is upon the Crown Court.

If after a committal for trial, but before arraignment at the Crown Court, there is an application for conditions of bail to be varied a magistrates' court has concurrent jurisdiction with the Crown Court to hear and determine the application (*R. v. Lincoln Magistrates' Court, ex p. Mawer* (1996) 160 J.P. 219).

IMPACT OF HUMAN RIGHTS ACT 1998

3–32   The timetable for bail applications set out in paragraphs 1–3 of Part IIA of Schedule 1 of the Bail Act 1976 will have to be read in the light of Article 5 of the Convention. This has been held to mean that the passage of time may require a court to hear a further bail application in order to ensure that the accused's rights under Article 5 are regularly reviewed (*Neumeister v. Austria (No. 1)* (1968) 1 E.H.R.R. 91). The exercise of discretion given to justices to hear renewed applications is summarised in §3–30, above would appear to comply with the Convention.

C. DUTIES OF A PERSON ADMITTED TO BAIL

3–33   A person granted bail has a duty to surrender to the custody of the court (or of the police if such a requirement has been made) at the time and place appointed for him to do so (s.3(1) and s.2(2)). If the accused is only a few minutes late in surrendering to custody then it has been said that the *de minimis* principle should apply (*R. v. Gateshead Justices, ex p. Usher and another* [1981] Crim.L.R. 491) although every case of lateness will depend on its own facts. Surrender to custody means that the accused should actually attend the court and surrender himself to the directions of the court. Surrender to custody does not necessarily involve physical constraint (such as surrender to a dock officer or security officer) but it does mean a situation in which the defendant is no longer free to come and go as he pleases (*R. v. Central Criminal Court, ex p. Guney* [1995] 1 W.L.R. 576). Once such procedure is complied with the person remains in the custody of the court, albeit that he has not surrendered to the dock, and notwithstanding that he is free to visit the court canteen or facilities generally (*D.P.P. v. Richards* [1988] Q.B. 701).

The judgment of Glidewell L.J. in *Richards*, above stated that magistrates' courts should consider ways of making it clear to those who have surrendered that they may not thereafter leave the court building without express consent. In magistrates' courts it is usual for trials and appearances to have fixed days and accordingly the "time and place" will be notified to the accused at the time the bail is granted.

D. BREACH OF BAIL

1. The Offence of Absconding whilst on Bail

3–34   It is an offence to fail to surrender to custody without reasonable cause (s.6(1)).

The offence is not committed if the person bailed has properly surrendered to custody but then leaves the court building without consent (*D.P.P. v. Richards*, above), although such behaviour might be deemed a contempt of court. If, however, the person arrives at the court building and does *not* surrender, and then leaves before his case is heard, the offence of absconding under section 6(1) is committed (*R. v. Reader* (1987) 84 Cr.App.R. 294).

Mistakes on the part of the bailed person as to the date for surrendering to custody caused by confusion or forgetfulness is not a reasonable cause for failing to surrender (*Laidlaw v. Atkinson, The Times*, August 2, 1986). If a bailed defendant fails to appear in the magistrates' court at the appointed time the court may issue a warrant for his arrest (s.7(1)).

It is extremely important that where a defendant is alleged to be in breach of bail that the offence under section 6(1) is put to him unambiguously and that he either admits it or denies it in clear terms. If it is admitted it is equally important that he be given the opportunity to put forward mitigating circumstances (*R. v. Watson* (1990) 12 Cr.App.R.(S.) 227).

2. Breaking Conditions of Bail

3–35   Where a person has broken a condition of bail, or there are reasonable grounds for believing that he will break a condition, he may be arrested and as soon as practicable, and in any event within 24 hours after his arrest, be brought before a justice of the peace for the petty sessions area in which he was arrested (s.7(3) and (4)). These provisions are absolute and the person arrested must be brought before a justice within the 24-hour period and not merely produced in the cells or the court precincts (*R. v. Governor of Glen Parva Young Offender Institution, ex p. G (a minor)* [1998] 2 All E.R. 295). It was held in that case that the legal consequence of failing to abide by the strict time limits in section 7(4) is that the court has no jurisdiction to hear the case, therefore the detainee must be released.

It follows that the court dealing with an alleged breach of conditions of bail will not necessarily be the same court which originally granted conditional bail. The power of the new court in these circumstances is to inquire into the matter and, if it is of the opinion that he has broken or is likely to break a condition of bail, either to readmit him to bail on the same or different conditions or to remand him in custody (s.7(5)).

Once the court has heard enough evidence to be of the opinion that a breach of bail has occurred there is specific power in the Bail Act to remand in custody, to re-admit to bail on the same terms, or to impose new conditions of bail (s.7(5)).

3–36   The nature of the proceedings under section 7 of the Bail Act 1976 have now been authoritatively explained by the Divisional Court in *R. v. Liverpool City*

Justices, ex p. D.P.P. [1992] 3 W.L.R. 20. The following general principles apply to hearings under section 7:

(i) The hearing is an informal one and strict rules of evidence do not apply, just as they do not apply in original applications for bail (see *Re Moles* [1981] Crim.L.R. 170, discussed at §3–27, above).

(ii) The inquiry into whether an accused who is brought before the court under section 7 should be admitted to bail must take place on the occasion when the accused is first brought before the court; there is no power to adjourn the proceedings.

(iii) The hearing may take place before a single justice because section 7(4) and (5) refers to "a justice of the peace," and a hearing under section 7 is not a trial.

(iv) Section 7 of the Bail Act 1976 requires a justice to form "an opinion" as to whether the conditions set out in the section apply. In doing so the justice would in fairness no doubt give the accused an opportunity to be heard.

3. Procedure on Breach of Bail

3–37   The procedure to be followed on breach of bail will depend on whether the accused has failed to appear having been bailed from a police station or whether he has absconded after being bailed by a court. If he had been bailed by the police then an information must be laid charging the accused with the offence specified in section 6(1) of the Bail Act 1976, and the time limits for the laying of informations will apply (*Murphy v. D.P.P.* [1990] 1 W.L.R. 601). However, if the accused absconded after being bailed by a magistrates' court then this will be tantamount to a defiance of a court order, and the court may initiate proceedings of its own motion and no time limits applicable to informations will apply (*Schiavo v. Anderton* [1987] Q.B. 20). The distinction has been explained in the following way: where a person bailed from a police station fails to appear there cannot be a defiance of a court order, and ... "[t]here does not exist the same compelling justification for the court to act by its own motion": *per* Lord Lane C.J. in *Practice Direction (Bail: failure to surrender)* [1987] 1 W.L.R. 79.

In both cases the prosecutor will conduct the proceedings and, where the matter is contested, call the evidence, but if the accused has absconded after being bailed by the court it is usual for the court itself to initiate the proceedings and invite the prosecutor to present the evidence.

It is mandatory for the court and the prosecution to follow the procedure set out in the *Practice Direction* and an individual magistrates' court may not depart from the procedure by adopting individual practices (*R. v. Teesside Magistrates' Court, ex p. Bujnowski* (1997) 161 J.P. 302).

Where the court proposes to deal with an accused for a Bail Act offence the accused's advocate should be invited to make specific submissions on sentence on the Bail Act charge, particularly if the court has in mind a consecutive sentence (*R. v. Woods* (1989) 11 Cr.App.R.(S.) 551).

Any trial should normally take place immediately following the disposal of the proceedings in respect of which bail was granted (*Practice Direction*, above). If a person on bail fails to surrender and a warrant is issued, but later he appears and offers an explanation for his non-appearance and is further remanded, justices sitting on the next occasion on which he appears have no jurisdiction to deal with him for a breach of the Bail Act. This is because by further remanding him, having accepted his explanation, justices were deemed to be excusing him (*France v. Dewsbury Magistrates' Court* [1988] Crim.L.R. 295).

4. Consequences for Sureties where there has been a Breach of Bail

3–38 Where any recognisance is conditioned for the appearance of a person before a magistrates' court and the accused fails to appear the court shall—

(a) declare the recognisance to be forfeited; and

(b) issue a summons to the surety requiring him to show cause why he should not be adjudged to pay the sum in which he is bound (MCA 1980, s.120(1A), as inserted by CDA 1998, s.55).

This amendment changes the old law whereby a recognisance was not forfeited until the surety had had the opportunity to make representations. The position now is that as soon as the accused has failed to appear the recognisance becomes due, with the caveat that the surety may make representations as to why either the whole or any part of the amount should not be paid.

If the surety fails to respond to the "show cause" notice the court may proceed in the absence of the surety providing the court is satisfied he was served with the summons (MCA 1980, s.120(1A)).

It follows that despite the declaration that a surety is forfeited the amount may not actually become payable until the surety has had the opportunity to be heard. Thus, the old case law setting out the considerations for the forfeiture of a recognisance remain relevant. The following principles, it is submitted, continue to apply:

(i) the starting point is that if an accused fails to surrender the recognisance should be paid because the real purpose of a surety was the force it should exert on the accused to attend his trial (*R. v. Southampton Justices, ex p. Corker* (1976) 120 S.J. 214);

(ii) any reduction in the amount of the recognisance should be confined to the really deserving cases and any reduction should be regarded as the exception rather than the rule (*R. v. Crown Court at Maidstone, ex p. Lever* [1995] 2 All E.R. 35, CA, Civ. Div.);

(iii) the burden of persuading the court that a recogniscance should not be paid (or that only a part should be paid) is upon the surety and it is a heavy one (*R. v. Uxbridge Justices, ex p. Heward-Mills* [1983] 1 W.L.R. 56);

(iv) lack of culpability on the part of the surety is not, in itself, a ground for holding the recognisance should not be paid (*R. v. Crown Court at Warwick, ex p. Smalley* 84 Cr.App.R. 51).

E. APPEALS IN RESPECT OF BAIL

3–39 The law and practice in relation to appeals in respect of bail decisions has seen a rapid development in recent years. With effect from June 27, 1994 the Bail

(Amendment) Act 1993 has permitted the prosecution, for the first time, to have a right of appeal against the grant of bail. With effect from April 10, 1995 the Criminal Justice and Public Order Act 1994 has permitted the police to grant conditional bail at the police station and has introduced a procedure for appeal to a magistrates' court in respect of the conditions imposed.

1. Appeal to the Magistrates' Court where Police Bail has been Granted

3–40   Section 27 of the Criminal Justice and Public Order Act 1994 has amended Part IV of the Police and Criminal Evidence Act 1984 to enable the police to release a person who has been charged at the police station on conditional bail. The purpose of this change is to reduce the number of persons being detained in police cells prior to their first appearance in the magistrates' court. The power given to the police enables a custody officer to impose conditions of bail on a person before that person has a duty to appear before a court. In order to deal with the possible misuse of this power the 1994 Act allowed a person to apply to another custody officer at the same police station to vary the conditions of bail (Bail Act 1976, s.3(8). In addition the 1994 Act provides a procedure for an appeal to a magistrates' court where a person is dissatisfied about conditions of bail imposed at a police station. Such an appeal will arise when the following circumstances exist:

Where a custody officer—

(a) grants bail to a person under Part IV of the Police and Criminal Evidence Act 1984 in criminal proceedings and imposes conditions, or

(b) varies, in relation to any person, conditions of bail in criminal proceedings under section 3(8) of the Bail Act 1976,

a magistrates' court may, on application by or on behalf of that person, grant bail or vary the conditions (MCA 1980, s.43B(1)).

The application must be made in writing, and must contain a statement of the grounds on which it is made, and it must be served on the clerk of the court of the appointed magistrates' court with a copy to the custody officer of the police station in question. The hearing must then be fixed no later than 72 hours after the receipt of the application, and a notice of the hearing must be sent by the clerk to the applicant, the prosecutor, and any surety (MCR 1981, r.84A).

When the court hears the application it may:

(i) grant bail on the same conditions as those imposed by the custody officer;

(ii) it may grant bail on different conditions (including more onerous conditions); or

(iii) it may remand the applicant in custody (MCA 1980, s.43B (2) and (3)).

There is therefore a risk that any person who seeks more generous conditions of bail from a magistrates' court than those imposed by the police may have more onerous conditions imposed or may have bail removed. In addition, it would appear that the respondent to the application is the prosecutor, invariably the Crown Prosecution Service, and not the custody officer who imposed the conditions. The prosecutor may take a different view from the custody officer and seek to persuade justices to remand the applicant in custody.

2. Appeal to the High Court

3–41   The High Court has overall jurisdiction over the conduct of proceedings in the magistrates' court and where the court withholds bail or imposes conditions of bail, the High Court may grant bail or vary the conditions (CJA 1967, s.22(1)). Despite the overall supervisory jurisdiction which the High Court undoubtedly has over proceedings in magistrates' courts all matters relating to appeals on questions of bail should be conducted under the above procedure and not by way of judicial review (*R. v. Epping and Harlow General Commissioners, ex p. Goldstone* [1983] 3 All E.R. 257).

An accused may appeal to the High Court at any stage of the proceedings, and the appeal may be against the refusal of bail or against the imposition of a particular condition of bail. The application must be commenced by summons before a judge in chambers to show cause why bail should not be granted, and this must be supported by an affidavit, usually sworn by the applicant's solicitor. The summons must be served, at least 24 hours before the hearing date, on the prosecution (RSC, Ord. 79, r. 9).

3. Appeal to the Crown Court

3–42   It is often more convenient to appeal against a refusal of bail to a local Crown Court. The Crown Court may grant bail to anyone who has:

(i)   been committed in custody to appear at that court;

(ii) been convicted and is appealing against conviction of sentence;

(iii) been remanded in custody and where a certificate of full argument has been issued (Supreme Court Act 1981, s.81(1) as amended by CJ and POA 1994, s.168(2) and Sched. 10, §48).

The details of the procedure are set out in *Practice Direction* issued by the Lord Chancellor's Department ((1983) 77 Cr.App.R. 69).

Although in practice there is a choice between appealing to the High Court or the Crown Court against a refusal of bail the jurisdiction of the High Court is separate and distinct from the Crown Court. This means that the High Court has jurisdiction even without a certificate of full argument. It also means that a High Court judge may (under the court's inherent jurisdiction) hear an application for bail after an application by the same person has been refused by the Crown Court (*R. v. Reading Crown Court, ex p. Malik* [1981] 1 Q.B. 451).

In addition, the High Court has power to consider an application to vary conditions of bail (including the amount of any surety) whereas the Crown Court may only entertain appeals against a refusal of bail.

4. Appeal by the Prosecution

3–43   An appeal by the prosecution against the grant of bail by a magistrates' court is permitted by the Bail (Amendment) Act 1993 which came into force on June 27, 1994. It allows the prosecution to appeal the grant of bail to the Crown Court, where a hearing may take place in chambers. References below are to the Bail (Amendment) Act 1993 unless otherwise stated.

The Act applies where:

(i) before bail was granted the prosecution made representations that it should not be granted (s.1(3));

(ii) the accused is charged with or convicted of an offence punishable with imprisonment of five years or more, or with an offence under section 12 or 12A of the Theft Act 1968 (taking a conveyance or aggravated vehicle-taking) (s.1(1)); and

(iii) the prosecution is conducted by or on behalf of the Director of Public Prosecutions, *i.e.* the Crown Prosecution Service, or by one of the prescribed authorities under the Act (s.1(2)). The prescribed authorities are; The Director of the Serious Fraud Office and any person designated under section 1(7) of the Criminal Justice Act 1987, The Secretary of State for Trade and Industry, The Commissioners of Customs and Excise, The Secretary of State for Social Security, The Post Office, and The Commissioners of Inland Revenue (Bail (Amendment) Act 1993 (Prescription of Prosecuting Authorities) Order 1994).

3–44   If these conditions apply and there is a bail hearing which results in the accused being granted bail, either conditional or unconditional, the prosecution may then and there give notice of their intention to appeal against the decison. The Act therefore permits a procedure whereby the prosecution may, by giving notice of an intention to appeal, deprive a person of the bail announced by the court.

It has been recognised by the Crown Prosecution Service that the Act confers "considerable power on the prosecutor" (Crown Prosecution Service Policy Circular, No. 11 of 1994). A public statement of guidance will be issued, but the Circular states that "[t]he right of appeal should be used only in cases of grave concern . . . and where there is a serious public interest involved".

Even if the use of the prosecutor's appeal is to be used sparingly, as the circular envisages, the concept of such an appeal is so novel that a new rule, rule 93A, has been inserted in the Magistrates' Courts Rules 1981 to allow the accused to be lawfully held in these circumstances (Magistrates' Courts (Bail) (Amendment) Rules 1994, r. 3(c)).

The Act sets out a procedure which is in two stages. The first, or interim, stage is the procedure to be followed after the prosecution have given an "oral notice" of appeal; the second stage may only arise if the prosecution have confirmed such an intention to appeal by the serving of a "written notice".

PROCEDURE FOLLOWING AN ORAL NOTICE

3–45   The oral notice must be given at the conclusion of the proceedings in which bail has been granted and before the release from custody of the person concerned (s.1(4)), and the court shall then remand the person concerned in custody (s.1(6)). The rules, inserted by The Magistrates' Courts (Bail) (Amendment) Rules 1994, provide as follows:

(i) the oral notice must be given to the clerk of the court and to the accused at the conclusion of the proceedings in which bail was granted and before the accused's release (MCR 1981, r. 93A(1)).

(ii) when such notice is given the clerk shall announce the time at which it was given (*ibid.*, r. 93A(2)).

(iii) a record of the fact of the oral notice and its time must be made in the register (*ibid.*, r. 93A(3)).

(iv) the accused shall be remanded in custody by a warrant for commitment provided for in the amended Magistrates' Courts (Forms) Rules (*ibid.*, r. 93A(4)).

The remand in custody under section 1(6) of the Act following an oral notice will last only until a "written notice" is served.

The words "at the conclusion of the proceedings" in r.93A(1) above, do not mean that the prosecution must give notice the very instant the proceedings end and a delay of five minutes before giving notice to the clerk does not breach the rule, even if the justices have left court (*R. v. Isleworth Crown Court, ex p. Clarke* [1998] 1 Cr.App.R. 257).

PROCEDURE FOLLOWING A WRITTEN NOTICE

3–46 A written notice of appeal must be served on the court and on the person concerned within two hours of the conclusion of the bail hearing (s.1(5)).

(i) the receipt of the written notice allows the court to issue a warrant of commitment until the appeal is heard or otherwise disposed of (MCR 1981, r. 93A (5)). The hearing of the appeal at the Crown Court must be commenced within 48 hours (s.1(8)).

(ii) a record of the receipt of the written notice must be made in the court register (MCR 1981, r.93A(6)).

(iii) the written notice, notes of the bail argument, and the particulars of the court remand dates must be provided to the Crown Court (MCR 1981, r. 93A(10)).

PROCEDURE WHERE WRITTEN NOTICE IS NOT GIVEN

3–47 If the prosecution fail to serve either or both of the written notices (*i.e.* one on the court and the other on the accused) within the period of two hours the appeal shall be deemed to have been disposed of (s.1(7)). This means that the clerk of the court must direct the release of the accused as soon as practicable on the terms of bail granted by the court (MCR 1981, r. 93A(7)).

The release of the accused will therefore follow automatically unless a written notice is served within two hours of the exact time of the giving of the oral notice. However, there is a further circumstance in which the accused's release may be ordered before the hearing of the appeal. The words "or otherwise disposed of" in section 1(7) allow for an abandonment by the prosecution of their wish to continue an appeal after the written notice has been served (Crown Court Rules 1982, r. 11A, as

inserted by the Crown Court (Amendment) Rules 1994, r. 4). Such a notice of abandonment must be served on the clerk of the magistrates' court concerned, and upon
receipt of the notice the clerk must order the release of the accused (MCR 1981,
r. 93A(8)).

G. RECONSIDERATION OF A BAIL DECISION

1. Introduction

3–48   Reconsideration of a bail decision is a power given to the prosecutor to
make an application to a magistrates' court for a previous bail decision made by that
court or by a custody officer at a police station to be reconsidered. The power is introduced by section 30 of the Criminal Justice and Public Order Act 1994 which inserts a
new section 5B to the Bail Act 1976. The conditions for the exercise of the power are:

  (i) the offence must be one triable on indictment only or triable either way
     (s.5B(2));

 (ii) the application must be based on information which was not available to the
     court or constable when the decision was taken (*ibid.*, s.5B(3)).

If these conditions apply the prosecutor may make an application for the previous
decision by a court or a constable to be reconsidered, and the court may—

 (a) vary the conditions of bail,

 (b) impose conditions in respect of bail which has been granted unconditionally,
     or

 (c) withhold bail (s.5B(1)(a), (b) and (c)).

3–49   The real purpose of giving the prosecution this new power is to enable a
court to review its bail decision if new information has come to light between the dates
of the accused's court appearances. On the first appearance of the accused at the
magistrates' court following the grant of police bail, the court may renew that bail on
the same or on different conditions or may remand the accused in custody. This is
because there is a general obligation upon the court to consider the accused's bail on
every occasion on which he appears or is brought before the court in criminal proceedings (s.4(2(a)). Thus, a prosecutor who disagreed with a decision of a custody
officer to release the accused on bail could object to bail at the accused's appearance
before justices irrespective of the power given in section 5B of the Act. In addition, a
magistrates' court has an inherent jurisdiction to remove bail if, exceptionally, new
circumstances have arisen to justify withholding bail (*R. v. Tower Bridge Magistrates'
Court, ex p. Gilbert* (1988) 152 J.P. 307). This inherent power may still be exercised
notwithstanding the new procedure under section 5B.

(i) Procedure on reconsideration application

3–50   The court may decide a reconsideration application whether or not the
accused appears before the court (s.5B(4)) and the decision may result in the accused
being arrested and thereafter remanded in custody (s.5B(6) and (7)). Reconsideration
applications are thus novel in that an accused's liberty may be curtailed without the

accused being before the court when the effective decision to curtail his liberty is taken. For this reason section 5B(9) of the Bail Act 1976 requires rules to be made to include provision for the notice of the prosecutor's application and the grounds for it to be given to the person affected, including the powers available to the court. The rules are made in the Magistrates' Courts (Amendment) Rules 1995, which insert a new rule 93B to the Magistrates' Courts Rules 1981.

Where the decision to admit the accused to bail was a police station the appropriate court for the hearing of a reconsideration application is a magistrates' court appointed by the custody office as the court before which the accused is to appear, or magistrates' court within the petty sessions area of the police station (MCR 1981, r. 93B(1)).

The prosecutor's application must be in writing, stating the grounds upon which it is made and must include the name of any surety (*ibid.*, r. 93B(2). The hearing of the application must then be fixed by the clerk of the court no later than 72 hours after receipt of the prosecutor's application (excluding Sundays and bank and public holidays) and notice of the hearing must be given to the accused, with a copy to the prosecutor and any surety (*ibid.*, r. 93B(3) and (4)).

The notice to the accused is critical for the reasons stated above and the following points should be noted:

(i) the notice must be in the prescribed form 153A in the Schedule of rule 93B (MCR 1981, r. 93B(3)),

(ii) service of the notice may be effected by delivering it to him (*ibid.*, r. 93B(5)),

(iii) the court may not take any decision to reconsider the accused's bail if he does not appear unless it is proved to the satisfaction of the court by an appropriate declaration that the accused was served with notice of the hearing (*ibid.*, r. 93B(6)). Service may be effected by personal delivery or by leaving the notice with some person at his last known place of abode (*ibid.*, r. 93B(8)).

It would seem that a reconsideration application is not appropriate if it is feared by the prosecutor that the accused has absconded because knowledge by the accused of the prosecutor's application is a pre-condition for the decision being made. If the accused has knowledge of the hearing he may make representations orally or in writing to the court (s.5B(9)(b)).

(ii) Decision of the Court on Reconsideration Application

3–51 Whether or not the accused appears the court must make a decision in accordance with section 4(1) and Schedule 1 of the Bail Act 1976 (s.5B(4)). This means that the presumption in favour of bail continues to apply at a reconsideration application.

Any decision to change the conditions of bail or to withhold bail must be based on new information which has come to light since the original decision was taken. Section 5B(3) of the Bail Act 1976 provides that "[n]o application for the reconsideration of a decision under this section shall be made unless it is based on information which was not available to the court or constable when the decision was taken". While section 5B(3) is a pre-condition for the making of the application, it is submitted that the court itself must be satisfied that the application relates to new material. The wording of section 5B(3) would appear to allow a prosecutor to make an application if the information had been known to him but not made "available to the court" when the original decision was taken. Thus, a prosecutor who negligently failed to make the court aware of certain facts at an earlier bail application could, theoretically, make a reconsideration application.

If the decision of the court is to withhold bail then the accused shall be remanded in custody if he is present before the court, or he must be ordered to surrender to the custody of the court if he is not (s.5B(5)(a) and (b)). An order under section 5B(5) gives a power of arrest without warrant (s.5B(7)). If the accused either surrenders to the court or is arrested and brought before the court then the consequence in either case is that the accused shall be remanded in custody (s.5B(6) and (8)). The combined effect of these provisions are that an accused who has knowledge of a reconsideration application but who chooses not to attend is at risk of having a decision to revoke his bail taken in his absence, and such a decision cannot be reversed if he subsequently surrenders or is later arrested. The Act is unambiguous that in each circumstance the accused shall be remanded in custody. Such a decision to remand in custody which is required if the conditions in sections 5B(6) and (8) are fulfilled will not apply, it is submitted, when the accused is produced on his following appearance. At that stage the normal provisions of the Bail Act 1976 will once again apply and the merits of a bail decision, in the light of the new information, may be argued by the prosecution and the defence.

G. SOME COMMON TERMS EXPLAINED

1. Recognisance

3–52 The Bail Act abolished personal recognisances for accused persons and provided instead for the offence of absconding whilst on bail. Accordingly an accused can never be asked to forfeit money (unless it is a "security," see, below) for failing to appear. Recognisances are preserved however for sureties and the court may order the whole or part of the amount of their recognisance or suretyship to be forfeited in the circumstances explained above.

2. Police Bail

3–53 It has always been the case that the police have power to grant an accused person bail pending his appearance in the magistrates' court or pending his later return to the police station for the completion of enquiries (*e.g.* while a substance suspected of being a prohibited drug is analysed). The words police bail may thus be used in two senses: release from the police station with a duty to appear at a magistrates' court on a later date, and release from the police station with a duty to attend the police station on a later date. The Criminal Justice and Public Order Act 1994 has introduced changes to enable the police to release those charged with an offence on conditional bail to attend a magistrates' court on a later date. These changes have been incorporated into the commentary in this chapter. Police bail in the sense of bail to return to the police station on a later date is beyond the scope of this chapter, but failure to answer such bail is now an arrestable offence (PACE 1984, s.46A, as inserted by CJ and POA 1994, s.29(1)).

3. Continuous Bail

3–54 This term is not defined in any statute but it is used with reference to the remand powers of magistrates defined in section 128 of the Magistrates' Courts Act 1980. In practice the court may order that bail be "continuous until committal" or "continuous until trial" which are two commonly used orders. This means that if sureties are taken at the time bail is first granted, and made continuous until committal, the sureties need not appear personally each time the accused is remanded (if he is remanded) in the intervening periods, although they would be required to attend again at the committal proceedings.

4. Variation of Bail

3–55   This means varying or changing the conditions of bail or adding conditions to bail since the grant of bail on an earlier occasion. Bail may be varied on an application to the court by the accused himself or the prosecutor. In practice it occurs when some supervening event makes an earlier condition impractical, for example when there is a condition of residence in one place and the accused changes his job which involves moving to a new address.

The jurisdiction to vary bail may be found in section 3(8) of the Bail Act 1976. During the period after a committal for trial to the Crown Court on bail but before the accused has surrendered to the Crown Court the magistrates' court and the Crown Court enjoy concurrent jurisdiction to hear an application to vary conditions of bail (*R. v. Lincoln Magistrates' Court, ex p. Mawer* [1995] Crim.L.R. 878).

It is good practice for a court when making a variation in bail which might affect a surety's willingness to continue as surety to decline to continue bail on the varied conditions unless the surety knows of the variation and agrees to continue as surety.

Variation cannot affect the validity of continuous bail, but if bail is made continuous it is good practice for the court to warn a surety that conditions may subsequently be varied (*R. v. Wells Street Magistrates' Court, ex p. Albanese* [1981] 3 W.L.R. 694).

5. Enlargement of Bail

3–56   This means continuing the bail of an accused in his absence when he is already on bail but cannot be present in court on the appointed day because of illness or accident. It also means continuing the bail of an accused if the court finds it cannot after all deal with the case on the appointed day. In such cases the court may simply enlarge or renew bail for the accused to appear on another date.

6. Security

3–57   The word Security has a wider meaning following the amendment to section 3(5) of the Bail Act introduced by section 54(1) of the Crime and Disorder Act 1998 (see paragraph 3–15, above). At the time of implementation of the Bail Act, a Home Office Circular (No. 206/1977) issued guidance as to what could constitute "security" at that time and stated that the word included cash, travellers cheques or any other article of value. It is submitted that the word is capable of carrying such a meaning following the 1998 amendment even though the circumstances whereby a security may be demanded have changed.

7. Certificate of Full Argument

3–58   It is the duty of the court to issue a certificate in the prescribed form when there has been a full application for bail and bail has been refused. If there are new circumstances entitling the accused's advocate to make a new application a certificate will similarly be issued stating the reason giving rise to the renewed application. The purpose of the certificate is to facilitate an application in the Crown Court for bail because both the accused and the Crown Court are entitled to know the precise reasons why bail was refused.

CHAPTER 4

Plea before Venue, Mode of Trial and Election for Trial

1. Introduction

4–01 Mode of trial is a key event in the process of criminal justice and over the years has excited much controversy. The Royal Commission on Criminal Justice, which reported in 1993, concluded that "magistrates send for trial a large number of cases that they could try themselves; while defendants opt for trial on the basis that they are going to plead not guilty but then usually plead guilty" (Cm. 2263, Chap. 6:12). The Royal Commission proposed a radical solution to this perceived anomaly – namely abolition of a defendant's right to jury trial and replacing this right by a decision taken by the court. Neither government which has been in power since 1993 has been prepared (at the time of writing) to take up so radical an idea, but in the Criminal Procedure and Investigations Act 1996 a modified reform, plea before venue, was introduced. While this change is, on its face, modest it has important implications for justices' sentencing powers, the role of the prosecution in the sentencing process and the obligation placed on the defence advocate to tender early advice on plea. For

93

these reasons many of the changes wrought by the introduction of plea before venue are discussed more fully elsewhere in this book.

The opportunity offered to an accused charged with an either way offence to plead guilty to it in the magistrates' court is an extra option to the traditional mode of trial procedure which is unaffected by this change; plea before venue does not replace mode of trial. Unless there is a plea of guilty mode of trial survives in its original form and this means that, with appropriate adjustments, the Mode of Trial Guidelines remain relevant even if the accused pleads guilty (*R. v. Warley Magistrates' Court, ex p. D.P.P.* [1998] 2 Cr.App.R. 307).

A. Plea before Venue

1. Procedure

4–02   The following procedure applies when the accused appears or is brought before the court on or after October 1, 1997 (CPIA 1996, s.49(6) and S.I. 1997, No. 2199).

In most circumstances the plea before venue procedure will take place in the accused's presence, although there is provision for it to occur in the accused's absence. This is dealt with in §4–10, below.

Subject to this exception the following procedure only applies if the accused has attained the age of 18 when he is brought before the court, and the accused is in court when the procedure is followed (MCA 1980, s.17A(1) and (2)).

  (i) the charge is read to the accused (if not already done) (*ibid.* s.17A(3)), and

  (ii) the court (invariably the clerk of the court) shall explain to the accused *in ordinary language* that he may indicate whether he wishes to plead guilty or not guilty (*ibid.*, s.17A(4)), and that if a guilty plea is indicated:

    (a) the court must proceed as if the indicated plea was a lawful plea of guilty in a summary trial and that the court will therefore hear the case and pass sentence (*ibid.*, s.17A(4(a) and 6(a) and (b)), and also

    (b) if an indicated plea is given he may be committed to the Crown Court for sentence in accordance with section 38 of the Magistrates' Courts Act 1980 (*ibid.*, s.17A(4(b)).

  (iii) having explained the forgoing the court shall formally ask the accused whether he pleads guilty or not guilty (*ibid.*, s.17A(5)).

  (iv) if the accused formally pleads guilty the court shall commence to hear the case as a guilty plea in summary proceedings (*ibid.*, s.17A(6)).

  (v) If the accused pleads not guilty or if the accused fails to indicate a plea of guilty the usual mode of trial procedures will apply (*ibid.*, s.17A(7) and (8)).

It is only if the above steps are followed that the taking of a plea of guilty and then proceeding to a summary trial in respect of an either way offence is lawful (*ibid.*, s.17A(9)).

2. Issues which arise from Plea before Venue

4–03   The apparently modest change to the traditional mode of trial procedure has important consequences for practice in the magistrates' court. The following points should be noted:

1. Although the procedure is sometimes described as the accused's indication of a guilty plea, by virtue of the wording in section 17A(4), such indication is in law a plea of guilty for the purposes of summary proceedings (*ibid.*, s.17A(6)(a) and (b)). This means that the duty of the court only to accept a plea which is unequivocal applies with equal force to the plea before venue procedure. For the duty of the court in respect of pleas of guilty which are, or may be, equivocal see §§4–33 to 4–37, below. If justices do not ensure that the plea is unequivocal and there is a committal for sentence to the Crown Court then particular difficulties may arise in seeking to put the matter right at the Crown Court (see *R. v. Rochdale Justices, ex p. Allwork* [1981] 3 All E. R. 434 and *R. v. Plymouth Justices, ex p. Hart* [1986] 1 Q.B. 950).

2. Plea before venue is conducted *before* the accused is entitled to primary disclosure of the prosecution case (CPIA 1996, s. 1(1)(b)). The procedure may not take place, without the accused's consent, until Advance Information is served (CLA 1977, s.48). For a full discussion of this topic see §§1–114 to 1–116, above.

3. The provisions must be read in the light of section 48 of the Criminal Procedure and Investigations Act 1996 (credit for early plea of guilty) (*R. v. Rafferty* [1998] Crim. L.R. 433). This means, in broad terms, that if an accused declines the opportunity of pleading guilty in the magistrates' court he may lose credit subsequently. For a full discussion of this topic see §§13–22 to 13–23, below.

4. Justices must be conscious of:

   (a) the Mode of Trial Guidelines;

   (b) the principles of concurrent and consecutive sentences where sentence is to be passed for more than one offence; and

   (c) the powers available to them to commit the offender to the Crown Court for sentence,

whenever an accused pleads guilty to an either way offence or offences under the plea before venue procedure (*R. v. Warley Magistrates' Court, ex p. D.P.P.* [1998] 2 Cr.App.R. 307).

For a full discussion of these topics see, respectively, Appendix I, §§13–59 *et seq.* and §§6–39 to 6–41, below.

5. If the decision whether of not to commit for sentence turns or may turn on the outcome of a *Newton* hearing, the court should proceed to conduct such a hearing before making the decision and the findings in the hearing should be recorded for the benefit of the Crown Court (*R. v. Warley Magistrates Court, ex p. D.P.P.*, above). For a discussion of *Newton* hearings see §§13–42 to 13–45, below.

4–04 It follows from the above that the plea before venue provisions cannot be seen in isolation and they impinge on many aspects of magistrates' court practice.

Practitioners will be conscious of their responsibilities with regard to advice on plea and justices must be conscious of their wide responsibilities with regard to sentencing principles. So far as the latter is concerned justices will not be assisted by the prosecution as to the seriousness of the offence (as they are at mode of trial) although it has been said that the prosecution should have the right to submit that an offender should be committed to the Crown Court for sentence (*R. v. Warley Magistrates Court, ex p. D.P.P.*, above).

B. Mode of Trial

1. Procedure

4–05 The procedure for determining mode of trial for offences triable either way is unaffected by the Criminal Procedure and Investigations Act 1996, subject to the point that it is specifically disapplied if the accused (or his representative) indicates a not guilty plea (see above). If the accused (or his representative) fails or refuses to indicate a plea it is taken to be an indication of a not guilty plea (MCA 1980, s.17A(7) and s.17B (3), as inserted by CPIA 1996, s.49(2)).

4–06 In most circumstances mode of trial will take place with the accused present in court but there is provision for the procedure to apply in his absence. This is dealt with in §4–09, below.

The procedure is as follows:

(a) The accused is identified and the charge is read to him (MCA 1980, s.19(2)(a)). At this stage he is not asked to plead to the charge.

(b) The accused shall be asked by the court whether he is aware that he is entitled to receive advance information of the prosecution case (CLA 1977, s.48 and the Magistrates' Courts (Advance Information) Rules 1985).

(c) The court shall first give the prosecution and then the accused an opportunity to make representations as to which mode of trial would be more suitable (MCA 1980, s.19(2)(b)). In practice the prosecution will give a short summary of the case highlighting the matters set out in (d), below.

(d) The court shall then consider:

   (1) the nature of the case;

   (2) whether the circumstances make the offence one of serious character;

   (3) whether the punishment which a magistrates' court would have power to inflict for it would be adequate; and

   (4) any other circumstances which appear to the court to make it more suitable for the offence to be tried in one way rather than the other (MCA 1980, s.19(3)).

(i) Considerations which apply to a Mode of Trial Decision

4–07 The purpose of the court being required to give consideration to the venue for trial is to avoid serious cases being tried summarily. Despite the importance of this general principle it was only recently that the Court of Appeal and the Divisional Court have given consideration to the need to achieve consistency in mode of trial decisions.

In October 1990 the Lord Chief Justice, Lord Lane, issued a comprehensive *Practice Note (Mode of Trial: Guidelines)* [1990] 1 W.L.R. 1439.

In 1995 Lord Taylor, the present Lord Chief Justice, issued revised Guidelines to reflect the changes to sentencing practice brought about by the Criminal Justice Act 1991 and the fact that the age limit for magistrates' courts' jurisdiction has been raised to 18.

Mode of Trial Guidelines are intended to encourage consistency amongst magistrates in making mode of trial decisions, although it is emphasised that justices have a duty to consider each case individually and on its particular facts. Broadly, it is envisaged that either way offences should be tried summarily unless there is some special feature of seriousness which is specified in the Guidelines. Special features have been specified for offences of burglary, theft and fraud, handling, social security frauds, offences of violence, sexual offences, drug offences, reckless driving and criminal damage. The revised Guidelines are set out in full in Appendix II.

4–08 The importance of complying with the provisions of section 19(3) of the Magistrates' Courts Act 1980 (see §4–06, above) and the National Mode of Trial Guidelines have been emphasised by the Divisional Court on more than one occasion (*R. v. Northampton Magistrates' Court, ex p. Commissioners of Customs and Excise* (1994) 158 J.P. 1083, *R. v. Flax Bourton Magistrates' Court, ex p. Customs and Excise* (1996) 160 J.P. 481 and *R. v. Warley Magistrates' Court, ex p. D.P.P., R. v. Staines Magistrates Court, ex p. D.P.P., R. v. Suffolk Magistrates' Court, ex p. D.P.P.* [1998] 2 Cr.App.R. 307). In each of these case justices had either accepted summary trial or proceeded to pass sentence in cases which were manifestly unsuitable for summary disposal. Although the Divisional Court will not lightly interfere with the discretion of justices in respect of their jurisdiction the High Court will do so if the decision of the magistrates' court can be described as "truly astonishing". This will apply to cases heard under the plea before venue procedure as well as the mode of trial procedure.

The fact that the case may involve issues of disclosure relating to public interest immunity is not, in itself, a ground for justices to decline summary trial (*R. v. Stipendiary Magistrate for Norfolk, ex p. Taylor* (1997) 161 J.P. 773). These observations would appear to conflict with those made *R. v. Bromley Justices, ex p. Smith* [1995] Crim. L.R. 248, and in so far as there is a conflict it is submitted that the view in *ex p. Taylor* is to be preferred.

Although justices have a discretion to commit for sentence after hearing the full facts under section 38 of the 1980 Act (and the decision under that section is a different one from that made at mode of trial stage) justices should nonetheless consider carefully before accepting jurisdiction in the first place (*R. v. Dover Magistrates' Court, ex p. Pamment* (1994) 15 Cr.App.R.(S.) 778). The considerations applicable to committal for sentence are discussed in §§6–39 to 6–41, below.

2. Conducting Mode of Trial in the absence of the Accused

4–09 In certain circumstances both mode of trial and plea before venue may take place in the absence of the accused, providing the accused is legally represented.

If the accused is absent for some good reason, such as illness, then section 23 of the 1980 Act provides for a modified form of mode of trial to take place. Such proceeding may only take place if:

(a) the absent accused has signified his consent to his legal representative for the proceedings to occur in his absence; and

(b) the court is satisfied there is good reason for so proceeding (MCA 1980, s.23(1)(a) and (b)).

In these circumstances the court may proceed as summarised in §§4–05 and 4–06, above and the court may determine that summary trial is suitable or not as the case may be, and if suitable the legal representative may elect trial on indictment on behalf of the absent accused (*ibid.*, s.23(3), (4) and (5)). It is to be noted that this modified form of mode of trial has no provision for the accused to be cautioned that if he consents to summary trial he may still be committed for sentence. For this reason, it is submitted that the justices should rarely conclude that there is "good reason" for proceeding in absence, unless the case is so manifestly suitable for summary disposal that neither the prosecution nor the court regard a further remand to obtain the accused's presence as necessary.

In addition, section 23 will apply if, by reason of the disorderly conduct of the accused, it is not practicable for mode of trial to be conducted in his presence (MCA 1980, s.18(3)). It should be noted that the combination of this provision with those in section 23 as a whole means that the court would have to be satisfied that there was good reason for proceeding in absence, even though by doing so the modified form of mode of trial would follow. It is submitted that it would be highly unusual for justices to permit a procedure to take place which omitted the committal for sentence caution simply because the accused misbehaved in court.

If the case involves criminal damage there is a further modification to mode of trial conducted in absence (MCA 1980, s.23(3)).

PLEA BEFORE VENUE IN ABSENCE

4–10   Section 17B of the 1980 Act (as inserted by CPIA 1996, s.49(2)) sets out the circumstances when plea before venue may occur in absence. They are broadly follow the circumstances described in section 18, and are:

(a) the accused is aged 18 or over,

(b) his is legally represented,

(c) the court considers by reason of the accused's disorderly conduct it is not practicable for plea before venue to be conducted in his presence, and

(d) the court considers that it should proceed in the absence of the accused (MCA 1980, s.17B (1) (a) to (d)).

If the court decides to proceed in this way the accused's legal representative has authority under the Act to indicate a guilty plea on behalf of the absent accused which has the same status as a guilty plea entered by the accused himself (*ibid.*, s.17B(2)(c)). The difference in the procedure is (as with mode of trial in absence) that there is no provision for a caution to be given that the absent accused may be committed for sentence, and if the representative indicates a not guilty plea the provisions of sections 18(3) and 23 of the Act (see above) will apply. It is submitted, therefore, that for the reasons set out above it will be rare when justices will be satisfied that the court should proceed to deal with plea before venue in absence.

3. Special Procedure for Criminal Damage and Aggravated Vehicle-Taking

(i) General Rule

4–11   The offences of criminal damage and aggravated vehicle-taking are offences triable either way (MCA 1980, s.17 and Sched. 1) and as such are offences which the value involved is relevant to mode of trial (MCA 1980, s.22(1) and Sched. 2).

Whenever an accused appears charged with such offences (and in the case of aggravated vehicle-taking damage is alleged, rather than dangerous driving) a preliminary question arises as to whether the value of the damage exceeds £5,000 (MCA 1980, s.22(1)). Value for these purposes means the cost of buying in the open market the property destroyed or damaged or, if beyond repair, what the property or vehicle would have cost to buy on the open market (MCA 1980, Sched. 2).

If it is clear that the value does not exceed £5,000 then the offence is triable summarily only (MCA 1980, s.22(2)). If it is clear that the value does exceed £5,000 then the offence is triable either way and the court must consider mode of trial and the accused is entitled to elect (MCA 1980, s.22(3)). If, however, it is not clear whether the value exceeds £5,000 the accused must be told in ordinary language: (i) that if he consents to summary trial he will definitely be tried that way, and (ii) that the maximum punishment available to the court is three months' imprisonment or a fine not exceeding level 4 on the standard scale (MCA 1980, s.22(5)). If after being told this the accused consents to summary trial there must be such a trial. If he does not consent the court must consider mode of trial and the accused will be entitled to elect jury trial (MCA 1980, s.22(6)).

(ii) Rule where more than one offence is charged

4–12 Where the accused is charged on the same occasion with two or more criminal damage offences (as defined in Sched. 2 to MCA 1980) of the same or similar character, then value means the aggregate of the series (MCA 1980, s.22(11)). It will not necessarily be the case therefore that an accused will be entitled to jury trial just because all the criminal damage charges he faces add up to more than £5,000. Before allowing an election the court must be satisfied that two or more criminal damage offences are charged on the same occasion, that they constitute a series of two or more offences of the same or similar character, and the aggregate values amount to more than £5,000.

4–13 If a number of defendants are involved collectively in an activity which results in damage exceeding £5,000 it is legitimate for the prosecution to lay individual charges of criminal damage against each defendant separately providing individual amounts of damage can be proved with clarity. If, as a result, the amount in each case is less than £5,000 each offence is summary only (*R. v. Salisbury Magistrates' Court, ex p. Martin* (1987) 84 Cr.App.R. 248).

(iii) Application of the above procedure to Plea before Venue

4–14 Where a single summary only criminal damage offence is founded on the same facts as an indictable offence or forms part of a series of offences which includes an indictable offence the criminal damage may be added to the indictment at the Crown Court (CJA 1988, s.40) but criminal damage is not an offence which may be committed to the Crown Court, with another indictable offence, under section 41 of the Criminal Justice Act 1988. This is because the procedure under section 41 applies only to summary only offences, and criminal damage is an either way offence. (For committal under s.41 of CJA 1988 see Chap. 6, below.)

4–15 The law stated in the previous paragraphs is that set out in sections 17, 19, 22 and 23 of the Magistrates' Courts Act 1980, and Schedule 2 of that Act as amended by section 2(1) of the Aggravated Vehicle-Taking Act 1992. Some, but not all of these provisions are affected by the implementation of section 49 of the Criminal Procedure and Investigations 1996 Act which inserted section 17A (plea before venue) into Part I of the 1980 Act (Criminal Jurisdiction and Procedure). The insertions and amendments made by the 1996 Act made no changes to sections 19, 22 and 23 of the 1980

Act. As a result there is no specific reference to plea before venue (the procedure in section 17A) in those unaffected provisions of the 1980 Act.

The consequence of this drafting is that the special procedure described in §§4–11 and 4–12, above would appear not to apply if the accused pleads guilty rather than not guilty to an offence of criminal damage or aggravated vehicle-taking because the special procedure applies only in mode of trial hearings and not to plea before venue hearings. It would seem, on this view, that an accused who pleaded guilty under section 17A would be liable to be committed for sentence, even if the value of the damage was small. On this view it would seem that Parliament has increased the potential penalty for an offence by introducing a procedural change only and not by explicit legislation.

4–16   It is submitted that this view would produce a perverse result which Parliament cannot have intended and is not a view which the drafting compels justices and practitioners to adopt. The reasons are as follows. Section 22(1) of the 1980 Act places a mandatory obligation upon the court to consider value in respect of the "offence charged by the information" and "where it is clear to the court that the value involved does not exceed the relevant sum, the court *shall* proceed as if the offence were triable only summarily" (s.22(2)). It may be strongly argued that the words "the offence charged by the information" in section 22(1) mean the specific charge in the case in question and not the general description of the offence. Accordingly, it is submitted that it is appropriate for the court to inquire of the prosecutor the value of the damage in the offence charged by the information. If the prosecutor contends that the value does not exceed the relevant sum then the court is obliged to proceed under section 22(2) of the 1980 Act whereby the court *shall* proceed as if the offence was summary only.

It is submitted that this inquiry is appropriate before the court proceeds to take a plea from the accused. Plainly, the provisions of section 17A were not intended to apply to proceedings which are purely summary in nature. It is further submitted that this view is unaffected by the decision in *R. v. Bristol Justices, ex p. Edgar* (1999) 163 J.P. 56 where the Divisional Court decided that an attempt to commit criminal damage of low value was an offence known to the law. In that case the Divisional Court held that the words "as if triable only summarily" in section 22(2) of the 1980 Act did not mean that Parliament had created a separate summary only offence of committing criminal damage of low value. Section 22(2) was a procedural provision which required the court to proceed *as if* the offence were triable only summarily if it was clear that the value of the damage was small. If, at a plea before venue hearing, the prosecutor contends that it is clear that the value is small the decision in *ex p. Edgar* does not inhibit the court from proceeding as if the case were triable only summarily. It is further submitted that the explicit re-drafting of the law in relation to sending for trial (see §§6–33 to 6–37, below) in section 52(3) of the Crime and Disorder Act 1998 puts the intentions of Parliament in this regard beyond doubt.

4. The Decision of the Court on Mode of Trial

(i) The decision to offer the accused summary trial

4–17   The decision of the court upon whether to offer the accused summary trial or to determine that the case is more suitable for trial on indictment follows immediately after the procedural steps summarised in §§4–05 and 4–06, above.

If, following those steps, and having considered the representations the court determines that summary trial is more suitable then the accused must be cautioned as follows:

(i) that despite the determination of suitability for summary trial he may elect trial by jury (MCA 1980, s.20(2)(a)), and

(ii) that if he tried summarily and convicted he may be committed to the Crown Court for sentence (*ibid.*, s.20(2)(b)).

The warning that the accused may be sentenced at the Crown Court even if he consents to summary trial is fundamental. The following form of words have been commended by the Divisional Court as being "crystal clear" (*R. v. Southampton Magistrates' Court, ex p. Sansome* [1999] 1 Cr.App.R.(S.) 112).

"It appears to the court more suitable that you be tried here. You may now consent to be tried by this court but if you wish, you may choose to be tried by a jury instead. If you are tried by this court and are found guilty this court may still send you to the Crown Court for sentence if it is of the opinion that a greater punishment should be inflicted for the offence than it has power to impose. Do you wish to be tried by this court or do you wish to be tried by a jury?"

4–18 If, after these steps have been given, the accused consents to be tried summarily then the court must proceed to summary trial (*ibid.*, s.23(3)(a)). The first procedural step in a summary trial is to ask the accused whether he pleads guilty or not guilty (MCA 1980, s.9(1)). Thus, even if the accused declines to enter a plea under the plea before venue procedure there is a further opportunity to do so at mode of trial stage, although a plea of guilty at this stage is, in practice, rare.

(ii) Decision to decline Summary Trial

4–19 If, after considering the matters set out in §4–06 above, the court considers that the case is more suitable for trial on indictment the accused must be so informed and the court will then proceed to a committal (MCA 1980, s.21).

The decision, under section 21 to proceed as examining justices does not mean that the committal actually commences on that occasion. It has been said that a committal hearing commences when justices begin to inquire into the case once the prosecution has opened the case or called a witness (*R. v. Worcester Magistrates' Court, ex p. Bell, Lester and Leavesly* [1994] Crim.L.R. 133).

(iii) The decision to discontinue a summary trial and proceed to a committal

4–20 If the court has begun to try a case summarily the court may, before the conclusion of the evidence for the prosecution, discontinue the summary trial and proceed to inquire into the case as examining justices (MCA 1980, s.25(2)).

The words "begun to try the case summarily" have been considered by the higher courts on a number of occasions.

4–21 The following general propositions apply to issues arising under section 25(2) of the 1980 Act:

(i) a fair and proper construction must be given to the words; trial means the holding of a trial without the court having a pre-conceived view of the result.

Accordingly, the provisions of section 25(2) may not be used a device in order to convert the proceedings immediately into a committal (*R. v. Birmingham Stipendiary Magistrate, ex p. Webb* (1992) 95 Cr.App.R. 75);

(ii) a trial is not a simple remand hearing, whereby the trial is adjourned to a different date following a plea of not guilty. Accordingly, at the adjourned hearing the court may not seek to use the provisions of section 25(2) straight away (*R. v. St. Helens Justices, ex p. Critchley* (1988) 152 J.P. 102);

(iii) a trial is not an occasion when the accused has enters a guilty plea because a court does not "try" a case when the accused pleads guilty (*R. v. Dudley Justices, ex p. Gillard* [1986] A.C. 442, HL);

(iv) if the accused has plead not guilty there must be something within the facts of the particular case to show that justices have begun to determine guilt or innocence before the trial has "begun". Such facts might be submissions of law on a preliminary issue which have a direct and immediate bearing on the conduct and content of the process of determining guilt or innocence. If such submissions reveal matters which, had justices known at the time of determining mode of trial, would have affected their decision then such submissions may found a proper use of section 25(2) (*R. v. Horseferry Road Magistrates' Court, ex p. K* [1996] 2 Cr.App.R. 574).

(v) The procedure may not be used in order, conveniently for the prosecution, to permit an accused to be tried together with a co-accused who had been committed for trial on a previous occasion (*R. v. Bradford Magistrates' Court, ex p. Grant* [1999] Crim L.R. 324).

(iv) Decision to change to summary trial after commencement of a committal

4–22   If the court has begun to inquire into the case as examining justices then at any time during the hearing the court may with the accused's consent and having heard representations from the parties, proceed to try the case summarily if the nature of the case permits it (MCA 1980, s.25(3)).

A magistrates' court may have begun to hear the case as a committal in two circumstances: (i) if the accused has declined to be tried summarily after the court has determined that the case is suitable for summary trial (MCA 1980, s.20(3)(b)), or (ii) if the court has determined that the case is unsuitable for summary trial (*ibid.*, s.21). If the court has begun a committal under (i) it is often sensible to allow the accused to change his mind and to consent to summary trial after all. This is because by allowing the accused to consent to summary trial the only decision which is being changed is the accused's own election and not the decision by the court as to mode of trial.

Different considerations will arise if the accused wishes to invoke the provisions of section 25(3) and the court is conducting a committal following a decision to decline summary trial under section 21. In these circumstances justices must allow the committal proceedings to continue to a point where there is information enabling them to consider whether, after all, the case is more suitable for summary trial (*R. v. Liverpool Justices, ex p. Crown Prosecution Service, Liverpool* 90 Cr.App.R. 261).

It was stated (*obiter*) in that case that the only circumstances where it could be envisaged that the mode of trial could be altered to summary trial before committal proceedings were commenced was where there was a change of circumstances since the original decision had been taken or there were circumstances existing at the time of the previous hearing which were not drawn to the attention of the court. However, this was not the factual situation which existed and accordingly it was not necessary to decide the point.

4–23 The above powers apply *only* to offences triable either way. Accordingly, where justices commenced committal proceedings for an offence contrary to section 18 of the Offences against the Person Act 1861 (triable only on indictment) but found there was a case to answer only on section 20 wounding (triable either way) section 25(3) did not apply because the only offence to which committal proceedings applied was triable on indictment only (*R. v. Cambridge Justices, ex p. Fraser* [1985] 1 W.L.R. 1391).

SPECIAL PROVISION FOR CASES UNDER THE CUSTOMS AND EXCISE ACTS

4–24 If the prosecution is conducted by HM Customs and Excise into any offence under the Customs and Excise Acts the provisions of section 25(3) may *not* be invoked without the consent of the Commissioners or, if the case was instituted by the Attorney-General, by the Attorney-General (Customs and Excise Management Act 1979, s.147(2)).

In addition there is a broad provisions permitting the prosecutor in a customs' case to appeal *any* decision made by justices in relation to the prosecution (*ibid.*, s.147(3)). The Divisional Court have held that this section permits an appeal against inappropriate mode of trial decisions by justices (*R. v. Commissioners of Customs and Excise, ex p. Wagstaff* [1998] Crim. L.R. 287) as well as too lenient a sentence (*R. v. H.M. Commissioners of Customs and Excise, ex p. Brunt* (1999) 163 J.P. 161).

C. ELECTION

1. Procedure

(i) Each accused must elect individually

4–25 Where more than one accused is before the court then the election must be put to each accused individually (*R. v. Brentwood Justices, ex p. Nicholls* [1992] 1 A.C. 1). In that case the House of Lords held that such individual election was the inevitable interpretation of the wording of section 20(3) of the Magistrates' Courts Act 1980, even though the consequence might be that one accused only might elect trial and others, jointly charged with the same offence might consent to summary trial. The House of Lords agreed with the observations of Lord Bridge in *Chief Constable of West Midlands v. Gillard* (see below) and held that it was not necessarily inimical to justice that two accused should be sentenced by different courts.

The consequences of the *Brentwood Justices* case have now been considered by the Divisional Court in *R. v. West Norfolk Justices, ex p. McMullen* (1993) 157 J.P. 461. In that case three defendants faced a joint charge of theft, and on the occasion of the mode of trial decision two accused appeared and one was absent. The prosecution represented the case suitable for summary trial, but the two accused elected jury trial. At a later date the absent accused was produced before the court and consented to summary trial. The prosecution then called some evidence, and invited the court to use its powers under section 25(2) of the Magistrates' Courts Act 1980 to discontinue the summary trial and to commit the accused to the Crown Court so that there could be a joint trial with his co-defendants who had already elected. (The procedure under s.25(2) is described at §§4–20 and 4–21, above.) The justices agreed, but the Divisional Court quashed the decision holding that while there was an unfettered discretion to discontinue a summary trial and to proceed to a committal under section 25(2), the discretion was subject to the *Wednesbury* principles that it should not be unreasonable, and it was unreasonable to use the procedure simply to avoid the difficulties posed for the prosecution by the *Brentwood Justices* case.

It is not permissible to circumvent the clear decisions in these cases by conducting a preliminary inquiry as to whether all the accused wish to elect trial (*R. v. Ipswich Justices, ex p. Callaghan* (1995) 159 J.P. 748). In that case three accused appeared for mode of trial proceedings and the prosecution indicated that the case was suitable for summary trial. Before considering the question of suitability under section 19 (see §4–06, above) the clerk asked whether any of the accused would elect trial. He was informed that two would so elect, and thereafter justices stated that the matter was not suitable for summary trial in respect of all three accused. The Divisional Court held that the clerk's inquiry was wrong (i) because the issues for consideration under sections 19 and 20 of the Act were separate and distinct, and (ii) because the inquiry deprived each individual accused of the right to consent to summary trial or to elect trial on indictment. The Divisional Court held that it was an inevitable conclusion of the decided cases cited above that two or more defendants charged jointly with a single offence could be tried before different courts (*R. v. Ipswich Justices, ex p. Callaghan*, above). For the same reasons the prosecutor may not invite justices to decline summary trial for an accused simply because another accused has elected to be tried on indictment in the same proceedings (*R. v. Wigan Magistrates' Court, ex p. Layland* [1995] Crim.L.R. 892).

It would seem, therefore, that whatever the practical need, on grounds of convenience and cost, for several accused to be tried together, the prosecution cannot prevent any individual accused who consents to summary trial actually being tried in the magistrates' court even though co-defendants may be tried on the same facts at the Crown Court.

4–26 It is mandatory for the accused to be put to his election when he is before the court on an either way offence and the court has determined that summary trial is suitable. Failure to observe the rules as to election will lead to a summary conviction being quashed (*R. v. Tottenham Justices, ex p. Arthur's Transport Services* [1981] Crim.L.R. 180).

The mandatory four steps must be undertaken in open court, invariably by the clerk, but no precise form of words is laid down providing ordinary language is used (MCA 1980, s.20). It is implicit in the steps laid down in section 20 of the Magistrates' Courts Act 1980 that the accused should apply his mind to them and understand the consequences. If he does not, or there is a doubt about it, there may be a later application to change the election. The circumstances when the court may change its determination as to mode of trial or when the accused may be allowed to change his election are dealt with below.

(ii) Changing election

4–27 It is not uncommon for an accused who has consented to summary trial, when first put to his election, later wishing to elect trial by jury. In deciding whether to allow an application to change an election justices have a discretion whether to allow or refuse the application but discretion must be exercised judicially. The following general principles have been held to apply.

(i) The court is not obliged to allow a change of election solely on the ground that the accused was unrepresented when originally making his election (*R. v. Lambeth Metropolitan Stipendiary Magistrate, ex p. Wright* [1974] Crim.L.R. 444).

(ii) The court is not obliged to allow a change of election if the accused seems to be vacillating from one view to another indefinitely (*R. v. West Bromwich Justices, ex p. Pearson* [1981] Crim.L.R. 709).

(iii) An accused ought not lightly to be deprived of a right to trial by jury (*R. v. Craske, ex p. Commr. of Police for the Metropolis* [1957] 2 Q.B. 591).

(iv) The central factor to which attention should be paid is the state of mind of the accused at the time he made his election. Did he properly understand the nature and significance of the choice which was put to him? Accordingly, where an unrepresented accused consented to summary trial and pleaded guilty he would be unlikely to direct his mind to where he wished to be tried and therefore unlikely to understand the nature and significance of his choice as to the mode of trial (*R. v. Birmingham Justices, ex p. Hodgson* [1985] Q.B. 1131).

(v) It is not a relevant consideration that an accused has become dissatisfied with the advice given to him by former solicitors when consenting to be tried summarily. Providing justices are satisfied that the accused's choice was an informed one they do not have to hear evidence from the former solicitors to determine in their own minds whether the advice to consent to summary trial was the proper advice (*R. v. Bourne Justices, ex p. Cope* (1989) 153 J.P. 161).

4–28 It does not matter whether the accused pleads guilty or not guilty after consenting to summary trial for the purposes of a later application to change the election. In *R. v. Birmingham Justices*, above, the accused pleaded guilty but was later advised that he had an arguable defence. In another case with similar facts an accused pleaded not guilty and later contended that he did not understand the choice between summary trial and jury trial. It was held that the stipendiary magistrate should have allowed a change of election because on the particular facts the original election was not an informed choice (*R. v. Highbury Corner Metropolitan Stipendiary Magistrate, ex p. Weekes* [1985] 1 Q.B. 1147). By the same reasoning if justices have exercised their discretion to allow an accused to change his plea from guilty to not guilty it is an inescapable conclusion that mode of trial proceedings should be started afresh (*R. v. Bow Street Magistrates' Court, ex p. Welcombe* (1992) 156 J.P. 609).

The procedure for deciding whether a change of election should be allowed is for the court to discover, usually from the clerk, what happened on the occasion when the original election was made. In addition the accused himself should have an opportunity to give evidence as to his reasons for wishing to change his election (*R. v. Forest Magistrates' Court, ex p. Spicer* (1989) 153 J.P. 81).

CHAPTER 5

Summary Trial

A. PRELIMINARIES

I. DISQUALIFICATION AND BIAS

1. Introduction

5–01 Disqualification is a category of circumstances, defined by statute and case law, defining the occcasions in which a justice should not sit. Bias is the word used to denote the circumstances generally where a fair trial may not be possible. The word has a wider meaning than obvious and transparent partiality, because by its nature bias is insidious: justices may genuinely believe they are impartial, although a mature examination of the facts by a superior court may reveal a contrary view. It is important that proceedings in magistrates' courts which handle the vast majority of criminal cases and for most citizens represent the face of criminal justice should be regularly and fairly conducted by an independent and unbiased tribunal (*R. v. Hereford Magistrates' Court, ex p. Rowlands and Ingram* (1997) 161 J.P. 258 *per* Lord Bingham C.J.).

The modern law on disqualification and bias is analysed and explained by the House of Lords in the leading case of *R. v. Gough* [1993] 2 W.L.R. 883.

The decision in *Gough* makes it clear that the justices' clerk, as well as the justice, is part of the judicial process, and therefore issues of disqualification and bias apply with equal force to the participation of the clerk in a case. For a full discussion of the judicial role of the clerk see §§11–70 *et seq.*, below.

There are certain circumstances when a justice should not begin to try an information listed before him or, when particular events occur, should not continue to try an information. Broadly there are three circumstances which may disqualify a justice from hearing a case:

(a) Statutory provisions which prohibit the participation of a justice.

(b) Circumstances which exist *before* the case commences which should disqualify a justice from the outset.

(c) Circumstances which arise during a trial which may lead to disqualification, the case being stopped, and the trial starting again before a different bench.

5–02   The general principles applicable to bias in magistrates' courts proceedings have been set out by Lord Bingham C.J. in *R. v. Hereford Magistrates' Court, ex p. Rowlands and Ingram* (1997) 161 J.P. 258 in a judgment which explained the effect of the House of Lords decision in *R. v. Gough*, above, on summary proceedings.

The test is whether there is a real danger of bias in that the decision maker might regard with favour or disfavour the case of a party in the sense that the decision maker is predisposed or prejudiced against one party's case for reasons unconnected with the merits of the case. Real means not without substance, more than a minimal risk, less than a probability. This formulation follows the one adopted in *R. v. Inner West London Coroner, ex p. Dellaglio and Another* (1995) 159 J.P. 133 which had explained the effect of *Gough* to judicial review of the decisions of inferior tribunals.

The famous aphorism that bias should be considered on the basis of whether justice had manifestly been seen to be done would now appear to apply only when the appearance of bias is such as to show a real danger of bias. As a result there is now a less stringent test to be applied when it is urged that justices should disqualify themselves on the grounds of actual or ostensible bias.

2. Statutory Prohibitions Upon Justices

5–03   If a justice is a member of a local authority (*i.e.* county, district or parish council including a joint authority) he must not sit in any proceedings brought by or against the authority of which he is a member (JPA 1997, s.66). The prohibition does not apply by reason only of proceedings being brought by a police officer (JPA 1997, s.66(5)), or to adjudicating on rating matters (JPA 1997, s.67), or control of pollution matters (Control of Pollution Act 1974, s.106).

A justice shall not take part in trying a contested summary trial if in the course of the same proceedings the justice has been informed during a bail application that the accused has one or more previous convictions (MCA 1980, s.42). This prohibition only applies to disqualification in contested cases, and only applies if the justice has learned of any previous convictions in the *same* proceedings. If, therefore, an habitual offender has previously been granted or refused bail in other proceedings it is not a bar to a justice trying him summarily in later proceedings.

3. Disqualification on Grounds of Natural Justice

(i) Direct pecuniary interest in the proceedings

5–04   Any direct pecuniary interest, however small, in the subject of inquiry, will disqualify a justice from sitting on a case (*R. v. Rand* (1866) L.R. 1 Q.B. 230). It is unnecessary to inquire whether such a justice will, in fact, be biased because the fact of the pecuniary interest offends against the principle that no man is to be a judge in his own cause (*Dimes v. Grand Junction Canal* (1853) 3 H.L.C. 759).

(ii) Direct interest in the subject-matter of the proceedings

5–05 The principle which disqualifies a justice automatically if he has a direct pecuniary interest in the proceedings applies with equal force if the justice has a direct interest in the subject of matter of the case before him (*R. v. Bow Street Metropolitan Stipendiary Magistrate, ex p. Pinochet Ugarte (No.2)* [1999] 2 W.L.R. 272). In that case the House of Lords held that there was no good reason for limiting automatic disqualification to that of direct pecuniary interest; if a judge had a relevant interest in the outcome of a case he should be automatically disqualified. This principle would not prohibit a justice sitting on a case involving a charity whose work interested him, but a justice should disqualify himself if he was a director of the charity or took an active role as trustee or director of the charity in question.

(iii) Indirect pecuniary interest in the proceedings

5–06 If a justice does not have a direct pecuniary or propriety interest, but has some indirect interest then he does not become disqualified unless there is a real like-lihood of bias. (*R. v. Camborne Justices, ex p. Pearce* [1955] 1 Q.B. 41). This test, now re-defined as the "real danger" test to ensure that the court is thinking in terms of possibility rather than probability of bias, has now been authoritatively approved by the House of Lords in *R. v. Gough* [1993] 2 W.L.R. 883. On these principles it has been held that a justice holding shares in a company should not sit when that company was being prosecuted (*R. v. Hammond* (1863) 27 J.P. 793) although a Crown Court judge was plainly not disqualified for trying an accused for robbery when one of the losers was a company in which he held shares (*R. v. Mulvihill* [1990] 1 W.L.R. 438).

(iv) Active connection with the proceedings

5–07 If it appears to a justice, having perused the court list, that he is known in the community for public work and by such work would be perceived to have a close connection with either the accused or the victim of the offence, he should either dis-qualify himself from hearing the case or at least declare his connection in open court. By such declaration the prosecution and the defence will have the opportunity of waiv-ing any objection or asking for the case to be tried by a different bench. Accordingly, where a co-opted member of an education authority and a governor of local schools was due to try a case where the victim was a school in a Weights and Measures Act offence she should have either disqualified herself or made known her connection (*R. v. Altrincham Justices, ex p. Pennington* [1975] Q.B. 549).

When a justice considers that there is a possibility of there appearing to be bias by his presence on the bench he should declare his interest at the outset to enable the parties to object if necessary (*R. v. Cambridge Justices, ex p. Yardline Ltd. and Bird* [1990] Crim.L.R. 733). In that case the Divisional Court quashed convictions arising out of a demolition of a listed building because a member of the Bench was employed as a consultant surveyor for the local authority conducting the prosecution.

(v) Knowledge of an accused's previous convictions

5–08 There is no absolute rule that a justice may never try an accused when he knows the accused is of bad character, because in a busy magistrates' court (particu-larly where a regular stipendiary is sitting) it is common for a magistrate sometimes to have knowledge of a defendant's record (*R. v. Metropolitan Stipendiary Magistrate, ex p. Gallagher* (1972) 136 J.P.N. 80). This general principle has been affirmed by the Divisional Court when, applying the test laid down in *R. v. Gough* (see §5–02, above) it was held that not every disclosure of previous convictions will give rise to a real danger of bias (*R. v. Harrow Youth Court, ex p. Prussia* (1997) 161 J.P. 258). In that case it was held that the fact that youth court justices might apprehend that the accused might fact more serious charges by virtue of his presence in the dock did not disqualify the bench from trying him. The implied or express disclosure of a pending charge should be distinguished from the disclosure of previous convictions shortly before or at the time of trial. For these reasons a justice should not proceed to try a case where previous convictions are disclosed in a way which might lead to bias, or a suggestion of bias, in the mind of the public. Accordingly, when in July the chairman of the Bench had presided when the accused was convicted of making threats to his wife, the same magistrate should not have tried the same accused a month later for a drink-driving offence (*R. v. Downham Market Justices, ex p. Nudd* (1988) 152 J.P. 511). Even when no suggestion of bias will arise in the minds of the public it is desirable as a matter of practice that a magistrate who has not dealt with an accused previously should try a contested case, but such desirability is not a proposition of law sufficient to deprive the magistrate of jurisdiction (*R. v. Metropolitan Stipendiary Magistrate, ex p. Gallagher* (*ante*)).

(vi) Prejudice

5–09 If in the course of hearing preliminary applications, for example for bail or legal aid, a magistrate conducts himself in such a way that a reasonable and fair-minded person would come to the conclusion that such bias had been shown against the accused that a fair trial in the future would be impossible then he should disqualify himself (*R. v. McLean, ex p. Aikens* (1975) 139 J.P. 261).

If in the course of a case the chairman of the bench makes a remark which can only be interpreted as a strong instinctive reaction towards believing police evidence then the chairman is biased and the conviction will be quashed (*R. v. Highgate Justices, ex p. Riley* [1996] R.T.R. 151).

It has been emphasised by the Divisional Court that some of the old cases on bias in the magistrates' court might, nowadays, have been decided differently following the test laid down in *Gough* (*R. v. Harrow Youth Court, ex p. Prussia* (1997) 161 J.P. 258). In particular, it has been held that a stipendiary magistrate need not disqualify himself on the grounds of bias from trying a case in which he had conducted a pre-trial *inter partes* hearing relating to disclosure (*R. v. Norfolk Stipendiary Magistrate, ex p. Taylor* (1997) 161 J.P. 773).

4. Disqualification on Grounds of Behaviour

5–10 The following are examples of when a justice becomes disqualified on grounds of behaviour, although obviously the list is not exhaustive.

(i) Mistake in procedure by the bench

5–11 If justices purport to convict the accused after hearing and rejecting submissions of no case to answer at the conclusion of the prosecution case, justices disqualify themselves from hearing the case further and the case should be re-listed before a different bench (*R. v. Midhurst Justices, ex p. Thompson* [1974] Q.B. 137).

(ii) Unjudicial conduct by the bench

5–12 If the chairman of the bench appears to be asleep during the proceedings, and application is made for the chairman to withdraw, the proper course is to accede to the application (*R. v. Weston-Super-Mare Justices, ex p. Taylor* [1981] Crim.L.R. 179).

If the chairman announces "Case Proved" before the accused or his advocate has had an opportunity to address the court, the proceedings are a nullity, even if the error is corrected and counsel is given an opportunity of making a final speech (*R. v. Marylebone Justices, ex p. Yasmin Farrag* [1981] Crim.L.R. 182).

It is improper for a chairman of the bench or a stipendiary magistrate to coerce the accused to reveal his defence to criminal charge during preliminary applications or hearings, even if the justice is not to try the case himself (*R. v. Horseferry Road Magistrates' Court, ex p. Hillier* (1998) 162 J.P. 783).

For other examples of the principle that the proceedings will be quashed if a reasonable and fair-minded person would think that a fair trial had not occurred see *R. v. Marylebone Magistrates' Court, ex p. Perry and Others* (1992) 156 J.P. 696, *R. v. Ely Justices, ex p. Burgess* (1993) 157 J.P. 484, and *R. v. Marylebone Magistrates' Court, ex p. Joseph, The Times,* May 7, 1993.

(iii) Unjudicial conduct by the clerk

5–13 If a reasonable and fair-minded person might think that a fair trial had not taken place because of the behaviour of the clerk, any conviction resulting therefrom is liable to be quashed (*R. v. Richmond and Gilling West Magistrates, ex p. Steel* [1993] Crim.L.R. 711). In that case the clerk of the court, on her own initiative, chose to warn the accused and a witness called on his behalf of the dangers of giving perjured evidence. In the case of the warning to the witness the Bench gave their approval. The Divisional Court held that the warnings were irregular because it suggested that the acccused and his witness might give perjured evidence, and that a fair trial was not seen to have been conducted.

5. Procedure when Disqualification or Bias Arises

(i) Duty of the clerk to avoid disqualification

5–14 The clerk who is responsible for preparing the court lists should use his good sense in avoiding justices seeing unrelated charges against the same defendant in the same list, but there is no rule of law requiring the clerk to do so. If there is a complaint the justices themselves should determine whether their knowledge of other charges in the list should cause them to disqualify themselves by reference to the test of ostensible bias discussed above (*R. v. Weston-Super-Mare Justices, ex p. Shaw* [1987] Q.B. 640).

(ii) Duty of justices to avoid disqualification

5–15 A justice should alert the clerk in advance if he is prohibited by statute from hearing a case or if he knows that he has recently tried the accused (*R. v. Downham Market Justices,* above). Further, a justice has a duty to peruse the names of the parties in the list to ascertain whether there is a close connection giving rise to disqualification (*R. v. Altrincham Justices,* above).

As soon as an issue of possible disqualification arises it should be raised and argued by the party objecting. If this procedure is followed and the parties consent to the trial continuing it is unlikely that a conviction will be subsequently quashed on appeal (*Telfer and Telfer v. D.P.P.* (1996) 160 J.P. 412). However, a justice is not bound to disqualify himself simply because an objection is raised. If he satisfies himself that justice can be done, and can be seen to be done, on the test set out above, he may continue to sit notwithstanding the objection (*R. v. Tooke* (1984) 148 J.P. 661).

If something occurs during a case which may give rise to disqualification, for example inadvertently observing the accused's criminal record, the justice should immediately alert the clerk. The clerk should then inform the parties as to what has occurred so that the accused may request a new trial before a different bench, or agree to continue with or without the justice in question continuing to sit (*R. v. Birmingham Justices, ex p. Robinson* (1986) 150, J.P. 1).

II. DECISIONS AFFECTING JOINT OR SEPARATE TRIALS

5–16   It often happens that an accused is charged with more than one offence and sometimes with a series of offences, or that several accused are charged with the same offence or with a variety of different offences. Where such charges arise out of the same police investigation or the same general incident it is usually the case, as a matter of convenience, that everybody appears initially in the magistrates' court together. There can be no objection to this practice for remand hearings, bail applications, committals or pleas of guilty. However, if the charges are contested and there is to be summary disposal, consideration has to be given to whether there should be joint or separate trials. This consideration will arise when (i) one accused is charged with more than one information, or (ii) where two or more accused are charged with separate informations. In addition consideration should be given to the question of joint or separate trials whenever an adult is charged with a juvenile. The rules as to the latter situation are different and are dealt with at §§5–21 *et seq.*, below.

1. General Rule

5–17   Where one defendant is charged with several informations or where two or more defendants are charged in separate informations, if the facts are connected and if the justices think it fit, the informations may be tried together. Justices should always ask themselves whether it would be fair and just to a defendant or defendants to allow a joint trial.

In applying this rule justices are entitled to follow the same principles as govern trials on indictment. This means that charges may be tried together if they are founded on the same facts or form or are part of a series of offences of the same or a similar character (Indictment Rules 1971, r. 9). Above all, justices should adapt their procedure for trying cases to suit contemporary needs and should not be tied down by technicalities (*Chief Constable of Norfolk v. Clayton* [1983] 2 A.C. 473, HL, at p. 489, *per* Lord Roskill).

This rule involves two points: (a) the facts must be connected, and (b) a joint trial must be just in all the circumstances.

(i) Charges must have a common factual origin

5–18   The law now is that the test of whether the facts are connected is not whether facts of each separate charge are identical in substance or virtually contemporaneous but whether the charges have a common factual origin (*R. v. Barrell and Wilson* (1979) 69 Cr.App.R. 250).

The rule that several informations may be tried together if they form a series of offences of the same or similar character means there has to be a nexus between the offences, that is to say a feature of similarity which enables the offences to be described as a series (*Ludlow v. Metropolitan Police Commissioner* [1979] A.C. 29).

EXAMPLES:

(1) Where an accused was charged with attempted theft from one public house and robbery from another public house both in Acton, West London 16 days apart the offences were similar both in fact and in law and could be tried together (*Ludlow v. Metropolitan Police Commissioner*, above).

(2) Where an accused was charged with assault occasioning actual bodily harm, possessing an offensive weapon and possessing a prohibited drug where the prosecution case was that the accused had taken a drug to put him in a frame of mind to commit the assault the charges could be tried together (*R. v. Conti* (1974) 58 Cr.App.R. 387).

(3) Where an accused was charged with dishonestly receiving photographic equipment in July and dishonestly receiving a credit card in September, where the origin of the stolen goods was different, the two offences could be tried together (*R. v. McGlinchey* (1984) 148 J.P. 73).

(4) Where an accused was charged with burglary and also criminal damage and the damage was not caused in the course of the burglary the two offences could *not* be tried together (*R. v. Hudson* (1952) 36 Cr.App.R. 94).

(5) Where an accused was charged with dangerous driving and using a driving licence with intent to deceive, the two offences could *not* be tried together (*R. v. Bogdal* [1982] R.T.R. 395).

(6) Where the accused was charged with reckless driving, criminal damage to a motor car, and assault occasioning actual bodily harm, these offences could *not* be tried together (*R. v. Marsh* (1986) 83 Cr.App.R. 165).

(ii) A joint trial must be just

5-19   It follows from these cases that it may often be necessary for justices to examine the facts alleged by the prosecution before ruling upon whether a joint trial would be just. For example, in *Conti* ((2), above) the decision would have been different if the drug had not been taken in order to put the accused in a frame of mind to commit the assault. This provided the nexus between the offences. Likewise in *Hudson* ((4), above) the decision would have been different if the criminal damage *had* been caused in order to commit the burglary.

Where the accused is charged with sexual offences against one or more children or young persons, the offences may be tried together providing there is a sufficient relationship between the events described in the evidence that the court can conclude that what happened to one victim provides strong enough support to the evidence of the second victim to make it just for the offences to be tried together (*D.P.P. v. P.* [1991] 2 A.C. 447). In that case, which involved an allegation of sexual abuse within a single family, the House of Lords said that the accused's joint trial at the Crown Court had not been unjust despite the prejudicial effect of more than one allegation of sexual abuse being tried at the same time.

2. Procedure for Deciding on Joint or Separate Trials

5-20   First, the prosecution and the defence should be asked by the court whether there is any objection to the charges being heard and determined together. If consent is forthcoming there is no problem. If consent is not forthcoming then justices should consider the rival submissions and (with advice from the clerk if necessary) rule as they think right in the interests of justice. Absence of consent, either express where the defendant is present or represented and objects, or necessarily brought about by his absence or the absence of representation, should not be an automatic bar to hearing more than one information at the same time or informations against more than one defendant charged on separate informations at the same time (*Chief Constable of Norfolk v. Clayton*, above, *per* Lord Roskill).

If a joint trial would be prejudicial or embarrassing to an accused because of some special feature then justices would be entitled to order separate trials (*Ludlow v. Metropolitan Police Commissioner*, above). If an accused does not consent to a joint trial justices should only order one if it is clearly just to the accused for there to be a joint trial (*Chief Constable of Norfolk v. Clayton*, above).

There is no power to order the simultaneous trial of cross-summonses even if there is consent (*R. v. Epsom Justices, ex p. Gibbons* [1984] Q.B. 574).

3. The Rule Concerning Joint and Separate Trials where an Adult is Charged with a Juvenile

(i) General rule—joint trial in magistrates' court

5–21 If an adult and a child or young person are jointly charged with the same offence the hearing is in the magistrates' court.

Similarly, if a juvenile is charged at the same time as an adult and either is charged with aiding, abetting, causing, procuring, allowing or permitting the other's offence or the juvenile is charged with an offence arising out of circumstances which are the same as, or connected with, those giving rise to an offence with which the adult is charged at the same time the hearing is in the magistrates' court (CYPA 1933, s.46(1) and CYPA 1963, s.18).

In all cases where a magistrates' court is dealing with a child or young person the court must consider whether to make an order under section 39 of the Children and Young Persons Act 1933 to protect the identity of the juvenile in any reports of the proceedings.

(ii) General rule is subject to powers and discretion to remit to youth court

5–22 If a juvenile and an adult appear together before a magistrates' court jointly charged with the same offence, and the hearing commences, if the adult pleads guilty and the juvenile pleads not guilty the court may remit the juvenile for trial in the youth court straight away before hearing any evidence (MCA 1980, s.29(2)(a)).

If the juvenile is tried in a magistrates' court and found guilty he must be remitted to the youth court to be sentenced unless the case can be properly dealt with by means of a fine, or an absolute or conditional discharge (Children and Young Persons Act 1969, s.7(8)).

The juvenile may also be remitted to the youth court without hearing evidence if the adult is committed for trial or discharged and the court agrees to summary trial of the juvenile and he pleads not guilty (MCA 1980, s.29(2)(b)). Without these provisions the trial of the juvenile would have to take place in the adult court in accordance with the general rule set out in §5–21, above.

(iii) Rule where adult elects trial at the Crown Court

5–23 If a juvenile and an adult are charged jointly with an either way offence, and the adult elects trial on indictment, the court must consider whether it is in the interests of justice to commit the juvenile for trial also (MCA 1980, s.24(1)). Such considerations will depend on all the circumstances of the case and it has been held that justices may be informed that the juvenile is of good character (*R. v. South Hackney Juvenile Court, ex p. R.B. (A Minor) and C.B. (A Minor)* (1984) 77 Cr.App.R. 294). Whether it is necessary in the interests of justice to commit the juvenile will depend on the considerations which apply to joint and separate trials generally, although there is an additional consideration concerning the gravity of the offence. Justices should consider committing the juvenile in grave cases because the Crown Court has wider sentencing powers than those possessed by the juvenile court (*R. v. Corcoran* (1986) 8 Cr.App.R. (S.) 118).

The court should consider, having read the charge and heard representations on both sides, whether a sentence greater than that which a youth court could pass might be imposed (*R. v. South Hackney Juvenile Court*, above). If the court does consider that it is in the interests of justice to commit the juvenile for trial it may also commit him in respect of any other indictable offence with which he is charged at the same time providing that offence arises out of circumstances which are the same as or connected with the original offence (MCA 1980, s.24(2)).

B. THE TENDERING OF A PLEA

5–24 The tendering of a plea may properly be said to be a matter which arises before trial because as a matter of practice a plea of not guilty is frequently tendered on a different occasion from that when the evidence is called. Furthermore, it has been said by the Divisional Court that the entering of a plea of "not guilty" does not mark the commencement of the trial, but merely establishes the need for a trial (*Quazi v. D.P.P.* [1988] Crim.L.R. 529) and *R. v. Horseferry Road Magistrate's Court, ex p. K* [1996] 2 Cr.App.R. 574). This is certainly the accepted practice in most magistrates' courts. The occasion on which a plea is tendered by the accused is an important procedural step, as a plea which is entered in error, or by mistake, or which is equivocal will have important consequences on the proceedings generally.

1. Plea of Guilty

5–25 A plea of guilty is a confession to the charge, and if the accused pleads guilty the court may convict him without hearing evidence (MCA 1980, s.9(3)). However, before sentencing the accused after a plea of guilty the plea must be accepted by the court in the sense that the court is satisfied:

  (a) that it is safe to act on the plea; and

  (b) that the accused really intended to put in a plea of guilty (*R. v. Blandford Justices, ex p. G.* [1967] 1 Q.B. 82).

A plea of guilty is properly made when an accused admits the offence in clear terms. The fact that he may subsequently dispute the amount of property stolen or the circumstances in which the offence was committed does not entitle the justices to enter a plea of not guilty. The proper course is to hear the case as a guilty plea and then to examine the areas of factual dispute, if it is necessary, in accordance with the principles of *R. v. Newton* (see §13–42, below) (*R. v. Telford Justices, ex p. Darlington* (1988) 87 Cr.App.R. 194).

(i) Plea of guilty must be voluntary

5–26 If a plea of guilty has been given under duress (*e.g.* where a wife may have committed an offence under coercion from her husband and the husband is standing in the dock beside her) then the plea is either equivocal or a nullity (*R. v. Huntingdon Crown Court, ex p. Jordan* [1981] Q.B. 857). Similarly, if a plea of guilty has been entered by an accused who is confused and did not appreciate the nature of the charge (*e.g.* pleading guilty to theft of motor cars in the mistaken belief that the charges he faced were unlawful taking of motor cars) the plea is equivocal or a nullity (*R. v. Phillips* [1982] 1 All E.R. 245).

5–27 Where the accused pleaded guilty to the wrong charge (murder instead of manslaughter) because the accused was misled by the inadequacies of an interpreter the trial was held to have been a nullity (*R. v. Iqbal Begum* (1991) 93 Cr.App.R. 96).

If an unequivocal plea of guilty is entered by an accused after previously indicating a not guilty plea it is wholly improper for the clerk of the court to ask the accused to give evidence as to why the change of plea had occurred with a view to establishing equivocality (*R. v. Eccles Justices, ex p. Fitzpatrick* (1989) 89 Cr.App.R. 324). Similarly, if a plea of guilty is unequivocal justices should not allow it to be withdrawn and a plea of not guilty substituted under the provisions of section 142 of the Magistrates' Courts Act 1980 (*R. v. Croydon Youth Court, ex p. D.P.P.* [1998] 2 Cr.App.R. 411). (For powers to rectify mistakes see §5–81, below).

(ii) Plea of guilty must be entered by the accused himself

5–28 It is not enough for a legal representative to enter a plea on the accused's behalf (*R. v. Wakefield Justices, ex p. Butterworth* (1969) 114 S.J. 30). If a plea entered by the accused himself is induced by a misunderstanding of the English language then the plea is not a proper plea (*R. v. Iqbal Begum*, above).

EXCEPTIONS:

5–29
(a) When an accused, charged in a summary information with an offence not punishable with more than three months' imprisonment, pleads guilty in his absence. In these circumstances if the clerk receives notification in writing purporting to be given by the accused or by a solicitor acting on his behalf then the court may dispose of the case as if the accused had appeared personally and pleaded guilty (MCA 1980, s.12).

(b) When a corporation wishes to plead guilty. In these circumstances a representative of the corporation may appear in court and plead on the corporation's behalf or, in the corporation's absence, a director or secretary of the corporation may plead guilty on the corporation's behalf (MCA 1980, s.12 and Sched. 3).

(iii) Quashing a conviction following a guilty plea

5–30 In general an accused may only appeal a conviction if he had pleaded not guilty in the first place (MCA 1980, s.108(1)). Thus there is deemed to be finality in the fact that a proper unequivocal plea has been entered (*R. v. Burton-Upon-Trent Justices, ex p. Woolley* (1995) 159 J.P. 183). In recent years there have been a number of cases where the Divisional Court has been asked to quash a conviction despite the fact that the accused had pleaded guilty. The circumstances in which the Divisional Court will intervene are strictly limited, and the broad principles may be stated as follows.

(a) In general the jurisdiction of the Divisional Court to quash a conviction following a plea of guilty is confined to cases where the plea was obtained by fraud, collusion or perjury on the part of the prosecution (*R. v. Burton-Upon-Trent Justices, ex p. Woolley* (1995) 159 J.P. 183).

(b) Where the prosecution is dependent on procedures entirely conducted by the police, or by the police in conjunction with an expert such as a doctor, the accused has no control of the procedures and a defendant may plead guilty relying wholly on the correctness of those procedures. In such a case the Divisional Court will, exceptionally, intervene if the procedures adopted by the police or the expert are shown to be manifestly false producing a result which induces a plea of guilty (*R. v. Bolton Justices, ex p. Scally* [1991] 1 Q.B. 537, and *R. v. Kingston-Upon-Thames Justices, ex p. Khana* [1986] R.T.R. 364).

(c) If no injustice has been caused to an accused, for example if an accused pleaded guilty to driving with excess alcohol when the procedures followed at the police station were not in accordance with those laid down in *D.P.P. v. Warren* [1993] A.C. 319, a plea of guilty will not be set aside even if the decision in *Warren* was not referred to by the prosecution (*R. v. Penrith Justices, ex p. Marks, The Times*, August 4, 1995).

(d) Where there is a failure by the prosecution to comply with the obligations of disclosure the defence might be ignorant of witnesses favourable to their case, and a plea of guilty might be based on such failure. In these circumstances the failure by the prosecution would amount to *suppressio veri* which had the same effect as *suggestio falsi* (*R. v. Leyland Justices, ex p. Hawthorn* [1979] Q.B. 283).

(e) Mere procedural impropriety on the part of the Bench or a plea of guilty resulting from poor advice from the accused's solicitors will not confer jurisdiction on the Divisional Court to intervene and quash the conviction (*R. v. Home Secretary, ex p. Al-Mehdawi* [1990] 1 A.C. 876).

2. Changing a Plea from Guilty to Not Guilty

5–31   A court may *consider* an application for an accused's plea to be changed from guilty to not guilty at any time before sentence, even if the case has been adjourned to a new date for sentence. This is because the word "conviction" denotes a judicial determination of a case which is the finding of guilt (or the acceptance of a plea) together with a sentence (*S. (an Infant) v. Manchester City Recorder* [1971] A.C. 481).

This principle is the same whether the accused is dealt with throughout by magistrates or whether he is committed to the Crown Court for sentence (*R. v. Mutford Justices, ex p. Harber* [1971] 2 Q.B. 291). Whether or not a court will allow a change of plea is entirely a matter of judicial discretion and should only be exercised in clear cases and very sparingly (*S. v. Manchester City Recorder*, above).

The court is entitled to take into account that the accused's likely reason for an application to change a plea from guilty to not guilty was a desire to avoid a custodial sentence. In such circumstances, in the court's discretion, an application to change a plea may be refused (*R. v. South Tameside Magistrates' Court, ex p. Rowland* (1984) 148 J.P. 202).

If discretion is exercised to allow an accused to change his plea from guilty to not guilty it is an inescapable conclusion that mode of trial proceedings be started afresh (*R. v. Bow Street Magistrates' Court, ex p. Welcombe* (1992) 156 J.P. 609).

3. Equivocal Plea

5–32   An equivocal plea is when, at the trial, the accused says "Guilty but ... " and adds a statement which showed he was really pleading not guilty. It is not a case of a defendant unequivocally pleading "Guilty" and then saying "I made a mistake" (*R. v. Durham Quarter Sessions, ex p. Virgo* [1952] 2 Q.B. 1, *per* Lord Goddard C.J.).

(i) Court has a duty to ensure a plea is not equivocal

5–33   The duty of the court to act on a plea of guilty only when it is satisfied that it is safe to do so (*R. v. Blandford Justices*, above) means that in practice the court's duty will differ depending upon whether the accused is represented or unrepresented, or whether he is absent.

(a) WHEN THE ACCUSED IS REPRESENTED

5–34   In cases where a defendant is legally represented and it becomes apparent that the lawyer has advised a plea of guilty under a mistaken view of the nature of the charge, justices should consider whether in the exercise of their discretion they should allow a change of plea on the grounds of equivocality. They are entitled to test the validity of the assertion that the sole reason for the plea was the lawyer's mistaken belief about the law (*P. Foster (Haulage) Ltd v. Roberts* [1978] 2 All E.R. 751).

It will, therefore, be a rare case where an argument for equivocality will succeed when the accused has had the benefit of legal advice. The growing use of "advance information" requests and the Duty Solicitor Scheme in magistrates' courts means that the accused is usually fully aware of the allegation against him.

(b) WHEN THE ACCUSED IS UNREPRESENTED

5–35   If the accused is unrepresented or is of tender years the accused himself may say something which casts doubt on the correctness of the plea. In those circumstances the court *must* refuse to accept the guilty plea and proceed as if the case were contested (*R. v. Blandford Justices*, above).

(c) WHEN AN ACCUSED IS ABSENT

5–36   If the accused pleads guilty by letter and there are several informations to be heard, the court must ensure that the plea of guilty applies to all the informations and not merely to one or some of the informations (*R. v. Burnham Justices, ex p. Ansorge* [1959] 1 W.L.R. 1041).

If the contents of the letter reveal a doubt about the plea the case must be re-listed as a contested matter. For a full account of the procedure to be followed when an accused is absent see §§1–30 *et seq.*, above.

(ii) Raising equivocal plea on appeal to the Crown Court

5–37   If an accused has pleaded guilty and has been sentenced in the magistrates' court but he later wishes to contend that the guilty plea was equivocal, the matter must be argued in the Crown Court. The magistrates' court no longer has jurisdiction, and the court is *functus officio* once sentence has been passed (see *S. v. Recorder of Manchester*, above). The court may not seek to re-open the matter under section 142 of the Magistrates' Courts Act 1980 because such applications only arise when the plea has been one of not guilty.

The procedure in such cases is as follows. First, the Crown Court must be satisfied that there is a prima facie case that the plea before the magistrates was equivocal, by hearing from the appellant. Only if there is such a prima facie case will the Crown Court embark on the second stage which is to hear evidence on affidavit from the clerk or the chairman of the Bench about what in fact happened at the magistrates' hearing. Only after hearing this evidence could the Crown Court be satisfied that an equivocal plea had been entered. If the court was so satisfied it should remit the case to the magistrates for a rehearing. However, the circumstances in which such a procedure *would* be adopted are likely to be out of the ordinary to say the least (*R. v. Rochdale Justices, ex p. Allwork* [1981] 3 All E.R. 434).

5–38   The reason why it would be very rare for such cases to be remitted is that if the magistrates have followed the procedure properly in relation to accepting a plea of guilty it is unlikely that the Crown Court would overturn the decision.

Secondly, magistrates become *functus officio* in relation to the question of plea once satisfied that it is safe to accept and act upon a guilty plea. Accordingly a case remitted for rehearing by the Crown Court without the clearest possible evidence could lead to an unseemly dispute between the two courts. Such an unseemly dispute may be avoided if the proper procedure laid down in *R. v. Rochdale Justices*, above, is followed. If it is followed the Crown Court has the power to direct a rehearing, and the magistrates' court has a corresponding duty to rehear the case as a not guilty plea (*R. v. Plymouth Justices, ex p. Hart* [1986] Q.B. 950).

4. Plea of Not Guilty

5–39   A plea of not guilty means that it is incumbent upon the prosecution to prove all the ingredients of the charge or summons. The court is obliged to hear evidence and the parties (MCA 1980, s.9). Unlike a plea of guilty, which is a confession, a plea of not guilty is not an assertion of innocence necessarily. The plea merely puts the prosecution to proof.

5. Special Pleas: *Autrefois Acquit* and *Autrefois Convict*

Principles

5–40   The principle of *autrefois convict* and *acquit* is that the accused may not be tried on a second occasion for a crime of which he has previously been convicted or acquitted, or for a crime which is substantially the same as the one for which he was previously convicted or acquitted (*Connelly v. D.P.P.* [1964] A.C. 1254).

It has been said that their Lordships speeches in *Connolly* establish two broad principles:

(i) that no man should be punished twice for an offence arising out of the same, or substantially the same, set of facts; and

(ii) that there should be no sequential trials for offences on an ascending scale of gravity (*R. v. Beedie* [1998] Q.B. 356).

Strictly the plea *autrefois acquit* or *autrefois convict* may only be raised in a trial on indictment, although the principles giving rise to such pleas are the same in the magistrates' court (*D.P.P. v. Porthouse* (1989) 89 Cr.App.R. 21). The question is whether the accused was previously convicted or acquitted on the same or substantially the same offence as the one for which he is before the court.

The meaning of previously convicted or acquitted is that the adjudication must have been by a properly constituted court, having jurisdiction to try the case, and that the accused must have been in jeopardy of conviction.

5–41   These principles have been authoritatively explained and applied by the Court of Appeal (Criminal Division) in *R. v. Dabhade* [1993] 2 W.L.R. 129. The court went on to explain the legal effect of charges being dropped, or new charges being preferred in substitution of old charges, on the doctrine of *autrefois acquit*:

(i) If a charge is summarily dismissed, because the prosecution recognise the difficulties which exist in prosecuting that charge, and a new charge is substituted, then the doctrine of *autrefois acquit* cannot arise (*Broadbent v. High* [1985] R.T.R. 359).

(ii) If a charge is dismissed without a hearing on the merits (for example because the prosecution are unable to proceed), then the doctrine of *autrefois acquit* does not strictly arise, although there is a well-known rule of practice that the prosecution may not institute fresh proceedings on the same or an essentially similar charge (*R. v. Pressick* [1978] Crim.L.R. 377).

The principles in *Connolly* apply when there has been a previous conviction or a previous acquittal. Thus, if there is an acquittal of a lesser offence which contains the same ingredients of a greater offence the accused cannot be convicted in a subsequent trial of the greater offence because such conviction would, in effect, reverse the acquittal of the lesser offence. However, that conclusion does not mean that in the *same* proceedings an accused must be found not guilty of the full offence if, on the particular facts, he was acquitted of an attempt to commit that offence (*R. v. Velasquez* [1996] 1 Cr.App.R. 155).

If, notwithstanding a previous acquittal, justices could have found the accused guilty of some other offence (not previously charged) and he is later charged with it a plea of *autrefois acquit* will fail. For example, if an accused is acquitted of theft there is no bar to subsequent proceedings for going equipped for theft. The ingredients of the two offences are different. Similarly an acquittal for being in charge of a motor vehicle with excess alcohol on the basis of the statutory defence (no likelihood of driving) did not necessarily involve an inevitable acquittal on a further charge of driving with excess alcohol based on an earlier occasion. Accordingly, the accused could not plead *autrefois acquit* when the prosecution issued a new summons based on that earlier incident (*R. v. Truro and South Powder Magistrates' Court, ex p. McCullagh* (1991) 155 J.P. 411).

5–42   The plea of *autrefois acquit* may not be raised simply because the prosecution choose to offer no evidence on a lesser charge which contains the same ingredients of a more serious charge upon which the Crown wishes to proceed (*D.P.P. v. Khan* [1997] R.T.R. 82). In that case the accused faced two charges arising out of the same incident, namely dangerous driving and careless driving. The Crown offered no evidence on the careless driving charge which was dismissed and the justices went on to convict of dangerous driving. The Divisional Court held the adjudication of not guilty to careless driving simply reflected the decision of the prosecution not to proceed on that charge and was not an acquittal on the merits. Accordingly, the plea of *autrefois acquit* did not apply. The reasoning of the Divisional Court in this case followed that of the Court of Appeal in *R. v. Brookes* [1995] Crim.L.R. 630.

For the same reasons a refusal of an adjournment by justices in a mode of trial hearing, followed by a decision by the prosecution to "offer no evidence" is not an acquittal entitling the accused to rely on *autrefois acquit* if the proceedings are revived (*R. v. Bradford Magistrates' Court, ex p. Daniel and another, The Independent,* June 16, 1997).

By contrast, if a properly constituted court has dismissed an information because the prosecution have no witnesses in court and a judicial exercise of discretion to refuse an adjournment has been made, there cannot be a second trial on a fresh information. This is because a dismissal of the charge was a trial on the *merits* in the sense that the accused was before the court and had been put in jeopardy of a conviction (*R. v. Swansea Justices, ex p. Purvis* (1981) 145 J.P. 252).

Examples

5–43 (i) If a previous conviction or acquittal had occurred because of some procedural irregularity, such as a conviction where the witnesses had been unsworn (*R. v. Marsham* (1912) 76 J.P. 284), then the accused was not in jeopardy because the proceedings were irregular. Similarly an accused was not in jeopardy of conviction if the wrong certificate relating to an excess alcohol charge was served originally, leading to an acquittal on a preliminary argument, and the prosecution were entitled to take out a fresh summons (*Williams v. D.P.P.* [1991] 1 W.L.R. 1160).

(ii) If the first information was so faulty (*e.g.* by combining particulars relating to both section 4 and section 5 of the Road Traffic Act 1988) that the accused could never have been convicted upon it, a plea of *autrefois acquit* could not be raised on a second, correctly worded, summons arising out of the same facts (*D.P.P. v. Porthouse*, above).

5–44 An accused who raises the plea of *autrefois convict* or *acquit* has the burden of proving to the court on the balance of probabilities that there has been a previous acquittal or conviction on the merits (*R. v. Coughlan and Young* (1976) 63 Cr.App.R. 33). While *autrefois convict* and *acquit* are technically pleas only available on indictment, a dismissal of an information has the same effect as an acquittal on indictment (MCA 1980, s.27) and the courts have applied the same principles to summary proceedings as for trials on indictment.

C. The Course of the Trial

1. The Prosecution Case

(i) Opening speech

5–45 Before calling the evidence the prosecutor may open the case (MCR 1981, r. 13(1)). The purpose of an opening address is to acquaint the court (who will not have any papers) of the nature of the case and to draw attention to the main issues which will arise in the evidence. There is no obligation on a prosecutor to open his case, and in simple and straightforward cases the prosecutor may wish to call the evidence without delivering an opening address.

(ii) Duty of the prosecution in calling witnesses

5–46 The duty of the prosecution in calling witness in a summary trial has now been comprehensively reviewed by the Divisional Court in *R. v. Haringey Justices, ex p. D.P.P.* [1996] 2 W.L.R. 114. The following general principles apply:

1. The prosecution has an unfettered discretion as to which witnesses should be called to prove the case at the stage in which the prosecution case is being prepared.

2. Thereafter, there is a distinction between summary only offences and offences triable either way.

3. If the offence is triable either way and advance information is served such service is the equivalent procedural step to the service of witness statements in the Crown Court.

4. The legal effect of service of witness statements is that the prosecution has a duty either to call the witness or to ensure that such witness attends court so that he may be called by the defence (*R. v. Oliva* [1965] 1 W.L.R. 1028).

5. Thereafter the following principles should apply:

   (i) the prosecution ought normally to call or offer to call all the witnesses who give direct evidence of the primary facts of the case, unless, for good reason the prosecutor regards the witness's evidence as unworthy of belief;

   (ii) it is for the prosecutor to decide which witnesses give direct evidence of the primary facts of the case;

   (iii) the prosecutor is the primary judge of whether or not a witness to the material events is incredible, or unworthy of belief. (It goes without saying that a prosecutor may not condemn a witness as incredible merely because he gives an account at variance with that of a larger number of witnesses, and one which is less favourable to the prosecution than that of the others);

   (iv) a prosecutor properly exercising his discretion in this way is not obliged to proffer a witness merely in order to give the defence material with which to attack the credit of other witnesses on whom the Crown relies.

6. The procedure stated above does not apply if the offence is summary only because specific obligations for trials of purely summary offences might make prosecutors reluctant to make voluntary disclosure of witness statements in those trials. The Divisional Court noted the absence of an obligation to provide advance information but commended the practice of often providing the defence with a courtesy bundle comprising a summary of the prosecution case or copies of witness statements.

7. In addition the above procedure does not apply if the prosecution wish to call a particular witness but, despite their best endeavours to secure the attendance of the witness, it is impossible for the prosecution to do so (*R. v. Cavanagh and Shaw* (1972) 56 Cr.App.R. 407). It has been said, in relation to a Crown Court trial, that these principles apply even if the prosecution have failed to follow the witness warning procedures precisely provided it was in the interests of justice generally for the trial to go ahead (*R. v. Gunden* [1997] Crim.L.R. 903). It is submitted that this latest case should have limited application in summary trials because justices are unlikely to be able to assess the issues in a case before the evidence is actually heard.

5–47 In *Haringey Justices*, above, the issue in the case was whether the CPS were properly entitled to decline to call a police officer in a summary trial who was under suspension for a wholly unrelated matter. The Divisional Court disapproved of the general policy statement of the CPS not to call such a witness if it was possible to proceed without his evidence. The Divisional Court held that such a policy was appropriate only if the suspended officer's evidence was peripheral or merely corroborative of other evidence. On the other hand if such a witness was effectively the complainant and central to the incident giving rise to the trial the proper course was to call the suspended officer. Once called the fact of the suspension should be elicited in evidence; he should be asked whether he admitted or denied the allegation giving rise to the suspension and there should be no cross-examination on the matters relating to the suspension.

(iii) Order of witnesses

5–48 The prosecutor has a discretion as to the order in which witnesses are called, although the usual practice is to call the evidence in chronological order as far as possible. It is a rule of practice that witnesses should remain outside court until called (*R. v. Bexley Justices, ex p. King* [1980] R.T.R. 49).

(iv) The swearing of witnesses

(a) GENERAL RULE

5–49 All evidence given before a magistrates' court shall be on oath (MCA 1980, s.98), unless the court admits the unsworn evidence of children. A witness who objects to being sworn may make an affirmation instead of taking the oath (Oaths Act 1978, s.8(1) and (3)).

The form of oath is prescribed by the Oaths Act 1978 and it may be summarised as follows: Christians are sworn on the New Testament, Jews on the Old Testament, Muslims on the Koran and Sikhs on their Holy Book the Adi Graath. Non-believers are permitted to affirm, and so also are believers if it is not practicable without inconvenience to administer an oath appropriate to their belief. In practice, this may arise if a holy book is not available in the courthouse. The purpose of taking an oath is that it should be binding on a witness's conscience. Therefore, if a Muslim witness mistakenly takes the oath using a New Testament Bible the evidence is not invalidated providing the court is satisfied of the following:

(i) that it was an oath which appeared to the court to be binding on the conscience of the witness, and

(ii) it was an oath which the witness himself considered to be binding on his conscience.

If on proper inquiry the court is so satisfied, such an oath is properly administered because section 1(3) of the Oaths Act 1978 provides that for persons who are neither Christians nor Jews the oath shall be administered in any lawful manner (*R. v. Kemble* [1990] 1 W.L.R. 1111).

(b) CHILDREN

5–50 The statutory provisions relating to the evidence of children has undergone rapid change. In the Criminal Justice Act 1988 substantial changes were introduced with the object of making the reception of the evidence of children easier, but these changes were then altered further by amendments added in the Criminal Justice Act 1991 and the Criminal Justice and Public Order Act 1994.

The present law is as follows:

(i)   a child's evidence in criminal proceedings shall be given unsworn;

(ii) a child's evidence shall be received unless it appears to the court that the child is incapable of giving intelligible testimony;

(iii) child means a person under 14 years of age (CJA 1988, s.33A(1), (2A), and (3).

The words "intelligible testimony" mean evidence that is capable of being understood (*R. v. Hampshire* [1996] Q.B. 1). It has been said (in the context of receiving evidence on video from a child) that the words also mean the child is able to understand questions and to answer them in a manner which is coherent and comprehensible (*D.P.P. v. M* [1997] 2 Cr.App.R. 70). For these purposes it would be rare for the court to receive expert evidence on the point (*G v. D.P.P.* [1997] 2 Cr.App.R. 83).

(v) The reading of statements, certificates and declarations

5–51   While the general rule is for oral testimony to be given on oath in order to prove a charge, there is scope for evidence to be read in certain circumstances. These circumstances have been created by statute with the object of saving time in trials. The most important of these statutory provisions are discussed below.

(a) SECTION 9 STATEMENTS

5–52   A statement made under section 9 of the Criminal Justice Act 1967 is admissible to the same extent as any oral evidence of the contents of the statement would be. The main conditions of admissibility of section 9 statements are that there is a declaration by the maker that the contents are true, that a copy is served on the opposing party before the hearing, and that there is no objection within seven days of the service to the statement being tendered in evidence (CJA 1967, s.9).

A statement admitted under section 9 is not conclusive of the matters stated in it. Accordingly justices are not bound to reject any live evidence given which may be in conflict with facts given in a section 9 statement, although it is bad practice for evidence which may be contentious to be given in section 9 form (*Lister v. Quaife* (1982) 75 Cr.App.R. 313).

(b) STATEMENTS OF WITNESSES IN FEAR

5–53   If a potential live witness is in fear, or is kept away from the court, there is provision for his statement to be read under the provisions of Part II of the Criminal Justice Act 1988. The statement must have been made to a police officer or some other person investigating the offence, but the statement does not have to be a formal statement within the meaning of section 102 of the Magistrates' Courts Act 1980 (CJA 1988, s.23(3)).

There are two issues which may arise when it is asserted that a witness is in fear. First, the witness may be absent and fail to attend court at all on the grounds of fear, and second the witness may appear in the witness box and then be unable to give evidence through fear. Both these matters have been considered in two cases, *Neill v. North Antrim Magistrates' Court* [1992] 1 W.L.R. 1220, and *R. v. Ashford Magistrates' Court, ex p. Hilden* [1993] 2 W.L.R. 529. In considering whether an absent witness is afraid the court may receive first-hand hearsay on the point. This means that a witness (usually a police officer) may give evidence that he saw and spoke to the witness who was afraid and whose demeanour was consistent with being in fear. However, the court may not receive second-hand hearsay. This means that a police officer may not give evidence that he spoke to somebody who said that the absent witness was too afraid to attend court (*Neill v. North Antrim Magistrates' Court*, above). For the importance of observing the rule excluding second-hand hearsay see *R. v. Wood and Fitzsimmons* [1998] Crim.L.R. 213 where it was held that the defence are entitled to cross-examine the deponent who gives evidence about a witness in fear.

5–54 Where a witness attends court and enters the witness box justices are entitled to decide that a witness does not give evidence through fear by observing the demeanour of the witness. It is not necessary for the witness to state that he is in fear nor necessary for the witness to have commenced giving evidence. If the conditions in section 23(3) of the Criminal Justice Act 1988 are met then the statement becomes admissible under section 26 of the Act even if justices have not read the statement, provided they are appraised of the contents of it and have enough information for leave to be granted for it to be admitted (*R. v. Ashford Magistrates' Court, ex p. Hilden*, above). For the same reasons justices may conclude that a witness is in fear after starting to give evidence and before the evidence is completed (*R. v. Waters* (1997) 161 J.P. 249).

There is wide discretion given to justices to refuse to allow such a statement to be read if it would cause unfairness to the accused. The detailed provisions setting out the issues which should govern this discretion are contained in section 25 of, and Schedule 2 to, the Criminal Justice Act 1988. If the court is invited to allow a statement of a witness in fear to be read the procedure is that the court must hear evidence on oath that the witness is, in fact, in fear either as a result of the offence itself, or of something said subsequently about the possibility of the witness testifying (*R. v. Acton Justices, ex p. McMullen; R. v. Tower Bridge Magistrates' Court, ex p. Lawlor* (1991) 92 Cr.App.R. 98). The court must be satisfied upon the criminal standard of proof that the witness is in fear, although the court need not be satisfied that the fear is based on reasonable grounds (*R. v. Acton Justices*, above). If, after conducting this preliminary inquiry, the court is satisfied that the witness is in fear, the court must then go on to consider whether, in the interests of justice, the statement should be admitted.

(c) CERTIFICATES

5–55 The automatic computer print-out showing the breath/alcohol level of a driver is admissible providing it is signed by the police officer administering the test and a copy is served on the accused at the time or not later than seven days before the hearing (RTOA 1988, s.16(1) and (2)). A certificate is also admissible to show that a particular motor vehicle was owned by a particular person or firm on a particular occasion (RTOA 1988, s.11).

This summary is not exhaustive, and it is beyond the scope of this book to discuss the full evidential conditions applicable to the reading of statements and certificates.

(vi) The agreement of facts

5–56 Instead of proving a particular fact by calling a witness, the parties by agreement may admit a particular fact and such admission of that fact shall be conclusive evidence in the proceedings (CJA 1967, s.10). In practice, such admissions are made when evidence of a formal nature has to be proved and the parties admit the evidence to save time and expense. If such admission is to be made it must be written down and signed by the party making the admission (MCR 1981, r. 71).

(vii) The production of exhibits

5–57 Real evidence, in the form of chattels or documents, often forms an important part of the prosecution case, in which case the real evidence is produced as an exhibit. The procedure is for the particular witness who found or came by the piece of real evidence to attend court with it and to produce it for inspection and examination by the court. However, there is no obligation upon the prosecution to produce every piece of real evidence resulting from a police investigation (*Hockin v. Alquist Brothers Ltd.* [1944] K.B. 120). For example, in a shoplifting case the prosecution are not obliged to produce the stolen articles if they are perishable, but a prosecution witness may properly give evidence of their existence at one time. In addition, where original exhibits are too large or unwieldy to be produced conveniently photographs of them may be admitted (*R. v. Uxbridge Justices, ex p. Sofaer* (1987) 85 Cr.App.R. 367).

5–58　While the rules relating to the admissibility of real evidence and exhibits is properly a matter of evidence (and therefore not fully discussed here), certain procedural matters should be mentioned:

(a) *Statutory instruments*

Unlike Acts of Parliament where the court may take judicial notice of their existence, subordinate legislation must be proved by the production of a copy printed by H.M. Stationery Office (Documentary Evidence Act 1868, s.2).

(b) *Bye-laws*

These may be proved by the production of a printed copy purporting to be made by the local authority making the bye-law and endorsed with a certificate signed by the proper officer of the authority (Local Government Act 1972, s.238).

(c) *Proceedings in the magistrates' court*

These may be proved by the production of a certified copy of the court register (MCR 1981, r. 68).

(d) *Tape-recorded police interviews*

The procedure for admitting the contents of a tape-recorded interview is now governed by Code of Practice E of the Police and Criminal Evidence Act 1984. In general terms the Code allows a written summary of the interview containing a balanced account of it to be prepared prior to trial and produced at the trial. The detailed procedure for the preparation of transcripts has been laid down in *Practice Direction (Crime: Tape Recording: Police Interviews)* [1989] 1 W.L.R. 631. If it is not possible for a summary to be agreed between prosecution and defence, the tape may be played in court. The procedure to be followed in these circumstances is similarly laid down in the *Practice Direction*, above.

(e) *Written confessions*

If the accused signs or initials an interview under caution, or otherwise adopts the contents as correct, the notes may be produced as an exhibit and placed before the justices (*R. v. Fenlon* (1980) 71 Cr.App.R. 307). If the accused does not sign the notes, even if contemporaneously recorded, they may not be produced as an exhibit (*R. v. Dillon* (1985) 149 J.P. 182). The only exception to this rule is that if the contemporaneous note is alleged by the defence to be a concoction, the notes could be produced as an exhibit in order to rebut that suggestion (*R. v. Sekhon* (1987) 85 Cr.App.R. 19).

(viii) The proof of confessions—trial-within-a-trial

5–59 The prosecution often rely on admissions or confessions made by the accused orally or in writing under caution. If the defence represent to the court that such a confession was, or may have been, obtained by oppression, or as a result of something said which may render the confession unreliable then the confession is not admissible unless a preliminary inquiry is made by the court. Such an inquiry is often called a "trial-within-a-trial" and it involves the prosecution satisfying the court beyond reasonable doubt that the confession was not obtained by oppression or as a result of some inducement (PACE 1984, s.76(2)).

There is an obvious difficulty about this procedure in a magistrates' court because justices are judges of both fact and law, and in order to rule whether a confession is admissible they must usually hear the contents of the disputed admissions. However, since the Police and Criminal Evidence Act 1984 came into force it is mandatory for justices to hold a trial-within-a-trial if requested (*R. v. Liverpool Juvenile Court, ex p. R.* [1987] 3 W.L.R. 224). The procedure is as follows:

(a) The defence must make a representation before the close of the prosecution case that the confession is not admissible. The representation must be a formal application and the court is not obliged to conduct an inquiry simply because of suggestions in cross-examination that the confession was obtained improperly.

(b) Once a defence representation has been made the prosecution must call evidence to prove beyond reasonable doubt that the confession was obtained in accordance with PACE 1984.

(c) The accused may give evidence confined to the question of admissibility only, and he may not be asked at this stage whether the confession is true (*Wong-Kam-ming v. R.* [1980] A.C. 247).

(d) At the conclusion of the trial-within-a-trial the justices must rule upon whether the confession is admissible or not.

(e) If the confession is ruled admissible it should never be necessary to call the prosecution witnesses who prove the confession again during the trial itself.

The reasons why this procedure is important is that the accused is entitled to have his confession excluded even if it is true, and this can only be achieved in a trial-within-a-trial, and secondly he is entitled to know the strength of the prosecution case against him before the Crown's case is closed, as this might affect his decision to give evidence or not. The defence are not obliged to request a preliminary inquiry on admissibility, and they are entitled to cast doubt on the reliability of any admissions during the trial (*R. v. Liverpool Juvenile Court, ex p. R.*, above).

5–60 If the application to exclude evidence under section 76 of the Police and Criminal Evidence Act 1984 also involves a submission that the evidence should be excluded under section 78 (the unfairness discretion) then it is appropriate for the above procedure to be followed (*Halawa v. Federation Against Copyright Theft* (1995) 159 J.P. 816). This is because applications under sections 76 and 78 may be made consecutively (*R. v. Allardice* (1988) 87 Cr.App.R. 380). There is no obligation to conduct a *voir dire* when the only issue raised is one based on section 78. This is because the issues under section 76 and section 78 of the 1984 Act are different, and accordingly there is no right on the part of the accused to have questions of discretionary exclusion of evidence determined in a trial-within-a-trial in summary proceedings (see "Rulings on Questions of Law" paragraph 5–73, below). However, despite this procedural rule justices have an overriding duty to ensure that summary trials are conducted fairly (*S.F.J. v. Chief Constable of Kent* [1982] Crim.L.R. 682). For this reason it has been said that there may be occasions when it would be fair to conduct a *voir dire* when an application relates only to the exclusion of evidence under section 78 because in general an accused should be able to have the opportunity to secure the exclusion of unfair evidence before he is required to testify on the main issue in the case. In these circumstances the procedure to be followed would be for the whole of the prosecution case to be heard, including the disputed evidence, before any trial-within-a-trial is held. This is because the question of excluding admissible evidence under section 78 must be decided "having regard to all the circumstances including the circumstances in which the evidence was obtained" (PACE 1984, s.78(1)) and fairness to the prosecution requires that the whole of the prosecution case should be before the court before justices apply their minds to section 78 (*Halawa v. Federation Against Copyright Theft (ante)*.

In that case it was stressed that such a procedure would not have to be adopted every time a point arose under section 78 and it would depend on the particular reason why an application to exlude unfair evidence was being made as to whether a *voir dire* should be held or not. It was suggested that the defence advocate should give the prosecution an idea of the nature of the application so that the court be informed and then decide whether, in the circumstances, a trial-within-a-trial should be held.

(ix) Dock identification in a summary trial

5–61   As a general rule a dock identification, in the sense that a witness is asked to look for the culprit in court, is highly undesirable because little weight can be attached to an identification in such circumstances (*R. v. Cartwright* 10 Cr.App.R. 219). Nowadays, the existence of the Codes of Practice under the Police and Criminal Evidence Act 1984 and the methods available for pre-trial identification mean that dock identifications rarely occur.

The above considerations do not mean, as a matter of strict law, that a dock identification is inadmissible and may never be permitted. In recent years the Divisional Court has taken a pragmatic approach to the difficulties which sometimes occur in summary proceedings which are not commenced by a charge and are not investigated by the police. The Divisional Court has held that while there is no logical distinction between proceedings in the Crown Court and those in the magistrates' court, justice would be impaired if in simple traffic summonses a defendant could escape conviction simply because no identification parade had been held (*Barnes v. Chief Constable of Durham* [1997] 2 Cr.App.R. 505).

For these reasons a first time identification in court might be the only way of proving a case and in such instances the following procedure should be followed:

(i) justices should first consider whether a dock identification is admissible. The answer is clear that it is admissible (*R. v. Horsham Justices, ex p. Bukhari* (1982) 74 Cr.App.R. 291);

(ii) justices should exercise a discretion whether or not to allow such an identification by applying the well known principle of whether the prejudicial effect of such a procedure was greater than its probative worth;

(iii) if the evidence was admitted justices should apply the principles set out in *R. v. Turnbull* [1977] Q.B. 224 in deciding what weight to attach to the evidence (*North Yorkshire Trading Standards Department v. Williams*, (1995) 159 J.P. 383).

2. Submission of Insufficient Evidence

5–62   At the conclusion of the prosecution case the defence may make a submission that there is no case to answer.

The following considerations apply to such a submission:

"A submission that there is no case to answer may properly be made and upheld:

(a) when there has been no evidence to prove an essential element in the alleged offence;

(b) when the evidence adduced by the prosecution has been so discredited as a result of cross examination or is so manifestly unreliable that no reasonable tribunal could safely convict on it.

Apart from these two situations a tribunal should not in general be called to reach a decision as to conviction or acquittal until the whole of the evidence which either side wishes to tender has been placed before it. If, however, a submission is made that there is no case to answer, the decision should depend not so much on whether the adjudicating tribunal (if compelled to do so) would at that stage convict or acquit but on whether the evidence is such that a reasonable tribunal might convict. If a reasonable tribunal might convict on the evidence so far laid before it, there is a case to answer." (*Practice Direction (Submission of No Case)* [1962] 1 W.L.R. 227.)

5–63   Since the *Practice Direction* guidance as to the proper approach for considerations submissions of no case on indictment has been issued by Lord Lane C.J. in *R. v. Galbraith* (1981) 73 Cr.App.R. 124. In that case Lord Lane referred to evidence which is of a tenuous character by reason of inherent weakness or vagueness or because it is inconsistent with other evidence. If, for any of these reasons, a judge at the Crown Court concludes that a jury could not properly convict on it then the submission of no case should be upheld. It is submitted that this guidance goes somewhat further than paragraph (b) of the *Practice Direction*. In so far as there may be a conflict between the two the guidance in *Galbraith* should, it is submitted, be preferred.

5–64   It has been said that it is desirable, as a general rule, for the attention of justices to be drawn to this Practice Direction before they make a decision whether to allow a submission of no case (*R. v. Barking and Dagenham Justices, ex p. D.P.P.* (1995) 159 J.P. 373). In that case the importance of distinguishing between the issues to be determined upon a submission of no case and those to be decided at the conclusion of a summary trial were emphasised. The dicta in *Brookes v. D.P.P.* [1994] 2 W.L.R. 381 to the effect that in committal proceedings the credibility of witnesses is not a consideration on determining a submission of no case to answer apply also to summary trials.

As to the procedure to be followed when a submission of no case to answer is made the Divisional Court in *R. v. Barking and Dagenham Justices*, above, made the following declaration: "[i]n circumstances where a magistrates' court is provisionally minded to dismiss an information prior to the start of the defence case, if any, either of its own motion or upon hearing a defence submission to that effect, it should not so rule without first calling upon the prosecution to address the court".

It follows that justices are obliged to apply a hypothetical and objective test of whether a reasonable tribunal might convict on the prosecution case, and not on whether they themselves would convict. Accordingly, it is not inconsistent for a Bench to rule that there is a case to answer on the above principles and then, if the defence calls no evidence, to dismiss the information.

It has been held that there is no obligation upon justices to give reasons when rejecting a submission of no case (*Harrison v. Department of Social Security* [1997] C.O.D. 220).

3. Procedure to Warn Accused of Effect of Silence at Trial

5–65   The provisions of section 35 of the Criminal Justice and Public Order Act 1994 (effect of accused's silence at trial) apply to all summary trials where the accused appears. By implication, although not by express drafting, the provisions will not apply to trials in absence, which are permitted under section 11 of the Magistrates' Courts Act 1980. It is submitted that section 35 of the 1994 Act only makes sense if it is read as applying to trials where the accused is present, and that trials conducted under section 11 of the 1980 Act will continue as if section 35 had not been enacted.

The procedure under section 35 must be observed whether the accused is legally represented or not, and a Practice Direction setting out the form of words to be used, depending upon whether the accused is represented or not, has been issued for proceedings in the Crown Court (*Practice Direction (Crown Court: Defendant's Evidence)* [1995] 1 W.L.R. 657). The Practice Direction cannot be followed precisely for trials in the magistrates' court because the role of the clerk of the court is quite different in summary proceedings. Accordingly, in the following paragraphs, the proper procedure to be followed in the magistrates' court is suggested having regard to the provisions of the Act, the Practice Direction and the exigencies of magistrates' court practice.

The observation of section 35 is mandatory and will apply to trials where the court begins to hear evidence but section 35(2) will *not* apply if:

(a) the accused's guilt is not in issue; or

(b) it appears to the court that the physical or mental condition of the accused makes it undesirable for him to give evidence (*ibid.*, s.35(1)(a) and (b)).

Section 35(2)(b) is a little difficult to understand because if the accused's mental or physical condition is such that it is undesirable for him to give evidence, it is presumably also undesirable for him to be on trial in the first place. Section 35(2)(a) is of greater relevance. It means that the procedure under section 35 need not be followed in the following circumstances:

(i) *Newton* hearings (see §13–42, below);

(ii) Binding Over hearings (see §§9–04 *et. seq*, below);

(iii) Special Reasons hearings (see §12–108, below).

(i) Procedure when the accused is legally represented

5–66   The requirements of section 35(2) do not apply if the legal representative of the accused informs the court that the accused will give evidence (CJ and POA 1994, s.35(1)). The accused is legally represented if represented by an authorised advocate or litigator, as defined by section 119(1) of the Courts and Legal Services Act 1991 (*ibid.*, s.38(1)). This sensible provision permits the mandatory obligation to follow the procedure under section 35(2) to be dispensed with if, at the conclusion of the prosecution case, the advocate for the accused announces to the court that his client will give evidence. It is implicit that the advocate will have advised his client of the consequences of refusing to answer any question once evidence has commenced.

If the advocate does not inform the court that his client will give evidence, or informs the court that his client will not give evidence then an appropriate warning should be given. It is submitted that the warning should be given by the clerk of the court, and not the chairman of the bench or the stipendiary magistrate, although there is no guidance in either the Act or the *Practice Direction* as to who should administer the warning. The warning should be as follows:

> "Have you advised your client that the stage has now been reached at which he may give evidence, and, if he chooses not to do so, or, having been sworn, without good cause refuses to answer any question, the [court] may draw inferences as appear proper from his failure to do so?"

This form of words is taken from the *Practice Direction* with the word "jury" omitted and the word "court" substituted.

If the advocate replies that the accused has been so advised, then the trial may proceed, but if the advocate replies that the accused has not been so advised then the clerk, or exceptionally, the chairman should direct the advocate to advise his client of the consequences, namely that the Court may draw an adverse inference, and the court should then adjourn briefly for such advice to be given.

(ii) Procedure when the accused is not legally represented

5–67   In all summary trials where the accused is unrepresented the court has a statutory duty under section 35(2) of the Act to "satisfy itself" that the accused is aware of the provisions of section 35 and the consequences which may flow from his failure to give evidence. A form of words to be used in the Crown Court in these circumstances has been set out in the *Practice Direction* (above). It is submitted that this form of words used cannot be used *ipsissima verba* in the magistrates' court because of the particular obligation of the clerk of the court to assist unrepresented defendants provided for in the Magistrates' Courts Rules 1981 (see generally "Duties and Function of the Clerk" in §11–70 *et seq.*, below). Accordingly, it is submitted that the following form of words, or a close approximation to them, which follow the words of the *Practice Direction* with particular regard to trials in the magistrates' court are appropriate if the accused is unrepresented:

> "You have heard the evidence against you. Now is the time for you to make your defence. You do not have to give evidence, but if you do your evidence must be on oath or affirmation and you may be cross examined like any other witness. If you do not give evidence, or having been sworn, without good cause refuse to answer any question the court may draw such inferences as appear proper. That means the magistrates [magistrate] may hold it against you. You may also call any witnesses whom you have arranged to attend court. Afterwards you may, if you wish, address the court by arguing your case from the dock, but what you say at that stage will not count as evidence. Do you want to give evidence?"

4. The Defence Case

(i) Opening speech

5–68   At the conclusion of the evidence for the prosecution, the accused may address the court, whether or not he calls evidence (MCR 1981, r. 13(2)). The right of the defence to make an opening speech is rarely exercised in practice because by opening the case the accused is deprived of making a closing speech at the conclusion of the evidence, unless the leave of the court is obtained (*ibid.*, r. 13(4) and (5)). Usually a defence advocate will not risk losing the opportunity of speaking last, at the end of the evidence, by making an opening speech and then having to seek leave to make a closing speech. If leave is granted then the prosecution also must be given the chance to address the court a second time (*ibid.*, r. 13(5)).

(ii) Order of witnesses

5–69   If the accused is to be called to give evidence he must give evidence before any other witness or witnesses unless the court in its discretion otherwise directs (PACE 1984, s.79). The reason for this is that the accused should not be able to tailor his evidence to fit in with what he has heard his witnesses say, nor should he have an advantage over witnesses for the prosecution who are kept out of court until they have given their evidence.

Where more than one accused is on trial then the first accused will give evidence followed by his witnesses, then the second accused followed by his witnesses and so on. The case of each accused is to be considered separately.

In practice, the statutory rule as to the order of witnesses is unlikely to be varied unless there is an expert witness or character witness whose evidence will not affect the account to be given by the accused. In such circumstances the discretion of the court may be sought to call witnesses out of order.

The accused has no right to make an unsworn statement from the dock (Criminal Justice Act 1982, s.72).

(iii) The reading of statements, certificates and declarations

5–70   The same rules apply to the defence case as apply to the prosecution case for the reading of statements and the agreement of facts. If defence witnesses' statements are to be read their evidence must conform to the provisions of section 9 of the Criminal Justice Act 1967 and must be served on the prosecution within the statutory period.

(iv) Evidence in Rebuttal of the Defence Case

5–71   At the conclusion of the evidence for the defence the prosecutor may call evidence to rebut that evidence (MCR 1981, r. 13(3)).

This rule is subject to the common law rule that all evidence probative of the accused's guilt should be called before the defence case begins. The exceptions to this rule (set out in rule 13(3), above) is when in the course of the defence case evidence arises which the prosecution could not have foreseen but which may be rebutted by other evidence. In such circumstances the proper procedure is for the prosecution to refer the court to the part of the defence case which was not foreseen, and to seek leave to call rebuttal evidence. The court has a discretion whether or not to allow such evidence to be called (*R. v. Scott* (1984) 79 Cr.App.R. 49).

Whether rebuttal evidence is allowed to be called will depend on:

(a) whether the defence evidence was completely unexpected, and

(b) whether that evidence went to the heart of the case and not to a peripheral, issue.

(v) Defence closing speech

5–72   If the defence has not opened the case the accused or his advocate may address the court at the conclusion of the defence evidence. Even if no defence evidence is called there is still a right to make a final speech (MCR 1981, r. 13(4)). Where the defence has made an opening speech, leave must be sought to make a second speech (see §5–68, above). If the prosecution is given leave to make a closing speech this shall be before the defence speech. The accused is always allowed the last word (*ibid.*, r. 13(6)).

If, during the trial, the accused has not given evidence it is not proper for an advocate to give any reasons for his client's failure to give evidence in a speech unless there has been evidence before the court to support such reasons (*R. v. Cowan and other appeals* [1995] 4 All E.R. 939).

The order of speeches in the magistrates' court is unaffected by the repeal of proviso (b) to section 1 of the Criminal Evidence Act 1898 (CJ and POA 1994, s.168(2), and (3) and Sched. 10, paras 2 and 11). This repeal enables the prosecution, in a trial on indictment, to comment on the fact that the accused has not given evidence, if that has been the case in the trial. However, the order of speeches in summary proceedings is strictly defined by the Magistrates' Courts Rules 1981, and unless the special circumstances defined above apply the prosecution do not have a final speech in a summary trial. Accordingly, if the accused has not given evidence the prosecution will be unable to comment on such fact unless, exceptionally leave is given, under the rules, for the prosecution to make a final speech.

5. Rulings on Questions of Law

5–73   As justices are judges of fact as well as of law there is no obvious way in which inadmissible evidence or other prejudicial material can be excluded without justices hearing for themselves the disputed material. The procedure at the Crown Court whereby the jury (who decide the facts) are sent away while the judge (who decides the law) makes rulings on the admissibility of evidence cannot apply in summary trials. Nonetheless, statutory provisions, particularly sections 76, 78 and 82 of the Police and Criminal Evidence Act 1984, and common law rules of evidence apply equally to trials in the Crown Court and in the magistrates' court (see *Vel v. Chief Constable of North Wales* (1987) 151 J.P. 510, and *R. v. Sang* [1980] A.C. 402).

For this reason uncertainties have arisen in the minds of practitioners and of justices about the correct procedure to be followed when a question of law arises for decision in the course of a summary trial and a number of cases on the point have been heard in the Divisional Court. The following general principles should be applied:

(i) There is an overriding duty of justices to ensure that the proceedings are just and fair to the accused and just and fair to the prosecution in the context of separating questions of law from questions of fact (*SFJ v. Chief Constable of Kent* [1982] Crim.L.R. 682).

(ii) An issue of law must, subject to (iii) and (iv) below, be decided as a separate issue from the main issue (namely the guilt or innocence of the accused) not as a trial-within-a-trial because justices are judges of law as well as of fact (*SFJ v. Chief Constable of Kent*, above).

(iii) If the question of law involves an application to exclude evidence of a confession under section 76 of the Police and Criminal Evidence Act 1984 there is an exception to the above rule because the 1984 Act requires that there should be a trial-within-a-trial (*R. v. Liverpool Juvenile Court, ex p. R.* [1987] 3 W.L.R. 224; see §5–54, above).

(iv) A trial-within-a-trial may also be appropriate, in certain circumstances, if there is an application to exclude evidence under section 78 of the Police and Criminal Evidence Act 1984 (*Halawa v. Federation Against Copyright Theft* (1995) 159 J.P. 816; see §5–60, above.)

(v) All other questions of law should be decided as and when they arise or justices may leave a decision on a question of law until the end of the hearing. The precise pocedure to be followed should be governed by the need to secure a hearing which is fair to both sides (*Vel v. Chief Constable of Wales* (1987) 151 J.P. 510).

It is submitted that the difficulty of laying down hard and fast rules about how a decision on a question of law should be tackled places a particular obligation on advocates to ensure that as far as possible justices are not prejudiced by hearing inadmissible evidence which should have been excluded by agreement before the commencement of the hearing. In deciding how the issue should be approached in a particular case the following procedure has been commended by the Divisional Court; justices are entitled to inquire whether the question of law involves only the circumstances in which the evidence was obtained. If this is so, then in most cases it would be appropriate for a *voir dire* to be held. On the other hand if the proceedings in a *voir dire* would or might be protracted and would introduce issues which would have to be examined during the remaining stages of the trial, then justices would be entitled to conclude that fairness did not require the holding of a trial-within-a-trial (*per* Ralph Gibson L.J. in *Halawa v. Federation Against Copyright Theft*, above).

5–74   Once a ruling of law has been made the decision should not be reversed, save in exceptional circumstances (*R. v. Sittingbourne Justices, ex p. Stickings and Another* (1996) 160 J.P. 801). In that case a clerk (not the Clerk to the Justices) had tendered certain advice which led to justices to rule that certain prosecution evidence was inadmissible. Before the trial continued on a later date the Clerk to the Justices, exercising his powers conferred under section 28(3) of the Justices of the Peace Act 1979, gave the justices further advice whereupon the earlier ruling was reversed and a new trial was ordered before a different bench. (The law set out in section 28(3) of the 1979 Act now appears in section 45(4), (5) and (6) of the Justice of the Peace Act 1997). The Divisional Court held that in the circumstances of that particular case it had been wrong for the CPS to have initiated the events which led to the reversal of the ruling, but that section 28(3) of the Act did permit the Clerk to the Justices to tender further advice. (For a further discussion of this topic see §11–71, below).

6. Discretion to Allow the Prosecution to Re-open their Case

5–75   There is a discretion to allow the prosecution to re-open their case, and to allow further evidence to be called after the close of the Crown's case. However, as a general rule, the prosecution must call all their evidence at the proper time.

The prosecution may not re-open their case to prove some essential part of the case after a submission by the defence has revealed an inherent weakness (*R. v. Gainsborough Justices, ex p. Green* (1983) 147 J.P. 434). An exception to this general rule exists where, after closing their case, they have failed to prove some technical matter about which there can be no serious dispute, for example the production of the regulations prohibiting learner drivers from using a motorway (*Royal v. Prescott-Clarke* (1966) 130 J.P. 274).

Other examples where the exception has been held to apply are: proving the consent of an authority to prosecute (*Price v. Humphries* [1958] 2 Q.B. 353); producing a certificate showing blood-alcohol levels in a drink-driving case (*Piggott v. Sims* [1973] R.T.R. 15); reading a section 9 statement (*Matthews v. Morris* (1981) 145 J.P. 262). An application to re-open the prosecution case should always be made before the defence case has closed. More recently it has been said (*obiter*) that in these days, 1998, an application to re-open to cure a point of continuity in the production of exhibits should be granted (*R. v. Horseferry Road Magistrates' Court, ex p. Hillier* (1998) 162 J.P. 783).

5–76   Where the court is invited to exercise its discretion to allow the prosecution to re-open their case the court should in general apply the same principles applicable to the calling of rebuttal evidence, namely: whether the defence evidence was completely unexpected and whether that evidence went to the heart of the case and not to a peripheral issue. However, in addition, there is a wider discretion to allow the Crown to re-open than applies to the calling of rebuttal evidence. While this wider discretion cannot be defined precisely it should be exercised only on the rarest of occasions (*R. v. Francis* [1990] 1 W.L.R. 1264), especially when the evidence is tendered after the case for the defendant has begun (*R. v. Munnery* (1992) 94 Cr.App.R. 164).

If there are a combination of circumstances which result in the prosecution being unable to call their evidence at the proper time (for example a witness arriving late because of a confusion about the location of the court house) the test is whether the defence case would have been conducted differently had the witness been called timeously (*James v. South Glamorgan County Council* (1994) 99 Cr.App.R. 321). In that case the Divisional Court refused to overturn the exercise of discretion allowing the prosecution to re-open their case by calling a witness who had been given a late warning and who did not know of the whereabouts of the court house. This resulted in his evidence being heard after the defence case had commenced, and the Divisional Court held that no injustice had been caused.

7. Power of Court to Call Witnesses

5–77   If none of the parties have called a particular witness there is a residuary discretion for justices to call a witness providing this discretion is not exercised after the defence has closed its case and not after the justices have retired to deliberate (*Webb v. Leadbetter* [1966] 1 W.L.R. 245).

It has been said that for trials on indictment the power of the court to call witnesses should rarely be exercised and then only to achieve justice and fairness. The power should not be used in order, in effect, to take over the prosecution (*R. v. Grafton* [1993] Q.B. 101). This general principle has been held to apply equally to summary proceedings (*R. v. Wellingborough Magistrates' Court, ex p. Francois* (1994) 158 J.P. 813). It is submitted the power should be exercised rarely, particularly as justices are judges of fact as well as law, but a circumstance in which it might be used is where the prosecution have wrongfully declined to call a witness themselves (*R. v. Haringey Justices, ex p. D.P.P.* [1996] 2 W.L.R. 114). (For the duties of the prosecution to call witnesses see §§5–46 and 5–47, above).

The exceptional circumstances in which it may have been right for justices to have called witnesses arose in *R. v. Haringey Justices, ex p. D.P.P.* [1996] 2 W.L.R. 114. In that case the prosecution had declined to call a police officer in a trial of a defendant charged with assault on police because the officer had been suspended pending a disciplinary hearing into an unrelated matter. The Divisional Court observed, having granted *certiorari* on other grounds, that it might have been appropriate for justices to have called the officer themselves rather than having dismissed the case on the grounds of abuse of process.

8. Power of Court to Attend a View

5–78   In appropriate cases justices may be invited to view the scene of an alleged offence, for example the view along a particular road in a traffic case. Justices are not bound to accede to such an application, but if it takes place the following procedure should be followed:

(i) both the prosecution and defence should be present or at least be given the opportunity of being present,

(ii) the view should take place before the conclusion of the evidence so that each party will have the opportunity of commenting on the features observed (*Parry v. Boyle* (1986) 83 Cr.App.R. 310), and

(iii) the accused himself, even if legally represented, should be permitted to be present. Failure to allow an accused to attend a view is fatal to the fairness of the proceedings generally (*R. v. Ely Justices, ex p. Burgess* (1993) 157 J.P. 484).

If the above procedure is not followed and a member of the bench attends the scene of an incident unofficially during an adjournment it does not necessarily mean that an irregularity has occurred. If the parties are content for the trial to proceed in the knowledge that the unofficial visit has happened and no prejudice is alleged the Divisional Court is unlikely to quash the conviction (*Telfer and Telfer v. D.P.P.* (1996) 160 J.P. 512).

9. No Power to Call Evidence after Justices have Retired

5–79   Once justices have retired to consider their verdict further evidence should only be admitted in the most exceptional circumstances (*Webb v. Leadbetter*, above, and *French Dairies (Sevenoaks) Ltd v. Davis* [1973] Crim.L.R. 630). It has been held that such exceptional circumstances did exist when a recorder hearing an appeal at a Crown Court asked a witness to refresh his memory as to evidence previously given. It was held that on the facts no injustice had been caused (*Phelan v. Back* [1972] 1 W.L.R. 273).

10. The Adjudication

5–80   Justices have a statutory duty either to convict the accused or to dismiss the information having heard the evidence and the parties (MCA 1980, s.9(2)).

An adjudication takes place the moment the decision is announced, and before it is recorded in the register. Once the decision, whether for conviction or acquittal, is reached justices are *functus officio* and the decision cannot be altered (*R. v. Essex Justices, ex p. Final* [1963] 2 Q.B. 816).

The statutory duty to convict or to acquit on the evidence is mandatory and must be strictly observed. For this reason a purported adjudication without hearing evidence is a nullity, unless the prosecution offer no evidence. It sometimes happens that such null adjudications occur because of the wrong tests being applied by justices to the granting of adjournments. The rules and procedure for the granting and refusal of adjournments is fully discussed in Chapter 2, above.

If there has been some error in the adjudication, for example announcing a final verdict after retiring to consider a submission of insufficient evidence, the court should order a rehearing before a differently constituted Bench (*R. v. Midhurst Justices, ex p. Thompson* (1974) 138 J.P. 359).

If there has been some obvious error in the adjudication such as the dismissal of an information when an accused has pleaded guilty it is appropriate, if the parties consent, for the justices, nonetheless, to exercise their discretion to sentence because otherwise judicial review proceedings may be inevitable. Where everyone is agreed that an adjudication is a nullity it is preferable for magistrates to put right their mistake themselves to save the parties the expense of proceedings for judicial review (*R. v. Leighton Buzzard Justices, ex p. D.P.P.* (1990) 154 J.P. 41).

Power to rectify a mistake after an adjudication

5–81   Where a person is convicted by a magistrates' court and it subsequently appears to the court that it would be in the interests of justice that the case should be heard again by different justices, the court may so direct (MCA 1980, s.142(2)). The court may also vary or rescind any sentence or other order if it appears to be in the interests of justice to do so (*ibid.*, s.142(1)).

This power to "re-open" may be exercised at any time, irrespective of the time which has elapsed since conviction or sentence, and the essential criterion governing the use of the power is the interests of justice. Mere delay in making an application for the court to re-open a case is not in itself a ground for refusing the application, but delay should be taken into account together with all the other relevant circumstances (*R. v. Ealing Justices, ex p. Sahota* (1998) 162 J.P. 73).

Most commonly, applications arise under section 142(2), the re-opening of convictions, often when an accused has been convicted previously in his absence. The Divisional Court has recognised that the power, as stated, is very wide and it should be regarded as a slip rule whereby mistakes can be rectified when it is plain that an injustice has been done (*R. v. Croydon Youth Court, ex p. D.P.P.* [1998] 2 Cr.App.R. 411). It is submitted that, in accordance with the reasoning in that case, the provisions of section 142 should not be used to set aside convictions as an alternative to pursing an appeal.

5–82   In deciding whether, in the court's discretion, a case which has been proved against an absent defendant should be re-opened justices are entitled to take the following matters into account:

(i)   whether the accused had failed to attend through his own fault or not;

(ii) whether a witness or witnesses would be inconvenienced by the ordering of a new trial; and

(iii) the fact that the accused had a right of appeal against the conviction to the Crown Court (*R. v. Gwent Magistrates' Court, ex p. Carey* (1996) 160 J.P. 61).

11. Passing Sentence

5–83   This section deals only with the procedure for passing sentence. The powers and principles for sentencing are dealt with fully in Part II.

(i) Duty to ascertain the accused's previous convictions and antecedent history

(a) WHEN THE DEFENDANT IS PRESENT

5–84 A *Practice Direction (Crime: Antecedents)* [1998] 1 Cr.App.R. 213, handed down by the Lord Chief Justice, which takes into account the provision of information to courts directly from the Police National Computer, now governs the procedure for ascertaining previous convictions. Much of the *Practice Direction* concerns practice at the Crown Court, but in the magistrates' court a Standard Format must be used showing previous convictions and recorded cautions and this should be submitted with the case file to the CPS.

When the list of previous convictions is produced the only appropriate question by the clerk (or the chairman of the bench) to the defence advocate is "have you seen this list?" because there is no professional obligation upon the defence to confirm or deny any particular previous conviction. This formulation was recently agreed between the Law Society's Criminal Law Committee and the Justices' Clerks Society.

If the defendant does not admit any relevant previous conviction it should not be disclosed to the court (*R. v. Sargeant* (1975) 60 Cr.App.R. 74). For this reason an unrepresented defendant should always be allowed to see, and agree, the list of previous convictions before the list is passed to the Bench.

(b) WHEN THE DEFENDANT IS ABSENT

5–85 If a defendant has been convicted in his absence the rules about the admissibility of previous convictions will depend on whether the case is a road traffic case or a non-traffic summary offence proved in absence. In road traffic cases previous convictions for endorsable and disqualifiable offences may be proved by producing the DVLA "print-out" (RTOA 1988, s.13).

In all other cases where there has been proof in absence previous summary (but not indictable) convictions may be cited by the prosecution if the defendant has been served personally or by registered post with a list at least seven days before the hearing (MCA 1980, s.104). The service of this notice is sometimes called a "notice to cite." If the prosecution cannot prove that such notice has been served the previous convictions may not be placed before the court.

(ii) Taking offences into consideration

5–86 A defendant who has committed more offences than those with which he was charged and convicted may ask that those offences be taken into consideration before sentence is passed. Such offences must be of the same general character as that with which the accused was convicted and the court must have jurisdiction to try them (*R. v. Davies* (1912) 7 Cr.App.R. 431).

PROCEDURE FOR TAKING OFFENCES INTO CONSIDERATION

5–87 Before the accused appears for his trial he should be served with a form setting out a list, together with brief details, of the offences he wishes to have taken into consideration. If he agrees the signed form (or a copy) should be placed before the court, and the chairman of the Bench should ask him, "Have you received and signed this list of other offences outstanding against you?" If he answers yes, he should be further asked "Do you admit those offences and wish them taken into consideration?"

The accused may then ask for all or some of them to be taken into consideration (*R. v. Marquis* (1951) 115 J.P. 329). If he does so unequivocally and voluntarily the court should announce when sentence is passed that the number of offences admitted is taken into consideration.

(iii) Pronouncing sentence

5–88 In January 1998 the Lord Chief Justice issued a Practice Direction to explain that when sentence is passed it is desirable that the practical effect of the sentence should be understood by the defendant, any victim and any member of the public who is present in court or who reads a full report of the proceedings (*Practice Direction (Custodial Sentences)* [1998] 1 Cr.App.R. 397). The Lord Chief Justice continued; [I]n future, whenever a custodial sentence is imposed on an offender, the court should explain the practical effect of the sentence in addition to complying with existing statutory requirements. This will be no more than an explanation; the sentence will be that pronounced in court".

The *Practice Direction* does not require a particular form of words to be used, but it should be stressed that the pronouncement relating to the practical effect of the sentence is *in addition* to statutory requirements. These statutory requirements are set out in §12–05, below.

The following form of words was suggested in the *Practice Direction* for custodial sentences of 12 months or less:

"The sentence is [   ] months.

You will serve half that sentence in prison/a young offender institution. After that time the rest of your sentence will be suspended and you will be released. Your release will not bring this sentence to an end. If after your release and before the end of the period covered by the sentence you commit any further offence, you may be ordered to return to custody to serve the balance of the original sentence outstanding at the date of the further offence, as well as being punished for that new offence.

Any time you have spent on remand in custody in connection with the offence[s] for which you are now being sentence will count as part of the sentence to be served unless it has already been counted."

(iv) Adjourning for reports

5–89 There are wide powers available to the court to adjourn the passing of sentence until a pre-sentence report, medical, mental or other reports are prepared. In some circumstances the court should obtain reports before passing sentence, and these are discussed fully at §§2–39, above, §§12–06 and 12–15, below. If the passing of sentence is adjourned until reports are prepared it is usual for the speech in mitigation to be reserved until the reports are prepared.

(v) Mitigation

5–90 It is contrary to the rules of natural justice for justices to pass sentence without giving the accused or his legal representative an opportunity to address the court on sentence (*R. v. Billericay Justices, ex p. Rumsey* [1978] Crim.L.R. 306). It is good practice for the court to read all the available reports before listening to mitigation.

(vi) *Varying or rescinding sentence*

5–91   A sentence may be varied or rescinded at any time after it has been passed if it appears to the court to be in the interests of justice to do so (MCA 1980, s.142(1), as amended by the Criminal Appeal 1955, s.26(2)). The significance of the 1995 amendment, which came into effect on January 1, 1996, is discussed in §5–81, above. The use of the power to vary or rescind sentence will arise where the court has inadvertently passed an invalid sentence or where the bench later consider that the sentence passed was too high or where the accused was sentenced in his absence and then mitigation is brought forward which changes the case. Although section 142 as amended allows a different bench from that which originally passed sentence to vary the sentence later, there will be some circumstances when justice can only be done by re-convening the original bench.

(vii) *Sentencing more than one offender*

5–92   Where several accused are charged with the same offence it is highly desirable that all are sentenced by the same court. Accordingly, where one accused pleads not guilty and his case is adjourned for trial at a later date but another accused pleads guilty, both should be sentenced together at the conclusion of the trial (*R. v. Weekes and Others* (1982) 74 Cr.App.R. 161).

If this procedure is not followed and widely different sentences are imposed by differently constituted courts on different offenders convicted of the same offence arguments about "disparity" may arise. Disparity means that one offender is left with a sense of grievance because of the difference or disparity between his sentence and a less severe one passed upon a co-accused.

While the Court of Appeal has shown great reluctance to accede to arguments based on disparity (see *R. v. Stroud* (1977) 65 Cr.App.R. 150) it is clearly desirable that the principles in *R. v. Weekes*, above, are followed whenever possible so that no lurking grievance may later be felt and that the Crown Court is not burdened with sentence appeals based on "disparity."

CHAPTER 6

Committal for Trial, Sending for Trial, Transfer to the Crown Court and Committal for Sentence

A. COMMITTAL FOR TRIAL

1. Introduction

6–01   Committal for trial is one of the most ancient procedures in the criminal law. It is the protection which prevents an accused standing trial before a jury unless there is a case for the accused to answer. Over the last thirty years great changes have taken place, which have gradually eroded the principle that witnesses should actually attest the case against an accused at a preliminary hearing. The latest changes made by section 47 and Schedule I of the Criminal Procedure and Investigations Act 1996 bring about, in a modified form, suggestions for reform proposed by the Royal Commission on Criminal Justice (Cm. 2263). The Commission's report was published in July 1993 and it was of the opinion that committal proceedings on the whole served no useful purpose and it recommended replacing them with an entirely administrative hearing called "Transfer for Trial". The mechanisms for such a system however were cumbersome and excessively bureaucratic and implementation was postponed while discussions took place with the professionals who were expected to make it work. It proved too difficult to make Transfer for Trial satisfactory and it was abandoned. At a late stage in the passage of the 1996 Act a reformed committal procedure was put in its place.

The opportunity has been used to make significant changes to committal proceedings. In summary the Act makes the following changes:

(i)   oral evidence at committals both from the prosecution and defence is abolished;

(ii) the definition of "evidence tendered" at committals is widened;

(iii) witness orders are abolished;

(iv) evidence tendered at committal may automatically be read at the Crown Court unless the defence positively give notice requiring the attendance of witnesses, and

(v)   the opportunity to make a submission of no case to answer is retained but such submission must be based on the contents of the evidence tendered in writing by the prosecution only.

The 1996 Act amends the Magistrates' Courts Act 1980 and therefore the original section numbers, familiar to many practitioners, are retained. Thus, a committal in which no legal submissions are made is still a "six-two" committal, and the other form of committal still a "six-one". References in this chapter to the 1980 Act are those which have been amended or inserted by Schedule 1 of the 1996 Act and references to the Magistrates' Courts Rules 1981 are those which are now amended by the Magistrates' Courts (Amendment) Rules 1997 (S.I. 1997, No. 706).

6–02 The committal procedure set out in the 1996 Act applies to alleged offences into which no criminal investigation had begun before April 1, 1997 (Criminal Procedure and Investigations Act 1996 (Commencement) (section 65 and Schedules 1 and 2 Order) 1997). The Divisional Court has held that complicated calculations, having regard to the date when a criminal investigation is said to have begun, are not appropriate when considering the application of the 1996 Act to proceedings in the magistrates' court (*R. v. Norfolk Stipendiary Magistrate, ex p. Keable* [1998] Crim.L.R. 510). In essence, the key date for consideration is the date on which the accused was charged with the offence giving rise to the committal. If the charge was on or after April 1, 1997 the law and practice set out in this Chapter will apply.

2. Procedure Common to all Committals

(i) The tendering of written evidence by the prosecution

6–03 The tendering of the evidence is, strictly, a separate and distinct procedural step from the formal committal. Evidence is tendered under the provisions of section 4 of the 1980 Act and, subject to specific statutory exceptions, the procedure must occur in the presence of the accused (MCA 1980, s.4(3)).

The exceptions are:

(a) that by reason of the disorderly conduct of the accused it is not practical for the evidence to be tendered in his presence; or

(b) that the accused cannot be present by reasons of health but is represented by a legal representative who has consented to the evidence being tendered in his absence (*ibid.*, s.4(4)(a) and (b)).

Written evidence is formally tendered when the prosecutor, or someone acting on his behalf, hands the written evidence to the clerk of the court on the occasion of the committal (MCA 1980, s.5A(2)(a)). This provision does not mean that a justice or a stipendiary magistrate may not see the evidence in advance of such formal tendering, particularly if the sufficiency of the evidence is in issue (*R. v. Colchester Stipendiary Magistrate, ex p. Beck* [1979] Q.B. 674).

Before the evidence is formally tendered a copy of any written statement defined in section 5B must be given to the defence (s.5B(2)(c)). Accompanying such service on the defence must be notice informing the accused of his right to object to the contents of the statements being read at trial (MCR 1981, r. 4B, as inserted by Magistrates' Courts (Amendment) Rules 1997, r. 3). The form of this notice should comply with the wording set out in rule 14A of the Magistrates' Courts (Forms) Rules 1981, as amended by the Magistrates' Courts (Forms) (Amendment) Rules 1997.

The essential change made by the 1996 Act is in the definition of what constitutes written evidence.

The only evidence admissible in committal proceedings is that falling within the definition of section 5A(3) of the Magistrates' Courts Act 1980. In nearly all cases this written evidence will be in the form of witness statements but there is no provision enabling the defence to object to the tendering of a witness statement and section 102 of the 1980 Act is repealed in full (CP and IA 1996, Sched. 5). In its place the formalities for the contents of written statements are redefined in the Act (MCA 1980, s.5A(2)(a) and (b)). If the defence wish to make a submission then the contents of the statement may be read aloud, and to this extent committals under section 6(1) of the 1980 Act are expressly preserved (see §6–12, below).

The categories of written evidence which may be tendered by the prosecution are exhaustively defined in section 5A to E of the amended 1980 Act. They are as follows:

(a) WRITTEN STATEMENTS

6–04   A written statement tendered in evidence is admissible by virtue of section 5A(3)(a) but such statement must comply with certain procedural formalities. These are set out in section 5B(2)(a) to (c) and section 5B(3) (a) to (c). In essence these provisions set out the familiar pre-conditions for the admissibility of a written statement in criminal proceedings which used to appear in section 102 of the 1980 Act. These are that the statement must be signed and must contain a declaration that the contents are true. Before such statements may be tendered a copy must be given to the defence (MCA 1980, s.5B(2)(c)). There is nothing in the Act which defines how long the defence must have had the copy of the statement before the prosecution are entitled to tender it in evidence. In practice it will be rare for justices to allow a statement to be tendered under section 5A(2) of the Act unless the defence have had a reasonable time in which to consider its contents.

Section 5F of the Act allows the prosecution to tender either the statement (s.5F(1)(a)) or a copy of it or a material part of it (s.5F(1)(b)). This is a convenient change enabling a committal to proceed even if, through an oversight, only a copy of a statement, not the original, is available. If such a copy is tendered, however, difficulties may be encountered at trial if the witness is to be cross-examined on the basis that the contents of the written statement is inconsistent with the witness's oral testimony. The rules made by the Criminal Procedure Act 1865 (*Denman's Act*) would suggest that it is obligatory for the witness to be shown his or her original statement before being confronted with its contents. It is submitted that in order not to prejudice the defence the prosecution should, for this reason, have the original statement available at the Crown Court even if a copy of it has been tendered for committal purposes.

(b) DOCUMENTS OR EXHIBITS REFERRED TO IN SUCH STATEMENTS

6–05   Documents or exhibits referred to in written statements are admissible by virtue of section 5A(3)(b), but there is no obligation upon the prosecution to tender every exhibit or document referred to in a statement. The question of whether exhibits should be disclosed will depend on issues of fairness generally (see §6–15, below). A document means anything in which information of any description is recorded (MCA 1980, s.5B(6)) and therefore could include a video-recording of a child's evidence. Such a video-recording may be tendered in evidence under the provisions of section 32A(10) of the Criminal Justice Act 1988. More commonly cases involving children where such a recording is made will be the subject of Transfer to the Crown Court (see §6–32, below).

(c) DEPOSITIONS AND EXHIBITS OF RELUCTANT WITNESSES TAKEN PRIOR TO COMMITTAL

6–06   Such depositions are admissible by virtue of section 5A(3)(c) and (d). The power of a magistrates' court to take a deposition prior to committal is a new power introduced by the 1996 Act and is discussed fully in §§6–15 to 6–20, below.

(d) DOCUMENTARY FIRST-HAND HEARSAY AND BUSINESS RECORDS

6–07   Such evidence is admissible by virtue of section 5A(3)(e). In practice such provisions will be rarely used, but in essence it allows for documentary first-hand hearsay and business records which comply with the provisions of sections 23 or 24 of the Criminal Justice Act 1988 to be tendered in committal proceedings. Before such evidence may be tendered the prosecutor must notify the court and the defence that he believes that such evidence *might* be admitted by the judge if the case came to trial and that the evidence is not available in any other way (MCA 1980, s.5D(2)(a) and (b)). The reason for this is that such evidence does not apply to committal proceedings as such (CP and IA 1996, s.47 and Schedule 1, paras 28–32). These considerations are considerations of evidential admissibility and are beyond the scope of this book to discuss in detail but see generally, Richard May, *Criminal Evidence* (4th ed., Sweet & Maxwell, 1999) Chapter 11.

(e) DOCUMENTS WHICH PROVE THEMSELVES

6–08 Such evidence is admissible by virtue of section 5A(3)(f). The definition of such evidence is given in abstract form in section 5E(a) to (e) and will comprise such things as evidence admitted under the Bankers Book Evidence Act 1879 or public documents which prove themselves under specific statutory enactment. The definition will also enable a certified copy of a magistrates' court register to be tendered, if it is necessary to do so to prove a conviction or other adjudication in a magistrates' court (MCR 1981, r. 68).

(ii) *Reminding the accused of his right to object to written evidence being read at trial*

6–09 An essential feature of a committal is a reminder by the clerk of the accused's right to object to written evidence being read at the trial, and thereby losing the right to cross-examine such witness orally (MCR 1981, r. 8, as substituted by Magistrates' Courts (Amendment) Rules 1997, r. 8).

Compliance with the provisions of rule 8, as amended, is important because section 68 and Schedule 2, para. 1 of the 1996 Act provides that evidence tendered at committal "may without further proof be read as evidence on the trial of the accused ... *unless* a party to the proceedings objects ..." The opportunity of objecting is provided by Schedule 2, para. 1(3)(c) of the 1996 Act. Unless the accused is warned that he is entitled to object, the Crown may be prohibited from reading any tendered witness statement at the trial. In practice the manner in which the evidence is to be presented at trial will normally be reviewed by a judge at a Plea and Directions Hearing at the Crown Court, prior to trial.

(iii) *The formal committal to the Crown Court*

6–10 The committal for trial under section 6 of the 1980 Act is a separate and distinct procedural step from the tendering of the evidence under section 4. Accordingly, the statutory limitations to proceeding in the absence of the accused set out in section 4(3) of the Act do not apply (*R. v. Liverpool City Magistrates' Court, ex p. Quantrell, The Times,* February 2, 1999). In that case the accused was ill on the occasion of the committal. The Divisional Court held that while justices were not obliged to proceed in the accused's absence there was no statutory prohibition upon them doing so.

The justice who is presiding over the committal must specify the Crown Court where the accused is to be tried. This will be the most convenient court where a High Court judge regularly sits if the offence is in Classes 1–3, and the most convenient location of the Crown Court if it is a Class 4 offence (MCA 1980, s.7 and *Practice Directions* [1995] 1 W.L.R. 1083 (as amended by *Practice Direction (Crown Court: Allocation of Business) (No. 2)* [1998] 1 W.L.R. 1244).

However, in addition the court is obliged to have regard to the convenience of the defence, the prosecution and the witnesses and the expediting of the trial in naming the Crown Court at a committal (MCA 1980, s.7). In practice these considerations will arise if there is some overwhelming local prejudice attaching to the accused where a trial in a local Crown Court would be undesirable or where there is a large backlog of work at the local Crown Court and there is a particular reason why there should be an early trial.

(iv) The committal must be on bail or in custody

6–11 The committing justice must specify whether the accused is to be admitted to bail or whether he is to be committed to stand his trial in custody (MCA 1980, s.6(3)). The considerations as to bail must be within the terms of the Bail Act 1976 as amended. For a detailed discussion on bail see Chapter 3.

3. Committals under section 6(1)

(i) Procedure

6–12 A committal under section 6(1) is one where a magistrates' court inquiring into an offence as examining justices considers the evidence. Such a committal must take place:

   (i) if the accused has no legal representative acting for him in the case, or

  (ii) if a legal representative acting for the accused has indicated to the court that he wishes to submit that there is no case for the accused to answer (MCA 1980, s.6(2)(a) and (b)).

The procedure to be followed in a "six-one" committal is as follows:

   (i) the prosecutor tenders the evidence in precisely the same as if the committal had been under section 6(2), with the proviso that—

     (a) the prosecutor may make an opening address to the court before the evidence is tendered (MCR 1981, r. 7(2));
     (b) the written evidence shall be read aloud, or if the court so directs summarised (*ibid.*, r. 7(3), and
     (c) the court may view any exhibits (*ibid.*, r. 7(4)).

  (ii) after the tendering of the evidence the court may hear any submission which the accused may wish to make as to whether there is sufficient evidence to put him on trial for any indictable offence (*ibid.*, r. 7(5)).

  (iii) The court shall allow the prosecutor to make a submission in reply, or shall allow the prosecutor to make submissions if no submission is made by the defence but the court is nevertheless minded not to commit for trial (*ibid.*, r. 7(6)(a) and (b)).

  (iv) The court shall then, if minded to commit for trial, remind the accused of his right to object to written evidence being read at trial (*ibid.*, r. 8). (see §6–09, above).

  (v) The court shall commit for trial (following the steps set out in §§6–10 to 6–11, above) if of the opinion there is sufficient evidence to put the accused on trial and shall discharge the accused if not of that opinion (MCA 1980, s.6(1)(a) and(b)).

6–13   Three points should be noted. First, the Rules in their presently amended form cure an ambiguity which had previously existed as to the order of speeches in committal proceedings and, in particular, the right of the prosecutor to reply to submissions. No such ambiguity exists in the amended rules, reflecting observations made by the Divisional Court in *R. v. Barking and Dagenham Justices, ex p. D.P.P.* [1995] Crim.L.R. 953 as to the potential for unfairness which had existed previously.

Secondly, the words "any indictable offence" in rule 7(5) mean any indictable offence which is disclosed on the evidence, not just the indictable offence with which the accused was charged when the committal proceedings commenced (*R. v. Cambridge Justices, ex p. Fraser* [1985] 1 W.L.R. 1391). Thus, the essential question at the conclusion of the evidence is not whether there is a case to answer the charge on which the accused originally appeared but whether there is a case to answer on the evidence presented. If so, the court must commit the accused for trial on a charge which reflects the evidence. If there is a possibility that the accused will be taken by surprise by a committal on an alternative charge justices must give the defence a proper opportunity of making representations (*R. v. Gloucester Magistrates' Court, ex p. Chung* 153 J.P. 75).

Finally, there is no provision for the calling of oral evidence either on behalf of the prosecution or the defence. Indeed, there is not even a provision enabling the accused to say anything in answer to the charge, as was the case under the original 1981 rules.

(ii) The test for whether the evidence is sufficient

6–14   The test for whether the prosecution evidence is sufficient to put the accused on trial is whether that evidence, taken at its highest, is such that a jury, properly directed, could convict upon it. The traditional and well-known authority of *R. v. Galbraith* [1981] 1 W.L.R. 1039 has only limited application to committal proceedings, it is submitted. In that case the judgment of Lord Lane C.J. posited a situation where evidence was of a tenuous character, or had within it inherent weaknesses or was inconsistent with other evidence. Such considerations may arise where oral evidence has been given and such evidence has been scrutinised in cross-examination (the usual situation in a trial on indictment). The prohibition upon oral evidence being called in committal proceedings and the fact that cross-examination is prohibited makes the application of the second part of the *Galbraith* guidance inappropriate to submissions at committal. The first part of that guidance, namely, that justices should not commit if there is no evidence that the accused committed the crime obviously is applicable.

In theory, justices are entitled, in considering whether there is a case for the accused to answer, to take into account his failure to mention any facts when questioned (CJ and POA 1994, s.34(2)(a) and (7)). In practice it would be unfair for justices to do so. The provisions relating to inferences from silence in committals were enacted in the 1994 Act at a time when oral evidence, cross-examination of such oral evidence and an opportunity for the accused himself to give evidence existed in such proceedings. As these procedures have now been abolished it would seem, on elementary principles, that the application of section 34 of the 1994 Act to committal hearings would be unjust.

4. Duty of the Prosecution in Committal Proceedings

6–15 It used to be said that the prosecution had a complete discretion as to which witnesses it chose to call when compelled by the defence to call oral evidence in a committal (*R. v. Epping and Harlow Justices, ex p. Massaro* [1973] 1 Q.B. 433). Since that case was decided the Divisional Court has been much more vigilant in its supervisory jurisdiction over magistrates' court procedure and modern tests of natural justice and fairness have evolved if the defence are taken by surprise or disadvantaged by the absence of a particular prosecution witness (see *R. v. Haringey Justices, ex p. D.P.P.*).

The law in relation to committal proceedings is that the prosecution have a duty to be fair and not to mislead the court by the choice of written statements chosen to be tendered (*Wilkinson v. Crown Prosecution Service* (1998) 162 J.P. 591). In that case it was held that providing the prosecution act fairly and do not contrive to produce a false picture by refusing to tender statements adverse to their case, the Crown have a discretion in deciding which statements to tender at a committal.

In relation to the tendering of exhibits the same general principles of fairness should be applied (*R. v. Central Criminal Court, ex p. Bebbehani* [1994] Crim.L.R. 352). In that case, decided under the pre-amended wording of section 6(2), it was said that if a reasonable prosecutor would be bound to realise that without showing the defence the exhibits the defence would be unable to make a decision as to whether there was a case to answer, there was a duty to make such exhibits available. It is submitted that the same principles should apply to committals under the 1996 Act. This does not mean, it is submitted, that the prosecution need formally tender such exhibits at the committal although in practice the prosecution would probably do so if the defence have seen them.

5. Special Evidential Rules for Committals

(i) Deposition from reluctant witness

6–16 Section 5A of the 1980 Act, as inserted by Schedule 1 of the 1996 Act, provides that one of the categories of admissible evidence tendered by the prosecution is a deposition taken in circumstances defined in the Act. This provision is novel and unusual and is intended to deal with the case of a witness who is known to be able to make a statement supporting the prosecution case but who will not voluntarily make such a statement. The somewhat complicated provisions permit a magistrates' court to issue a summons to the reluctant witness to attend court for the purpose of a deposition being taken. This procedure is envisaged to take place on an occasion *before* the committal hearing and thus is not an exception to the general rule that only written evidence may be tendered by the prosecution. The way in which this novel procedure is enacted is by the insertion of a new section, section 97A, to the familiar provisions of section 97 of the 1980 Act – the section which deals with witness summonses (CPIA 1996, s.47 and Schedule 1, para. 8).

CONDITIONS FOR THE OBTAINING OF A SUMMONS OR WARRANT

6–17 A justice of the peace must be satisfied–

(a) that a person in England and Wales is likely to be able to make on behalf of the prosecutor a written statement containing material evidence,

(b) the person will not voluntarily make the statement (or produce a document or exhibit), and

(c) the magistrates' court is the court concerned for the purposes of conducting a committal into an offence (MCA 1980, s.97A(1)(a), (b) and (c)).

If all three of the above conditions are satisfied a summons shall be directed to that person requiring him to attend at an appointed time for the purpose of his evidence being taken as a deposition (or for the purpose of his producing an exhibit) (*ibid.*, s.97A(2)).

A warrant for the arrest of the person may be issued if evidence on oath is given that it is probable that a summons would not procure the attendance of the person and that such person is in England and Wales (*ibid.*, s.97A(3) and (4)).

PROCEDURE FOR THE TAKING AND SERVICE OF THE DEPOSITION

6–18   The procedure is as follows:

 (i) When the reluctant witness attends the magistrates' court a justice of the peace shall cause his evidence to put into writing (MCR 1981, r. 4A(1)(a)).

 (ii) At the conclusion of the examination of the reluctant witness by the prosecutor the deposition must be signed by the witness (*ibid.*, r. 4A(2)).

(iii) If the witness refuses to provide a deposition (or to produce an exhibit) the consequences of such refusal must be explained to him and the witness must be asked to explain why he has so refused. Any refusal and explanation must be recorded in writing by the court (*ibid.*, r. 4A(1)(c) and (d)).

(iv) The court must send a copy of the deposition (together with any documentary exhibits) to the prosecutor as soon as reasonably practicable after the deposition is taken. This is a mandatory step, without which the condition of admissibility of the deposition subsequently is not met (MCA 1980, s.5C(1)(a) and s.97A(9)). The original deposition shall be retained by the court (MCR 1981, r. 3(4)).

 (v) The prosecutor shall, before the magistrates' court commences the committal, give a copy of the deposition to each of the other parties to the proceedings. This is a mandatory step, without which the condition of admissibility of the deposition is not met (MCA 1980, s.5C(1)(b) and (2)).

(vi) If there are any documentary exhibits referred to in the deposition they must be made available for inspection similarly, as a condition of admissibility (*ibid.*, s.5C(1)(c), and (3)).

CONSEQUENCES OF REFUSAL TO ATTEND OR TO PROVIDE A DEPOSITION

6–19   There are two consequencies:

 (i) If the reluctant witness refuses to attend the magistrates' court in answer to a summons, and a justice is satisfied by evidence on oath that he is likely to be able to make a statement (or produce an exhibit), and it is proved that the summons was served (together with conduct money), and it appears there is no just excuse for the failure to attend, a warrant may be issued (MCA 1980, s.97A(5) and (6)).

 (ii) If, having attended in response to a summons or warrant the reluctant witness refused without just excuse to have his evidence taken as a deposition the court may:

    (a) commit the witness to custody for a period not exceeding one month or
        until such time as the witness agrees to give a deposition (or produce the
        exhibit), and or
    (b) impose a fine not exceeding £2,500 (MCA 1980, s.97A(7)).

6–20 A number of points should be noted. First, the procedure under section 97A
may only be used if a justice is "satisfied" that a person is likely to be able to give
"material evidence". The consequences for the allegedly reluctant witness in refusing
to co-operate are potentially a sentence of imprisonment and it is submitted there
should be high degree of materiality involved. This inevitably will involve a justice
making a value judgment about the prosecution and its chances of success should it
proceed without the evidence being taken in a deposition.

Secondly, and more importantly it is unclear from the primary legislation and the
rules what the status of the proceedings under section 97A are. In one sense they
resemble an application (because the taking of a deposition is a preliminary stage
before a committal) but in another sense they resemble a full court hearing because the
prosecutor is present and there is the potential for penal consequences. It is submitted
that some assistance may be derived from the "mutual assistance" provisions in section 4 of the Criminal Justice (International Co-operation) Act 1990 and the rules
made thereunder. This Act allows a magistrates' court to obtain evidence in connection with criminal proceedings in a foreign jurisdiction. In rules made to accompany
the Act it is provided that in such proceedings the court may, if it thinks necessary in the
interests of justice, request that the public be excluded from the court while the evidence is being taken (Magistrates' Courts (Criminal Justice) (International Co-operation) Rules 1991, r. 8). No specific rules to this effect have been made by Parliament
to accompany section 97A but on general principles it would appear that the court
ought not to sit with the public excluded unless it is in the interests of justice to do so. In
practice it may well be the case, on the facts, that the public should be excluded because
the police do not take witness statements in those circumstances and it is intended that
a deposition should be in place of a witness statement.

It is similarly unclear whether the accused is entitled to be present if the court begins
the proceedings at least by sitting in open court. There would seem to be no positive
reason for the accused being present because his rights are preserved in the committal
proceedings themselves, should they occur. Under the Criminal Justice (International
Co-operation) Act 1990 this question does not arise, because in proceedings under
that Act the accused himself is in a foreign country.

(ii) Inadmissible evidence in committals

6–21 A Committal is not invalid simply because inadmissible evidence has been
received (*R. v. Norfolk Quarter Sessions, ex p. Brunson* [1953] 1 Q.B. 503). In theory,
therefore, there is no prohibition upon the prosecution tendering statements which
contain inadmissible material. Such a practice should not, however, occur following
the decision of the House of Lords in *Williams v. Bedwellty Justices* [1997] A.C. 225.
In that case their Lordships held that justices have a duty to consider whether evidence
tendered in a committal is admissible or inadmissible in the same way as such considerations may arise in a summary trial. If there is no admissible evidence upon which a
jury could convict the accused justices should not commit the accused for trial. It was
said in that case that if an issue as to admissibility arose justices would be well advised
to exclude the evidence only if such a course was plainly required on the facts.

If the evidence tendered contains evidence which is inadmissible together with evidence which is admissible, a committal for trial is not flawed merely because justices had considered some inadmissible material (*R. v. Ipswich Justices, ex p. Edwards* (1979) 143 J.P. 699). Similarly, if justices decline to rule upon questions of admissibility of evidence it is unlikely that the committal would be quashed on judicial review (*R. v. Oxford City Justices, ex p. Berry* [1988] Q.B. 507).

(iii) Confession evidence or unfair evidence

6–22   It is not possible for the admissibility of a confession to be challenged in committal proceedings nor for evidence to be excluded on the grounds of unfairness (CP and IA 1996, s.47 and Sched. 1, paras 25 and 26). These provisions of the 1996 Act deliberately disapply the application of sections 76 and 78 of the Police and Criminal Evidence Act 1984 to committals. As originally drafted section 76 of the 1984 Act applied to "any proceedings" although it had been doubted whether the draftsmen ever had in mind the possible impact on committal proceedings (*per* May L.J. in *R. v. Oxford Justices, ex p. Berry* [1988] Q.B. 507, at 512). The opportunity has now been taken in the Act to disapply section 76 of the 1984 Act to committals in accordance with the doubts voiced in *ex p. Berry*.

Similar considerations arise in relation to the removal of section 78 submissions from committal proceedings. This latest change reflects observations made by the Divisional Court in *R. v. King's Lynn Justices, ex p. Holland* (1992) 156 J.P. 825.

6. Publicity at Committals

(i) General rule

6–23   The only matters which may be reported or broadcast about committal proceedings are:

— the name, age and address of the accused and the charge or charges for which he was committed for trial,

— the identity of the court,

— the names of the examining justice or justices and counsel or solicitors in the case and the name of any witnesses,

— the decision by justices to commit for trial and the court to which he is committed,

— the arrangements about bail and whether the legal aid was granted (MCA 1980, s.8(4)).

These reporting restrictions apply automatically unless the accused or one of several accused apply for the restrictions to be lifted (MCA 1980, s.8(2)).

The general rule restricting the reporting or broadcasting of committal proceedings to those matters defined in section 8(4) of the Magistrates' Courts Act 1980 is intended to avoid a substantial risk of prejudice in the future (*R. v. Beaconsfield Magistrates' Court, ex p. Westminster Press Ltd* (1994) 158 J.P. 1055). Accordingly, justices should be slow to make any additional orders under the Contempt of Court Act 1981 postponing any reporting of a committal until the conclusion of the Crown Court trial.

For the circumstances in which it is proper to make an order prohibiting or postponing publicity see paragraphs 1–76 to 1–81, above.

Where several accused are to be committed and there is no agreement among them as to whether reporting restrictions should be lifted, the court should only lift the restrictions if it is in the interests of justice to do so. The burden of satisfying the justices about this lies with the accused who wishes to have the proceedings reported, and as it is paramount that all accused should have a fair trial, a powerful case should be made by the accused making the application (*R. v. Leeds Justices, ex p. Sykes* [1983] 1 W.L.R. 132). Failure to follow this procedure will make any lifting of reporting restrictions invalid (*R. v. Wirral Magistrates' Court, ex p. Meikle* (1990) 154 J.P. 1035).

The court should always explain to an accused (particularly if he is unrepresented) the rules about publicity and his right to have the restrictions removed (MCR 1981, r. 5).

The general prohibition on reporting applies only to committals. If therefore the accused is discharged the proceedings may be reported fully. Secondly, the prohibition applies only to the period between committal and trial. At the conclusion of the Crown Court trial the proceedings may be reported (MCA 1980, s.8(3)).

(ii) Special rule for sexual cases

6–24   Where the accused is charged with a rape offence or any sexual offence defined in the Sexual Offences (Amendment) Act 1992 the anonymity of the victim must be preserved (Sexual Offences (Amendment) Act 1976, s.4 and Sexual Offences (Amendment) Act 1992, s.1). The offence of rape is now defined to include vaginal or anal intercourse, and may be committed by a man upon another man otherwise than in circumstances of consensual buggery (Sexual Offences Act 1956, s.1(1), as amended by CJ and POA 1994, ss.142 and 143). The 1992 Act defines a sexual offence widely and it includes offences contrary to sections 2 to 7, 9, 10, 11, 12, 14, 15 and 16 of the Sexual Offences Act 1956, indecent conduct towards a child under the Indecency with Children Act 1960, incitement to commit incest under the Criminal Law Act 1977 or an incitement, attempt or conspiracy to commit any of the above offences (Sexual Offences (Amendment) Act 1992, s.2(2) as amended by CJ and POA 1994, s.168 and Sched. 9, para. 52).

The scheme of the 1992 Act is exactly the same as the 1976 Act, that is to say the Act gives protection to an alleged victim from the moment an allegation of a sexual offence is made, whether or not criminal proceedings in the magistrates' court follow. In addition, once a person is accused of any of the defined sexual offences, and the victim is a complainant, there is a prohibition against any publication or broadcast, throughout the complainant's lifetime, which might lead members of the public to identify the complainant.

The offences defined in the 1992 Act are triable either way, and therefore the Act applies in committal proceedings for any of those offences. In a committal for a rape offence the anonymity provisions continue to apply by virtue of the Sexual Offences (Amendment) Act 1976 which is still in force. However, the Sexual Offences (Amendment) Act 1992 will apply also to summary trials where any of the above listed offences are tried summarily. The effect of the new Act upon summary trial is discussed fully in §1–81, above.

There is no anonymity for defendants accused of any of the above offences, including rape. The anonymity of defendants in rape cases was abolished by section 158 of the Criminal Justice Act 1988.

7. Committal of juveniles

6–25   If a person under the age of 18 is charged jointly with an adult with an indictable offence (other than homicide) the court may commit both for trial if it is necessary in the interests of justice to do so (MCA 1980, s.24(1)(b)). This provision of the Magistrates' Courts Act has no application if the adult is discharged at the committal.

In such a situation the magistrates' court must, at the committal, go on to consider whether the charge remaining against the youth alone is a severe punishment case covered by section 24(1)(a) of the 1980 Act. This permits the court to commit the youth for trial if it ought to be possible for the Crown Court to sentence the youth under section 53 of the Children and Young Persons Act 1933 (*R. v. Haringey Justices, ex p. Fawzy* [1998] 1 Cr.App.R. 411). It was stressed in that case that section 24(1)(a) is permissive and not mandatory. The test is whether it is a *possible* severe punishment case. If it is then the youth may be committed alone to the Crown Court; if it is not he must be tried summarily.

If the court concludes that it is *not* a severe punishment case then the court should take a plea from the juvenile and then the case should be remitted to the Youth Court to be dealt with accordingly (MCA 1980, s.29(2) and C and YPA 1933, s.56). There is no express statutory provision which gives the magistrates' court power to refer the issue of possible severe punishment to the Youth Court in *committal* proceedings (C and YPA 1933, s.56(1)). Accordingly, in a committal if the adult is discharged the magistrates' court (and not the Youth Court) should decide whether a sentence under section 53 of the Children and Young Persons Act 1933 is a possible outcome or not.

6–26 The considerations for the application of section 24(1)(b) will depend on all the circumstances of the case and it has been held that justices may be informed that the juvenile is of good character (*R. v. South Hackney Juvenile Court, ex p. R.B. (a Minor) and C.B. (a Minor)* (1984) 77 Cr.App.R. 294). Whether it is necessary in the interests of justice to commit the juvenile will depend on the considerations which apply to joint and separate trial generally, although there is an additional consideration concerning the gravity of the offence. Justices should consider committing the juvenile in grave cases because the Crown Court has wider sentencing powers than those possessed by the magistrates' court (*R. v. Corcoran* (1986) 8 Cr.App.R.(S.) 118). If the court does consider it is in the interests of justice to commit the juvenile for trial it may also commit him in respect of any other indictable offence with which he is charged at the same time providing that offence arises out of circumstances which are the same as or connected with the original offence (MCA 1980, s.24(2)).

6–27 The meaning of the words "charged jointly" in section 24(1)(b) of the Magistrates' Courts Act 1980 were considered by the Divisional Court in *R. v. Peterborough Magistrates' Court, ex p. Allgood* (1995) 159 J.P. 627. In that case a juvenile was charged with allowing himself to be carried in a separate information from an adult who was charged with taking a motor vehicle in the aggravated form contrary to section 12A of the Theft Act 1968. It was held that while the offences were separate and distinct and had to be itemised as such they were part and parcel of an offence committed jointly. Although generally the words "charged jointly" would mean charged together, a different meaning applied to a charge under section 12A because, inevitably, only one person could drive at any one time. In the context of the crime alleged both defendants could be said to be "jointly charged", and accordingly the juvenile could be committed for trial with the adult under section 24. It is not necessary for the juvenile and the adult to be present in court on the same occasion for a decision to be taken to commit the juvenile for trial at the Crown Court under the MCA 1980, s.24(1)(b) (*R. v. Coventry City Magistrates, ex p. M.* (1992) 156 J.P. 809). In that case it was held that the decision to commit the juvenile under section 24(1)(b) could be taken by the youth court after a decision had been taken by a magistrates' court to commit the adult.

8. Power to Commit for Summary Offence in Certain Circumstances

6–28   Where a magistrates' court commits an accused to the Crown Court for trial in respect of an either way offence or a number of such offences it may also commit him for trial for any summary offence with which he is charged providing that offence:

(a) is punishable with imprisonment or involves obligatory or discretionary disqualification from driving, and

(b) arises out of circumstances which appear to the court to be the same as or connected with those giving rise to one or other of the either way offences (CJA 1988, s.41(1)).

The power only arises if the offence being committed to the Crown Court is an either way offence. It does not arise if that offence is indictable only. Secondly, it does not matter if the evidence relating to the summary only offence is not revealed in the depositions or written statements placed before the court. Providing the accused has been charged with the summary offences in question and the circumstances appear to the court to be connected with the either way offence or offences the court may commit the summary matters to the Crown Court (CJA 1988, s.41(1)).

The purpose of this new power is to allow the Crown Court to sentence the offender on the same occasion with a variety of offences (whether either way or summary only) which arise out of the same circumstances. However, the Crown Court may only deal with him if the summary offences are admitted. If they are denied, and the offences are to be tried, they will be sent back to the magistrates' court for trial (CJA 1988, s.41(7) and (8)).

In order that the magistrates' court may still be seized of the matter in the event of a not guilty plea at the Crown Court, the future trial of the information may technically be treated as an adjournment *sine die* (CJA 1988, s.41(1)).

B. Transfer to the Crown Court

1. Definition

6–29   The following may be made the subject of a notice of transfer to the Crown Court:

(i) serious or complex fraud (CJA 1987, s.4, as amended by CJ and POA 1994, s.168 and Sched. 9, para. 15).

(ii) a sexual offence involving violence or cruelty to a child (as defined in section 32(2) of the Criminal Justice Act 1988) in which a child is either the victim or a witness (CJA 1991, s.53).

In both statutes the procedure laid down is broadly the same, and although the role of the magistrates' court is limited there is scope for making an application for dismissal before a Crown Court judge which is similar to an application to discharge an accused in committal proceedings.

It had been the intention of Parliament to extend the transfer procedure to prosecutions brought under the War Crimes Act 1991, but no corresponding amendments had been made to section 2(2) of the Administration of Justice (Miscellaneous Provisions) Act 1933 and there remains a risk that any indictment preferred following transfer to the Crown Court in a war crimes case would be invalid. The application of transfer to the War Crimes Act 1991 was formally repealed by section 46 of the Criminal Procedure and Investigations Act 1996.

2. Procedure

6–30 First a decision to issue a Notice of Transfer must be made by the prosecution. In serious frauds this is a designated authority which means the Director of Public Prosecutions, the Director of the Serious Fraud Office, the Commissioners of Inland Revenue, the Commissioners of Customs and Excise, and the Secretary of State (CJA 1987, s.4(1)). In sexual cases involving children it is the Director of Public Prosecutions (CJA 1991, s.53(1)). Once a decision has been taken a notice of transfer must be issued under the Magistrates' Courts (Notice of Transfer) Rules 1988, or under Schedule 6 of the Criminal Justice Act 1991 and the functions of the magistrates' court shall cease (CJA 1987, s.4(1), CJA 1991, s.53(3)). This means that there is no obligation to conduct plea before venue or mode of trial proceedings for either way offences after the issue of a notice of transfer (*Brewer v. D.P.P.* [1995] Crim.L.R. 168). The decision to issue such a notice may not be questioned by any court nor may it be subject to appeal (CJA 1987, s.4(3), CJA 1991, s.53(4)). In the case of a serious or complex fraud which is to be transferred to the Crown Court there is no obligation to provide Advance Information under rule 4 of the Magistrates' Courts (Advance Information) Rules 1985 (*R. v. Serious Fraud Office, ex p. Maxwell (Kevin)*, *The Times*, October 9, 1992).

(i) Duties of the magistrates' court following a transfer notice

6–31 If the accused is in custody before the transfer notice is issued the magistrates' court has power to order that he remain in custody until such time as he is produced before the Crown Court (CJA 1987, s.5(3)(a)), and if he is on bail to renew his bail to the Crown Court (*ibid.*, s.5(3)(b)). These powers may be exercised without the accused being produced before the court if the accused gives his written consent and the court is satisfied he knows a transfer notice had been issued (CJA 1987, s.5(5)). The accused may apply for his existing terms of bail to be varied, and the magistrates' court retains this function to consider a variation of bail (Magistrates' Courts (Notice of Transfer) Rules 1988, r. 5). If, immediately before the transfer notice was issued, the accused was due to appear in the magistrates' court for a committal for trial, the committal is automatically cancelled and instead the accused must attend the Crown Court specified in the notice (CJA 1987, s.5(6) and (7)). For the purposes of the Criminal Procedure (Attendance of Witnesses) Act 1965 the magistrates' court from which the case was transferred shall be treated as examining magistrates (*ibid.*, s.5(8)). This provision, together with amendments to the Magistrates' Courts (Notice of Transfer) Rules 1998 made by the Magistrates' Courts (Notice of Transfer) Rules 1997, enables the formalities of transfer proceedings to be consistent with changes to committal proceedings brought about by the Criminal Procedure and Investigations Act 1996 (see, generally, Chapter 6, above).

The only other function of the magistrates' court is to consider the question of legal aid under the Legal Aid Act 1988, s.20, in the same way as if the court had committed the accused for trial (CJA 1987, s.4(1)).

Although the above references are to the Criminal Justice Act 1987, there are minor amendments to the wording of the 1987 Act contained in section 144 of the Criminal Justice Act 1988. In addition to the procedure laid down in Schedule 6 of the 1991 Act there are rules governing certain formalities called the Magistrates' Courts (Notice of Transfer) (Children's Evidence) Rules 1992.

(ii) Criteria for a transfer notice

(a) SERIOUS FRAUDS

6–32   A transfer notice may be issued if in the opinion of the designated authority the evidence in the case would be sufficient for the accused to be committed for trial and it is a fraud of such seriousness or complexity that it is appropriate that the management of the case should be taken over by the Crown Court without delay (CJA 1987, s.4(1)).

Although the decision to transfer a case to the Crown Court may be challenged by judicial review, the fact that the decision to transfer the case deprives the accused of a legitimate expectation of cross-examining witnesses in committal proceedings is not a ground for quashing a decision to transfer (*R. v. Salford Magistrates' Court, ex p. Gallagher* [1994] Crim.L.R. 374).

(b) CASES INVOLVING CHILDREN

A notice of transfer may be issued if in the opinion of the Director of Public Prosecutions the case should proceed without delay at the Crown Court for the purpose of avoiding prejudice to the welfare of the child (CJA 1991, s.53(1)).

C. SENDING INDICTABLE ONLY OFFENCES TO THE CROWN COURT

6–33   The sending for trial for indictable only offences is an entirely new – and at this stage experimental – procedure, introduced by section 51 of the Crime and Disorder Act 1998. The genesis for the concept was the Narey Report (*Review of Delay in the Criminal Justice System*) which concluded that too much time was spent processing indictable only offences in the magistrates' court. Section 51 of the 1998 Act allows such offences to be sent to the Crown Court forthwith, thus by-passing procedures of remand and committal for trial.

At present the sending for trial procedure is being used on a pilot basis in the following places: the petty sessions areas of Bromley; Croydon; and Sutton; Aberconwy; Arfon; Blackburn, Darwen and Ribble Valley; Burnley and Pendle; Colwyn; Corby; Daventry; Dyffryn Clwyd; Eifionydd and Pwllheli; Gateshead; Kettering; Meirionnydd; Newcastle-under-Lyme and Pirehill North; Newcastle-upon-Tyne; Northampton; Rhuddlan; Staffordshire Moorlands; Stoke-on-Trent; Towcester; Wellingborough; and Ynys Mon/Anglesey (Crime and Disorder Act (Commencement No. 2 and Transitional Provisions) Order 1998, Sched. 2, §§1 and 2).

(i) Conditions for sending for trial

6–34   Where an adult appears or is brought before a magistrates' court ("the court") charged with an offence triable only on indictment ("the indictable only offence"), the court shall send him forthwith to the Crown Court for trial for that offence, and for any either-way or summary offence with which he is charged which fulfils the requisite conditions set out below (CDA 1998, s.51(1)(a) and (b).

An offence fulfils the requisite conditions if it appears to the court to be related to the indictable only offence; and in the case of a summary offence, it is punishable with imprisonment or involves obligatory or discretionary disqualification from driving (*ibid.,* s.51(11)(a) and (b)).

Where an adult has been sent for trial under section 51(1) above and then subsequently appears charged with an either-way or summary only offence which fulfils the requisite conditions (see above) the court may send him forthwith to the Crown Court for trial for the either-way or summary only offence (*ibid.,* s.51(2)).

The Act makes special provision for the definition of "summary offence" if the offence is criminal damage or motor-vehicle taking. In these cases the offence is to be treated as being summary only if it is clear, having regard to any representations made by the prosecution, that the value does not exceed the relevant sum (*ibid.,* s.52(3)).

ADULT CO-ACCUSED

6–35 Where—

(a) the court sends an adult for trial under section 51(1) above;

(b) another adult appears or is brought before the court on the same or a subsequent occasion charged jointly with him with an either-way offence; and

(c) that offence appears to the court to be related to the indictable only offence;

the court shall where it is the same occasion, and may where it is a subsequent occasion, send the other adult forthwith to the Crown Court for trial for the either-way offence (*ibid.,* s.51(3)).

This provision is not mandatory but if the court does send such either-way offence to the Crown Court it may also at the same time send any other either-way or summary offence which fulfils the requisite conditions (*ibid.,* s.51(4)).

The words "appear to be related" in section 51(3) are different from the wording in section 41 of the 1988 Act (justifying a committal for sentence under that Act) and from those in rule 9 of the Indictment Rules 1971 (justifying joint trial on indictment).

YOUNG PERSONS AND CHILDREN WHO ARE CO-ACCUSED

6–36 Where—

(a) the court sends an adult for trial under section 51(1) or 51(3) above; and

(b) a child or young person appears or is brought before the court on the same or a subsequent occasion charged jointly with the adult or with an indictable offence for which the adult is sent for trial,

the court shall, if it considers it necessary in the interests of justice to do so, send the child or young person forthwith to the Crown Court for trial for the indictable offence (CDA 1998, s.51(5)). If these conditions are satisfied the court may at the same time send him to the Crown Court for trial for either-way or summary offence with which he is charged which fulfils the requisite conditions (*ibid.,* s.51(6)).

It is submitted that the words "necessary in the interests of justice to do so" should be interpreted in the same way as considerations arising under section 24 of the 1980 Act (committal of juveniles) where the same words appear. (See §§6–25 to 6–27, above).

(ii) *Procedure and formalities*

6–37 The Crime and Disorder Act 1998 has made provision for a number of familiar procedures of the magistrates' court to accompany sending for trial. These are:

- power to grant or to refuse bail (s.52(1));

- power of remand (s.52(5));

- application of disclosure provisions (s.119 and Schedule 8); and

- the power to send to the most convenient Crown Court (s.51(10)).

In addition there is a specific power for a deposition from a reluctant witness, as there is for committal proceedings (s.52(6) and Schedule 3).

The formalities of sending for trial are that the court shall specify in a notice the offence or offences for which a person is sent for trial under this section and the place at which he is to be tried; and a copy of the notice shall be served on the accused and given to the Crown Court (CDA 1998, s.51(7)).

D. COMMITTAL FOR SENTENCE

6–38   There are a number of circumstances in which a magistrates' court may commit an offender to be sentenced by the Crown Court. The most common reason for such a committal is when the court is of the opinion that its own powers of punishment are insufficient in respect of an either way offence, following a trial or a plea of guilty. There is also a power to commit for sentence after an indication of guilty plea. In addition the court may also commit for sentence in respect of Crown Court Community Orders, or if the offender is in breach of a Crown Court order, or if a restriction order is sought under the Mental Health Act 1983, or if a six month sentence in a Young Offenders Institution is insufficient for offenders under 18, or in respect of certain summary offences under the Criminal Justice Acts 1967 or 1988. The preconditions for a committal for sentence differ depending upon the grounds giving rise to the committal. The court must always have a statutory authority for a committal for sentence, and the committal must be in accordance with the provisions of the Act of Parliament in question.

1. Committal for Sentence after Summary Trial of an Either Way Offence

6–39   The power to commit for sentence has long been part of the jurisdiction of the magistrates' court and has been the subject of much legislative attention in recent years. The law is as follows:

(i) if an offender who is not less than 18 years of age is convicted (or pleads guilty) to an offence, and

(ii) the court is of the opinion—

    (a) that the offence or the combination of the offence and one or more other offences associated with it was so serious that greater punishment should be inflicted for the offence than the court has power to impose; or

    (b) in the case of a violent or sexual offence that a custodial sentence for a term longer than the court has power to impose is necessary to protect the public from serious harm from him, the court may commit the offender for sentence at the Crown Court (MCA 1980, s.38(1), 2(a) and (b), as substituted by CJA 1991, s.25(1), and CJ and POA 1994, s.168 and Sched. 9 para. 15).

6–40 The decision to commit for sentence is a separate and distinct decision from the mode of trial decision and justices should consider the words of section 38 and those words only when deciding whether or not to commit for sentence(*R. v. Sheffield Crown Court and Sheffield Stipendiary Magistrate, ex p. D.P.P.* (1994) 15 Cr.App.R.(S.) 768, *R. v. North Sefton Magistrates' Court, ex p. Marsh* (1995) 16 Cr.App.R.(S.) 401, and *R. v. Southampton Magistrates' Court, ex p. Sansome* [1997] 1 Cr.App.R.(S.) 112).

The law may be summarised as follows:

(i) section 38 has to be given its ordinary natural meaning. This is that a magistrates' court has power to commit for sentence if it is of the opinion that the offence or the combination of the offence and other offences associated with it is so serious that greater punishment should be inflicted for the offence than the court has power to impose;

(ii) this wording, which was changed significantly by the 1991 Act, means that the opinion that the offence or offences are so serious as to require a committal may be formed after jurisdiction had been accepted under section 19 of the Magistrates' Court Act 1980;

(iii) section 19 and section 38 relate to different stages in the proceedings and there is nothing unreasonable or illogical about permitting a court to form a different view at the stage when deciding whether or not to commit for sentence;

(iv) it would be illogical to apply any restrictions to the interpretation of section 38 because the restrictions which were explicit in the original wording are entirely absent from the new wording; and

(v) the fact that a Bench had, on an earlier occasion, requested the preparation of a pre-sentence report does not inhibit a subsequent Bench from making a decision to commit the offender for sentence unless the first Bench had specifically ruled out a committal for sentence.

The Development of the law in these respects is reflected in the latest National Mode of Trial Guidelines where the attention of justices is specifically drawn to the amended form of section 38 of the 1980 Act (see Appendix I, below).

SENTENCING PRACTICE FOR COMMITTAL FOR SENTENCE

6–41 The considerations which should properly be taken into account in deciding whether or not to commit the offender for sentence have been stated by the Divisional Court to be as follows:

(i) Pending appropriate revision the Mode of Trial Guidelines 1995 are still relevant as to whether or not it is appropriate to send the offender to the Crown Court (for Mode of Trial Guidelines see Appendix I, below).

(ii) Justices must have regard to the discount to be granted on a plea of guilty when deciding whether the punishment which it would have power to impose for any offence would be adequate. If, after discount, any offence ought to attract a sentence in excess of six months' imprisonment it follows that the requirements of section 38(2)(a) are satisfied, and the court must commit to the Crown Court for sentence. Sentences can only be made consecutive if in principle it is right to make them consecutive, not simply so as to arrive at a total within a 12 month maximum which seems appropriate for the case as a whole. If having made appropriate discount the court considers that an appropriate sentence can be imposed if it uses its sentencing powers to the full it should adopt that course.

(ii) If, taking the above into account, it is obvious that the offender should be committed for sentence this should be done straight away, without seeking a pre-sentence report or hearing in full the mitigation which may be sought to be advance.

(iii) There is nothing in the statutory provisions governing committal for sentence which should prevent the prosecutor from addressing the court as to its powers because sometimes a prosecutor will be in the best position of all in court to assist the court, for example as to the existence of a guideline decision on sentencing (*R. v. Warley Magistrates' Court, ex p. D.P.P., R. v. Staines Magistrates' Court, ex p. D.P.P., R. v. North East Suffolk Magistrates' Courts, ex p. D.P.P.* [1998] 2 Cr.App.R. 307).

NEWTON HEARINGS AND COMMITTAL FOR SENTENCE

6–42 A *Newton* hearing should be conducted in the magistrates' court prior to a committal for sentence if the decision whether or not to commit will depend on the outcome of such hearing (*R. v. Warley Magistrates' Court*, above). (For *Newton* hearing see §§13–42 to 13–45, below). If, having conducted a *Newton* hearing justices determine that the offender should be committed for sentence the findings of fact in the hearing should be recorded and sent to the Crown Court.

2. Committal for Sentence after Committal for Trial for a Related Offence

6–43 Where a defendant has indicated a plea of guilty to an either-way offence under the provisions of section 17A of the 1980 Act (plea before venue) but the defendant has been committed for trial for one or more related offences the court may commit the defendant for sentence for the either-way offence (MCA 1980, s.38A(2), as inserted by C(S)A 1997, s.51).

This latest amendment to section 38 of the 1980 Act permits all the offences facing a defendant to be dealt with on the same occasion by the Crown Court, however the magistrates' court does not need to be satisfied that its own powers of punishment would be insufficient in order to commit under section 38A.

Section 38A(4) requires the court to state whether or not it considers its powers sufficient. If the court does *not* state that, in its opinion, greater powers of punishment should be inflicted than the court has power to impose then the powers of the Crown Court are restricted to those of the magistrates' court (MCA s.38A(4)(a) and (b)). For this reason it may be wise for justices to state positively that in their opinion they *also* have power to commit under section 38(2) (committal for sentence for an either-way offence) and such positive statement is permitted by the wording of section 38A(4)(b)). In this way the powers of the Crown Court are not fettered.

Section 38A(3) permits the above decisions to be put back until the conclusion of committal proceedings for the offence or offences for which the defendant has elected trial.

3. Committal for Sentence for Purely Summary Offences

(i) Under the Criminal Justice Act 1967

6–44   The court has power to commit under section 56 of the Criminal Justice Act 1967 if the court is dealing with an offender for a purely summary offence on the same occasion as the offender is being committed to the Crown Court under another statutory provision for other offences. The summary offence must be either imprisonable or subject to penalty point endorsement and discretionary disqualification or the offender must be in breach of a suspended sentence imposed in a magistrates' court (CJA 1967, s.56). The powers of the Crown Court on sentence are limited to those of the magistrates' court.

It has been said that the purpose of a committal under section 56 is to allow one court to deal with an offender for all matters outstanding against him rather than having the sentencing decision split between two different courts (*R. v. Penfold* (1995) 16 Cr.App.R.(S.) 1016). In that case it was held that the power to commit under section 56 where the offender had committed a further offence when subject to a conditional discharge imposed at the Crown Court had been preserved notwithstanding the repeal of section 8(6) of the Powers of Criminal Courts Act 1973 by Schedule 13 of the Criminal Justice Act 1991. It was said in that case that if Parliament had intended to abolish the power of a magistrates' court to commit for sentence in these circumstances it would have done so specifically. This interpretation is consistent with the provisions of section 1B of the 1973 Act (see §6–52, below).

(ii) Under the Criminal Justice Act 1988

6–45   The court has power to commit under section 41 of the Criminal Justice Act 1988 for certain summary offences which arise out of the same facts or are connected with an offence which is being committed for trial. This power is discussed fully at §6–28, above. In essence a committal under section 41 is a committal with a view to sentence because, as is explained above, if the accused denies the offences they are remitted back to the magistrates' court for trial.

4. Committal for Sentence in Respect of Community Orders

6–46   The Criminal Justice Act 1991 has changed the law substantially in respect of the consequences to an offender when he appears before the court during the currency of a community order (which is defined in section 6(4) of the Act). The commission of a further offence is not sufficient in itself to give a court the power to deal with an offender. The court's powers now arise when an offender has failed to comply with a community order or there is an application for such order to be revoked. In addition there is a residual power to deal with an offender who has a custodial sentence imposed for a new offence while being subject to a community order. Where community orders have been made by the Crown Court there is a power to commit the offender to be dealt with by the Crown Court (WA 1991, Pt II, para. 3.3).

The importance of understanding the change brought about in the Criminal Justice Act 1991 that the commission of a further offence is not, in itself, a justification for committing an offender to be dealt with was underlined in *R. v. Adams* (1994) 15 Cr.App.R.(S.) 417. In that case the offender had been convicted of theft in the magistrates' court whilst subject to a probation order made at the Crown Court for burglary and theft, and had been committed to the Crown Court for sentence. The Court of Appeal (reconstituting itself as the Divisional Court) quashed the committal and emphasised the importance of court and practitioners adhering strictly to the powers set out in Schedule 2 to the Criminal Justice Act 1991. These powers are summarised in §§12–18 and 12–26, below.

COMMITTAL FOR FAILURE TO COMPLY WITH A COMMUNITY ORDER

6–47   Where a Probation Order or a Community Service Order has been made by the Crown Court, and it is proved to the satisfaction of a magistrates' court that the offender has failed without reasonable excuse to comply with any of the requirements of the order, the offender may be committed on bail or in custody to the Crown Court to be dealt with (CJA 1991, Sched. 2, Pt II, para. 3(3)). The Crown Court then has power to revoke the order and deal with the offender in any manner in which it could have dealt with him if he had just been convicted of the offence (*ibid.*, §4(1)). If the Crown Court is satisfied that the offender has wilfully and persistently failed to comply with the requirements it may impose a custodial sentence (see generally, §§12–18 and 12–26, below).

COMMITTAL ON APPLICATION FOR THE COMMUNITY ORDER TO BE REVOKED

6–48   Where a Probation order or Community Service Order has been made by the Crown Court, and the magistrates' court is satisfied on application of either the offender or the responsible officer that it would be in the interests of justice for the order to be revoked, the offender may be committed on bail or in custody to the Crown Court to be dealt with (CJA Sched 2. Pt III, para. 7(2)). The Crown Court then has the power to revoke the order and deal with the offender in any manner in which it could have dealt with him if he had just been convicted of the offence (*ibid.*, §8(1)).

COMMITTAL FOLLOWING A CUSTODIAL SENTENCE WHERE OFFENDER IS SUBJECT TO A CROWN COURT COMMUNITY ORDER

6–49   Where an offender is the subject of a Probation Order or a Community Service Order made by the Crown Court, and during the currency of such an order is convicted by a magistrates' court and a custodial sentence is imposed and it appears on application by the offender or the responsible officer that the community order should be revoked, the offender may be committed in custody or on bail to the Crown Court (CJA 1991, Sched. 2, Pt III, para. 9). The Crown Court then has the power to revoke the order if it is in the interests of justice to do so (*ibid.*, para. 10).

COMMITTAL WHERE A CROWN COURT ATTENDANCE CENTRE ORDER IS BREACHED

6–50   Where an offender is the subject of an Attendance Centre Order made by the Crown Court, and during the currency of such an order it appears that the offender has failed without reasonable excuse to attend the attendance centre or has breached the rules of such a centre, the offender may be committed on bail or in custody to the Crown Court to be dealt with (CJA 1982, s.19(3)). The Crown Court then has the power to revoke the order and deal with him in any manner in which it could have done if it had just made the order (*ibid.*, s.19(5)).

5. Committal for Sentence when the Offender is in Breach of a Crown Court Order

BREACH OF A SUSPENDED SENTENCE

6–51   Where an offender is convicted by a magistrates' court of an offence punishable with imprisonment, and the court is satisfied that the offence was committed during the operational period of a suspended sentence passed by the Crown Court, the offender may be committed on bail or in custody to the Crown Court to be dealt with (PCCA 1973, s.24(2)). The Crown Court then has the power to deal with the offender in a variety of ways (PCCA 1973, s.23(1)).

BREACH OF A CONDITIONAL DISCHARGE

6–52 Where an offender is convicted by a magistrates' court of an offence during the period of a conditional discharge made by the Crown Court the offender may be committed on bail or in custody to the Crown Court to be dealt with (PCCA, s.1B(5) as inserted by CJA 1991, Sched. 1). The Crown Court may then deal with the offender in any manner in which it could have dealt with him if he had just been convicted of the offence (*ibid.*, s.1B(6)).

6. Committal for Sentence of Prisoners Released on Licence who are Convicted of a Further Offence

6–53 Where a prisoner who has been sentenced to a term of imprisonment by any court on or after October 1, 1992, is convicted by a magistrates' court of a further offence punishable by imprisonment during the prisoner's release on licence, and the court determines to order him to be returned to prison to serve the unexpired part of the sentence, then if that period exceeds six months the offender may be committed on bail or in custody to the Crown Court to be dealt with (CJA 1991, s.40(3)). The Crown Court then has power to order the offender to be returned to custody for a period not exceeding the period between the date on which the new offence was committed and the end of the full term of the sentence (*ibid.*, s.40(2)).

The law and practice in relation to the use of section 40 of the 1991 Act has been the subject of a number of decisions in the Divisional Court and the Court of Appeal. The topic is discussed further in §§12–84 to 12–87, below.

7. Committal under the Mental Health Act with a View to Restriction

6–54 If a magistrates' court is satisfied generally that a Hospital Order should be made in respect of an offender (for Hospital Orders see "Mentally Disordered Offenders" at Chapter 7), but considers that a restriction order should be imposed in addition, and the offender is convicted of an offence punishable with imprisonment, then he must be committed to the Crown Court to be sentenced because only the Crown Court has power to impose a Restriction Order (MHA 1983, s.43(1)).

8. Committal of Juvenile with a View to Sentence in a Young Offender Institution for a Period of more than Six Months

6–55 Where an offender who is not less than 15 but under 18 years of age is convicted by a magistrates' court of an offence which carries a term of imprisonment of more than six months on indictment, the court may commit him in custody or on bail to the Crown Court to be sentenced if the court is of the opinion that a sentence greater than the court has power to impose should be passed (MCA 1980, s.37(1)).

Section 37 is to be repealed in full (from a date to be appointed) when Part IV of the Crime and Disorder Act 1998 is brought into force (CDA 1998, Sched. 10). Sections 73 to 79 of the 1998 Act will enable a youth court to pass a Detention and Training Order on an offender aged 15, 16 or 17, thus rendering redundant the power to commit for sentence under section 37 of the 1980 Act.

CHAPTER 7

Mentally Disordered Offenders

7–01   It is not uncommon for justices to encounter defendants who are suffering from some kind of mental disorder. This may range from insanity or unfitness to plead in its most severe form to severe impairment of intelligence in its least severe form.

The Government has recognised the particular difficulties facing the courts when confronted by the mentally ill, and has declared that wherever possible mentally disordered persons should receive care and treatment from the health and social services, rather than prosecution through the courts (Home Office Circular 66/90). The Code for Crown Prosecutors, issued pursuant to section 10 of the Prosecution of Offences Act 1985, endorses the spirit and objectives of this circular. Section 6.5(f) of the latest version of the Code, issued in June 1994, states, *inter alia*, "[t]he Crown Prosecution Service, where necessary, applies Home Office guidelines about how to deal with mentally disordered offenders. Crown Prosecutors must balance the desirability of diverting a defendant who is suffering from significant mental or physical ill health with the need to safeguard the general public". The Code for Crown Prosecutors is printed in full in Appendix II, below.

Despite this policy many magistrates' courts, particularly in urban areas, encounter mentally disturbed offenders regularly. Because of the procedural and sentencing diffi-

164

culties which arise when defendants are unable to comprehend the proceedings properly special rules exist which affect powers of remand, trial, committal and disposal. These rules are explained below.

1. Definitions

(i) Insanity

7–02   Insanity means that the defendant was, at the time of the commission of the act in question, labouring under a defect of reason, from disease of the mind, as not to know the nature and quality of the act he was doing; or if he did know it, he did not know it was wrong (*McNaghten's case* (1843) 10 Cl. & Fin. 200). This formulation, known as the McNaghten Rules, describes insanity in the legal sense and not in the medical or psychological sense because the Rules arose following replies by the judges in 1843 to abstract questions: *per* Lord Lane C.J. in *R. v. Hennessey* [1989] 1 W.L.R. 287. What the law regarded as insanity might be far removed from what might be regarded as insanity by a psychiatrist (*R. v. Burgess* [1991] 2 Q.B. 92).

The word "mind" in the McNaghten Rules means mental faculties of reason, memory and understanding and it does not matter whether the impairment is organic (*e.g.* epilepsy) or functional, whether permanent or transient, provided it subsisted at the time of commission of the act (*R. v. Sullivan* [1984] A.C. 156 (HL)).

Insanity is defence to a criminal charge under common law because insanity is merely a particular situation where *mens rea* is lacking (*R. v. Horseferry Road Magistrates' Court, ex p. K* [1996] 2 Cr.App.R. 574). For this reason insanity may be raised as a defence to a charge tried summarily even though there is no statutory provision allowing justices to give effect to a verdict of "not guilty by reason of insanity". This is because this procedure for a special verdict was introduced by statute and successive Acts of Parliament have addressed only the consequence of a special verdict being returned by a jury. It was recognised in *ex p. K* that there is a lacuna in the law in that the Mental Health Act 1983 makes no provision for a defendant to be committed to the Crown Court to be dealt with restrictively if justices have found that the common law of insanity has been made out.

INSANITY AND AUTOMATISM

7–03   There may be occasions when an accused puts his state of mind in issue before the court with a view to establishing a defence of automatism, that is to say that he did not know the nature and quality of his act because of something which did *not* amount to a defect of reason from disease of the mind. Here the defendant would be entitled to be acquitted if the criminal intent was not proved. However, whenever such defences are raised the court has a duty to consider whether the mental condition raised was caused by a disease, because if the cause is a disease of the mind insanity may arise.

An example of this principle occurred in the case of *R. v. Burgess*, above, where the accused claimed to have attacked his victim when sleepwalking and raised the defence of automatism. At his trial the Crown Court judge concluded, on the medical evidence presented, that if the accused was sleepwalking then it was insane automatism because it was an abnormality due to an internal factor, whether functional or organic, which had manifested itself in violence. The judge's ruling was upheld by the Court of Appeal and the jury's verdict of not guilty by reason of insanity was held to have been correct.

Where there is a malfunctioning of the mind caused by some external factor such as drugs, anaesthetics, alcohol or hypnotic influences then automatism and not insanity may properly arise (*R. v. Quick* [1973] 1 Q.B. 910). However, where the malfunctioning of the mind is caused by an inherent defect then such a case may fall within the McNaghten Rules.

AUTOMATISM AND HYPERGLYCAEMIA

7-04   It is particularly important to bear the above distinction in mind in the case of diabetes. Diabetes is an internal condition, an inherent defect, and if this produces hyperglycaemia or high blood sugar which results in automatism then this is insane automatism (*R. v. Hennessey* [1989] 1 W.L.R. 287).

Hyperglycaemia may be countered by the taking of insulin, which is an external factor, and this may result in hypoglycaemia, too little blood sugar. Where this is the case and the accused is being tried for an offence of specific intent, *i.e.* theft, the court would have to be satisfied that he had the necessary intent to commit the offence, and the effect of hypoglycaemia would be relevant to this issue (*R. v. Bingham* [1991] Crim.L.R. 433). However, the existence of hypoglycaemia must be relevant to an issue arising from the particular charge laid. If the offence is one of specific intent where the particular intent must accompany the act (*i.e.* dishonesty accompanying the act of appropriation in theft) the existence of hypoglycaemia is obviously relevant. It would not be relevant to a charge of dangerous driving where the accused was prone to hypoglycaemic episodes because such episodes could be reasonably foreseen before the accused got into his vehicle to drive it (*R. v. Marison* [1997] R.T.R. 457).

(ii) Unfitness to plead

7-05   The doctrine of unfitness to plead, which means that the accused is under such a disability that there should be a bar on his being tried, has no application in the magistrates' court. This is because the issue of unfitness to plead, as distinct from that of insanity, arises only when permitted under statute and the relevant law, contained in the Criminal Procedure (Insanity) Act 1964 and the Criminal Procedure (Insanity and Unfitness to Plead) Act 1991, applies only to proceedings in the Crown Court. If an accused has been charged with an either way offence he may be committed to the Crown Court for a jury to try the issue but there is no such power to send the accused to the Crown Court for an issue of unfitness to plead to be decided if the offence is triable only summarily (*R. v. Metropolitan Stipendiary Magistrate Tower Bridge, ex p. Antifowosi* (1985) 144 J.P. 752).

(iii) Mental disorder

7-06   This general term has been specifically defined as follows:

(a) *Mental disorder* meaning mental illness, arrested or incomplete development of mind, psychopathic disorder and any other disorder or disability of mind.

(b) *Severe mental impairment* meaning a state of arrested or incomplete development of mind which includes severe impairment of intelligence and social functioning and is associated with abnormally aggressive or seriously irresponsible conduct on the part of the person concerned.

(c) *Mental impairment* meaning a state of arrested or incomplete development of mind (not amounting to severe mental impairment) which includes significant impairment of intelligence and social functioning and is associated with abnormally aggressive or seriously irresponsible conduct on the part of the person concerned.

(d) *Psychopathic disorder* meaning a persistent disorder or disability of mind (whether or not including significant impairment of intelligence) which results in abnormally aggressive or seriously irresponsible conduct on the part of the person concerned (Mental Health Act 1983, s.1(2)).

IMPACT OF HUMAN RIGHTS ACT 1998

7–07   Article 5(1)(a) and (e) of the Convention is of importance in considering disposals which are available to the court for accused persons who are mentally ill. Article 5(1)(a) permits the lawful detention of persons after *conviction* by a competent court, and Article 5(1)(e) permits the lawful detention of persons of unsound mind. There is no precise equivalent in Strasbourg jurisprudence of making an order for detention without a conviction if the accused is proved to have committed the act giving rise to an offence (see generally §7–11, below). There is in Strasbourg jurisprudence an overlap between the provisions of Article 5(1)(a) and 5(1)(e). If the person is *convicted* and then detained in a mental institution Article 5(1)(a) will apply (*X. v. U.K.* (1981) 4 E.H.R.R. 188). If the person is not convicted and detained in a mental institution Article 5(1)(e) will apply (*Luberti v. Italy* 1984, unreported).

Article 5(1)(e) uses the term "person of unsound mind". In *Winterwerp v. Netherlands* (1979) 2 E.H.R.R. 387 it was held that it was for domestic jurisdictions to determine what constituted "unsound mind" but the words must mean more than behaviour which deviates from the norm, and the application of Article 5(1)(e) must depend on the developing state of psychiatric knowledge.

2. Summary of Procedure when Mental Disorder is Apparent or Suspected

7–08   It is important that the court should be made aware of suspected mental disorder at the earliest opportunity because the court will then be able to use statutory powers of particular application for the mentally disordered.

On *remand* the court will be able to request a medical report from the prison if the accused is in custody or make it a requirement that he have a medical examination if on bail (see Pre-Trial Remands, §7–09).

On *trial* the court need not be satisfied that the accused is guilty of all the ingredients of the offence charged providing the court is satisfied that he did the act or made the omission charged (see Special Procedure for Dealing with the Mentally Disordered without a Conviction, §7–10). Thereafter, the court has power further to remand for a medical examination before sentence and such a remand may be either under the provisions of the Mental Health Act 1983 or under the provisions of the Magistrates' Courts Act 1980 (see Powers to Remand the Mentally Disordered for Examination, §§7–14 to 7–16).

On *sentence*, in addition to the powers normally available, the court has power to make a Hospital or Guardianship Order or a psychiatric probation order (see Sentencing Mentally Disordered Offenders, §§7–17 to 7–23).

Finally, on *procedure* special rules exist for the reception of medical evidence without witnesses attending court (see Procedural Requirements for Receiving Medical Evidence, §7–24). Issues of insanity and unfitness to plead are strictly separate questions and a summary of the procedure to be adopted in those cases is set out in "Definitions" above. In all cases where complications of mental illness or disorder are likely to arise it is highly desirable that the accused should be given legal aid to be represented, whether he is in custody or on bail (*R. v. Blackwood* (1974) 59 Cr.App.R. 170).

3. Pre-Trial Remands

7–09   The general right to bail for persons accused of offences in the magistrates' court applies to the mentally disordered, although the court may impose a condition of bail that the accused makes himself available for a medical examination. The court may impose a requirement that the accused makes himself available for the purpose of enabling inquiries or a report to be made to assist the court in dealing with him for the offence (Bail Act 1976, s.3(6)(d)). Such a requirement is likely to be made if it is intimated to the court that the accused is or may be mentally disordered.

A mentally disordered defendant may equally be remanded in custody if the merits of the case generally justify such a remand. In this instance the court is entitled to inform the prison medical officer of the offence charged, the accused's previous record and medical history and the reasons which led the court to suspect that he is mentally abnormal, and to request that a report be prepared and supplied to the court. If it is necessary for the accused to be in hospital rather than in prison on remand, the Home Secretary may give directions for a transfer from prison to hospital if an accused needs urgent treatment (MHA 1983, s.48).

4. Special Procedure for Dealing with the Mentally Disordered Without a Conviction

7–10   There is a special procedure for disposing of a case involving the mentally disordered without a conviction. The procedure may arise in three circumstances:

   (i) on a summary trial;

   (ii) when remanding to a hospital for a report; and

   (iii) when making a Hospital or Guardianship Order.

(i) On a summary trial

7–11   If on a summary trial for an offence punishable with imprisonment the court is satisfied that the accused did the act or made the omission charged the court may further remand the accused with a view to disposal without convicting him (MCA 1980, s.30).

This means that if the court is satisfied that the external facts of an offence are made out (the *actus reus*) the court may use this power of further remand without being satisfied that the mental element of a particular crime such as intention, recklessness or dishonesty is proved. The purpose of this power is to enable the court to deal with an offender who might otherwise have had the charge against him dismissed because he did not have the capacity to apply his mind to the ingredients of the offence.

Before the court can exercise this power it must be of the opinion that an inquiry ought to be made into the accused's physical or mental condition before the method of dealing with him is determined (MCA 1980, s.30(1)). Clearly, if the court is in possession of a pre-trial report indicating mental disorder the court may use the power. Equally, if there is material in his background and antecedents suggesting mental abnormality the power may be used. However, it will be rare that such an unusual power will be adopted, and its use will require the consent of the offender's legal advisers (*R. v. Lincoln (Kesteven) Justices, ex p. O'Connor* [1983] 1 W.L.R. 335).

(ii) When remanding to a hospital for a report

7–12 The power to remand to a hospital for a report without a conviction arises under section 35 of the Mental Health Act 1983 and is fully discussed at §7–15, below.

(iii) When making a Hospital or Guardianship Order

7–13 This power arises under section 37 of the Mental Health Act 1983, and is fully discussed at §7–19, below.

The special procedure for dealing with an offender in any of the above ways *only* applies if the accused is charged with an offence punishable on summary conviction with imprisonment. If the offence charged is not imprisonable there is no alternative but to convict the accused according to law, that is, the court being satisfied the ingredients of the offence are proved, or to dismiss the charge.

5. Powers to Remand the Mentally Disordered for Examination

A remand for a medical examination may be either under the provisions of the Magistrates' Courts Act 1980 or under the Mental Health Act 1983.

(i) Remand under section 30 of the Magistrates' Courts Act 1980

7–14 This power will be appropriate when (a) no medical evidence is yet before the court, but the court is of the opinion that an inquiry should be made, and (b) when the examination can be conducted on bail (with conditions) or in custody. The power may be used if the court is of the opinion that a general inquiry ought to be made into the accused's mental condition and the court need not be satisfied by written or oral evidence before forming such an opinion. It arises only on a summary trial (MCA 1980, s.30). If the remand is in custody the court must send to the prison a statement of the reasons why the court is of the opinion that an inquiry ought to be made into his physical or mental condition (MCR 1981, r. 24).

The court may remand on bail, in which case the remand should not be for more than four weeks at a time, or in custody when the maximum period at a time is three weeks. If the remand is on bail the court must impose the general conditions under section 3(6) of the Bail Act as to medical examination, but in addition may require that the accused be examined by two practitioners, and that he attend such institutions and comply with such directions as the doctors direct (MCA 1980, s.30 (2)(a) and (b)). The purpose of making a Bail Act order is that if the accused fails to make himself available for an examination he may be arrested under the Bail Act, and the purpose of adding the requirement of two practitioners is that for certain sentencing purposes the evidence of two doctors is needed (see §7–19, below).

(ii) Remand under section 35 of the Mental Health Act 1983

7–15 This power may only be used when the following conditions apply: (a) when the court is satisfied on the written or oral evidence of a medical practitioner that there is reason to suspect the offender is suffering from mental illness, psychopathic disorder or mental impairment, whether severe or not, and (b) when a specified hospital should make a report, and that is impracticable for such a report to be made if the offender were on bail.

It follows that a court may not remand an accused to a hospital for examination unless the conditions in section 35 of the Mental Health Act 1983 are satisfied. In particular, the Act requires that a specific disorder is diagnosed, and that a hospital is willing to receive the accused either immediately or within seven days of the order. If any of these conditions are absent the court must use the remand powers of the Magistrates' Courts Act if a medical examination is sought. The use of the power will be rare and should only be adopted with the consent of the accused's legal advisers (*R. v. Lincoln (Kesteven) Justices, ex p. O'Connor* [1983] 1 W.L.R. 335).

While the power to remand under the Magistrates' Courts Act arises only on a summary trial, an accused may consent at any time to the powers under section 35 of the Mental Health Act 1983 being used. This means that the power could be used before a trial or on a remand if the accused consented.

The period of a remand under section 35 must not be for more than 28 days at a time, nor for more than 12 weeks in all. The court may at any time terminate the remand, and the accused may himself apply for a termination if he has privately instructed a doctor to recommend a termination (MHA 1983, s.35(7) and (8)).

(iii) Consequences if the conditions of the remand are not complied with

7–16 When the court requires that an accused be examined by two practitioners, and that he attend such institutions and comply with such directions as the doctors direct (MCA 1980, s.30), the court must also attach specific Bail Act conditions with respect to medical examination. It follows that the provisions of the Bail Act 1976 will then apply to the arrest without warrant of an offender who fails to comply with bail conditions, and the court will have power to deal with him under the Bail Act. No such powers exist under the Mental Health Act, but there is provision for the arrest of an offender who absconds from the specified hospital or who absconds when being conveyed to or from the hospital. The arrest may be without warrant and the offender must then be brought back before the court. He may then be remanded in custody (MHA 1983, s.35(10)).

6. Sentencing Mentally Disordered Offenders

7–17 It has always been the case that a magistrates' court is not precluded from passing a custodial sentence upon an offender simply because the offender is mentally disordered. The restrictions upon the passing of custodial sentences under the Criminal Justice Act 1991 apply generally to the mentally ill, and there are additional requirements which must be satisfied before a mentally ill offender may be given a custodial sentence. These are explained fully below. The other sentencing options open to the court are the making of a Hospital or Guardianship Order or a Probation Order with a condition of treatment. It is important to remember that justices have no power to attach a Restriction Order confining the offender to hospital for a specified time (see "Effect of a Hospital Order", below). If, therefore, the court is dealing with an either way offence and it appears from the nature of the offence that a Restriction Order might be appropriate the court should decline jurisdiction.

The special sentencing options for the mentally disordered are as follows.

(i) Custodial sentence

7–18 The substantive and procedural requirements for the passing of a custodial sentence laid down in the Criminal Justice Act 1991 apply to all offenders whether or not they are mentally disordered (see paragraphs 12–04 to 12–12, below). However, those provisions of the Act, even if satisfied, do not require the court to pass a custodial sentence on a mentally disordered offender (CJA 1991, s.28(4)(a)). Equally, if the court considers that the criteria of the Act are satisfied in respect of the offence or offences committed the court may still pass a custodial sentence if it considers such sentence to be the most appropriate in all the cirumstances (*ibid.*, s.28(4)(b)).

More important than these provisions are those contained in section 4 of the 1991 Act which provide that the court must obtain and consider a medical report on an offender who is or appears to be mentally disordered before a custodial sentence is passed (CJA 1991, s.4(1)). Having obtained the report the court must then consider—

(a) any information which relates to his mental condition (whether in a medical or pre-sentence report or otherwise); and

(b) the likely effect of such a sentence on that condition and on any treatment that may be available for it (CJA 1991, s.4(3)).

This is an important provision because until the 1991 Act the effect of a prison sentence on the mental condition of an offender was not a relevant consideration and it was assumed that any mentally disordered prisoner could be removed administratively from prison to a hospital under section 48 of the Mental Health Act 1983. Section 4 of the 1991 Act requires the court to consider the likely effect of the sentence before it is imposed. Clearly the purpose of the 1991 legislation is to try and reduce the number of mentally ill offenders being sent to prison.

(ii) Hospital Order

7–19 The court may make a Hospital Order in respect of an offender who is convicted of an offence punishable on summary conviction with imprisonment or in respect of an offender whom the court is satisfied did the act or omission charged.

Before making the order the court must be satisfied on the written or oral evidence of two registered medical practitioners that the offender is suffering from mental illness, psychopathic disorder, severe mental impairment or mental impairment, and that the mental disorder is of a degree which makes it appropriate for him to be detained in hospital for treatment, and in the case of psychopathic disorder or mental impairment the treatment is likely to alleviate or prevent a deterioration in the condition.

The court must be of the opinion, having regard to all the circumstances, including the offence, antecedents, and other available methods of disposal, that the most suitable method of disposal is a Hospital Order.

The court must be satisfied on written or oral evidence that the arrangements have been made for the offender's immediate admission or that he can be admitted within 28 days of the making of the order (MHA 1983, s.37).

All the above conditions must apply before a Hospital Order is made, although the use of section 37 procedure does not necessarily have to arise on a summary trial. If the accused is charged with an offence triable either way and the accused elects trial on indictment, a section 37 Order may still be made because the accused is still before a magistrates' court charged with an act or omission as an offence (*R. v. Ramsgate Justices, ex p. Kazmarek* (1984) 80 Cr.App.R. 366). Similarly, an order may be made if the accused was unable to consent to summary trial (*R. v. Lincoln Justices*, above). The power may not be used if the accused is charged with an offence triable exclusively on indictment because a pre-condition for invoking the provisions of section 37 is that the court would have power to convict the accused as stated in section 37(3) of the Act (*R. v. Chippenham Magistrates' Court, ex p. Thompson* (1996) 160 J.P. 207).

EFFECT OF A HOSPITAL ORDER

7–20   A Hospital Order made by a magistrates' court is the only authority for the patient's detention for one year in the first instance. Unlike the sentencing powers in the Crown Court there is no power to make a Restriction Order. This means that the patient's case can be reviewed and he can be discharged at any time. In addition, the patient may appeal at certain intervals to a mental health review tribunal. Once a patient is discharged he is no longer liable to recall, and powers of arrest in respect of a patient who is absent without leave are restricted (*R. v. Gardiner* [1967] 1 W.L.R. 464).

If the court is of the view that because of the nature of the offence, the offender's antecedents and the risk of further offences being committed if he is set at large a Restriction Order *should* be attached to a Hospital Order, the offender should be committed to the Crown Court for sentence (MHA 1983, s.43).

It may not always be appropriate, however, to use the powers of the Mental Health Act in a committal for sentence because if the Crown Court is of the opinion that a Restriction Order is not appropriate sentencing powers are limited to those available to magistrates. Accordingly, if justices are of the view that greater punishment should be imposed than they have power to inflict unless a Hospital Order with a Restriction Order is made, the offender should be committed for sentence under section 38 of the Magistrates' Courts Act 1980 (MHA 1983, s.43(4)).

(iii) Guardianship order

7–21   A Guardianship Order means that the offender is placed under the guardianship of a local social services authority or under the guardianship of some specified person approved by a social services authority. The purpose of guardianship is primarily to ensure that the offender receives care and protection rather than medical treatment (Home Office Circular 66/90).

Such an order is a direct alternative to a Hospital Order and is likely to be imposed in practice when treatment under a Probation Order is for some reason not appropriate and a Hospital Order is not warranted.

Before making the order the court must be satisfied that the offender's mental disorder is of a nature and degree which warrants his reception into guardianship and in addition the conditions as to imprisonable offences and the necessary medical evidence are the same as for Hospital Orders (see §7–18, (a), (b), and (c), above). Finally, the social services authority or specified person must be willing to accept the offender (MHA 1983, s.37).

A Hospital or Guardianship Order may not be combined with imprisonment or detention, or with a fine or probation, but any other ancillary orders which may lawfully be imposed for the offence may be made (MHA 1983, s.37(8)).

(iv) Interim Hospital Order

7–22   If the court is not sure whether to make a Hospital Order the court may, before making the order or dealing with the offender in some other way, make an Interim Hospital Order. The pre-conditions for making the Interim Order are similar to the first pre-conditions of a Hospital Order (see §7–18, (a), (b) and (c)) and the effect of an Interim Order is as follows. The offender is authorised to be admitted to a specified hospital for a period not exceeding 12 weeks, although this may be renewed for further periods of not more than 28 days at a time, with medical evidence, for a maximum period of six months.

The court may convert an Interim Order into a Full Order providing the required conditions are satisfied without the offender being produced providing he is legally represented at the time (MHA 1983, s.38).

(v) Probation with a condition of treatment

7–23 A court may make a Probation Order with a requirement as to treatment for a mental condition if such an order is in the interests of securing the rehabilitation of the offender or of protecting the public from harm or of preventing the commission of further offences (PCCA 1973, s.3(1), as substituted by CJA 1991, s.9). Such an order is a Community Sentence under the Criminal Justice Act 1991 and, therefore, the provisions of sections 6 and 7 of the Act must also apply) see paragraphs 12–11—12–19, below). Providing the criteria of the Act with respect to community sentences apply, and the offender consents, a condition of treatment may be attached to a Probation Order (PCCA 1973, Sched. 1A, para. 5, as inserted by CJA 1991, Sched. I, Pt II). Before such an order is made the court must be satisfied on the evidence of a suitably qualified medical practitioner that the offender's condition is susceptible to treatment but a Hospital or Guardianship order is not warranted (*ibid.*, §5(1)).

7. Procedural Requirements for Receiving Medical Evidence

7–24 Before the remand powers under section 35, or the making of Interim or Full Hospital Orders under section 37 and section 38 of the Mental Health Act 1983 can be exercised the court must be satisfied upon medical evidence. Special procedural rules for the reception of such evidence have been made which are as follows:

(i) the court may receive the written evidence of a medical practitioner approved by the Secretary of State as having special experience in the diagnosis or treatment of mental disorder;

(ii) such written evidence may be received if it is signed without further proof that the signatory has the requisite qualifications or authority, although the court may require him to attend to give oral evidence;

(iii) if the court receives the written evidence a copy must be given to the counsel or solicitor representing the accused, or if he is unrepresented the substance of the report must be disclosed to him;

(iv) the accused or his legal representatives are entitled to require the signatory of the report to attend to give evidence;

(v) the accused or his representatives may call evidence to rebut the evidence contained in the report (MHA 1983, s.54).

CHAPTER 8

Costs

1. Introduction

8–01 The law relating to costs is contained in the Prosecution of Offences Act 1985, as amended, the Costs in Criminal Cases (General) Regulations 1986 and the Costs in Criminal Cases (General) (Amendment) Regulations 1991.

The power to award costs in the magistrates' court depends entirely on these provisions and there is no inherent, common law, jurisdiction to award costs (*R. v. Coventry Magistrates' Court, ex p. CPS* (1996) 160 J.P. 741). In addition to the statute and the regulations there is a comprehensive *Practice Direction* handed down by the Lord Chief Justice which consolidates earlier Directions, and gives directions on how the amended regulations should be applied (*Practice Direction (Crime: Costs)* [1991] 1 W.L.R. 498).

References in this chapter are to the Act and the Regulations unless otherwise stated.

8–02 The general scheme of the POA 1985 may be summarised as follows:

(i) a successful defendant, acquitted of an either way or summary offence may recover his costs from central funds but *not* against the prosecution (s.16);

(ii) a public authority prosecutor (*i.e.* the Crown Prosecution Service) cannot recover costs from central funds (s.17);

174

(iii) the prosecution *may* recover costs from a defendant but only if he is found guilty and only if the amount of costs is specified at the time (s.17);

(iv) *any* party to criminal proceedings who has incurred costs because of an unnecessary or improper act or omission by another party may be compensated in costs by that other party (s.19);

(v) in certain circumstances a legal representative may be ordered to pay costs or have costs disallowed if costs have been wasted as a result of improper, unreasonable or negligent acts (s.19A).

Subject to the statutory provisions and Practice Directions issued on costs the award of costs is a matter of discretion and there is no appeal to the Crown Court by an accused against an order of costs (MCA 1980, s.108(3)(b)). The discretion must be exercised judicially and the general supervisory jurisdiction of the Divisional Court to the orders of inferior tribunals applies to awards of costs in the magistrates' court.

8–03   Whenever a court is considering the question of costs the following general principles should be observed.

 (i) An order for costs should never exceed a sum which, having regard to the defendant's means and any other financial penalty imposed, was reasonable (*R. v. Northallerton Magistrates' Court, ex p. Dove, The Times*, June 17, 1999).

(ii) If an accused is in a position to pay the prosecution costs in addition to another penalty there is no reason in principle why he should not do so (*R. v. F. Howe and Son (Engineering) Ltd* [1999] 2 All E.R. 249). If a prosecution has been lengthy and expensive it may be appropriate to award a high sum in costs even if a modest penalty is imposed for the offence (*Cozens v. Hobbs* [1999] C.O.D. 24).

(iii) Providing the award of costs is not an undue burden on the accused there is no reason in principle why a long period should not be allowed to discharge the payment of the costs (*R. v. Olliver and Olliver* (1989) 11 Cr.App.R.(S.) 10).

(iv) An order for costs should not exceed the sum which the prosecutor had actually and reasonably incurred (*R. v. Northallerton Magistrates' Court*, above).

 (v) The purpose of a costs order is to compensate the prosecutor, not punish the accused (*R. v. Northallerton Magistrates' Court*, above).

(vi) In the ordinary way an order for costs should not be grossly disproportionate to any fine imposed, although there is no requirement that a costs order should stand in an arithmetical relationship to a financial penalty (*R. v. Northallerton Magistrates' Court*, above).

2. Defence Costs

(i) General rule

8–04   An order for costs in favour of the accused, called a "Defendant's Costs Order," may be made in the following circumstances:

(a) where an information is not proceeded with;

(b) where examining justices do not commit for trial;

(c) where on a summary trial the information is dismissed (s.16(1)).

Under this power a Defendant's Costs Order may be made if a prosecution is withdrawn (*R. v. Bolton Justices, ex p. Wildish* (1983) 147 J.P. 309), or if it is discontinued (*D.P.P. v. Denning* [1991] 3 W.L.R. 235), or if the prosecution are unable to proceed because their summonses were laid out of time (*Patel v. Blakey* (1987) 151 J.P. 532) in addition to the general power to award costs if an information is dismissed on the merits. Justices nevertheless have a wide discretion as to (a) whether to award to costs, and (b) what the amount awarded should be.

(ii) General principles governing the exercise of discretion

8–05 The following principles set out in the latest Practice Direction, *Practice Direction (Crime: Costs)* [1991] 1 W.L.R. 498, should be applied.

A Defendant's Costs Order should normally be made unless there are positive reasons for not doing so, and examples of such reasons are:

(a) the defendant's own conduct has brought suspicion on himself and misled the prosecution into thinking that the case against him is stronger than it is;

(b) there is ample evidence to support a conviction but the defendant is acquitted on a technicality which has no merit;

(c) where the defendant is convicted on some charges but acquitted on others the court may exercise its discretion to make a Defendant's Costs Order but may order that only part of the costs incurred be paid. Where the court considers that it would be inappropriate that the defendant recover all of the costs properly incurred, the amount must be specified in the order.

It is not an acquittal "on a technicality" where an accused is found not guilty on an excess alcohol charge because the police had failed to follow correctly the statutory procedure for obtaining blood or urine samples (*Wareing v. D.P.P.* (1990) 154 J.P. 443).

If, in the exercise of the court's discretion, proper regard is not paid to the terms of a Practice Direction on costs, the Divisional Court has power to remit a decision back to the court with a direction to reconsider an award of costs in the light of the guidelines (*R. v. Horseferry Road Justices, ex p. Underwoods (Cash Chemists) Ltd* (1985) 81 Cr.App.R. 334).

(iii) Discretion as to the amount of costs

8–06 The general rule is that the amount of a defendant's costs should be the amount reasonably sufficient to compensate him for any expenses properly incurred in the proceedings (s.16(6)). However, the court may order the disallowance of costs out of central funds not properly incurred or may direct the determining officer to consider whether or not specific items have been properly incurred. Costs not properly incurred are those of work unreasonably done, for example if the case has been conducted unreasonably as to incur unjustified expense, or costs have been wasted (*Practice Direction (Crime: Costs)*, above). In a plain case it may be more appropriate to make a wasted costs order (see §8–14, below).

However, when an accused is acquitted on all charges the court should normally order the repayments of his legal aid contributions and remit any unpaid instalments due under the order, unless there are circumstances which make such a course inappropriate (*Practice Direction (Crime: Costs)*, above). (If there are no proceedings because charges are dropped the costs are those "in or about the defence" (s.16(10)). The quantum, or amount, of such costs is discussed at §§ 8–20 *et seq.*, below. This rule is subject to two exceptions as follows.

(a) If the court makes a Defendant's Costs Order but is of the opinion that there are circumstances which make it inappropriate to order the full amount the court may assess what it considers to be a just and reasonable amount, and specify that amount instead (s.16(7)).

(b) If the defendant is legally aided the expenses incurred under the Legal Aid Order should be disregarded (s.16(8)). In practice, this means that on a personal basis a successful legally aided defendant will recover only his out-of-pocket expenses, such as travel.

If a solicitor is acting for himself in criminal proceedings and he is awarded costs from central funds, such costs will mean a solicitor's fees and disbursements incurred in the conduct of the case (*R. v. Stafford Stone and Eccleshall Magistrates' Court, ex p. Robinson* [1988] 1 W.L.R. 369).

3. Prosecution Costs

(i) General rule

8–07   In the case of prosecutions conducted by a public authority the court has no power to award prosecution costs from central funds (s.17).

A public authority means the Crown Prosecution Service, a police force, a local authority, a government department or body receiving money provided by Parliament, or a nationalised industry (s.17(6)).

If such a prosecution is unsuccessful the public authority is left to pay its own costs. If the prosecution results in a conviction the accused may be ordered to pay such costs of the prosecution as the court considers just and reasonable (s.18(1)). (Where the court has imposed a sum not exceeding £5.00 to be paid in a fine, forfeiture or compensation costs should not generally be awarded: s.18(4).)

8–08   The words "just and reasonable" in section 18(1) may (depending on the circumstances) include the costs of the investigation into the offence as well as the costs of the presentation of the case in court (*R. v. Associated Octel Ltd* [1997] Crim.L.R. 144). This decision affirms a principle decided in *Neville v. Gardner Merchant Ltd* (1983) 5 Cr.App.R.(S.) 349 and the Court disapproved of an earlier decision, *R. v. Seymour* (1987) 9 Cr.App.R.(S.) 395 to the contrary effect. It now seems clear, from the reasoning in all these cases, that the costs of the investigation may be recovered if the investigation is carried out by the *same* body which presents the prosecution in court. In *Associated Octel* the investigation and the prosecution had been conducted throughout by the Health and Safety Executive, whereas in *Seymour* the investigation had been conducted by English Heritage and the prosecution by the Crown Prosecution Service. The decision in *Associated Octel* would therefore not be applicable to the majority of cases which are investigated by the police and conducted by the Crown Prosecution Service.

8–09   Where proceedings are conducted under section 12 of the Magistrates' Courts Act 1980 (written pleas of guilty in the absence of the accused) the prosecution may state their intention to apply for administrative costs in the documents sent to the accused containing the statement of facts, providing the amount is clearly specified. It is then the duty of the clerk in reading the statement of facts to the justices to draw their attention to the application (*R. v. Coventry City Justices, ex p. D.P.P.* [1991] 1 W.L.R. 1153).

EXCEPTION TO GENERAL RULE

8–10   The above rule does not apply to private prosecutions in proceedings in respect of an indictable offence. A private prosecutor is entitled to costs from central funds whether or not the accused is convicted summarily of the indictable offence (s.17(1)). In practice this exception will most often apply when a prosecution is begun privately, but then taken over by the Crown Prosecution Service. The private prosecutor may recover his costs from central funds up to the time that the case is taken over (s.17(5)).

In the *Practice Direction (Crime: Costs)*, above, it was stated that an order for the payment of a private prosecutor's costs from central funds should be made unless there was good reason for not doing so, for example where proceedings have been instituted or continued without good cause.

(ii) Costs against the accused

8–11   If the accused is convicted in a summary trial in a magistrates' court he may be ordered to pay such costs of the prosecution as the court considers just and reasonable (s.18(1)). The amount of such costs must be specified in the order (s.18(3)).

An order under section 18 should be made where the court is satisfied that the offender has the means and the ability to pay (*Practice Direction (Crime: Costs)*, above). Merely because the accused has pleaded guilty is no reason for not applying the POA 1985 and the *Practice Direction*, although it is a factor which the court can take into account in assessing the amount of costs (*R. v. Maher* [1983] Q.B. 784).

4. Costs Incurred by an Improper Act of Another

8–12   The power to award costs in these circumstances extends only to the parties to the proceedings and not any legal representative, and the power arises under section 19(1) of the POA 1985 and the Costs in Criminal Cases (General) Regulations 1986. Regulation 3 provides that if at any time during criminal proceedings the court is satisfied that costs have been incurred by one party as a result of an unnecessary or improper act or omission by, or on behalf of, another party to the proceedings, the court may, after hearing the parties, order that all or part of the costs so incurred to be paid by the other party. Any award of costs made under this paragraph must be specified, and the court must take into account any other costs order, including any Legal Aid Order, which has been made.

This important provision gives the court a wide discretionary power to compensate a party (whether the prosecution or the defence) who has incurred costs as a result of delay, incompetence, or some improper behaviour by the other party. If this is the defence then the party concerned must be the accused himself and not his legal representative. If the court is of the view that the improper act or omission is the fault of solicitor or counsel an award cannot be made under this provision, but in other provisions explained below.

8–13   If the fault lies with the prosecution then it is submitted the words should mean those collectively responsible for the prosecution, whether the police or the Crown Prosecution Service. This was the interpretation given to the words "the prosecution" in section 22(3) of the POA 1985 (custody time limits) in *R. v. Birmingham Crown Court, ex p. Ricketts* [1991] R.T.R. 105 (see §2–23, above) and it is submitted the same meaning should apply when construing section 19(1).

An award of costs under regulation 3 may be made at any time during the proceedings (s.19(2)). Therefore, the court may make an award at the time the improper act has come to light, and need not wait until the final outcome of the case.

5. Wasted Costs

8–14   Under the powers introduced by the Courts and Legal Services Act 1990, s.111, the Prosecution of Offences Act 1985 has been amended to enable a magistrates' court to disallow legal aid costs or to order the legal or other representative to bear the costs which are wasted. Wasted costs means any costs incurred as a result of any improper unreasonable or negligent act or omission on the part of a representative which, in the light of any such act or omission occurring after they were incurred, the court considers it unreasonable to expect that party to pay (POA 1985, s.19A).

This is a wide power enabling the court to disallow legal aid costs, or to order the negligent representative to compensate his own client for wasted costs or to pay the other side's costs caused by the negligence. If a wasted costs order is merited it is irrelevant that the client of the legal representative concerned is legally aided (*Practice Direction (Crime: Costs)*, above). Clearly the court should exercise these wide powers judicially, as has been said in respect of any discretionary award of costs (*R. v. Highgate Justices, ex p. Petrou* [1954] 1 W.L.R. 485).

The amendment deliberately uses the words "legal or other representative" to include persons other than a solicitor or barrister exercising a right to conduct litigation under Part II of the Courts and Legal Services Act 1990 (when the provisions are in force), but also to include an informant conducting his own prosecution. It is not clear whether the word "representative" and "party" have the same meaning when applied to the prosecution generally but it is submitted that the purpose of the amendment to section 19 is to make the legal corps of the prosecution (*i.e.* the CPS or prosecuting body) responsible rather than a particular solicitor or barrister within the prosecution service.

(i)   Guidelines for the award of wasted costs

8–15   Guidelines for the award of costs where there has been an improper, unreasonable or negligent act have been given by the Court of Appeal (Civil Division) in *Ridehalgh v. Horsefield and Another*; *Allen v. Unigate Dairies Ltd*; *Roberts v. Coverties (Asphalters) Ltd*; *Philex plc v. Golban*; *Watson v. Watson*; *Antonelli and others v. Wade Gery Farr* [1994] 3 W.L.R. 482. In the judgment it was stated that while the conduct of criminal cases often raise different questions and depended on different circumstances it was hoped that the judgment might give guidance which would be of value to criminal courts. It has subsequently been held that the judgment in that Case is relevant to criminal cases (In *Re a Barrister (Wasted Costs Order) (No. 4 of 1992)*, *The Times*, March 15, 1994).

The judgment of the Court of Appeal in *Ridelagh v. Horsefield*, above, stated that the mischief against which the wasted costs legislation was aimed was the causing of loss and expense to litigants by their or the other side's lawyers. The Court further stated that the three-stage process recommended in *Re a Barrister (Wasted Costs*

Order) (No. 1 of 1991) [1992] 3 W.L.R. 662, summarised in §8.18 below, was right.

The Court went on to consider the meaning of the words improper, unreasonable and negligent.

  (i) Improper covers, but is not confined to, conduct which may ordinarily be held to justify disbarment, striking off, suspension or other serious professional penalty, but it is not limited to that. It could include conduct which would be regarded as improper according to the consensus of professional, including judicial, opinion whether or not it violated the letter of the professional code.

 (ii) Unreasonable means conduct which is vexatious, designed to harass the other side rather than advance the resolution of the case and it makes no difference if such conduct is the product of excessive zeal and not improper motive. The acid test is whether the conduct permitted of a reasonable explanation.

(iii) Negligent means failure to act with the competence reasonably expected of ordinary members of the profession, and does not have a narrow legalistic meaning of an actionable breach of duty.

APPLICATION TO ADVOCACY IN COURT

8–16   The Court of Appeal recognised that there was some distinction to be made between preparation and written work before a case commenced and advocacy in court. This was because (a) the decision in *Rondel v. Worsley* [1969] 1 A.C. 191 had held that a barrister or solicitor was immune from an action in negligence by a client in respect of conduct in court and pre-trial work immediately connected with it and (b) advocates in court inevitably had to make decisions quickly and mistakes would be made.

Although such a distinction could be made there was no doubt that the Courts and Legal Services Act 1990 applied to conduct in court which was improper, unreasonable or negligent and that such behaviour could make an advocate liable to a wasted costs order. However, although the legislation plainly applied to advocacy in court it did not follow that public interest considerations, on which the immunity was founded, were to be regarded as irrelevant or lacking in weight. Far from it. Any judge invited to make or to contemplate making such an order must make allowance for the fact that an advocate in court had to make decisions quickly and under pressure and that mistakes would inevitably be made. "It was only when, with all allowances made, an advocate's conduct of court proceedings was quite plainly unjustifiable that it could be appropriate to make a wasted costs order against him" (*per* Sir Thomas Bingham M.R.).

DISCRETION

8–17   Discretion in respect of making or contemplating making a wasted costs order arises (i) at the stage of the initial application when a representative is invited to show cause why an order should not be made and (ii) at the final stage.

In considering discretion at the first stage the court is entitled to consider the costs of the inquiry compared with the costs claimed and sometimes the procedure for an inquiry as to whether wasted costs had been incurred would not be justified. In the final stage a court is not bound to make an order even if satisfied that a legal representative has acted improperly, unreasonably or negligently.

(ii) Procedure for wasted costs orders

8–18   Whenever a Wasted Costs Order is contemplated, the court must be alert to the problems which can arise and the hearing must be conducted only in accordance with the statutory rules and the *Practice Direction (Crime: Costs)* [1991] 1 W.L.R. 498 (see §8–05, above). A careful study of the Practice Direction should always be made before a Wasted Costs Order is made (*Re a Barrister (Wasted Costs Order) (No. 1 of 1991)* [1992] 3 W.L.R. 662). In that case the Court of Appeal (Criminal Division) issued guidelines as to the practice and procedure to be adopted when a Wasted Costs Order was being contemplated by the court. The guidelines are as follows:

"(1) There is a clear need for any judge or court intending to exercise the wasted costs jurisdiction to formulate carefully and concisely the complaint and grounds upon which such an order may be sought. These measures are draconian, and, as in contempt proceedings, the grounds must be clear and particular.

(2) (Not applicable in the magistrates' court).

(3) A defendant involved in a case where such proceedings are contemplated should be present if, after discussion with counsel, it is thought that his interests may be affected. And he should certainly be present and represented if the matter might affect the course of his trial. Regulation 3B(2) of the Costs in Criminal Cases (General) (Amendment) Regulations 1991 furthermore requires that before a Wasted Costs Order is made "the court shall allow the legal or other representative and any party to the proceedings to make representations". There may be cases where it may be appropriate for counsel for the Crown to be present.

(4) A three-stage test or approach is recommended when a Wasted Costs Order is contemplated.

(i) Has there been an improper, unreasonable or negligent act or omission?
(ii) As a result, have any costs been incurred by a party?
(iii) If the answers to (i) and (ii) are "Yes"; should the court exercise its discretion to disallow or order the representative to meet the whole or any part of the relevant costs, and if so what specific sum is involved?

(5) It is inappropriate to propose any deal or settlement, such as was suggested in the present case, that the representative might forgo fees. The judge should formally state his complaint, in chambers, and invite the representative to make his own comments. After any other party has been heard the judge should give his formal ruling. Discursive conversations such as took palce in the present case may be unfair and should certainly not take place.

(6) As was indicated above the judge must specify the sum to be disallowed or ordered. Alternatively, the relevant available procedure should be substituted, should it be impossible to fix the sum."

In paragraph 5 above there is a reference to a complaint being made "in chambers." It is submitted that in the magistrates' court this should mean in the courtroom itself, but in circumstances where the public are excluded.

8–19   A Wasted Costs Order may be made at the time that the improper, unreasonable or negligent act occurs, or the court may postpone the making of an order until the end of the case if, for example, the likely amount is not readily available, or there is a possibility of conflict between the representatives as to the apportionment of blame, or the legal representative concerned is unable to make full representations because of a possible conflict with his duty to his client (*Practice Direction*, above).

6. Costs which may be Covered by an Award

8–20   The following categories are a summary of the costs which may be covered by an award under the provisions of sections 16, 17, 18 and 19 of the POA 1985. The summary is not intended to be comprehensive.

(i) Legal Costs

8–21   Legal costs mean the work that is actually and reasonably done and the disbursements actually and reasonably incurred, taking into account all the relevant circumstances of the case, including the nature, importance, complexity or difficulty of the work and the time involved (Legal Aid in Criminal and Care Proceedings (Costs) Regulations 1989). However, for certain work the Regulations lay down a standard rate of remuneration. The type of work for which standard fees are payable has now been greatly extended by the Legal Aid in Criminal and Care Proceedings (Costs) (Amendment) Regulations 1993 and under these regulations a considerable amount of the work done in the magistrates' court will be covered by standard fees. Where leading counsel has appeared for the defence in the magistrates' court and defence costs are awarded from central funds the question for the clerk in determining costs is whether it was reasonable in the circumstances for leading counsel to have been instructed (*R. v. Dudley Magistrates' Court, ex p. Power City Stores* (1990) 154 J.P. 654).

(ii) Personal expenses for defendant or prosecutor

8–22   A subsistence and travel allowance may be claimed. The subsistence allowance will depend on the amounts from time to time agreed between the Lord Chancellor's Department and the Treasury. Travel allowance usually means travel by private car, public transport, or second class rail travel. Such allowances may be claimed under the Costs in Criminal Cases (General) Regulations 1986 and these Regulations specify the circumstances when other forms of travel may be claimed.

(iii) Witness Expenses

8–23   The amount allowed in costs for a witness will depend on the category of the witness. No expenses may be claimed for purely character witnesses, nor police and prison officers giving evidence in their occupational capacity. All other witnesses may be entitled to an allowance, although the amount allowed will depend upon whether the witness follows a profession, is an expert witness, is a medical practitioner, is an interpreter, or is simply a witness of fact outside the above categories. Generally, loss of earnings, travel and subsistence will be allowed and further additional allowances may be made for witnesses in special categories. Entitlement to an allowance does not depend on whether the witness actually gave evidence, providing the witness was present in the court building and properly attending in order to give evidence.

Full details of the above summary may be found in the Costs in Criminal Cases (General) Regulations 1986, and the Notes of Guidance issued to Justices' Clerks under the Regulations.

7. Procedure for Claiming Costs

(i) Prosecution costs

8–24 Where the prosecution is a public authority the amount of costs claimed against an accused must be specified at the time the claim is made. If the court regards the amount claimed as just and reasonable it may order the accused to pay such costs at the time sentence is passed. This sum then becomes enforceable as if it were a summary conviction (Administration of Justice Act 1970, s.41(1)). The above rules apply whether an accused is ordered to pay prosecution costs following summary conviction or as a result of an unnecessary or improper act or omission.

PUBLIC AUTHORITIES

8–25 The following procedure should, save in cases where standard costs are claimed, be followed:

(i) the prosecution should serve on the defence, at the earliest time, full details of its costs, so as to give the defence a proper opportunity to consider them and make representations on them, if appropriate;

(ii) if there is dispute about the whole or any part of the costs claimed the defence should give the court notice of such objections so that the court could understand the area of dispute. There is no provision for the taxation of prosecution costs in these circumstances (*R. v. Associated Octel Ltd* [1997] Crim.L.R. 144).

PRIVATE INDIVIDUALS

8–26 If the prosecution is *not* a public authority then in addition to being able to claim costs against the accused the prosecutor may claim costs from central funds in respect of indictable offences. In this case, the procedure is either (a) for an amount to be agreed by the prosecutor and the court and be specified in the order, or (b) for an amount to be "taxed" or determined by the clerk to the justices unless the court considers it inappropriate for the prosecutor to recover the full costs. If it is inappropriate for the full costs to be recovered the court may assess a just and reasonable amount and then specify it in the order (s.17(3) and (4)).

(ii) Defence costs

8–27 The procedure for claiming defence costs is either to agree an amount in court and have the amount specified in a court order or to have the costs "taxed" or determined by the clerk to the justices subject to an exception where less than full costs are to be awarded.

If it is appropriate for a Defendant's Costs Order to be made then if the defence agree the amount may be specified in the order by the court at the conclusion of the proceedings (s.16(9)). If the amount is not agreed the amount of costs must be determined by the appropriate authority which in the magistrates' court is the justices' clerk or a deputy appointed on his behalf (reg. 5 (2)). This will involve a claim submitted in writing within three months of the order setting out the amount claimed. The justices' clerk will then determine the actual amount which is reasonable to be paid from central funds. For obvious reasons, if defence costs can be agreed they will be paid more quickly than if a determination has to be made. There is no power to award interest on a Costs Order in favour of a successful defendant in criminal proceedings because the

Judgments Act 1838 applies only to civil cases (*Westminster City Council v. Wingrove (Lord Chancellor intervening)* [1991] 1 Q.B. 652).

The exception to these rules is where the court makes a Defendant's Costs Order but is of the opinion that it is inappropriate for the full amount to be recovered. Here the court must assess an amount which in its opinion is just and reasonable and then specify it in the order (s.16(7)).

CHAPTER 9

Binding Over Orders

1. Introduction

9–01   A Binding Over Order has been defined as an acknowledgement by the person bound over of his indebtedness to the Queen in the sum fixed by the court. The sum fixed has the condition that it shall have no effect if in the meantime the person bound keeps the peace (*Veater v. Glennon* [1981] 1 W.L.R. 567, in which the judgment of Lord Lane C.J. reviewed "Dalton's Country Justice" and Blackstone's Commentaries).

The essence of a bind over is that the person bound accepts the obligation to keep the peace or to be of good behaviour and when justices bind a person over they are administering preventive justice.

9–02   This concept that a breach of the peace may be prevented by the making of an order is a unique legal concept and a breach of the peace is not a criminal offence as such. It follows that when a bind over is made there is neither a conviction nor a sentence. It would be anomalous if, for this reason alone, there was no procedure for an appeal against the making of a binding over order. This anomaly was remedied by Parliament in the Magistrates' Courts (Appeals from Binding Over Orders) Act 1956 which allows a person aggrieved by the order appealing to the Crown Court.

Although the question of whether a bind over is civil or criminal in nature has been the subject of some historical debate it is plainly a criminal matter for the purposes of the Human Rights Act 1998 (see §9–18 below and Chapter 24, below).

Origins

9–03 It has been said that the jurisdiction of justices in making a binding over order is not immediately easy to trace or grasp (*R. v. Clerkenwell Magistrate, ex p. Hooper* [1998] 1 W.L.R. 806, *per* Mance J.) and its origins are shrouded in mystery. The Justices of the Peace Act 1361 almost certainly placed on a statutory footing powers which were already excercised by justices. Such is the antiquity of the concept of bind over that its propriety cannot be questioned (*Lansbury v. Riley* [1914] 3 K.B. 229).

For these reasons binding over survives and Parliament has from time to time made provision for this ancient concept to be incorporated into modern practice. The current statutory provision (in addition to the 1361 Act which has never been repealed) is section 115 of the Magistrates' Courts Act 1980. Superior courts of record such as the Crown Court were given statutory authority to make binding over orders by section 1(7) of the Justices of the Peace Act 1968.

Although modern statutes incorporated the broad notion of a bind over Parliament has never legislated for the procedure to be followed when a bind over is contemplated. Procedure was something which traditionally justices themselves regulated and it is only in recent years that the Divisional Court has subjected binding over to mature legal analysis.

2. Jurisdiction

(i) General principles

9–04 The foundation for exercising the power to bind over under the 1361 Act is the fear in the minds of justices of a future breach of the peace.

It follows that it is not necessary for justices to make a finding of fact that a breach of the peace has in fact occurred before exercising the power to bind a defendant over, providing the facts found show that there was behaviour of a kind likely to provoke violence (*R. v. Morpeth Ward Justices, ex p. Ward and Others* (1992) 95 Cr.App.R. 215). In that case the Divisional Court held that justices had been correct to bind defendants over who were demonstrating against hunting, and who had been the subject of a complaint under the MCA 1980, s.115 because the facts showed that the manner of the demonstration was likely to provoke the huntsmen into violence.

Although the jurisdiction of the court depends upon a perception of future behaviour there must be material before the court giving rise to such a fear (*R. v. Marylebone Metropolitan Stipendiary Magistrate, ex p. Okunnu* (1988) 87 Cr.App.R. 295). In that case the defendant had been charged with possession of a small quantity of cannabis and had elected trial by jury. At the commencement of committal proceedings the prosecution indicated that they would be prepared to offer no evidence if the defendant agreed to be bound over. The defendant consented but maintained he was innocent of any offence. The stipendiary magistrate refused to make a Binding Over Order on the grounds that he had no jurisdiction to do so, and his decision was upheld by the Divisional Court.

This case underlines another important rule relating to bind overs: a defendant cannot confer jurisdiction on the court simply by consenting to be bound over (*R. v. South West London Magistrates' Court, ex p. Brown* [1974] Crim.L.R. 313).

(ii) Meaning of future breach of the peace

9–05 The fear of future violence need not necessarily be a fear that the defendant will commit or threaten the violence; it is sufficient if the conduct of the defendant is such that the natural consequences of it would be violence from a third party (*Percy v. D.P.P.* [1995] 1 W.L.R. 1382).

A breach of the peace has been defined as harm actually done or likely to be done to a person, or in his presence to his property, or if a person is in fear of being so harmed through an assault, an affray, a riot, a unlawful assembly or other disturbance (*R. v. Howell* [1982] Q.B. 416). Such a breach of the peace may occur in private premises as well as in public (*McConnell v. Chief Constable of the Greater Manchester Police* [1990] 1 W.L.R. 364, CA (Civ.Div.)).

(iii) Consent

9–06 It was once thought that consent by the person whom justices proposed to bind over was a pre-condition to the making of the order (*R. v. South Molton Justices, ex p. Ankerson* [1989] 1 W.L.R. 40) but this has now been authoritatively held not to be legally correct (*R. v. Lincoln Crown Court, ex p. Jude* [1998] 1 Cr.App.R. 130). In that case the Divisional Court, in a reserved judgment, held that the Justices of the Peace Act 1361 and the Justices of the Peace Act 1968 were both silent on the question of consent. The 1361 Act specifically used the word "require" in relation to justices' jurisdiction and therefore, as a matter of law, consent was not a pre-condition to the making of an order. The court then went on to consider the circumstances in which the court should allow representations to be made before an order is announced. The procedure for allowing representations is discussed in §9–08, below.

(iv) Standard of proof required

9–07 As recently as 1981 the Divisional Court found itself unable to state with confidence whether binding over was criminal or civil in nature (*Veater v. Glennon* [1981] 1 W.L.R. 567). Since then the preponderance of judicial opinion is that justices exercise criminal, not civil, jurisdiction when making bind over orders (*R. v. Bolton Justices, ex p. Gruere* (1986) 150 J.P. 190, and *R. v. Coventry Magistrates' Court, ex p. CPS* (1996) 160 J.P. 741).

It follows from this analysis that the standard of proof when exercising jurisdiction under the 1361 Act is the criminal standard of proof, namely proof beyond a reasonable doubt that a bind over is necessary to prevent a future breach of the peace (*Percy v. D.P.P.* [1995] 1 W.L.R. 1382). It was held in that case that there must be real risk, and not a mere possibility of a risk, of future violence before a bind over could be contemplated.

More difficult considerations arise if binding over proceedings are initiated by complaint under section 115 of the Magistrates' Courts Act 1980 (see §9–09, below) because such proceedings would appear to be unequivocally civil. It has now been held that a complaint brought under this section must be proved to the criminal standard also (*D.P.P. v. Speede, R. v. Collins and Santos* [1998] 2 Cr.App.R. 108). It is submitted that this decision is plainly consistent with modern practice because sometimes a person is described as being "charged" with a breach of the peace and is brought to court from a police station, even though the written material before the court may refer to section 115 of the 1980 Act. To classify such proceedings as civil in these circumstances would seem to be perverse (see *R. v. Coventry Magistrates' Court, ex p. CPS* (1996) 160 J.P. 741).

(v) Requirement to allow representations to be made

9–08   The question of whether the court must allow representations to be made against the making of a binding over order will depend on the precise nature of the proceedings.

The law may be summarised as follows:

(i)   If the person whom justices propose to bind over is a complainant or a witness in a criminal trial such a person *must* be given an opportunity to make representations about it (*Sheldon v. Broomfield Justices* [1964] 2 Q.B. 573, and *R. v. Hendon Justices, ex p. Gorchein* [1973] 1 W.L.R. 1502).

(ii)   If the person is the defendant and the order is contemplated during the course of the trial he *must* be given the opportunity to make representations (*R. v. South Molton Justices, ex p. Ankerson* [1989] 1 W.L.R. 40).

(iii)   If the person is the defendant and he has been *acquitted* after a trial it is courteous and good practice for him to be allowed to make representations, but it is not mandatory (*R. v. Woking Justices, ex p. Gosage* [1973] 1 Q.B. 448).

(iv)   If the person is an unconvicted defendant who has created a disturbance in the face of the court there is no obligation upon justices to hear representations (*R. v. North London Metropolitan Magistrate, ex p. Haywood and Brown* [1973] 1 W.L.R. 965) *unless* justices ask for a recognisance which is plainly not a just and reasonable one (*R. v. Clerkenwell Magistrate, ex p. Hooper* [1998] 1 W.L.R. 806).

(v)   If the person is a defendant who has been *convicted* after a trial there is no obligation upon justices to allow representations to be made before a binding over order is made, providing the proper conditions for the making of an order apply to the facts of the case (*R. v. Lincoln Crown Court, ex p. Jude* [1998] 1 Cr.App.R. 130).

(vi) Differences between bind over under the 1361 Act and a bind over following a complaint

9–09   Theoretically, there is a distinction to be made between a binding over order imposed under the 1361 Act, which may be described as ancient, inherent jurisdiction and a bind over made following a complaint laid under section 115 of the Magistrates' Courts Act 1980. In recent years, when successive judgments of the Divisional Court have scrutinised bind overs in the context of natural justice and modern practice, the distinction has become less clear. This is because bind over orders are undoubtedly criminal and not civil in nature (see §9–07, above and commentary on the Human Rights Act 1998 in Chapter 24, below).

The blurring of the distinction between the two theoretical types of bind over was highlighted in *R. v. Coventry Magistrates' Court, ex p. CPS* (1996) 160 J.P. 741 when it was held that a person charged at a police station with a breach of the peace should be treated by the court as if a complaint had been laid under section 115. Thus, a person is validly before the court if produced following an arrest for a breach of the peace even if there is no specific complaint laid (*D.P.P. v. Speede, R. v. Collins and Santos* [1998] 2 Cr.App.R. 108).

For these reasons the court is seldom troubled about the precise origins of a case if presented with a defendant against whom a binding over is sought. The issues which matter are not the origins of the case but the material presented which is said to justify the order.

9–10   In some circumstances (particularly if a private individual commences proceedings in which a bind over is sought) the distinction between the two may be important. The following points should be noted:

    (i) if a person is produced before the court as if a complaint had been laid he must be given an opportunity of giving evidence and calling witnesses (*R. v. Aubrey Fletcher, ex p. Thompson* [1969] 1 W.L.R. 872);

    (ii) if justices proceed in the absence of a defendant who has not previously appeared the court must be satisfied that the summons was served, and may only issue a warrant for the arrest of an absent defendant if the provisions of section 55(2) and (3) of the Magistrates' Courts Act 1980 is strictly complied with (*D.P.P. v. Speede* [1998] 2 Cr.App.R. 108).

3. Terms of the Order

9–11   The obscure wording of the 1361 Act and the various later commentaries on it has included the concept of a bind over to keep the peace "and be of good behaviour". It is submitted that the concept of a bind over which contemplates future "good behaviour" has its roots in a number of old cases where the court had bound defendants over whose behaviour was mischievous or suspicious (see, for example, *R. v. Sandbach, ex p. Williams* [1935] 2 K.B. 192 and *R. v. County of London Quarter Sessions, ex p. Commissioner of Metropolitan Police* (1948) 112 J.P. 118). It is submitted that such reasoning is contary to modern jurisprudence, and would not conform to the strict requirements of a fear of future violence, based on material clearly evident in the proceedings. Providing the court is sure that a bind over is necessary there would appear to be nothing objectionable in making an order "to keep the peace *and* be of good behaviour", even though, strictly, the latter words are surplusage.

The following principles should be observed when a Binding Over Order is made.

(i) A binding over order may be with or without sureties

9–12   It is a matter of discretion whether the person to be bound is required to produce sureties for his future behaviour or not. The question will depend upon the facts and circumstances of the individual case.

If a person is committed to prison because he cannot find sureties the court may later dispense with sureties or reduce the amount after hearing fresh evidence (MCA 1980, s.118).

(ii) The amount of any recognisance must be reasonable

9–13   The person to be bound must be allowed to make representations as to his means or the court itself must make inquiries about means because a recognisance in a relatively large sum could cause injustice (*R. v. Central Criminal Court, ex p. Boulding* [1984] Q.B. 813 and *R. v. Atkinson* (1988) 10 Cr.App.R.(S.) 470).

(iii) A binding over order should be for a finite period

9–14   The length of the period is within the discretion of the court, although the usual period is one of six or 12 months in the magistrates' court.

The terms of the order may be different if, exceptionally, proceedings are commenced by complaint under the provisions of section 115 of the Magistrates' Courts Act 1980. Such proceedings are rare nowadays, but the 1980 Act states that where a complaint is proved the court may make an order requiring the defendant to enter into a recogniscance (with or without sureties) "to keep the peace or to be of good behaviour towards the complainant". It would seem, therefore, that the 1980 Act permits the making of a bind over following a complaint requiring the defendant to be of good behaviour only. Such an order would be contrary to the modern perception of the nature of Binding Over Orders as explained in the case of *Percy v. D.P.P.* [1995] 1 W.L.R. 1382, although the words of the statute are clear and unambiguous. An order made under section 115, however, is confined to future behaviour relating to the complainant only, whereas the concept of breach of the peace under inherent jurisdiction relates to an acknowledgement by the person bound to keep the peace towards the community at large.

4. Breach of the Order

(i) Consequences if a person refuses to be bound

9–15   A Binding Over Order is an obligation entered into by the person bound and a court may not force the obligation on an unwilling person. However, if a court is satisfied that a Binding Over Order should be made and the person refuses to be bound, the court may impose imprisonment unless the person is under the age of 18 (*Veater v. Glennon* [1981] 1 W.L.R. 567). This is because the decision in *Veater v. Glennon* must now be read in the light of section 9 of the Criminal Justice Act 1982 (detention of persons in default or contempt), which has itself been amended by CJA 1991, s.63(5), substituting the age of 18 for that of 17.

There is power to imprison persons aged over 18 but under 21 for refusing to be bound over because such a refusal is a "kindred offence" within section 12(1) of the Contempt of Court Act 1981 (*Howley v. Oxford* and *Chief Constable of the Surrey Constabulary v. Ridley & Steel* [1985] Crim.L.R. 724 and 725).

If a defendant refuses to be bound following a complaint under section 115 the maximum sentence is six months, or an equivalent sentence for a person aged 18 to 21 (MCA 1980, s.115(3)).

The fact that there is no power to imprison a juvenile does not prevent a juvenile consenting to be bound over (*Conlan v. Oxford* (1984) 148 J.P. 97), nor does it prevent a court imposing a Binding Over Order on a juvenile (*Veater v. Glennon*, above).

(ii) Consequences if a person breaches the peace during the period of the order

9–16   The only consequence of a breach of the order is forfeiture of the recognisance and/or any surety or sureties.

There must be a complaint before the court, and there must be clear evidence of what the original obligation was, and what the alleged breach amounts to. The person subject to the complaint must be allowed to make representations and call evidence or witnesses (*R. v. McGregor* (1945) 109 J.P. 136).

It has been said that the court should be satisfied on the civil standard of proof that a binding over order has been breached (*R. v. Marlow Justices, ex p. O'Sullivan* [1984] Q.B. 381). It is submitted that this proposition must now be doubted in the light of more recent Divisional Court authority which has classified bind over proceedings as criminal in nature as well as the autonomous meaning of criminal charge required by the European Convention on Human Rights (see generally below and Chapter 24, below).

Section 55 of the Crime and Disorder Act 1998 has amended section 120 of the Magistrates' Courts Act 1980 with respect to the law on forfeiting recognisances. In respect of sureties in binding over proceedings the law is unchanged because the discretion of justices to forfeit such a surety is preserved (MCA 1980, s.120(1)(a) and (2)(a) and (b), as amended by CDA 1998, s.55). This discretion does not apply if the surety is taken in bail proceedings and the accused fails to attend on bail (see §3–38 above).

9–17   In addition to these general provisions, there is specific provision for a surety to be able to bring to the attention of the court the fact that the person bound has been guilty or is about to be guilty of conduct constituting a breach of his recognisance (MCA 1980, s.116). The surety shall make a complaint, and justices may issue a warrant for the arrest of the principal to be brought before the court. Once before the court the principal may be ordered to enter into a new recognisance with or without sureties to keep the peace or to be of good behaviour, or the original recognisance may be forfeited (MCA 1980, s.116(2)).

IMPACT OF HUMAN RIGHTS ACT 1998

9–18   The particular character of binding over proceedings is rooted in antiquity and originates from a time when fundamental human rights and freedoms were largely unrecognised. For this reason bind overs are difficult to fit into a code of rights such as the Convention. The Convention sets out a number of fundamental rights and freedoms including freedom of expression (Article 10) and freedom of assembly and association (Article 11). Most of the recent domestic decisions on binding over decided in the Divisional Court have concerned applicants who have been endeavouring to exercise these rights. It follows that the complexity which sometimes arises in bind over cases is unlikely to be reduced when the 1998 Act is implemented.

The European Court considered the impact of Convention rights on binding over proceedings in a case brought by five applicants in 1998. The case, *Steel v. United Kingdom* ((ref.00024838/94, decided on September 23, 1998) [1998] Crim. L.R. 893), is complicated because the Court found there to be breaches of the Convention in respect of some applicants but not others. In summary the case of *Steel v. United Kingdom* established the following principles:

   (i) the law on breach of the peace had been established with sufficient clarity by United Kingdom courts over recent years for a person to appreciate the consequences, namely arrest, of acting in a manner which would be likely to cause, or provoke, violence;

   (ii) if a protest is entirely peaceful then the law did not permit an arrest;

   (iii) detention after a lawful arrest for a breach of the peace fell within the scope of Article 5(1)(b);

   (iv) the restrictions on the right to freedom and expression under Article 10 were not disproportionate if a person was detained following a refusal to be bound over if there was a danger of disorder and physical injury occurring by the person who refused to be bound.

The last of these points is of particular importance because the Convention requires the *substance* and not merely the procedural formality of the case to be scrutinised. Thus, if a person refused to be bound over imprisonment in default would not appear to be justified if such an action was disproportionate to the behaviour giving rise to the proceedings.

9–19   A second respect in which Binding Over Orders may receive renewed attention following implementation of the Human Rights Act 1998 concerns the conduct giving rise to the arrest in the first place. In *Arrowsmith v. UK* (1975) 3 E.H.R.R. 218 the applicant, a pacifist campaigner, had been arrested for a breach of the peace when distributing leaflets at an Army Base in Wiltshire which urged soldiers not to fight in Northern Ireland. She was subsequently prosecuted for offences contrary to the Incitement to Disaffection Act 1934 and convicted. Her application to the European Court that her rights under Article 9 (freedom of thought, conscience and religion) had been infringed failed because she was not exercising rights of belief by urging soldiers to desert. Secondly, the Court paid regard to the fact that she was later convicted of a substantive criminal offence. The decision in *Arrowsmith* would not necessarily be of assistance in a case of a peaceful protest which was disruptive, but falling short of violence or a threat of violence, particularly if no substantive offences were later charged.

If a protest is peaceful a police officer would not be acting in the execution of his duty if he arrested such a person on the grounds that a breach of the peace had occurred (*Redmond-Bate v. D.P.P., The Times*, July 29, 1999). In that case the defendant had been preaching on the steps of a cathedral, and some passers by were showing hostility to the preaching. The Divisional Court quashed the defendant's conviction for obstructing the officer when making the arrest after unsuccessfully trying to stop the preaching. The Divisional Court, citing Articles 9 and 10 of the Convention, held that a breach of the peace should not be predicted simply because speeches in public might be considered offensive, irritating heretical or unwelcome. "Freedom only to speak inoffensively was not a freedom worth having" (*per* Sedley L.J.).

For these reasons the conclusions of the Law Commission (Report No. 22 Cm. 2439, 1994) that the Binding Over laws fall short of the due process enshrined in Convention law may become the subject of renewed argument after the Human Rights Act 1998 is implemented.

CHAPTER 10

Misbehaviour and Contempt of Court

1. Introduction

10–01 Sometimes the proceedings in the magistrates' court are interrupted by incidents of noise, minor violence or misbehaviour either from an accused in the dock or from observers in the public gallery. Sometimes also the proper functioning of the court is disturbed because a witness refuses to give evidence or there is an attempt to interfere with a witness or an advocate. Occasionally a magistrate himself may be insulted or made fun of. All such incidents, if they interfere with the administration of the law, may amount to a contempt and a magistrates' court now has a power to punish contempt. It has been said that the "course of justice must not be deflected or interfered with. Those who strike at it strike at the very foundations of our society": *per* Lord Denning M.R. in *Morris v. Crown Office* [1970] 2 Q.B. 114 at p. 122. More recently it has been said that abuse or insults directed at a judge are usually of very short duration and judges should not be so conscious of their own dignity that action has to be taken in all cases (*R. v. Powell*, 98 Cr.App.R., 224).

A magistrates' court did not have specific powers to punish for contempt until the coming into force of the Contempt of Court Act 1981. Now, the power to imprison a contemnor exists with the inherent powers of a justice to regulate the proceedings of the court, such as binding over, closing of the court and the issuing of summonses. In addition, there are specific statutory provisions regulating conduct in court such as the prohibition of photography and tape-recording, and the power to deal with a witness who refuses to give evidence. Finally, there is a specific offence of intimidation, punishable by six months' imprisonment created for the first time by section 51 of the Criminal Justice and Public Order Act 1994.

2. Categories of Contempt

(i) Contempt amounting to insults, interruptions or misbehaviour

10–02 The words insult, interruption and misbehaviour are vital to the power of a magistrates' court to punish for contempt because not being a superior court of record having inherent powers to punish contemnors, a magistrates' court may only punish under the statutory provisions of the Contempt of Court Act 1981.

Section 12(1) of the Act provides that it is a contempt where a person:

   (a) wilfully insults the justice or justices, any witness or officer of the court or any solicitor or counsel having business in the court, during his or their sitting or attendance in court or in going to or returning from the court, or

   (b) wilfully interrupts the proceedings of the court or otherwise misbehaves in court.

The words in section 12(1)(b) mean the wilful interruption of the proceedings in court, whether this results from acts done within the court or whether they are brought to a standstill by acts from outside. The mental element necessary is that the contempt should be deliberate and the contemnor must either intend to interrupt the proceedings or be reckless as to whether his acts would interrupt the proceedings (*Bodden v. Commissioner of Police of the Metropolis* [1990] 2 Q.B. 397).

In any such case the court may order that the offender be taken into custody and detained until the rising of the court and, if it thinks fit, commit the offender to custody for a specified period not exceeding one month or impose a fine not exceeding £2,500, or both (CCA 1981, s.12(2)).

(a) Meaning of insult

10–03 Whether a particular remark is an insult will depend on the facts and circumstances of each case. For example, shouting from the public gallery that the judge was biased has been held to be insulting (*R. v. Hill* [1986] Crim.L.R. 457). However, the following words addressed to a judge, "You are a humourless automaton. Why don't you self-destruct?" were held not to be insulting (*Balogh v. St. Albans Crown Court* [1975] 1 Q.B. 73). In that case Lord Denning M.R. said that insults were best treated with disdain unless they were gross and scandalous and judges should be slow to use contempt powers when insults were directed against themselves.

Paradoxically, an insult to a witness or other party to the proceedings may be treated more seriously as the intention may be to undermine the confidence of the witness or party in giving evidence. Such conduct may be punished even if it occurs when the witness is going into or returning from the court (CCA 1981, s.12(1)(a)). However, "insult" must be given its ordinary English meaning. Accordingly, a threat of violence made to a witness in the precincts of the court is not an "insult" entitling the court to use powers under section 12 of the 1981 Act (*R. v. Havant Justices, ex p. Palmer* (1985) 149 J.P. 609).

(b) Meaning of misbehaviour

10–04 Although the word has not been judicially interpreted under the 1981 Act it is submitted it has the same meaning as a contempt in the face of the court which has been defined as a gross interference with the course of justice in a case that was being tried, about to be tried, or just over, whether or not it was witnessed by the judge (*Balogh v. St. Albans Crown Court*, above).

EXAMPLES:

10–05

(i) Assault. It is a contempt for anybody to commit an assault on a person, whether a magistrate, party, witness or legal representative (*Parashuram v. The King Emperor* [1945] A.C. 264).

(ii) Disruption. The singing of songs and shouting of slogans in court by members of the public (*Morris v. Crown Office*, above), the distribution of leaflets in the public gallery inciting others to picket the courts (*Lecointe v. Central Criminal Court* (1973) (unreported)), or deliberate tactics of disruption by a defendant in respect of court procedure (*R. v. Aquarius* (1974) 59 Cr.App.R. 165).

(iii) Disrespectful behaviour. Mere discourtesy or the showing of disrespect is not in itself a contempt (*Weston v. Central Criminal Court* [1977] 1 Q.B. 32) unless it is such as to impair the authority of the court such as swearing, shouting, and protestations of innocence by a defendant following his conviction (*R. v. Logan* [1974] Crim.L.R. 609). A wolf-whistle from the public gallery of a court obviously directed at a female in the well of the court has been held to amount to a contempt (*R. v. Powell* (1994) 98 Cr.App.R. 224).

The court must be careful to distinguish between behaviour which is offensive, rude, uncivilised and wholly reprehensible but which nevertheless falls short of behaviour giving rise to the court's jurisdiction (*R. v. Runting* (1989) 89 Cr.App.R. 243). This reasoning has been applied to summary proceedings where the Divisional Court has held that justices were wholly wrong to have committed a solicitor for contempt after the listing arrangements in the court had been criticised in vigorous terms (*R. v. Tamworth Justices, ex p. Walsh* [1994] C.O.D. 277).

(ii) Use of tape recorders in court

10–06 It is a contempt to use in court, or to bring into court for use, any tape recorder or other instrument for recording sound except with the leave of the court, unless it is for the purpose of making official transcripts of the proceedings (CCA 1981, s.9).

A Practice Direction has been issued by the Lord Chief Justice giving guidance as to when the leave of the court might be given. (*Practice Direction (Tape Recorders)* [1981] 1 W.L.R. 1526). It is not summarised because it is unlikely to be of particular relevance in the magistrates' court.

The penalty for breaching section 9 is one month's imprisonment or a fine not exceeding £2,500 (CCA 1981, s.14).

It is not clear what the necessary *mens rea* for the offence of using a tape-recorder under section 9 of the Contempt of Court Act is. If the offender is dealt with for this infraction under section 12 of the Act it has been held that the contempt must be wilful (*Re Hooker* [1993] C.O.D. 190).

(iii) Photographs in court

10–07 There is a prohibition on any person taking or attempting to take any photograph with a view to publication or making a sketch of any magistrate, justice or witness or party to any proceedings before the court. A person contravening this prohibition is liable to a fine not exceeding level 3 on the standard scale (CJA 1925, s.41 as amended by CJA 1982, s.38).

(iv) Contempt by witnesses

10–08 If a witness before a magistrates' court refuses without just excuse to be sworn or give evidence or to produce any document or thing the court may commit him to custody for a period not exceeding one month or impose a fine not exceeding £2,500 (MCA 1980, s.97(4).

In considering "just excuse" for failing to give evidence it has been held that duress may be a defence to a witness who refuses to testify (*R. v. K.* (1984) 148 J.P. 410). Similarly, a witness's well-founded fear of attack if he was to give evidence will amount to a defence (*R. v. Lewis (James John)* (1993) 96 Cr.App.R. 412).

3. Methods of Dealing with Contempt

10–09 There are a number of ways in which the court may deal with a contempt. The decision as to which method is adopted will depend upon (a) the nature of the contempt, (b) whether prompt action is needed to deal with it, and (c) whether the contempt is also an offence defined by the statute where a penalty is prescribed.

When the Human Rights Act 1998 is brought into force the law and practice of contempt will be subject to the European Convention on Human Rights. For this reason alternatives to the imposition of punishment for contempt should be explored before the ultimate sanction of deprivation of liberty is used. Even though the Contempt of Court Act 1981 has provided for a specific punishment to be imposed (for example for the offence of playing a tape-recorder in court, see §10–06, above) it is desirable that alternative means of dealing with the matter should be used whenever possible. In the above instance justices should consider ordering the tape-recording to cease and to invite the contemnor to surrender his tape. Similarly, if a witness refuses to be sworn then the matter should be explored sensitively before a prosecution under the Contempt of Court Act 1981 is contemplated.

(i) Dealing with contempt as a substantive offence

10–10 This procedure will be appropriate if there is strong *prima facie* evidence of an offence having been committed. Most commonly, these will be offences of assault or criminal damage, or possibly offences contrary to sections 3 or 4 of the Public Order Act 1986. The advantage of dealing with gross and obvious contempts in this way is that the alleged contemnor will be dealt with in proceedings which conform to the European Convention of Human Rights, namely by an independent and impartial tribunal, not the tribunal who witnessed the contempt.

(ii) Summary punishment

10–11 A court is entitled in clear cases to punish the contemnor immediately by ordering him to be placed in custody for a finite period. When the court uses this power it is called a summary power because the usual procedural steps of information, trial and adjudication are dispensed with. The justification for inflicting immediate punishment is the protection of the administration of justice and the need to put an immediate stop to the contempt (*R. v. Davies* [1906] 1 K.B. 32). However, it has been recognised that the power is draconian and should only be used when it is necessary to ensure that proceedings which are in progress or about to start can be brought to end without disturbance (*Balogh v. St. Albans Crown Court*, above).

It follows that swift summary punishment is usually appropriate only when the court is faced with gross and obvious disruption which cannot be dealt with in any other way (*e.g.* by clearing the public gallery). Even when the court is faced with such behaviour justices should always give the alleged contemnor an opportunity to reflect on his position and if necessary obtain legal advice before the issue of contempt is finally decided (*R. v. Tamworth Magistrates' Court, ex p. Walsh* [1994] C.O.D. 277). The importance of these principles has been underlined in two other cases, *R. v. Newbury Justices, ex p. du Pont* (1984) 148 J.P. 248) and *R. v. Selby Justices, ex p. Frame* [1992] 1 Q.B. 72.

If the proceedings are being disrupted from outside (*e.g.* by a protestor making such a noise that the court cannot function) justices may order an officer of the court to bring the protestor before them with a view to exercising powers under section 12(2) of the Contempt of Court Act 1981. However, such action may only be taken if there are reasonable grounds for believing that the proceedings are being interrupted wilfully, and therefore it will be prudent to issue a warning so that the person interrupting the court is aware of the effect of his actions (*Bodden v. Commissioner of Police of the Metropolis* [1990] 2 Q.B. 397).

10–12 It has been said that the imprisonment of a contemnor is not a conviction (*R. v. Newbury Justices, ex p. Du Pont* (1984) 148 J.P. 248). For these reasons there is no power to place a contemnor on probation (*R. v. Palmer* [1992] 1 W.L.R. 568). In that case the Court of Appeal (Criminal Division), *per* Glidewell L.J., expressed the hope that Parliament might consider giving the courts a power to place contemnors on probation.

PROCEDURE FOR IMPOSING SUMMARY PUNISHMENT

10–13 The wording of section 12 of the Contempt of Court Act 1981 envisages a two-stage process: the immediate "detention" of the contemnor, and the later discretionary custodial sentence as punishment (CCA 1981, s.12(2)). In the period between the detention and sentence the contemnor may apologise, and it allows time for the contemnor to receive legal representation. Such a contemnor is now entitled to legal aid, without a means test, if it is in the interests of justice to grant it (Legal Aid Act 1988, s.29). It is submitted that in view of the above authorities it will nearly always be in the interests of justice to allow a contemnor to be represented.

If the court is considering exercising the powers given in section 12 of the Contempt of Court Act 1981—namely fining or imprisoning the contemnor—the court must not act too quickly. The following principles should always be borne in mind:

(a) there should be time for reflection rather than a spur of the moment decision;

(b) if it is possible for the contemnor to have some legal advice he should be given that opportunity;

(c) before the court imposes any penalty the contemnor should be given an opportunity of apologising (*R. v. Moran* (1985) 81 Cr.App.R. 51).

These points have been specifically approved as having application in the magistrates' court (*R. v. Pateley Bridge Magistrates' Court, ex p. Percy* [1994] C.O.D. 453).

SPECIAL PROCEDURE IF THE CONTEMNOR IS UNDER 21

10–14 There is power to order the detention of an offender aged from 18 to 20 for contempt of court in the same way as an offender over 21 may be summarily sentenced to a term of imprisonment (CJA 1982, s.9(1)). However, this power may not be used unless the court is of the opinion that no other method of dealing with him is appropriate, and in forming such opinion the court:

(a) shall take into account all such information about the circumstances of the default or contempt (including any aggravating or mitigating factors) as is available to it; and

(b) may take into account any information about that person which is before it (CJA 1982, s.1(5) as substituted by CJA 1991, Sched. 11, para. 30). In addition there is an obligation to state the reasons why no method other than detention is imposed in open court and record them in the court register (*ibid.*).

If the contemnor is under the age of 18 there is no power to order detention because the provisions of section 9 of the 1982 Act are now limited to those over the age of 18 by virtue of section 63(5) of the Criminal Justice Act 1991 (*R. v. Byas* [1995] Crim.L.R. 439).

10–15   It is essential that if the court exercises the power of summary punishment, justice is seen to be done and that the contemnor has a fair trial and the normal rules of evidence should still be applied (*R. v. Shokoya, The Times*, June 10, 1992). In that case it was held that a Crown Court judge had been wrong to consider hearsay evidence in a summary contempt hearing. Where, in contempt proceedings, a judge failed to allow counsel representing the contemnor to examine his client properly in chief, and gave the impression that he was using the occasion as an example to others, there would not be a fair trial (*R. v. Renshaw* [1989] Crim. L.R. 811). In that case the Court of Appeal (Criminal Division) quashed a contempt conviction imposed by a Crown Court judge, and similar conduct by justices might lead to the conviction being quashed on judicial review.

SENTENCING CONSIDERATIONS IN SUMMARY PUNISHMENT

10–16   If the contempt consists of a deliberate attempt to interfere with the administration of justice, for example by seeking to influence a juror during a criminal trial, a short immediate sentence of imprisonment is appropriate (*R. v. Owen* [1976] 1 W.L.R. 840). If the contempt is something which is potentially offensive or insulting but nevertheless an interference with the administration of justice, detention in the court cells may be an appropriate penalty (*R. v. Powell* (1994) 98 Cr.App.R. 224). Abuse or an insult directed at a judge or magistrate should not always attract contempt proceedings (*Balogh v. St. Albans Crown Court* [1975] 1 Q.B. 73), but if the contempt was in the nature of vulgar abuse a sentence of 14 days' imprisonment has been held to be appropriate (*R. v. McDonald* (1990) 12 Cr.App.R.(S.) 44).

(iii) Alternatives to summary punishment, fine or imprisonment

(a) ORDERING THE CONTEMNOR TO LEAVE

10–17   If the accused himself is responsible for the disorder and it is not practical for the proceedings to continue in his presence he may be ordered to leave under the provisions of the Magistrates' Courts Act 1980 if the proceedings are committal proceedings (MCA 1980, s.4(4)) and the same power probably also exists in respect of summary trials (*R. v. Abrahams* (1895) 21 V.L.R. 343). In either event section 12 of the Contempt of Court Act 1981 allows a police officer or officer of the court to remove him. If the contemnor is a member of the public the court may also order his removal, and if further disruption is reasonably anticipated, order that the public be excluded for the remainder of the trial (*R. v. Denbigh Justices, ex p. Williams* [1974] Q.B. 759). The power to remove a person from the court will apply also to an advocate, whether a barrister or a solicitor, if the conduct of the advocate is grossly disrespectful but falls short of a contempt (*R. v. Tamworth Justices, ex p. Walsh, The Times*, March 3, 1994). It is submitted that the use of this draconian power will be rare, and in *ex p. Walsh* the Divisional Court opined that removal from the court was only one of a number of ways of dealing with the particular problem which had arisen in that case.

(b) ISSUING A SUMMONS

10–18　If a gross and obvious contempt occurs in the sight and hearing of justices which prima facie is a criminal offence, for example assault, a summons may be issued immediately to enable the matter to be tried (*R. v. Butt* (1957) 41 Cr.App.R. 82).

(c) BINDING OVER

10–19　Where the misbehaviour gives rise to a breach of the peace the contemnor may be bound over (*R. v. North London Metropolitan Magistrate, ex p. Haywood* [1973] 1 W.L.R. 965). For a detailed discussion of the use of Binding Over Orders see Chapter 9. However, a Binding Over Order may not be used unless there is a fear that a future breach of the peace may occur. Mere disturbance in court is not of itself a ground for imposing a Binding Over Order (*R. v. Ipswich Crown Court, ex p. Eris* [1989] C.O.D. 345).

It is submitted that the use of justices' powers of binding over should be used with considerable discretion. In *ex p. Eris* the Divisional Court quashed the Binding Over Order and since then the Divisional Court has further limited the circumstances in which bind overs are considered appropriate. In addition the combination of inherent powers to punish for contempt and powers, dating from 1361, to order a bind over have important implications after the Human Rights Act 1998 is implemented. See §9–18, above.

4. Effect on the Proceedings when Disruption Occurs

10–20　The object of the powers to deal with contempt is to prevent the course of justice being deflected or interfered with. It follows that a contemnor should not be allowed so to frustrate traditional procedures that he may be allowed to claim later, on appeal, that he was denied natural justice. If, therefore, an accused is ordered to leave court because of his behaviour he may not be able to claim later that he was denied a fair trial by being prevented from cross-examining witnesses. An accused's rights in a criminal trial are conditional on him using those rights for proper purposes. Accordingly, if a consequence of an accused's contempt is that he is unable to call witnesses or make a closing address to the court because he has been removed, the trial is not invalidated (*R. v. Morley* [1988] Q.B. 601).

The same principles apply to committal proceedings. If an accused behaves in such a way during a committal, for example by shouting and raving in court, that the clerk forgets to inform him of his right (which then existed) to call evidence at the conclusion of the prosecution case, the committal is not invalid (*R. v. Barnet Magistrates' Court, ex p. Wood* [1993] Crim.L.R. 78). In that case the accused had repeatedly interrupted the evidence of a prosecution witness and had to be removed, and then he dismissed his solicitor and represented himself. Thereafter, he was persistently abusive and disruptive and the clerk had difficulty in making herself heard when the formal committal to the Crown Court took place. The incident took place under previous committal rules and the Divisional Court held that while in normal circumstances a failure to comply with rule 7 of the Magistrates' Courts Rules 1981 would be fatal to a committal in this case no prejudice had occurred because on the facts there was plainly a case to answer.

5. The Offence of Intimidation

10–21   There is an offence, punishable upon summary conviction with six months' imprisonment, of intimidation (CJ and POA 1994, s.51(1)). The offence is principally intended to provide greater protection to witnesses, but applies also to persons assisting in the investigation of an offence. A further, separate offence of reprisal is created by section 51(2) of the 1994 Act which is not discussed below as it falls outside the context of this Chapter.

The offence is committed if a person does to another person—

(a) an act which intimidates, and is intended to intimidate, that other person;

(b) knowing or believing that the other person is assisting in the investigation of an offence, or is a witness or potential witness [or a juror or potential juror] in proceedings for an offence; and

(c) intending thereby to cause the investigation or the course of justice to be obstructed, perverted or interfered with (CJ and POA 1994, s.51(1)).

A person who is guilty of such an offence is liable on summary conviction to imprisonment for a term not exceeding six months or a fine not exceeding the statutory maximum or both (*ibid.*, s.51(6)(b)).

The offence is in addition to, and not in derogation of, any offence subsisting at common law (*ibid.* s.51(11)). In the magistrates' court there is no common law offence of contempt, and therefore the power to punish acts of intimidation towards witnesses in criminal proceedings is a new power given to justices by the 1994 Act. The offence is triable either way and where evidence of intimidation exists the offence should be charged and prosecuted in the normal way. Because the accused has a right of election at the Crown Court an act of intimidation towards a witness in summary proceedings may eventually be tried in the Crown Court.

IMPACT OF HUMAN RIGHTS ACT 1998

10–22   When the summary powers of contempt are adopted justices may be acting as judge, witness, prosecutor or perhaps victim in the proceedings. Thus, the use of the procedure "omits many of the procedures to which the accused is ordinarily entitled and for this reason it has been repeatedly stated that the judge should choose to adopt it only in case of real need" (*R. v. Griffin* (1989) 88 Cr.App.R. 63, *per* Mustill L.J.).

For these reasons the protection offered by English common law procedures relating to summary trial and the protection provided by Article 6 of the Convention are absent. This does not mean that use of the summary power to punish contempt is prohibited by the Convention because frequently contemnors are interfering with the exercise of the rights of others, usually the accused on trial. Nonetheless, any use of the summary power to punish for contempt must be examined in the light of the provisions of the Convention.

Article 5 of the Convention states that no one shall be deprived of his liberty save in the following cases and in accordance with a procedure prescribed by law. The case applicable to a deprivation of liberty following a contempt of court is Article 5(b) which permits the lawful detention of a person for the non-compliance with the lawful order of the court or to secure the fulfilment of any obligation prescribed by law.

10–23   Convention jurisprudence provides that when a detention under Article 5 occurs the decision should not be arbitrary (*Winterwerp v. Netherlands* (1979) 2 E.H.R.R. 387). It follows that the following matters discussed in this Chapter are of particular importance:

(i) alternatives to deprivation of liberty should be explored, and be seen to be explored lest the contemnor feels a punishment has been inflicted arbitrarily (see §10–17, above);

(ii) an opportunity for reflection, the offer of legal advice and the opportunity of an apology should be given (see §10–13, above).

It is submitted that these procedures may assume the force of law once the 1998 Act is in force. Although there is no precise authority which affirms that English law complies with the Convention in contempt proceedings it is unlikely that the procedures fail to comply with Convention principles providing imprisonment for contempt is used only as a last resort. If the only way to uphold another Convention right, namely the right of an accused to a fair trial under Article 6, is to punish a person interfering with that right it would seem that common law contempt procedures do comply with Convention principles.

CHAPTER 11

Professional Duties

11–01 The administration of criminal justice requires high standards of probity and integrity from those who appear in the courts in a professional capacity. In order to foster and maintain these standards both the Law Society and the General Council of the Bar have issued codes of conduct for solicitors and barristers who appear as advocates. These codes go to the heart of court procedure because without them justice itself suffers. In addition, the Code for Crown Prosecutors has now been issued as a public declaration of the principles upon which the Crown Prosecution Service will exercise its functions. This is reproduced in Appendix II.

Despite the importance of the codes governing solicitors and barristers, they are often not closely read by practitioners, and magistrates are sometimes ignorant of them. Accordingly they are reproduced below where they are relevant to the preparation of cases or appearance in the magistrates' court. The extracts are reproduced with the kind permission of the Law Society and the General Council of the Bar who respectively hold the copyright in the Guide and Code of Conduct.

In addition to the professional duties of advocates the role of the clerk is of great importance in the conduct of proceedings in court. His role in criminal trials and his function generally is often misunderstood, largely perhaps because a magistrates' court clerk holds a unique place in court practice: he is neither advocate nor tribunal of fact or law and yet he may play an active role in the conduct of criminal cases. For this reason, and because of the amount of judicial *dicta* from the Divisional Court on the role of the clerk, his duties and functions are included also in this chapter.

A. PROFESSIONAL DUTIES OF A SOLICITOR

11–02 The following paragraphs are reproduced from the seventh edition of *The Guide to the Professional Conduct of Solicitors* published by the Law Society in June 1996. This latest Guide follows recent legislation, notably the Courts and Legal Services Act 1990 and changes generated by the Law Society itself. Paragraph numbers in bold have been inserted for the purposes of this book. All others appear as they do in *The Guide to the Professional Conduct of Solicitors*.

Chapter 1: Obtaining Instructions

Solicitor's independence and client's freedom of choice

11–03 It is fundamental to the relationship which exists between solicitor and client that a solicitor should be able to give impartial and frank advice to the client, free from any external or adverse pressures or interests which would destroy or weaken the solicitor's professional independence or the fiduciary relationship with the client or the client's freedom of choice.

1. A solicitor who suspects that a potential client has been improperly influenced in the choice of solicitor must satisfy himself or herself that the client's freedom of choice has not been restricted. Improper influence can come from the solicitor or from a third party.

2. A solicitor must not allow clients to override the solicitor's professional judgment, for example by insisting on the solicitor acting in a way which is contrary to law or to a rule or principle of professional conduct.

3. Gifts to potential clients, particularly those who are accused of criminal offences, or to people connected with them, in order to persuade them to become or remain the solicitor's clients, may amount to a breach of rule 1 of the Solicitors' Practice Rules 1990. Such gifts could compromise or impair the independence and integrity of the solicitor and the good repute of the solicitor and the solicitors' profession. The Criminal Law Committee strongly advise solicitors that neither they nor their representatives should directly or indirectly make a gift to a person who is accused of a criminal offence except by way of refreshments or cigarettes for the client's immediate consumption in the solicitor's presence."

NOTE: Rule 1 of the Solicitors' Practice Rules 1990 states:

"A solicitor shall not do anything in the course of practising as a solicitor, or permit another person to do anything on his or her behalf, which compromises or impairs or is likely to compromise or impair any of the following:

   (a) the solicitor's independence or integrity;
   (b) a person's freedom to instruct a solicitor of his choice;
   (c) the solicitor's duty to act in the best interests of the client;
   (d) the good repute of the solicitor or of the solicitors' profession;
   (e) the solicitor's proper standard of work;
   (f) the solicitor's duty to the court."

Chapter 15: Conflict of Interests

"15.01 When instructions must be refused

11–04 A solicitor or firm of solicitors should not accept instructions to act for two or more clients where there is a conflict or a significant risk of a conflict between the interests of those clients.

1. Where a solicitor already acts for one client and is asked to act for another client whose interests conflict or appear likely to conflict with those of the first client, the solicitor must refuse to act for the second client.

2. Disclosure of the conflicting interest to the client or potential client does not permit the instruction to be accepted by the solicitor, even where the client consents.

[paragraphs 3 and 4 omitted.]

15.02 Relevant confidential information

11–05 If a solicitor or firm of solicitors has acquired relevant confidential information concerning a former client during the course of acting for that client, the solicitor or the firm must not accept instructions to act against the client.

1. Any knowledge acquired by a solicitor whilst acting for the former client is

confidential and cannot be disclosed without that client's consent. ... However, a solicitor is under a duty to the present client to inform the client of all matters which are material to the retainer. ... Consequently, a solicitor in possession of confidential information concerning a former client which is or might be relevant, is put in an impossible position and cannot act against that client.

[paragraphs 2–8 omitted.]

15.03 Conflict arising between two or more current clients

11–06 A solicitor or firm of solicitors must not continue to act for two or more clients where a conflict of interests arises between those clients.

1. If a solicitor has already accepted instructions from two clients in a matter or related matters and a conflict subsequently arises between the interests of those clients, the solicitor must cease to act for both clients. A solicitor may only continue to represent one client if not in possession of relevant confidential knowledge concerning the other obtained whilst acting for the other. Even in such a case it would be prudent to confirm that the other party does not object. [Further paragraphs applicable to practice in the Crown Court are not printed.]

2. Where a solicitor acts for two or more co-defendants in criminal proceedings, and one or more of them changes his or her plea, the solicitor must consider carefully whether it is proper to continue to represent any of them. In reaching a decision, the solicitor must bear in mind that if his or her duty of disclosure to the retained client or clients conflicts with his or her duty of confidentiality to the other client or clients, the solicitor must cease to act for all of them. Before agreeing to continue to represent one client the solicitor must, therefore, examine carefully whether there is any information in his or her possession relating to the other clients which may be relevant to the retained client (see *R. v. Ataou* [1988] Q.B. 798).

3. Following the amalgamation of two or more firms, the clients of the individual firms will, as a result of an express or implied change of retainer, become clients of the new firm; care must be taken to ensure that the interests of the clients of the new firm do not conflict. If they do, the firm must cease to act for both clients unless they are able, within the terms of Commentary 1, to continue to act for one. In certain exceptional circumstances the amalgamated firm may continue to act for one client after erecting a 'Chinese wall'... Further guidance can be found in Annex 15A. [Not printed.]

4. It is doubtful whether, in circumstances other than where there has been an amalgamation of two or more firms, a 'Chinese wall' can be erected so that a firm can continue to represent the interests of two clients whose interests conflict. The courts have expressed doubts on whether an impregnable wall can ever be created because of the practical difficulties of ensuring the absolute confidentiality of each client's affairs (see *Re a firm of solicitors* [1992] 1 All E.R. 353)."

Chapter 20: Relations with the Bar, other lawyers and professional agents

"20.03 Instructing a counsel or other advocate

11–07 When instructing counsel or other advocate, it is the solicitor's responsibility to ensure so far as practicable, that adequate instructions, supporting statements and documents are sent in good time.

20.04 Attending counsel at court

11–08 Where counsel has been instructed, his instructing solicitor is under a duty to attend or arrange for the attendance of a responsible representative throughout the proceedings, save that attendance may be dispensed with in the magistrates' court or in certain categories of Crown Court proceeding where, in either case, the solicitor is satisfied that it is reasonable in the particular circumstances of the case that counsel be unattended and, in particular, that the interests of the client and the interests of justice will not be prejudiced.

[Sub-paragraphs 1–3 in relation to attendance on counsel in the Crown Court omitted.]

4. The Council, when considering any complaint that principle 20.04 has not been observed, will take into account all the practical difficulties.

20.05 Solicitors' responsibility to clients

11–09 Solicitors may not abrogate their responsibility to clients by instructing counsel or other advocate.

1. A solicitor should take care in the selection of suitable counsel or other advocate and must, when considering the advice of counsel or other advocate, ensure that it contains no obvious errors. If the advice conflicts with previous advice it may be necessary to seek clarification.

2. Solicitors must use their best endeavours to ensure that the barrister or other advocate carries out instructions within a reasonable time and that the claim does not become statute barred or liable to be struck out for want of prosecution. Where appropriate a solicitor must ask for the return of the papers in order to instruct another barrister or other advocate.

3. The Bar's code requires that where a barrister has received instructions and it is or becomes apparent that the work cannot be done within a reasonable time, the barrister should inform the instructing solicitor forthwith. Where a brief has been delivered, immediately that there is an appreciable risk that the barrister may not be able to undertake the case, the brief should be returned in sufficient time to allow another barrister to be engaged and to master the brief."

Chapter 21: Litigation and Advocacy

21.01 Practice rule 16A (solicitors acting as advocates)

11–10 "Any solicitor acting as advocate shall at all times comply with the Law Society's Code for Advocacy."

21.02 Solicitors acting as advocates—additional guidance

11–11

1. The Advocacy Code applies to advocacy before any court and not merely to advocacy in the higher courts or advocacy under extended rights of audience.

2. The Advocacy Code appears at Annex 21A (see §§11–27, below). Guidance on paragraph 4.1(e) of the Code (not accepting brief where solicitor responsible for course of action) appears at Annex 21D [omitted].

3. Paragraph 3.3 of the Advocacy Code refers to the British Code of Advertising Practice. This now forms part of the British Codes of Advertising and Sales Promotion. Relevant extracts appear at Annex 21B [omitted].

21.03 Practice rule 16B (choice of advocate)

11–12

"(1) A solicitor shall not make it a condition of providing litigation services that advocacy services shall also be provided by that solicitor or by the solicitor's firm or the solicitor's agent.

(2) A solicitor who provides both litigation and advocacy services shall as soon as practicable after receiving instructions and from time to time consider and advise the client whether having regard to the circumstances including:

  (i) the gravity, complexity and likely cost of the case;

  (ii) the nature of the solicitor's practice;

  (iii) the solicitor's ability and experience;

  (iv) the solicitor's relationship with the client;

the best interests of the client would be served by the solicitor, another advocate from the solicitor's firm, or some other advocate providing the advocacy services."

[21.04–21.06 omitted.]

21.07 Duty not to mislead court

11–13 Solicitors who act in litigation, whilst under a duty to do their best for their client, must never deceive or mislead the court.

1. Principle **21.07** applies equally to proceedings before tribunals and inquiries as well as to proceedings before the court.

2. See also paragraph 2.2 of the Advocacy Code, (Annex 21A at §11–27, below).

3. Although a solicitor is entitled to take every point, technical or otherwise, that is fairly arguable on behalf of the client, the court must be advised of relevant cases and statutory provisions by the advocates on both sides; if one of them omits a case or provision or makes an incorrect reference to a case or provision, it is the duty of the other to draw attention to it even if it assists the opponent's case. See also paragraph 7.1(c) of the Advocacy Code at §11–33, below.

21.08 Improper allegations

11–14 A solicitor must not make or instruct an advocate to make an allegation which is intended only to insult, degrade or annoy the other side, the witness or any other person.

1. Principle 21.08 would also preclude a solicitor from making or instructing an advocate to make an allegation which is merely scandalous.

2. In any litigation, a solicitor should, if possible, avoid the naming in open court of persons who are neither parties nor witnesses if their characters would thereby be impugned. The court should be invited to receive in writing the names, addresses and other details of such third parties.

3. A solicitor should not, in a plea in mitigation, make or instruct counsel to make an allegation which is likely to vilify or insult any person, without first being satisfied that there are reasonable grounds for making the statement.

21.09 Private communications with judge

11–15   Except when making an application to the court, a solicitor must not discuss the merits of the case with a judge, magistrate or other adjudicator before whom a case is pending or may be heard, unless invited to do so in the presence of the solicitor or counsel for the other side or party.

1. If a written communication is to be made to the judge, magistrate or other adjudicator at any time, the solicitor should at the same time deliver a copy of it to his or her professional adversary or to the opposing party if not legally represented. Where oral communication is proper, prior notice to the other party or that party's solicitor or counsel should be given.

2. Where, after a hearing, judgment is reserved and a relevant point of law is subsequently discovered, a solicitor who intends to bring it to the judge's attention should inform the advocate on the other side, who should not oppose this course of action, though that advocate knows that the point of law is against him or her.

21.10 Interviewing witnesses

11–16   It is permissible for a solicitor acting for any party to interview and take statements from any witness or prospective witness at any stage in the proceedings, whether or not that witness has been interviewed or called as a witness by another party.

1. Principle 21.10 stems from the fact that there is no property in a witness and applies both before and after the witness has given evidence at the hearing.

2. A solicitor must not, of course, tamper with the evidence of a witness or attempt to suborn the witness into changing evidence. Once a witness has given evidence, the case must be very unusual in which a solicitor acting for the other side needs to interview that witness without seeking to persuade the witness to change evidence.

3. A solicitor should be aware that in seeking to exercise the right to interview a witness who has already been called by the other side or who to the solicitor's knowledge is likely to be called by them, the solicitor may well be exposed to the suggestion that he or she has improperly tampered with the evidence. This may be so particularly where the witness subsequently changes his or her evidence. It is wise in these circumstances for such solicitor to offer to interview the witness in the presence of a representative of the other side.

4. In interviewing an expert witness or professional agent instructed by the other side there should be no attempt to induce the witness to disclose privileged information. In these circumstances also it would be wise to offer to interview the witness in the presence of the other solicitor's representative.

5. As a general rule, it is not improper for a solicitor to advise a witness from whom a statement is being sought that he or she need not make such a statement. The advice that the solicitor should give must depend upon the client's interests and the circumstances of the case.

6. A solicitor must not, without leave of the court, or without the consent of counsel or solicitor for the other party, discuss the case with a witness, whether or not the witness is the client, whilst the witness is in the course of giving evidence. This prohibition covers the whole of the relevant time including adjournments and weekends.

21.11 Payments to witnesses

11–17 A solicitor must not make or offer to make payments to a witness contingent upon the nature of the evidence given or upon the outcome of a case.

1. There is no objection to the payment of reasonable expenses to witnesses and reasonable compensation for loss of time attending court. In the case of an expert witness, there is an implied obligation to pay a reasonable fee ...

2. The obligation includes witnesses who have been subpoenaed where they have been invited to give evidence and have agreed to do so. Therefore, a solicitor who does not wish to accept such responsibility should make this clear to the witness in advance. In criminal cases in the Crown Court all witnesses other than expert witnesses can obtain payment of their fees and expenses, within the limits of the statutory scale, from the Court Office. It is good practice to inform such witnesses of this and to agree in advance whether the solicitor will accept responsibility for any sum in excess of such scale.

3. In legal aid cases, whether civil or criminal, a solicitor should draw the attention of the witnesses to the fact of legal aid and that the witnesses' fees and disbursements will have to be taxed or assessed and that only such amounts can be paid to the witness. A solicitor should expressly disclaim personal responsibility for payment of fees beyond those allowed on taxation or assessment. It should be noted that:

    (a) prior authority is not mandatory;
    (b) Area Committees do not have the power to grant prior authority for the costs of tendering expert evidence in criminal cases;
    (c) witness expenses are not payable under a criminal legal aid order unless the court directs that they may not be paid from Central Funds (see *Practice Direction on Costs in Criminal Proceedings*, May 3, 1991 [1991] 2 All E.R. 924).

21.12 Solicitor called as witness

11–18 A solicitor must not accept instructions to act as advocate for a client if it is clear that he or she or a member of the firm will be called as a witness on behalf of the client, unless the evidence is purely formal.

1. A solicitor must exercise judgment as to whether to cease acting where he or she:

    (a) has already accepted instructions as advocate and then becomes aware that he or she or a member of the firm will be called as a witness on behalf of the client; or

  (b) is instructed to act as litigator and knows that he or she must give evidence.

2. The circumstances in which a solicitor should continue to act as advocate, or as a litigator, must be extremely rare where it is likely that he or she will be called to give evidence other than that which is purely formal.

3. It may be possible for a solicitor to continue to act as an advocate if a member of the firm will be called to give evidence as to events witnessed whilst advising or assisting a client, for example at a police station or at an identification parade. In exercising judgment, the solicitor should consider the nature of evidence to be given, its importance to the case overall and the difficulties faced by the client if the solicitor were to cease to act. The decision should be taken in the interests of justice as a whole and not solely in the interests of the client. See also paragraph 4.1(d) of the Advocacy Code (Annex 21A at p.349).

21.13 Client's perjury

11–19 Where a client, prior to or in the course of any proceedings, admits to his or her solicitor that the client has committed perjury or misled the court in any material matter in continuing proceedings in relation to those proceedings, the solicitor must decline to act further in the proceedings, unless the client agrees fully to disclose his or her conduct to the court.

21.14 Duty to obey court

11–20 A solicitor must comply with any order of the court which the court can properly make requiring the solicitor or the firm to take or refrain from taking some particular course of action; equally, a solicitor is bound to honour an undertaking given to any court or tribunal.

1. A breach of Principle 21.14 may amount to contempt of court.

2. A solicitor must not aid and abet a client where the client refuses to obey a lawful court order.

3. The Society has issued guidance as to the steps a solicitor should take to secure the attendance of his client at the Crown Court for trial...

21.15 Solicitor standing bail

11–21 It is undesirable for a solicitor to offer to stand bail for a person for whom the solicitor or any partner is acting as solicitor or agent.

It is unlawful for any person, including a solicitor, to be a party to a bargain to indemnify a surety for bail.

21.16 Tapes and videos of children's evidence

11–22 When solicitors act in the defence or prosecution of an accused and have in their possession a copy of an audio or video recording of a child witness, which has been identified as having been prepared to be admitted in evidence at a criminal trial in accordance with section 54 of the Criminal Justice Act 1991, they must comply with the Council statement on access to recordings of a child witness's evidence dated November 25, 1992.

The Council statement and recorded form of undertaking, together with practice notes, are set out in Annex 21E, p.363.

21.17 Court dress

11–23 A solicitor appearing in court as an advocate should appear duly robed where this is customary and must always wear suitable clothing.

1. Whilst it is proper for a solicitor or firm of solicitors to act as solicitors in a matter where the solicitor or the firm have an interest, they must, when engaged in such litigation, sue or appear as litigants in person. If they appear before the court in such a capacity, they should not be robed, so that it is clear that they are not acting as professional advocates.

2. Where a solicitor, an employee or the firm is one of a number of plaintiffs or defendants, the firm is permitted to go on the record as the solicitors, but a solicitor or employee who is a party to the litigation should not appear as a professional advocate on behalf of the parties either in chambers or in open court. If the solicitor does appear he or she must not be robed; the alternative being for the litigants to be represented by some other person who can act as a professional advocate.

3. [Not printed.]

21.18 Statements to the press

11–24 A solicitor who on the client's instructions gives a statement to the press must not become in contempt of court by publishing any statement which is calculated to interfere with the fair trial of a case which has not been concluded.

"21.19 Solicitor for prosecution

11–25 Whilst a solicitor prosecuting a criminal case must ensure that every material point is made which supports the prosecution, the evidence must be presented dispassionately and with scrupulous fairness.

1. The prosecutor should state all relevant facts and should limit expressions of opinion to those fairly required to present the case. He or she should reveal any mitigating circumstances; and should inform the court of its sentencing powers if invited to do so and whenever it appears to be under a misapprehension about those powers.

2. If a prosecutor obtains evidence which he or she does not intend to use but which may assist the defence, the prosecutor must supply particulars of witnesses to the defence, but is not obliged to supply copies of the statements made by those witnesses. If, however, he knows of a credible witness who can speak to material facts which tend to show the accused to be innocent, he or she must either call that witness or make the statement available to the defence. Further, if the prosecutor knows, not of a credible witness, but a witness whom he or she does not accept as credible, the prosecutor should tell the defence about the witness so that they can call that person if they wish. The prosecutor must reveal to the defence factual evidence of which he or she has knowledge and which is inconsistent with that which he, as prosecutor, has presented or proposes to present to the court.

3. The prosecutor must reveal all relevant cases and statutory provisions known to him or her whether it be for or against the prosecution's case. This is so whether or not the prosecutor has been called upon to argue the point in question (see Principle 22.01)."

"21.20 Solicitor for defence

11–26 A solicitor who appears in court for the defence in a criminal case is under a duty to say on behalf of the client what the client should properly say for himself or herself if the client possessed the requisite skill and knowledge. The solicitor has a concurrent duty to ensure that the prosecution discharges the onus placed upon it to prove the guilt of the accused.

1. Unlike the advocate for the prosecution, a solicitor who appears for the defendant is under no duty of disclosure to the prosecution or the court, save that he or she is bound to reveal all relevant cases and statutory provisions. Moreover, save in exceptional and specific circumstances, the client's privilege precludes the solicitor from making a disclosure of privileged material without the client's consent. Consequently, the solicitor must not, without instructions, disclose facts known to him or her regarding the client's character or antecedents nor must the solicitor correct any information which may be given to the court by the prosecution if the correction would be to the client's detriment. The solicitor must not, however, knowingly put forward or let the client put forward false information with intent to mislead the court. Similarly, the solicitor must not indicate the agreement with information that the prosecution puts forward which the solicitor knows to be false...

2. It is an implied term of the retainer that the advocate is free to present the client's case at the trial or hearing in such a way as he or she considers appropriate. If the client's express instructions do not permit the solicitor to present the case in a manner which the solicitor considers to be the most appropriate, then unless the instructions are varied, the solicitor may withdraw from the case after seeking the approval of the court to that course, but without disclosing matters which are protected by the client's privilege.

3. If the client instructs the solicitor that he or she is not guilty, the solicitor must put before the court the client's defence, even if the client decides not to give evidence and must, in any event, put the prosecution to proof. Whilst a solicitor may present a technical defence which is available to the client, he or she must never fabricate a defence on the facts.

4. In general, there is no duty upon a solicitor to enquire in every case as to whether the client is telling the truth. However, where instructions or other information are such as should put the solicitor upon enquiry, he or she must, where practicable, check the truth of what the client says to the extent that such statements will be relied upon before the court, or in pleadings or affidavits.

5. Where, prior to the commencement or during the course of the proceedings, a client admits to the solicitor that he or she is guilty of the charge, the solicitor must decline to act in the proceedings if the client insists on giving evidence in the witness box in denial of guilt or requires the making of a statement asserting his or her innocence. The advocate who acts for a client who has admitted guilt but has pleaded not guilty (as the client entitled), is under a duty to put the

prosecution to proof of its case and may submit that there is insufficient evidence to justify a conviction. Further, the advocate may advance any defence open to the client, other than protesting the client's innocence or suggesting, expressly or by implication, that someone other than the client committed the offence.

6. If, either before or during the course of proceedings, the client makes statements to the solicitor which are inconsistent, this is not of itself a ground for the solicitor to refuse to act further on behalf of the client. Only where it is clear that the client is attempting to put forward false evidence to the court should the solicitor cease to act. In other circumstances, it would be for the court, and not the solicitor, to assess the truth or otherwise of the client's statement.

7. If the client wishes to plead guilty, but at the same time asserts the truth of facts which, if true, would or could lead to an acquittal, the solicitor should use his or her best endeavours to persuade the client to plead not guilty. However, if the client insists on pleading guilty, despite being advised that such a plea may or will restrict the ambit of any plea in mitigation or appeal, then the solicitor is not prevented from continuing to act in accordance with the client's instructions, doing the best he or she can. The solicitor will not, in mitigation, be entitled to suggest that the facts are such that the ingredients of the offence have not been established."

Annex 21A

Law Society's Code for Advocacy

PART I—INTRODUCTION

11–27 1.1 For the purpose of maintaining the proper and efficient administration of justice this Code sets out the principles and standards to be observed by all solicitor advocates when acting as such. These obligations are in addition to and do not replace those imposed by law or required by other Law Society rules.

1.2 In this Code except where otherwise indicated:

"the Act" means the Courts and Legal Services Act 1990 and where the context permits includes any orders or regulations made pursuant to powers conferred thereby;

"advocacy services" means advocacy services as defined in section 119 of the Act;

"advocate" means an authorised advocate as defined in section 119 of the Act;

"brief" means instructions to an advocate to appear in person at or before a court;

"client" means the lay client and also (in the case of an advocate with a professional intermediary) the professional client and where the context permits includes a prospective client;

"court" means:

   (i) any court of record (the House of Lords, the Court of Appeal, the High Court, the Crown Court, county courts, magistrates' courts, coroners' courts);

  (ii) any tribunal which the Council on Tribunals is under a duty to keep under review;

 (iii) any court martial; and

 (iv) a statutory inquiry within the meaning of section 19(1) of the Tribunals and Inquiries Act 1971;

"litigator" means an authorised litigator as defined in section 119 of the Act;

"member" in relation to any authorised body means a member as defined in section 119 of the Act;

"rules of conduct" means rules of conduct as defined in section 27(9) of the Act.

PART II—FUNDAMENTAL PRINCIPLES

11–28 2.1 Advocates must not:

(a) engage in conduct whether in pursuit of their profession or otherwise which is:

  (i) dishonest or otherwise discreditable to an advocate;
  (ii) prejudicial to the administration of justice; or
  (iii) likely to diminish public confidence in the legal profession or the administration of justice or otherwise bring the legal profession into disrepute;

(b) engage directly or indirectly in any occupation if their association with that occupation may adversely affect the reputation of advocates or prejudice their ability to attend properly to the interests of clients.

2.2 Advocates have an overriding duty to the court to ensure in the public interest that the proper and efficient administration of justice is achieved: they must assist the court in the administration of justice and must not deceive or knowingly or recklessly mislead the court.

2.3 Advocates:

(a) must promote and protect fearlessly and by all proper and lawful means the clients' best interests and do so without regard to their own interests or to any consequences to themselves or to any other person (including professional clients or fellow advocates or members of the legal profession);

(b) subject only to compliance with the specific provisions of Legal Aid Regulations owe their primary duty:

  (i) as between their lay client and their professional client; and
  (ii) as between the legal aid authorities and the lay client,

  to the lay client and must not permit the legal aid authorities or professional clients to limit their discretion as to how the interests of the lay client can best be served;

(c) must act towards clients at all times in good faith.

2.4.1 Advocates must not in relation to any other person (including a client or another advocate) on grounds of race, ethnic origin, gender, religion, sexual orientation or political persuasion treat that person for any purpose less favourably than they would treat other such persons.

2.4.2 Advocates must not decline to accept instructions to act as such:

(a) on grounds relating to the race, colour, ethnic or national origins, creed, gender or sexual orientation of the client;

(b) on the grounds that the nature of the case is objectionable to the advocate or to any section of the public;

(c) on the grounds that the conduct, opinions or beliefs of the client are unacceptable to the advocate or to any section of the public;

(d) on any ground relating to the source of any financial support which may properly be given to the client for the proceedings in question (for example on the grounds that such support will be available under the Legal Aid Act 1988).

2.5 Nothing in this Code is to be taken as requiring an advocate to accept instructions if there are reasonable grounds for the advocate to consider that having regard to:

(i) the circumstances of the case;

(ii) the nature of the advocate's practice; or

(iii) the advocate's experience and standing;

the advocate is not being offered a proper fee.

2.6 Advocates must not:

(a) permit their absolute independence and freedom from external pressures to be compromised;

(b) do anything (for example accept a present) in such circumstances as may lead to any inference that their independence may be compromised;

(c) compromise their professional standards in order to please their clients, the court or a third party;

(d) except as permitted by the Act, accept a brief on terms that payment of fees shall depend upon or be related to or postponed on account of the outcome of the case or of any hearing.

2.7 Advocates are individually and personally responsible for their own conduct and for professional work: they must exercise their own personal judgment in all their professional activities and must not delegate such responsibility to another advocate.

PART III—ORGANISATION OF THE ADVOCATE'S PRACTICE

11–29 3.1 Advocates must have or have ready access to library facilities which are adequate having regard to the nature of their practice.

3.2 Advocates must take all steps which it is reasonable in the circumstances to take to ensure that:

(a) their practices are administered competently and efficiently and properly staffed having regard to the nature of the practice;

(b) proper records are kept;

(c) all employees and staff in the practice:

(i) carry out their duties in a correct and efficient manner; and
(ii) are made clearly aware of such provisions of this Code as may affect or be relevant to the performance of their duties.

3.3 Advocates may engage in any advertising or promotion in connection with their practice which conforms to the British Code of Advertising Practice (and such advertising or promotion may include photographs or other illustrations of the advocate, statements of rates and methods of charging, statements about the nature and extent of the advocate's services and with that client's express written consent the name of any client) but advertising or promotion must not:

(a) be inaccurate or likely to mislead;

(b) be likely to diminish public confidence in the legal profession or the adminis-tration of justice or otherwise bring the legal profession into disrepute;

(c) make comparison with or criticisms of other advocates;

(d) include statements about the advocate's success rate;

(e) indicate or imply any willingness to accept a brief, or any intention to restrict the persons from whom a brief may be accepted otherwise than in accordance with this Code;

(f) be so frequent or obtrusive as to cause justifiable annoyance to those to whom it is directed.

PART IV—THE DECISION TO APPEAR

11–30 4.1 Advocates must not accept any brief if to do so would cause them to be professionally embarrassed and for this purpose advocates will be professionally embarrassed:

(a) if they lack sufficient experience or competence to handle the matter, or if their experience of advocacy in the relevant court or proceedings has been so infrequent or so remote in time as to prejudice their competence;

(b) if having regard to their other professional commitments they will be unable to do or will not have adequate time and opportunity to prepare that which they are required to do;

(c) if the brief seeks to limit the ordinary authority or discretion of an advocate in the conduct of proceedings in court or to impose on an advocate an obligation to act otherwise than in conformity with the provisions of this Code;

(d) if the matter is one in which they have reason to believe that they are likely to be witnesses or in which, whether by reason of any connection of the advocate (or of any partner or other associate of the advocate) with the client or with the court or a member of it or otherwise, it will be difficult for them to maintain professional independence or the administration of justice might be or appear to be prejudiced;

(e) if they have been responsible for deciding on a course of action and the legality of that action is in dispute in the proceedings; if they are company directors and the company is a party to the proceedings;

(f) if there is or appears to be some conflict or a significant risk of some conflict either between the interests of the advocate (or of any partner or other associ-ate of the advocate) and some other person or between the interests of any one or more of their clients;

(g) if the matter is one in which there is a risk of a breach of confidences entrusted to them (or to any partner or other associate) by another client or where the knowledge which they possess of the affairs of another client would give an undue advantage to the new client.

4.2 Queen's Counsel are not obliged to accept a brief to act without a junior if they consider that the interests of the lay client require that a junior should also be instructed.

4.3.1 Advocates (whether or not they are also litigators and whether they are instructed on their own or with another advocate) must in the case of each brief consider whether consistently with the proper and efficient administration of justice and having regard to:

  (i) the circumstances including the gravity, complexity and likely cost of the case;

 (ii) the nature of their practice;

(iii) their ability, experience and seniority;

(iv) their relationship with the client;

the best interests of the client would be served by instructing or continuing to instruct them in that matter.

4.3.2 Where more than one advocate is instructed in any matter each advocate must in particular consider whether the best interests of the client would be served by:

 (a) the advocate representing the client together with the other advocate or advocates; or

 (b) the advocate representing the client without the other advocate or advocates; or

 (c) the client instructing only the other advocate or advocates; or

 (d) the client instructing some other advocate.

4.3.3 If they consider that the best interests of the client would not be served by their continuing to represent the client (together with any other advocate instructed with them) advocates must immediately advise the lay client accordingly.

PART V—WITHDRAWAL FROM A CASE

11–31   5.1 Advocates must cease to act and return any brief:

 (a) if continuing to act would cause them to be professionally embarrassed within the meaning of paragraph 4.1 provided that if they would be professionally embarrassed only because it appears to them that they are likely to be witnesses on a material question of fact they may retire or withdraw only if they can do so without jeopardising the clients' interests;

 (b) if having accepted a brief on behalf of more than one client there is or appears to be:

    (i) a conflict or a significant risk of a conflict between the interests of any one or more of such clients; or

   (ii) a risk of a breach of confidence;

and the clients do not all consent to them continuing to act;

(c) if in any legally aided case (whether civil or criminal) it has become apparent to them that legal aid has been wrongly obtained by false or inaccurate information and action to remedy the situation is not immediately taken by the client;

(d) if the circumstances set out in Regulation 67 of the Civil Legal Aid (General) Regulations 1989 arise at a time when it is impracticable for the Area Committee to meet in time to prevent an abuse of the Legal Aid Fund;

(e) if the client refuses to authorise them to make some disclosure to the court which their duty to the court requires them to make;

(f) if having become aware during the course of a case of the existence of a document which should have been but has not been disclosed on discovery the client fails forthwith to disclose it,

(g) if having come into possession of a document belonging to another party by some means other than the normal and proper channels and having read it before they realise that it ought to have been returned unread to the person entitled to possession of it they would thereby be embarrassed in the discharge of their duties by their knowledge of the contents of the document provided that they may retire or withdraw only if they can do so without jeopardising the client's interests.

5.2 Advocates may withdraw from a case where they are satisfied that:

(a) the brief has been withdrawn or their retainer terminated;

(b) their professional conduct is being impugned; or

(c) there is some other substantial reason for so doing.

5.3 Advocates must not:

(a) cease to act or return a brief without having first explained to their client their reasons for doing so;

(b) return a brief to another advocate without the consent of the client;

(c) return a brief which they have accepted and for which a fixed date has been obtained or (except with the consent of the client and where appropriate the court) break any other professional engagement so as to enable them to attend a social or non-professional engagement;

(d) save as provided above return any brief or withdraw from a case in such a way or in such circumstances that their client may be unable to find other legal assistance in time to prevent prejudice being suffered by the client.

PART VI—CONDUCT OF WORK: THE CLIENT

11–32   6.1 Advocates:

(a) must in all their professional activities be courteous and act promptly, conscientiously, diligently and with reasonable competence and take all reasonable and practicable steps to avoid unnecessary expense or waste of the court's time and to ensure that professional engagements are fulfilled;

(b) must not undertake any task which:

    (i) they know or ought to know they are not competent to handle;

    (ii) they do not have adequate time and opportunity to prepare for or perform; or

    (iii) they cannot discharge within a reasonable time having regard to the pressure of other work;

(c) must read all briefs delivered to them expeditiously;

(d) must have regard to any relevant written standards adopted by the Law Society for the conduct of professional work;

(e) must inform the client forthwith:

    (i) if it becomes apparent that they will not be able to do the work within a reasonable time after receipt of instructions;

    (ii) if there is an appreciable risk that they may not be able to undertake a brief or fulfil any other professional engagement which they have accepted.

6.2 Whether or not the relation of advocate and client continues, advocates must preserve the confidentiality of their clients' affairs and must not without the prior consent of the client or as permitted by law lend or reveal the contents of the papers in any brief to or communicate to any third person (other than an associate or any of the staff in their practice who need to know it for the performance of their duties) information which has been entrusted to them in confidence or use such information to their clients' detriment or to their own or another client's advantage.

6.3 Advocates must not in relation to any current matter in which they are or have been briefed offer their personal views or opinions to or in any news or current affairs media upon the facts of or the issues arising in that matter.

6.4 Advocates who form the view that there is a conflict of interest between their lay client and their professional client must advise that it would be in the lay client's interest to instruct another professional adviser and such advice must be given either in writing or at a conference at which both the professional client and the lay client are present.

6.5 Advocates must not when interviewing a witness out of court:

(a) place witnesses who are being interviewed under any pressure to provide other than a truthful account of their evidence;

(b) rehearse, practise or coach witnesses in relation to their evidence or the way in which they should give it.

6.6 Advocates must not devise facts which will assist in advancing their client's case and must not draft any originating process, pleading, affidavit, witness statement or notice of appeal containing:

(a) any statement of fact or contention (as the case may be) which is not supported by the client or by their brief or instructions;

(b) any contention which they do not consider to be properly arguable;

(c) any allegation of fraud unless they have clear instructions to make such allegation and have before them reasonably credible material which as it stands establishes a prima facie case of fraud;

(d) in the case of an affidavit or witness statement any statement of fact other than the evidence which in substance according to their instructions the advocate reasonably believes the witness would give if the evidence contained in the affidavit or witness statement were being given *viva voce*;

provided that nothing in this paragraph shall prevent an advocate drafting a pleading, affidavit or witness statement containing specific facts, matters or contentions included by the advocate subject to the client's confirmation as to their accuracy.

PART VII—CONDUCT OF WORK: THE COURT

11–33 7.1 Advocates when conducting proceedings at court:

(a) are personally responsible for the conduct and presentation of their case and must exercise personal judgment upon the substance and purpose of statements made and questions asked;

(b) must not unless invited to do so by the court or when appearing before a tribunal where it is their duty to do so assert a personal opinion on the facts or the law;

(c) must ensure that the court is informed of all relevant decisions and legislative provisions of which they are aware whether the effect is favourable or unfavourable towards the contention for which they argue and must bring any procedural irregularity to the attention of the court during the hearing and not reserve such matter to be raised on appeal;

(d) must not adduce evidence obtained otherwise than from or through their client or devise facts which will assist in advancing their client's case;

(e) must not make statements or ask questions which are merely scandalous or intended or calculated only to vilify, insult or annoy either a witness or some other person;

(f) must if possible avoid the naming in open court of third parties whose character would thereby be impugned;

(g) must not by assertion in a speech impugn a witness whom they have had an opportunity to cross-examine unless in cross-examination they have given the witness an opportunity to answer the allegation;

(h) must not suggest that a witness or other person is guilty of crime, fraud or misconduct or attribute to another person the crime or conduct of which their client is accused unless such allegations go to a matter in issue (including the credibility of the witness) which is material to their client's case and which appear to them to be supported by reasonable grounds.

PART VIII—COMMUNICATIONS WITH CLIENTS

11–34 8.1 Advocates must have proper lines of communications. When instructed by a litigator they are normally entitled to rely on the litigator to communicate with the client. When instructed direct by a representative of the client who is not a litigator, they should ensure that the representative is properly authorised.

8.2 Where there is any reason to doubt the propriety of any action or proposed course of action, advocates should satisfy themselves that the client has received and understood any warnings or advice which it may be appropriate to offer. Where the client is a public or corporate body, this duty may include ensuring that the council, the board of directors, the governing body or others in positions of like authority have received the warnings or advice and that consequent instructions have their approval.

Annex 1B

Solicitors' Anti-Discrimination Rule 1995

11–35 *Rule dated January 18, 1995 made by the Council of the Law Society with the concurrence of the Master of the Rolls under section 31 of the Solicitors Act 1974 and section 9 of the Administration of Justice Act 1985, regulating the professional conduct of solicitors and recognised bodies in England and Wales.*

(1) Solicitors must not discriminate on grounds of race, sex or sexual orientation, and must not discriminate unfairly or unreasonably on grounds of disability, in their professional dealings with clients, staff, other solicitors, barristers or other persons.

(2) Principal solicitors in private practice must operate a policy dealing with the avoidance of such discrimination, and solicitors with management responsibilities in employed practice must use reasonable endeavours to secure the operation of such a policy.

(3) Principal solicitors in private who have not developed and adopted their own policy dealing with the avoidance of such discrimination will be deemed to have adopted the model anti-discrimination policy for the time being promoted for such purposes by the Law Society.

(4) Paragraph (1) applies to a recognised body as it applies to a solicitor, and paragraphs (2) and (3) apply to a recognised body as they apply to a principal solicitor in private practice.

(5) This rule comes into force on July 18, 1995.

B. PROFESSIONAL DUTIES OF A BARRISTER

11–36 The following paragraphs are reproduced from the Code of Conduct of the Bar of England and Wales adopted by the Bar Council in January 1990, with amendments effective from October 22, 1990, March 12, 1994, March 16, 1991 and September 1994. The amendment made in September 1994 is especially significant in that recognition is specifically given to the victim of a criminal offence. The Code came into force on March 31, 1990. This comprehensive revised Code was adopted in anticipation of the Courts and Legal Services Act 1990, which came into force on November 1, 1990. On September 24, 1997 the Professional Conduct and Complaints Committee of the Bar Council issued guidance as to the duties of counsel in relation to the preparation of defence statements pursuant to the Criminal Procedure and Investigations Act 1996. This is reproduced in §11–68, below. As with the guidelines for solicitors only the paragraphs which are relevant to the preparation of cases and the appearance in the magistrates' court are reproduced in full. The paragraph numbers refer to the original Code, although cross-headings are added to assist easy reference to the points in issue.

"Part I—Preliminary

11–37 101.1 This Code (which save as provided in §1001 replaces all earlier Codes) was adopted by the Bar Council on January 27, 1990 and save as provided in §1002 will come into force on March 31, 1990.

101.2 Amendments and additions to this Code may be made by Resolution of the Bar Council which shall be operative upon such date as the Resolution shall appoint. Amendments and additions will be published from time to time in such manner as the Bar Council may determine.

GENERAL PURPOSE OF THE CODE

11–38   102 The general purpose of this Code is to provide the standards of conduct on the part of barristers which are appropriate in the interests of justice in England and Wales (and so far as applicable elsewhere) and in particular:

(a) in relation to barristers in independent practice to provide common and enforceable requirements and prohibitions which together preserve and enhance the strength and competitiveness of the independent Bar as a whole in the public interest by requiring such barristers:

   (i) to be completely independent in conduct and in professional standing as sole practitioners;

  (ii) to act only as consultants instructed by solicitors and other approved professional persons;

 (iii) to acknowledge a public obligation based on the paramount need for access to justice to act for any client (whether legally aided or not) in cases within his field of practice;

(b) in relation to employed barristers to make appropriately similar provision taking into account the fact that such barristers are employed to provide legal services to and may therefore act only on behalf of their employer."

"Part II—Fundamental Principles

APPLICABLE TO ALL BARRISTERS

11–39   201 A barrister must have regard to paragraph 102 and must not:

(a) engage in conduct whether in pursuit of his profession or otherwise which is:

   (i) dishonest or otherwise discreditable to a barrister;

  (ii) prejudicial to the administration of justice; or

 (iii) likely to diminish public confidence in the legal profession or the administration of justice or otherwise bring the legal profession into disrepute;

(b) engage directly or indirectly in any occupation if his association with that occupation may adversely affect the reputation of the Bar or in the case of a practising barrister prejudice his ability to attend properly to the interests of his clients.

NOTE: A barrister employed by the Crown Prosecution Service ought not to rely on policy considerations of the Service nor on recommendations of a Working Group on Pre-Trial Issues to avoid fundamental duties of assisting the court in the administration of justice (*R. v. Highbury Corner Magistrates' Court, ex p. O'Donoghue* (1997) 161 J.P. 217). In that case the Lord Chief Justice stated, *obiter*, in the course of judicial review proceedings, that the CPS were at fault in failing to comply with an order of a magistrates' court for reasons connected with "policy considerations" for pre-trial preparation.

APPLICABLE TO PRACTISING BARRISTERS

11–40 202 A practising barrister has an overriding duty to the Court to ensure in the public interest that the proper and efficient administration of justice is achieved; he must assist the Court in the administration of justice and must not deceive or knowingly or recklessly mislead the Court.

203 A practising barrister:

(a) must promote and protect fearlessly and by all proper and lawful means his lay client's best interests and do so without regard to his own interests or to any consequences to himself or to any other person (including his professional client or fellow members of the legal profession);

(b) subject only to compliance with the specific provisions of Legal Aid Regulations owes his primary duty:

(i) as between his lay client and his professional client; and
(ii) as between the Legal Aid Fund and his lay client;

to his lay client and must not permit the Legal Aid Fund or his professional client to limit his discretion as to how the interests of his lay client can be best served;

(c) must act towards his lay client and his professional client at all times in good faith.

204 A practising barrister must not in relation to any other person (including a lay client or a professional client or another barrister or a pupil or a student member of an Inn of Court) on grounds of race, ethnic origin, sex, religion or political persuasion treat that person for any purposes less favourably than he would treat other such persons.

205 A practising barrister must not:

(a) permit his absolute independence, integrity and freedom from external pressures to be compromised;

(b) do anything (for example, accept a present) in such circumstances as may lead to any inference that his independence may be compromised;

(c) compromise his professional standards in order to please his client the court or a third party.

206 A practising barrister is individually and personally responsible for his own conduct and for his professional work: he must exercise his own personal judgment in all his professional activities and must not if he is a barrister in independent practice delegate such responsibility to another barrister or agree to assume responsibility for the professional work of another barrister.

207 A practising barrister must not:

(a) enter into a professional partnership with another barrister or enter into a professional partnership or any other form of unincorporated association with any person other than a barrister;

(b) be a member of a firm or be employed or engaged by any person, firm or company which is either wholly or in part a device whereby the barrister himself (with or without others) is intended directly or indirectly to supply legal services to the public or a section of the public;

(c) have a seat in the office of any person (other than his employer in the case of an employed barrister) entitled to instruct him;

(d) give a commission or present or lend any money for any professional purpose to or save as a fee in accordance with the provisions of this Code accept any money by way of loan or otherwise from any person (other than his employer in the case of an employed barrister) entitled to instruct him.

APPLICABLE TO BARRISTERS IN INDEPENDENT PRACTICE

11–41   208 A barrister in independent practice must make his practice in England and Wales or in the Courts of the European Community his primary occupation and must hold himself out as being and must be willing at all times in return for the payment of fees to render legal services to the public generally in England and Wales.

209 A barrister in independent practice must comply with the "Cab-rank rule" and accordingly except only as otherwise provided in paragraphs 501, 502 and 503 he must in any field in which he professes to practise in relation to work appropriate to his experience and seniority and irrespective of whether his client is paying privately or is legally aided or otherwise publicly funded:

(a) accept any brief to appear before a court in which he professes to practise;

(b) accept any instructions;

(c) act for any person on whose behalf he is briefed or instructed;

and do so irrespective of (i) the party on whose behalf he is briefed or instructed (ii) the nature of the case and (iii) any belief or opinion which he may have formed as to the character reputation cause conduct guilt or innocence of that person.

210 A barrister in independent practice whether or not he is acting for a fee:

(a) may supply legal services only if he is briefed or instructed by a professional client;

(b) must not when acting in a professional capacity enter into contractual relations relating to the services to be provided by him with any person other than his professional client;

provided that a barrister may without the intervention of a professional client accept a brief or instructions with or without fee directly from and represent another barrister on that other barrister's appeal as to his fees before a taxing master.

211 Except as permitted by the Act a barrister in independent practice must not accept a brief or instructions on terms that payment of fees shall depend upon or be related to or postponed on account of the outcome of the case or of any hearing."

Part III—Barristers in Independent Practice

FEES AND REMUNERATION

11–42 308 A barrister in independent practice may charge for any work undertaken by him (whether or not it involves an appearance in court) on any basis or by any method he thinks fit which does not infringe paragraph 211 but must not represent any person authority or organisation for a fixed salary or at a fixed fee for advising or otherwise acting over a fixed period irrespective of the amount of work he does provided that a barrister may accept a brief to conduct a list of cases in any Court on the basis of a single agreed fee for a session or half-session.

309.1 A barrister in independent practice who receives fees in respect of work done by another barrister must himself and without delegating the responsibility to anyone else forthwith pay the whole of the fee in respect of that work to that other barrister.

309.2 A barrister in independent practice who arranges for another barrister to undertake work on his behalf (other than a person who has asked to do the work in order to increase his own skill or experience) must himself and without delegating the responsibility to anyone else:

(a) pay proper financial remuneration for the work done;

(b) make payment within a reasonable time and if possible within three months after the work has been done unless otherwise agreed in advance with the other barrister.

Part V—Briefs and Instructions to Practising Barristers

Acceptance of briefs and instructions and application of the "Cab-rank Rule"

11–43 501 A practising barrister must not accept any brief or instructions if to do so would cause him to be professionally embarrassed and for this purpose a barrister will be professionally embarrassed:

(a) if he lacks sufficient experience or competence to handle the matter;

(b) if having regard to his other professional commitments he will be unable to do or will not have adequate time and opportunity to prepare that which he is required to do;

(c) if the brief or instructions seek to limit the ordinary authority or discretion of a barrister in the conduct of proceedings in Court or to impose on a barrister an obligation to do any excepted work (except as permitted by the Overseas Practice Rules or in the case of an employed barrister by paragraph 405) or to act otherwise than in conformity with the provisions of this Code;

(d) if the matter is one in which he has reason to believe that he is likely to be a witness or in which whether by reason of any connection of his with the client or with the Court or a member of it or otherwise it will be difficult for him to maintain professional independence or the administration of justice might be or appear to be prejudiced;

(e) if there is or appears to be some conflict or a significant risk of some conflict either between the interests of the barrister and some other person or between the interest of any one or more of his clients;

(f) if the matter is one in which there is a risk of a breach of confidences entrusted to him by another client or where the knowledge which he possesses of the affairs of another client would give an undue advantage to the new client;

(g) if he is a barrister in independent practice in a privately funded matter if the brief or instructions are delivered by a solicitor or firm of solicitors in respect of whom a Withdrawal of Credit Direction has been issued by the Chairman of the Bar pursuant to the Terms of Work on which Barristers Offer their Services to Solicitors and the Withdrawal of Credit Scheme 1988 unless the brief or instructions are accompanied by payment of an agreed fee or the barrister agrees in advance to accept no fee for such work or has obtained the consent of the Chairman of the Bar;

(h) if he is a barrister in independent practice in a Direct Professional Access matter or an Overseas matter unless he has previously informed BMIF that he intends to accept Direct Professional Access work or Overseas work (as the case may be) and has paid the appropriate insurance premium.

NOTE: This part of the Code has been the subject of judicial comment. The words "appear to be prejudiced" in 501(d) and "risk" in 501(e) were emphasised by the Court of Appeal in *R. v. Dann* [1997] Crim.L.R. 46. In that case the Court of Appeal (Criminal Division) considered that such emphasis was necessary when considering whether breaches of the Code bore on the fairness of the proceedings generally. The judgment of the Court went on state that it was essential that barristers and barrister's chambers had procedures for ensuring that instructions would not be accepted where there might be some infringement of the Code. It has also been said that the words "professionally embarrassed" are capable of arising when the receipt of a brief late will entail an inability to grasp submissions and lead to embarrassing pauses during oral argument (*Antonelli and Others v. Wade Grey Farr (a Firm), The Times,* December 29, 1992). In that case the order of the trial judge to make a Wasted Costs Order against counsel who had accepted the late brief was quashed on appeal.

502 A barrister in independent practice is not obliged to accept a brief or instructions:

(a) requiring him to do anything other than during the course of his ordinary working year;

(b) other than at a fee which is proper having regard to the complexity, length and difficulty of the case and to his ability experience and seniority; and any instructions or brief in a legally aided matter shall for this purpose be deemed to be at a proper professional fee;

(c) if the expenses which will be incurred are likely to be unreasonably high in relation to the fee likely to be paid and are not to be paid additionally to such fee;

(d) save in the case of legal aid work:

    (i) unless and until his fees are agreed;

    (ii) if having required his fees to be paid before he accepts the brief or instructions to which the fees relate those fees are not paid;

(e) in a Direct Professional Access matter unless he has previously notified BMIF that he intends to accept Direct Professional Access work and has paid the appropriate insurance premium;

(f) in an overseas matter.

503 A Queen's Counsel in independent practice is not obliged to accept a brief or instructions:

(a) to settle alone any document of a kind generally settled only by or in conjunction with a junior;

(b) to act without a junior if he considers that the interests of the lay client require that a junior should also be instructed.

503A.1 A practising barrister (whether he is instructed on his own or with another advocate) must in the case of each brief and if he is a barrister in independent practice also in the case of all instructions consider whether consistently with the proper and efficient administration of justice and having regard to:

(i) the circumstances (including in particular the gravity complexity and likely cost) of the case;

(ii) the nature of his practice;

(iii) his ability experience and seniority; and

(iv) his relationship with his client;

the best interests of the client would be served by instructing or continuing to instruct him in that matter.

503A.2 Where more than one advocate is instructed in any matter each barrister must in particular consider whether the best interests of the client would be served by:

(a) his representing the client together with the other advocate or advocates; or

(b) his representing the client without the other advocate or advocates; or

(c) the client instructing only the other advocate or advocates; or

(d) the client instructing some other advocate.

503A.3 Unless he considers that the best interests of the client would be served by his continuing to represent the client (together with any other advocate instructed with him) a barrister must immediately advise the client accordingly.

WITHDRAWAL FROM A CASE AND RETURN OF BRIEF OR INSTRUCTIONS

11–44 504 A practising barrister must cease to act and if he is a barrister in independent practice must return any brief or instructions:

(a) if continuing to act would cause him to be professionally embarrassed within the meaning of paragraph 501, provided that if he would be professionally embarrassed only because it appears to him that he is likely to be a witness on a material question of fact he may retire or withdraw only if he can do so without jeopardising his client's interests;

(b) if having accepted a brief or instructions on behalf of more than one client there is or appears to be:

(i) a conflict or a significant risk of a conflict between the interests of any one or more of such clients; or

(ii) a risk of a breach of confidence;

and the clients do not all consent to him continuing to act;

(c) if in any legally aided case (whether civil or criminal) it has become apparent to him that legal aid has been wrongly obtained by false or inaccurate information and action to remedy the situation is not immediately taken by his client;

(d) if the circumstances set out in Regulation 67 of the Civil Legal Aid (General) Regulations 1989 arise at a time when it is impracticable for the Area Committee to meet in time to prevent an abuse of the Legal Aid Fund;

(e) if the client refuses to authorise him to make some disclosure to the court which his duty to the court requires him to make;

(f) if having become aware during the course of a case of the existence of a document which should have been but has not been disclosed on discovery the client fails forthwith to disclose it;

(g) if having come into possession of a document belonging to another party by some means other than the normal and proper channels and having read it before he realises that it ought to have been returned unread to the person entitled to possession of it he would thereby be embarrassed in the discharge of his duties by his knowledge of the contents of the document provided that he may retire or withdraw only if he can do so without jeopardising his client's interests.

11–45 505 Subject to paragraph 506 a practising barrister may withdraw from a case where he is satisfied that:

(a) his brief or instructions have been withdrawn;

(b) his professional conduct is being impugned; or

(c) there is some other substantial reason for so doing.

506 A practising barrister must not:

(a) cease to act or return a brief or instructions without having first explained to his professional client his reasons for doing so;

(b) return a brief or instructions to another barrister without the consent of his professional client or his representative;

(c) if he is a barrister in independent practice return a brief which he has accepted and for which a fixed date has been obtained or (except with the consent of his lay client and where appropriate the Court) break any other professional engagement so as to enable him to attend a social or non-professional engagement;

(d) except as provided in paragraph 504 return any brief or instructions or withdraw from a case in such a way or in such circumstances that his client may be unable to find other legal assistance in time to prevent prejudice being suffered by the client."

NOTE: This part of the Code has been the subject of judicial comment. In his judgment in *R. v. Sutton Justices, ex p. D.P.P.* [1992] 2 All E.R. 129, Brooke J. stated that the Code of Conduct imposed a personal responsibility on counsel who accepted the brief and members of the Criminal Bar should recognise that they had this personal responsibility if they were to avoid disciplinary complaints against them.

In particular paragraphs 505 and 506, which dealt with the withdrawal by counsel from a case, and the late return of briefs, ought to be clearly understood by every barrister who holds himself out to practise in the criminal courts and by his or her clerk. He added that if lay justices or indeed any court are concerned that arrangements for the late return of a brief has led to a problem it is open to them to send a complaint to the Professional Conduct Committee of the Bar Council. Unless complaints are made there is no effective way of ensuring that causes of difficulty in justices' courts can be mitigated.

The substantive principles of the case are discussed at §2–33, above). It concerned the premature dismissal of an information by justices when counsel instructed for the prosecution was late in arriving at court. This had occurred in part because the clerk to counsel originally instructed returned the brief to a clerk in another set of chambers who did not ensure that the new counsel was aware of his obligations until it was too late for him to attend court on time. The Divisional Court decided on the facts that the justices had been wrong to dismiss the informations, but Brooke J. drew attention to the Code of Conduct in assisting justices to understand the professional standards required from lawyers appearing in their courts.

Part VI—Conduct of Work by Practising Barristers

GENERAL

11–46   601 A practising barrister:

(a) must in all his professional activities be courteous and act promptly conscientiously diligently and with reasonable competence and take all reasonable and practicable steps to avoid unnecessary expense or waste of the Court's time and to ensure that professional engagements are fulfilled;

(b) must not undertake any task which:

  (i) he knows or ought to know he is not competent to handle;

  (ii) he does not have adequate time and opportunity to prepare for or perform; or

  (iii) he cannot discharge within a reasonable time having regard to the pressure of other work;

(c) must read all briefs and instructions delivered to him expeditiously;

(d) must have regard to the relevant Written Standards for the conduct of Professional Work (reproduced in Annex H);

(e) must inform his professional client forthwith and subject to paragraph 506 return the instructions or brief to the professional client or to another barrister acceptable to the professional client:

  (i) if it becomes apparent to him that he will not be able to do the work within a reasonable time after receipt of instructions;

  (ii) if there is an appreciable risk that he may not be able to undertake a brief or fulfil any other professional engagement which he has accepted.

602 [Not printed.]

Confidentiality

11–47   603 Whether or not the relation of counsel and client continues a practising barrister must preserve the confidentiality of his lay client's affairs and must not, without the prior consent of his lay client or as permitted by law, lend or reveal the contents of the papers in any brief or instructions to or communicate to any third person (other than a devil, his pupil or any of the staff of his chambers who need to know it for the performance of their duties) information which has been entrusted to him in confidence or use such information to his lay client's detriment or to his own or another client's advantage.

Media comment

11–48   604 A practising barrister must not in relation to any current matter:

(i) in which if he is a barrister in independent practice he is or has been briefed or instructed; or

(ii) in which if he is an employed barrister he is to appear or has appeared as an advocate;

comment to or in any news or current affairs media upon the facts of or the issues arising in the matter.

Conflicts between professional and lay clients

11–49   605 If a barrister in independent practice forms the view that there is a conflict of interest between his lay client and his professional client he must advise that it would be in the lay client's interest to instruct another professional adviser and such advice must be given either in writing or at a conference at which both the professional client and the lay client are present.

Contact with witnesses

11–50   607 A practising barrister must not out of Court:

(a) place a witness under any pressure to provide other than a truthful account of his evidence;

(b) rehearse, practise or coach a witness in relation to his evidence or the way in which he should give it.

Conduct at court

11–51   608 Provided that he is satisfied that the interests of the lay client and the interests of justice will not be prejudiced, a practising barrister to whom a brief has been delivered may agree with his professional client that attendance by the professional client and his representative may be dispensed with for all or part of any hearing:

(a) in a Magistrates' Court or a county court;

(b) provided that he has been supplied with any necessary proofs of evidence in any other Court.

609 Notwithstanding that neither his professional client nor his representative is present a practising barrister who has been briefed in a case may:

(a) if the attendance of his professional client has been dispensed with pursuant to paragraph 608; or

(b) if he arrives at Court and neither the professional client nor his representative is in attendance and there are no other grounds on which to request an adjournment and no practicable alternative;

conduct the case on behalf of the lay client and if necessary interview witnesses and take proofs of evidence.

610 A practising barrister when conducting proceedings at Court:

(a) is personally responsible for the conduct and presentation of his case and must exercise personal judgment upon the substance and purpose of statements made and questions asked;

(b) must not unless invited to do so by the Court or when appearing before a tribunal where it is his duty to do so assert a personal opinion of the facts or the law;

(c) must ensure that the Court is informed of all relevant decisions and legislative provisions of which he is aware whether the effect is favourable or unfavourable towards the contention for which he argues and must bring any procedural irregularity to the attention of the Court during the hearing and not reserve such matter to be raised on appeal;

(d) must not adduce evidence obtained otherwise than from or through his professional client or devise facts which will assist in advancing his lay client's case;

(e) must not make statements or ask questions which are merely scandalous or intended or calculated only to vilify, insult or annoy either a witness or some other person;

(f) must if possible avoid the naming in open Court of third parties whose character would thereby be impugned;

(g) must not by assertion in a speech impugn a witness whom he has had an opportunity to cross-examine unless in cross-examination he has given the witness an opportunity to answer the allegation;

"(h) must not suggest that a victim, witness or any other person guilty of crime, fraud or misconduct or make any defamatory aspersion on he conduct of any other person or attribute to another person the crime or conduct of which his lay client is accused unless such allegations go to a matter in issue (including the credibility of the witness) which is material to his lay client's case and which appear to him to be supported by reasonable grounds."

ANNEX H

Written Standards for the Conduct of Professional Work

(i) *General standards*

INTRODUCTION

11–52 1.1 These Standards are intended as a guide to the way in which a barrister should carry out his work. They consist in part of matters which are dealt with expressly in the Code of Conduct and in part of statements of good practice. They must therefore be read in conjunction with the Code of Conduct, and are to be taken into account in determining whether or not a barrister has committed a disciplinary offence. They apply to employed barristers as well as to barristers in independent practice, except where this would be inappropriate. In addition to these General Standards, there are Standards which apply specifically to the conduct of criminal cases.

GENERAL

11–53 2.1 The work which is within the ordinary scope of a barrister's practice consists of advocacy, drafting pleadings and other legal documents and advising on questions of law. A barrister acts only on the instructions of a professional client, and does not carry out any work by way of the management, administration or general conduct of a lay client's affairs, nor the management, administration or general conduct of litigation nor the receipt or handling of clients' money.

2.2 It is a fundamental principle which applies to all work undertaken by a barrister that a barrister is under a duty to act for any client (whether legally aided or not) in cases within his field of practice. The rules which embody this principle and the exceptions to it are set out in paragraphs 203, 501, 502 and 503 of the Code of Conduct.

ACCEPTANCE OF WORK

11–54 3.1 As soon as practicable after receipt of any brief or instructions a barrister should satisfy himself that there is no reason why he ought to decline to accept it.

3.2 A barrister is not considered to have accepted a brief or instructions unless he has had an opportunity to consider it and has expressly accepted it.

3.3 A barrister should always be alert to the possibility of a conflict of interests. If the conflict is between the interests of his lay client and his professional client, the conflict must be resolved in favour of the lay client. Where there is a conflict between the lay client and the Legal Aid Fund, the conflict must be resolved in favour of the lay client, subject only to compliance with the provisions of the Legal Aid Regulations.

3.4 If after a barrister has accepted a brief or instructions on behalf of more than one lay client, there is or appears to be a conflict or a significant risk of a conflict between the interests of any one or more of such clients, he must not continue to act for any client unless all such clients give their consent to his so acting.

3.5 Even if there is no conflict of interest, when a barrister has accepted a brief or instructions for any party in any proceedings, he should not accept a brief or instructions in respect of an appeal or further stage of the proceedings for any other party without obtaining the prior consent of the original client.

3.6 A barrister must not accept any brief or instructions if the matter is one in which he has reason to believe that he is likely to be a witness. If, however, having accepted a brief or instructions, it later appears that he is likely to be a witness in the case on a material question of fact, he may retire or withdraw only if he can do so without jeopardising his client's interests.

3.7 A barrister should not appear as a barrister:

(a) in any matter in which he is a party or has a significant pecuniary interest;

(b) either for or against any local authority, firm or organisation of which he is a member or in which he has directly or indirectly a significant pecuniary interest;

(c) either for or against any company of which he is a director, secretary or officer or in which he has directly or indirectly a significant pecuniary interest.

3.8 Apart from cases in which there is a conflict of interests, a barrister must not accept any brief or instructions if to do so would cause him to be otherwise professionally embarassed: paragraph 501 of the Code of Conduct sets out the general principles applicable to such situations.

WITHDRAWAL FROM A CASE AND RETURN OF BRIEF OR INSTRUCTIONS

11–55   4.1 When a barrister has accepted a brief for the defence of a person charged with a serious criminal offence, he should so far as reasonably practicable ensure that the risk of a conflicting professional engagement does not arise.

4.2 The circumstances in which a barrister must withdraw from a case or return his brief or instructions are set out in paragraph 504 of the Code of Conduct; the circumstances in which he is permitted to do so are set out in paragraph 505; the circumstances in which he must not do so are set out in paragraph 506.

CONDUCT OF WORK

11–56   5.1 A barrister must at all times promote and protect fearlessly and by all proper and lawful means his lay client's best interests.

5.2 A barrister must assist the Court in the administration of justice and, as part of this obligation and the obligation to use only proper and lawful means to promote and protect the interests of his client, must not deceive or knowingly or recklessly mislead the Court.

5.3 A barrister is at all times individually and personally responsible for his own conduct and for his professional work both in Court and out of Court.

5.4 A barrister must in all his professional activities act promptly, conscientiously, diligently and with reasonable competence and must take all reasonable and practicable steps to ensure that professional engagements are fulfilled. He must not undertake any task which:

(a) he knows or ought to know he is not competent to handle;

(b) he does not have adequate time and opportunity to prepare for or perform; or

(c) he cannot discharge within a reasonable time having regard to the pressure of other work.

5.5 A barrister must at all times be courteous to the Court and to all those with whom he has professional dealings.

5.6 In relation to instructions to advise or draft documents, a barrister should ensure that the advice or document is provided within such time as has been agreed with the professional client, or otherwise within a reasonable time after receipt of the relevant instructions. If it becomes apparent to the barrister that he will not be able to do the work within that time, he must inform his professional client forthwith.

5.7 Generally, a barrister should ensure that advice which he gives is practical, appropriate to the needs and circumstances of the particular client, and clearly and comprehensibly expressed.

5.8 A barrister must exercise his own personal judgment upon the substance and purpose of any advice he gives or any document he drafts. He must not devise facts which will assist in advancing his lay client's case and must not draft any originating process, pleading, affidavit, witness statement or notice of appeal containing:

(a) any statement of fact or contention (as the case may be) which is not supported by his lay client or by his brief or instructions;

(b) any contention which he does not consider to be properly arguable;

(c) any allegation of fraud unless he has clear instructions to make such an allegation and has before him reasonably credible material which as it stands establishes a prima facie case of fraud; or

(d) in the case of an affidavit or witness statement, any statement of fact other than the evidence which in substance according to his instructions, the barrister reasonably believes the witness would give if the evidence contained in the affidavit or witness statement were being given *viva voce*.

5.9 A barrister should be available on reasonable notice for a conference prior to the day of hearing of any case in which he is briefed; and if no such conference takes place then the barrister should be available for a conference on the day of the hearing.

5.10 (The code applicable to "General Standards" here reproduces Code 610A, which may be found in §11–18, above).

5.11 A barrister must take all reasonable and practicable steps to avoid unnecessary expense or waste of the Court's time. He should, when asked, inform the Court of the probable length of his case; and he should also inform the Court of any developments which affect information already provided.

5.12 In Court a barrister's personal appearance should be decorous, and his dress, when robes are worn, should be compatible with them.

WITNESSES

11–57 6.1.1 The rules which define and regulate the barrister's functions in relation to the preparation of evidence and contact with witnesses are set out in paragraphs 501(c), 606, 607, 608, 609, and 901 of the Code of Conduct.

6.1.2 There is no longer any rule which prevents a barrister from having contact with any witness.

6.1.3 In particular, there is no longer any rule in any case (including contested cases in the Crown Court) which prevents a barrister from having contact with a witness whom he may expect to call and examine in chief, with a view to introducing himself to the witness, explaining the court's procedure (and in particular the procedure for giving evidence), and answering any questions on procedure which the witness may have.

6.1.4 It is a responsibility of a barrister, especially when the witness is nervous, vulnerable or apparently the victim of criminal or similar conduct, to ensure that those facing unfamiliar court procedures are put as much at ease as possible.

DISCUSSING THE EVIDENCE WITH WITNESSES

11–58 6.2.1 Different considerations apply in relation to contact with witnesses for the purpose of interviewing them or discussing with them (either individually or together) the substance of their evidence or the evidence of other witnesses.

6.2.2 Although there is no longer any rule which prevents a barrister from having contact with witnesses for such purposes a barrister should exercise his discretion and consider very carefully whether and to what extent such contact is appropriate, bearing in mind in particular that it is not the barrister's function (but that of his professional client) to investigate and collect evidence.

6.2.3 The guiding principle must be the obligation of counsel to promote and protect his lay client's best interests so far as that is consistent with the law and with counsel's overriding duty to the court (Code of Conduct, paragraphs 202, 203).

6.2.4 A barrister should be alert to the risks that any discussion of the substance of a case with a witness may lead to suspicions of coaching, and thus tend to diminish the value of the witness's evidence in the eyes of the court, or may place the barrister in a position of professional embarrassment, for example if he thereby becomes himself a witness in the case. These dangers are most likely to occur if such discussion takes place:

(a) before the barrister has been supplied with a proof of the witness's evidence; or

(b) in the absence of the barrister's professional client or his representative.

A barrister should also be alert to the fact that, even in the absence of any wish or intention to do so, authority figures do subconsciously influence lay witnesses. Discussion of the substance of the case may unwittingly contaminate the witness's evidence.

6.2.5 There is particular danger where such discussions:

(a) take place in the presence of more than one witness of fact; or

(b) involve the disclosure to one witness of fact of the factual evidence of another witness.

6.2.6 Whilst there is no rule that any longer prevents a barrister from taking a witness statement in civil cases (for cases in the Crown Court see below), there is a distinction between the settling of a witness statement and taking a witness statement. Save in exceptional circumstances, it is not appropriate for a barrister who has taken witness statements, as opposed to settling witness statements prepared by others, to act as counsel in that case because it risks undermining the independence of the barrister as an advocate. The cab rank rule does not require a barrister to agree to undertake the task of taking witness statements.

6.2.7 There is no rule which prevents a barrister from exchanging common courtesies with the other side's witnesses. However, a barrister should not discuss the substance of the case or any evidence with the other side's witnesses except in rare and exceptional circumstances and then only with the prior knowledge of his opponent.

CRIMINAL CASES IN THE CROWN COURT (NOT PRINTED)

DOCUMENTS

11–59 7.1 A barrister should not obtain or seek to obtain a document, or knowledge of the contents of a document, belonging to another party other than by means of the normal and proper channels for obtaining such documents or such knowledge.

7.2 If a barrister comes into possession of a document belonging to another party by some means other than the normal and proper channels (for example, if the document has come into his possession in consequence of a mistake or inadvertence by another person or if the document appears to belong to another party, or to be a copy of such a document, and to be privileged from discovery or otherwise to be one which ought not to be in the possession of his professional or lay client) he should:

(a) where appropriate make enquiries of his professional client in order to ascertain the circumstances in which the document was obtained by his professional or lay client; and

(b) unless satisfied that the document has been properly obtained in the ordinary course of events at once return the document unread to the person entitled to possession of it.

7.3.1 If having come into possession of such a document the barrister reads it before he realises that he ought not to, and would be embarrassed in the discharge of his duties by his knowledge of the contents of the document, then provided he can do so without prejudice to his lay client he must return his brief or instructions and explain to his professional client why he has done so.

7.3.2 If, however, to return his brief or instructions would prejudice his lay client (for example, by reason of the proximity of the trial) he should not return his brief or instructions and should, unless the Court otherwise orders, make such use of the document as will be in his client's interests. He should inform his opponent of his knowledge of the document and of the circumstances, so far as known to him, in which the document was obtained and of his intention to use it. In the event of objection to the use of such document it is for the Court to determine what use, if any, may be made of it.

7.4 If during the course of a case a barrister becomes aware of the existence of a document which should have been but has not been disclosed on discovery he should advise his professional client to disclose it forthwith; and if it is not then disclosed, he must withdraw from the case.

ADMINISTRATION OF PRACTICE

11–60 8.1 A barrister must ensure that his practice is properly and efficiently administered in accordance with the provisions of paragraph 303 of the Code of Conduct.

8.2 A barrister should ensure that he is able to provide his professional client with full and proper details of and appropriate justification for fees which have been incurred, and a proper assessment of any work to be done, so that both the lay client and the professional client are able to determine the level of any financial commitment which has been incurred or may be incurred.

(ii) Standards applicable to criminal cases

INTRODUCTION

11–61 10 These standards are to be read together with the General Standards and the Code of Conduct. They are intended as a guide to those matters which specifically relate to practice in the criminal Courts. They are not an alternative to the General Standards, which apply to all work carried out by a barrister. Particular reference is made to those paragraphs in the General Standards relating to the general conduct of a case (5.8), conduct in Court (5.10), discussion with witnesses (6.1, 6.2) and the use of documents belonging to other parties (7.1, 7.2, 7.3), which are not repeated in these standards.

RESPONSIBILITIES OF PROSECUTING COUNSEL

11–62 11.1 Prosecuting counsel should not attempt to obtain a conviction by all means at his command. He should not regard himself as appearing for a party. He should lay before the Court fairly and impartially the whole of the facts which comprise the case for the prosecution and should assist the Court on all matters of law applicable to the case.

11.2 Prosecuting counsel should bear in mind at all times whilst he is instructed that he is responsible for the presentation and general conduct of the case and that it is his duty to ensure that all relevant evidence is either presented by the prosecution or made available to the defence.

11.3 Prosecuting counsel should, when instructions are delivered to him, read them expeditiously and, where instructed to do so, advise or confer on all aspects of the case well before its commencement.

11.4 In relation to cases tried in the Crown Court [omitted].

11.5 Paragraphs 6 to 6.34 of the Written Standards for the Conduct of Professional Work refer.

11.6 Prosecuting counsel should at all times have regard to the report of Mr Justice Farquharson's Committee on the role of Prosecuting Counsel. In particular, he should have regard to the following recommendations of the Farquharson Committee:

(a) Where counsel has taken a decision on a matter of policy with which his professional client has not agreed, it would be appropriate for him to submit to the Attorney-General a written report of all the circumstances, including his reasons for disagreeing with those who instructed him;

(b) When counsel has had an opportunity to prepare his brief and to confer with those instructing him, but at the last moment before trial unexpectedly advises that the case should not proceed or that pleas to lesser offences should be accepted, and his professional client does not accept such advice, counsel should apply for an adjournment if instructed to do so;

(c) Subject to the above, it is for prosecuting counsel to decide whether to offer no evidence on a particular count or on the indictment as a whole and whether to accept pleas to a lesser count or counts.

11.7 It is the duty of prosecuting counsel to assist the Court at the conclusion of the summing-up by drawing attention to any apparent errors or omissions of fact or law.

11.8 In relation to sentence, prosecuting counsel:

(a) should not attempt by advocacy to influence the Court with regard to sentence: if, however, a defendant is unrepresented it is proper to inform the Court of any mitigating circumstances about which counsel is instructed;

(b) should be in a position to assist the Court if requested as to any statutory provisions relevant to the offence or the offender and as to any relevant guidelines as to sentence laid down by the Court of Appeal;

(c) should bring any such matters as are referred to in (b) above to the attention of the Court if in the opinion of prosecuting counsel the Court has erred;

(d) should bring to the attention of the Court any appropriate compensation, forfeiture and restitution matters which may arise on conviction, for example pursuant to sections 35–42 of the Powers of Criminal Courts Act 1973 and the Drug Trafficking Offences Act 1986;

(e) should draw the attention of the defence to any assertion of material fact made in mitigation which the prosecution believes to be untrue: if the defence persist in that assertion, prosecuting counsel should invite the Court to consider requiring the issue to be determined by the calling of evidence in accordance with the decision of the Court of Appeal in *R. v. Newton* (1983) 77 Cr.App.R. 13.

NOTE: The responsibilities of prosecuting counsel in relation to assisting the court as to sentencing powers have been the subject of judicial comment (see particularly *R. v. Komsta and Murphy* (1990) 12 Cr.App.R.(S.) 63, *R. v. Hartley* [1993] Crim.L.R. 230, and *R. v. Brown* [1996] Crim.L.R. 134).

RESPONSIBILITIES OF DEFENCE COUNSEL

11–63 12.1 When defending a client on a criminal charge, a barrister must endeavour to protect his client from conviction except by a competent tribunal and upon legally admissible evidence sufficient to support a conviction for the offence charged. 12.2 A barrister acting for the defence:

(a) should satisfy himself, if he is briefed to represent more than one defendant, that no conflict of interest is likely to arise;

(b) should arrange a conference and if necessary a series of conferences with his professional and lay clients;

(c) should consider whether any enquiries or further enquiries are necessary and, if so, should advise in writing as soon as possible;

(d) should consider whether any witnesses for the defence are required and, if so, which;

(e) should consider whether a Notice of Alibi is required and, if so, should draft an appropriate notice;

(f) should consider whether it would be appropriate to call expert evidence for the defence and, if so, have regard to the rules of the Crown Court in relation to notifying the prosecution of the contents of the evidence to be given;

(g) should ensure that he has sufficient instructions for the purpose of deciding which prosecution witnesses should be cross-examined, and should then ensure that no other witnesses remain fully bound at the request of the defendant and request his professional client to inform the Crown Prosecution Service of those who can be conditionally bound;

(h) should consider whether any admissions can be made with a view to saving time and expense at trial, with the aim of admitting as much evidence as can properly be admitted in accordance with the barrister's duty to his client;

(i) should consider what admissions can properly be requested from the prosecution;

(j) should decide what exhibits, if any, which have not been or cannot be copied he wishes to examine, and should ensure that appropriate arrangements are made to examine them as promptly as possible so that there is no undue delay in the trial.

12.3 A barrister acting for a defendant should advise his lay client generally about his plea. In doing so he may, if necessary, express his advice in strong terms. He must, however, make it clear that the client has complete freedom of choice and that the responsibility for the plea is the client's.

12.4 A barrister acting for a defendant should advise his client as to whether or not to give evidence in his own defence but the decision must be taken by the client himself.

12.5 Where a defendant tells his counsel that he did not commit the offence with which he is charged but nevertheless insists on pleading guilty to it for reasons of his own, counsel must continue to represent him, but only after he has advised what the consequences will be and that what can be submitted in mitigation can only be on the basis that the client is guilty.

CONFESSIONS OF GUILT

11–64 13.1 In considering the duty of counsel retained to defend a person charged with an offence who confesses to his counsel that he did commit the offence charged, it is essential to bear the following points clearly in mind:

(a) that every punishable crime is a breach of common or statute law committed by a person of sound mind and understanding;

(b) that the issue in a criminal trial is always whether the defendant is guilty of the offence charged, never whether he is innocent;

(c) that the burden of proof rests on the prosecution.

13.2 It follows that the mere fact that a person charged with a crime has confessed to his counsel that he did commit the offence charged is no bar to that barrister appearing or continuing to appear in his defence, nor indeed does such a confession release the barrister from his imperative duty to do all that he honourably can for his client.

13.3 Such a confession, however, imposes very strict limitations on the conduct of the defence, a barrister must not assert as true that which he knows to be false. He must not connive at, much less attempt to substantiate, a fraud.

13.4 While, therefore, it would be right to take any objections to the competency of the Court, to the form of the indictment, to the admissibility of any evidence or to the evidence admitted, it would be wrong to suggest that some other person had committed the offence charged, or to call any evidence which the barrister must know to be false having regard to the confession, such, for instance, as evidence in support of an alibi. In other words, a barrister must not (whether by called [*sic*] the defendant or otherwise) set up an affirmative case inconsistent with the confession made to him.

13.5 A more difficult question is within what limits may counsel attack the evidence for the prosecution either by cross-examination or in his speech to the tribunal charged with the decision of the facts. No clearer rule can be laid down than this, that he is entitled to test the evidence given by each individual witness and to argue that the evidence taken as a whole is insufficient to amount to proof that the defendant is guilty of the offence charged. Further than this he ought not to go.

13.6 The foregoing is based on the assumption that the defendant has made a clear confession that he did commit the offence charged, and does not profess to deal with the very difficult questions which may present themselves to a barrister when a series of inconsistent statements are made to him by the defendant before or during the proceedings; nor does it deal with the questions which may arise where statements are made by the defendant which point almost irresistibly to the conclusion that the defendant is guilty but do not amount to a clear confession. Statements of this kind may inhibit the defence, but questions arising on them can only be answered after careful consideration of the actual circumstances of the particular case.

GENERAL

11–65 14.1 Both prosecuting and defence counsel:

(a) should ensure that the listing officer receives in good time their best estimate of the likely length of the trial (including whether or not there is to be a plea of guilty) and should ensure that the listing officer is given early notice of any change of such estimate or possible adjournment;

(b) should take all reasonable and practicable steps to ensure that the case is properly prepared and ready for trial by the time that it is first listed;

(c) should ensure that arrangements have been made in adequate time for witnesses to attend Court as and when required and should plan, so far as possible, for sufficient witnesses to be available to occupy the full Court day;

(d) should, if a witness (for example a doctor) can only attend Court at a certain time during the trial without great inconvenience to himself, try to arrange for that witness to be accommodated by raising the matter with the trial Judge and with his opponent;

(e) should take all necessary steps to comply with the *Practice Direction (Crime: Tape Recording of Police Interviews)* [1989] 1 W.L.R. 631.

VIDEO RECORDINGS

11–66 15.1 When a barrister instructed and acting for the prosecution or the defence of an accused has in his possession a copy of a video recording of a child witness which has been identified as having been prepared to be admitted in evidence at a criminal trial in accordance with section 54 of the Criminal Justice Act 1991, he must have regard to the following duties and obligations:

(a) Upon receipt of the recording, a written record of the date and time and from whom the recording was received must be made and a receipt must be given.

(b) The recording and its contents must be used only for the proper preparation of the prosecution or defence case or of an appeal against conviction and/or sentence, as the case may be, and the barrister must not make or permit any disclosure of the recording or its contents to any person except when, in his opinion, it is in the interests of his proper preparation of that case.

(c) The barrister must not make or permit any other person to make a copy of the recording, nor release the recording to the accused, and must ensure that:

(i) when not in transit or in use, the recording is always kept in a locked or secure place, and:

    (ii) when in transit, the recording is kept safe and secure at all times and is not left unattended, especially in vehicles or otherwise.

(d) Proper preparation of the case may involve viewing the recording in the presence of the accused. If this is the case, viewing should be done:

    (i) if the accused is in custody, only in the prison or other custodial institution where he is being held, in the presence of the barrister and/or his instructing solicitor;

    (ii) if the accused is on bail, at the solicitor's office or in counsel's chambers or elsewhere in the presence of the barrister and/or his instructing solicitor.

(e) The recording must be returned to the solicitor as soon as practicable after the conclusion of the barrister's role in the case. A written record of the date and time despatched and to whom the recording was delivered for despatch must be made.

ATTENDANCE OF COUNSEL AT COURT

11–67 16.1 Prosecuting counsel should be present throughout the trial, including the summing-up and the return of the jury. He may not absent himself without leave of the Court; but, if two or more barristers appear for the prosecution, the attendance of one is sufficient.

16.2.1 Defence counsel should ensure that the defendant is never left unrepresented at any stage of his trial.

16.2.2 Where a defendant is represented by one barrister, that barrister should normally be present throughout the trial and should only absent himself in exceptional circumstances which could not reasonably be expected to foresee and provided that:

(a) he has obtained the consent of the professional client (or his representative) and the lay client; and

(b) a competent deputy takes his place.

16.2.3 Where a defendant is represented by two barristers, neither may absent himself except for good reason and then only when the consent of the professional client (or his representative) and of the lay client has been obtained, or when the case is legally aided and the barrister thinks it necessary to do so in order to avoid unnecessary public expense.

16.2.4 These rules are subject to modification in respect of lengthy trials involving numerous defendants. In such trials, where after the conclusion of the opening speech by the prosecution defending counsel is satisfied that during a specific part of the trial there is no serious possibility that events will occur which will relate to his client, he may with the consent of the professional client (or his representative) and of the lay client absent himself for that part of the trial. He should also inform the judge. In this event it is his duty:

(a) to arrange for other defending counsel to guard the interests of his client;

(b) to keep himself informed throughout of the progress of the trial and in particular of any development which could affect his client; and

(c) not to accept any other commitment which would render it impracticable for him to make himself available at reasonable notice if the interests of his client so require.

16.3.1 If during the course of a criminal trial and prior to final sentence the defendant voluntarily absconds and the barrister's professional client, in accordance with the ruling of the Law Society, withdraws from the case, then the barrister too should withdraw. If the trial judge requests the barrister to remain to assist the Court, the barrister has an absolute discretion whether to do so or not. If he does remain, he should act on the basis that his instructions are withdrawn and he will not be entitled to use any material contained in his brief save for such part as has already been established in evidence before the Court. He should request the trial judge to instruct the jury that this is the basis on which he is prepared to assist the Court.

16.3.2 If for any reason the barrister's professional client does not withdraw from the case, the barrister retains an absolute discretion whether to continue to act. If he does continue, he should conduct the case as if his client were still present in Court but had decided not to give evidence and on the basis of any instruction he has received. He will be free to use any material contained in his brief and may cross-examine witnesses called for the prosecution and call witnesses for the defence.

Preparation of Defence Case Statements

11–68   On September 24, 1997, the Professional Conduct and Complaints Committee of the Bar Council approved guidance as to the duties of counsel in relation to the preparation of defence statements pursuant to the Criminal Procedure and Investigations Act 1996. The guidance is as follows:

1. It is becoming increasingly common for solicitors to instruct counsel to draft or settle defence case statements, required under section 5 of the Criminal Procedure and Investigations Act 1996. Often these instructions are given to counsel with no or little previous involvement in the case shortly before the expiry of the time limit.

(i) the time limit for compliance is short—14 days from service of prosecution material or a statement that there is none; the permitted grounds for an extension of time are limited;

(ii) the contents of the defence case statement are obviously of great importance to the defendant; an inaccurate or inadequate statement of the defence could have serious repercussions for the defendant, if the trial judge permits "appropriate" comment;

(iii) whilst it will the (*sic*) natural instinct of most defence counsel to keep the defence case statement short, a short and anodyne statement may be insufficient to trigger any obligation on the prosecution to give secondary disclosure of prosecution material.

3. Normally it will be more appropriate for instructing solicitors to draft the defence case statement, since typically counsel will have had little involvement at this stage.

4. However, there is nothing unprofessional about counsel drafting or settling a defence case statement, although it must be appreciated that there is no provision in the current regulations for graduated fees allowing for counsel to be paid a separate fee for this work.

11–69   This most unsatisfactory situation (which has arisen, as a result of the 1996 Act, since the graduated fees regulations were negotiated) is being addressed urgently by the Legal Aid and Fees Committee. A barrister has no obligation to accept work for which he will not be paid. The absence of a fee will justify refusal of the instructions by counsel who are not to be retained for the trial and are simply asked to do no more than draft or settle the defence case statement. Where counsel is retained for the trial, rule 502(b) of the Code of Conduct deems instructions in a legally aided matter to be at a proper fee and counsel would not be justified in refusing to draft or settle a defence case statement on the sole ground that there is no separate fee payable for this work.

5. Many members of the Bar will nevertheless feel that, in the interests of their lay client and or of good relations with instructing solicitors, they cannot refuse the work, even where they would otherwise be entitled to do so. Those who do so need to recognise the crucial importance of:

(i) obtaining all prosecution statements and documentary exhibits;

(ii) getting instructions from the lay client, from a properly signed proof and preferably a conference. Those instructions need to explain the general nature of the defence, to indicate the matters on which issue is taken with the prosecution and to give an explanation of the reason for taking issue. They must also give details of any alibi defence, sufficient to give the information required by section 5(7) of the 1996 Act;

(iii) getting statements from other material witnesses;

(iv) ensuring that the client realises the importance of the defence case statement and the potential adverse consequences of an inaccurate or inadequate statement;

(v) getting proper informed approval for the draft from the client. This is particularly important, given the risks of professional embarrassment if the client seeks to disown the statement during the course of the trial, perhaps when the trial is not going well or when under severe pressure in cross-examination. Counsel ought to insist on getting written acknowledgement from the lay client that:

(a) he understands the importance of the accuracy and adequacy of the defence case statement for this case;

(b) he has had the opportunity of considering the contents of the statement carefully and approves it.

This may often mean having a conference with the lay client to explain the defence case statement and to get informed approval, although in straightforward cases where counsel has confidence in the instructing solicitor, this could be left to the solicitor. Where this latter course is taken, a short written advice (which can be in a standard form) as to the importance of obtaining the written acknowledgement before service of the statement should accompany the draft defence case statement. A careful record should be kept of work done and advice given;

(vi) if there is inadequate time, counsel should ask the instructing solicitor to apply for an extension of time. This needs to be considered at a very early stage, since the application must be made before the expiry of the time limit.

6. It follows that counsel ought not to accept any instructions to draft or settle a defence case statement unless given the opportunity and adequate time to gain proper familiarity with the case and to comply with the fundamental requirements set out above. In short there is no halfway house. If instructions are accepted, then the professional obligations on counsel are considerable.

C. Duties and Function of the Clerk

11–70 The principal duties of the clerk of the court are to advise the justices on matters of law, or mixed questions of fact and law and to advise on practice and procedure. In addition, the clerk should assist unrepresented defendants, take notes of evidence and advise on sentence when appropriate and ensure that justices are not prejudiced by the preparation of court lists. These duties are described below.

1. Advice to Justices on Law, Practice and Procedure

11–71 The functions of a justices' clerk include giving advice to the justices to whom he is clerk, at their request about law, practice or procedure on questions arising in connection with the discharge of their functions, including questions arising when the clerk is not personally attending on them (JPA 1997, s.45(4)). In addition, a justices' clerk may, at any time when he thinks he should do so, bring to the attention of those justices any point of law, practice or procedure that is or may be involved in any question so arising (*ibid.*, s.45(5)). The Justices of the Peace Act 1997 is a consolidating statute and the powers referred to repeat exactly those set out in the Justices of the Peace Act 1979, now repealed.

It has been held that these are broad powers because they entitle the justices' clerk himself or herself to give further advice to justices even if those justices have been given advice already by another clerk (*R. v. Sittingbourne Justices, ex p. Stickings and Another* (1996) 160 J.P. 801). It was held in that case that the intervention by the clerk to the justices at a resumed hearing of a summary trial, previously adjourned part-heard, to tender further advice in respect of the justices' ruling earlier was permissible. It was stressed by the Divisional Court that such a course should be regarded as the exception rather than the rule.

The independence of justices' clerks in respect of advice given to justices, which was specifically preserved by the Police and Magistrates' Courts Act 1994, is now to be found in section 48 of the Justices of the Peace Act 1997.

The governing enactment, now consolidated in the 1997 Act, does not define or in any respect limit the powers and duties of a justices' clerk (JPA 1997, s.45(7)(b)), and the judiciary have further defined and explained the clerk's function in practice directions and in cases. The latest and most succinct, *Practice Direction (Justices: Clerk to Court)* [1981] 1 W.L.R. 1163, was given by Lord Lane C.J. and is set out below so far as criminal proceedings are concerned.

11–72

"1. A justices' clerk is responsible to the justices for the performance of any of the functions set out below by any member of his staff acting as court clerk and may be called in to advise the justices even when he is not personally sitting with the justices as clerk to the court.

2. It shall be the responsibility of the justices' clerk to advise the justices as follows:

    (a) on questions of law or of mixed law and fact;
    (b) as to matters of practice and procedure.

3. If it appears to him necessary to do so, or he is so requested by the justices, the justices' clerk has the responsibility to:

    (a) refresh the justices' memory as to any matter of evidence and to draw attention to any issues involved in the matters before the court;
    (b) advise the justices generally on the range of penalties which the law allows

them to impose and on any guidance relevant to the choice of penalty provided by the law, the decisions of the superior courts or other authorities. If no request for advice has been made by the justices, the justices' clerk shall discharge his responsibility in court in the presence of the parties.

4. The way in which the justices' clerk should perform his functions should be stated as follows: (a) The justices are entitled to the advice of their clerk when they retire in order that the clerk may fulfil his responsibility outlined above; (b) Some justices may prefer to take their own notes of evidence. There is, however, no obligation on them to do so. Whether they do so or not, there is nothing to prevent them from enlisting the aid of their clerk and his notes if they are in any doubt as to the evidence which has been given; (c) If the justices wish to consult their clerk solely about the evidence or his notes of it, this should ordinarily and certainly in simple cases be done in open court. The object is to avoid any suspicion that the clerk has been involved in deciding issues of fact."

11–73 The importance of the role of the clerk in the administration of justice, and the need for justice to be seen to be done, has been restated and examined in a number of recent cases. The famous dictum of Lord Hewart C.J. that "justice should not only be done, but should manifestly and undoubtedly be seen to be done" in *R. v. Sussex Justices, ex p. McCarthy* [1924] 1 K.B. 256 was uttered in the context of a case concerning the impartiality of a clerk's advice. More recently, when Lord Hewart's dictum came under scrutiny by the House of Lords in *R. v. Gough* [1993] 2 W.L.R. 883, the judicial role of the clerk in criminal cases in the magistrates' court was explained. The clerk of the court "is part of the judicial process in the magistrates' court" (*per* Lord Woolf, at p. 905) and therefore the clerk himself has a duty to ensure justice is done and that justice is seen to be done.

Because the clerk is part of the judicial process it is wise for a clerk who is required to sit with justices on a particular case to have regard to issues of disqualification and bias which may make participation in that case a denial of justice. These issuses (as they affect justices) are discussed fully in §§5–17 *et seq.*, above. In *R. v. Gough* it was said by their Lordships that whenever such issues affected, or might be seen to affect, a clerk, then that clerk should not sit in case his advice was called for. If in such circumstances his advice was called for, it would be inferred later that the clerk's actual or perceived bias had infected the justices adversely.

11–74 In order to give effect to the principle that justice must be seen to be done the trend in recent years has been for advice on matters of law to be given to justices by the clerk in open court (*R. v. Eccles Justices, ex p. Fitzpatrick* (1989) 89 Cr.App.R. 324), although there is no strict obligation to do so (*R. v. Uxbridge Magistrates' Court, ex p. Smith* (1985) 149 J.P. 620 and *Practice Direction (Justices: Clerk to Court) above*). Indeed the speeches in *R. v. Gough*, above, assumed that the practice was for the clerk to give advice to justices privately if invited to do so (*per* Lord Goff of Chieveley at p. 898). However, the vigilance of the Divisional Court is such that the practice of giving advice privately may lead to the impression that a clerk, however well-intentioned, was participating in the decision-making process (*R. v. Eccles Justices, ex p. Farelly* (1993) 157 J.P. 77). Further difficulties may arise if justices wish to seek the advice of a more senior clerk than the one who was in court after they have retired. If this is the case, it is undesirable that further advice is given without the legal submissions being repeated in that clerk's presence in open court. This is because it is important that fairness to both sides actually takes place, and is seen to take place, in open court (*R. v. Chichester Justices, ex p. D.P.P.* (1993) 157 J.P. 1049).

For these reasons a clerk should never leave his place unless invited to do so (*R. v. East Kerrier Justices, ex p. Mundy* [1952] 2 K.B. 719). It is implicit in the invitation that there is a real and not an obvious point of law involved, and justices themselves have a responsibility not to draw their clerk into discussion unnecessarily (*R. v. Guildford Justices, ex p. Harding* (1981) 145 J.P. 174). Such unnecessary discussion can be avoided if the advice is given in open court and seen to be given. For a recent example of where the Divisional Court has quashed a conviction when the principles stated in this §were not followed see *R. v. Birmingham Magistrates, ex p. Ahmed* [1995] Crim.L.R. 503.

11–75 The superior courts are unlikely to interfere with a decision reached by justices if the principles of openness, discussed above, are followed. However, even if there is no actual unfairness resulting from the actions of the clerk, a conviction is liable to be quashed if there is apparent unfairness. Thus, if a clerk gives a warning to the defendant and his witnesses of the dangers of giving perjured evidence, and such warning is not given also to the prosecutions witnesses, a reasonable and fair-minded person might think the trial was unfair (*R. v. Richmond and Gilling West Magistrates, ex p. Steel* [1993] Crim.L.R. 711).

If a question arises as to whether the participation of a clerk in a case may be challenged, the test is whether there was a real danger, meaning a possibility, of bias, in the sense that the clerk may have regarded with favour or disfavour the case of a party before the court. If the advice of the clerk had been given to justices privately the Divisional Court would be entitled to infer that there was a real danger that the clerk's advice had infected the minds of the justices (*R. v. Gough* [1993] 2 W.L.R. 883).

In this formulation the House of Lords preferred the test in *R. v. Camborne Justices, ex p. Pearce* [1955] 1 Q.B. 41 (the real likelihood test) rather than that propounded by Lord Hewart C.J. in *R. v. Sussex Justices, ex p. McCarthy* [1924] 1 K.B. 256 (the reasonable suspicion test). However, despite the apparent difference between the two tests the House of Lords was of the opinion that there was little difference in reality: "if a reasonable person with the relevant knowledge thinks that there might well be bias, then there is in his opinion a real likelihood of bias" (*per* Lord Goff of Chieveley at p. 901).

2. Taking Notes of Evidence

11–76 The clerk must be in a position to comply with the responsibility to "refresh the justices' memory on any matter of evidence" (see *Practice Direction* at §11–28, above). Because of this obligation it is the invariable practice of the clerk to take a note of at least the most important parts of the proceedings. However, there has not been a formal obligation upon the clerk to do so until very recently. There is now a duty upon the clerk to take a note of full argument in bail applications (MCR 1981, r. 90A, as inserted by the Magistrates' Courts (Miscellaneous Amendments) Rules 1993, r. 3(f)).

If a clerk has taken notes then it has been stated that a reasonable request by a party for a copy of such notes ought not to be refused, but there is no rule of law requiring a clerk to supply them: (*R. v. Clerk to Highbury Corner Justices, ex p. Hussein* (1987) 84 Cr.App.R. 112). If, however, a legal aid order is made in respect of an appeal against conviction to the Crown Court, a clerk must supply a copy of any notes if the solicitor assigned requests them (Legal Aid in Criminal Proceedings (General) Regulations 1968, reg. 16). Under the Magistrates' Courts Rules a clerk must send any notes with documents on a committal for sentence, committal for a Hospital Order with restrictions, or if sentence is remitted to another magistrates' court (MCR 1981, rr. 17, 18 and 19).

3. Assistance to Parties who are Unrepresented

11–77 If a party, whether prosecution or defence, is unrepresented and the party is not competent to examine witnesses, this function may be conducted by the clerk. Although this was always a rule of practice, this duty has now been added to the Magistrates' Courts Rules 1981. If an unrepresented defendant makes assertions instead of asking questions during cross-examination the clerk has a duty to put such assertions in the form of questions in order to bring out or clear up any point arising in those assertions (MCR 1981 r. 13A, as inserted by the Magistrates' Courts (Miscellaneous Amendments) Rules 1993, r. 3(b)).

In the case of a defendant who is unrepresented there is a further duty upon the clerk to ensure that his case is not prejudiced by conduct which might put his bad character in evidence. If such a course is anticipated by the nature of questions asked by an accused in person, the proper course is for the prosecution to ask for a short adjournment so that the clerk may explain to an accused the risk he runs if he persists in the line of questioning (*R. v. Weston-Super-Mare Justices, ex p. Townsend* (1968) 132 J.P. 526).

A further duty to assist an unrepresented defendant arises under section 35 of the Criminal Justice and Public Order Act 1994 where an inference adverse to a defendant may be drawn if he does not give evidence. For this reason there is a particular obligation upon the clerk to ensure that an unrepresented defendant fully understands the consequences of not giving evidence. This matter is fully discussed in §5–63, above.

4. Preparing Court Register Sheets which will not Induce Bias

11–78 Where a particular defendant is due to appear before justices on a number of different and unconnected charges but the Bench are to try him on one of those charges, a clerk should ensure that the court list before the justices does not contain charges other than those on which the court is to adjudicate (*R. v. Liverpool City Justices, ex p. Topping* [1983] 1 W.L.R. 119), but there is no rule of law requiring him to do so (*R. v. Weston-Super-Mare Justices, ex p. Shaw* [1987] Q.B. 640).

5. Assisting in Applications for an Adjournment

11–79 It frequently happens that either the prosecution or the defence apply for the adjournment of a summary trial when justices expect to hear a contested case. Where such application is made by the prosecution, justices can decide the merits of the application with only minimal assistance from the clerk on the principles which generally apply to adjournments (see §§2–26 *et seq.*, above). More difficult problems may arise when the defence apply for an adjournment because the defence have no duty to disclose their case in advance, and therefore a defence advocate may be inhibited from revealing the true reasons for the application in the presence of the prosecution and the Bench who may have to hear the case if an adjournment is refused. In these circumstances it has been held that it is a proper function of the clerk to inquire of the defence, privately, what prejudice will result if an adjournment is refused, and then advise the Bench accordingly (*R. v. Bracknell Justices, ex p. Hughes* (1990) 154 J.P. 46).

Part II

Sentencing

CHAPTER 12

Summary of Sentencing Powers, Ancillary Orders and Procedural Steps in Sentencing

Introduction

12–01   The Criminal Justice Act 1991 and the Powers of Criminal Courts Act 1973 are the principal statutes governing sentencing powers and procedures. This remains the case in 1999 despite the fact that these statutes have themselves been amended by later legislation. In this Chapter references to these Acts do not include references to the amending statute unless such amendments have occurred very recently, namely in Acts passed in 1997 and 1998.

In some cases new sentencing law is made by the creation of specific new powers in separate Acts of Parliament, for example the Restraining Order created by the Protection from Harassment Act 1997. In these instances references are to the Act in question.

The Human Rights Act 1998, which is not yet in force, has the capability of affecting sentencing law and practice and this is discussed separately in Chapter 24, below.

COMMENCEMENT

12–02   Section 5 of the Protection from Harassment Act 1997 (Restraining Orders) came into force on June 16, 1997 (Protection from Harassment Act 1997 (Commencement)(No. 1) Order 1997).

Sections 1–6 of the Sex Offenders Act 1997 (Notification Requirement) came into force on September 1, 1997 (Sex Offenders Act 1997 (Commencement) Order 1997).

Section 2 of the Crime (Sentences) Act 1997 (indictable only Class A drug trafficking offence carrying a minimum sentence) came into force on October 1, 1997 in respect of a fresh offence (but not a previous offence) committed on or after that date (Crime (Sentences) Act 1997 (Commencement No. 2 and Transitional Provisions) Order 1997).

Section 38 of the Crime (Sentences) Act 1997 (abolition of the need to obtain consent or willingness to comply with a community sentence) applies in respect of offences committed on or after October 1, 1997 (Crime (Sentences) Act 1997 (Commencement No. 2 and Transitional Provisions) Order 1997).

Section 37 of the Crime (Sentences) Act 1997 (persistent petty offenders) came into force on January 1, 1998 (*ibid.*).

Section 3 of the Crime (Sentences) Act 1997, as prospectively amended by CDA 1998, s.106 and Sched. 7, para. 49, (indictable only domestic burglary offence carrying a minimum sentence) came into force on September 30, 1998 but will apply only if all offences are committed after that date (Crime and Disorder Act 1998 (Commencement No. 2 and Transitional Provisions) Order 1998).

Section 2 of the Crime and Disorder Act 1998 (Sex Offender Orders) came into force on December 1, 1998 (Magistrates' Courts (Sex Offender and Anti-social Behaviour Orders) Rules 1998), and Crime and Disorder Act 1998 (Commencement No. 2 and Transitional Provisions) Order 1998).

Section 1 of the Crime and Disorder Act 1998 came into force on April 1, 1999 (Magistrates' Courts (Sex Offender and Anti-social Behaviour Orders) Rules 1998), and Crime and Disorder Act 1998 (Commencement No. 3 and Transitional Provisions) Order 1998).

TRANSITIONAL PROVISIONS

12–03   The Crime (Sentences) Act 1997 made a number of amendments to existing legislation. Those affecting magistrates' courts practice included the abolition of the need for the consent of the offender before the making of a Probation Order or a Community Service Order (C(S)A 1997, s.38). This, in turn, required a large number of consequential amendments to pre-existing legislation involving breaches and revocation of community orders. Before most of the 1997 Act was brought into effect Parliament passed the Crime and Disorder Act 1998 which introduced a new community sentence, the Drug Treatment and Testing Order. This change involved a similarly large number of minor and consequential amendments to pre-existing legislation. The effect of two statutes bringing about change to sentencing practice being passed within short periods of time has been complicated. In short, the 1998 Act prospectively amended many of the changes envisaged in the 1997 Act and these were brought into force at various periods during 1998. Unless stated to the contrary (where pilot schemes are in operation) the provisions set out in this Chapter are in force.

A. CUSTODIAL MEASURES

1. Custodial Sentences

(i) Powers

12–04   (a) A court shall not pass a custodial sentence on an offender unless:

(1) the offence, or the combination of the offence and one or more offences associated with it, was so serious that only a custodial sentence can be justified for the offence (CJA 1991, s.1(2)(a)); or

(2) the offence is a violent or sexual offence, and only a custodial sentence would be adequate to protect the public from serious harm from the offender (*ibid.*, s.1(2)(b)); or

Nothing in subsection (2) above shall prevent the court from passing a custodial sentence on an offender if he fails to express his willingness to comply with—

(1) a requirement which is proposed by the court to be included in a probation order [or a supervision order] which requires an expression of such willingness; or

(2) a requirement which is proposed to be included in a drug treatment and testing order under section 61(6) of the Crime and Disorder Act 1998 (CJA 1991, s.1(3)(a) and (b), as amended by CDA 1998, s.119 and Sched. 8, para. 72).

(b) The length of the custodial sentence shall be—

(1) for such term (not exceeding the permitted maximum) as is commensurate with the seriousness of the offence, or the combination of the offence and one or more offences associated with it; or

(2) where the offence is a violent or sexual offence, for such longer term (not exceeding the maximum) as is necessary to protect the public from serious harm from the offender (CJA 1991, s.2(2)(a) and (b)).

(c) The permitted maximum is not more than six months for any one offence (MCA 1980, s.31) or not more than 12 months where two or more offences triable either way are tried summarily with the accused's consent (*ibid.*, s.133).

(d) In considering the seriousness of any offence, the court may take into account any previous convictions of the offender or any failure of his to respond to previous sentences (CJA 1991, s.29(1)).

(e) In considering the seriousness of any offence committed while the offender was on bail, the court shall treat the fact that it was committed in those circumstances as an aggravating factor (*ibid.*, s.29(2)).

(f) The court may take into account any matters which are relevant in mitigation of sentence (*ibid.*, s.28(1)), and in particular nothing shall prevent a court from mitigating any penalty included in a sentence by taking into account any other penalty included in that sentence, nor where an offender is convicted of numerous offences of applying any rule as to the totality of sentences (*ibid.*, s.28(2)(a) and (b)).

DEFINITIONS

12–05   An offence is *associated with* another if (a) the offender is convicted of it in the same proceedings, or (if convicted earlier) is sentenced for it at the same time as the other offence, or (b) he asks for it to be taken into consideration when being sentenced for the other offence (CJA 1991, s.31(2)). This means that an earlier suspended sentence of which the offender is in breach is not an associated offence (*R. v. Crawford* (1993) 14 Cr.App.R.(S.) 782), but an earlier offence for which a conditional discharge was imposed is an associated offence if the offender is in breach and the court passes a sentence in respect of it (*R. v. Godfrey* (1993) 14 Cr.App.R.(S.) 804).

Violent offence means an offence which leads, or is intended to lead, to a person's death or to physical injury to a person and includes arson.

Sexual offence means all offences under the Sexual Offences Act 1956 (except for homosexual acts on merchant ships, living off the earnings of prostitution, controlling a prostitute, or brothel offences); an offence under the Indecency with Children Act 1960 or the Protection of Children Act 1978; burglary with intent to commit rape; an offence under section 128 of the Mental Health Act 1959; an offence under section 54 of the Criminal Law Act 1977; any conspiracy, incitement or attempt to commit any of the above offences (CJA 1991, s.31(1)).

(ii) Procedure

12–06   (a) Before forming an opinion as to whether an offence is either so serious that only a custodial sentence can be justified, or that it is a violent or sexual offence, the court must obtain and consider a pre-sentence report (CJA 1991, s.3(1)).

Paragraph (a) above does not apply if, in the circumstances of the case, the court is of the opinion that it is unnecessary to obtain a pre-sentence report (*ibid.* s.3(2).

(b) In forming an opinion as to whether the offence or (as the case may be) the offence and other offences associated with it is so serious, the court may consider the circumstances of the offence (including any aggravating and mitigating factors), and if the offence is a violent or sexual one the court may also consider any information about the offender which is available to it (*ibid.*, s.3(3)).

(c) When passing a custodial sentence the court must state in open court that it is of the opinion that the offence is within the category of section 1(2)(a) of the Act ("so serious") or section 1(2)(b) ("violent or sexual") and why it is of that opinion (*ibid.*, s.1(4)(a)).

(d) In any event the court must explain to the offender in ordinary language why a custodial sentence is being passed (*ibid.*, s.1(4)(b)).

In stating an opinion under section 1(4)(a), above, it is desirable to use the words of the statute. If the words of the statute are not used, it is necessary in addition for the offender to be addressed in ordinary language as to why a custodial sentence is being passed (*R. v. Baverstock* [1993] 1 W.L.R. 202).

(e) Such a reason must be entered in the court register (*ibid.*, s.1(5)).

(f) If a sentence longer than one commensurate with the seriousness of the offence is passed for a violent or sexual offence, the court must state in open court why it is of the opinion that this is necessary and explain to the offender in open court why such a longer sentence is being passed (*ibid.*, s.2(3)(a) and (b)).

(g) A custodial sentence shall not be passed on an offender not previously so sentenced unless he has applied for legal aid and been refused on the grounds of means, or having been informed of his right to apply for legal aid and had the opportunity to do so, has refused or failed to apply (PCCA 1973, s.21(1) and (2)).

(h) An explanation of the practical effects of the custodial sentence should be given at the time that the sentence is passed (*Practice Direction (Custodial Sentences)* [1998] 1 Cr.App.R. 397).

DEFINITION

12–07 A *pre-sentence report* is a report in writing made by a probation officer or social worker to assist the court in determining the most suitable method of dealing with an offender. It contains information as to such matters as conform with the agreed national standards (CJA 1991, s.3(5)).

(iii) Special provisions for custodial sentences

(a) AGE OF THE OFFENDER

12–08 (a) A court shall not pass a sentence of imprisonment on an offender under the age of 21 (CJA 1982, s.1(1)).

(b) For offenders under the age of 21 the restrictions upon the length of a custodial sentence in a Young Offender Institution are as follows:

— where the offender is under the age of 18 the minimum period which may be imposed is two months;

— where the offender is aged 15, 16 or 17 the maximum period is 12 months;

— where the offender is under 21 but over 18 the minimum period is 21 days (CJA 1982, ss1A, 1B).

(b) MENTALLY DISORDERED OFFENDERS

(a) Where an offender is or appears to be mentally disordered the court shall obtain and consider a medical report before passing a custodial sentence (CJA 1991, s.4(1)).

(b) Before passing a custodial sentence the court must consider any information before it which relates to his mental condition (whether in a medical report, pre-sentence report or otherwise) and also the likely effect of such a sentence on that condition and any treatment which may be available for it (*ibid.*, s.4(3)).

(iv) Combining custodial sentences with other orders

12–09 (a) A custodial sentence may be combined with a fine and with Compensation, Restitution and Forfeiture Orders.

(b) A sentence of imprisonment should not be imposed on the same occasion as a suspended sentence imposed for another offence (*R. v. Sapiano* (1968) 112 S.J. 799) or a Probation Order imposed for another offence (*R. v. Emmet* (1968) 53 Cr.App.R. 203).

2. Suspended Sentence of Imprisonment

(i) Powers

12–10   (a) A court which imposes a sentence of imprisonment may order that the sentence shall not take effect unless, during a period (called the operational period), being not less than one year and not more than two years from the date of the order, the offender commits another offence punishable with imprisonment (PCCA 1973, s.22(1)).

(b) A court shall not deal with an offender by means of a suspended sentence unless:

(1) the case is one in which a sentence of imprisonment is appropriate in any event; and

(2) suspending the sentence can be justified by the exceptional circumstances of the case (PCCA 1973, s.22(2), as substituted by CJA 1991, s.5).

For the meaning of "exceptional circumstances" see §§13–53 to 13–56, below.

(c) In deciding whether a sentence of imprisonment is appropriate in any event, the power to impose a custodial sentence, set out at §12–04, above, must exist, and the procedural steps for the imposition of a custodial sentence set out at §12–05, above, must be followed.

(d) In addition, when a court passes a suspended sentence it must consider whether the circumstances of the case are such as to warrant the imposition of a fine or the making of a Compensation Order as well as the suspended sentence of imprisonment (*ibid.*, s.22(2A), as substituted by CJA 1991, s.5).

(ii) Procedure

(a) PROCEDURE ON MAKING THE ORDER

12–11   On passing a suspended sentence of imprisonment a court must explain to the offender in ordinary language his liability to have the term of imprisonment activated if a further offence is committed during the operational period (PCCA 1973, s.23).

(b) PROCEDURE ON BREACH: ACTIVATION OF SUSPENDED SENTENCE

1. A magistrates' court only has power to activate a suspended sentence imposed by the same or another magistrates' court, not one imposed by the Crown Court (PCCA 1973, s.24).

If an offender is convicted by a magistrates' court of an offence punishable with imprisonment and the offender is thereby in breach of a suspended sentence imposed by the Crown Court he should be committed for sentence to the Crown Court at the location where the suspended sentence was imposed (*Practice Direction (Crown Court Business: Classification and Allocation)* [1995] 1 W.L.R. 1083).

2. Where an offender has committed another offence punishable by imprisonment during the operational period of a suspended sentence imposed by a magistrates' court the court must deal with him in respect of the suspended sentence unless the court is of the opinion that it would be unjust to do so (PCCA 1973, s.23).

3. The ways in which the court may deal with him are (a) ordering the suspended sentence to take effect with the original term unaltered, (b) ordering a lesser term than

the original term to take effect, or (c) making no order in respect of the suspended sentence (PCCA 1973, s.23).

4. The court must order the original term to take effect unaltered *unless* it would be unjust to do so in all the circumstances, including the facts of the subsequent offence, and where it is of that opinion the court shall state its reasons (PCCA 1973, s.23 as amended by CJA 1982).

5. When a suspended sentence is activated, with or without alteration, a court may order that the sentence take effect immediately or take effect consecutive to another term (PCCA 1973, s.23).

(iii) Combining a suspended sentence with other orders

12–12   (a) A suspended sentence of imprisonment may be combined with a fine and with Compensation, Restitution and Forfeiture Orders.

(b) A suspended sentence should not be imposed on the same occasion as imprisonment for another offence (*R. v. Sapiano*, above).

(c) A suspended sentence should not be imposed on the same occasion as a Probation Order is made for another offence (PCCA 1973, s.22(3)).

B. COMMUNITY SENTENCES

DEFINITION

12–13   (a) A *community sentence* is a sentence which consists of or includes one or more community orders (CJA 1991, s.6(1)).

(b) A *Community Order* means any of the following:

— a Probation Order,

— a Community Service Order,

— a Combination Order,

— a Curfew Order,

— an Attendance Centre Order,

— a Drug Treatment and Testing Order.

(i) Powers—general

12–14   (a) A court shall not pass a community sentence unless it is of the opinion that the offence, or the combination of the offence and one or more offences associated with it, was serious enough to warrant such a sentence (CJA 1991, s.6(1)).

(b) The restrictions on liberty imposed by the order or orders shall be such as in the opinion of the court are commensurate with the seriousness of the offence, or the combination of the offence and one or more offences associated with it (*ibid.*, s.6(2)(b)).

(c) In forming an opinion as is mentioned above a court shall take into account all such information about the circumstances of the offence or (as the case may be) of the offence and other offences associated with it (including aggravating and mitigating factors) as is available to it (*ibid.*, s.7(1)).

(d) In considering the seriousness of any offence, the court may take into account any previous convictions of the offender or any failure of his to respond to previous sentences (*ibid.*, s.29(1)).

(e) In considering the seriousness of any offence committed while the offender was on bail, the court shall treat the fact that it was committed in those circumstances as an aggravating factor (*ibid.*, s.29(2)).

(f) Nothing shall prevent a court from taking into account any matters which are relevant to mitigation of sentence (*ibid.*, s.28(1)), nor from mitigating any penalty included in an offender's sentence by taking into account any other penalty in that sentence, nor in the case of an offender convicted of multiple offences from applying any rule as to the totality of sentence (*ibid.*, s.28(2)).

(ii) Procedure—general

12–15 (a) The particular order or orders comprising or forming part of the community sentence must be the most suitable for the offender (CJA 1991, s.6(2)(a)).

(b) In forming the above opinion the court may take into account any information about the offender which is before it (*ibid.*, s.7(2)).

(c) Before forming an opinion as to the suitability of the offender for:

— a Probation Order which includes additional requirements,

— a Community Service Order, or

— a Combination Order,

the court shall obtain and consider a pre-sentence report (*ibid.*, s.7(3)). Paragraph (c) above does not apply if, in the circumstances of the case, the court is of the opinion that it is unnecessary to obtain a pre-sentence report (*ibid.*, s.7(3A) as inserted by CJ and POA 1994, s.168 Sched. 9, para. 40). A *pre-sentence report* is a report in writing made by a probation officer or social worker to assist the court in determining the most suitable method of dealing with an offender. It contains information as to such matters as conform with the agreed national standards (*ibid.*, s.3(5)).

1. Probation Order

(i) Powers

12–16 (a) A court may make a Probation Order in respect of an offender over the age of 16 for a period of not less than six months nor more than three years if it is of the opinion that a Probation Order is desirable in the interests of:

— securing the rehabilitation of the offender, or

— protecting the public from harm or preventing the commission by him of further offences (PCCA 1973, s.2(1), as substituted by CJA 1991, s.8(1)).

(b) In addition, the court may require the offender to comply with such additional requirements included in a Probation Order as are authorised by Schedule 1A of the Act (PCCA 1973, s.3, as substituted by CJA 1991, s.9). The additional requirements are:

(1) requirements as to residence;

(2) requirements as to activities, etc.;

(3) requirements as to attendance at probation centre;

(4) requirements for sexual offenders;

(5) requirements as to treatment for mental condition, etc.;

(6) requirements as to treatment for drug or alcohol dependency (PCCA 1973, Sched. 1A, as inserted by CJA 1991, Sched. 1, Pt II, and s.9(2)).

(c) A court may not include a requirement that the offender comply with a condition of treatment for a mental condition or that the offender comply with a condition of treatment for drugs or alcohol dependency unless the offender has expressed his willingness to comply with such a requirement (PCCA 1973, Sched. 1A, as amended by C(S)A 1997, s.38(3) and (4)).

(ii) Procedure

12–17 (a) Before making the order the court must explain to the offender in ordinary language:

— the effect of the order including any additional requirements;

— the consequences which may follow if he fails to comply with any requirements of the order; and

— the fact that the court has power to review the order on application of the offender or the supervising officer.

(PCCA 1973, s.2(3), as amended by C(S)A 1997, s.38(2)(a)).

BREACH OF PROBATION ORDER

12–18 (a) If it is proved that an offender has failed without reasonable excuse to comply with the requirements of the order the court may:

(1) impose a fine not exceeding £1,000;

(2) make a Community Service Order not exceeding 60 hours in aggregate;

(3) if the offender is over 16 and under 21 make an Attendance Centre Order;

(4) if the order was made by a magistrates' court, deal with the offender in any manner in which it could deal with him if he had just been convicted by the court of the offence (CJA 1991, Sched. 2, Pt II, paras 3(1) and 6(3)(a)).

The court should proceed to hear an information alleging a breach of a community order notwithstanding that a notice of appeal has been lodged against the making of the original order (*Greater Manchester Probation Committee v. Bent* (1996) 160 J.P. 297).

(b) In dealing with an offender under (a)(4) above, the court:

(1) shall take into account the extent to which the offender has complied with the requirements of the relevant order; and

(2) in the case of an offender who has wilfully and persistently failed to comply with those requirements may impose a custodial sentence nothwithstanding anything in section 1(2) of the Criminal Justice Act 1991 (*ibid.*, para. 3(2), as substituted by C(S)A 1997, s.55 and Sched. 4, §15(11)); and

(3) where a magistrates' court deals with the offender as above it shall revoke the relevant order if it is still in force (*ibid.*, para. 2A, as inserted by CDA 1998, ss106 and 119 and Sched. 8, paras 96(2) and(3)).

(c) If the order was made by the Crown Court the offender may be committed on bail or in custody to be dealt with by the Crown Court (*ibid.*, §3(3)).

AMENDMENT OF PROBATION ORDER

12–19 (a) The supervising court may, on application by the probation officer or the probationer, amend a Probation Order by cancelling a requirement or by inserting a requirement, providing the total period of probation is not reduced nor extended beyond three years from the date of the original order. No new requirement relating to mental treatment or to treatment for drug or alcohol dependency may be inserted unless made within three months of the original order (CJA 1991, Sched. 2, Pt IV, para.13).

(b) If a probationer is being treated by a medical practitioner as a condition of probation, and the medical practitioner is of the opinion that the period of treatment should be extended, or different treatment is necessary, or that the probationer is not susceptible to treatment, or no longer requires treatment, or the medical practitioner is for any reason unwilling to continue the treatment, the medical practitioner may apply to the court in writing for the conditions of probation to be varied or cancelled (*ibid.*, §14).

REVOCATION OF PROBATION ORDER

12–20 (a) If, on application by the offender or the supervising officer, it appears that because of circumstances which have arisen since the order was made that it is in the interests of justice:

(1) that the order should be revoked; or

(2) that the offender should be dealt with in some other way;

the court may either simply revoke the order or revoke the order and deal with the offender in any manner in which it could have dealt with him if he had just been convicted by the court of the offence. If the order was made by the Crown Court, the magistrates may commit him on bail or in custody to be brought before the Crown Court (CJA 1991, Sched. 2, Pt III, paras 7(1) and (2) (as amended by CDA 1998, s.64(5) and Sched. 4, paras 1–6).

(b) The circumstances in which a Probation Order may be revoked under para. 7(2)(a) above shall include the offender's making good progress or responding satisfactorily to supervision (*ibid.*, §7(3)).

(c) If the court decides to revoke the order and deal with the offender in some other way, it must take into account the extent to which the offender has complied with the requirements of the original order (*ibid.*, §7(4)).

(d) If, during the period of a Probation Order, the offender receives a custodial sentence, and it appears in the interests of justice to do so, the court may revoke the order, and if the order was made by the Crown Court commit him on bail or in custody to be dealt with by the Crown Court (*ibid.*, para. 9(1) and (2)).

REVOCATION OF PROBATION ORDER AND SUBSTITUTION OF CONDITIONAL DISCHARGE

12–21   In addition to the powers summarised above a magistrates' court may, in dealing with an application to revoke a probation order, impose a conditional discharge in substitution for the probation order, and if so the period of the order shall begin on the date on which it was made and shall end on the date when the original probation order would have ended.

An application for such a substitution may be made in the offender's absence by the responsible officer if the officer produces a statement by the offender that he understands the effect of a conditional discharge (CJA 1991, Sched. 2, para. 8A, as inserted by CDA 1998, s.106 and Sched. 7, para. 46(11)).

(iii) Combining probation with other orders

12–22   (a) A Probation Order may not be combined with a Community Service Order (CJA 1991, s.6(3)). If a Community Service Order is to accompany a period of supervision the court must make a Combination Order (see §12–30, below).

(b) A Probation Order should not be made on the same occasion as a suspended sentence is imposed for another offence (PCCA 1973, s.22(3)).

(c) A Probation Order may be combined with a Compensation Order or Restitution Order or with any form of sentence unless prohibited. A Probation Order is a sentence whether made before or after October 1, 1992 (CJA 1991, ss6(1) and 29(3)).

2. Community Service Order

(i) Powers

12–23   (a) A court may make a Community Service Order where an offender over the age of 16 is convicted of an offence punishable with imprisonment. The number of hours to be worked must be specified in the order and they must not in aggregate be less than 40 nor more than 240 (PCCA 1973, s.14 as amended by CJA 1991, s.10).

(b) A court shall not make the order unless the court, having heard (if it thinks necessary) a probation officer or social worker, is satisfied that the offender is a suitable person to perform work under the order (PCCA 1973, s.14(2) as amended by C(S)A 1997, s.38(2)(b).

(c) The work required to be performed under the order must be completed within 12 months of the order being made (PCCA 1973, s.15(2)).

COMMUNITY SERVICE ORDER FOR PERSISTENT PETTY OFFENDERS

12–24   If a person has been convicted by a magistrates' court and the court would be minded to impose a fine for the offence, and the court is satisfied:

   (i) that one or more fines imposed on the offender in respect of one or more previous offences have not been paid; and

(ii) if a fine were imposed in an amount commensurate with the seriousness of the offence, the offender would not have the means to pay it;

the court may impose a Community Service Order instead of imposing a fine (C(S)A 1997, s.37(1) and (2)).

(ii) Procedure

12–25   (a) Before making the order the court must explain to the offender in ordinary language:

— the purpose and effect of the order and the requirements of reporting to an officer and of informing him of any change of address;

— the consequences if he fails without reasonable excuse to comply with any of the requirements; and

— the powers of the court on application by a probation officer or the offender to revoke the order and substitute some other sentence (PCCA 1973, s.14(2) as amended by C(S)A 1997, s.38(2)(b)).

BREACH OF COMMUNITY SERVICE ORDER

12–26   (a) If it is proved that an offender has failed without reasonable excuse to comply with the requirements of the order the court may:

(1)   impose a fine not exceeding £1,000;

(2)   make a new Community Service Order not exceeding the maximum number of hours permitted under the Act;

(3)   if the offender is over 16 and under 21 make an Attendance Centre Order;

(4)   if the order was made by a magistrates' court, revoke the order and deal with the offender in any manner in which it could deal with him if he had just been convicted by the court of the offence (CJA 1991, Sched. 2, Pt II, paras 3(1) and 6(3)(b)).

(b) In dealing with an offender under (a)(4) above, the court:

(1)   shall take into account the extent to which the offender has complied with the order; and

(2)   in the case of an offender who has wilfully and persistently failed to comply with those requirements may impose a custodial sentence nothwithstanding anything in section 1(2) of the Criminal Justice Act 1991 (*ibid.*, para. 3(2), as substituted by C(S)A 1997, s.55 and Sched. 4, para. 15(11)).

(c) If the order was made by the Crown Court the offender may be committed on bail or in custody to be dealt with by the Crown Court (*ibid.*, para. 3(3)).

REVOCATION OF COMMUNITY SERVICE ORDER

12–27   (a) If on application by the offender or the supervising officer it appears that because of circumstances which have arisen since the order was made that it is in the interests of justice:

(1) that the order should be revoked, or

(2) that the offender should be dealt with in some other way,

the court may either simply revoke the order or revoke the order and deal with the offender in any manner in which it could have dealt with him if he had just been convicted by the court of the offence. If the order was made by the Crown Court, the magistrates' court may commit him on bail or in custody to be brought before the Crown Court (CJA 1991, Sched. 2, Pt III, §7(1) and (2)(a) and (b) as amended by CDA 1998, s.64(5) and Sched. 4 paras 1–6).

(b) If the court decides to revoke the order and deal with the offender in some other way, it must take into account the extent to which the offender has complied with the original order (*ibid.*, para. 7(4)).

(c) If, during the period of a Community Service Order, the offender receives a custodial sentence, and it appears in the interests of justice to do so, the court may revoke the order, or if the order was made by the Crown Court commit him on bail or in custody to be dealt with by the Crown Court (*ibid.*, paras 9(1) and (2)).

EXTENSION OF COMMUNITY SERVICE ORDER

12–28   If on application of the offender of the supervising officer it appears in the interests of justice to do so, the court may extend the period of 12 months in which the Community Service Order is to be performed (CJA 1991, Sched. 2, Pt IV, §15).

(iii) Combining a Community Service Order with other Orders

12–29   (a) A Community Service Order may not be combined with a Probation Order (CJA 1991, s.6(3)). If a Community Service Order is to accompany a period of supervision the court must make a Combination Order (see below).

(b) A Community Service Order may be combined with a Compensation and Restitution Order.

3. Combination Order

(i) Powers

12–30   (a) A court may make a Combination Order, that is to say an order requiring an offender to be under the supervision of a probation officer for a period of not less than 12 months nor more than three years, as well as performing unpaid work for a period of not less than 40 and not more than 100 hours, if the offender is over the age of 16 and is convicted of an offence punishable with imprisonment, providing the court is of the opinion that such an order is in the interests of:

— securing the rehabilitation of the offender; or

— protecting the public from harm from him or preventing the commission of further offences (CJA 1991, s.11(1) and (2)).

(b) A court shall not make the order unless the court, having heard (if it thinks necessary) a probation officer or social worker, is satisfied that the offender is a suitable person to perform work under the order (PCCA 1973, s.14(2) as amended by C(S)A 1997, s.38(2)(b)).

(ii) Procedure

12–31 Before making the order the court must explain to the offender in ordinary language:

(a) the purpose and effect of the order and the requirements of reporting to an officer and of informing him of any change of address;

(b) the consequences if he fails without reasonable excuse to comply with any of the requirements of the order; and

(c) the powers the court on application by the offender or the probation officer to revoke the order and substitute some other sentence (PCCA 1973, ss2 and 14 as amended by CJA 1991, s.11(3)).

BREACH OF COMBINATION ORDER

12–32 (a) If it is proved that an offender has failed without reasonable excuse to comply with the requirements of the order the court may:

(1) impose a fine not exceeding £1,000;

(2) make a Community Service Order not exceeding 60 hours in aggregate;

(3) if the offender is over 16 and under 21 make an Attendance Centre Order;

(4) if the order was made by a magistrates' court, revoke the order and deal with the offender in any manner in which it could deal with him if he had just been convicted by the court of the offence (CJA 1991, Sched. 2, Part 11, paras 3(1) and 6(3)(a)).

(b) In dealing with an offender under (4) above, the court:

(1) shall take into account the extent to which the offender has complied with the order; and

(2) in the case of an offender who has wilfully and persistently failed to comply with those requirements may impose a custodial sentence nothwithstanding anything in section 1(2) of the Criminal Justice Act 1991 (*ibid.*, para. 3(2), as substituted by C(S)A 1997, s.55 and Sched. 4, para. 15(11)).

(c) If the order was made by the Crown Court the offender may be committed on bail or in custody to be dealt with by the Crown Court (*ibid.*, para. 3(3)).

REVOCATION OF A COMBINATION ORDER

12–33 (a) If on application by the offender or the supervising officer it appears that because of circumstances which have arisen since the order was made that it is in the interests of justice:

(1) that the order should be revoked; or

(2) that the offender should be dealt with in some other way,

the court may either simply revoke the order or revoke the order and deal with the offender in any manner in which it could have dealt with him if he had just been convicted by the court of the offence. If the order was made by the Crown Court, the magistrates may commit him on bail or in custody to be brought before the Crown Court (CJA 1991, Sched. 2, Pt III, §7(1) and (2), as amended by CDA 1998, s.64(5) and Sched. 4 paras 1–6).

(b) If the court decides to revoke the order and deal with the offender in some other way, it must take into account the extent to which the offender has complied with the original order (*ibid.*, para. 7(4)).

(c) If, during the period of a Combination Order, the offender receives a custodial sentence, and it appears in the interests of justice to do so the court may revoke the order, or if the order was made by the Crown Court commit him on bail or in custody to be dealt wih by the Crown Court (*ibid.*, paras 9(1) and (2)).

4. Curfew Order

12–34 A Curfew Order is a Community Order as defined in the Criminal Justice Act 1991 (CJA 1991, s.6(4)), and the precise nature of a Curfew Order is defined in sections 12 and 13 of the 1991 Act. With effect from January 9, 1995 these sections were brought into force in a form as amended by the Criminal Justice and Public Order Act 1994, s.168 and Sched. 9, para. 41 (Commencement Order No. 2).

Paragraph 41 adds a new subsection to section 12 of the Criminal Justice Act 1991, the effect of which is to prohibit a court from making a Curfew Order unless the Secretary of State has notified the court that arrangements exist for monitoring the offender's whereabouts are available in the area specified in the Order (CJA 1991, s.12(4A)). This means that the electronic monitoring of an offender's whereabouts provided for in section 13 of the 1991 Act may not occur unless and until suitable arrangements have been made, and the Secretary of State permits, by statutory instrument, the making of a Curfew Order in a particular area.

The Secretary of State has announced that Berkshire, Cambridgeshire, Greater Manchester, the London Boroughs of Barnet, Brent, Ealing, Enfield, Haringey, Harrow, Hillingdon or Hounslow, Norfolk, Suffolk and West Yorkshire to be trial areas for Curfew Orders.

In view of the fact that the use of a Curfew Order is limited to so few magistrates' courts at present the provisions of section 12 and 13 are not summarised.

5. Attendance Centre Order

(i) Powers

12–35 (a) A court may make an Attendance Centre Order in respect of an offender under the age of 21 convicted of an offence punishable with imprisonment, or on a person under the age of 21 who has failed to comply with a probation order under Pt II of Schedule 2 of the Criminal Justice Act 1991 (CJA 1982, s.17(1)).

(b) Before making the order the court must have been notified that an attendance centre is available to receive the offender and that it is reasonably accessible to him (*ibid.*).

(c) The aggregate number of hours shall not exceed 12 unless in all the circumstances 12 would be inadequate, in which case the number of hours shall not exceed 24 if the offender is under 16 or 36 where the offender is over 16 and under 21 (CJA 1982, s.17(5)).

(ii) Procedure

(a) PROCEDURE WHEN THERE IS A BREACH OF THE ORDER OR THE ATTENDANCE CENTRE'S RULES ARE BROKEN

12–36 1. Where the court which made the order, or a court in the area where the centre is situated, is satisfied that an offender has failed without reasonable excuse to attend the centre, or has broken the rules after attending, the court may revoke the order and deal with the offender in any manner in which he could have been dealt with originally (*ibid.*, s.19).

2. If the order was made by the Crown Court and a breach set out above is proved, the offender should be committed to the Crown Court together with a certificate from the magistrates' court setting out the particulars of the breach (*ibid.*).

(b) PROCEDURE FOR VARYING OR DISCHARGING THE ORDER

1. The court which made the original order, or a court in the area where the centre is situated, may alter the centre specified in the order if the offender has changed his address or vary the time of the first attendance at the centre (*ibid.*, s.18).

2. The offender or the officer in charge of the centre may apply to a court local to the centre or the court which made the original order for the order to be discharged (*ibid.*).

6. Drug Treatment and Testing Order

12–37 A Drug Treatment and Testing Order is a community order for the purposes of the Criminal Justice Act 1991 (CDA 1998, s.61(4)). Section 61 of the Crime and Disorder Act 1998 introduces the order for offenders who are dependent on or have a propensity to misuse drugs and where such condition is susceptible to treatment.

The Secretary of State has announced that pilot schemes for the use of the order will take place in Merseyside (Liverpool), South-East London (Croydon) and Gloucestershire.

In view of the fact that the use of a Drug Treatment and Testing Order is limited to so few magistrates' courts at present the provisions of sections 61 to 64 of the Crime and Disorder Act 1998 are not summarised.

C. FINANCIAL PENALTIES

(i) Powers

12–38 (a) The maximum fines which may be imposed are as follows:

— for an adult convicted of an offence triable either way, £5,000 (MCA 1980, s.32(9), as amended by CJA 1991, s.17(2)(c)).

— for a young person convicted of any offence, £1,000 (MCA 1980, ss24(3), and 36, as amended by CJA 1991, s.17(2)(a)).

— for a child convicted of any offence, £250 (MCA 1980, s.24(4), as amended by CJA 1991, s.17(2)(b)).

(b) The maximum fine which may be imposed for a summary offfence where the level of fine is prescribed by statute, or for an either way offence punishable with a fine not exceeding the statutory maximum, is as follows:

level 1	£200
level 2	£500
level 3	£1,000
level 4	£2,500
level 5	£5,000

(CJA 1982, s.37(2) as substituted by CJA 1991, s.17(1)).

(c) Before fixing the amount of any fine on an offender who is an individual a court shall inquire into his financial circumstances (CJA 1991, s.18(1), as amended by CJ and POA 1994, s.168 and Sched. 9, para. 42).

(d) The amount of any fine fixed by a court shall be such as, in the opinion of the court, reflects the seriousness of the offence (*ibid.*, s.18(2)).

(e) In fixing the amount of any fine, a court shall take into account the circumstances of the case including, among other things, the financial circumstances of the offender as far as they are known, or appear, to the court whether taking into account those financial circumstances has the effect of increasing or reducing the amount of the fine (*ibid.*, s.18(3) and (5)).

(f) The court may take into account any matters which are relevant in mitigation of sentence (*ibid.*, s.28(1)), and in particular nothing shall prevent a court from mitigating any penalty included in that sentence, nor, where an offender is convicted of numerous offences, of applying any rule as to the totality of sentences (*ibid.*, s.28(2)(a) and (b)).

(g) In considering the seriousness of any offence, the court may take into account any previous convictions or any failure of the offender to respond to previous sentences (*ibid.*, s.29(1)).

(h) In considering the seriousness of any offence committed while the offender was on bail, the court shall treat the fact that it was committed in those circumstances as an aggravating factor (*ibid.*, s.29(2)).

(ii) Procedure

MAKING A FINANCIAL CIRCUMSTANCES ORDER

12–39 (a) The court may, before sentencing an offender who is an individual, make an order requiring him to give to the court, within such period as may be specified, such statement of his financial circumstances as the court may require. Such an order is called a Financial Circumstances Order (CJA 1991, s.20(1) and (1C) as amended by CJ and POA 1994, s.168 and Sched. 9, para. 41).

(b) An offender who fails without reasonable excuse to comply with a Financial Circumstances Order commits an offence (*ibid.*, s.20(2)).

(c) If an offender in furnishing a statement of his financial circumstances makes a statement which he knows to be false in a material particular; recklessly furnishes a statement which he knows to be false in a material particular; or knowingly fails to disclose any material fact he commits an offence punishable with three months' imprisonment or a fine on level 4 or both (CJA 1991, s.20A, as inserted by CJ and POA 1994, s.168 and Sched. 9, para. 43).

(d) Where an offender has indicated that he wishes to plead guilty without appearing before the court, the court may still make a Financial Circumstances Order in respect of him (*ibid.*, s.20(1A)).

ALLOWING TIME TO PAY

12–40 (a) When imposing a fine a court may: require immediate payment; allow time for payment; or order payment by instalments (MCA 1980, s.75).

(1) If the court requires immediate payment it may order the offender to be searched and any money found applied to the payment of the fine (MCA 1980, s.80).

(2) If the court allows time for payment or payment by instalments it may fix, in the defendant's presence, a day on which if any part of the fine or any instalment then due remains unpaid the offender must appear before the court again (MCA 1980, s.86).

(b) A court may not on the occasion of imposing a fine impose an alternative of imprisonment in default unless:

(1) in the case of an offence punishable with imprisonment the offender appears to the court to have sufficient means to pay the fine forthwith; or

(2) it appears to the court he is unlikely to remain long enough at a place of abode in the United Kingdom to enable payment to be enforced by other methods; or

(3) if on the occasion the fine is imposed the offender is also sentenced in respect of another offence to custody or he is already serving a sentence of custody (MCA 1980, s.82).

(c) Where a fine is imposed on a child or young person the court must order the fine to be paid by the parent or guardian of the juvenile unless either the parent or guardian cannot be found or it would be unreasonable to make the order in all the circumstances (Children and Young Persons Act 1933, s.55).

(d) Where the offender is on income support the court may apply to the Secretary of State for the fine to be deducted from any amounts paid to the offender in income support (CJA 1991, s.24 and Fines (Deductions from Income Support) Regulations 1992). Minor amendments have been made to section 24 of the 1991 Act (CJ and POA 1994, s.47(3)).

The importance of complying with these statutory provisions has been emphasised by the Divisional Court in *R. v. Oldham Justices, ex p. Canley* [1996] 1 All E.R. 414.

D. MISCELLANEOUS MEASURES

1. Absolute and Conditional Discharge

(i) Powers

12–41   (a) A court may impose an absolute or conditional discharge on an offender of any age if, having regard to the nature of the offence and the character of the offender, (1) it is inexpedient to inflict punishment, and (2) a Probation Order is not appropriate. The condition of a conditional discharge is that the offender commits no offence during the period of the order, which must not exceed three years (PCCA 1973, s.1A).

With effect from February 3, 1995 a conditional discharge imposed after September 30, 1992 shall be treated as a conviction and a sentence and an absolute discharge imposed after that date shall be treated as a conviction (CJA 1991, s.29(5) and (6)).

(ii) Procedure

(a) PROCEDURE ON MAKING A CONDITIONAL DISCHARGE

12–42   Before making the order the court must explain to the offender in ordinary language the effect of the order and explain also that if he commits another offence during the period of the conditional discharge he will be liable to be sentenced for the original offence (*ibid.*, s.1A(3)).

(b) PROCEDURE WHEN A FURTHER OFFENCE IS COMMITTED

1. If an offender subject to a conditional discharge commits a further offence during the period of the conditional discharge the court may terminate the order to deal with the offender in any way it could have done for the original offence.

2. Unless the court dealing with the offender in this way is the court which originally made the order, the consent of that court must be obtained before any action on the breach can be taken.

3. If the conditional discharge was made by the Crown Court then the offender should be committed to the Crown Court to be dealt with for the original offence together with any other offences of which the offender has been convicted by the committing court (PCCA 1973, s.8 and CJA 1967, s.56).

4. Before any of the above steps may be taken the subsequent conviction must be put to the offender and admitted or the court must be satisfied that a further offence has been committed (*ibid.*, s.1B(1)).

(iii) Combining absolute and conditional discharge with other orders

12–43   (a) An absolute or conditional discharge may be combined with a Compensation or Restitution Order.

(b) An absolute or conditional discharge may be combined with a suspended sentence, a fine or a Community Service Order imposed on the same occasion for another offence (*R. v. Bainbridge* (1979) 1 Cr.App.R.(S.) 36).

2. Deferment of Sentence

(i) Powers

12–44 (a) A court may defer passing sentence on any offender for a period of six months if, having a regard to the nature of the offence and the circumstances of the offender, it is in the interests of justice to do so for the purpose of enabling the court to assess his conduct after conviction including, where appropriate, the making of reparation for the offence or any change in circumstances (PCCA 1973, s.1).

(b) The deferring of sentence includes the deferring of any ancillary orders such as disqualification, compensation or restitution (*R. v. Dwyer* (1974) 60 Cr.App.R. 39).

(ii) Procedure

(a) Procedure on making the order

12–45 1. The offender must consent to his sentence being deferred (PCCA 1973, s.1(3)).

2. The court should make it clear to the offender when making the order the particular purpose the court has in mind for making the deferment, and the steps the court expects the offender to take during the period of deferment. These should be recorded in the register (*R. v. George* [1984] 1 W.L.R. 1082).

3. The period of the deferment should be specified.

(b) Procedure when the case is relisted on the deferred date

1. Where possible the same Bench should deal with the offender on the deferred date. Where this is not possible the purpose of the deferment and the requirements, if any, upon the offender should be ascertained and made known to the new Bench (*R. v. Gurney* [1974] Crim.L.R. 472).

2. The court may pass any sentence and impose any ancillary orders which the court deferring sentence could itself have passed (PCCA 1973, s.1(8)(a)), but an offender is entitled to expect that a custodial sentence will not be imposed if he has substantially conformed or attempted to conform with the expectations of the deferring court (*R. v. George*, above).

(c) Procedure when a further offence is committed during the deferred period

1. The court which has deferred sentence may deal with an offender before the expiration of the period of deferment if in the meantime he is convicted by any court of any offence (PCCA 1973, s.1(4)).

2. A court convicting an offender of an offence may also deal with him in respect of the offence for which sentence was deferred unless the sentence was originally deferred by the Crown Court (PCCA 1973, s.4(A)).

3. Where a magistrates' court deals with an offender whose offence was committed during a period of deferment from the Crown Court the offender should be committed to the Crown Court for sentence.

(iii) Combining a deferred sentence with other orders

12–46 All other orders should be combined (if appropriate) at the time sentence is imposed at the end of the period of deferment, and the lawful combinations will depend upon which sentence is then imposed.

E. Ancillary Orders

1. Compensation Orders

(i) Powers

12–47　(a) A court may make a Compensation Order requiring an offender convicted of an offence to pay compensation for any personal injury, loss or damage resulting from that offence, or any other offence, taken into consideration, of not more than £5,000 and if it does not make such an order in a case when it is empowered to do so the court shall give reasons when passing sentence, which must be recorded in the register (PCCA 1973, s.35 and MCR 1981, r.66(10A)).

(b) If the injury, loss or damage is due to an accident arising from the presence of a motor vehicle on a road a Compensation Order may only be made (1) in respect of damage resulting from an offence under the Theft Act 1968, or (2) in respect of injury loss or damage which is caused when the offender himself is uninsured and when the Motor Insurers' Bureau will not compensate the victim (*ibid*. s.35(3)). It has been held that the proper interpretation of section 35(3)(b) of the Act (compensation is not payable under any arrangements to which the Secretary of State is a party) is that the maximum amount of compensation which may be awarded by justices is £175 because under that agreement the Motor Insurers Bureau are not required to pay the first £175 of any such damage (*R. v. Scott* [1995] R.T.R. 40, and *R. v. Austin* [1996] R.T.R. 414).

(c) The amount of compensation arising from an accident on a road in circumstances defined above may include compensating the victim for the loss or reduction of any preferential rates of insurance attributable to the accident (*ibid*. s.35(3)).

(d) The maximum amount which may be awarded by way of compensation is £5,000 for each offence for which the offender is convicted. If the offender asks for further offences to be taken into consideration the maximum compensation for those offences is the total permissible for offences for which he is convicted, less the amount actually awarded in respect of those offences (MCA 1980, s.40, as amended by CJA 1991, s.17(3) and Sched. 4).

(ii) Procedure

12–48　(a) In determining whether to make a Compensation Order, and the amount of such order, the court must take into account the means of the offender as far as they appear or are known to the court (PCCA 1973, s.35(4)).

(b) If it is appropriate to impose a fine as well as compensation but the offender has insufficient means to pay both the court must give preference to compensation (PCCA 1973, s.35(4A)).

(iii) Review of Compensation Orders

12–49　(a) The court which has the function of enforcing a Compensation Order may discharge the order, or reduce the amount to be paid, before the compensation is paid in full but after the time limits for an appeal have expired if the offender makes an application and any of the following circumstances apply:

(1) the injury loss or damage in respect of which the order was made has been held in civil proceedings to be less than it was taken to be for the purpose of the order;

(2) the order was in respect of property and it has been recovered by the victim;

(3) the means of the offender is insufficient to satisfy both a Confiscation Order (see §12–52, below) and a Compensation Order made in the same proceedings;

(4) the offender has suffered a substantial reduction in his means which was unexpected at the time when the order was made and his means seem unlikely to increase for a considerable period (PCCA 1973, s.37 as amended by CJA 1988, s.105).

(b) An application for a review of a Compensation Order must be made by complaint, and the court must then issue a summons directed to the person for whose benefit the order was made requiring him to show cause why the order should not be amended or revoked (MCR 1981, r.104).

(iv) Combining a Compensation Order with other sentences

12–50 (a) A Compensation Order may be combined with any lawful sentence for the offence.

(b) A Compensation Order should only be combined with imprisonment if there is little risk of the offender re-offending after his release in order to pay the compensation (*R. v. Wilkinson* [1980] 1 W.L.R. 396).

2. Restitution Orders

(i) Powers

12–51 (a) A court which convicts a person of any offence involving stolen goods, or which takes such an offence into consideration, may:

(1) order anyone having possession or control of the goods to restore them to a person entitled to them; or

(2) order any other goods directly or indirectly representing the original stolen goods to be delivered by the convicted person to an applicant entitled to them; or

(3) order any money found on the convicted person not exceeding the value of the stolen goods to be paid to a person entitled to them (Theft Act 1968, s.28).

(b) A court shall not exercise the above powers unless the relevant facts appear sufficiently clear from the evidence given at the trial, including the available documents and admissions (Theft Act 1968, s.28(4)).

(ii) Procedure

12–52 (a) The power may only be exercised in respect of money found on the offender at the time of his arrest, and not recovered prior to his arrest (*R. v. Hinde* (1977) 64 Cr.App.R. 213).

(b) An order should only be made in simple and straightforward cases where the rights of third parties in respect of the goods are not likely to be affected (*R. v. Ferguson* [1970] 1 W.L.R. 1246).

(c) The property which is to be made the subject of a Restitution Order must relate to the offence of which the accused is convicted (*R. v. Parker* [1970] 1 W.L.R. 1003).

3. Deprivation of Property and Forfeiture

(i) Powers

(a) UNDER SECTION 43 OF THE POWERS OF CRIMINAL COURTS ACT 1973

12–53 1. When a court convicts an offender, it may make an order forfeiting any property which has been lawfully seized from him or was in his possession or control at the time of his arrest providing the property in question: (i) has been used for the purpose of committing or facilitating the commission of an offence, or was intended by him to be used for that purpose; or (ii) the offence itself consists of his being in unlawful possession of the property in question (PCCA 1973, s.43).

2. In considering whether to make such an order the court shall have regard to the value of the property and the likely financial and other effects on the offender of the making of the order, taken together with any other the court contemplates making (*ibid.*).

3. Where an offender is convicted of: (i) an offence punishable with imprisonment under RTA 1988, or (ii) manslaughter, or (iii) wanton and furious driving, and such offence has been committed either by driving, attempting to drive, or being in charge of a vehicle, or the offender has failed to provide a breath or blood sample, or has failed to stop or report an accident after so driving, then the vehicle used shall be regarded as having been used for the purpose of facilitating an offence (PCCA 1973, s.43(1B) and (1C), as inserted by RTA 1991, s.36).

(b) UNDER PARTICULAR STATUTES

12–54 1. The Misuse of Drugs Act 1971. A court which convicts an offender of any offence under the Misuse of Drugs Act 1971, or a drug trafficking offence as defined in section 38(1) of the Drug Trafficking Offences Act 1986, may make a Forfeiture Order in respect of any tangible property if the court is satisfied it relates to the offence (Misuse of Drugs Act 1971, s.27(1) as amended by CJA 1988, s.70).

If the property to be forfeited may belong to some person other than the offender, the court must give that person an opportunity to make representations (MDA 1971, s.27(2)). Upon making the order the property will be destroyed or dealt with in such manner as the court may order.

2. The Prevention of Crime Act 1953. A court which convicts an offender of having an offensive weapon may order that the weapon be forfeited (Prevention of Crime Act 1953, s.1(2)).

3. The Obscene Publications Act 1964. A court *shall* order the forfeiture of any articles seized under the Obscene Publications Act 1959 if an offender is then convicted of having them for publication for gain under section 2 of that Act, providing that the order shall not take effect until the time limit for any appeal has expired (Obscene Publications Act 1964, s.1).

4. The Firearms Act 1968. A court which convicts an offender of an offence under the Firearms Act (other than an offence relating to air weapons) may order any firearm or ammunition found in his possession to be forfeit; or a court which convicts an

offender of *any* offence, and he is sentenced to imprisonment or detention as a young offender and has a firearm or ammunition in his possession, may make a Forfeiture Order in respect of the firearm or ammunition (Firearms Act 1968, s.52(1)(a)).

In all instances where it is proposed to make a Forfeiture Order the above statutory provisions must be strictly applied. Accordingly, the court must be satisfied that the property has been used by the offender to commit the offence, and not used by some other person to commit the offence (*R. v. Slater* [1986] 1 W.L.R. 1340). Secondly, the property must relate to an offence for which the offender is convicted and not some future, intended offence (*R. v. Llewellyn* (1985) 7 Cr.App.R.(S.) 225).

(ii) Procedure

12–55 (a) Upon making the order the property will be taken into the possession of the police (PCCA 1973, s.43(3)).

(b) An order should only be made in simple and straightforward cases, and not where there is an issue that the property is subject to joint ownership or some other encumbrance, such as hire-purchase (*R. v. Troth* (1979) 71 Cr.App.R. 1).

(c) Even when the issue appears simple and straightforward some evidence must be placed before the court by the prosecution to enable the court to make the proper and necessary investigations before making the order (*R. v. Pemberton* (1982) 4 Cr.App.R. (S.) 328).

(d) If the offender disputes that the property proposed to be forfeited relates to the offence for which he has been convicted he must be allowed to call evidence on the issue (*R. v. Churcher* (1986) 8 Cr.App.R.(S.) 94).

(iii) Combining Forfeiture Orders with other penalties

12–56 (a) A Forfeiture Order may be combined with any other penalty the court is entitled to impose for the offence.

(b) In respect of the general powers under section 43 of the Powers of Criminal Courts Act 1973 (as amended by CJA 1988) a Forfeiture Order may be imposed without restrictions on forfeiture in any enactment contained in an Act before the coming into force of the Criminal Justice Act 1988 (CJA 1988, s.69).

4. Confiscation Orders

(i) Powers

12–57 If a court convicts an offender of a scheduled offence (see below), or such offence is taken into consideration and the court is satisfied that he has benefited by obtaining property or deriving a pecuniary advantage as a result of or in connection with such offence the court may confiscate that benefit if it is £10,000 or more (CJA 1988, s.71(1), (3), (4), (5) and (6)).

The scheduled offences are:

(a) offences relating to sex establishments under the Local Government (Miscellaneous Provisions) Act 1982;

(b) supplying or possessing video recording of unclassified work under the Video Recording Act 1984;

(c) use of unlicensed premises under the Cinemas Act 1985 (CJA 1988, s.71 and Sched. 4).

(d) offences relating to the making, dealing or using illicit recordings or the making or dealing with infringing articles under the Copyright, Designs and Patents Act 1988;

(e) an offence under section 92(1), (2) or (3) of the Trade Marks Act 1994;

(f) an offence under section 114(1) of the Social Security Administration Act 1992.

(g) an offence relating to the unauthorised use of trade marks in relation to goods under the Trade Marks Act 1994.

A Confiscation Order may only be contemplated in relation to offences summarised under (d) and (e) above if the offence was committed on or after January 1, 1996 (CJA 1988, s.71(3), and Criminal Justice Act 1988 (Confiscation Orders) Order 1995).

(ii) Procedure

12–58   The procedural steps which must be taken before a Confiscation Order may be made are complicated, and have recently been changed by the Proceeds of Crime Act 1995 which will apply to all offences committed on or after November 1, 1995. After this date a magistrates' court may make assumptions about the origins of the offender's property for the purpose of calculating benefit obtained (CJA 1988, s.72A, as inserted by the Proceeds of Crime Act 1995, s.2). If the offence was committed before November 1, 1995 the original section 72 of the 1988 Act will apply. As orders under this legislation are likely to be rare in the magistrates' court the procedure for making a Confiscation Order are not set out in full. They are described in sections 72 to 88 of the Criminal Justice Act 1988 as amended by sections 1 to 12 of the Proceeds of Crime Act 1995.

5. Exclusion Orders

(i) Offence committed on licensed premises

(a) Powers

12–59   1. A court which convicts a person of an offence committed on licensed premises and is satisfied that in committing the offence the offender resorted to violence or offered or threatened to resort to violence may prohibit him from entering those premises, or any other specified licensed premises, for a period of not less than three months and not more than two years without the express consent of the licensee (Licensed Premises (Exclusion of Certain Persons) Act 1980, s.1).

2. An Exclusion Order may be made in addition to any other sentence imposed for the offence of which the offender is convicted.

3. An Exclusion Order is designed for those who in general make nuisances of themselves in public houses and, therefore, is not appropriate for offenders of mature years and persons of good character (*R. v. Grady* (1990) 12 Cr.App.R.(S.) 152).

(b) PROCEDURE IF EXCLUSION ORDER IS NOT COMPLIED WITH

12–60 If it is proved that an offender subject to an Exclusion Order has entered premises in breach of the order he may be fined an amount not exceeding level 3 or sent to prison for a term not exceeding one month (LP (E of CP)A 1980, s.2).

(ii) Offence committed in connection with football matches

(a) POWERS

12–61 1. A court which convicts a person of an offence connected with football (for definition see below) during a period relevant to an association football match may make an Exclusion Order prohibiting the offender from attending any prescribed football match for any period of not less than three months, providing the court is satisfied that the making of the order would help to prevent violence or disorder at the prescribed football matches (Public Order Act 1986, ss.30, 31).

A prescribed football match is defined as a match at which at least one of the sides is a Premier League or Football League club; an international match; a match in the European champion Clubs Cup; a match in the European Cup Winners Cup; a match in the UEFA Cup (Public Order (Football Exclusion) (Amendment) Order 1992).

Offence connected with football means:

(a) any offence committed at the ground, or while entering or attempting to enter the ground in the two hours before the match, or leaving the ground up to one hour after it, providing the match is prescribed by the Home Secretary; or

(b) an offence involving the threat of violence to the person or property or disorderly conduct or racial hatred on a journey to and from any association football match; or

(c) an offence committed on the journey in breach of the Sporting Events (Control of Alcohol) Act 1985 (POA 1986, s.31).

2. An Exclusion Order must be combined with some other penalty (including a Probation Order or an absolute or conditional discharge) (POA 1986, s.30(2)).

3. A court making an Exclusion Order may also order that the offender be photographed on application by the prosecution (POA 1986, s.35).

(b) PROCEDURE IF EXCLUSION ORDER IS NOT COMPLIED WITH

12–62 If it is proved that an offender subject to an Exclusion Order has entered premises in breach of the order he may be fined an amount not exceeding level 3 or sent to prison for a term not exceeding one month (POA 1986, s.32(3)).

(c) TERMINATION OF ORDER

An offender may apply to the court to terminate the order after it has been in force for one year (POA 1986, s.33).

6. Recommendation for Deportation

(i) Powers

12–63 1. A court may recommend for deportation any person over the age of 17 who is not a British citizen who is convicted of an offence punishable with imprisonment, provided the offender is not a Commonwealth or Irish citizen who was ordinarily resident in the United Kingdom before January 1, 1973 and who at the time of his conviction had been ordinarily resident in the United Kingdom for the preceding five years (Immigration Act 1971, s.3(b) and s.7(1)).

2. In the case of offenders who are EEC Nationals the court must be satisfied that the offender's continued presence represents a "genuine and sufficiently serious threat to the requirements of public policy affecting one of the fundamental interests of society" (*Re Bouchereau* [1978] Q.B. 732—a case in the European Court of Justice interpreting Article 48 of the EEC Treaty).

(ii) Procedure

12–64 1. Before a court is able to make a recommendation for deportation the offender must have been given at least seven days' notice in writing (IA 1971, s.6(2)).

2. Unless the court directs otherwise the offender will be detained in custody pending the Home Secretary's decision (IA 1971, Sched. 3). The court may direct otherwise and admit the offender to bail.

3. A court should grant legal aid, subject to means, to an offender when the court is contemplating a recommendation for deportation (*R. v. Edgehill* [1963] 1 Q.B. 593).

4. In the case of an EEC national reasons must be given in open court as to why a recommendation for deportation is being made (*R. v. Secretary of State, ex p. Santillo* [1981] Q.B. 778; a decision of the European Court of Justice).

(iii) Combining a recommendation for deportation with other sentences or orders

12–65 A recommendation for deportation may be combined with any other lawful sentence or order for the offence imposed on the same occasion.

7. Order Applying the Proceeds of Forfeited Property

Powers

12–66 (a) A court which has made a Forfeiture Order (see §12–53, above) for an offence which has resulted in personal injury loss or damage (or where such an offence is taken into consideration) may also make an order that any proceeds which arise from the disposal of the property, and which do not exceed a sum specified by the court shall be paid to the victim.

(b) Such an order may only be made when the court would have made a Compensation Order for not less than the specified amount but for the inadequacy of the means of the offender.

(c) For the purposes of any claims under the Police (Property) Act 1897, if the property in question is in the possession of the police, a claimant to it must satisfy the court that he had not consented to the offender having possession of the property or that he did not know or have reason to believe that the property was likely to be used for the purpose of committing an offence. In any event a claim under the Police (Property) Act shall not be made before six months have expired since the making of the order (PCCA 1973, s.43A).

8. Restriction Orders

(i) Powers

12–67   (a) A court which convicts a person of a relevant football-related offence (for definition see below) may make a Restriction Order for a period of two years (or five years if immediate imprisonment is imposed) requiring the offender to report to a specified police station at such time as to prevent his attendance at football matches being played outside England and Wales which are designated by the Secretary of State, providing the court is satisfied that the making of the order would help to prevent violence or disorder at or in connection with designated football matches (Football Spectators Act 1989, ss15 and 16).

A designated football match is any match played at Wembley Stadium, the National Stadium in Cardiff or at any sports ground in England and Wales which is registered with the Football League or the Football Association Premier League as the home ground of a club which is a member of either league at the time the match is played (Football Spectators (Designation of Football Matches in England and Wales) Order 1993).

Relevant offence means any of the following offences committed at a designated football match or while the offender was entering or leaving the ground:

(1) an offence under section 5 or Pt III of the Public Order Act 1986;

(2) an offence involving the use or threat of violence towards a person or property;

or any of the following offences committed on a journey to or from a designated football match where the court has made a declaration that the offence related to football:

(1) an offence under section 12 of the Licensing Act 1872;

(2) an offence under section 91(1) of the Criminal Justice Act 1967;

(3) an offence under section 1 of the Sporting Events (Control of Alcohol) Act 1985;

(4) an offence under section 5 or Pt III of the Public Order Act 1986;

(5) an offence involving the use or threat of violence towards a person or property;

(6) an offence under sections 4 or 5 of the Road Traffic Act 1988;

(7) an offence under sections 2, 3 or 4 of the Football (Offences) Act 1991;

or an offence under section 2 of the Sporting Events (Control of Alcohol Act) 1985 committed while entering or trying to enter the ground of a designated football match (FSA 1989, Sched. 1).

Matches played outside England and Wales are national or U.E.F.A. games or any game played abroad by a team in the Football League or F.A. Premier League (Football Spectators (Designation of Football Matches outside England and Wales) Order 1990, as amended by the Sports Grounds and Football (Amendment of Various Orders) Order 1992).

(b) A Restriction Order made for an offence committed in this country under section 15 must be combined with some other penalty (including a Probation Order or absolute or conditional discharge, or an Exclusion Order made under the Public Order Act 1986) (FSA 1989, s.15(3)).

(c) Where the relevant offence is committed on a journey to or from a match a Restriction Order may only be made if the court issues a declaration of relevance that the offence related to football, and the prosecution must serve a notice on the accused signifying their intentions of submitting that the offence related to football at least five days before the hearing.

(ii) Procedure

(a) PROCEDURE ON MAKING THE ORDER

12–68   1. The court must make a declaration of relevance that the offence related to football matches. Such a declaration may not be made unless the prosecution has given notice to the defendant at least five days prior to the first day of the trial in which it was proposed to show that the offence related to football matches, unless the defendant waives his right to notice and the court considers that the interests of justice do not require such notice to be given (FSA 1989, s.23(1) and (2)).

2. The court shall explain to the offender the effect of the order in ordinary language namely:

(a) that the purpose of the order is to make it impossible for him to attend certain football matches outside England and Wales by making him report to a police station whenever such matches take place;

(b) that to fail to report without reasonable excuse is a criminal offence;

(c) that the offender must report initially within five days of the making of the order (or release from custody) to the stated police station (FSA 1989, s.15(6)).

(b) PROCEDURE IF RESTRICTION ORDER IS NOT COMPLIED WITH

If an offender fails without reasonable excuse to comply with a Restriction Order he commits an offence punishable with one month's imprisonment or a fine not exceeding level 3 on the standard scale (FSA 1989, s.16(4) and (5)).

(c) TERMINATION OF THE ORDER

Where an order has been in force for at least one year the offender may apply to the court which originally made the order to have it terminated. The court must then have regard to his character, his conduct since the order was made, the nature of the offence which led to the Restriction Order, and any other circumstances of the case. If the application is refused no further application may be made for six months (FSA 1989, s.17).

9. Anti-Social Behaviour Order

(i) Powers

12–69 1. An application for an anti-social behaviour order may be made by a relevant authority if it appears to the authority that the following conditions are fulfilled with respect to any person aged 10 or over, namely—

(a) that the person has acted since the commencement date, in an anti-social manner, that is to say, in a manner that caused or was likely to cause harassment, alarm or distress to one or more persons not of the same household as himself; and

(b) that such an order is necessary to protect persons in that local government area in that harassment, alarm and distress was caused or was likely to be caused from further anti-social acts by him (CDA 1998, s.1(1)(a) and (b)).

2. If, on such an application, it is proved that the conditions mentioned in subsection (1) above are fulfilled, the magistrates' court may make an order under this section (an "anti-social behaviour order") which prohibits the defendant from doing anything described in the order (*ibid.*, s.1(4)).

3. For the purpose of determining whether the condition mentioned in subsection (1)(a) above is fulfilled, the court shall disregard any act of the defendant which he shows was reasonable in the circumstances (*ibid.*, s.1(5)).

4. The prohibitions that may be imposed by an anti-social behaviour order are those necessary for the purpose of protecting from further anti-social acts by the defendant:

(a) persons in the local government area; and

(b) persons in any adjoining local government area specified in the application for the order (*ibid.*, s.1(6)).

BREACH OF THE ORDER

12–70 If without reasonable excuse a person does anything which he is prohibited from doing by an anti-social behaviour order, he shall be liable:

(a) on summary conviction, to imprisonment for a term not exceeding six months or to a fine not exceeding the statutory maximum, or to both; or

(b) on conviction on indictment, to imprisonment for a term not exceeding five years or to a fine, or to both (with the proviso that a court may not impose a Conditional Discharge (CDA 1998, s.1(10) and (11)).

DISCHARGE OF THE ORDER

12–71 The applicant or the defendant may apply by complaint to the court which made an anti-social behaviour order for it to be varied or discharged by a further order but no application may be made before the end of a period of two years from the date on which the order is served on the defendant (CDA 1998, s.1(8) and (9)).

(ii) Procedure

12–72 An application for an anti-social behaviour order must be made by complaint to a magistrates' court in whose commission area the anti-social behaviour occurred (CDA 1998, s.1(3)).

The application must be in the form set out in Schedule 4 of the Magistrates' Courts (Sex Offender and Anti-social Behaviour) Rules 1998.

An application may not be made unless the relevant authority has consulted the other relevant authority (CDA 1998, s.1(2)).

The standard of proof on an application is the civil standard of proof.

DEFINITIONS

12–73

- Relevant authority means the council for the local government area or the chief officer of police any part of whose police area lies within that area (CDA 1998, s.1(1)).
- Local government area means a London borough, county borough, county, city of London, Isle of Wight and Isles of Scily (*ibid.*, s.1(12)).

10. Sex Offender Order

(i) Powers

12–74   (a) A complaint may be made by a chief officer of police to a magistrates' court if it appears to him that the following conditions are fulfilled—

(i) that the person is a sex offender; and

(ii) that the person has acted, since the relevant date, in such a way as to give reasonable cause to believe that an order under this section is necessary to protect the public from serious harm from him (CDA 1998, s.2(1) and (2)).

(b) If, on such an application, it is proved (on the balance of probabilities) that the above conditions fulfilled, the court may make an order which prohibits the defendant from doing anything described in the order (*ibid.*, s.2(3)).

(c) The prohibitions that may be imposed by a sex offender order are those necessary for the purpose of protecting the public from serious harm from the defendant (*ibid.*, s.2(4)).

(d) A sex offender order shall have effect for a period (not less than five years) specified in the order or until further order; and while such an order has effect, Part I of the Sex Offenders Act 1997 shall have effect as if:

(i) the defendant were subject to the notification requirements of that Part; and

(ii) in relation to the defendant, the relevant date (within the meaning of that Part) were the date of service of the order (*ibid.*, s.2(5)).

BREACH OF THE ORDER

12–75   If without reasonable excuse a person does anything which he is prohibited from doing by a sex offender order, he shall be liable:

(i) on summary conviction, to imprisonment for a term not exceeding six months or to a fine not exceeding the statutory maximum, or to both; or

(ii) on conviction on indictment, to imprisonment for a term not exceeding five years or to a fine, or to both.

Where a person is convicted of an offence under subsection (8) above, it shall not be open to the court by or before which he is so convicted to make an order under subsection (1)(b) (conditional discharge) of section 1A of the 1973 Act in respect of the offence (CDA 1998, s.2(8) and (9)).

DISCHARGE OF THE ORDER

12-76 The applicant or the defendant may apply by complaint to the court which made a sex offender order for it to be varied or discharged by a further order but except with the consent of both parties, no sex offender order shall be discharged before the end of the period of five years beginning with the date of service of the order (CDA 1998, s.2(6) and (7)).

DEFINITIONS

12-77 A sex offender is a person who has been convicted (or found not guilty by reason of insanity) of an offence to which Part I of the Sex Offenders Act 1997 applies (CDA 1998, s.3(1)).

(ii) Procedure

12-78

(a) The application must be made by a complaint.

(b) It must be proved that the offender is a sex offender.

(c) It must be proved that the conduct of the offender gives rise to a reasonable belief that an order is necessary to protect the public from serious harm.

(d) The standard of proof is the civil standard.

11. Sex Offender Notification Requirement

12-79 If an offender is convicted of any offence to which the Sex Offenders Act 1997 applies the court may state in open court that the offender has been so convicted (Sex Offenders Act 1997, s.5(2). Such a statement is not a sentence but the court may certify the fact that the offender has been convicted of an offence to which the Act applies (*ibid.*, s.5(2)(b)).

The Act is relevant in magistrates' courts proceedings only if there has been a conviction following a summary trial or a conviction following a guilty plea to a sexual offence which is triable either way and is an offence in Schedule 1 of the 1997 Act.

There is a requirement upon the offender, independent of any sentence imposed by the court, to comply with "notification requirements" in relation to his name and his home address or change of address. Such notification requirement is not strictly a penalty and therefore it is not appropriate to reduce a sentence simply because the Act imposes a burden of registration (*Att.-Gen.'s Reference No. 50 of 1997 (R. v. Victor)* [1998] 2 Cr.App.R.(S.) 155).

12. Restraining Order

12-80 If an offender has been convicted of an offence contrary to section 2 or section 4 of the Protection from Harassment Act 1997 the court may (as well as sentencing him or dealing with him in any other way) make a Restraining Order (Protection from Harassment Act 1997, s.5(1)).

A Restraining Order is an order prohibiting the offender from doing anything described in the order which is conduct which:

(a) amounts to harassment, or

(b) will cause a fear of violence,

for the purpose of protecting the victim of the offence (*ibid.*, s.5(2)(a) and (b)).

The order may be made for a specified period or until further order (*ibid.*, s.5(3)).

It has been stated, in a Circular issued by the Home Office, that the contents of the order are at the discretion of the court provided the court is satisfied that the conditions are necessary to protect the victim or any other person named in the order from harassment or the fear of violence (HO 34/1997).

Breach of the Order

12–81 If without reasonable excuse the defendant does anything which he is prohibited from doing by a Restraining Order he is guilty of an offence and liable to imprisonment for a term not exceeding the statutory maximum (or a fine or both) if convicted summarily or a sentence not exceeding five years if convicted on indictment (*ibid.*, s.5(6)).

F. Orders in Respect of Prisoners Released on Licence

1. Breach of Licence Condition

(a) Original offence committed before January 1, 1999

12–82 (a) Where a short-term prisoner, that is to say a prisoner serving a sentence of less than four years imposed after October 1, 1992 and before January 1, 1999 is released on licence and fails to comply with the conditions of the licence he commits an offence and may be fined an amount not exceeding level 3 on the standard scale (CJA 1991, s.33(5) and s.38(1)).

(b) In addition the court may suspend the licence for a period not exceeding six months, and order the prisoner to be recalled to prison for the period during which the licence is suspended (*ibid.*, s.38(2)).

(b) Original offence committed on or after January 1, 1999

12–83 The above provisions will not apply if the original offence (for which the offender is before the court) was committed on or before January 1, 1999 (CDA 1998, s.103(2)).

Offenders in this category will in future be subject to recall by the Parole Board and the courts will have no further involvement in allegations relating to breach of licence conditions (*ibid.*, s.103(3)).

2. Commission of Further Offence During Licence

Powers

12–84 The Criminal Justice Act 1991 makes provision for the return to custody of an offender convicted of a new offence after his release from a previous sentence but before the final term of that sentence has expired.

If, before the date on which he would (but for his release) have served his sentence in full, an offender commits an offence punishable with imprisonment; and whether before or after that date, he is convicted of a new offence then (subject to magistrates' courts powers) the court before which the offender is convicted of the new offence may, whether or not it passes any other sentence on him, order him to be returned to prison for the whole or any part of the period which:

(a) begins with the date of the order; and

(b) is equal in length to the period between the date on which the new offence was committed and the date mentioned in subsection (1) above (CJA 1991, s.40(1) and (2)).

A magistrates' court:

(a) shall not have power to order a person to whom this section applies to be returned to prison for a period of more than six months; but

(b) subject to section 25 of the Criminal Justice and Public Order Act 1991 may commit him in custody or on bail to the Crown Court for sentence and the Crown Court (*ibid.*, s.40(3)) as amended by CDA 1998, ss106 and 119 and Sched. 7, para. 43).

The period for which a person is ordered to be returned to prison:

(a) shall be taken to be a sentence of imprisonment for the purposes of this Part (of the Criminal Justice Act 1991),

(b) shall, as the court may direct, either be served before and be followed by, or be served concurrently with, the sentence imposed for the new offence; and

(c) in either case, shall be disregarded in determining the appropriate length of that sentence (*ibid.*, s.40(4)(a), (b) and (c)).

Where the new offence is found to have been committed over a period of two or more days, or at some time during a period of two or more days, it shall be taken for the purposes of this section to have been committed on the last of those days (*ibid.*, s.40(5), as inserted by CDA 1998, ss106 and 119 and Sched.8, para. 85).

12–85   The following general points should be noted.

1. The words "short term prisoner" (*i.e.* one serving a sentence of four years or less (CJA 1991, s.33(5)) include sentence served in a young offender institution.

2. The new offence must be one punishable with imprisonment and *committed* within the full term of the sentence. It is the date of the commission of the new offence which is relevant, not the date on which the court invokes the provisions of section 40.

3. The court should disregard the fact that the offender may be returned to prison when fixing the length of the new sentence (s.40(4)(c)).

4. In calculating whether the new offence was committed within the full term the court should allow for time spent in custody on remand in deciding whether the offence was committed within the full term of the original sentence (CJA 1967, s.67).

5. The power is discretionary: the court may return the offender to serve the whole of the remaining term (subject to the restrictions set out in s.40(3)) or a lesser term.

6. The period ordered under section 40 must be served *before* any new sentence imposed for the new offence or concurrently with it; it may not be ordered to be served consecutively (s.40(4)(b)). Unless the order is announced in this way the sentence will be unlawful (*R. v. Clerkenwell Magistrates' Court, ex p. Feeley* [1996] 2 Cr.App.R.(S.) 309).

7. The requirement to impose a new sentence to be served consecutively to any period ordered under section 40 is unaffected by section 102 of the Crime and Disorder Act 1998 because an order to return is taken to be a sentence of imprisonment by virtue of the wording of section 40(4)(a) of the 1991 Act (*R. v. Lowe, R. v. Leask* [1999] Crim.L.R. 423.

8. An offender ordered to be returned under section 40 is entitled to be released unconditionally after having served half the term imposed, if that term is for a period of 12 months or less if the new offence was committed on or after September 30, 1998 (CJA, s.40A, as inserted by CDA 1998, s.105 and s.120(1) and Sched.9, para, 14).

12–86   The deliberate wording in section 40(2) that "the court ... may ... order him to be returned to prison" means that an order under section 40(3) is not a sentence of imprisonment restricted by section 133 of the Magistrates' Courts Act 1980. Accordingly, the statutory limit as to the length of a prison sentence applicable to magistrates' courts is not relevant (*R. v. Worthing and District Justices, ex p. Varley* (1998) 1 Cr.App.R.(S.) 175). In that case justices had imposed the maximum sentence (six months) for the new offence and ordered the offender to be returned to prison to serve the outstanding term of 128 days which was ordered to be served first. The Divisional Court held that the order under section 40 was an order continuing the old sentence imposed at the Crown Court not a new sentence: accordingly, the restrictions on the length of a custodial sentence laid down in section 133 of the Magistrates' Courts Act 1980 did not apply.

12–87   It has been held that the wording of section 40(3) means that if the offender has committed a new summary only offence during the unexpired period of a sentence imposed by the Crown Court justices should commit the whole matter to be dealt with by the Crown Court if the new offence was one of any gravity or there was a significant period of the whole term left unexpired (*R. v. Harrow Justices, ex p. Jordan* [1997] 1 W.L.R. 84). The same principle will obviously apply if the new offence is one triable either way. It was also held in that case that the wording of section 40(3) equally allowed the magistrates' court to deal with the whole matter, but justices may not pass sentence for the new offence and commit the offender to the Crown Court to be dealt with under section 40. The interpretation of section 40 has not proved to be easy and the correctness of the decision in *ex p. Jordan* was challenged in a later case, *R. v. Burton-On-Trent Justices, ex p. Smith* (1997) 161 J.P. 741. It was held that *ex p. Jordan* had been correctly decided. It has also been held that justices may commit under section 40(3) if the offender has committed a new summary only offence whilst subject to recall of a sentence imposed by the Crown Court for an either way offence, even though the power of the Crown Court to sentence for the new offence would be limited to six months' imprisonment (*R. v. Russell* [1998] 2 Cr.App.R.(S.) 375).

SENTENCING PRINCIPLES

12–88   When justices are faced with a decision whether to make an order under section 40 they should first decide what the appropriate sentence should be for the new offence, disregarding the fact that the offender was liable to recall. Having made that decision justices should then have regard to the nature and extent of any progress made by the offender since his release in considering whether to make an order under section

40. Finally, applying the totaltity principle, justices should decide whether, if a return to prison is ordered, it should be served before or concurrently with the sentence for the new offence (*R. v. Taylor* [1998] 1 Cr.App.R.(S.) 312).

G. Disqualification, Penalty Points and Endorsement of Driving Licences

1. Introduction

12–89   The Road Traffic Act 1991, which came into force on July 1, 1992, and the Aggravated Vehicle-Taking Act 1992, which came into force on April 1, 1992, have each made changes to the law and procedure affecting road traffic cases. Both Acts are amending Acts to existing legislation. Part 1 of the Road Traffic Act 1991 amends the Road Traffic Act 1988 and the Road Traffic Offenders Act 1988, and the Aggravated Vehicle-Taking Act 1992 amends the Theft Act 1968. For this reason the references will, in the main, refer to the principal Act in question.

(a) New offences

12–90   The Road Traffic Act 1991 creates a number of new offences, some of which are triable on indictment only and not included in this summary.

The principal new offences triable summarily, or either way, are:

(1)   dangerous driving (replacing reckless driving),

(2)   causing danger to road users,

(3)   construction and use offences.

The Aggravated Vehicle-Taking Act 1992 creates the new offence of taking a vehicle, or allowing oneself to be carried in a taken vehicle, which then causes damage or injury or is driven dangerously.

It is beyond the scope of this book to discuss the details of these offences, and they are mentioned in order to assist the reader in understanding the changes to sentencing powers and procedure.

(b) New penalties

12–91   Substantial new penalties are introduced in the new Acts for the offences of dangerous driving, taking a motor vehicle without consent, aggravated motor vehicle-taking, driving without insurance and failing to stop after an accident. In addition the Road Traffic Act 1991 makes changes to the number of penalty points which must be imposed in respect of a number of offences. These are discussed fully at §12–104, below.

2. Obligatory Disqualification

(a) Obligatory disqualification for a minimum period of 12 months

12–92   Disqualifications must be imposed upon an offender for at least 12 months (RTOA 1988, s.34) when he is convicted of the following offences:

1.   driving or attempting to drive whilst unfit through drink or drugs;

2.   driving or attempting to drive with excess alcohol;

3. failing or refusing to provide a specimen for laboratory analysis (RTOA 1988, s.34);

4. dangerous driving; and

5. aggravated vehicle-taking (RTOA 1988, Sched. 2, as amended by RTA 1991, s.26 and Sched. 2 and Aggravated Vehicle-Taking Act 1992, s.3).

(b) Obligatory disqualification for a minimum period of three years

12–93 Disqualification must be imposed upon an offender for at least three years when he is convicted of driving or attempting to drive whilst unfit or with excess alcohol or with failing to provide a specimen for laboratory analysis, if within the previous 10 years he has been convicted of any of those offences.

The only ground for avoiding disqualification for the mandatory minimum period in the above cases is if there are special reasons for not disqualifying or special reasons for disqualifying for a shorter period. (For the meaning of special reasons see below, §12–108.)

(c) Obligatory disqualification for varying periods when the offender has 12 or more points endorsed on his licence

12–94 Where an offender is convicted of an endorsable offence and the penalty points to be taken into account number 12 or more, the offender must be disqualified as follows:

1. six months if no previous disqualification is to be taken into account;

2. 12 months if one previous disqualification is to be taken into account;

3. two years if more than one previous disqualification is to be taken into account;

unless there are mitigating circumstances which are not excluded from consideration (RTOA 1988, s.35).

Disqualification in this context is sometimes called "totting up." (For the meaning of "totting up" see §12–103, below.) A disqualification *to be taken into account* means one imposed within three years of the latest offence under consideration by the court (RTOA 1988, s.35(2)). However, such disqualification shall only be taken into account if there are also 12 or more penalty points.

The only grounds for avoiding obligatory disqualification for the appropriate period are (i) special reasons for not disqualifying at all, or (ii) mitigating circumstances entitling the court to reduce the mandatory period or not to disqualify at all.

For *penalty points to be taken into account* and *penalty points disqualification* see §§12–99 to 12–101.

For *special reasons* see §12–108.

For *mitigating circumstances* see §12–109.

Endorsable offence means one defined in Schedule 2 of the Road Traffic Offenders Act 1988, as amended by Schedule 2 of the Road Traffic Act 1991.

The new, amended, list of such offences and their respective penalty points is set out in the table at §12–101, below.

(d) Obligatory disqualification until new test is passed

12–95 Where an offender is convicted of dangerous driving the court must, in addition to the mandatory 12 months' disqualification for the offence, also disqualify the offender until he has passed an extended driving test (RTOA 1988, s.36(1), as substituted by RTA 1991, s.32). The words "extended driving test" have a different meaning to the traditional "test of competence to drive" (*ibid.*, s.36(5)), and will therefore involve a more rigorous examination. This new duty to order a new driving test also applies to the more serious driving offences triable only on indictment (*ibid.*, s.36(2)).

3. Discretionary Disqualification

(a) Discretionary disqualification where penalty points are mandatory

12–96   A discretionary power to disqualify exists in respect of a conviction for any offence for which endorsement is obligatory and which appears in the table at §12–101, below (RTOA 1988, s.34(2), as amended by RTA 1991, s.29).

The range of penalty points applicable to individual offences has been considerably revised by the Road Traffic Act 1991 and the table reflects these revisions.

The 1991 Act alters the law on discretionary disqualification in the following way. The court may only exercise its discretion to disqualify for a particular offence when the offender is not liable for disqualification under "totting up." Where an offender is liable for "totting up" then he must be disqualified only under section 35 of the Act (the "totting up" section (*ibid.*, s.34(2)(a))).

The significance of this change is explained fully below.

(b) Discretionary disqualification where penalty points may not be imposed

12–97   Under the 1991 Act the court may not assign penalty points (or disqualify under the "totting up" provisions) for the offences of taking a motor vehicle without consent, stealing a motor vehicle or going equipped for the theft of a motor vehicle. However, the court does have a discretionary power to disqualify an offender convicted of any of these offences (Pt. II of Sched. 2 of RTOA 1988, as amended by RTA 1991, s.26 and Sched. 2).

A discretionary power to disqualify also exists where an offender has been convicted of common assault and the assault was committed by the driving of a motor vehicle (PCCA 1973, s.44(1A) and (2A)).

(c) Interim disqualification

12–98   Where a court:

(1) commits an offender for sentence at the Crown Court, or

(2) remits an offender for sentence to another magistrates' court, or

(3) defers passing sentence, or

(4) adjourns passing sentence in order to prepare reports,

and the offence carries obligatory or discretionary disqualification, the court may order the offender to be disqualified in the interim until sentence is passed (RTOA 1988, s.26(1) and (2), as substituted by RTA 1991, s.25).

Such an interim disqualification may only last for a maximum period of six months and will then automatically expire if it has not already ceased to have effect (*ibid.*, s.26(4)).

The procedure for passing an interim disqualification is for the court to require the offender to surrender his licence, or to post it to the court immediately (*ibid.*, s.26(7)).

If the sentencing court dealing with the offender imposes a sentence of disqualification, the length of such an order must be treated as reduced by the period of the interim disqualification (*ibid.*, s.26(12)).

4. Penalty Points

General rule

(a) INDIVIDUAL OFFENCE

12–99 A court which convicts of an offence involving obligatory endorsement must impose (i) the number of penalty points the offence attracts, or (ii) where there is a range of numbers, a number within the range (RTOA 1988, s.28(1), as substituted by RTA 1991, s.27).

(b) TWO OR MORE OFFENCES

12–100 Where the offender is convicted (whether on the same occasion or not) of two or more offences committed on the same occasion, the number of points should be attributed to the offence carrying the highest number, unless the court states its reasons, and records them in the register, for not following this rule (*ibid.*, s.28(4), (5) and (6)).

Therefore, the 1991 Act has diverged from the previous rule which was that the court should invariably attach the points to the most serious offence when an offender was convicted of more than one offence. Now the court may "if it thinks fit" impose points on all the offences (*ibid.*, s.28(5)), but only when there is good reason to do so (*ibid.*, s.28(6)). The good reason for imposing penalty points for more than one offence committed on the same occasion will be rare, but will apply when the maximum number of points available for any individual offence is insufficient to reflect the gravity of the offending behaviour.

Secondly, the 1991 Act provides that the rule applies even if the offender is convicted on different occasions for offences occurring at the same time. For this reason there is specific provision for the penalty points imposed on the later occasion to be restricted to comply with the obligation to impose points for the offence attracting the highest number (*ibid.*, s.28(4)).

(c) FIXED PENALTY

12–101 Where an offender is convicted without a court hearing (the "fixed penalty" system) and the offence attracts a range of points (for example, speeding), then the number of points imposed under the system must be the lowest of the range (*ibid.*, s.28(3)).

The importance of this change is that the new Act gives the Secretary of State power to alter the number and range of penalty points by statutory instrument (*ibid.*, s.28(7)).

5. "Totting Up"

12–102 "Totting up" is the colloquial expression for the rule under which an offender has his past penalty points added to the penalty points imposed for the present offence for the purposes of disqualification, where the number of points is 12 or more.

The new Act makes a number of changes to the law. It provides that where an offender is convicted of an offence involving obligatory endorsement, the number of points to be taken into account is:

(a) those attributed to the present offence, disregarding any mandatory or discretionary disqualification imposed; and

(b) those already on the licence relating to the period of three years immediately preceding the date of the new offence unless any of the offences were committed more than three years before any other offence or unless the offender has in the meantime been disqualified under section 35 of the Act (see §12–70, above) (RTOA 1988, s.29(1), as substituted by RTA 1991, s.28).

TABLE OF PENALTY POINTS

12–103

Being in charge of a motor vehicle when unfit or with alcohol above the prescribed limit	10
Failing or refusing to provide a specimen for analysis when the offender was not driving or attempting to drive	10
Failing to stop after an accident	5–10
Failing to report an accident	5–10
Using (or causing or permitting the use of) a motor vehicle whilst uninsured	6–8
Driving whilst disqualified	6
Careless or inconsiderate driving	3–9
Driving after making a false declaration as to physical fitness	3–6
Driving after notification of physical fitness	3–6
Driving after licence has been revoked on grounds of disability	3–6
Driving otherwise than in accordance with a licence	3–6
Exceeding a speed limit	3–6
Failing to provide a preliminary specimen for a breath test	4
Failing to comply with traffic lights or traffic directions	3
Contravention of construction and use regulations	3
Contravention of pedestrian crossing regulations	3
Contravention of traffic regulations on special roads	3
Driving with uncorrected defective eyesight or refusing to submit to an eyesight test	3
Using a vehicle in a dangerous condition	3
Driving whilst under age	2
Failing to comply with the conditions of a licence	2

NOTE: If there are special reasons for not disqualifying for an offence attracting obligatory disqualification then the notional penalty points for assessing future liability shall be 3–11, depending upon the seriousness of the offence.

This amendment removes the anomaly whereby a person who was disqualified for a specific offence could be simultaneously disqualified under the "totting up" procedure.

The change also has an effect on "wiping the slate clean." In the past when an offender was disqualified, he received his licence back at the end of the period of disqualification free from any of the earlier penalty points: as a result the disqualification was said to have "wiped the slate clean." Under the 1991 Act where an offender is disqualified under "totting up" this will continue to be the case, but where the offender is disqualified for the new offence, and he already has points on his licence, these points will remain until they expire through time.

This change is brought about by section 29 of the new Act, which amends RTOA 1988, s.34(2) in the following way:

"Where a person is convicted of an offence involving discretionary disqualification, and either—

(a) the penalty points to be taken into account on that occasion number fewer than 12, or

(b) the offence is not one involving obligatory endorsement, the court may order him to be disqualified for such period as the court thinks fit."

Where the penalty points to be taken into account on that occasion number 12 or more, then the offender is only disqualified under section 35 of the 1988 Act ("totting up"), and not for the new offence as well.

6. Penalties

(a) DANGEROUS DRIVING

12–104 The maximum penalty for dangerous driving in six months' imprisonment and/or the statutory maximum fine, a mandatory disqualification for a minimum period of 12 months and disqualification until an extended driving test is passed.

The provisions relating to a compulsory new driving test for those convicted of dangerous driving is described at §12–95, above.

If there are special reasons for not disqualifying for the offence, then the penalty points to be imposed are in the range of 3–11.

(b) AGGRAVATED VEHICLE-TAKING

12–105 The maximum penalty for aggravated vehicle-taking is six months' imprisonment and/or the statutory maximum fine and a mandatory disqualification for a minimum period of 12 months. In addition, special new rules relating to "special reasons" apply to this offence. These are discussed fully at §12–108, below.

If there are special reasons then the penalty points to be imposed are in the range of 3–11.

(c) FAILING TO STOP AFTER AN ACCIDENT (OR FAILING TO REPORT AN ACCIDENT)

12–106 This offence is now punishable with a maximum six months' imprisonment and/or the statutory maximum fine, with discretionary disqualification and a range of penalty points of 5–10.

(d) Using a vehicle whilst uninsured

12–107   The maximum fine for this offence is increased to the statutory maximum.

(e) Theft or attempted theft of a vehicle, taking a vehicle without consent, or going equipped to steal a vehicle

Penalty point endorsement for these offences is abolished.

7. Special Reasons

12–108   A special reason means a mitigating or extenuating circumstance, not amounting to a defence in law to the charge, but directly connected with the commission of the offence and one which the court ought properly to take into account when imposing sentence (*Whittal v. Kirby* [1946] 1 All E.R. 552).

The application of this principle to different factual circumstances is dealt with in *Stone's Justices Manual* and specialist books on road traffic law.

The onus of establishing special reasons is on the party who raises them and the standard of proof is the balance of probabilities (*Jones v. English* [1951] 2 All E.R. 853).

Special rule for aggravated vehicle-taking offences

12–109   If an offender is convicted of aggravated vehicle-taking he will not be allowed to put forward the fact that he did not drive the vehicle at a particular time or at all as a special reason for avoiding the mandatory disqualification (RTOA 1988, s.34(1A), as inserted by the Aggravating Vehicle-Taking Act 1992, s.3(2)).

8. Mitigating Circumstances

12–110   A mitigating circumstance is any circumstance which is not one which alleges the offence is not serious, nor one which causes hardship unless the hardship is exceptional, nor one upon which the offender has relied in the previous three years (RTOA 1988, s.35(4)). This means that the court must be satisfied that there would be exceptional hardship to the offender if he were to be disqualified for the minimum statutory period. If the court is so satisfied it may reduce the period of disqualification or not disqualify at all (*ibid.*, s.35(1)).

The application of section 35 of the Road Traffic Offenders Act 1988 will depend on the facts and circumstances of the case including considerations of general sentencing policy (*R. v. Thomas* [1983] 3 All E.R. 756).

The onus of establishing mitigating circumstances is on the party who raises them and the standard of proof is on the balance of probabilities (*Jones v. English* [1951] 2 All E.R. 853).

9. Alternative Verdicts

12–111   Section 24 of the Road Traffic Offenders Act 1984, as substituted by section 24 of the Road Traffic Act 1991 allows the court to convict of alternative offences in the manner shown below:

Offence charged	Alternative
section 2 (dangerous driving)	section 3 (careless or inconsiderate driving)
section 4(1) (driving or attempting to drive when unfit through drink or drugs)	section 4(2) (being in charge of a vehicle when unfit through drink or drugs)
section 5(1)(a) (driving or attempting to drive with excess alcohol in breath, blood or urine)	section 5(1)(b) (being in charge of a vehicle with excess alcohol in breath, blood or urine)
section 28 (dangerous cycling)	section 29 (careless or inconsiderate cycling)

10. Procedural Steps

12–112   (a) A court may not disqualify an offender in his absence unless he has been given the opportunity of attending an adjourned hearing (MCA 1980, s.11(4)).

(b) All orders for disqualification commence from the moment the order is pronounced and cannot run consecutively to any other order or to an order of imprisonment.

(c) A court may endorse an offender's licence with penalty points in his absence provided the licence has been sent to the court. If it has not been sent the court may order its production, and failure thereafter to produce it will mean that the licence is suspended (RTOA 1988, s.27(3)).

(d) If the court finds that there are special reasons or mitigating circumstances the reasons or circumstances must be announced in open court and entered on the court register (*ibid.*, s.47(2)).

CHAPTER 13

General Sentencing Practice

A. General Principles

1. The Purpose of Sentencing

13–01   The purposes of criminal sentencing have traditionally been said to be retribution, deterrence and rehabilitation (*per* Lord Bingham C.J. in an address to the Police Foundation, July 10, 1997). In this address Lord Bingham reiterated the essential and fundamental concepts of sentencing which have been adopted by Judges and magistrates for many years. In a booklet published jointly by the Home Office and the Judicial Studies Board in 1990, *The Sentence of the Court,* it was stated that there were three ways in which the courts could punish and prevent crime: deterring potential offenders by a fear of punishment; preventing the particularly dangerous from offending by putting them out of circulation; influencing offenders not to offend again (HMSO 1990, para. 3.2).

In 1991 Parliament attempted, by introducing the Criminal Justice Act 1991, to replace these three traditional purposes with a single objective of sentencing, namely just deserts. In a White Paper *Crime, Justice and Protecting the Public* (Cm. 965) which preceded the Act it was stated that "punishment in proportion to the seriousness of the crime . . . should be the principal focus for sentencing decisions" (*ibid.*, §2.2). This aim, known as the aim of proportionality or just deserts, was the central idea in the White Paper and became the main feature of the Criminal Justice Act 1991.

It was not long before it became clear that the provisions of the 1991 Act did not, and could not, satisfy the public. The emphatic concentration on the single principle of just deserts in the Act meant that an offender's previous record of offending had to be ignored in all but the most exceptional cases. In 1993 Parliament modified the principle of just deserts considerably by amending the 1991 Act to allow courts to take into account previous convictions in assessing the seriousness of an offence (CJA 1991, s.29(1), as substituted by CJA 1993, s.66(6)). In the same year Lord Taylor C.J. ruled that the Act did not exclude an element of deterrence being assessed when punishment for an offence was imposed (*R. v. Cuningham* [1993] 1 W.L.R. 183).

The combination of Parliament's own amendment and judgments from the Court of Appeal have considerably diluted the central purpose of the 1991 Act and concepts which existed before the passing of the Act have been revived. Thus, Lord Bingham reiterated the traditional concepts of retribution, deterrence and rehabilitation in his address quoted above. In another speech Lord Bingham stated that all, or almost all, sentences are imposed for the purpose of protecting the public. Such protection may be achieved either by curing a defendant from his propensity to offend, or by deterring him and others from offending, or both (Speech to the National Probation Convention, November 12, 1997).

Although the Criminal Justice Act 1991 is a shadow of its former self it has had and will continue to have a major effect towards achieving rationality and consistency in sentencing. This is because the Act provides a statutory framework within which all sentencing decisions must be taken. The essential feature is that it is the concept of seriousness which governs the decision whether a custodial or non-custodial sentence should be passed.

2. The Concept of Seriousness

(i) General considerations

13–02 The requirement that a court may not ordinarily pass a custodial sentence unless the offence (or the combination of the offence and one or more offences associated with it) is so serious that only such as a sentence can be justified for it has been described as "fundamental" (*R. v. Brewster* [1998] 1 Cr.App.R. 220). It is the central concept of the 1991 Act, even though the word "serious" is not defined in the Act.

The only attempt to categorise offences is the distinction between a "serious" offence and a "violent or sexual offence." Theoretically, a custodial sentence may be passed on a violent or sexual offender even if the offence committed is not a serious one (ss1(2)(b) and 2(2)(b)). However, almost all violent or sexual offences are also serious, and the distinction is really aimed at the length of the custodial sentence appropriate for the violent and sexual offender. This is discussed below at §§13–46 *et seq.*, below).

The concept of seriousness is the foundation of the sentencing structure of the 1991 Act. At every stage of the sentencing process the court is required to consider what it means. It governs the qualification for the imposition of a custodial sentence (s.1(2)(a)), a community sentence (s.6(1)), and a fine (s.18(2)). It governs the length of a custodial sentence (s.2(2)(a)) and the type of community sentence to be ordered (s.6(2)(b)) and is the criterion for protecting the public from a dangerous offender (s.1(2)(b)), and for a committal for sentence (MCA 1980 s.38). The Act cannot be applied or understood without an analysis of what seriousness means.

13–03 At one time Judges in the Court of Appeal were reluctant to embark on a definition of seriousness other than the somewhat vague and entirely subjective rationalisation of seriousness in the mind of right-thinking members of the public. The Court of Appeal (Criminal Division) has now, in a judgment of Lord Bingham C.J., given guidance on the factors to be taken into account (*R. v. Howells and other appeals* [1999] 1 All E.R. 50). The judgment has recognised the subjective nature of sentencing in that each sentencer would form his or her own judgment of what justice required and that it would be dangerous to lay down prescriptive rules governing the exercise of that judgment. Any guidance on seriousness therefore will necessarily be subject to exceptions and qualifications. With that caveat, the following guidance was given by the Lord Chief Justice:

(a) FACTORS RELATING TO THE OFFENCE

13–04   1. It is usually helpful to begin by considering the defendant's criminal *intention* and the nature and extent of any injury or damage caused to the victim. All things being equal an offence which was deliberate and premeditated would usually be more serious than one which was spontaneous and unpremeditated or which involved an excessive response to provocation.

2. An offence which inflicts personal injury or mental trauma, particularly if permanent, is usually more serious than one which inflicts financial loss.

3. Previous convictions and the defendant's failure to respond to previous sentences may be taken into account.

4. It will be an aggravating factor if the offence was committed on bail.

(b) FACTORS RELATING TO THE OFFENDER

13–05   1. A plea of guilty tendered at the earliest opportunity accompanied by hard evidence of genuine remorse.

2. A genuine self-motivated determination to address addiction when an offence was fuelled by drink or drugs.

3. Youth and immaturity would often justify a less rigorous penalty than that appropriate to an adult.

4. Some measure of leniency would normally be extended to offenders of previous good character, the more so if there was evidence of positive good character such as a solid employment record or faithful discharge of family duties as opposed to a mere absence of previous convictions.

5. There would be a greater reluctance to impose a custodial sentence when the offender had never previously served such a sentence.

13–06   In addition the Court of Appeal has stated that as the purpose of imposing a custodial sentence is to punish and deter the words "commensurate with the seriousness of the offence" in section 2(2)(a) of the 1991 Act mean commensurate with the punishment and deterrence which the punishment of the offence requires. In considering such questions the court is entitled to have regard to the prevalence of the offence (*R. v. Cunningham* [1993] 1 W.L.R. 183). Thus, if pickpocketing is a prevalent offence in a particular locality it is permissible for justices to take that into account in assessing the seriousness of the offence (*R. v. Smith and Read* [1997] 1 Cr.App.R.(S.) 342).

The decision in *Cunningham*, above, together with another, *R. v. Cox* [1993] 1 W.L.R. 188, established another important aspect of the sentencing structure of the 1991 Act.

In its original form the Criminal Justice Act 1991 stated that with the exception of offences triable only on indictment a court was obliged to obtain and consider a presentence before forming an opinion either that the offence was so serious that only a custodial sentence could be justified or before forming an opinion as to the suitability of an offender for a community penalty. The clear purpose of the legislation was to make the contents of a pre-sentence report, which received a statutory definition in section 3(5) of the Act, an integral part of the sentencing decision. The exception to this principle was confined only to the very serious offences triable exclusively on indictment where a tariff sentence or a deterrent punishment would be unlikely to be affected by anything said in a pre-sentence report.

In an amendment introduced in the Criminal Justice and Public Order Act 1994 this exception now applies to all cases. The law is that the obligation to obtain and consider a pre-sentence before forming an opinion as to seriousness does not apply if, in the circumstances of the case, the court is of the opinion that it is unnecessary to obtain a report (CJA 1991, s.3(1) and (2) as amended). It is submitted that it will only be proper for the court to pass a custodial sentence without considering a report if there is some material before the court, either in the obvious and transparent seriousness of the offence or in the nature of the offender's previous history, which would entitle the court to conclude that it is unnecessary to obtain a report. The court must direct its mind to the issue of whether in the circumstances of the particular case it is unnecessary to obtain a report. Only if this question is determined affirmatively will it be permissible for the court to dispense with a report before making a final decision as to seriousness.

13–07 Seriousness is a threshold which has to be reached before a custodial or a community sentence can be passed. The fact that the sentencing court is of the opinion that an offence is "so serious" that only a custodial sentence can be justified (s.1(2)(a)), or "serious enough" to warrant a community sentence (s.6(1)) does not mean necessarily that such sentences must be passed. The decision as to which sentence must in the end be passed will depend upon many factors, particularly the offender's personal mitigation. The seriousness test is a pre-condition for the consideration of a particular type of sentence. If the threshold for that type of sentence is reached, the court must go on to consider the offender's mitigation, and decide what particular sentence to pass in his case.

> D, aged 19, pleaded guilty to handling stolen goods, common assault and theft. Held: The combination of the offences of theft and handling stolen goods was such that only a custodial sentence could be justified, but the fact that the criteria for imposing a custodial sentence had been reached did not oblige the court actually to pass such a sentence. (In this case a custodial sentence imposed at the Crown Court was upheld.) (*R. v. Baverstock* [1993] 1 W.L.R. 202.)

(ii) Seriousness and the pre-sentence report

13–08 Although the 1991 Act intended the consideration of a pre-sentence report to be an integral part of the process of considering seriousness, the contents of such a report will rarely, if ever, be of assistance on the facts of the case. This is because the offender will often gloss over the more incriminating aspects of his behaviour to the probation officer. For this reason it has been said that sentencers will not normally pay any attention to the account of the crime contained in a pre-sentence report (*R. v. Tolera* [1998] Crim.L.R. 426, *per* Lord Bingham C.J.).

(iii) Aggravating and mitigating factors

13–09 The 1991 Act provides that an offence may be more or less serious depending upon the presence of aggravating or mitigating factors. The Act requires the court to take into account all such information about the offence, or the offence and any associated offences (including aggravating and mitigating factors) before forming an opinion as to whether the offence is either "so serious" as to warrant a custodial sentence, or "serious enough" for a community sentence (ss3(3) and 7(1)).

The only definition of the word "aggravating" occurs in section 29(2), which states that if an offence was committed on bail the court must treat that fact as an aggravating factor. This definition appears in the amendments to the Act introduced by the Criminal Justice Act 1993. It is not clear why parliament has chosen to single out an offence on bail as an aggravating factor. As long ago as 1973, Lord Widgery C.J. said it would be a very wrong form of sentencing to give people the idea that they could commit an offence on bail and not receive an additional penalty for it (*R. v. Young* [1973] Crim.L.R. 585).

The word aggravating must relate to the *offence* and not the offender.

13–10 The Court of Appeal has on a number of occasions identified factors which aggravate particular offences. These include:

(i) aggravating factors of burglary (*R. v. Brewster and others* [1998] 1 Cr.App.R. 220 (see paragraph 16–02, below);

(ii) aggravating factors of dangerous driving (*R. v. Boswell* (1984) 9 Cr.App.R. (S.) 277) (see paragraph 22–03, below);

(iii) aggravating factors of breach of trust, theft (*R. v. Barrick* (1985) 7 Cr.App.R.(S.) 142) (see paragraph 17–02, below);

(iv) aggravating factors of sexual offences (see generally Chapter 19, below).

More recently Parliament has stated that racial motivation in the commission of an offence shall be treated as an aggravating factor (CDA 1998, s.82(2)). This is dealt with fully below.

In addition, the Court of Appeal has in the past identified particular features of offences generally which are aggravating. For example, an offence aimed at an elderly or vulnerable victim (*R. v. Allen and Bennett* (1988) 10 Cr.App.R.(S.) 466 and *R. v. Flynn and Flynn* (1993) 14 Cr.App.R.(S.) 422), or where an attack is racially motivated (*R. v. Alderson* (1989) 11 Cr.App.R.(S.) 301). It is submitted that all of these matters would be considered to be aggravating factors within the meaning of sections 3(3) and 7(1).

While it is mitigation that an offender has pleaded guilty (see §§13–22 and 13–23, below) it is never an aggravating factor that an accused has contested the charge, and sentence should never be increased because of the way a defence was conducted (*R. v. Scott* (1983) 5 Cr.App.R.(S.) 197).

(iv) Racial motivation as an aggravating factor

13–11 The Crime and Disorder Act 1998 has put on a statutory basis the considerations which should apply when racial motivation exists. First, in Part II of the Act, Parliament has created a number of racially aggravated offences for which greater powers of punishment have been prescribed for sentences passed in the Crown Court. Secondly, in Part IV of the Act, Parliament has required sentencers to regard racial aggravation as an aggravating factor for all remaining offences (CDA 1998, s.82).

This radical approach reflects the intention of the government (announced in a consultation document *Racial Violence and Harassment* published by the Home Office in September 1997) that the criminal law should be adequate to protect victims of crime which is motivated by intentions amounting to racial hatred. It remains to be seen whether the good intentions of the government in this regard will be achieved by the legislation.

The Act contains a broad definition of what is meant by racially aggravated. An offence is racially aggravated if:

(a) at the time of committing the offence, or immediately before or after doing so, the offender demonstrates towards the victim of the offence hostility based on the victim's membership (or presumed membership) of a racial group; or

(b) the offence is motivated (wholly or partly) by hostility towards members of a racial group based on their membership of that group (CDA 1998, s.28(1)).

This definition will apply also to all other crimes if sentence is to be increased on the grounds of racial aggravation under section 82 (CDA 1998, s.82(3)).

Section 82 provides that where section 28 applies the court:

(a) shall treat that fact as an aggravating factor (that is to say, a factor that increases the seriousness of the offence); and

(b) shall state in open court that the offence was so aggravated (CDA 1998, s.82(2)).

Racially aggravated offences

13–12 The following either way offences are capable of being charged as racially aggravated crimes for which, in the Crown Court, a higher penalty is available: malicious wounding or causing grievous bodily harm (CDA 1998, s.29(1)(a) and (b)), criminal damage (*ibid.*, s.30(1)) and harassment which puts a person in fear of violence (*ibid.*, s.32(1)(b)).

The following offences, which in their original form are purely summary, are capable of being charged as racially aggravated crimes: common assault (CDA 1998, s.29(1)(c)), offences under section 4 and 4A of the Public Order Act 1986 (*ibid.*, s.31(1)(a), (b) and (c)) and simple harassment (*ibid.*, s.32(1)(a)).

If these offences are charged in their aggravated form they become offences triable either way (CDA 1998, s.29(3)); s.31(4), and s. 32(3)).

The purely summary only offence of causing harassment, alarm and distress under section 5 of the Public Order Act 1986 is capable of being charged in a racially aggravated and the penalty is increased from a fine on level 3 to one on level 4 (CDA 1998, s.31(5)).

In respect of the offences triable either way justices will have a difficult task in weighing the precise nature of the aggravating feature if the accused is convicted or pleads guilty to such an offence. Is the aggravating factor such that the offender should be committed to the Crown Court for sentence, or are summary powers of punishment sufficient, albeit that a greater sentence may need to be imposed to reflect the aggravating factor? This question arose for consideration in *R. v. Miller* [1999] Crim.L.R. 590 when justices committed an offender (with a bad criminal record) for sentence at the Crown Court after he had pleaded guilty to the offence of racially aggravated threatening words and behaviour. He was sentenced to 18 months' imprisonment at the Crown Court and the Court of Appeal held, in dismissing the appeal, that Parliament regarded racial aggravation as a very significant factor.

The Crime and Disorder Act 1998 has not provided greater powers of punishment if the offence is racially aggravated for proceedings in the magistrates' court. Justices are not prevented from imposing a higher penalty than they might otherwise have imposed to reflect the aggravating feature of the offence but they are not bound to do so. Sections 29 to 32 of the Act do not *require* the court to treat racial motivation as an aggravating factor as is the case for all remaining offences by virtue of section 82 (see §13–11, above). Presumably Parliament thought it unnecessary to make such a requirement having increased the penalties, but such drafting only applies to cases in the Crown Court.

There are other difficulties in applying the intentions of Parliament to proceedings in the magistrates' court. If the accused is not convicted of the offence charged in its racially aggravated form there is no provision for a conviction to take place for the simple offence, because there is no power for justices to return an alternative verdict. This restriction will no doubt discourage prosecutors from charging an offence in its aggravated form only. If such a decision results in the accused pleading guilty to or being convicted of the simple offence then justices may not pass sentence on the basis that the offence was racially aggravated (*R. v. Ajit Singh* (1981) 3 Cr.App.R.(S) 380). Further, any offender who has pleaded guilty is entitled to credit for a plea of guilty (see §13–22, below).

Plainly, if the offence is either way and the offender pleads guilty or is convicted then justices may legitimately use their powers to commit the offender for sentence at the Crown Court.

INCREASE IN SENTENCE FOR RACIAL AGGRAVATION GENERALLY

13–13   There is an important principle of sentencing that a racial element accompanying an offence of violence is a gravely aggravating feature (*Att.-Gen.'s Reference (Nos 29, 30 and 31 of 1994)* (1995) 16 Cr.App.R.(S.) 698, *per* Lord Taylor C.J.) Section 82 of the Crime and Disorder Act 1998 puts into statutory form this principle and extends it in the following manner:

   (i) racial aggravation applies to *all* offences other than those created under section 29 to 32 of the Act,

  (ii) the court is *required* to treat racial aggravation as a fact increasing the seriousness of the offence, and

 (iii) the court is *required* to state in open court that the offence was so aggravated (CDA 1988, s.82(1)and(2)).

It is a matter for justices to determine on the facts of the case in question whether the offence has been committed in circumstances defined in section 82(1) and (2). The Act is silent as to the procedure to be followed in making such a determination but it is submitted that justices must be sure beyond a reasonable doubt that the elements defined in section 82 are made out. In addition, the statement in open court must presumably state which of the particular elements defined in section 82 are proved.

In making the determination it is legitimate to hold a *Newton* hearing in order to determine whether or not the offence was racially aggravated (*R. v. Craney and Corbett* [1996] 2 Cr.App.R.(S.) 336). (For *Newton* hearings see §13–42, below).

(v) Mitigating factors

13–14   In deciding whether an offence is "so serious" that only a custodial sentence may be justified or is "serious enough" for a community penalty the court shall take into account all the circumstances of the offence (or associated offences) including "mitigating factors" (CJA 1991, s. 3(3) and 7(1)). Thus, mitigating factors in the 1991 Act relate only to the offence or offences before the court, and is a separate and distinct matter from general mitigation which is considered relevant in reducing the sentence. Mitigation is discussed fully below in §§13–21 to 13–25.

As mitigation invariably attaches to the offender's personal circumstances, or the fact that there has been a plea of guilty, there has been less explicit guidance from the Court of Appeal as to factors which mitigate particular offences. However, the Court of Appeal did outline a number of mitigating features of the offence of obtaining money dishonestly from the Department of Social Security. These were given in *R. v. Stewart and Others* (1987) 9 Cr.App.R.(S.) 135 (see paragraph 17–11, below).

An obvious example of there being mitigation on the facts is where an offence is committed under provocation. Provocation is not a defence to offences of violence (other than murder) but it frequently provides cogent mitigation. If the provocation is considerable it may be enough to provide exceptional circumstances for suspending a sentence of imprisonment in an appropriate case (see *R. v. Huntley* [1993] Crim.L.R. 721). Suspended sentences are dealt with at §§13–53 *et seq.*, below. The other common circumstance where there is mitigation on the facts is where a number of offenders are convicted of the same offence, and the court has to distinguish the relative involvement of each offender.

(vi) Associated offences

13–15 In considering seriousness for the purpose of a custodial or community sentence the court may consider the offence and one or more offences associated with it (ss 1(2)(a), and 6(1)). The words "one or more offences associated with it" were inserted by section 66 of the Criminal Justice Act 1993, and substantially change the intentions of the Act.

The Act, as originally drafted, allowed the court to consider the offence and only one other associated offence for the purpose of assessing seriousness This was to prevent the court from aggregating a number of individual offences, not serious in themselves, in order to pass a custodial or community sentence. The new wording of the Act allows the court to do precisely that, providing that all the offences before the court are "associated offences." The words do not mean similar offences, or offences of comparable seriousness or even offences of the same or similar character. An offence is associated with another if:

(a) the offender is convicted of it in the proceedings in which he is convicted of the other offence, or (if convicted earlier) is sentenced for it at the same time as that offence, or

(b) the offender asks for the offence to be taken into consideration (CJA 1991, s.31(2)).

13–16 Prior to the CJA 1993 amendments, where an offender was due to be sentenced on the same occasion for numerous offences the court could consider only two of them for the purposes of considering the custody threshold (or the community sentence threshold). Now all the offences may be aggregated, and if the offender has previous convictions these may also be taken into account (see "Previous Convictions", below). This is a significant and important departure from the original intentions of the Act which enjoined the courts to ignore previous convictions unless certain circumstances applied and to consider only two offences for the purposes of the seriousness threshold.

The effect of these changes is that more offenders probably receive custodial sentences than the 1991 Act intended. For those who thought that the Act as originally drafted forced the courts to have a blinkered or artificial view of persistent offending, the changes have been welcome. For those who supported the scheme of the 1991 Act which was to divert petty offenders from the "universities of crime" (prisons) the changes have been viewed with dismay.

(vii) Previous convictions

13–17 The question of whether a court was able to take previous convictions into account when sentencing proved to be one of the most controversial aspects of the 1991 Act. It was the original intention of the Act that previous convictions had to be ignored as being irrelevant, unless certain particular circumstances, defined in the old section 29(2), applied. The interaction of the old provisions of section 29(1) and 29(2) caused great difficulty of interpretation and a certain artificiality of application.

The law now states that in considering the seriousness of any offence, the court may take into account any previous convictions of the offender or any failure of his to respond to previous sentences (CJA 1991, s.29(1)). Clearly, this provision must be interpreted in the light of the provisions of Part I of the Act generally, and the court must still concentrate on the seriousness of the offence as the primary consideration. This approach is consistent with established sentencing practice laid down in numerous decisions of the Court of Appeal. "The sentence should reflect the seriousness of the crime committed. Even when a man has got a long record of crimes, he must be sentenced for the offences he has committed" (*R. v. Galloway* (1979) 1 Cr.App.R.(S.) 311).

13–18 Applying this principle it would not be correct for a sentence longer than the seriousness of the offence warrants to be imposed (unless the offence is a violent or sexual one) because of some factor unconnected with the offence, such as the offender's record. The way in which the court should have regard to an offender's previous record was expressed authoritatively by the Court of Appeal in the following way:

> "No prisoner is to be sentenced for the offences which he has committed in the past and for which he has already been punished. The proper way to look at the matter is to decide a sentence which is appropriate for the offence for which the prisoner is before the court. Then in deciding whether that sentence should be imposed or whether the court can extend properly some leniency to the prisoner, the court must have regard to those matters which tell in his favour, and equally to those matters which tell against him; in particular his record of previous convictions" (*R. v. Queen* (1981) 3 Cr.App.R.(S.) 245 at 246).

(viii) Specimen charges

13–19 Where an offender is convicted of an offence or offences which the prosecution allege to be representative of other criminal conduct of the same kind committed on other occasions the court may not take into account such other criminal conduct in order to increase sentence unless the offender specifically admits the conduct or asks for it to be taken into consideration (*R. v. Canavan, Kidd and Shaw* [1998] 1 Cr.App.R. 79).

In that case the Court of Appeal, in a judgment of Lord Bingham C.J. reviewed conflicting dicta on sentencing for "sample charges". The Court of Appeal (Criminal Division) has now authoritatively stated that as a matter of principle an offender may only be sentenced for offences for which he has been convicted, or admitted in a plea of guilty or asked to be taken into consideration. This principle applies even if, on the facts, a conviction for a single offence necessarily involves the commission of other offences. In the judgment of the Court in *Canavan, Kidd and Shaw* this conclusion is consistent with the wording of sections 1, 2, 3 and 31 of the Criminal Justice Act 1991. Such a conclusion does not mean, however, that the court may not take into account acts done in the course of committing the offence or offences charged, even if such acts might have been separately charged.

Plainly, in the light of this decision it is important for the prosecution to charge a sufficient number of charges to represent a pattern of offending (if that is the allegation) or to prepare a full list of offences to be taken into consideration.

> D was convicted at the Crown Court on nine counts of obtaining property by deception to the value of £2,500. The prosecution alleged that such counts represented conduct over a two year period when property to the value of £30,000 had been dishonestly obtained and was so sentenced. Held: Applying *Canavan* D should only have been sentenced in respect of £2,500 (*R. v. Rosenburg* [1998] Crim.L.R. 94)

(ix) Seriousness and the Sentencing Advisory Panel

13–20 Section 80 of the Crime and Disorder Act 1998, which was implemented on July 1, 1999, requires the Court of Appeal (Criminal Division) to consider, in each case before it, whether to frame guidelines as to sentencing with the object, *inter alia*, of promoting consistency in sentencing and promoting confidence in the criminal justice system. If the Court proposes either to frame or revise guidelines it must inform the Sentencing Advisory Panel of its intention. The Panel then has a duty to discuss those intentions within a wider context, to formulate its own views and to communicate those views to the Court of Appeal (CDA 1998, s.81).

3. Mitigation

13–21 The plea in mitigation of penalty has been such an important part of criminal jurisprudence that it has now been incorporated into statute. The Criminal Justice Act 1991 lays down that nothing shall prevent a court from mitigating an offender's sentence by taking into account any such matters as, in the opinion of the court, are relevant in mitigation of sentence (CJA 1991, s.28(1)).

This provision is so broadly stated that, within the limits of relevance, the court is able to consider almost anything which is advanced on an offender's behalf to reduce the sentence. It should be stressed that mitigation under section 28 is something which is considered after the consideration of the threshold of seriousness (including aggravating and mitigating factors of the offence) but before the sentence is announed. The mitigating factors which relate to the concept of seriousness have already been discussed (see paragraph 13–14, above). Mitigation under section 28 is something which might enable a court not to impose a custodial sentence even if the threshold of seriousness for custody has been reached.

This important distinction, between the aggravating and mitigating factors of an offence which must be considered for the question of seriousness and the mitigation which may reduce a deserved custodial sentence to some other disposal, may be illustrated in the following examples:

> D, aged 19, pleaded guilty to a dwelling house burglary, and the sentencer had to consider whether the offence was "so serious that a noncustodial sentence for it

[could not] be justified" under the CJA 1982, s.1(4A)(c). The sentencer decided to defer sentence, but D committed a further offence during the deferment and fell to be sentenced for the burglary. It was argued that the burglary offence could not have been considered by the sentencer to have been "so serious" because sentence was deferred. Held: The argument was false. An offence mght be "so serious", although because of the offender's personal circumstances and mitigation it would not be appropriate actually to impose the sentence. Eighteen months' youth detention imposed at the crown court reduced to 12 months' (*R. v. Bray* (1992) 12 Cr.App.R.(S.) 705).

D1 and D2 pleaded guilty to dwelling house burglary. D1 was sentenced to 12 months' youth detention and D2 consented to a community sentence. Held: D2 had the benefit of a previous good character which was not the case for D1. The fact that the offence was "so serious" as to pass the custody threshold did not mean that such a sentence had to be imposed because section 28 of the 1991 Act overrode the other provisions of the Act (*R. v. Reynolds* [1993] Crim.L.R. 467).

Section 28 of the Act provides wide scope for the consideration of mitigation. The traditional categories of mitigation may be summarised as follows.

(i) Plea of Guilty

13–22 The rule that a reduction in sentence may be imposed after a guilty plea has now been put on a statutory basis. Section 48 of the Criminal Justice and Public Order Act 1994 provides as follows:
(1) In determining what sentence to pass on an offender who has pleaded guilty to an offence in proceedings before that or another court a court shall take into account—

(a) the stage in the proceedings for the offence at which the offender indicated his intention to plead guilty, and

(b) the circumstances in which this indication was given.

(2) If, as a result of taking into account any matter referred to in subsection (1) above, the court imposes a punishment on the offender which is less severe than the punishment it would otherwise have imposed, it shall state in open court that it has done so, (CJ and POA 1994, s.48(1)(a) and (b) and s.48(2)).

The section allows the court to take into account:

(i) the fact that there has been a plea of guilty (s.48(1));

(ii) the occasion of the plea, or indication of a plea (s.48(1)(a)); and

(iii) the circumstances of the plea (s.48(1)(b)).

This new statutory formulation of the matters to which the court may, but not must, take into account is intended to give the sentencer greater discretion in giving a discount for a plea because a plea at a late stage may not attract such a discount as a plea indicated at an early stage. This formulation follows the reasoning of the Royal Commission which suggested a system of "graduated discounts" whereby the most generous discount would be given to a defendant who indicated a plea on the occasion the prosecution papers were served, and the least generous discount would apply to a defendant who only pleaded guilty on the day of the trial.

The intentions of the Royal Commission in this respect have been given explicit statutory force by the procedure for "plea before venue" inserted into the Magistrates' Courts Act by section 49 of the Criminal Procedure and Investigations Act 1996. For the effects of discount for a plea indicated in these circumstances see generally *R. v. Rafferty* [1998] 2 Cr.App.R.(S.) 449.

13–23 Section 48(2) obliges the sentencer to state in open court that credit has been given to an offender who has pleaded guilty, but there is no absolute requirement to pass a lower sentence following a plea. Section 48(2) allows the court to pass a sentence which is not "less severe than the punishment it would otherwise have imposed". In this wording section 48 preserves the common law practice in relation to the circumstances when credit may not be given for a guilty plea. However, it is highly desirable that whenever a sentence is passed following a guilty plea that the court should state whether or not credit has been given under section 48 (*R. v. Fearon* [1996] Crim.L.R. 212).

The Court of Appeal has said that a sentencer is not obliged to reduce a sentence following a plea if:

(i) the protection of the public makes a long sentence or the maximum sentence necessary,

(ii) where the offender delayed tendering his plea until the last moment, and

(iii) where the evidence was overwhelming and a plea of guilty was inevitable (*R. v. Costen* (1989) 11 Cr.App.R.(S.) 182).

For a recent example where it has been re-stated that little weight need be given to the fact of a guilty plea when, on the evidence, a guilty plea is inevitable see *R. v. Landy* (1995) 16 Cr.App.R.(S.) 908.

In addition where an offender has absconded for a considerable period of time before being apprehended on a warrant the behaviour undermines the reason for a discount which might otherwise be given for a plea of guilty (*R. v. Byrne* [1997] 1 Cr.App.R.(S.) 164).

It has been said (in a case decided before section 48 came into force) that in the case of a young offender the invariable practice should be to provide some discount for a plea of guilty save in the most exceptional circumstances (*R. v. Murphy* (1994) 15 Cr.App.R.(S.) 320).

An offender is still entitled to credit for a plea of guilty even if he later gives evidence for a co-accused and, in the court's view, has told lies in that evidence (*R. v. Lawless* [1998] 2 Cr.App.R.(S.) 176).

(ii) Offender's personal circumstances

13–24 There is no exhaustive list of the matters relevant to mitigation which a court is entitled to take into account. The factual circumstances of individual cases are infinitely variable. The following is a summary of the sort of circumstances which have been urged with sufficient regularity for them to have been approved by the Court of Appeal.

(a) the offence was committed when the accused was under great emotional stress, or financial stress for which he was not himself directly responsible;

(b) the background of the accused—the accused is very old or very young, or has taken part in an act of unusual bravery and heroism relating to saving human life in the past;

(c) the effect of a custodial offence on others—the wife and child of the accused being seriously injured in a road accident would suffer unusual hardship if the accused were in custody, or the children of the accused might become seriously disturbed and delinquent if the accused were in custody;

(d) the special consequences of a custodial sentence for an accused—losing a substantial service pension, or being discharged from military service following a conviction for a relatively minor offence;

(e) the conduct of the accused since the commission of the offence—providing the police with valuable information such as the supplier of drugs in a drugs case or the activities of others in the same criminal conduct as the accused.

In addition the Court of Appeal has frequently stressed that the facts of a particular case may provide relevant mitigation. Under the sentencing structure of the Criminal Justice Act 1991 this aspect of mitigation ("mitigating factors") should have been considered at the stage when the court is weighing up the threshold of seriousness (see §§13–02 *et seq.*, above).

(iii) Good character

13–25 An offender's previous good character has always been considered to be relevant mitigation because it shows that offending has not been a regular or persistent activity. In addition, by explicitly recognising and giving credit in sentencing to the offender of good character, the court is able to distinguish such an offender from one with bad character.

Despite the infelicitous and confusing wording of the original section 29(1) of the Criminal Justice Act 1991 the mitigation of good character was retained in the Act. The case of *R. v. Reynolds* (cited at §13–21, above) where an offender of good character received a community sentence while his co-accused, of bad character, received a custodial sentence, is confirmation of this fact. For another example of this general principle see *R. v. Quirke* (1992) 4 Cr.App.R.(S.) 187.

Regrettably, the principle that there is a progressive loss of mitigation for the offender of bad character compared to the one of good character was greatly misunderstood by sentencers in the period immediately after October, 1992. As a result it was assumed by some that the original provisions of section 29(1) prohibited a court from distinguishing between offenders of good and bad character. This was not, it is submitted, the case, but the perception that section 29(1) was defective persuaded the government to alter radically that part of the Act. As has been explained above (see §§13–17 and 13–18, above) the court may now take into account previous convictions in considering seriousness If previous convictions may make the new offence more serious, it obviously follows that the absence of previous convictions may also be a relevant circumstance. Although as a matter of logic the absence of previous convictions cannot affect the seriousness or otherwise of the offence, good character may affect the penalty for the offence.

(iv) Mitigation which is not relevant

13–26 Section 28 of the Act allows the court to take into account "relevant" mitigation. While it is difficult to envisage circumstances in which the court would expressly refuse to hear particular matters advanced on the accused's behalf, there are certain matters which the Court of Appeal has stated are not relevant. These are:

(a) a comparison with the sentences which other offenders have received from other courts for the same offence. If such sentences were unduly lenient, it is not relevant mitigation to urge such leniency for the offender before the court (*R. v. Large* (1981) 3 Cr.App.R.(S.) 80);

(b) in the absence of special circumstances, that the accused committed the offence when under the influence of drink (*R. v. Bradley* (1980) 2 Cr.App.R.(S.) 12);

(c) that the offence was committed when the accused was addicted, whether to drink, drugs, gambling, fast cars or anything else (*R. v. Lawrence* [1989] Crim.L.R. 309);

(d) that at the time of sentence the accused was HIV positive, unless the condition was immediately life-threatening (*R. v. Moore* (1990) 12 Cr.App.R.(S.) 384).

(e) that an accomplice was sentenced to a shorter sentence for the same offence in a foreign jurisdiction (*R. v. Lillie* (1994) 16 Cr.App.R.(S.) 534).

MITIGATION AND DEROGATORY ASSERTIONS

13–27   If in the course of mitigation an assertion derogatory to a person's character is made (for instance, because it suggests that his conduct has been criminal, immoral or improper) *and* that the assertion is false or irrelevant to the sentence the court may make an order (CPIA 1996, s.58 (4) and (7)). The effect of such an order is to prevent the derogatory assertion being reported in the media (*ibid.*, s.59).

An order may be made only if there are "substantial grounds for believing" that a derogatory assertion has been made (*ibid.*, s.58(4)) and only if "there is a real possibility" that the assertion made will turn out to be false or irrelevant (*ibid.*, s.58(3)).

The way in which sections 58 and 59 of the 1996 are drafted do not make the task of justices easy. Plainly, the sections must be read in the light of the important general principle that proceedings in magistrates' courts must be open to press and public and that cases may be fairly reported (see §1–76, above). On the other hand, if an accused has pleaded guilty the victim is seldom present in court and mitigation by the accused sometimes casts aspersions on the motives and behaviour of others. In practice, it will be difficult for the court to conclude that assertions made in mitigation are either factually false or irrelevant. Section 58(8) of the Act permits the court to postpone making the order until the conclusion of the case or "as soon as reasonably practical after making the determination" (s.58(8)(a)). Presumably, the intention of Parliament was that by this stage the court would have determined the relevance of any derogatory assertion, although it would not necessarily follow that the truth of such assertion would be determined without hearing representations to the contrary.

The Code of Conduct of the Bar (Standards Applicable to Criminal Cases, Code 11.8(e)) place a duty on prosecuting counsel to "draw the attention of the defence to any assertion of material fact made in mitigation which the prosecution believes to be untrue". The Code then suggests that a *Newton* hearing may be appropriate if the assertion is persisted in. (See §11–62, above). This duty appeared in the Code before sections 58 and 59 of the 1996 Act were brought into force, and the intentions of Parliament now appear to be that the victim of a derogatory assertion should be given further protection by the making of an order. There is nothing in the 1996 Act to suggest that a *Newton* hearing must take place before an order is made.

4. The Totality Principle

13–28   The principle of totality is one which must be applied where the offender is sentenced on the same occasion for multiple offences. The principle means that the court cannot impose a proportionate sentence for each offence, and make such sentences consecutive even though proper to do so, if the resulting sentence is disproportionate to the criminal behaviour. "The court must look at the totality of the criminal behaviour and ask itself what is the appropriate sentence for all the offences" (*per* Lawton L.J. in *R. v. Barton* [1973] 1 W.L.R. 115). The application of the principle may be illustrated in the following examples:

> D, aged 49 with numerous previous convictions for obtaining property by deception, pleaded guilty in the magistrates' court to three charges of obtaining property by deception to the value of about £200. He was committed for sentence to the Crown Court where he was sentenced to three years' imprisonment on each charge, consecutive, making nine years in all. Held: The sentence was utterly wrong in principle. Although the defendant was a plausible rogue with many previous convictions, the sentence was out of proportion to the offences he had committed. The appropriate sentence should have been one of 12, 15 or 18 months' imprisonment (*R. v. Cooper* (1983) 5 Cr.App.R.(S.) 295).

> D, a haulage contractor, pleaded guilty to 10 offences of using an overweight goods vehicle where the degree of overweight varied between 15 and 25 per cent. Held: The decision of the justices (upheld in the Crown Court) to apply a formula of a £400 fine as a starting point and a further £20 for each one per cent by which the overweight was exceeded, producing a total fine of £7,600, was wholly wrong. The Divisional Court quashed the sentence as being so far beyond the normal discretionary limits that it contained errors of law. A fine of £1,300 was substituted (*R. v. Chelmsford Crown Court, ex p. Birchall* (1989) 11 Cr.App.R.(S.) 510).

This principle (which as the above examples show applies to all sentences including fines) has statutory weight because the Criminal Justice Act 1991 states that nothing in the Act shall prevent a court in the case of an offender who is convicted of one or more offence, from mitigating his sentence by applying any rule of law as to the totality of sentences (CJA 1991, s.28(2)(b)). Although the totality principle is a rule of sentencing practice, and so not strictly a rule of law, it is clear that the guidance of the Court of Appeal on totality should continue to apply under the 1991 Act.

6. The Proportionate Sentence

13–29   Proportionality is a principle which relates to the actual sentence passed by the court. It has been stressed that the concept of seriousness is in part an abstract concept, a theoretical threshold which must be reached in the sentencer's mind before a sentence within that category of seriousness can be contemplated. The fact that, conceptually, an offence is so serious that only a custodial sentence can be justified for it does not mean automatically that such a sentence must be passed. Whether such a sentence is passed will depend upon many other factors—the offender's personal mitigation, good character, the contents of the pre-sentence report and so on. Once all of these factors have been considered, and the court determines the sentence, such sentence must be a proportionate one (unless the offence is violent or sexual, see §§13–48 *et seq.*, below).

Before the proportionate sentence is decided the factors discussed in this chapter must be weighed: the nature of the offence including other associated offences, previous convictions, personal mitigation and the totality principle. Next, the court must consider what penalties will comprise the sentence, for example, imprisonment combined with a Compensation Order, a fine combined with a period of disqualification. Where more than one penalty is contemplated, the court may mitigate the severity of an individual penalty by taking into account that that penalty is to be included in the total sentence. Section 28 of the Criminal Justice Act 1991 provides that nothing shall prevent the court from mitigating any penalty included in an offender's sentence by taking into account any other penalty included in that sentence (CJA 1991, s.28(2)(a)).

When the court has weighed all of these factors, the principle of proportionality shall apply as follows.

CUSTODIAL SENTENCE

13–30 The proportionate custodial sentence is one which is commensurate with the seriousness of the offence, or the combination of the offence and one or more offences associated with it (CJA 1991, s.2(2)(a)).

There is an exception to this rule in the case of the violent or sexual offender (see paragraph 13–48, below).

The importance of the principle of proportionality is that courts are prohibited from passing long custodial sentences as a means of locking up those who prefer life in prison (*R. v. Cohen* (1984) 6 Cr.App.R.(S.) 131), or as a welfare disposal when other agencies have failed (*R. v. Coombes* (1981) 3 Cr.App.R.(S.) 300). Even if the offender himself considers a custodial sentence a suitable and attractive disposal the court may not impose such a sentence if it would be out of proportion. In the case of *Cooper* (cited at paragraph 13–28, above) the appellant did not appeal against his nine-year sentence, and his appeal was pursued by the Official Solicitor on his behalf.

COMMUNITY SENTENCES

13–31 Different considerations of proportionality apply to community sentences. The particular community sentence must be commensurate with the seriousness of the offence or the combination of the offence and one or more offences associated with it (as with custodial sentences), but in addition the sentence must be the most suitable for the offender (CJA 1991, s.6(2)). Thus, the court is entitled to consider, in weighing proportionality, whether a long or short Probation Order should be made, or whether it is suitable for the offender to perform a large number or small number of hours of Community Service. A community sentence may, thus, be a proportionate sentence if the gravity of the offence suggested a Probation Order, but because of the circumstances of the offender, it was considered more suitable that a Community Service Order were made. The resulting community sentence would be a proportionate sentence under the Act.

FINANCIAL PENALTIES

13–32 A further difference in the application of the principle of proportionality attaches to the fixing of fines. While the amount of the fine shall be commensurate with the seriousness of the offence (strict proportionality) the court shall take into account the financial circumstances of the offender (whether it has the effect of increasing or reducing the amount of the fine) (CJA 1991, s.18(2), (3) and (5)). Thus, the proportionate fine is one which reflects culpability and wealth.

More detailed discussion of custodial sentences, community sentences and financial penalties appears later in this Chapter.

B. The Relevance of "Guideline" Cases

13–33   The chapters in Part II which deal with sentencing for individual offences often cite what are described as "Guideline Cases." This description has the approval of the Court of Appeal, as indeed such cases are intended to provide guidance to sentencers as to the offences which should attract a particular type of penalty. However, guidance from the Court of Appeal cannot be binding, nor can sentencing cases generally fetter the exercise of judicial discretion. The relevance of "Guideline Case" is described below.

1. Guideline Cases Generally

13–34   The status of the guideline case was described in a judgment of the Court of Appeal in the following way:

> "... the appropriate sentence is a matter for the discretion of the sentencing judge. It follows that decisions on sentencing are not binding authorities in the sense that decisions of the Court of Appeal on points of substantive law are binding both on this court and on lower courts. Indeed they could not be, since the circumstances of the offence and of the offender present an almost infinite variety from case to case. As in any breach of the law which depends on judicial discretion, decisions on sentencing are no more than examples of how the court has dealt with a particular offender in relation to a particular offence. As such they may be useful as an aid to uniformity of sentence for a particular category of crime, but they are not authoritative in the strict sense. Occasionally the court suggests guidelines for sentencers dealing with a particular category of offence or a particular type of offender. ... However, the sentencer retains his discretion within the guidelines, or even to depart from them if the particular circumstances of the case justify departure. The vast majority of decisions of the court are concerned with the facts and circumstances of the particular case before it and are directed to the appropriate sentence in that case. Each case depends on its own facts": *per* Dunn L.J. in *R. v. de Havilland* (1983) 5 Cr.App.R.(S.) 109.

The status of the guideline case has been further explained by the Court of Appeal as follows:

> "The decisions of the Court of Appeal were no more than guidelines to judges who had the task of sentencing in the Crown Court. Within the guidelines there was a great deal of flexibility, and the Court recognised that a sentencing judge would take into account many factors in arriving at a proper sentence. The judge might have in mind that a particular crime was too prevalent in the area, and that stiffer sentences were called for, or that the offence had a particularly distressing effect on the victim, or that the offender had behaved in a particularly vicious manner. Nevertheless, a judge when sentencing must pay attention to the guidance given by the Court of Appeal and sentences should be broadly in line with guideline cases, unless there were factors applicable to the particular case which required the judge to depart from the normal level of sentence. In such special cases the judge should indicate clearly the factor or factors which in his judgment

allowed a departure from the tariff set by the Court of Appeal. What the judge must not do is to state that he is applying some personal tariff of his own because he considers the accepted range of sentences to be too high or too low" *per* Roch L.J. in *R. v. Johnson* [1994] Crim.L.R. 537."

2. Guidelines on Custodial Sentences

13–35 Guidance on the imposition and the length of custodial sentences was given by Lord Lane C.J. in *R. v. Bibi* (1980) 71 Cr.App.R. 360. Clearly there have been considerable developments since then, not least of which is the Criminal Justice Act 1991 which places the imposition of a custodial sentence within a statutory framework. However, it is submitted that the following general guidance continues to be relevant, and should be borne in mind by sentencers.

"... sentencing courts must be particularly careful to examine each case to ensure, if an immediate custodial sentence is necessary, that the sentence is as short as possible, consistent only with the duty to protect the interests of the public and to punish and deter the criminal.

Many offenders can be dealt with equally justly and effectively by a sentence of six or nine months' imprisonment as by one of 18 months or three years. We have in mind not only the obvious case of the first offender for whom any prison sentence however short may be an adequate punishment and deterrent, but other types of case as well.

The less serious types of factory or shopbreaking; the minor cases of sexual indecency; the more petty frauds where small amounts of money are involved; the fringe participants in more serious crime: all these are examples of cases where the short sentence would be appropriate.

There are, on the other hand, some offences for which, generally speaking, only the medium or longer sentences will be appropriate. For example, most robberies; most offences involving serious violence; use of a weapon to wound; burglary of private dwelling-houses; planned crime for wholesale profit; active large scale trafficking in dangerous drugs. These are only examples. It would be impossible to set out a catalogue of those offences which do and those which do not merit more severe treatment. So much will, obviously, depend upon the circumstances of each individual offender and each individual offence.

What the court can and should do is to ask itself whether there is any compelling reason why a short sentence should not be passed. We are not aiming at uniformity of sentence; that would be impossible. We are aiming at uniformity of approach."

13–36 The observations in *Bibi* continue to have validity in the context of present day prison overcrowding (*R. v. Ollererenshaw* [1999] 1 Cr.App.R.(S.) 65, *per* Rose L.J. (Vice-President of the Court of Appeal, Criminal Division). In that case it was said that where a court was contemplating a custodial sentence of 12 months or less it should generally ask itself whether an even shorter period might be equally effective.

Some caution should be used, it is submitted, in applying these principles too strictly in the magistrates' court because justices may, for offences triable either way, commit the offender for sentence at the Crown Court. If, in respect of a single offence or for a number of offences for which concurrent sentences are appropriate, a sentence of six months' imprisonment is justified, the offender ought not to be committed for sentence (*R. v. Warley Magistrates' Court, ex p. D.P.P.* [1998] 2 Cr.App.R. 307). In making this decision justices ought not to apply routinely the reasoning in *Ollerenshaw* because the decision not to commit for sentence is made on the basis that the maximum powers available to justices should be used.

3. The Application of Guideline Cases to the Magistrates' Court

13–37   There are particular difficulties about applying Court of Appeal guidelines in the magistrates' court. The maximum sentence for any single offence triable summarily is six months imprisonment, even though a very wide range of indictable offences may be tried summarily with the accused's consent. Accordingly the range of sentencing choice if there is to be a custodial sentence is a very narrow one, and where the Court of Appeal has indicated that a "short" custodial sentence is appropriate, there is rarely an indication as to whether such sentence should be three, four or six months.

Secondly, the actual sentence which is substituted on appeal from the Crown Court often reflects the time already spent in custody by the appellant before the appeal is heard. It is, therefore, sometimes misleading to pay particular regard to the number of months ordered to be served by the Court of Appeal in individual cases.

The third reason for approaching the Court of Appeal decisions with caution is that rarely are they intended to assist magistrates directly in sentencing. All the cases are appeals from the Crown Court, where the sentence of a Crown Court judge or recorder is upheld or overturned. Parliament has deliberately made powers of punishment greater in the Crown Court than in the magistrates' court for a wide range of offences. (For example, burglary is punishable with 14 years in the Crown Court, and six months in the magistrates' court.) The range of sentences, or tariff, is therefore likely to be higher in the Crown Court than for the same offence tried in the magistrates' court. Unless the Court of Appeal specifically indicates that guidance is intended for magistrates as well as Crown Court judges the decisions should be read with care.

Finally, decisions reached in magistrates' courts are nearly always collective, with a Bench of three conferring over a sentence, and this collective decision is itself a product of meetings of magistrates when Bench policy will have been discussed. The value of such collective decision is that the levels and the type of crime may vary widely from one area to another. A magistrates' court in the West End of London where wealthy thieves persistently steal from large stores may treat shoplifters differently from a deprived Petty Sessional Division with high unemployment. The prevalence of an offence in a particular locality is a legitimate matter to be considered in weighing the seriousness of a particular offence (*R. v. Cunningham* [1993] 1 W.L.R. 183).

In many respects the value of the guidelines from the Court of Appeal is in assisting decisions about Mode of Trial, as the sentencing powers of the magistrates' court are a highly relevant consideration whenever summary trial is considered suitable.

For these reasons the decisions set out in this book cannot be binding. They were never intended to be binding. The value of the decisions is that they help to promote consistency in sentencing and to highlight the relevant considerations which should be taken into account before a sentence is passed.

C. Establishing the Factual Basis for Sentencing

1. General rule

13–38   It is a fundamental principle of sentencing that an offender may only be sentenced for an offence (or offences) for which he has been convicted or which he has admitted by a plea of guilty, not for offences possibly disclosed in the evidence.

D pleaded guilty to driving whilst disqualified, possession of cannabis resin and driving whilst unfit through drugs. He had been arrested following a piece of erratic driving. The sentencer had indicated when passing sentence that the main cause of the erratic driving had been D's consumption of cannabis whist driving. As a result a sentence of three years' imprisonment had been imposed for possession of cannabis. Held: It was not permissible to pass sentence as if D had been convicted of the offence of dangerous driving. D should have been sentenced only for the criminality revealed in the offences for which he pleaded guilty (*R. v. O'Prey* [1999] Crim.L.R. 233).

(i) Sentence following conviction after a trial

13–39   Where there has been a trial and the court convicts the accused justices are entitled to pass sentence on the basis of the facts found to be proved in the trial (*R. v. Tolera* [1999] 1 Cr.App.R. 29). The corollary of this rule is that the offender must not be sentenced on the basis of facts which were not proved in the trial but which may have formed part of the prosecution case. The obligation to pass sentence only on the facts of the case does not mean that the court must ignore the consequences to the victim of an offence because a more serious charge could have been preferred (*R. v. Nottingham Crown Court, ex p. D.P.P.* (1996) 160 J.P. 78).

If the accused has been convicted of some offences and found not guilty of others he should only be sentence for the offences for which he was convicted.

(ii) Sentence following a plea of guilty

13–40   (a) The general rule is that following a plea of guilty the factual basis for the sentence will be those facts opened by the prosecution. If the defence did not accept those facts for the purpose of sentence it should be made quite clear before sentence is passed and a written statement of the factual basis urged by the defence should be handed to the prosecution. The prosecution should then consider whether a *Newton* hearing was necessary (see §13–42, below, or whether the facts could be presented incorporating the written statement provided by the defence (*R. v. Tolera* [1998] Crim.L.R. 425).

(b) In any event the prosecution must present a version of the facts which is either true or which contains matters which the Crown are unable to challenge (*R. v. Tolera,* above, *R. v. Beswick* (1996) 160 J.P. 337).

(c) If, in the course of mitigation, facts are advanced by the offender which the prosecution is unable to challenge, but equally unable to accept (either because they are inherently improbable or because it defies common sense) the court may require the defendant to give evidence on the issues (*R. v. Tolera,* above). If this course is followed the court may accept or reject the defendant's evidence, even if it is not challenged by the prosecution (*R. v. Connell* (1983) 5 Cr.App.R.(S.) 360).

PROCEDURE WHEN MITIGATION RAISES ISSUES UNKNOWN TO THE PROSECUTION

13–41   Occasionally the defence will advance matters of fact about the offence or the background to the commission of the offence of which the prosecution has no knowledge. Sometimes this is raised in the version of events provided by the offender in the pre-sentence report and sometimes it is raised by the advocate during a speech in mitigation.

In ordinary circumstances justices should pay no attention to a version of facts contained in a pre-sentence report if it conflicts with the prosecution case (*R. v. Tolera* [1998] Crim.L.R. 425). If the defence advocate specifically relies on a version put forward in such a report the matter should, if necessary, be resolved by calling evidence.

Where a version of the facts is raised for the first time by an advocate the court should determine whether such matters may be categorised as extraneous mitigation which does not contradict the prosecution case but simply purports to explain the background to the offence. In such a case a *Newton* hearing has been held not to be necessary (*R. v. Broderick* (1993) 15 Cr.App.R.(S.) 476). On the other hand if the mitigation goes directly to the facts and circumstances of the offence itself, the defendant is obliged to make good the mitigation by calling evidence (*R. v. Guppy and Marsh* (1994) 16 Cr.App.R.(S.) 25). If evidence is called in these circumstances the burden is upon the defence to establish the factual basis on the balance of probabilities and the prosecution does not have to disprove it.

It has been held that an exception to the rule that it is for the defence to make good the mitigation on the balance of probabilities is when the defence asserts the offence was committed under some compulsion falling short of duress. Here the onus is on the prosecution to rebut such a suggestion (*R. v. Kerrigan* (1993) 14 Cr.App.R.(S.) 179).

If the prosecution is unable to challenge the factual basis of mitigation advanced, but the court regards it as inherently improbable the court may require that the mitigation is given on oath. The role of the prosecution in this situation would be to test the evidence in order to assist the court (*R. v. Tolera*, above).

2. *Newton* Hearings

(i) General rule

13–42   Occasionally the factual dispute between the prosecution and the defence is so substantial that in order to pass sentence the court will have to resolve the dispute by hearing evidence. This procedure has become known as the rule in *R. v. Newton* (1983) 77 Cr.App.R. 13, because it was in that case that the procedure was first given judicial approval by the Court of Appeal. In *Newton* the accused pleaded guilty to buggery with his wife which the prosecution said was without her consent, although in mitigation the accused said it was with consent. The Lord Chief Justice Lord Lane stated that "it was about as sharp a divergence of fact as could possibly have been imagined" and then set out the choices which were open to the court when faced with such circumstances.

(a)   (Only relevant where facts have been decided by a jury.)

(b)   The court may hear evidence on one side and another and come to its own conclusion on the issue which is at the root of the problem.

(c)   The court may hear no evidence but listen to submissions . . . but where there is a substantial conflict between the two sides the court must come down on the side of the defendant.

Since *Newton* was decided the Court of Appeal has sought to restrict the circumstances in which the court should hear evidence to the minimum, and there are a number of instances when the court is not obliged to hear evidence even though there is a dispute between prosecution and defence. If the court does hear evidence then a strict application of the rules of procedure, such as the burden of proof, and of evidence must apply before the court can reach conclusions adverse to the accused (*R. v. Gandy* (1990) 11 Cr.App.R.(S.) 564).

(ii) Procedure

13–43 If there is a dispute about relevant facts which may affect sentence it is the duty of the defending advocate to make this clear to the prosecution at the outset and for the court to be informed so that justices can consider whether it is necessary to order a *Newton* hearing (*R. v. Gardener* (1993) 15 Cr.App.R.(S.) 667). If there is a dispute, or a possible dispute as to the facts it is desirable that this should be resolved before the case is adjourned for the preparation of a pre-sentence report (*R. v. McFarlane* (1995) 16 Cr.App.R.(S.) 315). Even if neither the prosecution nor the defence request a *Newton* hearing or draw the attention of the court to a dispute on the facts there is a residual duty upon the court to initiate an inquiry if there is a substantial conflict between the respective versions put forward (*R. v. Costley* (1989) 11 Cr.App.R.(S.) 357).

Even if the accused's evidence in a *Newton* hearing is rejected he must still be given some credit by virtue of the guilty plea (*R. v. Williams (Timothy)* (1990) 12 Cr.App.R.(S.) 415). In practice the credit given in these circumstances will be less than that which would have been given without the hearing.

Examples where a *Newton* hearing has been considered appropriate

13–44 (i) Where, in a case of violence, the mitigation is based on alleged provocation by the victim, it will be necessary to explore this by hearing evidence (*R. v. Costley* (1989) 11 Cr.App.R.(S.) 357).

(ii) Where it is important to establish accurately what the offender did during an incident of violent disorder, *e.g.* whether he was kicking or punching or merely lending encouragement and support (*R. v. Jackson-Crisp* (1989) 11 Cr.App.R.(S.) 267).

(iii) Where a guilty plea has been entered on a certain basis and that basis is accepted by the prosecution justices are not entitled to pass sentence on a basis of greater culpability than that implied by the pleas without conducting a *Newton* hearing (*R. v. Yorkshire Water Services Ltd* (1995) 16 Cr.App.R.(S.) 280).

(iv) It has been said, *obiter*, that where an offender has pleaded guilty to common assault but there remains a dispute about the nature of any consequential injuries caused thereby a *Newton* hearing may be the only appropriate way of determining the question (*R. v. Nottingham Crown Court, ex p. D.P.P.* (1996) 160 J.P. 78).

Circumstances when a *Newton* hearing is not necessary

13–45 (i) A *Newton* hearing is not necessary if in the view of the court the version being put forward by the accused is wholly implausible or manifestly false (*R. v. Hawkins* (1985) 7 Cr.App.R.(S.) 351, and *R. v. Mudd* (1988) 10 Cr.App.R.(S.) 22).

(ii) The procedure suggested in *Newton* does not mean that in every case where there is a factual dispute the court must hear evidence before rejecting the defence version.

> D, who had 12 previous convictions for driving whilst disqualified, pleaded guilty to two cases of driving whilst disqualified and asserted in mitigation that in relation to one case he had contacted the DVLC at Swansea, and been told he was at liberty to drive. Held: The court was fully entitled to reject the submissions put forward having regard to the number of times the accused had previously been disqualified (*R. v. Walton* (1987) 9 Cr.App.R.(S.) 107).

(iii) The procedure suggested in *Newton* does not apply if the disputed facts are not enough materially to affect the court's judgment.

D pleaded guilty to two charges of theft (shoplifting) and one of common assault, and there was a factual dispute as to the precise circumstances of the assault on the security officer who chased the accused. Held: Where there is only a divergence of degree of a minor character between the prosecution and defence it is not necessarily appropriate for any trial of an issue to take place (*R. v. Bent* (1986) 8 Cr.App.R.(S.) 19).

(iv) There is no need to hold a *Newton* hearing where the accused disputes the inferences to be drawn from the facts outlined by the prosecution, rather than the facts themselves (*R. v. Nadim Mirza* (1993) 14 Cr.App.R.(S.) 64)).

D. CUSTODIAL SENTENCES

1. General Principles

13–46   As a broad general principle it is necessary to bear in mind that *all* criminal sentences are intended to protect the public whether by punishing the offender or reforming him or by deterring him or others *(R. v. Howells and other cases* (1998) 162 J.P. 731, *per* Lord Bingham C.J.). For this reason custodial sentences must be seen in the broad context of sentencing generally, and the further observations of Lord Bingham in this case are set out fully in §§13–04 and 13–05, above.

Where a custodial sentence is justified the sentence should be no longer than the penal purpose which the court had in mind (*R. v. Howells*, above). Secondly, before a custodial sentence may be imposed the statutory criteria laid down by the Criminal Justice Act 1991 must apply. In essence this means that a custodial sentence may only be imposed if the offence is so serious that a non-custodial penalty cannot be justified.

(i) The "So Serious" test

13–47   The criteria of seriousness in section 1(2)(a) of the Criminal Justice Act 1991 applies to all offenders who appear before the magistrates' court, and, therefore, the view at one time that an offence which was "so serious" for an adult might not be "so serious" for a young offender (*R. v. Scott (Tracy)* (1990) 12 Cr.App.R.(S.) 23) no longer applies. Secondly, the threshold of seriousness under the 1991 Act may be lower than that under section 1(4A) of the 1982 Act because seriousness is in some respects a theoretical concept which does not automatically trigger the imposition of a custodial sentence (see §§13–07 *et seq.*, above).

Confirmation that the threshold of seriousness under the Act is relatively low may be seen in a number of decisions of the Court of Appeal, for example *R. v. Keogh* (1993) 15 Cr.App.R.(S.) 279 (obtaining property by deception) and *R. v. Foster* (1993) 15 Cr.App.R.(S.) 340 (making off without payment). These cases are discussed in more detail in Chapter 16, below, and in later chapters consideration is given to whether particular offences have been regarded as "so serious" in judgments by the Court of Appeal. Whenever the court is of the opinion that an offence is "so serious" that a custodial sentence must be imposed for it, the court must state why it is of that opinion, and must explain that reasoning to the offender (CJA 1991, s.1(4)). The precise procedural steps in sentencing are described at §§12–04 to 12–06, above, and these steps are a reminder of the central place that the concept of seriousness has in the scheme of the 1991 Act. The concept is of such fundamental importance that readers should have regard   to   §§13–02   to   13–20   of   this   chapter,   the   application   of the concept to particular offences in later chapters, as well as to the procedural steps in sentencing set out in Chapter 12, in order to understand the meaning of "so serious."

(ii) The violent or sexual offender

13–48 There is a distinction in the 1991 Act between a proportionate sentence imposed on the grounds of seriousness, and a sentence for "such longer term" as is necessary in the case of a violent or sexual offender (CJA 1991, s.2(2)(b)). This distinction between the dangerous offender who should be sentenced for a long term on the grounds of prevention and public protection and the non-violent offender has been long-established in sentencing practice. A violent offence is defined in the Criminal Justice Act 1991 as an offence which leads, or is intended to lead, to a person's death or to physical injury to a person, and includes an offence which is required to be charged as arson (whether or not it would otherwise fall within this definition) (*ibid.*, s.31(1)). The reference to arson is especially important as the following examples illustrate:

> D, with 11 previous convictions for criminal damage, and who suffered from psychiatric depression, pleaded guilty to setting fire to furniture and bedding in his flat which was on an upper floor of a block. Held: There was a duty to protect the public from the actions of a man who could be dangerous. Seven years' imprisonment imposed at the Crown Court upheld by the Court of Appeal (*R. v. Compton* (1983) 5 Cr.App.R.(S.) 411).

> D, aged 24, who had a long history of psychiatric disorder which rendered him incapable of coping in open society, pleaded guilty to arson by setting fire to a curtain in a mental hospital. He was not acceptable as a patient in a hospital following the incident. Held: The danger to the public was great and a long term of imprisonment, six years, was justified on the basis of danger to himself and to others (*R. v. Gouws* (1981) 3 Cr.App.R.(S.) 325).

13–49 The distinction between the sexual or violent offender who may be expected to receive a longer sentence than the non-violent offender is further underlined by the provisions contained in sections 58 to 60 of the Crime and Disorder Act 1998. These provisions (which provide for extended licence periods for dangerous offenders) do not directly affect the magistrates' court, but read in combination with the Sex Offenders Act 1997 reveal a clear determination by Parliament to provide a distinct sentencing regime for those characterised as violent or sexual offenders.

Parliament's intentions in this regard follows traditional sentencing principles handed down by the Court of Appeal which, on the whole, have stated that violence is more serious than offences involving only property.

The long sentences which, traditionally, have been passed for offenders who are deemed to be dangerous have taken into account the offender's previous convictions. An isolated offence of arson may not indicate that the offender is a danger to the public, but repetitive offending of such character may show that the public need to be protected. For this reason the Criminal Justice Act 1991 expressly permitted the court to take into account any information about the offender (*i.e.* previous convictions) before forming an opinion as to whether the public needed protection (CJA 1991, s.3(3)(b)). This distinction between considering previous convictions for dangerous offenders but not for other offenders is now of less importance following the amendment to section 29(1) by the CJA 1993, although the weight attached to previous offences of a violent or sexual nature may be greater than for a non-violent offender.

13–50   Before a sentence longer than one commensurate with seriousness can be passed for a violent or sexual offender, the court must be of the opinion that such a sentence is necessary to protect the public from serious harm from the offender (CJA 1991, s.2(2)(b)). This means protecting the public from death or serious personal injury, whether physical or psychological, occasioned by further such offences committed by the offender (*ibid.* s.31(3)). Thus, the court must, in relation to the facts of the case and the nature of previous convictions, be of the view that there is a danger of the offender committing similar crimes in the future. As a matter of practice such sentencing decisions are likely to be confined to the Crown Court where offences of gravity such as rape, arson with intent, or wounding with intent must be tried. However, the magistrates' court may sometimes be faced with a decision on sentence under sections 1(2)(b), 2(2)(b) and 3(3)(b), as the following examples illustrate:

> D, aged 25, pleaded guilty to unlawful wounding by attacking a female bar assistant with a knife causing a one centimetre cut in her arm, requiring three stitches. Held: D had a number of previous convictions and a drug addiction which demonstrated that he was prone to violence when under the influence of either drink or drugs. A longer than commensurate sentence, namely four years' imprisonment, was justified to protect the public (*R. v. Coull* (1993) 15 Cr.App.R.(S.) 305).

> D, who had no previous convictions, pleaded guilty at the Crown Court to two charges of assault occasioning actual bodily harm to his wife. On the first occasion he punched her about the head, arms and body, pulled her up the stairs by her hair and hit her on the leg with a stick. On the second occasion he punched her a number of times. It was accepted by D that these were not the only incidents. Held: A longer than normal sentence might be imposed to protect a single member of the public and, applying *Att.-Gen.'s Reference No. 34 of 1992 (R. v. Oxford)* 15 Cr.App.R.(S.) 167, the fact that D was of previous good character was not a bar to imposing a sentence under CJA 1991, s.2(2)(b). Four years' imprisonment imposed at the Crown Court reduced to three years' by the Court of Appeal (*R. v. Nicholas* (1993) 15 Cr.App.R.(S.) 381).

> D, aged 27 with a number of previous convictions for offences of violence, assaulted three members of staff at a shop when apprehended for shoplifting by a head-butt which caused the victim's glasses to shatter and intrude into the eye, a kick to the groin to a female staff member and attempt to grab the genitals of a male. Whilst on bail for the above offences he was again arrested for shoplifting and he bit the arresting police officer's leg, leaving bite marks. Held: A total sentence of five years' imprisonment (two years' for the first incident, and three years' consecutive for the second) imposed under section 2(2)(b) upheld by the Court of Appeal: the offender's record and the facts of the instant offences showed that the public needed to be protected (*R. v. Ely* (1994) 15 Cr.App.R.(S.) 881).

13–51   Such considerations as to whether a violent offence requires a sentence to be passed under section 2(2)(b) of the 1991 Act will usually arise when the court is considering its powers to commit the offender for sentence to the Crown Court. These powers are discussed fully in paragraph 6–38 *et. seq.*, above. Section 38(2)(b) of the Magistrates' Courts Act 1980, as substituted by amendments introduced by the Criminal Justice Act 1991 and the Criminal Justice and Public Order Act 1994, does not restrict the powers of the court to offenders who are aged 21 or over.

(ii) Offender who does not consent to conditions of a community sentence

13–52 In the Criminal Justice Act 1991 as originally drafted an offender had to express his consent to the imposition of a community sentence, and there was a proviso in the Act enabling the court to impose a custodial sentence on an offender to whom a community penalty was proposed but who refused to consent to it. Section 38 of the Crime (Sentences) Act 1997 effectively abolished the need for an offender to consent to a simple community penalty, although a willingness to comply with the conditions of a community sentence were preserved in some circumstances (see §§12–04, above). The amendments to the 1991 Act made necessary by this change have since been further amended by section 119 and Schedule 8, para. 72 of the Crime and Disorder Act 1998. The effect of these changes is as follows:

(a) a court may pass a custodial sentence on an offender if he fails to express his willingness to comply with a requirement which is proposed to be included in a probation order; and

(b) a court may pass a custodial sentence on an offender if he fails to express his willingness to comply with the requirements of a Drug Treatment and Testing Order under section 61(6) of the Crime and Disorder Act 1998 (CJA 1991, s.1(3)).

Section 1(3) of the 1991 Act in this latest amended form makes no reference to Community Service Orders which used to require the consent of the offender before they could be imposed. A Community Service Order may now be made without obtaining the offender's consent, although there must be some evidence before the court that the offender is fit and suitable for such an order. If it appears later that the offender deceived the court into passing such a sentence by pretending to be fit when he was not there is no bar on the court imposing a custodial sentence in revocation proceedings (*R. v. Hammon* [1998] 2 Cr.App.R.(S) 202). (For revocation of a Community Service Order see §12–27, above).

2. Suspended Sentence of Imprisonment

(i) Imposition of suspended sentence

13–53 The circumstances in which a suspended sentence may be imposed were intended to be restricted by the Criminal Justice Act 1991 because the purpose of that Act was to give effect to the theory of "just deserts" which required every offender to be punished, whether in custody, or in the community or by a financial penalty. Accordingly the government considered that an offender who was given a suspended sentence had not been punished at all, indeed might be regarded as having been let off completely (Cm. 965, para. 3.22).

As a result of this thinking a deserved custodial sentence may only be suspended if such a course can be justified by "the exceptional circumstances of the case" (PCCA 1973, s.22(2)(b), as substituted by CJA 1991, s.5(1)). In addition if the court imposes a suspended sentence it must consider also whether it is appropriate to impose a fine or a Compensation Order (PCCA 1973, s.22(2A), as inserted by CJA 1991, s.5(1)). Presumably, this requirement was put into the 1991 Act to avoid the accusation that an offender who had been given a suspended sentence had been "let off."

13–54 It is difficult to state precisely what is meant by "exceptional circumstances" because every case will depend on its own facts, but the words do not mean factors which are common to many cases, such as youth, good character or an early plea of guilty (*R. v. Okinikan* [1993] 1 W.L.R. 173). It has been said that the words are of such wide construction to allow the court to take into account all the circumstances of the offence and the offender (*R. v. Lowery* (1992) 14 Cr.App.R.(S.) 485) including general matters of personal mitigation (*R. v. Weston* [1995] Crim.L.R. 900). It is submitted that in general terms the Court of Appeal has shown a willingness to approve of the passing of suspended sentences in circumstances which Parliament probably did not envisage as exceptional and it has been acknowledged that the Court of Appeal is now prepared to take a broad view of the words (per Rougier J. In *R. v. Edney* (1994) 15 Cr.App.R.(S.) 889).

Examples of exceptional circumstances

13–55

  (i) If the desirability of reuniting a family following cogent representations from a local authority is of such importance then that may override what is otherwise the gravity of the offence providing exceptional circumstances for suspending the sentence (*R. v. Cameron* (1993) 14 Cr.App.R.(S.) 801).

  (ii) If the offender is elderly and suffers from serious health problems that has been held as an exceptional circumstance (*R. v. Ullah Khan* (1993) 15 App.R.(S.) 78).

  (iii) If the offender is the carer of her elderly mother and part of the reason for stealing money was to spend it on the care of her mother that has been held to be an exceptional circumstance (*R. v. Edney* (1994) 15 Cr.App.R.(S.) 889).

  (iv) If in a breach of trust theft the offender had voluntarily paid back some of the money prior to being sentenced and there was a reasonable expectation that the remainder could be repaid in short time that has been held to be an exceptional circumstance (*R. v. Kondal* (1995) 16 Cr.App.R.(S.) 845).

  (v) If there is significant provocation preceding an incident of violence that has been held to amount to exceptional circumstances (*R. v. Brodkin* (1995) 16 Cr.App.R.(S.) 78).

  (vi) If there is cogent medical evidence that the offender's young child is so ill as to be unlikely to survive the period of the sentence that has been held to amount to an exceptional circumstance (*R. v. Bellikli* [1998] 1 Cr.App.R.(S.) 135).

13–56   It must be stressed that such examples cannot provide a precedent for the meaning and interpretation of the words "exceptional circumstances". In addition, such examples were taken from decisions in the Court of Appeal where a suspended sentence has been substituted for an immediate sentence of imprisonment imposed at the Crown Court. Where an offender has already served part of a sentence prior to the hearing of an appeal, a decision to substitute a community penalty at that stage might offend the principle of double jeopardy (see *Att.-Gen.'s Reference (No. 2 of 1989)* (1989) 11 Cr.App.R.(S.) 481). Every case depends on its own facts, and it will not be every offender whose circumstances contain some or all of the above factors where a conclusion that exceptional circumstances will be reached.

(ii) Activation of suspended sentence

13–57   It has been said that where a new offence is not so serious as to merit a custodial sentence it was generally inappropriate to activate an offender's suspended sentence (see *R. v. McElhorne* (1983) 5 Cr.App.R.(S.) 53, *R. v. Brooks* (1991) 12 Cr.App.R.(S.) 756, *R. v. Bexley, Summers and Harrison* (1992) 14 Cr.App.R.(S.) 462, and *R. v. Bee* (1993) 14 Cr.App.R.(S.) 703)). However, this line of cases does not establish an invariable rule. In *R. v. Evans* (1993) 14 Cr.App.R.(S.) 751 the Court of Appeal quashed a sentence of imprisonment imposed at the Crown Court for an offence committed during the operational period of a suspended sentence, but did not quash the activation of the suspended sentence. Section 23 of the Powers of Criminal Courts Act 1973 remains in force and the Court of Appeal did not consider, in that case, that it was unjust for the suspended sentence to be activated. It has also been held that while it was often inappropriate to activate a suspended sentence when the new offence did not, in itself, justify custody, there was no absolute prohibition on doing so (*R. v. McQuillan* (1993) 15 Cr.App.R.(S.) 159). Accordingly, where the new offence was not so serious as to merit a custodial sentence, there was no automatic conclusion that an existing suspended sentence could not be activated. In such circumstances it was not wrong in principle for the court to activate the suspended sentence, while passing no separate penalty for the new offence (*R. v. Calladine* (1993) 15 Cr.App.R.(S.) 345).

The reasoning in *R. v. McQuillan* and *R. v. Calladine* has been followed in *R. v. Stacey* (1993) 15 Cr.App.R.(S.) 585.

> D, who was the subject of a suspended sentence of 18 months, committed a further offence of handling some stolen tools, to the value of £120, during the operational period of the suspended sentence. Held: The court should first consider whether the new offence was so serious that only a custodial sentence could be justified, and in this case the answer was no; however that did not preclude the court from then going on to consider whether it was appropriate to activate the suspended sentence, and the activation of the suspended sentence by the Crown Court had been correct, albeit that the Court of Appeal reduced the period to nine months (*R. v. Stacey* (1993) 15 Cr.App.R.(S.) 585).

13–58 A particular difficulty of statutory interpretation in relation to the activation of a suspended sentence has been encountered where the new offence committed by an offender subject to a suspended sentence merits only a conditional discharge. In a judgment which considered the relevant legislative history the Court of Appeal has held in *R. v. Moore* (1994) 16 Cr.App.R.(S.) 748 that despite the literal interpretation of section 1C of the Powers of Criminal Courts Act 1973 (as inserted by Schedule 2 of the Criminal Justice Act 1991) it was plainly not the legislative intention of the 1991 Act as a whole that minor offending should trigger a custodial sentence, and that a purposeful construction led to the conclusion that *R. v. Tarry* (1970) 54 Cr.App.R. 322 was still good law. The matter is further complicated for practitioners in the magistrates' court because both cases arose upon a committal for sentence and turned strictly on the powers of the Crown Court in those circumstances.

3. Concurrent and Consecutive Terms of Imprisonment

(i) General rule

13–59 A magistrates' court may not impose on the same occasion consecutive sentences in respect of two of more offences triable either way which in aggregate exceed 12 months (MCA 1980, s.133(2)). This rule is subject to specific exceptions set out below, as are the rules of general sentencing practice.

EXCEPTIONS TO GENERAL RULE

13–60   1. A magistrates' court may order any sentence of imprisonment or detention in a young offender institution to commence at the expiration of any custodial sentence imposed by any other court (MCA 1980, s.133(1)). In effect, this allows a court to impose a consecutive sentence to the sentence the offender is already serving.

2. A magistrates' court may activate a suspended sentence in addition to any other term of imprisonment imposed consecutively and such activation may exceed the permitted statutory maximum (*R. v. Chamberlain* (1991) 156 J.P. 440).

3. A magistrates' court may order an offender's return to custody under section 40 of the Criminal Justice Act 1991 in addition to any custodial sentence imposed for the new offence, and the total term may exceed the statutory maximum (*R. v. Worthing and District Justices, ex p. Varley* (1998) 1 Cr.App.R.(S.) 175).

Consecutive terms of imprisonment are to be treated as a single term for the purpose of licence and early release if:

(a) the sentences were passed on the same occasion; or

(b) where they were passed on different occasions there has been a continuous period of custody between those occasions (CJA 1991, s.51(1), as substituted by CDA 1998, s.101(1)).

In addition, the provisions in respect of the imposition of consecutive sentences are now subject to section 102 of the Crime and Disorder Act (CDA 1998, s.119 and Sched.8, para. 46). This provision does not alter the law in respect of the imposition of consecutive terms of imprisonment in the magistrates' court.

(ii) General sentencing practice

13–61   In general terms consecutive sentences are appropriate if the offender has committed two or more quite separate and unconnected offences on separate occasions but concurrent sentences should be imposed in respect of offences which arise out of a single incident (*Att.-Gen.'s Reference (No. 1 of 1990)* 12 Cr.App.R.(S.) 245).

This rule is no more than a general statement of broad principle and no hard and fast rules apply. Providing the totality of the sentence imposed is proportionate it may not matter whether short consecutive sentences are imposed for a series of offences or whether the sentence is expressed in concurrent terms (*R. v. Lawrence (Justin)* [1990] R.T.R. 45).

Subject to these general observations justices ought not to impose consecutive sentences merely in order to avoid committing the offender for sentence at the Crown Court (*R. v. Warley Magistrates' Court, ex p. D.P.P.* [1998] 2 Cr.App.R. 307). In that case it was said that justices should consider whether for any one offence or series of offences for which in principle concurrent sentences would be appropriate a sentence of more than six months would be justified. If it is or may be justified the offender should be committed for sentence at the Crown Court.

An offence committed whilst on bail is a specific aggravating feature (CJA 1991 s.29(2)), and for this reason it has long been recognised that an offence committed on bail should generally attract a consecutive sentence (*R. v. Young* [1973] Crim.L.R. 585).

E. Community Sentences

(i) The making of a Community Order

13–62 A community sentence is one which consists of one or more Community Orders, defined in section 6 of the Criminal Justice Act 1991.

The imposition of a community sentence requires the court to apply the general sentencing structure of the Act in exactly the same way as is required when a custodial sentence is imposed. However, there is an important difference in principle between a custodial sentence and a community sentence. In the case of a community sentence the court is obliged to consider which order or orders comprising the community sentence is, or taken together are, the most suitable for the offender (CJA 1991, s.6(2)(a)). The consideration of the suitability of an offender for a custodial sentence does not arise under the Act, with the possible exception of the consideration of a custodial sentence for a mentally ill offender (see Chapter 7, above). The suitability of the offender for a community sentence is crucial to the sentencing consideration if a community penalty is to be contemplated. For this reason the approach to sentencing for a Combination Order, Community Service Order, or a Probation Order should be considered (it is submitted) in the following way.

(i)   Is the offence, or the combination of the offence and one or more offences associated with it, serious enough to warrant such a sentence? (CJA 1991, s.6(1)).

(ii) If so, which partiuclar *type* of community sentence is commensurate with seriousness? (*ibid.*, s.6(2)(b)).

(iii) In forming an opinion for the above, the court may consider the seriousness of the offence or offences (*ibid.*, s.7(1)) and may take into account previous convictions or failure to respond to previous sentences (*ibid.*, s.29(1)).

(iv) Having considered seriousness, the court must then consider which particular order or orders are the most suitable for the offender (*ibid.*, s.6(2)(a)), and in so doing may take into account any information about the offender (*ibid.*, s.7(2)).

(v)   Finally, the court must obtain and consider a pre-sentence report in order to form an opinion as to suitability for a particular community order (with the exception of an Attendance Centre Order) (*ibid.*, s.7(3)) unless the court is of the opinion that it is unnecessary to obtain such a report (*ibid.*, s.7(3)(a)).

A pre-sentence report is a report which should assist the court in determining the most suitable method of dealing with an offender (*ibid.*, s.3(5)(a)). If, therefore, the court has determined that the offence is serious enough for a community penalty in principle, the pre-sentence report will be highly material and relevant in suggesting which particular community order should be imposed. For these reasons it is submitted that the circumstances when the court will consider passing a community penalty without obtaining and considering a report will be extremely rare. Section 7(3)(a) has been inserted to provide consistency with the amended provisions of section 3(2) of the 1991 Act, but its use in practice will be unusual.

Section 29 of the Act allows the court to take into account any previous convictions or failure to respond to previous sentences for the purpose of weighing seriousness In applying this rule a conviction in respect of which a Probation Order was made, whether before or after October 1, 1992, shall count as a conviction, and a Probation

Order made before or after October 1, 1992 shall be treated as a sentence (CJA 1991, s.29(3) and (4)).

An absolute and a conditional discharge shall also count as a sentence if imposed after September 30, 1992, and an absolute discharge (in addition to a conditional discharge and a probation order) shall count as a conviction if imposed after that date (CJA 1991, s.29(5) and (6) as inserted by CJ and POA 1994, para. 44 of Sched. 9).

(ii) Breach of a Community Order

13–63   The detailed provisions relating to breaches of community orders are set out in §§12–18 and 12–26, above. A number of points of general sentencing practice should be noted.

First, a magistrates' court has no power to revoke an existing probation order when passing sentence for a new offence and re-sentence the offender for the offence for which he had been placed on probation. This is because the enforcement of community order is now governed by Schedule 2 of the Criminal Justice Act 1991, and this Schedule confines the power to revoke and re-sentence to the Crown Court (*R. v. Ipswich Justices, ex p. Best* [1993] Crim.L.R. 473).

Secondly, the commission of a further offence by an offender who is subject to a Probation or a Community Service Order does not, of itself, put the offender in breach of the order.

Thirdly, the amendments to section 29 of the Act provide that a Probation Order ranks as a sentence and a conviction, whether imposed before or after October 1, 1992 (CJA 1991, ss29(3) and (4)). The relevance of this change is that the court is able to take into account previous convictions and the failure by the offender to respond to previous sentences in weighing seriousness (*ibid.*, s.29(1)). Accordingly, an offender who commits an offence while on probation may thereby make the new offence more serious, although the fact of the new offence does not breach the order.

While a magistrates' court has no power to revoke a community order upon conviction of a new offence, the court does have power to revoke an order and deal with the offender for the original offence if he has wilfully and persistently failed to comply with the requirements of the order. This power arises in section 1(3) of the Act and Schedule 2, para. 3. In exercising this power the court must take into account the extent to which the offender has complied with the requirements of the original order (*ibid.*, Sched. 2, para. 3(2)). Thus, the Act endorses the general sentencing principle that an offender should be given credit for the hours performed during community service if a custodial sentence is to be imposed on breach (*R. v. Baines* (1983) 5 Cr.App.R.(S.) 264, *R. v. Whittingham* (1986) 8 Cr.App.R.(S.) 116), but the Act extends this principle to all community sentences. Therefore if, for example, an offender has completed two years of a three year Probation Order then the court must give him credit for this in assessing the severity of the new order, say a Community Service Order. In this example the number of hours ordered to be served in the new Community Service Order would have to take account of the partial success of the previous Probation Order.

13–64   Where the court is exercising its power under section 1(3) and Schedule 2 to the Criminal Justice Act 1991 (sentencing an offender who has wilfully and persistently failed to comply with a Community Service Order) there is no obligation to obtain and consider a new pre-sentence report before sentence is passed (*R. v. Meredith* (1994) 158 J.P. 322). The court will have, of course, the original pre-sentence report prepared for the occasion on which the community penalty was imposed, and also the "breach report" informing the court of the circumstances in which the order was not complied with.

It has been said that if the original Community Service Order was made as an alternative to a custodial sentence it may be inevitable that a custodial sentence is imposed for an offender who wilfully disobeys that order (*R. v. Davey* (1994) 15 Cr.App.R.(S.) 852).

The Act contemplates that an offender should only be at risk of being re-sentenced for the original offence if there has been a "wilful" and "persistent" failure to comply with the original order. An isolated lapse in observing the requirements of a Community Order will not render the offender liable to a new sentence.

F. FINANCIAL PENALTIES

13–65   As with custodial and community sentences a punishment by way of a fine should reflect the seriousness of the offence, but the court may consider also the means of the offender, even if this results in a higher fine than was originally contemplated.

Before a fine can be contemplated the court must have determined that the offence was not serious enough for either custody or a community penalty, or if these theoretical thresholds were reached, that the personal mitigation of the offender is such that the seriousness of the offence is considerably reduced. If the court considers the offence may be punished with a fine, it must first inquire into the financial circumstances of the offender (CJA 1991, s.18(1)), and this may be done by making a Financial Circumstances Order, requiring the offender to furnish the court with a statement of his means (*ibid.*, s.20). A minor amendment introduced in the 1994 Act confines this procedure to the occasion where the offender is an individual and not a company or a body corporate (CJ and POA 1994, s.168 and Sched. 9, para. 42). This amendment will make little difference to daily practice in the magistrates' court.

Next the court must fix a fine which reflects the circumstances of the case, but in so doing must take into account the offender's means, whether or not this has the effect of increasing or reducing the amount of the fine (*ibid.*, s.18(3) and (5)). Thus, seriousness may be a combination of the elements of the offence (and any previous convictions and mitigating circumstances) and the wealth of the offender. It has been said that the circumstances of the case may include the fact that the offender had served a period in custody on remand before being sentenced, and as such was a circumstance which might reduce the level of a fine (*R. v. Warden* (1996) 160 J.P. 363). This formulation, which was brought about by the abolition of unit fines by the substantial amendments to the 1991 Act in section 65 and Schedule 3 of the 1993 Act, is a compromise between the traditional sentencing principles applicable to fines and the unit fine principle. While the unit fine formula provided a rigid (and in practice largely unworkable) structure, the present compromise allows the wealthy offender to be ordered to pay more, thus preserving an essential element of the unit fine approach while restoring greater discretion to the sentencer.

13–66   Traditionally the court was obliged to consider what level of fine was merited for the seriousness of the offence, and then to reduce that amount if the offender could not afford to pay it (*R. v. Cleminson* (1985) 7 Cr.App.R.(S.) 128). Now the court must consider the means of the offender and the seriousness of the offence and fix a fine which is an appropriate punishment. It is submitted that the following general sentencing principles will continue to apply:

(i) where a fine is ordered to be paid in instalments, the period of repayment must not be an undue burden upon the offender (*R. v. Olliver and Olliver* (1989) 11 Cr.App.R.(S.) 10).

(ii) where there are multiple offences, the court should not apply a rigid multiplier to produce a fine which offends against the "totality principle" (*R. v. Chelmsford Crown Court, ex p. Birchall* (1989) 11 Cr.App.R.(S.) 510). (The facts of this case are summarised at paragraph 13–28, above.)

G. DEFERMENT OF SENTENCE

13–67   Guidelines as to the procedure and the circumstances whereby it may be appropriate to defer sentence have been laid down by Lord Lane C.J. in *R. v. George* [1984] 1 W.L.R. 1082.

PROCEDURE WHEN DEFERRING SENTENCE

13–68

"The consent of the defendant must of course be obtained ... The court should make it clear ... what the particular purposes are which the court has in mind under section 1(1) of the [Powers of Criminal Courts Act] 1973, and what conduct ... is expected of [the accused] during the deferment. The deferring court should make a careful note of the purposes for which the sentence is being deferred and what steps, if any, it expects the accused to take during the period of deferment" (at p. 1085).

PURPOSE OF DEFERMENT

13–69

"The purpose of deferment is to enable the court to take into account the defendant's conduct after conviction or any change in circumstances and then only if it is the interests of justice to exercise the power... The power is not to be used as an easy way out for a court which is unable to make up its mind" (at p. 1084).

"A deferment of sentence [rather than a short Probation Order] will be more appropriate where the conduct required of the defendant is not sufficiently specific to be made the subject of a condition imposed as part of a Probation Order ... [or] where the steps to be taken by the defendant could not of their nature be the subject of a condition ... It is unnecessary and undesirable to attempt an exhaustive definition of the circumstances in which the procedure should be employed" (at pp. 1085, 1086).

TASK OF THE COURT WHICH DEALS WITH THE ACCUSED AT THE EXPIRATION OF THE PERIOD OF DEFERMENT

13–70

"First the purpose of the deferment and any requirement imposed by the deferring court must be ascertained. Secondly, the court must determine if the defendant has substantially conformed or attempted to conform with the proper expectations of the deferring court ... If he has, then the defendant may legitimately expect that an immediate custodial sentence will not be imposed. If he has not, then the court should be careful to state with precision in what respects he has failed": (at p. 1085).

It is wrong in principle for the court to defer sentence as an easy way out when the court is unable to make up its mind as to the correct sentence. "This court wishes to make it clear that deferring sentence is not to be regarded as another soft option which is available to judges who find it difficult to bring themselves to pass a sentence": *per* Lawton L.J. in *R. v. Burgess*, July 18, 1974.

If the offender has conformed to the expectations of the deferring court, the court which eventually passes sentence should ignore the fact that there are unresolved further charges pending against the offender (*R. v. Aquilina* (1989) 11 Cr.App.R.(S.) 431).

If the offender has not conformed to the expectations of the deferring court, the court which passes sentence is not precluded from deciding that the offence is so serious that only a custodial sentence can be justified merely because another court had deferred sentence (*R. v. Bray* (1991) 12 Cr.App.R.(S.) 705). Although *Bray* was a decision under section 1(4A) of the Criminal Justice Act 1982, the reasoning will apply to sentences passed under the Criminal Justice Act 1991 (see *R. v. Baverstock* [1993] 1 W.L.R. 202).

H. ANCILLARY ORDERS

1. Compensation Orders

(i) General principles

13–71   When deciding whether or not to make a Compensation Order under section 35 of the Powers of Criminal Courts Act 1973 (and in deciding on reasons for not making a Compensation Order), the court should bear in mind the following considerations. Such an order should not be made unless (i) the most careful enquiry is made by the court into the capacity of a defendant to pay compensation; (ii) when the court has satisfied itself that there is some capacity to pay, it should ensure, if it is minded to give time to a defendant to pay, that that time is not excessive; (iii) the order must be precise in its terms, *i.e.* if it is to be met by the payments in instalments, then those payments must be ordered to begin and end at a specified time in total fulfilment of the gross amount of the Compensation Order (*R. v. Scott (formerly Lutta)* (1986) 83 Cr.App.R. 221).

Compensation should not be regarded as an additional penalty where in civil proceedings judgment in the victim's favour could be obtained independently of any sentence in a criminal court. A Compensation Order is a cheap, speedy and summary method of ensuring a victim is compensated if funds are available (*R. v. Dorten* (1988) 152 J.P. 197).

13–72   If there is a real issue as to whether the person claiming compensation has suffered any loss, a court may not make a Compensation Order without evidence proving the sum claimed.

> D pleaded guilty to stealing goods from tents at a campsite. There was an application by the prosecution for compensation in respect of goods stolen and still alleged to be missing. D maintained that all the goods he stole were recovered by the police. The prosecution application was made with reference to the contents of witness statements, the accuracy of which was not accepted by the defence. The justices ordered that half the amount claimed, namely £164, should be paid as compensation. Held: A court had no jurisdiction to make a compensation order without receiving any evidence where there are real issues raised whether the claimants have suffered any, and if so what, loss Justice required that D should

have an opportunity to test the grounds on which the order was to be made against him. The Compensation Order would be quashed (*R. v. Horsham Justices, ex p. Richards* [1985] 1 W.L.R. 986).

Similar difficulties may occur where losses said to be suffered by an insurance company, following an offence, cannot be proved (*R. v. Watson* (1990) 12 Cr.App.R.(S.) 508 and *R. v. White* [1996] Cr.App.R.(S.) 58).

A Compensation Order should not be made where difficult issues of law or fact arise in the evidence.

> D pleaded guilty to obtaining unemployment benefit without being so entitled, and, in addition to fining him, the justices made a Compensation Order by endeavouring to calculate what D would have been entitled to in supplementary benefit and then deducting this from the amount wrongly claimed. Held: Courts should not be invited to make Compensation Orders on evidence out of which difficult questions of law or fact arose. The process of making a Compensation Order should be a very simple one. Justices should decline to make the order unless it was based on very simply stated propositions which had been agreed or which were simple to resolve. There might be circumstances in which it would be proper for a court making a Compensation Order to take account of the fact that the offender would have been entitled to supplementary benefit, but only where there was no issue between the parties as to whether that course should be taken and the amount was not in dispute (*Hyde v. Emery* (1984) 6 Cr.App.R.(S.) 206).

(ii) Compensation and specimen charges

13–73   The amount of compensation which may be awarded is limited to the loss or damage resulting from the charges giving rise to the conviction or the plea of guilty or any other offences which the offender asks to be taken into consideration (*R. v. Crutchley and Tonks* (1993) 15 Cr.App.R.(S.) 627). This principle derives from the plain meaning of section 35 of the Powers of Criminal Courts Act 1973, and the principle must be applied strictly. Accordingly, an offender cannot confer jurisdiction upon the court to permit a Compensation Order to be made in a sum greater than that disclosed in the charges unless such admission is in the form of other offences taken into consideration (*R. v. Hose* (1995) 16 Cr.App.R.(S.) 682).

(iii) Compensation and personal injury

13–74   A Compensation Order may be made in respect of any personal injury resulting from the offence (PCCA 1973, s.35(1)). The words "personal injury" clearly cover identifiable injury, such as cuts, bruising, grazes, etc. but may also include pain and suffering resulting from a common assault where no physical injury is visible. In addition, it has been held that the words are wide enough to include terror and anxiety experienced during the commission of a criminal offence.

It has been said that an award of compensation for personal injury is an inherently difficult jurisdiction and justices must satisfy themselves as to the proper evidential basis before imposing an order (*R. v. Smith (Andrew)* [1998] 2 Cr.App.R.(S.) 400. In that case a judge fell into error by assuming an injury would be permanent when no evidential basis for such an assumption existed on the facts.

There must be some causal connection between the offence committed and the injury suffered (*R. v. Derby* (1990) 12 Cr.App.R.(S.) 502), but the offence does not have to be the sole cause (*R. v. Corbett* [1992] Crim.L.R. 833). Where personal injury is disputed by the defence, some evidence of it should be produced (*R. v. Chorley Justices, ex p. Jones* (1990) 154 J.P. 420), but proof is unnecessary if injury is admitted (*R. v. Cornwell* (1979) 1 Cr.App.R.(S.) 19).

The causal connection need not be a direct connection. If, therefore, in the course of an affray or violent disorder there is a chain of events in which the offender, with others, participates in violence which results in injury, a Compensation Order may be made even though an individual offender cannot be shown himself to have caused particular injuries (*R. v. Taylor, R. v. Guertjens* [1993] Crim.L.R. 317).

(iv) Combining a Compensation Order with imprisonment

13–75 A Compensation Order should not be combined with an immediate custodial sentence if its effect would be to subject the offender on his discharge to a financial burden which he would not be able to meet from available resources and which might encourage him to commit further offences in order to pay the compensation (*R. v. Panayioutou* (1989) 11 Cr.App.R.(S.) 535).

It is not generally appropriate to combine a Compensation Order with an immediate sentence of imprisonment which is a "significant" one (*R. v. Gill* (1992) 13 Cr.App.R. (S.) 36, and *R. v. Clark* (1992) 13 Cr.App.R. 124). In those cases a "significant" sentence was one of 12 months' and 15 months' imprisonment respectively. If, however, the court has determined upon the proper sentence which reflects the seriousness of the offence, it is wrong for the court to indicate that such sentence might be reduced if the offender was able to pay compensation (*R. v. Barney* (1989) 11 Cr.App.R.(S.) 448).

(v) Procedure for making a Compensation Order

13–76 If the court considers that a Compensation Order may be appropriate this view should be made known to the accused or his advocate so that the matter may be properly and fairly investigated before any order is made (*R. v. Stanley* (1989) 11 Cr.App.R.(S.) 446). The court should be satisfied that any compensation ordered to be paid will be paid by the accused himself (*R. v. Mortimer* (1977) 121 S.J. 334). It has been said (*obiter*) that only in rare circumstances should the court accept an undetaking from another party to pay compensation on an offender's behalf, as the enforcement of such an undertaking is virtually impossible (*Att.-Gen. v. Mantoura* (1993) 157 J.P. 317). A Compensation Order should not be made before taking into account the offender's means to pay (*R. v. Bolden* (1987) 9 Cr.App.R.(S.) 83), and should not be such that it would take the offender an excessive period to pay (*R. v. Bagga* (1989) 11 Cr.App.R.(S.) 497).

2. Recommendations for Deportation

(i) General rule

13–77 The general guidelines for making recommendations for deportation, which are not rigid rules of law and to which there might be exceptions, depending on the evidence, have been laid down by the Court of Appeal in *R. v. Nazari* [1980] 1 W.L.R. 1366. The guidelines may be summarised as follows.

(i) The court must consider first whether the offender's continued presence in the United Kingdom is to its detriment. This will depend upon the nature of the offence, and the criminal record of the offender.

(ii) Once the court has determined that it is correct in principle to make a recommendation for deportation, the court must ignore the political system in the offender's country of origin. The court is deemed to have no knowledge of political systems in other countries. The Home Secretary is able to take such matters into account in deciding whether or not to accede to the court's recommendation.

(iii) The court is able to take into account the effect of deportation upon the offender's family or upon others who may be dependent upon the offender.

Examples

13–78 A minor case of unlawful sexual intercourse (by a 19-year-old on a 15-year-old) does not justify a recommendation (*R. v. Ariquat* (1981) 3 Cr.App.R.(S.) 83). A persistent offender may be a potential detriment to the country (*R. v. Alman*, unreported, November 8, 1971). An offender who has previously been the subject of a recommendation, although the recommendation was reversed on appeal to the Crown Court, and who then re-offended may be a potential hazard justifyng a further recommendation (*R. v. Letizia*, unreported, June 8, 1976).

> D, who was an Iranian citizen, was convicted of importing opium. He called evidence that he might face the death penalty if he was returned to Iran. Held: It is for the Home Secretary, on receiving the court's recommendation, and not for the court itself, to consider the political systems which operate in other countries and whether it would be unduly harsh to send him back to his country of origin. Recommendation upheld (*R. v. Nazari*, above).

> D, who was Spanish with two children born in this country, was convicted of conspiracy to rob and aggravated burglary. D's wife wished to stand by him but was convinced that the children who spoke English at their schools had a better future in England. Held: The case showed the dilemma of punishing innocent people because the wife will have to make a heartrending choice of whether to go with her husband or look after the interests of her children. Recommendation quashed (*R. v. Fernandez*, heard in appeal of *R. v. Nazari*, above).

> D, an Iranian of previous good character, was convicted of fraudulent trading in a company which amassed debts of £400,000 and where a prison sentence of two years was imposed for the offence. Held: The offence was sufficiently serious to merit a recommendation for deportation (*R. v. Kouyoumdjian* (1990) 12 Cr.App.R.(S.) 35).

(ii) Recommendation for deportation when the offender is already in breach of immigration rules

13–79 The general rule is that a recommendation for deportation should be decided independently of the offender's status under the Immigration Act 1971 (*R. v. Nunu* (1991) 12 Cr.App.R.(S.) 752).

If, therefore, the offender had originally gained admission lawfully but had thereafter remained in breach of the immigration conditions, for example, overstaying, a recommendation may not be appropriate (*R. v. Akan* [1973] 1 Q.B. 491). Similarly, if a minor offence has been committed by an offender who had gone through a "marriage of convenience" in order to attempt to remain in the United Kingdom, the court should consider only whether the principles in *Nazari*, above, applied, and should not consider the sham marriage (*R. v. Nunu*, above).

The only exception to this rule is where the original entry to the United Kingdom had been obtained by fraud, for example by using a forged passport. In such a case a recommendation for deportation would usually be appropriate (*R. v. Uddin* [1971] Crim. L.R. 663).

(iii) Recommendation for deportation when the accused is an E.C. national

13–80

(a) The court is entitled to have regard to the accused's background when considering the primary question of whether his continued presence in the United Kingdom is a genuine and sufficiently serious threat to the requirements of public policy affecting one of the fundamental interests of society. Accordingly, if the accused was in the United Kingdom because he was a Nazi, and such an organisation as proscribed in West Germany, the court is entitled to consider the ruthlessness with which members of such parties seek to achieve their aims in considering whether to make a recommendation for deportation (*R. v. Kraus* (1982) 4 Cr.App.R.(S.) 113).

(b) A conviction for an offence which is so serious as to justify an immediate custodial sentence, *e.g.* unlawful wounding with a beer glass, is not in itself a reason for recommendation for deportation upon an E.C. national (*R. v. Compassi* (1987) 9 Cr.App.R.(S.) 270).

(c) The court must try and strike a balance between the possibility of the offender committing further offences and the harm that would be done to his dependants if he was deported. Applying this principle a recommendation for deportation on a Spanish citizen who had been in this country for 14 years with two previous convictions was quashed following a further conviction for theft from an hotel (*R. v. Cravioto* (1990) 12 Cr.App.R.(S.) 71). It was said in that case that where the effect upon family and relatives upon deportation would be serious it is particularly important that the principles in *R. v. Nazari*, above, be applied scrupulously.

(d) Where a German citizen, of previous good character, was convicted of one act of indecent assault on an 11-year-old boy it was held that before a recommendation for deportation could be made the court would have to be satisfied of the danger of further breaches of the law against children. In that case the Court of Appeal quashed a recommendation made by the Crown Court (*R. v. Spura* (1988) 10 Cr.App.R.(S.) 376).

3. Disqualification from Driving

13–81 Although the period of disqualification is within the discretion of the court, it has been said that very long periods of disqualification defeat their object because they discourage young men from leading honest working lives which may require the use of a motor car (*R. v. Scott* (1989) 11 Cr.App.R.(S.) 248). In addition, a long period of disqualification may tempt an offender who is frustrated by being unable to drive lawfully into a cycle of crime (*R. v. Fazal* [1999] 1 Cr.App.R.(S.) 152).

It is not appropriate to impose a lifetime disqualification from driving in the absence of psychiatric evidence or evidence from the offender's previous record that he will be a danger to the public indefinitely (*R. v. King (Phillip)* (1992) 13 Cr.App.R.(S.) 668).

It is a proper consideration to have regard to the offender's prospects of employment when considering the length of disqualification to be imposed.

D, aged 23, was convicted of dangerous driving and sentenced in the Crown Court to 18 months' imprisonment and disqualified from driving for a period of five years. Held: D was of an age when a long period of disqualification would have a serious effect on his future prospects of employment and combined with a sentence of imprisonment was excessive. Five years' disqualification reduced to 2 years together with an order under RTOA 1988, s.36(1) by the Court of Appeal (*R. v. Callum* [1995] R.T.R. 246).

D, aged 33, who had a bad criminal record for driving while disqualified, was given 12 months' imprisonment and disqualified for five years for driving while disqualified. Held: Because of the grave handicap the period of disqualification would have on his efforts to rehabilitate himself after release, the period of disqualification was reduced to two years (the minimum, on facts, provided by law) (*R. v. West* (1986) 8 Cr.App.R.(S.) 266).

The statutory provision in the Road Traffic Offenders Act 1988, s.36, enabling a court, in its discretion to disqualify a driver until he passes a further driving test should only be used when the offender is ordinarily lacking in competence to drive and should not be used as a punishment (*Hughes v. Challes* (1984) 5 Cr.App.R.(S.) 374, *R. v. Peat* (1984) 6 Cr.App.R.(S.) 311, and *R. v. Buckley* (1988) 10 Cr.App.R.(S.) 477).

13–82   The use of a disqualification from driving until a new driving test is passed may properly form part of a sentence where there is reason to think that the driver is lacking competence to drive. In determining whether to make such an order "the court shall have regard to the safety of road users" (R.T.O.A. 1988, s.36(6)). The use of the power was approved in the following circumstances.

D, aged 23 with numerous driving convictions, who had never passed a driving test, pleaded guilty to driving without due care and attention which included skidding while turning a corner, passing a give way sign without stopping, in a manner which caused other vehicles to swerve and at an excessive speed. Held: While the power should not be used as an additional punishment (see *R. v. Buckley*, above, it was permissible to use the power where there was reason to think that the driver lacked competence to drive, and in this case the driving was grossly incompetent. The order of the Crown Court to disqualify until a new test was passed was properly made (*R. v. Miller* (1994) 15 Cr.App.R.(S.) 505).

The provisions of the Road Traffic Offenders Act 1988 provide for a mandatory disqualification until a new driving test is passed in dangerous driving cases (RTOA 1988, s.36(1), as substituted by RTA 1991, s.32).

4. Deprivation of Property

13–83   The magistrates' court has the power to deprive an offender of his rights over property used to commit an offence or intended to be used in the commission of an offence (PCCA, s.43).

The court must first be satisfied that there has been a deliberate use of the property for the purposes of committing the offence. Secondly, the property must have been in the possession or under the control of the offender at the time of his apprehension or at the time the summons for the offence was issued. Thirdly, the court must consider both the value of the property itself and the likely financial effect on the offender of an order for forfeiture. Lastly, the court must consider the making of the order in the context of the total penalty imposed for the offence in order to maintain the principle of proportionality (*R. v. Highbury Corner Metropolitan Stipendiary Magistrate, ex p. Di Matteo* [1991] 1 W.L.R. 1374 and *R. v. Joyce* (1989) 11 Cr.App.R.(S.) 253).

Providing these principles are followed, a forfeiture order may be made in respect of a wide variety of offences. For example, it could be used to deprive an offender of money if it was found to be working capital for future drug dealing (*R. v. O'Farrell* (1988) 10 Cr.App.R.(S.) 74), or a car in the case of reckless driving (*R. v. Bramble* (1984) 6 Cr.App.R.(S.) 80), or driving while disqualified (*R. v. Highbury Corner Metropolitan Stipendiary Magistrate*, above).

The power may only be used when there is a direct connection between the offence and the property. If, therefore, an offender had indecently assaulted his victim by dragging her towards his car it would not be right to deprive the offender of his rights over the car (*R. v. McDonald* (1990) 12 Cr.App.R.(S.) 408).

I. ABSOLUTE AND CONDITIONAL DISCHARGE

1. Absolute Discharge

13–84 An absolute discharge is appropriate where the circumstances of the offence, and the offender's involvement in it, are so exceptional that no order other than a finding and a recording of guilt is called for. In practice the pronouncement of an absolute discharge is rare.

2. Conditional Discharge

13–85 This is a more common disposal and is usually imposed: (a) when the facts of the offence absolve the offender from moral blame; or (b) when the offender is of previous good character and the facts of the case and the mitigation are such that the court does not wish to take away the offender's good character. If the offender commits a further offence during the period of the discharge he, of course, then becomes liable to be sentenced for the original offence and thereby loses his good character.

This traditional sentencing principle has been given express recognition in section 29(3) and (4) of the Criminal Justice Act 1991, which provides that a conditional discharge is a sentence and also a conviction, whether the conditional discharge was imposed before or after October 1, 1992. Thus, the court may take a previous conditional discharge into account in assessing the seriousness of any new offence committed during the period of discharge; it counts as a previous conviction (CJA 1991, s.29(1)). It is also an associated offence for the purposes of assessing seriousness under section 1(2)(a) of the Act if the court passes a sentence to mark the breach (*R. v. Godfrey* (1993) 14 Cr.App.R.(S.) 804).

CHAPTER 14

Offences Against the Person

1. Unlawful Wounding and Inflicting Grievous Bodily Harm

14–01   Cases involving injury caused by a weapon such as a knife or a bottle are regarded as being very serious indeed and plainly fall within the criteria of section 1(2)(a) or (b) of the Criminal Justice Act 1991. If considerable injury is caused to the victim without a weapon being used, such as kicking on the ground and stamping on the head, the conduct must be visited by a custodial sentence, save in the most exceptional circumstances (*Att.-Gen.'s Reference (No. 10 of 1992) (R. v. Cooper)* (1993) 15 Cr.App.R.(S.)1). Such cases invariably attract custodial sentences of longer than six months, and accordingly, justices should consider carefully whether it is appropriate to accept jurisdiction in such cases: (*R. v. Fox* (1980) 2 Cr.App.R.(S.) 188; *R. v. Ajit Singh* (1981) 3 Cr.App.R.(S.) 180; *R. v. Jones* (1984) 6 Cr.App.R.(S.) 55; *R. v. Wright* (1989) 11 Cr.App.R.(S.) 63.)

2. Assault Occasioning Actual Bodily Harm

14–02   The offence of assault occasioning actual bodily harm is almost always an offence which is so serious that only a custodial sentence can be justified under the Criminal Justice Act 1991, s.1(2)(a), even where the offence is considered suitable for summary trial. The offence will usually merit an immediate custodial sentence even if there is a plea of guilty and even if the injuries are caused without the use of a weapon and without kicking (*R. v. Mellor* (1994) 16 Cr.App.R.(S.) 230).

> D, of previous bad character, attempted to jump the taxi queue at a railway station late at night and punched the victim, who tried to prevent him entering the taxi, in the nose causing a fracture. Held: Unprovoked, loutish and drunken behaviour in the street which results in an assault causing actual bodily harm

requires a short custodial sentence commensurate with the violence actually used. Six months' imprisonment (on a plea) imposed at the Crown Court reduced to four months' by the Court of Appeal (*R. v. Marples* [1998] 1 Cr.App.R.(S.) 335).

D, aged 26 and of good character, had drunk about nine pints of Guinness when he struck the victim in the face and then kicked him on the ground causing bruising to the face and jaw and a cut to the eyebrow which required stitching. Held: An unprovoked, gratuitous and drunken attack on an innocent victim, particularly when it involved repeated blows, was an offence clearly within the ambit of the CJA 1991, s.1(2)(a). The sentence of six months' imprisonment imposed at the Crown Court was reduced to three months to reflect the fact that the offence was out of character and that the injuries were relatively minor (*R. v. Audit* [1993] Crim. L.R. 627).

D, a woman aged 21 of good character, had had an argument with the victim in a restaurant, and then outside the restaurant had hit her with two blows to the face causing black eyes and a fracture to the nose. Held: Two vicious blows to the face which caused a fracture was so serious that only a custodial sentence could be justified for the offence, but a short sharp sentence was all that was required. Six months' imprisonment imposed at the Crown Court reduced to 28 days (*R. v. Graham* [1993] Crim.L.R. 628).

D, aged 31 with previous convictions for offences of violence, pleaded guilty to punching a victim in the face with a single blow causing a fracture to the cheek bone and a badly swollen right eye following an argument in a public house. Held: Such a deliberate offence was so serious that only a custodial sentence was justified. 12 months' imprisonment imposed at the Crown Court reduced to six months' by the Court of Appeal (*R. v. Blewitt* (1994) 15 Cr.App.R.(S.) 132).

14–03 Identical consideration will apply if the offender is under 21 and of previous good character,

D1, aged 18 and D2, aged 17, both of previous good character and who had been drinking pleaded guilty to repeatedly kicking and punching the victim, who was a complete stranger, in the street. Apparently, the offenders had considered the victim was staring at them. The victim suffered a severe black eye. Held: Such incidents give rise to considerable public concern and cannot be tolerated. They must attract, and be understood to attract, severe punishment. In view of the offenders' ages and previous good character the sentence of six months' youth detention was reduced to 2 months' in each case by the Court of Appeal (*R. v. Robson and Howard* (1998) 162 J.P. 731).

D, aged 20 and of good character, had drunk six pints of lager in a public house, and went to the lavatory where he saw the victim, aged 45, who was jostled by D and another youth. D then hit the victim in the face, pulled his jacket over his head and continued to hit him causing a fractured nose and other minor facial injuries. Held: As D had himself suffered a broken nose in the incident, which was a sort of punishment, a sentence of 12 months' youth detention imposed at the Crown Court would be reduced to six months (*R. v. Tooke* (1990) 90 Cr.App.R. 417).

Assaults between motorists

14–04   "Offences in which one vehicle driver leaves his vehicle and assaults the driver of another vehicle causing serious injury are on the increase ... such offences should be visited with immediate sentences of imprisonment, even though the defendant is a person of hitherto good character" (*R. v. Remblance* (1992) 13 Cr.App.R.(S.) 388).

Since that dicta, exemplified in the examples cited below, it has been said that, if anything, the climate of opinion in relation to "road rage" violence has hardened and that some of the sentences upheld in the past might nowadays be considered too low (*R. v. Hunt* [1997] 1 Cr.App.R.(S.) 414).

EXAMPLES

14–05

D, who claimed that his car had been clipped by a bus, confronted the bus driver and assaulted him by punching him once in the face causing bruising and a small cut. Held: Such incidents are far too common, and are unpleasant for those involved and spectators. As there was only one blow and no persistent violence a sentence of four months' imprisonment imposed at the Crown Court would be reduced to six weeks (*R. v. Atkins* (1993) 14 Cr.App.R.(S.) 146).

D1, aged 25, and his brother D2, a mortgage broker aged 27, both of good character, were in a car on a Sunday outing when, after "an immature driving episode," D1 punched one victim on the nose and D2 inflicted minor injuries with a riding crop he had taken from the car on another victim. Held: Gross behaviour involving violence between motorists must be visited by a custodial sentence but it should be as short as possible for offenders of good character. Eight weeks and six weeks respectively substituted for four months and three months imposed at the Crown Court (*R. v. Ord and Ord* (1990) 12 Cr.App.R.(S.) 12).

D, aged 27, when driving to work, followed the victim in his car through a number of roads after the victim had allegedly pulled out in front of him. When the two cars were then forced to stop at traffic lights D went over to the victim's car punched him several times in the face and then partially dragged the victim from his car. Held: While an immediate sentence of imprisonment was perfectly proper, three months was substituted for nine months imposed at the Crown Court (*R. v. Smith* (1989) 11 Cr.App.R.(S.) 444).

14–06   Even if the assault between motorists does not amount to actual bodily harm, and consists only of a common assault, a short custodial sentence is justified.

D, aged 37 with previous convictions, got out of his car and pushed the victim in the chest over a dispute in the road earlier. Held: Such behaviour will not be tolerated. Violence between motorists will in the vast majority of cases involve a custodial sentence in order to underline the importance of preventing violence and to ensure that people think before they resort to aggressive contact with other motorists. 14 days' imprisonment imposed as the Crown Court reduced to 7 days' by the Court of Appeal (*R. v. Fenton* (1994) 15 Cr.App.R.(S) 628).

3. Assault upon persons in authority

(i) Public transport employees

14–07

D was involved in an incident with a passenger when boarding a bus which attracted the attention of the conductor, who was then threatened with a pool cue and pushed by D. He was convicted of common assault upon the bus conductor. Held: It is clearly the duty of the courts to extend to conductors and drivers such protection as they can. One measure of protection which they can and should extend is to impress upon defendants in cases such as this that the penalty for using violence of any kind towards such persons will be met by immediate prison sentences. Six months' imprisonment was fully justified (*R. v. Tremlett* (1983) 5 Cr.App.R.(S.) 199).

(ii) Traffic wardens

14–08 Traffic Wardens deserve the protection of the courts from assault when carrying out their duties.

D assaulted a female traffic warden causing actual bodily harm because she was attempting to place a parking ticket on his car. Held: Three months' immediate imprisonment was substituted for six months imposed at the Crown Court (*R. v. Robertson* (1990) 12 Cr.App.R.(S.) 278).

Where a car is deliberately driven at a traffic warden with the intention of frightening the warden, but the consequence of the driving is that the warden is hit and injury is caused a sentence of six months' imprisonment imposed at the Crown Court has been upheld by the Court of Appeal (*R. v. Charlton* (1995) 16 Cr.App.R.(S.) 703).

(iii) Licensees of public houses

14–09

D, aged 38 and of good character, pleaded guilty to assaulting the licensee by grabbing him by the throat and kicking him after being rebuked for eating his own food in the bar. Held: The seriousness of the offence outweighed the mitigation arising from D's personal circumstances. Three months' imprisonment imposed by the Crown Court upheld by the Court of Appeal (*R. v. Percival* (1988) 10 Cr.App.R.(S.) 450).

D, a woman aged 19, refused to leave a public house when asked to by the female licensee and then attacked the licensee knocking out a tooth. Held: The courts are determined to stop violence on those like licensees who hold jobs which expose them to risk of violence. Four months [imprisonment] was not wrong in principle (*R. v. Williams* (1980) 2 Cr.App.R.(S.) 150).

D, aged 20, without a record for violence, was one of four youths making a nuisance of themselves on the forecourt of an Indian restaurant. When asked to leave by the proprietor the youths abused him and later D returned with a jack handle which he used to strike the proprietor on the arm causing actual bodily harm. Held: Those who commit disgraceful incidents of this kind should know, and so should their friends, that substantial sentences may follow. Five months' youth custody, upheld by the Court of Appeal (*R. v. English* (1985) 7 Cr.App.R.(S.) 65).

14–10 A brawl in a public house, which was spontaneous, and involved the throwing of a chair, is likely to attract an immediate custodial sentence even though no actual injury is caused to the victim.

> D pleaded guilty to common assault for throwing a chair across a room in a public house which did not actually injure the licensee. Held: Nine months' imprisonment imposed at the Crown Court upheld by Court of Appeal. (*R. v. Cachia* (1980) 2 Cr.App.R.(S.) 60.)

> *NOTE:* Common assault is now triable only summarily (CJA 1988, s.39).

4. Assaults upon Police

14–11 A custodial sentence is almost always inevitable for an assault on a constable which causes actual bodily harm when the constable is acting in the execution of his duty. The principle that a custodial sentence is inevitable (save in the most exceptional circumstances) where a police officer is injured in an assault was recently restated by the Court of Appeal in *R. v. Roughsedge (Att.-Gen.'s Ref. (No. 7 of 1993))* [1994] R.T.R. 322.

It has been said that police officers performing a public duty in circumstances where they are only too likely to encounter bad temper and unreasonableness deserve such protection as the courts can give (*R. v. Fletcher* [1998] 1 Cr.App.R.(S.) 7).

> D caused bruising to a police officer when being arrested for using threatening behaviour outside a dance hall. Held: Six months' imprisonment was not too long (*R. v. Bird* (1979) 1 Cr.App.R.(S.) 348).

> D punched a police officer in the face when being arrested for shoplifting and punched another officer at the police station. Held: Six months' imprisonment was not too long (*R. v. Bradley* (1980) 2 Cr.App.R.(S.) 12).

> D punched a police officer in the eye when his friend was being arrested for causing a disturbance in a discotheque. Held: Three months' imprisonment and £300 compensation was not too great (*R. v. McGrath* (1990) 12 Cr.App.R.(S.) 204).

Even if actual bodily harm is not caused, a custodial sentence is usually inevitable for a deliberate assault upon an officer.

> D, aged 20 with several previous convictions, including one for violent disorder, assaulted two police officers after being arrested for a drink-drive offence. Held: In the context of the circumstances surrounding the assaults each offence was "so serious that a non-custodial sentence cannot be justified for it" (CJA 1982, s.1(4A)) (*R. v. Rhoades* (1989) 11 Cr.App.R.(S.) 538).

5. Violence Towards Children

Guideline case

R. v. Durkin (1989) 11 Cr.App.R.(S.) 313.

14–12 Lord Lane C.J., in this case, stated that where children are victims of violence there are four matters which should be considered:

(i) it is necessary to punish someone who commits this sort of offence;

(ii) it is necessary to provide some sort of expiation of the offence for the offender;

(iii) public conscience must be satisfied; and

(iv) others must be deterred by making it clear that such behaviour would result in condign punishment, unless, on the facts, there is a sudden loss of temper in which case deterrence is not a factor.

14–13 One of the most important considerations is the degree and persistence of the attacks. Whereas one act arising out of momentary loss of control was to some degree forgiveable, a series of assaults could excite little sympathy.

D, a single parent living in stressful circumstances, pleaded guilty to persistently beating her two-and-a-half-year-old daughter with a buckled belt causing a fractured rib and elbow and scarring of the thorax, abdomen and legs. Held: 18 months' imprisonment, with 12 months to serve and the balance held in suspense imposed at the Crown Court, upheld by the Court of Appeal (*R. v. Gayle* (1989) 11 Cr.App.R.(S.) 538).

NOTE: Partially suspended sentences have since been abolished (CJA 1991, s.5(2)(b)).

14–14 Where a single incident amounted to actual bodily harm, without severe connotations, shorter sentences have been imposed and upheld.

D, aged 22 and of good character, pleaded guilty to assaulting his three-month-old daughter by striking her around the eyes with the back of his hand causing bruises. Held: D was in a stable relationship and no reason for the offence was evident. Nine months' imprisonment at the Crown Court upheld by the Court of Appeal (*R. v. Jeffrey* (1989) 11 Cr.App.R.(S.) 265).

D, aged 22 with previous convictions but none for violence, struck his three-year-old step-daughter twice with his hand on each side of the face so hard that bruises showed the imprint of his hand. Held: An immediate prison sentence to reflect the seriousness of the case was merited, but as the incident was an isolated one, a sentence of four months was substituted for 18 months imposed at the Crown Court (*R. v. Todd* (1990) 12 Cr.App.R.(S.) 14).

D, aged 25, pleaded guilty to assault occasioning actual bodily harm of his two-year-old son by kicking him on his bottom causing him to hit his head on a cabinet resulting in bruising. Held: No sentence other than an immediate custodial sentence was appropriate. Four months' imprisonment imposed at the Crown Court upheld by the Court of Appeal (*R. v. Howard* (1992) 13 Cr.App.R.(S.) 720).

14–15 Where the offender is a mother whose self-control has snapped or is clinically depressed, a sentence of imprisonment may not be appropriate.

D, aged 25 and of good character, pleaded guilty to punching her four-year-old daughter in the stomach about four times causing bruises. Held: Sentence should have been passed on the basis that D had admitted a single incident of violence by a mother whose self-control had snapped. A two-year Probation Order substituted for imprisonment imposed at the Crown Court (*R. v. Ralf* (1989) 11 Cr.App.R.(S.) 121).

D, aged 20, of previous good character, pleaded guilty to inflicting grievous bodily harm on her child aged two months. On one occasion she hit the baby causing a flake fracture to the leg, and on the second occasion twisted her leg causing a fractured femur. Held: The offence had been committed when D was probably suffering from a panic disorder and post-natel depression but by the time sentence was passed had made a good recovery and had married and the child was no longer at risk. A probation order could be substituted for a sentence of six months' detention imposed at the Crown Court (*R. v. Black* [1996] 2 Cr.App.R.(S.) 66).

The reasoning in the above cases has been applied in the case of a mother who was plainly under considerable stress (*R. v. Glover (Julie)* (1993) 14 Cr.App.R.(S.) 261).

CHAPTER 15

Offences Against Public Order

15–01 Offences in the category of public order crimes are those of violent disorder, affray, and assaults committed in public places. It has been said that such offences are so variable and cover such a wide area of behaviour that it is difficult to formulate a helpful sentencing framework (Lord Lane C.J. in *R. v. Keys and Others* (1986) 8 Cr.App.R.(S.) 30). This is particularly true in the magistrates' court because most public order crimes are triable either way, and justices will have to consider first whether to accept jurisdiction when public order offenders are before the court. Guidelines on the considerations to be followed when deciding on mode of trial are set out in Appendix I, and such considerations are a starting point when considering the range of sentences to be imposed.

1. General Considerations

15–02 (a) The fact that other offenders were not apprehended is irrelevant. The fact that others, involved in the same public violence, might have received heavier sentences if apprehended, or that others equally involved were never arrested is not a reason for not imposing the proper sentence (*R. v. Caird* (1970) 54 Cr.App.R. 499).

(b) The political views of the offender are not relevant. The court is not concerned whether violence originates from gang rivalry or from political motives (*R. v. Caird*, above).

(c) The location of violence is not relevant. It does not matter whether the public violence has taken place in a first class hotel or whether it has occurred in public places frequented by the less privileged (*R. v. Caird*, above).

(d) A distinction may be drawn between planned violence and spontaneous violence. An affray which is planned is very serious and will usually attract a substantial term of imprisonment, but an affray which is spontaneous is much less serious (*R. v. Annett and Moore* (1980) 2 Cr.App.R.(S.) 318).

2. Violent Disorder

15–03 Violent disorder is an offence created by section 2 of the Public Order Act 1986. It most closely resembles the old common law offence of Unlawful Assembly which was triable only on indictment, although Parliament has specifically made violent disorder an either way offence. It must be presumed therefore that Parliament must have envisaged that there were some cases of violent disorder which were suitable for justices to deal with. Such cases are likely in practice to be those which on the facts are only slightly more serious than cases of threatening behaviour, because on indictment the jury are entitled to convict in the alternative of threatening behaviour. There is some similarity between the offences, although in the magistrates' court justices do not have the option of convicting in the alternative if the offence of violent disorder is not fully made out.

In sentencing for violent disorder the principal consideration is not any individual act of violence which may have occurred, but the use of violence in circumstances where so many people are present as to inspire fear in the general public (*R. v. Tomlinson and Others* (1993) 157 J.P. 695). It has been said that the *gravemen* of violent disorder is that three or more persons are present using or threatening violence, and thus it may properly be described as "mob violence" (*R. v. Coote* (1993) 14 Cr.App.R. (S.) 40).

15–04 If the violent disorder is premeditated and weapons are taken on an expedition to cause violence, sentences of 12 months or two years are appropriate (*R. v. Vanes and Vanes* (1989) 11 Cr.App.R.(S.) 147).

At common law violent disorder which was racially motivated merited a long sentence to reflect this aggravating feature (*R. v. Alderson* (1989) 11 Cr.App.R.(S.) 301). It is now obligatory to treat racially motivated violent disorder as an aggravating factor by virtue of section 82 of the Crime and Disorder Act 1998. (See generally §§13–11, above.

If the violent disorder involves groups of youths of eight to 10 or more, fighting and kicking in a town centre late at night, a sentence of 12 months' imprisonment has been considered appropriate (*R. v. Jackson-Crisp* (1989) 11 Cr.App.R.(S.) 257).

15–05 For these reasons, it is submitted, it will be rare for justices to accept jurisdiction in violent disorder cases, although summary disposal may be appropriate if none of the aggravating features mentioned above are present.

> D1, aged 21 of good character, D2, aged 24 with previous convictions for violence, and D3, aged 19 of good character, took part in a poll tax demonstration which ended in scuffling and shouting which caused fear to the general public. During the incident D1 threw a two pence piece at an office building, D2 threw a stone, and D3 collected and threw some half bricks. Held: A sentence of four months' imprisonment on D1 upheld, and sentences on D2 and D3 varied to six months' imprisonment and youth custody respectively (*R. v. Tomlinson and Others* (1993) 157 J.P. 695).

> D1, aged 21 and with previous convictions for theft and criminal damage and D2,

aged 19 and with convictions for dishonesty, pleaded guilty to violent disorder in a shopping centre. Fighting had broken out between a number of youths and D1 interfered with the arrest of one such youth and caused criminal damage to a police van. D2 struck an officer during the mêlée surrounding the incident. Held: Such prevalent and disgraceful conduct was too serious to justify a non-custodial sentence. Four months' imprisonment for D1 and three months' youth detention for D2 were substituted for longer sentences imposed at the Crown Court (*R. v. Cotter and Farrell* (1989) 11 Cr.App.R.(S.) 102).

15–06
D, of previous good character who was in employment, pleaded guilty to involving himself in a violent crowd outside night club and punching and exchanging punches with another man. Other offenders were also sentenced in respect of more serious incidents. Held: A distinction could be made between D and the other offenders. D's involvement was spontaneous, no weapon was used and no injury was caused. A short Community Service order would be adequate punishment. Six months' imprisonment imposed by the Crown Court quashed by the Court of Appeal (*R. v. Shanoor* (1998) 162 J.P. 731).

NOTE: The offence of violent disorder is committed when three or more persons use or threaten violence and their conduct *taken together* would cause another to fear for his personal safety. D's plea of guilty was therefore inevitable but in this case the presence of CCTV cameras meant that D's individual acts could be isolated for the purpose of sentence. It would seem that in the absence of such surveillance evidence a *Newton* hearing might be appropriate to determine the precise part played by an offender when joint or crowd violence is prosecuted.

3. Affray

15–07 Affray is defined in section 3 of the Public Order Act 1986 and it closely resembles the former common law offence of affray. Like violent disorder it is an either way offence, whereas under common law affray was triable only on indictment. Premeditated affrays will not be suitable for summary trial, but even spontaneous affrays have attracted sentences of longer than six months in the Crown Court and such sentences have been upheld by the Court of Appeal.

An affray in a restaurant, involving customers and waiters with chair legs being used as weapons which lasted a relatively short time attracted a sentence of two years' imprisonment (reduced to nine months on appeal) for an offender of good character (*R. v. Kin Sun Chu* (1987) 9 Cr.App.R.(S.) 377).

At common law an affray which was racially motivated merited a deterrent element in the sentence (*R. v. Miller* [1998] 2 Cr.App.R.(S.) 398). It is now obligatory to treat a racially motivated affray as an aggravating factor by virtue of section 82 of the Crime and Disorder Act 1998. (See generally §§13–11, above).

15–08 If the affray involves an attack by more than one offender on a single victim in the street which is unprovoked and involves kicking there is a risk of serious injury and the activity is highly dangerous. For these reasons the sentencing powers of justices' would be insufficient (*R. v. Miller* [1998] 2 Cr.App.R.(S.) 398).

If none of these aggravating features is present and the offender enters a timely plea of guilty the sentencing powers of the magistrates' court are likely to be sufficient to deal with the case (*R. v. Fox* [1999] 1 Cr.App.R.(S.) 332). In that case the Court of

Appeal reduced a sentence of nine months' imprisonment imposed at the Crown Court to one of four months', but it is submitted a community sentence might have been appropriate on the facts of that case.

Affray in public houses

15–09   Fighting in public houses even without weapons when fists were used, and beer glasses, stools and billiard balls and cues were thrown so that a number of people were frightened and hurt but not seriously injured called for deterrent sentences. Sentences of two years' imprisonment, or 18 months and 21 months where there had been pleas of guilty, were considered appropriate for a spontaneous affray which had occurred in a public house between groups of youths on a stag night (*R. v. Anderson* (1985) 7 Cr.App.R.(S.) 210).

A brawl in a public house, which was spontaneous and involved the throwing of a chair, is likely to attract an immediate custodial sentence even though no actual injury is caused to the victim.

> D pleaded guilty to common assault for throwing a chair across a room in a public house which did not actually injure the licensee. Held: Nine months' imprisonment imposed at the Crown Court was upheld. (*R. v. Cachia* (1980) 2 Cr.App.R. (S.) 60).

> *NOTE*: Common Assault is now triable only summarily (CJA 1988, s.39).

An affray in an Indian restaurant by men who had previously been banned by the owner involving threats to use knives merited 12 months' imprisonment (*R. v. Whalley and Vincent* (1989) 11 Cr.App.R.(S.) 405).

4. Violence Connected with Football

(i) Introduction

15–10   Since the mid-1980s there has been particular concern in Parliament and in the courts about the phenomenon commonly known as "football hooliganism." As a result, a number of statutes were passed aimed specifically at this problem, creating summary offences, and in addition the Court of Appeal issued guidance on sentence for football related offences. The legislation may be summarised as follows.

(a) SPORTING EVENTS (CONTROL OF ALCOHOL, ETC.) ACT 1985

15–11   This prohibits public drunkenness at or on the way to football matches and outlaws the possession of fireworks at a match.

(b) PUBLIC ORDER ACT 1986

15–12   This Act introduced Exclusion Orders, preventing offenders attending football fixtures after certain public order offences connected with football are committed.

(c) FOOTBALL SPECTATORS ACT 1989

15–13   This allows a court to restrict an offender convicted of a football related offence from attending a match abroad and instead requires him to report to his local police station.

(d) FOOTBALL (OFFENCES) ACT 1991

15–14 This Act (which came into force on August 10, 1991) creates new summary offences of throwing an object, chanting indecent or racialist slogans, or invading the pitch at a football match. Offenders convicted under this Act may be made subject to an exclusion or restriction order.

Exclusion Orders and Restriction Orders are explained fully in Chapter 12, above.

(ii) Guideline case

15–15 *R. v. Wood* (1984) 6 Cr.App.R.(S.) 2.

> "The time has come for the courts to impose sentences which may deter those who are minded to use violence at or near football grounds. Unless there are exceptional mitigating circumstances—and it is not easy to see what they could be— youths between the ages of 17 and 21 who are convicted of any offence involving violence towards police officers or others trying to maintain order or to spectators who are not themselves involved in the violence should receive a custodial sentence. In most cases a short detention centre order should be adequate [*]; but if any weapon has been used or a disabling injury was caused or there is evidence that the convicted youth is addicted to the use of violence, a youth custody order would be appropriate.[*] If the injury should be such as to amount to grievous bodily harm, as is likely to arise from stabbing, a longish sentence may be necessary": (*per* Lawton L.J., at p. 5).

> [*] A Detention Centre Order was, before the Criminal Justice Act 1988, a sentence of less than four months, and youth custody was a sentence of more than four months.

Since this judgment was given the courts have additional powers to deal with football related offences under the Public Order Act 1986 (see §12–61, above).

> D, aged 21, with a criminal record including convictions and Binding Over Orders for public order offences, was among a large group of youths in a town centre precinct celebrating their team's promotion to the First Division. There was a police presence and general disorder and D was among a group who kicked and punched a police officer who briefly became unconscious and was later off duty for a period. Held: Deterrent sentences are necessary where mobs of youths, usually inflamed by drink, assault police officers. Two years' imprisonment imposed at the Crown Court upheld by the Court of Appeal (*R. v. Nawrot* (1988) 10 Cr.App.R. (S.) 239).

(iii) Assault by players on the field

15–16 Unlawful violence by a player on the field during the course of a game is likely to attract an immediate custodial sentence.

> D, with a criminal record including convictions for violence, struck an opponent on the jaw, fracturing it, during a football match after he claimed the opponent fouled him in a late tackle. Held: Incidents of this kind, on or off the field, cannot be tolerated because they give football a bad name. A sentence of immediate imprisonment was necessary. Eight months imposed at the Crown Court was reduced to six months (*R. v. Birkin* (1988) 10 Cr.App.R. (S.) 303).

D, aged 26, punched an opponent in the face during a match causing blurred vision. Later a fractured cheekbone was diagnosed. Held: It was an unprovoked assault of the utmost seriousness and six months' imprisonment imposed at the Crown Court upheld by the Court of Appeal (*R. v. Davies* (1990) 12 Cr.App.R. (S.) 308).

D, aged 31 with two minor convictions, punched an opponent in the jaw during a match causing a fracture in two places. Held: Justice required an immediate custodial sentence, but it was a momentary loss of self-control and 28 days' imprisonment was substituted for three months imposed at the Crown Court (*R. v. Lincoln* (1990) 12 Cr.App.R.(S.) 250).

(iv) Violence by spectators

15–17 Spectators who invade a football pitch during or immediately following a match and who participate in group violence on the pitch should receive an immediate custodial sentence.

D1, aged 27, and D2, aged 32, each with previous convictions were among a group of about 50 supporters who invaded a football league match causing the match to be held up for about five minutes. The incident resulted in 39 prosecutions which collectively had caused fear to players and spectators. D1 pushed a player and was escorted from the field but returned in a second wave of pitch invaders. D2 occupied the pitch and caused fear to players who were trying to escape. Each pleaded guilty to affray. Held: Violence at football matches causes fear to players who may be the target and does damage to efforts made by soccer's governing bodies to eliminate disorder and crowd threats. Four months' imprisonment imposed at the Crown Court was entirely appropriate but D2's sentence was exceptionally suspended by the Court of Appeal (*R. v. Pollinger and Pearson* [1999] 1 Cr.App.R.(S.) 128).

5. Offensive Weapons

(i) Introduction

15–18 The law on offensive weapons has been created almost exclusively by statute on occasions when Parliament has felt it necessary to respond to public anxiety about the carrying of weapons in public places. In addition to the creation of offences Parliament has, on occasions, increased the penalties available for offences in response to public anxiety.

In 1953 Parliament reacted to the wave of "Teddy boy" offences involving knuckle-dusters by passing the Prevention of Crime Act 1953. This created the offence of possessing an offensive weapon which was committed either by carrying a weapon offensive *per se* or by carrying an article which was intended to be used offensively. The offence is triable either way and was punishable with two years' imprisonment on indictment and three months' imprisonment on summary conviction. In 1988 this was increased to the statutory maximum (CJA 1988, s.46) and in 1996 the penalty on indictment was increased to four years' imprisonment (Offensive Weapons Act 1996, s.2(1)). In 1961 the manufacture and sale of flick knives was prohibited (Restriction of Weapons Act 1961, s.1).

In 1988, following widespread public disquiet about the number of offences involving the carrying of knives, Parliament created an offence of strict liability which prohibited the carrying of a knife or sharply pointed instrument in a public place (CJA 1988, s.139). This offence is known as "carrying a bladed article". The offence was punishable with a fine only if sentence was passed in the magistrates' court, but in 1996 the penalty was increased to one of six months' imprisonment (Offensive Weapons Act 1996, s.3(1)). Also in 1988 Parliament prohibited the sale of knuckledusters, swordsticks, push daggers and other specifically designed weapons (CJA 1988, s.141).

Finally, in 1997 Parliament passed the Knives Act 1997 which prohibited the selling or offering for sale of knives which are suitable for combat (Knives Act 1997, s.1). This offence is punishable with six months' imprisonment in the magistrates' court.

The conclusions to be drawn from these somewhat overlapping statutory provisions are that the same penalties are available in the magistrates' court for a wide variety of offences, whereas in the Crown Court some attempt has been made to distinguish the more serious from the less serious type of offence. The following §§ indicate that the Court of Appeal has attempted to make some distinctions on grounds of seriousness between the numerous offences on weapons created by Parliament.

(ii) Carrying an offensive weapon

FLICK KNIVES

15–19

D, aged 44 of good character, was convicted of possessing a flick knife as an offensive weapon after it was found concealed in a bag which D had with him in the street. D told the arresting officer that the area was dangerous because everybody had a knife. Held: The offence was so serious that only a custodial sentence could be justified. Six months' imprisonment imposed by the Crown Court reduced to three months' by the Court of Appeal (*R. v. Buzzer* [1996] 2 Cr.App.R. (S.) 271).

LOCK KNIVES

15–20

D, with a bad record of previous convictions, was stopped in the street and a lock knife was found in his possession. His companion, also of bad character, was found to be in possession of a metal cosh. Held: nine months' imprisonment imposed at the Crown Court reduced to three months' by the Court of Appeal (*R. v. Magee and Flavin* (1990) 12 Cr.App.R.(S.) 493).

KITCHEN KNIVES

15–21

D, aged 24, with two previous convictions for possession of an offensive weapon, was convicted of possession of a domestic vegetable knife which he admitted he had for causing injury. Held: While six months' imprisonment could be considered too long for the possession of such a knife in some cases, in the circumstances of this particular case the sentence was appropriate (*R. v. Shorter* (1988) 10 Cr.App.R.(S.) 4).

(iii) Carrying a bladed article

15–22 If the facts reveal no more than the simple carrying of a bladed article with no accompanying aggressive behaviour a custodial sentence is not justified following a plea of guilty.

D pleaded guilty to possession of a sheaf knife which was found concealed beneath his jacket when he was searched after leaving a public house. Held: The appropriate penalty in such a case should be a community penalty. Two months' imprisonment imposed at the Crown Court (without the consideration of a pre-sentence report) quashed by the Court of Appeal (*R. v. Datsun* [1999] 1 Cr.App.R.(S.) 84).

6. Firearms

15–23   The Firearms Act 1968 proscribes a wide variety of behaviour in relation to the acquisition, possession and use of firearms and some offences set out in that Act are triable either way. The principal offences justices may encounter are: (i) possession of a firearm or ammunition without a certificate; (ii) possession of a shotgun without a certificate; (iii) possession of firearm as a prohibited person, and (iv) possession of a firearm in a public place.

In a guideline case, *R. v. Avis and others* [1998] 2 Cr.App.R.(S.) 178, Lord Bingham C.J. stated that the unlawful possession and use of firearms should be recognised as a grave source of danger to society and that Parliament had increased the maximum penalties for firearms offences in the Firearms (Amendment) Act 1994. Accordingly, there was a clear public need to discourage the unlawful possession of firearms both real and imitation. It was stated in *Avis* that only where the offence charged represented a minor infringement of the law should the case be dealt with summarily. Cases other than minor infringements should be treated seriously.

While the guidance in *Avis* contained no specific relevance to the powers of justices to commit for sentence (in the event of plea before venue) or to decline jurisdiction it is submitted that justices should rarely, if ever, contemplate passing sentence in a firearms case unless it comes within the category minor infringement.

EXAMPLE

15–24

D, aged 38 of good character, had purchased various parts which, when fitted together, made a perfectly operative sten machine gun, although D had not intended either to assemble the parts or to use the gun. He pleaded guilty to two offences of possession of a prohibited weapon and one offence of possession of a firearm without a certificate. Held: A custodial sentence for offences of this type was inevitable. Six months' imprisonment imposed at the Crown Court reduced to two months' by the Court of Appeal (*R. v. Hedges* [1998] 1 Cr.App.R.(S.) 35).

7. Criminal Damage

15–25   Serious cases of criminal damage, that is to say those cases which cannot easily be disposed of by a fine and a Compensation Order, are often committed by offenders under the age of 21. Often such offences are committed in a group context, frequently after consuming alcohol. In the past, under the criterion of section 1(4A) of the Criminal Justice Act 1982, many such cases were considered so serious that a non-custodial sentence could not be justified. It is submitted that a similar view will continue to be taken under the criteria of the Criminal Justice Act 1991.

EXAMPLES

15–26

D, aged 17, with two minor previous convictions, pleaded guilty to three counts of criminal damage comprising the spraying of graffiti with aerosol to London

Underground trains and asked for 28 similar offences to be taken into consideration. The cost of repairing the damage to one train so sprayed was £650. Held: Two months' detention in a Young Offender Institution imposed at the Crown Court upheld by the Court of Appeal because any right-thinking member of the public would conclude that an offence causing £650 worth of wanton damage was so serious as to make a non-custodial sentence unjustified (*R. v. Hurren* (1990) 90 Cr.App.R. 60).

D, aged under 21 and of good character, together with others had had a great deal to drink before getting on a train at 3.30 in the morning. On the train they broke a window, damaged a lavatory bowl with a fire extinguisher, set fire to a newspaper and removed seat cushions. The cost of the damage was estimated at £2,000. Held: This is precisely the kind of case which the public believes ought to be dealt with by a custodial sentence. Twelve months' youth custody imposed at the Crown Court upheld by the Court of Appeal (*R. v. Hough* (1986) 8 Cr.App.R.(S.) 359).

D1–4, aged between 15 and 17 and of good character, had consumed a great deal of alcohol at a late night party and then systematically slashed the tyres of about 18 parked cars with a lock knife. The cost of the damage was estimated at about £1,000. Held: Despite offers to pay compensation and the effect of a custodial sentence on schooling and careers, an immediate custodial sentence is not only proper but absolutely required. Sentences of three months in a detention centre were substituted for six months' youth custody imposed at the Crown Court (*R. v. Travis and Others* (1985) 7 Cr.App.R.(S.) 149).

15–27 If the criminal damage is a revenge attack it may be an offence which is "so serious."

D, aged 20, caused damage to furniture and fittings to the value of £1,384 in the home of his former girlfriend's parents after the relationship had been terminated. Held: The circumstances of the offence were "so serious" that a non-custodial sentence could not be justified. The sentence of three months' youth detention imposed at the Crown Court upheld by the Court of Appeal (*R. v. Hunter* (1990) 12 Cr.App.R.(S.) 358).

Where criminal damage is caused in the course of a wider public order disturbance and the defendant is found not guilty of public order offences but admits damaging the roof of a motor car to a cost of £300 it has been held that a Community Service Order of 70 hours was appropriate for a youth aged 20 of good character (*R. v. Fenton* (1988) 10 Cr.App.R.(S.) 250).

The fact that criminal damage is caused for a political motive does not mean that an immediate custodial sentence is inappropriate in certain circumstances.

D, who felt strongly about the political situation in South Africa, daubed paint over glass doors and surrounding walls of South Africa House in London at considerable cost. Held: Deliberate flouting of the law cannot be excused by the motives for which it was committed. The rule of law had to be maintained and 14 days' imprisonment imposed at the Crown Court was upheld by the Court of Appeal, notwithstanding that conditional discharges had been imposed on other offenders under 21 (because of the statutory restrictions upon imposing custodial sentences on those under 21) (*R. v. Bowles* (1988) 10 Cr.App.R.(S.) 146).

D, a married woman, who did voluntary work for the Citizens Advice Bureau, was convicted of cutting the fence at Greenham Common Air Base as part of a protest against Cruise missiles. She had a number of previous convictions for the same offence in the same circumstances including a suspended sentence of which she was not in breach. At the Crown Court she stated she would refuse to pay a financial penalty. Held: In the circumstances there was no penalty other than a custodial sentence which was appropriate, but of the 12 months imposed at the Crown Court six were ordered to be held in suspense and six ordered to be served immediately (*R. v. Francis* (1985) 7 Cr.App.R.(S.) 222).

IMPACT OF HUMAN RIGHTS ACT 1998

15–28   It is submitted that these decisions will have to be considered in the light of the European Convention on Human Rights when the Human Rights Act 1998 is implemented. The determination of any criminal charge under Article 6 of the Convention means the whole of the proceedings including the sentence (*Eckle v. Germany* (1982) 5 E.H.R.R. 1). See, generally, §24–23, below. In the above two cases each offender was expressing a political cause, albeit violently, and therefore Articles, 9, 10 and 11 of the Convention arise for consideration. In addition, the distinction made between an adult and juvenile offenders made in *Bowles* is no longer applicable and the reasoning in *Francis* that a custodial sentence could be justified if an offender refused to pay a fine is no longer applicable following the Criminal Justice Act 1991.

For these reasons the *dicta* on sentencing for offences which arise from the exercise of political protest may not have persuasive force any longer.

8. Threatening or Provoking Violence

15–29   The purely summary offence of threatening or provoking violence contrary to section 4 of the Public Order Act 1986 is punishable with six months' imprisonment, although it may not be an offence which is "so serious."

D, aged 19 and with at least one previous conviction, faced two charges of threatening behaviour. In the first incident he was involved in violence in a car park having been asked to leave a public house. In the second incident, four months later, he was involved in fighting outside an off-licence when the proprietor had complained about the behaviour of his friends. Held: The circumstances of each offence were not so serious that a non-custodial sentence could not be justified. A long Community Service Order was appropriate (*R. v. Pearson* (1989) 11 Cr.App.R.(S.) 391).

CHAPTER 16

Burglary, Theft and Counterfeiting

A. BURGLARY

1. Residential Burglaries

16–01 In general terms, unless the circumstances are quite exceptional, sentences of between two and four years' imprisonment have been considered necessary by the Court of Appeal for the offence of dwelling house burglary. See, for example, *R. v. Mincher* (1990) 12 Cr.App.R.(S.) 592, *R. v. Bosanquet* (1991) 12 Cr.App.R.(S.) 646, *R. v. Gayle* [1991] 1 Cr.App.R.(S.) 378 and *R. v. Browon and Samuels* [1996] 1 Cr.App.R.(S.) 319.

It has been said that the offence of house burglary is an offence against the person as well as being an offence of dishonesty (*R. v. Mussell and Others* [1991] 1 W.L.R. 187, *per* Lord Lane C.J.) and that the public are not likely to be protected against burglars if lenient sentences are imposed (*R. v. Smith and Woollard* (1987) 67 Cr. App. R. 211, *per* Lawton L.J.).

For these reasons it will be rare for any case of dwelling house burglary to be suitable for disposal in the magistrates' court, but in the Guideline Case of *Brewster* (quoted below) it is not invariably the case that a custodial sentence must be imposed for the offence of house burglary. In his judgment Lord Bingham C.J. gave the example of an impulsive act whereby the offender stole a bottle of milk by putting his hand through an open window, or where a can of petrol was stolen from an outhouse. Cases which fall into this category may, it is submitted, be suitable for sentence in the magistrates' court in the absence of aggravating features, but in general, justices should decline to pass sentence for this offence.

Guideline case

16–02   *R. v. Brewster and others* [1998] 1 Cr.App.R. 220.

Domestic burglary is, and always has been, regarded as a very serious offence. It may involve considerable loss to the victim. Even when it does not, the victim may lose possessions of particular value to him or her. To those who are insured, the receipt of financial compensation does not replace what is lost. But many victims are uninsured; because they may have fewer possessions, they are the more seriously injured by the loss of those they do have.

The loss of material possessions is, however, only part (and often a minor part) of the reason why domestic burglary is a serious offence. Most people, perfectly legitimately, attach importance to the privacy and security of their own homes. That an intruder should break in or enter, for his own dishonest purposes, leaves the victim with a sense of violation and insecurity. Even where the victim is unaware, at the time, that the burglar is in the house, it can be a frightening experience to learn that a burglary has taken place; and it is all the more frightening if the victim confronts or hears the burglar. Generally speaking, it is more frightening if the victim is in the house when the burglary takes place, and if the intrusion takes place at night; but that does not mean that the offence is not serious if the victim returns to an empty house during the daytime to find that it has been burgled.

The seriousness of the offence can vary almost infinitely from case to case. It may involve an impulsive act involving an object of little value (reaching through a window to take a bottle of milk, or stealing a can of petrol from an outhouse). At the other end of the spectrum it may involve a professional, planned organisation, directed at objects of high value. Or the offence may be deliberatley directed at the elderly, the disabled or the sick; and it may involve repeated burglaries of the same premises. It may sometimes be accompanied by acts of wanton vandalism.

The record of the offender is of more significance in the case of domestic burglary than in the case of some other crimes. There are some professional burglars whose records show that from an early age they have behaved as predators preying on their fellow citizens, returning to their trade almost as soon as each prison sentence has been served. Such defendants must continue to receive substantial terms of imprisonment. There are, however, other domestic burglars whose activities are of a different character, and whose careers may lack any element of persistence or deliberation. They are entitled to more lenient treatment.

It is common knowledge that many domestic burglars are drug addicts who burgle and steal in order to raise money to satisfy their craving for drugs. This is often an expensive craving, and it is not uncommon to learn that addicts commit a burglary, or even several burglaries, each day, often preying on houses in less affluent areas of the country. But to the victim of burglary the motivation of the burglar may well be of secondary interest. Self-induced addiction cannot be relied on as mitigation. The courts will not be easily persuaded that an addicted offender is genuinely determined and able to conquer his addiction.

Generally speaking, domestic burglaries are the more serious if they are of occupied houses at night; if they are the result of professionl planning, organisation or execution; if they are targeted at the elderly, the disabled and the sick; if there are repeated visits to the same premises; if they are committed by persistent offenders; if they are accompanied by vandalism or any wanton injury to the victim; if they are shown to have a seriously traumatic effect on the victim; if the offender operates as one of a group; if goods of high value (whether actual or sentimental) are targeted or taken; if force is used or threatened; if there is a pattern of repeat offending. It mitigates the seriousness of an offence if the offender pleads guilty, particularly if the plea is indicted at an early stage and there is hard evidence of genuine regret and remorse.

We are indebted to counsel for referring us to a very large number of sentencing decisions on domestic burglary over the past 20 years. But the decisions have to a very large extent turned on the facts of individual cases and the circumstances of individual offenders; they have often been influenced by the legislation in force at the time. While, therefore, the decisions have identified the aggravating and mitigating factors mentioned above, they do not fall into neat groups or lend themselves to the derivation of any precise arithmetical tariff. We do not think any detailed review of the cases will prove helpful. But we should mention *Edwards and Brandy, The Times*, July 1, 1996. The first appellant pleaded guilty to burglary of an unoccupied dwelling-house at night and was sentenced to four years' imprisonment. The second appellant was convicted of two burglaries of occupied dwelling-houses at night and was sentenced on these counts to a total of seven years. Both had long records of persistent offending of this kind. Having reviewed authorities on the burglary of unoccupied dwelling-houses the Court concluded that in a contested case the normal sentence was about three years, and with the benefit of a plea of guilty about two. Where the house was occupied the Court was tentatively of the opinion that the normal sentence would be four years or more in a contested case and that, if mitigated by a plea of guilty, it would not normally attract a sentence of less than three years. The Court accordingly, quashed the sentences imposed and substituted sentences of three years and five years respectively.

We have four reservations about this decision. First, we question whether adequate weight was given to the fact that, judging by their records, both appellants were dedicated professional burglars. Secondly, while entry to a house which is not occupied reduces the risk of confrontation and generally makes the burglary less frightening to the owner, it may also be evidence of careful planning and preparation. Thirdly, it places too much emphasis on past cases and seeks to establish sentencing brackets where none is possible or desirable. Fourthly, the demarcation between occupied and unoccupied houses is not clear cut. Read more literally than the court intended, *Edwards and Brandy*, above, could, we think, be understood as making too sharp a distinction between occupied and unoccupied houses and as pointing towards what might, in some cases, be too low a level of sentence.

Overall, the cases show:

(1) that burglary of a dwelling-house, occupied or unoccupied, is not necessarily and in all cases an offence of such seriousness that a non-custodial sentence cannot be justified;

(2) that the decision whether a custodial sentence is required, and if so the length of such sentence, is heavily dependent on the aggravating and mitigating features mentioned above and, usually to a lesser extent, the personal circumstances of the offender;

(3) that the courts, particularly the higher courts, have generally reflected in their sentences the abhorrence with which the public regard those who burgle the houses of others.

16–03   For the reasons set out in the judgment in *R. v. Brewster and Others*, above, cases of residential burglary will nearly always be unsuitable for summary trial. Decisions from the Court of Appeal have repeatedly stated that sentences of longer than six months' imprisonment are appropriate, in the absence of exceptional circumstances, for offenders convicted of dwelling house burglary. The following example is only an illustration of the approach to sentence adopted by the Court of Appeal consistently over many years.

> D1 and D2, each of previous good character, who pleaded guilty, gained access to a house in a rural area which was unoccupied during the day and were apprehended before anything was taken. Held: The sentence which should have been passed was the shortest possible proper sentence. Eighteen months' imprisonment imposed at the Crown Court reduced to 12 months' by the Court of Appeal (*R. v. Fogarty and Mahoney* (1991) 13 Cr.App.R.(S.) 328).

2. Burglary of Shops and Small Business Premises

16–04 These cases are in a different category because it is unlikely that the distress, worry and fear suffered by the victim will be the same as that often suffered by householders. Thus, the burglary of an unoccupied office by night involving the theft of a fax machine may not justify a custodial sentence (*R. v. Carlton* [1993] Crim.L.R. 981). However, burglary of shops and small business premises which have professional hallmarks is an offence which is so serious that only a custodial sentence may be justified under the criteria of the Criminal Justice Act 1991.

> D1 aged 28, and D2 aged 20 and of good character, each pleaded guilty to burglary of a shop by removing bricks and then taking property to the value of £600. Burglary kit, a hammer, a crowbar and a radio scanner were later found in D1's car. Held: The circumstances of the burglary were such that only a custodial sentence could be justified. Twenty-one months' imprisonment for D1 and six months' youth detention for D2 substituted for longer sentences imposed at the Crown Court (*R. v. Dorries and Dorries* [1993] Crim. L.R. 408).

> D pleaded guilty to the entering of a record shop by removing slates from an outhouse. He was apprehended when the alarm was activated. Held: He should receive the shortest possible sentence that could properly be passed in the circumstances. Six months was substituted for nine months imposed at the Crown Court (*R. v. Bleasdale* (1984) 6 Cr.App.R.(S.) 177).

It follows that whether magistrates accept jurisdiction in non- residential burglary cases will depend upon the precise circumstances of "the less serious types of factory or shopbreaking."

16–05 A non-residential burglary is not necessarily an offence which is so serious that custody is inevitable.

> D1 and D2, both aged 21, attempted to enter a public house through the roof and had with them a sledgehammer in order to disconnect the alarms if entry was gained. Held: A Community Service Order of 100 hours was appropriate (*R. v. Hollingworth and Young* (1990) 12 Cr.App.R.(S.) 81).

If the burglary is non-residential, but nonetheless committed in a residential area the offence may be so serious that only a custodial sentence can be justified.

> D was convicted of attempted burglary of a garage of a bungalow at night. Held: An offence of burglary or attempted burglary in a residential area at night

is an offence "so serious" that only custody can be justified. Nine months' imprisonment imposed at the Crown Court upheld by the Court of Appeal (*R. v. Nicholson* (1994) 15 Cr.App.R.(S.) 226).

B. THEFT

16–06 The offence of theft differs widely depending upon the particular circumstances; it may consist of the most minor piece of spontaneous shoplifting or the most devious appropriation bordering on fraud. For a general discussion of "seriousness" under the Criminal Justice Act 1991, see paragraphs 13–02 to 13–11, above. When considering the seriousness of theft courts should apply the dicta in *R. v. Howells and other appeals* [1999] 1 All E.R. 50 (see §§13–02 *et seq.*, above). Accordingly, the decisions in *R. v. Keogh* (1993) 15 Cr.App.R.(S.) 279 (shoplifting) and *R. v. Costello* (1993) 14 Cr.App.R.(S.) 240 (theft from telephone boxes) must now be read in the light of *Howells*. The element of pre-planning and the loss to the victim are also factors which may properly be taken into account in deciding seriousness (*R. v. Foster* (1993) 15 Cr.App.R.(S.) 340). In that case a short custodial sentence was upheld by the Court of Appeal where deliberate and pre-arranged "taxi-bilking" has occurred. The following are some decisions and reasoning of the Court of Appeal involving the most common types of theft.

1. Shoplifting

16–07 It has been said that where an offender commits a petty offence of shoplifting, theft of goods worth £3.50, and there is evidence that the offender has psychiatric problems, then the offence comes "nowhere near the threshold of seriousness to justify a custodial sentence" (*R. v. Bond (Wendy)* (1994) 15 Cr.App.R.(S.) 430). It has also been held in the Court of Appeal that an act of shoplifting which involved pushing a trolley through an unsupervised exit of a supermarket was not so serious that only a custodial sentence could be justified (*R. v. Crawford* (1993) 157 J.P. 667).

D, aged 22, pleaded guilty to shoplifting in that she admitted acting in concert with two women (who subsequently absconded) to steal goods to the value of £449 from a department store by concealing them in a bag beneath clothing. Held: D had voluntarily returned from abroad to face her court appearance and in all the circumstances a Community Service Order would have been appropriate. Six months' imprisonment imposed at the Crown Court quashed by the Court of Appeal (*R. v. Glowacki* (1998) 162 J.P. 731).

However, where the offence of shoplifting is the result of a planned expedition to steal and a sizeable quantity of goods are stolen the offence may well be so serious that only a custodial sentence can be justified (*R. v. Bailey* (1994) 15 Cr.App.R.(S.) 277). In that case the Court of Appeal upheld a sentence of 12 months' imprisonment because there were aggravating features in that the offence was committed whilst on bail, the offence was prevalent in the locality and there had been no plea of guilty.

The other circumstances which may justify the imposition of a custodial sentence for shoplifting is where the offender is a persistent thief or has failed to respond to previous sentences (CJA 1991, s.29(1)). The amended section 29 of the Act allows the court to take previous convictions into account in weighing seriousness. In the absence of aggravating features (see *R. v. Bailey*, above) or a persistent history of shoplifting offending it would seem that the offence of shoplifting is not, in itself, an offence so serious that no sentence other than a custodial sentence can be justified for it.

2. Pickpocketing

16–08   It has been held in *R. v. Cunningham* [1993] 1 W.L.R. 183, that the prevalence of an offence is a relevant factor in determining its seriousness. Consequently, if pickpocketing is particularly prevalent in a locality a custodial sentence may be justified for the offence under the criteria of the Criminal Justice Act 1991. Further, a deterrent element is a proper aspect of sentencing for crimes which are prevalent or unpleasant (*R. v. Smith and Read* [1997] 1 Cr.App.R.(S.) 342). In that case sentences of 18 months' imprisonment for attempted theft (pickpocketing) from women's handbags in central London was reduced to 12 months' by the Court of Appeal. On the London underground and on London buses the offence is regarded as very prevalent (*R. v. Spencer and Carby* (1995) 16 Cr.App.(S.) 482).

3. Credit Card Theft

16–09   In deciding the seriousness of theft where credit cards are involved, the court is entitled to look at the consequences of the theft, namely the dishonest use of the cards to obtain property by deception. The case of *R. v. Bumrungpruik*, below, was decided under the Criminal Justice Act 1982 s.1(4A)(c) when the court was required to consider each offence in isolation. Under the amended provisions of section 1(2)(a) of the Criminal Justice Act 1991 the court is entitled to consider the seriousness of the offence or the combination of the offence and other offences associated with it. It would seem obvious, therefore, that the reasoning in *Bumrungpruik* is going to apply to sentences passed under the 1991 Act.

> D, aged 19, with no previous convictions, pleaded guilty to five offences of theft and five offences of obtaining property by deception and asked for a further 159 similar offences to be taken into consideration. The total value of the goods dishonestly obtained amounted to £11,000. Held: While each individual offence had to be considered, and the court could not observe what happened afterwards and reflect back as to whether a single offence was "so serious," nevertheless in judging the seriousness of an individual theft the court could consider the offender's purpose. In this case D's purpose was to obtain goods by stealing credit cards. By way of example, if a cheque book was stolen in order to provide paper to light a fire the offence might be less serious than the theft of a cheque book in order to pass forged cheques. Nine months' detention in a young offender institution imposed at the Crown Court upheld by the Court of Appeal (*R. v. Bumrungpruik* (1992) 14 Cr.App.R.(S.) 98).

C. COUNTERFEITING

1. Offences involving Counterfeit Currency

16–10   The forgery of notes or the possession of forged notes with the intention of passing them as genuine are serious offences which attract substantial sentences of imprisonment. Only in exceptional circumstances have lesser offences involving counterfeiting been dealt with by shorter sentences. Forgery of banknotes—three years' imprisonment (*R. v. Lister* (1982) 4 Cr.App.R.(S.) 331). Counterfeiting 50 pence pieces—18 months' imprisonment (*R. v. Lee* (1981) 3 Cr.App.R.(S.) 275). Possession of counterfeit currency—two years' imprisonment (*R. v. Turner* (1982) 4 Cr.App.R.(S.) 367). The forgery of notes or the possession of forged notes with the intention of passing them as genuine have in the past been considered so serious that substantial sentences of imprisonment are appropriate. It is submitted that under the criteria of the 1991 Act the same considerations will apply.

> "The issue of counterfeit notes undermines the whole economy... [Custodial sentences imposed on those tendering counterfeit currency] indicate to others who are minded to make cheap and easy profit by the acceptance of counterfeit notes, that it is simply not worth the candle. If they do choose to have counterfeit notes ... they are going to get some considerable punishment": *per* Lord Lane C.J. in *R. v. Howard* (1985) 7 Cr.App.R.(S.) 320 at 322.

16–11   An immediate custodial sentence of six months' imprisonment has been considered necessary in the case of tendering a counterfeit £20 note in a shop (*R. v. Dickens* (1993) 14 Cr.App.R.(S.) 76) and a sentence of nine months' imprisonment has been considered appropriate for the tendering of nine counterfeit £10 notes in a restaurant (*R. v. Simmonds* (1995) 16 Cr.App.R.(S.) 898).

Examples of the serious view taken of counterfeiting offences appear in the following cases.

> D, aged 25, attempted to buy a gramophone record in a shop with a forged £50 note. Held: This particular offence was at the lower end of the spectrum but in the absence of exceptional circumstances an immediate custodial sentence is necessary in all cases involving the tendering or passing of forged banknotes. (*R. v. Sardar Shah* (1987) 9 Cr.App.R.(S.) 167).

> D, aged 31 and of good character, was convicted of passing two £10 Bank of England notes knowing or believing them to be counterfeit on two occasions on the same day. Held: As the forgers of counterfeit notes rely on others to pass them into circulation an immediate custodial sentence is necessary in all cases unless there are exceptional circumstances. Twelve months' imprisonment imposed at the Crown Court reduced to three months on appeal (*R. v. Wake* (1992) 13 Cr.App.R.(S.) 422).

2. Offences involving Counterfeit Goods

16–12   If the offender is a market trader dealing in clothing which are counterfeit, that is to say goods purporting to bear a well-known trade mark such as Calvin Klein or Levi Strauss, the offence passes the custody threshold (*R. v. Rafiq Adam* [1998] 2 Cr.App.R.(S.) 403). In that case the Court of Appeal upheld a sentence of three months' imprisonment imposed at the Crown Court because a custodial sentence was necessary to deter others.

CHAPTER 17

Fraud

17–01 There is no criminal offence, as such, known as fraud. The concept of a fraud is the use of false representations dishonestly to obtain an unjust advantage or to injure the rights of another. Where fraud occurs the accused may be charged with a variety of offences. In considering sentence it is not the precise offence charged which is the key to the proper sentence, but the purpose and object of the fraud, the way it was carried out, the position of trust (if any) of the fraudster, the harm done, and the benefit gained.

The magistrates' court is unlikely to be invited to deal with serious fraud, such as banking and long term fraud nor with any fraud where the loss in any single offence exceeds £5,000. However, there are many frauds which may be dealt with in the magistrates' court and they may be broadly categorised as follows:

1. frauds involving breach of trust;

2. frauds involving the DSS;

3. frauds involving insurance companies;

4. frauds in relation to share applications.

1. Frauds Involving Breach of Trust

(i) Guideline case

R. v. Barrick (1985) 7 Cr.App.R.(S.) 142.

17–02 The Guidance in *Barrick* has been revised to take into account inflation and the following extract from the judgment of Lord Lane C.J. in *Barrick* is printed as revised by the judgment of Rose L.J. in *R. v. Clark (Trevor)* [1998] 2 Cr.App.R.(S.) 95.

"The type of case with which we are concerned is where a person in a position of trust, for example, an accountant, solicitor, bank employee or postman has used that privileged and trusted position to defraud his partners or clients or employers or the general public of sizeable sums of money. He will usually, ... be a person of hitherto impeccable character. It is practically certain ... that he will never offend again and, in the nature of things, he will never again in his life be able to secure similar employment with all that that means in terms of disgrace for himself and hardship for himself and also for his family. .... We can see no proper basis for distinguishing between cases of this kind simply on the basis of the defendant's occupation. Professional men should expect to be punished as severely as the others; in some cases more severely. ... In general a term of immediate imprisonment is inevitable, save in very exceptional circumstances or where the amount of money obtained is small. Where the amount is not small, but less than £17,500, terms of imprisonment from the very short up to 21 months will be appropriate ...

17–03   The guidelines then continued for cases where larger sums were involved, and where it would be inappropriate for magistrates to assume jurisdiction. The Lord Chief Justice then highlighted a number of features in breach of trust cases which the court would no doubt wish to have regard before determining what the proper level of sentence should be. They are as follows:

"(i)   the quality and degree of trust reposed in the offender, including his rank;

(ii)   the period over which the fraud or the thefts have been perpetrated;

(iii)   the use to which the money or property dishonestly taken was put;

(iv)   the effect upon the victim;

(v)   the impact of the offences on the public and public confidence;

(vi)   the effect on fellow employees or partners;

(vii)   the effect on the offender himself;

(viii)   his own history;

(ix)   those matters of mitigation special to [the offender], such as illness; being placed under great strain by excessive responsibility or the like; where, as sometimes happened, there has been a long delay, say over two years, between his being confronted with his dishonesty by his professional body or the police and the start of his trial; finally any help given by him to the police" (per Lord Lane C.J., at p. 147).

17–04   It has been said that the guidelines in *Barrick*, above, should not be departed from unless there is some specially unusual feature about the case (*R. v. Matthews* (1986) 8 Cr.App.R.(S.) 204).

More recently it has been said that even if the amount stolen is very small, a theft by a person placed in a responsible position by an employer is an offence which necessarily and properly will attract a short custodial sentence (*R. v. McCormick* (1995) 16 Cr.App.R.(S.) 134).

While a short sentence could be imposed for thefts up to £10,000 it is unlikely that magistrates will accept jurisdiction if the sums exceed £6,000.

D, a despatch foreman for a printing company, stole £6,000 over a period of 18 months by claiming reimbursement of sums purportedly spent on postage. Held: A sentence of 12 months (the maximum possible in a magistrates' court) was considered appropriate (*R. v. Brinley* (1986) Cr.App.R.(S.) 105).

17–05   In a number of reported sentencing decisions of the Court of Appeal before October 1, 1992, a suspended sentence of imprisonment was considered appropriate in breach of trust cases where it was felt it was unlikely that the defendant would re-offend (see, for example, *R. v. Boggs (Tracy)* (1990) 12 Cr.App.R.(S.) 39). Under the 1991 Act a suspended sentence should only be imposed if it can be justified by the exceptional circumstances of the case (PCCA 1973, s.22(2)(b), as substituted by CJA 1991, s.5(1)). Strictly, the statutory obligation to impose either a custodial sentence or a community penalty unless the circumstances justifying suspending a prison sentence are exceptional should mean that the option of passing a suspended sentence in deserving cases of breach of trust theft will disappear. Recent decisions from the Court of Appeal (Criminal Division) have indicated this is not necessarily the case (see §§13–53 *et seq.*, above). Despite what appears to be a broad view of the words "exceptional circumstances" an immediate sentence of imprisonment is often inevitable when the facts indicate that the *Barrick* guidelines apply.

D, a sub-postmistress, falsified post office records to conceal the removal of £2,250 over a two-year period. Held: The sentence of four months' imprisonment imposed at the Crown Court could not be faulted, and four months' must be regarded as a short sentence in a breach of trust case but for compassionate reasons the sentence was reduced by the Court of Appeal to two months to allow D's immediate release (*R. v. Robinson* [1993] Crim.L.R. 404).

(ii) Breach of trust by cashiers

17–06

D was a till cashier at a supermarket who stole sums of £100 on 17 separate occasions by falsifying the till record and stealing cash. Held: Two months' imprisonment was appropriate (*R. v. Bagnall* (1985) 7 Cr.App.R.(S.) 40).

(iii) Breach of trust by postal workers

17–07

D, a young woman of good character, was employed as a postwoman for a period of 12 months during which she "systematically" stole postal packets containing cheque cards, some of which she used dishonestly herself. The total loss was in the region of £1,000. Held: The sanctity of the mail is a very important matter, 12 months' imprisonment imposed at the Crown Court upheld by the Court of Appeal (*R. v. Traille* (1989) 11 Cr.App.R.(S.) 265).

D, aged 20 with one previous conviction for dishonesty, stole a postal packet containing a pocket calculator valued at £11 while working as a postman. Held: While a custodial sentence was inevitable six months imposed at the Crown Court was too long and a sentence (two-and-a-half months) to secure his immediate release was substituted (*R. v. Bartley* (1989) 11 Cr.App.R.(S.) 3).

(iv) Sentences where the sums of money are very small

17–08

D, who was the deputy manager of a supermarket and had responsibility for securing the premises, stole £5. Held: While the court must take a serious view, non-violent petty offenders should not take up valuable space in prison. The sentence should be as short as possible and two months' imprisonment was the proper sentence (*R. v. Upton* (1980) 2 Cr.App.R.(S.) 182).

D, who was the manageress of a branch of a hardwares store in a large business, stole a sunbed worth £25 and on a separate occasion a sprinkler worth £6. Held: Comparatively speaking this was a trivial instance of breach of trust and where a defendant was of good character and had given loyal service it was appropriate to impose a fine or a conditional discharge (*R. v. Sutton* (1984) 6 Cr.App.R.(S.) 70).

(v) Other examples of breach of trust sentences

17–09

D was a woman of good character employed by a firm of estate agents who had responsibility for handling money received from the building society, her firm's principal. She stole £1,300 over a five-month period. Held: The clang of the prison gates in this case would be a deterrent and a punishment and three months was appropriate (*R. v. Weston* (1980) 2 Cr.App.R.(S.) 191).

D was an honorary official of a community centre who stole £350 in cash (about a third of the amount passing through his hands) over a two-and-a-half year period. Held: Although D was of good character this was a straightforward breach of trust case calling for a short sentence. Four months' imprisonment was appropriate (*R. v. Chatfield* (1985) 7 Cr.App.R.(S.) 262).

Confirmation that the reasoning in the above cases continues under the criteria of the Criminal Justice Act 1991 is provided by the following example.

17–10

D, aged 18, and of previous good character, stole goods to the value of £1,500 over a period of two to three months from his employers whilst working as a warehouse assistant, on occasions covering up the theft by issuing forged receipts. Held: Such offending was so serious that only a custodial sentence could be justified. Three months' youth detention imposed at the Crown Court varied only because D had been on bail pending his appeal (*R. v. Hill* (1993) 14 Cr.App.R.(S.) 556).

2. Frauds Involving the DSS

17–11 Sentencing guidelines in cases involving fraudulent claims for welfare benefits from the Department of Social Security and other Government departments were given by Lord Lane C.J. in *R. v. Stewart and Others* (1987) 9 Cr.App.R.(S.) 135.

"... the run of the mill offence is almost certain to be before the magistrates ... [and] ... it will only be the apparently more serious cases which will come before the Crown Court. These offences involve the dishonest abstraction of honest taxpayers' money and are not to be treated lightly. They are easy to commit and difficult and expensive to track down. However it must be remembered that they are non-violent, non-sexual and non-frightening crimes. ... [The carefully organised frauds by professional fraudsmen who] have selected the welfare departments as an easy target ... and have made a profitable business [bear little relation to the average offender in this area] ... the sentence [in these cases] will depend on an almost infinite variety of factors .... As a first step it may be advisable for the court to enquire what steps the department propose to take to recover their loss from the offender. Other considerations which may affect the decision of the court are:

(i) a guilty plea;

(ii) the amount involved and the length of time over which the defalcations were persisted in (bearing in mind that a large total might in fact represent a very small amount weekly);

(iii) the circumstances in which the offences began (*e.g.* there is a plain difference between a legitimate claim which is false owing to a change of situation and on the other hand a claim which is false from the very beginning);

(iv) The use to which the money is put (the provision of household necessities is more venial than spending money on unnecessary luxury);

(v) previous character;

(vi) matters special to the offender, such as illness, disability, family difficulties, etc.;

(vii) any voluntary repayment of the amounts overpaid" (at pp. 138–139).

17–12 The Lord Chief Justice then went on to consider the sentencing principles laid down in *R. v. Clarke* (1982) 4 Cr.App.R.(S.) 197, a case which is no longer directly relevant in the light of the Criminal Justice Act 1991. The following part of the guidelines in *Stewart* continue to be relevant.

"If immediate imprisonment is necessary, a short term of up to about nine or 12 months will usually be sufficient in a contested case where the overpayment is less than, say, £10,000. ...

So far as compensation is concerned, we would add this. Where no immediate custodial sentence is imposed, and the amount of overpayment is below, say, £1,000 or thereabouts, a Compensation Order is often of value. This will usually only be the case when the defendant is in work. Counsel for the Crown must be equipped with the relevant information to enable the Court to come to a proper conclusion on [the] matter" (at pp. 139–140).

NOTE: Where a court now passes a suspended sentence, it must consider whether, in addition, a fine or a Compensation Order should also be imposed (PCCA 1973, s.22(2A).

17–13 The following cases are examples of the application of the guideline principles and were individual appeals heard in the case of *R. v. Stewart*, above.

(i) D, who was married with a large family to support, falsely claimed a total of £5,600 to which he was not entitled over a two-year period by way of unemployment benefit. He could have become entitled to supplementary benefit if he had gone about things properly. Held: Community Service might have been appropriate but six months' imprisonment was substituted for 30 months to allow his immediate release.

(ii) D, an Iranian citizen, falsely claimed supplementary benefit and housing benefit amounting in all to £3,000 over a 20-month period. Held: Six months' imprisonment was appropriate.

(iii) D, of previous good character who suffered from epilepsy and anxiety neurosis, was overpaid some £7,000 over a four-year period when the DSS mistakenly failed to act upon his change of circumstances. Held: Six months' imprisonment suspended for two years was appropriate.

(iv) D, aged 50 of previous good character, was overpaid £4,700 over a five-year period when he failed to disclose his wife had obtained employment. The money was used to pay debts. Held: A Community Service Order was appropriate.

FURTHER EXAMPLES

17–14

D, of previous good character, pleaded guilty to specimen offences relating to the obtaining of nearly £11,000 worth of benefit to which he was not entitled over a period of four years. He asked for 88 similar offences to be taken into consideration. Held: Applying the guidelines in *Stewart*, adjusted for inflation, a total sentence of 10 months' imprisonment was appropriate having regard to D's personal circumstances (*R. v.Ellison* [1998] 2 Cr.App.R.(S.) 382).

D, a woman aged 46, with two previous convictions for fraud including one on the DSS for which she received community service, claimed supplementary benefit relating to mortgage commitments by forgery. The claim was false as she was not a single divorced woman with a mortgage because she had married her lodger and then sold the house to him. Held: 12 months' imprisonment imposed at the Crown Court was not manifestly excessive nor wrong in principle (*R. v. Rea* (1987) 9 Cr.App.R.(S.) 364).

D, with previous convictions for dishonesty, obtained £1,030 supplementary benefit fraudulently over a seven-month period and received also free accommodation by fraud. He was working at the time the false claims were made. Held: Six months' imprisonment substituted for nine months imposed at the Crown Court (*R. v. Baffour-Acheampong* (1986) 8 Cr.App.R.(S.) 313).

D, aged 26 and of good character, pleaded guilty to a fraud on the DSS over a five-month period and to obtaining £2,040 by continuing dishonestly to collect his father's pension after his father's death. Held: A suspended sentence of imprisonment and a Compensation Order of £500 was substituted for an immediate sentence of imprisonment imposed at the Crown Court (*R. v. Miah* (1989) 11 Cr.App.R.(S.) 163).

3. Frauds on Insurance Companies

17–15 It has been held that fraud upon an insurance company is an offence "so serious" that no sentence other than a custodial sentence can be justified for the offence (*R. v. Dover* (1995) 16 Cr.App.R.(S.) 61).

There appears to be no difference in the attitude of the Court of Appeal (Criminal Division) to the gravity of this type of fraud since the implementation of the Criminal Justice Act 1991, as the following examples illustrate.

> D, a serving police officer of exemplary character who was the victim of a burglary, made an insurance claim for the loss which was false in that he added to the list of stolen property, items which had not been stolen to the value of some £900. Held: Having regard to the pleas of guilty and the mitigating circumstances four months' imprisonment substituted for six months' imposed at the Crown Court (*R. v. Thomas* (1995) 16 Cr.App.R.(S.) 539).

> D1 arranged with D2 for his car to be burnt out, and then made a fraudulent claim for £800 from the insurers. Held: This type of insurance swindle called for imprisonment which might, where there was a guilty plea, be suspended. Even where it is unlikely that the offence would be repeated a short immediate sentence is not wrong in principle. Four months and three months respectively (remainder in suspense) to be served immediately, substituted for 12 months and nine months respectively (*R. v. Hussain and Mugal* (1983) 5 Cr.App.R.(S.) 330).

> D faked a burglary of his own shop and made a fraudulent insurance claim in the sum of £5,000. Held: Six months' imprisonment imposed at the Crown Court upheld by the Court of Appeal (*R. v. Ahmed* (1988) 10 Cr.App.R.(S.) 73).

> D, aged 41 and of good character, made a false claim in respect of a burglary and gained £3,300 and later attempted to make a further false claim. Held: a total of six months' imprisonment together with costs and compensation imposed at the Crown Court upheld by the Court of Appeal (*R. v. Michael* (1990) 12 Cr.App.R. (S.) 223).

4. Fraud in Relation to Multiple Share Applications

17–16

> D, a self-employed businessman aged 44 and of good character, pleaded guilty to making 93 multiple applications for shares over a 10-month period using a number of different names and addresses which could have yielded a profit of over £60,000 but which in fact yielded £5,000. Held: The fraud was a serious one because it involved several share issues, was persisted in over a long period of time, and compromised several people, including employees in whose names the applications were made. An immediate sentence of six months' imprisonment imposed at the Crown Court was entirely appropriate (*R. v. Griffiths* (1989) 11 Cr.App.R.(S.) 216).

CHAPTER 18

Offences Connected with Pornography

1. Having Obscene Articles for Publication for Gain

(i) General principles

18–01 If the offender is an owner or supplier of explicit pornography which is sold in shop premises a sentence of imprisonment should be imposed to show the court's disapproval of the activity. Organisers and wholesalers should be treated more seriously than retailers, and offenders in the former categories should be sentenced in the Crown Court.

Retailers should expect to receive a short immediate sentence of imprisonment, although the length of the sentence will depend to a degree on the nature of the material.

On the other hand, if a legitimate newsagent happens to have the odd pornographic publication for sale amongst many other publications then a custodial sentence need not be imposed (*R. v. Holloway* (1982) 4 Cr.App.R.(S.) 128).

More recently it has been said that if the offender is a retailer and the pornography in question involves sexual acts of consenting adults, and not children or animals, sentence should be passed in the magistrates' court (*R. v.Tunnicliffe, R. v. Greenwood, The Times,* December 16, 1998 (Transcript No. 9807142/W5)).

(ii) Organisers

18–02 If the defendant is neither a first offender (because the charges reveal a persistent course of conduct) nor a persistent offender (because for practical purposes he is of good character) but occupies an important place in the pornographic trade the appropriate sentence is between 12 and 15 months' imprisonment.

D, aged 49, was engaged in a pornography business from February until July

1982 and paid £480 per week in rent for his Soho premises. Pornographic magazines and videos were sold. He pleaded guilty to one indictment of eight counts
and was convicted of a second indictment of nine counts at the Crown Court.
Held: 12 to 15 months' imprisonment was appropriate (*R. v. Zampa* (1984) 6
Cr.App.R.(S.) 110).

(iii) Wholesalers

18–03 A sentence of longer than six months' imprisonment has been upheld on a
wholesaler who supplied pornographic video tapes to shops in Soho (*R. v. Vella*
(1984) 6 Cr.App.R.(S.) 373).

(iv) Retailers

18–04 Where the obscene material is grossly exploitive of women, depicting simu-
lated acts of rape or torture a sentence of six months' imprisonment has been considered appropriate.

> D, aged 36, pleaded guilty to six counts of having obscene articles for gain, which
> were video films, advertised for hire from her private address, of hard-core por-
> nography depicting acts of violence, torture and simulated acts of rape. Held:
> Applying *R. v. Holloway* (1982) 4 Cr.App.R.(S.) 128 (the "Guideline" case sum-
> marised at paragraph 18–01, above) the offence was a serious one. The serious-
> ness lay in the exploitation of human beings for profit and the sexual satisfaction
> of others. Six months' imprisonment substituted for nine months' imposed at the
> Crown Court (*R. v. Edwards (Angela)* (1992) 13 Cr.App.R.(S.) 662).

18–05 Where the obscene material is not exploitive in that the activities involve
consenting adults an immediate custodial sentence is nevertheless justified.

> D, aged 50 without relevant previous convictions, was convicted of possessing
> one obscene video tape for publication for gain. He had worked as an assistant in
> an unlicensed sex shop for four months and was aware that he was liable for
> prosecution if the shop was raided. Held: The sentence of three months' imprison-
> ment for one video alone imposed at the Crown Court upheld by the Court of
> Appeal (*R. v. Pace* [1998] 1 Cr.App.R.(S.) 121).

> D1, of good character, worked as a shop assistant and D2,without relevant pre-
> vious convictions, performed a supervisory role in the shop management of prem-
> ises offering for hire and sale pornographic magazines and videos depicting
> consenting adults performing obscene acts. Held: Applying *Holloway* and *Pace*,
> above, an immediate custodial sentence was appropriate, but the court should
> impose the shortest possible custodial sentence consistent with the court's public
> duty. Two months' imprisonment imposed on D1 reduced to 28 days and three
> months imposed on D2 reduced to six weeks by the Court of Appeal (*R. v. Tunni-
> cliffe and Greenwood, The Times*, December 16, 1998).

18–06 It has been said (*obiter*) that there may be circumstances, particularly
where the offender is of previous good character, where it is not necessary to impose an
immediate custodial sentence for the offence of possession of obscene articles for publication for gain (*R. v. Tunnicliffe and Greenwood*, above).

2. Procuring the Sending of Obscene Material through the Post

18–07   If the offence involves neither direct corruption nor the commercial exploitation of pornography and the offender is of previous good character a custodial sentence need not be imposed.

> D, aged 38 and effectively of good character, pleaded guilty to procuring the sending from abroad of a video depicting sex scenes involving children and thereafter sending the material through the post to another. Held: As the offences did not in themselves involve corruption and as D was of good character and the offences did not fall into the category where a sentence of imprisonment was required for a first offender, the appropriate sentence was a financial penalty (*R. v. Littleford* (1984) 6 Cr.App.R.(S.) 272).

The reasoning in *R. v. Littleford*, above, has been further applied recently when it was said by the Court of Appeal that where the material was not corrupting and the criminality could not be described as wicked the appropriate penalty was a financial one (*R. v. Holt* (1995) 16 Cr.App.R.(S.) 510).

3. Importing Obscene Publications

Guideline case

18–08   *R. v. Nooy and Schyff* (1982) 4 Cr.App.R.(S.) 308.

> "[T]his court, in the case of *Holloway* (1982) 4 Cr.App.R.(S.) 128 said that where inside the United Kingdom obscene material is distributed for gain on a commercial basis, custodial sentences should be the norm. It follows in our judgment that the same approach should apply where indecent and obscene material is imported into the United Kingdom for the purpose of commerce.

> This court starts off, in the circumstances of this case, there clearly being commercial importation, with thinking that the normal sentence should be one of loss of liberty. The problem arises as to the length of the sentence.

> The facts of the case are of a familiar kind. We have had considerable experience now of facts of this kind in relation to the importation of dangerous drugs. This is just a variation, in relation to filth which may very well poison the minds of the young, of the problems which arise with regard to the importation of dangerous drugs. The organisers of this filthy trade are very seldom caught. They are usually to be found on the Continent or in the Americas. They take great care to ensure that they do not expose themselves to the risks which are attendant upon unlawful importation. Our experience has been that they tend to keep a lookout for people in need of money and of hitherto good character. The reason they choose such people is obvious, because they can persuade such people that if they are arrested in the United Kingdom, they will have substantial grounds which can be put forward in mitigation of penalty" (at p. 309).

> "As I indicated at the beginning of this judgment, the public interest in this realm calls for the law and the courts to do everything they reasonably can to stop this kind of filth coming into the United Kingdom with the danger that it may corrupt our young. This court is determined that that should be the policy of the law. This,

as far as we can judge from the earlier cases which have been drawn to our attention, is the first one in which severe sentences have been passed for importing this
kind of material into the United Kingdom. Apparently in the past sentences of
three months and one month have been thought appropriate. We do not consider
such sentences are appropriate now and in the foreseeable future. If sentences of
that kind are imposed, those who make vast profits out of the importation of
pornography may be prepared to take risks. The word should go round the Conti-
nent of Europe and the Americas that importing on a commercial basis indecent
and obscene matter into the United Kingdom is nearly as hazardous an operation
as importing dangerous drugs. Those who are caught, whether they are the organisers, or whether they are mere carriers or helpers, should expect to get, and, in our
judgment, should get, severe sentences. The sentences imposed in this case should
not be regarded as the normal kind of sentence imposed. This case should go out
as a warning as to what can happen, and in the future even severer sentences may
properly be passed. Those who pass them should bear in mind that the law allows
substantial fines as well as loss of liberty. One of the best ways of discouraging this
trade is to take the profit out of it" (*per* Lawton L.J., at p. 311).

(For the above reasons the court upheld sentences of nine months' and 18 months'
imprisonment respectively on two offenders who had been concerned in the importation of books, magazines and videos with a total value of £137,655.)

18–09   Further guidance as to the sentencing considerations which apply to the
importation of pornographic material was given by Lord Lane C.J. in *R. v. Rolt* (1984)
6 Cr.App.R.(S.) 117, where he said that the matters to be taken into consideration
when considering the proper sentence to be imposed are:

   (i) the quantity and street value of the pornographic material;

   (ii) the position of the defendant in the hierarchy of distribution;

   (iii) the amount of profit the defendant is likely to make;

   (iv) the affront to public decency.

18–10   If there is a large quantity of material (6,000 magazines plus cassettes and
films) which is sado-masochistic, or depicts children or animals engaged in sexual acts,
a deterrent sentence may be imposed. Twelve months' imprisonment reduced from 18
months imposed at the Crown Court only because of consequential financial hardship
unforeseen by the Crown Court recorder (*R. v. Rolt*, above).

D was an agent for persons in Copenhagen who imported hard-core pornographic books, films and catalogues into the United Kingdom over a period of
several months. Held: The importation of substantial quantities of hard-core pornographic material into this country can only properly be dealt with by an
immediate term of imprisonment. Six months' imprisonment imposed at the
Crown Court was upheld by the Court of Appeal (*R. v. Kweller* (1981) 3
Cr.App.R.(S.) 9).

CHAPTER 19

Sexual Offences

1. Unlawful Sexual Intercourse

19–01 The magistrates' court may only deal with this offence when the girl is aged 13, 14 or 15. Unlawful sexual intercourse with a girl under the age of 13, or intercourse with a defective or incest, may only be tried on indictment.

Guideline case

19–02 *R. v. Taylor and Others* [1977] 1 W.L.R. 612.

In this leading case the Court of Appeal drew the distinction between a youth who has a "virtuous" relationship with a girl under the age of 16, and a much older man who abuses his position of trust for sexual gratification. The judgment then went on to review the history and social context of the law which is intended to protect young girls.

> "It is of some interest to remind everyone what that law is. For over 700 years now, the law of this country has concerned itself on various occasions with deciding what offences should be committed, if any, when men have sexual intercourse with young girls. As long ago as 1576 it was enacted by Parliament that it was a misdemeanour for a man to have intercourse with a girl under the age of 12. That was the law until 1875, when Parliament raised the age to 13. In 1885, Parliament raised the age to 16. One of the reasons given at the time for raising the age was to make it more difficult for young girls to drift into prostitution. In 1922, Parliament again considered the law relating to sexual intercourse with young girls. Far from relaxing it, it made it more severe because the 1885 statute had made it a defence for any man to say that, on reasonable grounds, he believed the girl to be over 16. That defence, by the 1922 Act, was restricted to young men under the age of 24.

That is not the end of the story. In 1956, Parliament looked at the whole range of sexual offences. It repealed the old statutes and re-enacted them in the Sexual Offences Act, 1956. It follows that the law which we are applying is not a law dating back to Victorian times; it is a law which a recent Parliament decided should be enforced. In our judgment, it is the duty of the courts to enforce it. This court said that last year in the case of *R. v. Rathbone* [1976] Crim.L.R. 521; it says the same in this case. Like all laws, this one must be enforced with mercy. As I have already said, the range of guilt is so wide that there is ample room for both mercy and severity. In case it should be thought that, at the present time the law in England reflects Victorian concepts of morality, it is not without relevance to point out that in most countries of the world the age of consent is 16. It is 16 in Scotland, Italy, Germany, Norway, Canada, New Zealand and South Africa, and in many of the United States of America. In the U.S.S.R. it is 18. The only country of importance of which I know where the age is under 16 is Denmark, where it is 15.

How then should the court approach this case? We are very conscious indeed in making our decision that the girl was a wanton. She approached these men. They in no way started her corruption, although the way they encouraged her to behave increased the degree to which she was debauched. The law exists for the protection of girls. It is particularly necessary in the case of wanton girls because, as was pointed out in argument, it is this type of girl who wanders away from her home and her village to the local town and from the local town to London. The evil which these men were doing was to confirm her in her wantonness. That, in our judgment, is the very type of conduct which Parliament intended should be stopped. It can only be stopped by custodial sentences taking immediate effect" (*per* Lawton L.J., at pp. 615–616).

(In that case the Court of Appeal upheld sentences of four months' and two months' imprisonment imposed on offenders aged 26, 27 and 28, who each pleaded guilty to sample counts of unlawful sexual intercourse with a girl aged 14 who was described as wanton and had not been corrupted.)

If the defendant is the step-father of the victim or occupies a position *in loco parentis* to the girl, sentences of 18 months or two years have been upheld by the Court of Appeal (*R. v. Lindley* (1980) 2 Cr.App.R. (S.) 3, *R. v. Mellor* [1981] 1 W.L.R. 1044, *R.v. Hogg* (1982) 4 Cr.App.R. (S.) 191).

19–03 If the defendant is in a position of authority or trust in relation to the girl, and is considerably older (*e.g.*, a school-teacher), sentences of 15 and 18 months' imprisonment imposed at the Crown Court have been upheld by the Court of Appeal (*R. v. Usher* (1980) 2 Cr.App.R.(S.) 123; *R. v. Dewar* (1986) 8 Cr.App.R.(S.) 311).

19–04 Lower sentences have been considered appropriate where there is no element of exploitation and the court is satisfied that the girl was willing.

D, aged 30 and of good character, pleaded guilty to sample counts in an indictment reflecting sexual intercourse with a girl over a period of 18 months beginning when she was 14. Held: While the first act of intercourse was seduction, thereafter D was more foolish than really wicked. Nine months' imprisonment was substituted for 18 months imposed at the Crown Court (*R. v. Harding* (1979) 1 Cr.App.R.(S.) 160).

D, aged 29 with a bad criminal record, pleaded guilty to one act of unlawful sexual intercourse with a girl aged 14 years and 10 months who stayed in D's flat after running away from home. She had had previous sexual experience and looked older than her true age. Held: Such a case was at the bottom end of the scale and six months' imprisonment was substituted for nine months imposed at the Crown Court (*R. v. Cooke* (1979) 1 Cr.App.R.(S.) 325).

19–05   A custodial sentence is not wrong in principle where the offender is under 21 and the girl is aged 15 and is a willing participant.

D1, aged 20, and D2, aged 18, both of good character, committed the offence after consuming alcohol and watching pornographic videos and the circumstances were described as squalid and distasteful. Held: (applying *R. v. Taylor,* above) nine months' youth custody imposed at the Crown Court after a trial in which they were acquitted of rape was neither manifestly excessive nor wrong in principle (*R. v. Forrest and Gray* (1984) 6 Cr.App.R.(S.) 268).

19–06   If the defendant and the girl are both in the same general age group, the girl is willing, and there are no aggravating circumstances, it is wrong to impose a custodial sentence (*R. v. O'Grady* (1978) 66 Cr.App.R. 279).

2. Indecent Assault on a Female

(i) Cases considered too serious for summary disposal

19–07   Where the assault is upon a young child, particularly if there has been more than one incident, and the accused is a relative or is trusted by the victim or the victim's parents, substantial sentences of imprisonment in excess of magistrates' courts powers are invariably imposed (*R. v. Ware* (1981) 3 Cr.App.R.(S.) 152, *R. v. Turner* (1983) 5 Cr.App.R.(S.) 254).

19–08   It has been emphasised by the Court of Appeal that in 1985 Parliament increased the maximum sentence for indecent assault on a female to 10 years' imprisonment (*R. v. L* [1999] 1 Cr.App.R. 117). In that case the Court said that generally the personal circumstances of the offender would have to take second place behind the plain duty of the courts to protect the victim of sexual attack and to reflect the clear intention of Parliament that indecent assault is to be met with greater severity than may have been the case in former years.

D, a pet-shop owner, was convicted on one charge of touching the breast and bottom and on another of touching the vagina over clothing of a 15-year-old victim who worked in his shop on work-experience placement. Held: It was a bad case and had the following aggravating features; (i) the offence was repeated despite the victim's protestations; (ii) D knew the victim was only 15 years of age; and (iii) D held a position of responsibility towards the victim. In the ordinary course of events a sentence of 12 months' imprisonment would be merited. Eight months' imprisonment substituted for a fine of £250 plus costs imposed at the Crown Court, having regard to the principle of double-jeopardy (*Att.-Gen.'s Reference No. 25 of 1997, R. v. Williams* [1998] 1 Cr.App.R.(S.) 310).

19–09   Even if the victim is not a child, and she consented to the assault, the offence remains a serious one if the accused was in a position of trust (*e.g.* a school-teacher).

D, aged 34, was the school-teacher of the victim aged 15 who was a willing participant in sexual intimacy on a number of occasions which did not amount to sexual intercourse. Held: Girls of such an age who find themselves falling in love with their teachers should be protected against themselves. It was D's duty to discourage her, but he had in fact encouraged her infatuation in a grave breach of trust. 12 months' imprisonment imposed at the Crown Court upheld by the Court of Appeal (*R. v. Seaman* (1982) 4 Cr.App.R.(S.) 108).

19–10   Where the assault is accompanied by violence, a substantial sentence is likely to be imposed.

D, a complete stranger to the victim, aged 16, followed her on foot at night in the street and seized her between her legs, and then punched her occasioning actual bodily harm. Held: The courts must do what they can to keep the streets safe by imposing substantial periods of imprisonment on those who commit offences of this kind. Two years' imprisonment imposed at the Crown Court upheld by the Court of Appeal (*R. v. Wintle* (1987) 9 Cr.App.R.(S.) 262).

19–11   Where the indecency is of an obvious and gross character, for example inserting a finger into the vagina or ejaculating on a young child, the case will similarly be unsuitable for summary disposal (*R. v. Gibbons* (1987) 9 Cr.App.R.(S.) 238, and *R. v. Whitelock* (1989) 11 Cr.App.R.(S.) 439).

(ii) Cases suitable for summary disposal

19–12   If the assault is an isolated incident, and the indecent circumstances are not of a grossly offensive character, and the victim is not of tender years, shorter sentences consistent with magistrates' powers have been considered suitable by the Court of Appeal.

EXAMPLES

19–13

D, aged 46, of good character, was a neighbour of the victim, a girl aged 12, and her family. He visited the victim's home for a purely innocent reason and he found the victim and a 12-year-old friend alone looking after a young baby. There was apparently conversation of a sexual nature and D pulled the victim on to his knee, pulled her knickers down and placed his face on her stomach. Held: While the behaviour was disgraceful it was at the lower end of the scale. It was an isolated incident, a case of a middle-aged man giving way to a sexual impulse which he should have been able to control. He had pleaded guilty and spared the girls the distressing experience of having to give evidence. Three months' imprisonment substituted for nine months imposed at the Crown Court (*R. v. Cank* (1985) 7 Cr.App.R.(S.) 99).

D, aged 40, had been drinking heavily when he arrived home and met by accident the victim, aged 12, whom he knew. There was conversation of a sexual nature and he rubbed the victim's breasts over her clothing. Held: The incident was isolated and out of character where there had been a loss of self-control because of drink. No physical injury had been caused to the victim. Six months' imprisonment substituted for 30 months imposed at the Crown Court (*R. v. Merrick* (1986) 8 Cr. App. R.(S.) 283).

D, aged 39, was the manager of a public house and the victim, aged 13, had gone to the public house to buy sweets. She was touched over her clothes in the area of her breasts and vagina and her legs were stroked. Held: Any indecent assault on a girl in her early teens is a serious offence and not one the court can overlook, but because of the guilty plea and the nature of the offence a sentence of 12 months was reduced to allow his release after serving an effective term of imprisonment of four months (*R. v. Long* (1980) 2 Cr.App.R.(S.) 8).

19–14 Where the indecent assault occurs on an underground train and involves rubbing against a female causing obvious distress to the victim a very short custodial sentence is justified even if the offender is of previous good character.

D, aged 18 with previous convictions but none for indecency, deliberately rubbed his groin against a young woman on an underground train. Held: Such conduct is thoroughly degrading to the victim and an immediate custodial sentence was justified. Three months' imprisonment substituted for six months' imposed at the Crown Court (*R. v. Townsend* (1995) 16 Cr.App.R.(S.) 553).

D, aged 34 and of good character, was convicted of pressing his clothed erect penis against a female passenger on an underground train and persisted in his conduct despite the victim's efforts to distance herself from him. There was evidence that D had sought out his victim. Held: such an offence causes distress and is highly unpleasant and in the circumstances a custodial sentence was appropriate. A short prison sentence is what is needed for a first offender. Six months' imprisonment imposed at the Crown Court reduced to three months' by the Court of Appeal (*R. v. Tanyidiz* [1998] 1 Cr.App.R.(S.) 362).

D, aged 62 and of good character, was convicted of moving his hand (which was in his pocket) against the victim's private parts on an underground train, rubbing his upper arm against her breast and pressing his body close to the victim who was standing with her back to a glass partition. Held: for a sustained and unpleasant assault the sentence of three months' imprisonment imposed at the Crown Court was fully justified (*R. v. Yazbek* [1998] 1 Cr.App.R.(S.) 406).

3. Indecent Assault on a Male

19–15 Where the assault is upon a young boy, particularly where there has been more than one incident, and the accused is trusted by the victim or the victim's parents, substantial sentences of imprisonment are invariably imposed.

Even if the assault in question is over the victim's clothing, if the accused is in a position of trust and the victim is under 16 years of age sentences of 12 months or more have been imposed and upheld by the Court of Appeal.

D, aged 47 and of good character, was a church choir-master who invited a chorister aged 15 to his home where he asked the boy to rub himself to obtain an erection, and D took photographs and then himself seized the boy's genitals. Held: Such an offence rightly disturbs and alarms the public. Children must be protected and D grossly abused a position of trust. Twelve months' imprisonment imposed at the Crown Court was upheld by the Court of Appeal (*R. v. Rhodes* (1985) 7 Cr.App.R.(S.) 341).

D, aged 40, was the coach of a boys' Under 13 football team. The victim's parents agreed that D could coach their son aged 12-and-a-half. When the boy was at D's home with parental consent, D squeezed the area of the boy's genitals over his clothing. D was convicted after a trial. Held: A breach of trust of this kind is a matter of gravity. It involved serious conduct. 12 months' imprisonment was the appropriate sentence (*R. v. Smith* (1987) 9 Cr.App.R.(S.) 228).

4. Indecent Assault by a Female on a Male

19–16　If the nature of the offence is serious and horrifying then the court may pass a sentence which reflects society's disapproval.

> D, aged 20, pleaded guilty to indecently assaulting the three-year-old son of a neighbour by masturbating him, biting his penis, and inserting a finger into his anus. Held: As it is a matter of general knowledge that the public are concerned about child abuse, and there is discussion as to how to stop the sexual abuse of young children, the courts can only assure the public that particular behaviour meets with society's disapproval by custodial sentences. That is sometimes called the retributive factor. A sentence of 12 months' youth custody imposed at the Crown Court was upheld in the Court of Appeal (*R. v. Hancock* (1986) 8 Cr.App.R.(S.) 159).

> D, aged 28 and of good character, pleaded guilty to indecently assaulting a 10-year-old boy over a three-week period by engaging in sexual intercourse and oral sex with the boy. Held: The Crown Court judge was correct to approach the case as one of child abuse and nine months' imprisonment was not excessive (*R. v. Sant* (1989) 11 Cr.App.R.(S.) 441).

19–17　If the assault by a female involved consensual sexual intercourse but none-theless involved a breach of trust the same principles applicable to sentencing a male for unlawful sexual intercourse will apply.

> D, aged 27 and a school teacher of previous good character, formed an affection-ate relationship with a 13-year-old pupil which developed into a consensual sex-ual relationship which lasted six or seven weeks. Held: The offence involved deceit because the trust imposed on teachers by the parents of children is immense. The offence was so serious that a custodial sentence was inevitable. Twelve months' imprisonment imposed at the Crown Court upheld by the Court of Appeal (*R. v. Tozer* (1994) 15 Cr.App.R.(S.) 807).

5. Gross Indecency

19–18　Consensual homosexual activities are not to be regarded with the serious-ness that they once were, but if the offence of gross indecency involves video recorded orgies of homosexual acts being performed in the presence of others (albeit not made for a commercial motive) the offence is more serious than a single consensual act in a public lavatory (*R. v. T and others* [1999] Crim.L.R. 432). In that case the Court of Appeal considered that the offence was "serious enough" for a community penalty.

In general, offenders using public lavatories and behaving in a grossly indecent way do not get sent to prison, they are generally fined.

> "Conduct of this kind in public conveniences is a nuisance to the public. It makes members of the public reluctant to use those conveniences. Courts by their sen-tences have got to do their best to stop this kind of conduct. Experience has shown

that for the majority of first offenders an appearance before the court, coupled with a monetary penalty, stops any repetition of the offence, at least in public lavatories. On the other hand, occasionally those who are convicted persist in this kind of behaviour and when they do prison sentences may be appropriate": *per* Lawton L.J. in *R. v. Morgan and Dockerty*, September 28, 1978.

D1 and D2, of previous good character, committed an act of gross indecency in an alleyway at 3.20 a.m. in West London. Held: A £50 fine on each was appropriate (*R. v. Clayton and Restrepo* (1981) 3 Cr.App.R.(S.) 67).

6. Persistent Importuning for an Immoral Purpose

19–19

D had been observed importuning males and then importuned a plain clothes police officer in an area of London frequented by homosexuals. Held: A fine of £100 was appropriate (*R. v. Gray* (1981) 3 Cr.App.R.(S.) 363).

CHAPTER 20

Offences Connected with Prostitution

Living on the Earnings of Prostitution

20–01   "In the absence of any evidence of coercion, whether physical or mental, or of corruption, ... two years' imprisonment is probably adequate. Anything exceeding two years should be reserved for a case where there is an element of coercion or there is some strong evidence of corruption": *per* Lawton L.J. in *R. v. Farrugia* (1979) 69 Cr.App.R. 108.

> D, aged 59, deliberately set up a business which involved a brothel and an escort agency with 40 girls operating a call-girl system. Held: Two years' imprisonment imposed at the Crown Court upheld by the Court of Appeal (*R. v. Smith (David)* (1993) 14 Cr.App.R.(S.) 708).

> D was the leaseholder of premises in Soho, who was observed for a period of 11 days by police. Prostitution was carried on at the premises and D controlled those activities. Held: The guidelines in *R. v. Farrugia*, above, were appropriate to the facts of this case and a sentence of 18 months' imprisonment was substituted for one of three years imposed at the Crown Court (*R. v. Hall* (1987) 9 Cr.App.R.(S.) 121).

A sentence of 15 months' imprisonment was considered appropriate for an offender of bad character who had received £10,000 over a period of 14 months from the earnings of prostitution (*R. v. Smyle* (1990) 12 Cr.App.R.(S.) 256).

20–02   If, however, the prostitute was carrying on her own business without pressure being placed upon her by the accused a more lenient view may be taken.

> D lived off the earnings of Miss P, who was a prostitute before he met her, and Miss P was observed to be soliciting on various occasions between the end of April and the beginning of May.
> The magistrates' court accepted jurisdiction but D was committed for sentence to the Crown Court because he had a previous conviction for the same offence. Held: Nine months' imprisonment was substituted for 18 months imposed at the Crown Court (*R. v. Turay* (1983) 147 J.P. 735).

> D, aged 33, with previous convictions but none for this offence, had a stable

relationship with Miss P, a prostitute with many convictions before the relationship with D was formed. Miss P earned a substantial income as a prostitute and this contributed to D's own high standard of living. Held: Although there was no corruption or coercion it was a serious offence calling for immediate imprisonment. Four months' imprisonment coupled with a fine of £1,500 was substituted for nine months and a fine of £5,000 imposed at the Crown Court (*R. v. Charlery* (1988) 10 Cr.App.R.(S.) 53).

20–03   The guidelines in *R. v. Farrugia*, above, have been held to apply to a case when the conviction arose from the running of an escort agency which was a front for prostitution. The reasoning was that such immoral activity is injurious to the public interest because it encourages and leads to the concentration of prostitutes in particular areas like blocks of flats and hotels. This tends to lower the general tone of the area and the premises (*R. v. El-Gazzar* (1986) 8 Cr.App.R.(S.) 182).

D, aged 48, of previous good character, was convicted of living off the immoral earnings of a number of prostitutes by managing, with others, two brothels in which he played an active part and received good profits. Held: Applying the guidance in *R. v. Farrugia*, above, the sentence of nine months' imprisonment imposed at the Crown Court was a moderate sentence for such type of offending (*R. v. Kirk* (1995) 16 Cr.App.R.(S.) 895).

20–04   The guidelines in *R. v. Farrugia*, above, have *not* been applied where premises exist lawfully for one commercial purpose, *e.g.* as a sauna bath, but where sexual services are also unlawfully offered.

D, aged 41, helped run premises known as "Experience Sauna" which was advertised as giving health massage and sauna bath, but also provided services of a sexual nature short of full sexual intercourse for which the girls were paid an extra fee which benefited D. The girls willingly offered sexual services, and D knew of their activities. Held: A sentence not greater than six months should have been imposed, together with a fine (the fine was in fact quashed on examination of D's financial circumstances) (*R. v. Hilton* (1982) 4 Cr.App.R.(S.) 184).

D1 was the landlord of two massage parlours which were run as brothels and D2 received money from this activity. Held: While the case of *R. v. Hilton*, above should not be regarded as a guideline case, there was no corruption of the girls and a short immediate sentence of three months' imprisonment would be adequate, together with an order for costs (*R. v. Jackson and Sullivan* (1982) 4 Cr.App.R. (S.) 286).

D1, aged 48, who had a bad criminal record, and D2, his son aged 27, of good character, both ran a massage parlour which offered sexual services from girls who participated willingly without coercion from D1 or D2. Held: The cases of *R. v. Hilton* and *R. v. Jackson and Sullivan*, above, quite plainly established the basis upon which the court is to impose sentences where there is no corruption, coercion or pressure on the clientele to accept the services. The appropriate disposal in such circumstances is a short immediate sentence of imprisonment. Sentences of four months and three months respectively were substituted for 12 months (six suspended) and two years imposed at the Crown Court (*R. v. Russell and Russell* (1985) 7 Cr.App.R.(S.) 257).

20–05 A longer sentence may be imposed if a brothel (or disorderly house) is kept in residential premises and equipment and films to cater for a variety of sexual tastes are kept. If such activity is charged under section 23 of the Sexual Offences Act 1956 the maximum sentence is six months, and it is not wrong in principle for such a sentence to be passed in a case where there are aggravating features (see the judgment of Lawton L.J. in *R. v. Payne (Cynthia)* (1980) 2 Cr.App.R.(S.) 161).

CHAPTER 21

Dangerous Drugs

1. Generally

Guideline case

21–01   *R. v. Aramah* (1983) 76 Cr.App.R. 190.

"*Class 'A' Drugs and particularly Heroin and Morphine*:

It is common knowledge that these are the most dangerous of all the addictive drugs for a number of reasons: first of all, they are easy to handle. Small parcels can be made up into huge numbers of doses. Secondly, the profits are so enormous that they attract the worst type of criminal. Many of such criminals may think, and indeed do think, that it is less dangerous and more profitable to traffic in heroin or morphine than it is to rob a bank. It does not require much imagination to realise the consequential evils of corruption and bribery which the huge profits are likely to produce. This factor is also important when considering the advisability of granting bail. Sums which to the ordinary person, and indeed the ordinary defendant, might seem enormous are often trivial for the trafficker in drugs.

The two main sources of supply are South-East Asia and South-West Asia. These two sources are in competition, one with the other, and with the stakes so high, this may be a fruitful source of violence and internecine strife. Fourthly, the heroin taker, once addicted (and it takes very little experimentation with the drug to produce addiction), has to obtain supplies of the drug to satisfy the terrible craving. It may take anything up to hundreds of pounds a week to buy enough heroin to satisfy the craving, depending upon the degree of addiction of the person involved. The only way, it is obvious, in which sums of this order can be obtained is by resorting to crime. This in its turn may be trafficking in the drug itself and disseminating accordingly its use still further.

Fifthly, and lastly, and we have purposely left it for the last because it is the most horrifying aspect, comes the degradation and suffering and not infrequently the death which the drug brings to the addict. It is not difficult to understand why in

381

some parts of the world traffickers in heroin in any substantial quantity are sentenced to death and executed.

Consequently, anything which the courts of this country can do by way of deterrent sentences on those found guilty of crimes involving these Class "A" drugs should be done.

Then I turn to the importation of Heroin, Morphine and so on: Large scale importation, that is where the street value of the consignment is in the order of £100,000 or more, sentences of seven years and upwards are appropriate. There will be cases where the values are of the order of £1 million or more, in which case the offence should be visited by sentences of 12 to 14 years. It will seldom be that an importer of any appreciable amount of the drug will deserve less than four years.

This, however, is one area in which it is particularly important that offenders should be encouraged to give information to the police, and a confession of guilt, coupled with considerable assistance to the police can properly be marked by a substantial reduction in what would otherwise be the proper sentence.

Next, supplying heroin, morphine, etc.: It goes without saying that the sentence will largely depend on the degree of involvement, the amount of trafficking and the value of the drug being handled. It is seldom that a sentence of less than three years will be justified and the nearer the source of supply the defendant is shown to be, the heavier will be the sentence. There may well be cases where sentences similar to those appropriate to large scale importers may be necessary. It is however unhappily all too seldom that those big fish amongst the suppliers get caught.

Possession of heroin, morphine, etc.: (Simple possession): It is at this level that the circumstances of the individual offender become of much greater importance. Indeed the possible variety of considerations is so wide, including often those of a medical nature, that we feel it impossible to lay down any practical guidelines. On the other hand the maximum penalty for simple possession of Class "A" drugs is seven years' imprisonment and/or a fine, and there will be very many cases where deprivation of liberty is both proper and expedient.

Class "B" Drugs, particularly Cannabis:

21-02   We select this from amongst the Class "B" drugs as being the drug most likely to be exercising the minds of the courts.

Importation of cannabis: Importation of very small amounts for personal use can be dealt with as if it were simple possession, with which we will deal later. Otherwise importation of amounts up to about 20 kilogrammes of herbal cannabis, or the equivalent in cannabis resin or cannabis oil, will, save in the most exceptional cases, attract sentences of between 18 months and three years, with the lowest ranges reserved for pleas of guilty in cases where there has been small profit to the offender. The good character of the courier (as he usually is) is of less importance than the good character of the defendant in other cases. The reason for this is, it is well known that the large scale operator looks for couriers of good character and for people of a sort which is likely to exercise the sympathy of the court if they are detected and arrested. Consequently, one will frequently find students and sick and elderly people are used as couriers for two reasons: first of all they are vulnerable to suggestion and vulnerable to the offer of quick profit, and secondly, it is felt that the courts may be moved to misplaced sympathy in their case. There are few, if any, occasions when anything other than an immediate custodial sentence is proper in this type of importation.

Medium quantities over 20 kilogrammes will attract sentences of three to six years' imprisonment, depending upon the amount involved, and all the other circumstances of the case.

Large scale or wholesale importation of massive quantities will justify sentences in the region of 10 years' imprisonment for those playing other than a subordinate role.

Supply of cannabis: Here again the supply of massive quantities will justify sentences in the region of 10 years for those playing anything more than a subordinate role. Otherwise the bracket should be between one to four years' imprisonment, depending upon the scale of the operation. Supplying a number of small sellers—wholesaling if you like—comes at the top of the bracket. At the lower end will be the retailer of a small amount to a consumer. Where there is no commercial motive (for example, where cannabis is supplied at a party), the offence may well be serious enough to justify a custodial sentence.

Possession of cannabis: When only small amounts are involved being for personal use, the offence can often be met by a fine. If the history shows however a persisting flouting of the law, imprisonment may become necessary.

We turn now to apply those principles in so far as relevant to the present case. This was importation of a very large quantity of cannabis, 59 kilogrammes, the value of which, as I have already stated, was between £100,000 and £135,000. It seems to us that this was at the top of the range. There is no feature of the case which we can discover as a mitigating feature. The case was contested. Consequently, unlike the cases where there has been a plea of guilty, no discount can on this account be given to him. The fact that this man had been warned in the past, when he was convicted in 1972 of a very similar offence and then sent to prison for three years, shows that he is flouting the law. In those circumstances it seems to us that the sentence of six years was entirely appropriate" (*per* Lord Lane C.J., at pp. 191–193).

21–03   Since the judgment in *R. v. Aramah* the maximum sentence for importation was increased by the Controlled Drugs (Penalties) Act 1985 from 14 years to life imprisonment. This change was reflected in the judgment of Lord Lane C.J. in *R. v. Bilinski* (1987) 9 Cr.App.R.(S.) 1, when dealing with an appeal against sentence in an importation case. However, the revised guidelines, following *Bilinski*, above, do not affect the type of case likely to be dealt with in the magistrates' court.

The guidelines for cannabis offences in *R. v. Aramah* (1983) 76 Cr.App.R. 190 have been reaffirmed in *R. v. Hedley* (1990) 90 Cr.App.R. 70.

Since the guidance case of *R. v. Bilinski* (1987) 9 Cr.App.R.(S.) 1, the Court of Appeal has further considered the basis upon which the value of drugs should be assessed for the purposes of sentence. It has now been authoritatively held that for cases of importation or distribution of Class "A" drugs the yardstick should be the weight of the consignment and not its street value (*R. v. Arangure, Aroyewumi, Bioshugen, Littlefield and Gould* (1994) 99 Cr.App.R. 347). As with the dicta in *Bilinski*, above, this new guideline is not likely to affect the type of case dealt with in the magistrates' court. The same criteria apply to the drug Ecstasy (*R. v. Warren, R. v. Beeley* (1996) 1 Cr.App.R.(S.) 223.

In the case of LSD the relevant pointer was the number of impregnated squares to be marketed (*R. v. Hurley* [1998] 1 Cr.App.R.(S.) 299).

2. Possession of a Class "A" Drug with Intent to Supply

21–04 The guidelines in *R. v. Aramah* indicate that it will hardly ever be suitable for the magistrates' court to accept jurisdiction in cases of possession of a Class "A" drug with intent to supply. Even when it is said that the accused only supplied small quantities to a small circle of friends, or that there was a supply to finance the accused's own addiction, the Court of Appeal have approved the imposition of substantial sentences of imprisonment.

> "It is perfectly plain and common knowledge that one of the most vicious aspects of this type of addiction and trading is its ability to perpetuate itself, because in order to feed an addiction very large sums of money are required to purchase the drug, and that means that those who wish to finance the addiction have to resort to crime of one sort or another. One of the sorts of crime to which they turn is the purchase and supply at great profit of heroin and other drugs to other people who are addicted or who are going to be addicted. That is one of the most pernicious features of this terrible trade which results in, as can be seen from this case, not merely the loss of weight but misery, degradation and eventually death, let alone what it may cause to the families of these young people—and they are all young people—who are addicted in this manner": *per* Lord Lane C.J. in *R. v. France* (1984) 6 Cr.App.R.(S.) 283.

EXAMPLES

21–05

D pleaded guilty to supplying heroin on a modest scale in order to obtain money to buy drugs for himself. Held: Even if there is a place available at a drug rehabilitation centre, a non-custodial disposal would be out of character with the range of dispositions established by the Court of Appeal. Four years' imprisonment substituted for six years imposed by the Court of Appeal (*R. v. Gee* (1984) 6 Cr.App.R. (S.) 86).

D pleaded guilty to possessing 534 milligrammes of heroin with intent to supply on the basis that he sold the drug in small consignments only to those already addicted within a small circle over a four-week period. Held: Four years' imprisonment substituted for six years imposed by the Crown Court (*R. v. Guiney* (1985) 7 Cr.App.R.(S.) 200).

D, aged 28 and of good character, pleaded guilty to possession of 10.7 grammes of powder containing heroin with intent to supply to others, the 10.7 grammes being part of a consignment he had bought for £600. Held: 30 months' imprisonment imposed by the Crown Court upheld by the Court of Appeal (*R. v. Eliot* (1988) 10 Cr.App.R.(S.) 454).

D, aged 28 and of good character, was convicted of possessing 17.9 grammes of cocaine (street value £1,000) with intent to supply. Held: Three years' imprisonment imposed at the Crown Court upheld by the Court of Appeal (*R. v. Atkins* (1981) 3 Cr.App.R.(S.) 257).

D, aged 31, was convicted of possession of 27 tablets of MDMA (Ecstasy) with intent to supply outside a "rave". Held: As Parliament had chosen to classify MDMA as a Class "A" drug it was on a par with heroin or cocaine, and applying the guideline in *Aramah* (1983) and *Bilinski* (1987) the sentence of 4 years' imprisonment imposed at the Crown Court was entirely correct (*R. v. Jones* (1994) 15 Cr.App.R.(S.) 856).

Permitting premises to be used for the smoking of opium

21–06

D, aged 46 and with previous convictions for drug related offences, pleaded guilty to allowing his premises to be used for the smoking of opium. Held: Any criminal conduct which facilitates the use of a Class "A" drug is serious. Fifteen months' imprisonment imposed at the Crown Court reduced to six months (*R. v. Gregory* (1993) 14 Cr.App.R.(S.) 403).

3. Simple Possession of a Class "A" Drug

21–07   "It is at this level that the circumstances of the individual offender become of much greater importance. Indeed the possible variety of considerations is so wide, including often those of a medical nature, that we feel it impossible to lay down any practical guidelines. On the other hand the maximum penalty for simple possession of Class 'A' drugs is seven years' imprisonment and/or a fine, and there will be very many cases where deprivation of liberty is both proper and expedient": *per* Lord Lane C.J. in *R. v. Aramah*, above.

D1 and D2, both aged 22 and each with a previous conviction for a drugs offence, pleaded guilty to possession of heroin. It was unquestionably for their personal use and both were addicts. Held: The case of *R. v. Aramah*, above shows that where possession of heroin is involved the sentence may differ widely according to the circumstances and it is impossible to lay down precise guidelines for such cases. In the particular circumstances of the facts of this particular case a sentence of three months' immediate imprisonment was substituted for one of nine months, with six held in suspense, imposed at the Crown Court (*R. v. Long and Smith* (1984) 6 Cr.App.R.(S.) 115).

21–08

D, aged 34 and of good character, who ran his own company, was convicted of possessing a bag weighing 13.6 grammes containing 25 per cent cocaine hydrochloride with a street value of about £800. Held: A sentence of eight months' imprisonment, with six held in suspense and two to serve, and a fine of £4,000 was upheld by the Court of Appeal notwithstanding the harm the publicity of a conviction had done to D's business, and the fact that he had raised money for charity. The court observed that D could not claim he had been driven to drugs through the boredom of unemployment nor could he claim that, as an educated man, he was unaware of the risks that he ran (*R. v. Diamond* (1985) 7 Cr.App.R.(S.) 152).

D, aged 32 and with a bad criminal record but without previous convictions for drug-related offences, pleaded guilty to possession of 5.6 grammes of cocaine. Held: The just and proper sentence for simple possession of cocaine, being the first offence of its kind, was three months' imprisonment (three months substituted for 30 months imposed at the Crown Court) (*R. v. Layton* (1988) 10 Cr.App.R.(S.) 109).

D, aged 34 and with seven previous convictions mostly for drug-related offences, pleaded guilty to possession of 283 milligrammes of heroin. Held: Six months' imprisonment was substituted for 12 months imposed at the Crown Court (*R. v. Lutzo* (1989) 11 Cr.App.R.(S.) 495).

D, aged 26, with previous convictions for possession of cannabis, was convicted of possession of seven small pieces of "crack" cocaine, amounting to 1.69 grammes. Held: "Crack" cocaine is highly addictive and leads to serious crime. Six months' imprisonment imposed at the Crown Court upheld by the Court of Appeal (*R. v. Scarlett* (1995) 16 Cr.App.R.(S.) 745).

D, aged 19 of previous good character, pleaded guilty to possession of nine wraps of "crack" cocaine being 1.5 grammes with an estimated value of £200, and possession of 16 ecstasy tablets with an estimated value of £350. Held: It was proper to look at the two offences together and to conclude that in combination they were offences "so serious" that a non-custodial sentence could not be justified. Eighteen months' imprisonment imposed at the Crown Court reduced to a sentence of 3 months' by the Court of Appeal (*R. v. Cox* (1994) 15 Cr.App.R.(S.) 216).

4. Possession of a Class "B" Drug with Intent to Supply

21–09

"... the supply of massive quantities will justify sentences in the region of 10 years for those playing anything more than a subordinate role. Otherwise the bracket should be between one and four years' imprisonment, depending upon the scale of the operation. Supplying a number of small sellers—wholesaling if you like—comes at the top of the bracket. At the lower end will be the retailer of a small amount to a consumer. When there is no commercial motive (for example, where cannabis is supplied at a party), the offence may well be serious enough to justify a custodial sentence": *per* Lord Lane C.J. in *R. v. Aramah*, above.

21–10   The bracket of one to four years' imprisonment imposed for possession with intent to supply means that in most instances offences of this type should not be sentenced in the magistrates' court as the following examples illustrate.

EXAMPLES

(i) If the amount of cannabis or cannabis resin is about one kilogramme it is not a case which comes at the bottom end of the scale and a sentence of 15 months' imprisonment has been considered appropriate for possession with intent to supply (*R. v. MacDonald* (1983) 5 Cr.App.R.(S.) 22).

(ii) If there is evidence of dealing in cannabis over a considerable period of time, and profit in the region of £100 per week to the supplier a sentence of 21 months' imprisonment has been considered appropriate (*R. v. Hill* (1988) 10 Cr.App.R.(S.) 150).

(iii) For possession with intent to supply at the top end of the scale of retail dealing a sentence of 30 months' imprisonment has been considered appropriate (*R. v. Daley* (1989) 11 Cr.App.R.(S.) 243).

(iv) A sentence of 12 months' imprisonment has been upheld for possession of 5.8

grammes of cannabis resin with intent to supply (*R. v. Friend* (1993) 14 Cr.App.R.(S.) 77).

21–11 It is only if the offence of commercial supply is at the very lowest end of the scale that it may be suitable for sentence to be passed in the magistrates' court.

Examples

D, with no previous convictions for drug-related offences, was convicted after a trial of selling three grammes of cannabis to another man for £10. D was not in possession of any of the familiar drug dealing paraphanalia. Held: Twelve months' imprisonment imposed at the Crown Court was too long; six months' substituted by the Court of Appeal (*R. v. Weeks* (1992) 14 Cr.App.R.(S.) 94).

D, aged 19 of previous good character, was convicted of possessing 39.6 grammes of cannabis which were in eight wraps of silver foil. Held: D was peddling cannabis on a small scale and as such a non-custodial sentence could not be jusitified. Six months' youth detention imposed at the Crown Court reduced to three months' by the Court of Appeal (*R. v. Black* (1992) 13 Cr.App.R.(S.) 262)

21–12 The dicta in *Aramah* is not explicit as to what is meant by "commercial motive". It has now been clarified that any supply in exchange for money even at the very bottom of the scale will merit a custodial sentence.

D, aged 20 and university student of previous good character, pleaded guilty to supplying five ounces of cannabis over a four week period to his friends providing a profit of £20 per ounce. Held: It is important that people know, whether they are university students or others, that if they choose to dabble in supplying drugs, even on a small scale they are likely to lose their liberty. Six months' youth detention imposed at the Crown Court reduce to two months' by the Court of Appeal (*R. v. Roberts* [1998] 1 Cr.App.R.(S.) 155).

Where the supply of cannabis is on a small scale (the supply of three grammes valued at £10) a sentence of six months' imprisonment has been considered appropriate (*R. v. Weeks* (1993) 14 Cr.App.R.(S.) 94).

Supplying cannabis to a prisoner

21–13 Where drugs are smuggled into a prison with the intention of supplying a prisoner a sentence of 12 months' may be expected even on a plea of guilty.

D, aged 22 with previous convictions including a conviction for possessing cannabis, pleaded guilty to taking 1.91 grammes of cannabis into a prison with the intention of supplying it to a friend who was an inmate. Held: Smuggling drugs into prison had become more prevalent since 1992 when, in (*R. v. Savage* (1993) 14 Cr.App.R.(S.) 409), the Court had upheld a sentence of six months' imprisonment for such an offence. The problem is such nowadays that the offence should always be treated seriously, even if the amount of the drugs is small. Twelve months' imprisonment imposed at the Crown Court upheld as being correct in principle following a plea of guilty (*R. v. Farooqi* [1999] 1 Cr.App.R.(S.) 379).

5. Simple Possession of a Class "B" Drug

21–14

> "When only small amounts are involved being for personal use, the offence can often be met by a fine. If the history shows however a persisting flouting of the law, imprisonment may become necessary": *per* Lord Lane C.J. in *R. v. Aramah*, above.

Although a continual flouting of the law in respect of possession of cannabis may leave the courts with no alternative but to impose a custodial sentence, a second offence of possession of cannabis does not justify a departure from the general principle that a fine is the appropriate penalty (*R. v. Robertson-Coupar and Baxendale* (1982) 4 Cr.App.R.(S.) 150).

If, on the other hand, a persistent offender in relation to cannabis with a large number of previous convictions is convicted of simple possession of a small quantity of cannabis (3.83 grammes) a short immediate sentence of imprisonment is not wrong in principle (*R. v. Osborne* (1982) 4 Cr.App.R.(S.) 262).

6. Cultivation of Cannabis

21–15   Production of cannabis is to be regarded more severely than simple possession, particularly because the penalty, on indictment, is higher for cultivation than for simple possession.

> D, aged 22 and with no previous convictions for drugs offences, pleaded guilty to cultivating three cannabis plants in his flat in order to produce cannabis for his personal use. Held: The sentence of three months' imprisonment imposed at the Crown Court was perfectly correct (*R. v. Case* (1992) 13 Cr.App.R.(S.) 20).

> D, aged 55 and of previous good character, pleaded guilty to producing cannabis on the basis that the production provided for his personal use of two ounces of cannabis per week with the remainder being supplied to a small circle of friends without payment. Held: The element of non-commercial supply was an aggravating feature of the offence of cultivation. Twelve months' imprisonment imposed at the Crown Court reduced to six months' by the Court of Appeal (*R. v. Bennett* [1998] 1 Cr.App.R.(S.) 429).

CHAPTER 22

Offences Connected with Motor Vehicles

22–01 Criminal offences which are committed with the use of motor vehicles have been regarded with mounting seriousness by both parliament and the courts. The Road Traffic Act 1991 created a number of new offences and the Aggravated Vehicle-Taking Act 1992 created a new offence, punishable by imprisonment. In the Criminal Justice Act 1993 the penalty for causing death by dangerous driving was increased from five to 10 years, and the Court of Appeal has consistently approved severe penalties for serious offending which involves the use of cars (see, *e.g., Att.-Gen.'s Reference (No. 37 of 1992)*, (1993) 15 Cr.App.R.(S.) 71, and *Att.-Gen.'s Reference (No. 14 of 1993)* (1993) 15 Cr.App.R.(S.) 640. In a number of reported sentencing decisions in the Court of Appeal a trend towards more serious penalties can be discerned for motor vehicle offending which is triable summarily. The following §§are an attempt to reflect these developments.

1. Dangerous Driving

22–02 The Road Traffic Act 1991 (which amends substantially the Road Traffic Act 1988) states that the penalty for dangerous driving must include a mandatory disqualification for a minimum period of 12 months, and the offender must be ordered to pass an extended driving test before his licence may be restored. In these respects the penalties for dangerous driving are more severe than those for the old offence of reckless driving, although, like reckless driving, the new offence carries six months' imprisonment and a fine not exceeding level 5.

(i) Guideline case

22–03 *R. v. Boswell* (1984) 9 Cr.App.R.(S.) 277.

The Court of Appeal (Criminal Division) in a judgment of Lord Lane C.J. gave guidance on the factors which would aggravate or mitigate the offence of *reckless* driving which, it is submitted, remain relevant to the offence of dangerous driving.

Aggravating features

(i) the consumption of alcohol or drugs, whether it is a couple of drinks or "a motorised pub crawl";

(ii) the driver who races: competitive driving against another vehicle on the public highway, grossly excessive speed, showing off;

(iii) the driver who disregards warnings from his passengers;

(iv) prolonged, persistent and deliberate course of very bad driving (a person who over a lengthy stretch of road ignores traffic signals, jumps red lights), passing other vehicles on the wrong side, driving with excessive speed, driving on the pavement and so on;

(v) offences committed at the same time as related offences, that is to say driving without ever having held a licence, driving whilst disqualified, driving without supervision whilst still a learner and so on;

(vi) previous convictions for motoring offences, particularly offences which involve bad driving or the consumption of excessive alcohol before driving. In other words the man who demonstrates that he is determined to continue driving badly despite past experience;

(vii) behaviour at the time of the offence, for example failure to stop or the driver who tries to throw the victim off the bonnet by swerving in order to escape.

Mitigating features

22–04

(i) a piece of driving which might be described in the vernacular as a "one off," a momentary reckless error of judgment, briefly dozing off at the wheel;

(ii) a good driving record;

(iii) a plea of guilty;

(iv) the effect on the defendant if he is genuinely shocked or remorseful.

22–05 It has been stressed that *Boswell* was decided within a statutory framework for sentencing which no longer applies (see §22–01, above). Since the decision in *Boswell* the maxima penlties have been increased for a number of offences to reflect public concern, particularly where death results (*R .v. Simmonds* [1999] Crim.L.R. 421).

The guidance in *Boswell* has provided the background upon which the Court of Appeal have decided appeals in cases of dangerous driving and the following general principles may be derived from recent cases.

If the dangerous driving is "particularly atrocious" (gross speed to avoid detection by pursuing police vehicle) and is combined with driving with excess alcohol and driving without insurance a sentence of nine months' imprisonment has been held to be appropriate (*R. v. Templeton* [1996] 1 Cr.App.R.(S.) 380).

22–06 If the dangerous driving is less gross (erratic driving and driving after a tyre burst) but is combined with driving with excess alcohol a sentence of six months' imprisonment has been held to be appropriate in the public interest following a trial (*R. v. Nicholls* [1998] 2 Cr.App.R.(S.) 296).

If, in similar circumstances, the offender pleads guilty, a lesser sentence may be imposed to reflect the credit for a plea of guilty.

> D, aged 30, with a substantial criminal record, pleaded guilty to dangerous driving involving the following: having been stopped by a police officer who suspected D of drinking (on good grounds) D decamped and drove away from the police officer at speed and then crossed two "give way" junctions without stopping. The car was later abandoned and D could not be breath tested. Held: There was a clear risk to the public aggravated by the fact that D had been drinking. Four months' imprisonment imposed at the Crown Court upheld by the Court Appeal (*R. v. Ashby* (1998) 162 J.P. 731).

22–07 Where the only aggravating feature present is speed an immediate custodial sentence may not be necessary.

> D, aged 42 and with a good driving record, was convicted of reckless driving by driving at 85 mph in a 60 mph area and colliding with a police car parked in a lay-by after skidding to avoid a police checkpoint. Held: As none of the aggravating features, except speed, were present a prison sentence was not appropriate and a fine of £750 with a 12 month disqualification was substituted for 28 days' imprisonment imposed at the Crown Court (*R. v. Elwood-Wade* (1990) 12 Cr.App.R.(S.) 51).

NOTE: This was a case of reckless driving.

2. Careless Driving

22–08 In straightforward cases of careless or inconsiderate driving the sentence is invariably a fine, together with the imposition of penalty points to reflect the gravity of the offence and disqualification is discretionary in bad cases.

22–09 Where the careless driving causes death different sentencing considerations arise. The court should regard the consequence of death as an aggravating factor of the offence (*R. v. Simmonds* [1999] Crim. L.R.421). In that case the Court of Appeal emphasised that the current statutory framework for road traffic offences showed that there was parliamentary and public concern at death on the roads and Parliament had legislated for an enhanced statutory sentencing bracket for certain offences where death resulted from an act of driving. Accordingly, it is now anomalous for a court to wholly disregard the consequence of death where the offender has been charged with careless driving. In another case, *R. v. Morling* [1998] 1 Cr.App.R.(S.) 421, it was stressed that the attitude of the Court of Appeal towards the careless driving of motor vehicles had hardened in recent years.

EXAMPLES

22–10
> D, age 63 and of good character, missed his turning to a motorway and executed a "U" turn on a minor road to regain his route. In doing so he failed to see a motorcyclist approaching at a normal speed and despite D's efforts to evade a collision the motorcyclist collided with the D's car causing the rider's death. Held: A fine of

£1,000 and a disqualification of 12 months' imposed at the Crown Court following D's plea of guilty to careless driving upheld by the Court of Appeal. While culpability remains the primary sentencing consideration the sentencing judge was entitled to have regard to the death; although the fine exceeded the Magistrates' Association Guidelines it was not excessive and neither was the period of disqualification (*R. v. Simmonds*, above).

D, aged 23, drove a van too fast on a bend in darkness and bad weather conditions and hit an approaching vehicle head on. Held: It was not a prolonged piece of bad driving but it was appropriate when examining culpability for the carelessness to have regard to the consequences which was the death of the other driver and his passenger. Twelve months' disqualification imposed at the Crown Court reduced to five months by the Court of Appeal (*R. v. Johnson* [1998] 2 Cr.App.R.(S.) 453).

D, of mature years, and a professional driver, drove a tractor without lights pulling a trailer without a flashing amber light on a piece of dual carriageway, that was not lit, at a speed of 14 miles per hour. A car approaching the trailer at 60 miles per hour swerved and a serious collision resulting in death occurred. D was acquitted of causing death by dangerous driving but convicted of careless driving by a jury at the Crown Court. Held: It was serious act of negligence not to have the required lights on because of the consequences which might follow and were different from other serious lapses of concentration. A fine of £500 and a disqualification for 12 months upheld by the Court of Appeal (*R. v. Morling*, above).

22–11   If the facts of the careless driving show that there is good reason to believe that the offender lacks competence to drive then it may be appropriate to disqualify until a new driving test is passed under section 36 of the Road Traffic Offenders Act 1988 because the amendment to that section in section 32 of the Road Traffic Act 1991 requires the court to have regard to the safety of road users (*R. v. Miller* (1993) 15 Cr.App.R.(S.) 505).

3. Driving with Excess Alcohol

22–12   Since the enactment of the Criminal Law Act 1977 the offence of driving with excess alcohol has been triable only summarily, and as a result there have been few opportunities in recent years for the Court of Appeal to give guidance on the appropriate level of sentence for drink-driving offending. Prior to 1977 there were a number of cases in which it was stated that where the level of alcohol was substantially above the permitted legal limit a custodial sentence was entirely proper and ought not to be interfered with on appeal (see, for example, *R. v. Tupa* [1974] R.T.R. 153, and *R. v. Horton* [1974] R.T.R. 399). This approach to the seriousness of driving with high levels of alcohol in the body has been reflected also in the sentencing guidance for indictable offences where the driver has committed an offence with a motor vehicle having consumed alcohol in large quantities (see, for example, *R. v. Vickers* (*Att. Gen's Reference No. 42 of 1994*) 16 Cr.App.R.(S.) 742).

It has only been very recently that the Court of Appeal has had the opportunity to make specific observations to the sentencing principles which should apply to offences of drinking and driving which are tried exclusively in the magistrates' court. It has now been authoritatively stated that the level of penalties suggested by the Magistrates' Association are sound and appropriate, and accordngly where the offender has 100 microgrammes of alcohol or more per 100 millilitres of breath consideration should be given to the imposition of a custodial sentence (*R. v. Shoult* [1996] 2 Cr.App.R.(S.) 234). It was emphasised in that case that the Association's suggested penalties were only a guide and that each case had to be considered individually on its own merits.

4. Taking a Motor Vehicle without Consent

22–13   The offence of unlawfully taking a motor vehicle is typically committed by offenders under 21, and under earlier legislation it was necessary to consider whether the offence was so serious that a custodial sentence was inevitable (CJA 1982, s.1(4A)). Under the Criminal Justice Act 1991 there is no distinction made between offenders who are under 21 and those who are over 21, and it is submitted that the considerations applying to the examples in paragraph 22–15, below, will continue to apply under the 1991 Act.

22–14   If the offence is combined with other offences arising out of the same circumstances the offence of unlawful taking of a motor vehicle may justify a custodial sentence coupled with a substantial period of disqualification.

D, who was aged 19 and disqualified from driving, took a motor vehicle without consent and drove it recklessly and at high speeds for 18 miles. He was apprehended only after a collision. Held: The court had to consider the safety of the public and the offender had to be disqualified for a sufficiently long period to give him the opportunity to mature so that he does not yield to the temptation of engaging in this disgraceful form of endangering the public. 12 months' youth custody and disqualification from driving for four years imposed at the Crown Court was upheld by the Court of Appeal. (*R. v. Gibbons* (1987) 9 Cr.App.R.(S.) 21).

D, aged 18, was involved with others in taking several cars in the course of one evening, driving around in them at high speeds in a city centre and crashing them. One car was damaged beyond repair. D later told the police he had committed the offence "for a bit of fun." Held: The Crown Court judge was correct in concluding that the offences were so serious that a non-custodial sentence could not be justified because, in addition to the unlawful taking, the cars had been deliberately damaged. Four months' detention imposed at the Crown Court upheld by the Court of Appeal (*R. v. Jeary* (1986) 8 Cr.App.R.(S.) 49).

5. Aggravated Vehicle-Taking

22–15   Guidance on sentencing for the offence of aggravated motor vehicle-taking has been given by Lord Taylor C.J. in *R. v. Bird* (1992) 14 Cr.App.R.(S.) 343. This new offence, which provides for greater punishment than for simple motor vehicle-taking if the offence is accompanied by dangerous driving or if damage is caused to a person or property, came into force on April 1, 1992. The most important matter to consider is the culpability of the driver. To this extent the element of dangerous driving is more serious than if damage alone is caused, because damage is often a question of chance.

Aggravating features primarily involve considerations of how bad the dangerous driving was and for what length of time it took place, and to a lesser extent the amount of damage or injury. The youth of the offender is a less significant piece of mitigation than in some other offences because the new offence is aimed at young offenders. Where drink played a part then that too would affect the dangerousness of the driving.

In the appeal of *R. v. Bird* the Court of Appeal reduced a sentence of 15 months' youth detention to one of 12 months, where the appellant, aged 17, had driven for 18 miles at speed and on the wrong side of the road, going through a red traffic light before colliding with a police car and slightly injuring a police officer. The court emphasised that the reduction in sentence was influenced by the change in the law brought about by the Criminal Justice Act 1991 which reduced the maximum sentence for an offender aged 17 to 12 months' youth detention.

22–16   While the most important matter for consideration in sentence is the manner of the driving there is culpability also in being a passenger because the purpose of the legislation is to deter a very prevalent form of activity and there is little mitigation in the fact that the offender was merely a passenger (*R. v. Sealey* (1993) 15 Cr.App.R. (S.) 189). In that case the Court of Appeal upheld a sentence of nine months' imprisonment together with a disqualification from driving for two years on a passenger in a motor vehicle which had been taken unlawfully and then driven dangerously.

If the circumstances of the offence also involve driving with excess alcohol a sentence of over six months' imprisonment may be appropriate.

> D, aged 21, of previous good character, took a car and drove it at excessive speed, thereby losing control and colliding with a wall causing a pedestrian personal injury. D was found to have 58 microgrammes of alcohol in 100 millilitres of breath after his arrest. Held: As the driving was not over a considerable length of time, and in the light of the plea of guilty and the offender's previous good character nine months' imprisonment was substituted for 15 months' imposed at the Crown Court (*R. v. Timothy* (1995) 16 Cr.App.R.(S.) 1028).

22–17   It has been specifically held that the offence of aggravated vehicle-taking is an offence which is "so serious" that only a custodial sentence may be justified for the offence.

> D, aged 20, took a motor vehicle from a car showroom on the pretext of wishing to test-drive the car, and whilst on the road drove too fast and injured a child pedestrian. Held: The offence was so serious that only a custodial sentence could be justified. Twelve months' youth detention imposed at the Crown Court reduced to six months' by the Court of Appeal (*R. v. Marron* (1993) 14 Cr.App.R.(S.) 615).

CHAPTER 23

Miscellaneous Offences

1. Evading Excise Duty

23–01   The offence of evading excise duty by smuggling drink and tobacco is sufficiently serious that a deterrent element in sentencing is called for, and offenders who evade significant amounts of duty should expect to go to prison. Where the duty evaded does not exceed £10,000 the case is suitable for summary disposal. In addition justices should consider their powers to make a Deprivation Order under section 43 of the Powers of Criminal Courts Act 1973, and/or an order of disqualification from driving under section 44 of that Act (*R. v. Dosanjh* [1999] 1 Cr.App.R.(S.) 107).

> D, aged 46 of virtually good character, pleaded guilty to two offences of evading duty, namely 20,000 cigarettes, 10 kilos of hand rolling tobacco and 500 cigars, 115 litres of beer and 40 litres of spirits which had been purchased duty free for sale to friends and family. The duty evaded amounted to £10,000 effected in the course of 10 trips to the continent. Held: Twelve months' imprisonment imposed at the Crown Court reduced to nine months' by the Court of Appeal (*R. v. Ollerenshaw* [1999] 1 Cr.App.R.(S.) 65).

2. Offences under Health and Safety Regulations

23–02   Guidance has been given by the Court of Appeal when a company or firm had committed offences contrary to safety regulations and death or serious injury is caused to an employee (*R. v. F. Howe and Son (Engineering) Ltd* [1999] 2 All E.R. 249). The guidance has been described by the Lord Chief Justice, Lord Bingham, as providing a clear and correct statement of the relevant principles (*R. v. Rollow Screw Rivet Co. Ltd, The Times,* April 29, 1999).

In *R. v. Howe and Son,* the Court of Appeal observed that disquiet had been expressed about the level of fines imposed in the magistrates' court which, on average, were less than one-third of the maximum. In the Court's view there had been an increasing recognition in recent years of the seriousness of health and safety offences. The guidance is a follows.

1. It was necessary, on the facts of each individual case, to assess how far short of the appropriate standard the defendant fell.

2. It was often a matter of chance whether death or serious injury resulted but generally death should be regarded as an aggravating factor.

3. The financial penalty should reflect the public disquiet at the unnecessary loss of life.

4. The size of the defendant company is not relevant to the degree of care required to maintain safety standards.

5. Considerations as to whether the offence was an isolated breach or one which had continued over a period was often relevant.

PARTICULAR AGGRAVATING FEATURES

23–03
  (i) failure to heed warnings;

  (ii) deliberately running a risk to save money or enhance profit.

PARTICULAR MITIGATING FACTORS

23–04
  (i) prompt admission of responsibility and a timely plea of guilty;

  (ii) steps taken to remedy the deficiency;

  (iii) a good safety record.

In that case the company, F. Howe and Son (Engineering) Ltd, was a modest company with a turnover of £355,000; the net profit was £26,969 p.a. and neither director of the company received an income in excess of £20,000 p.a. The Court of Appeal reduced to £22,500 a fine of £55,000 imposed at the Crown Court, justices having declined jurisdiction.

Even if the company was a small one where the directors were also the shareholders, the penalty should make clear that it was the directors who bore responsibility and this could not be shuffled off to the shareholders (*R. v. Rollow Screw and Rivet Co. Ltd*, above).

3. Harassment

(a) HARASSMENT UNDER THE PROTECTION FROM HARASSMENT ACT 1997

23–05   The Court of Appeal has given the following general guidance on the principles to be followed when sentence is to be passed for offences under the Protection from Harassment Act 1997. The Act provides for sentence to be passed in two circumstances:

  (i) the original offence, which may consist of harassment which is not violent in nature (PHA 1997, s.2), or which may be accompanied by violence or a threat of violence (*ibid.*, s.4), and

(ii) the breach of a restraining order which is a separate offence in itself (*ibid.*, s.5).

Accordingly, the primary considerations are:

(i) is the offence contrary to section 2 or section 4?, and

(ii) is sentence to be passed in the context of a breach of a court order? (*R. v. Liddle, R. v. Hayes, The Times,* May 26, 1999).

In the above context the following sentencing consideration should apply:

(i) the seriousness of the conduct in question;

(ii) whether the conduct was persistent;

(iii) the effect on the victim, whether physical or psychological including the level of risk posed to the victim or the children of the victim;

(iv) the mental health of the offender; whether he was willing to undergo treatment or receive help from the probation service; and

(v) whether the offender had shown remorse and pleaded guilty.

In the consolidated appeals of *R. v. Liddle* and *R. v. Hayes*, above, the Court of Appeal were concerned in each case with offences contrary to section 5 of the Act (breach of a restraining order). The Court considered that for a first offence a short, sharp sentence might be appropriate, but for a second or subsequent offence a sentence of the order of 15 months' imprisonment might be necessary on a plea of guilty and in the region of three years or upwards for a contested case.

(b) Harassment contrary to the Protection from Eviction Act 1977

23–06 It is virtually certain that an offender who is guilty under this legislation of harassing a tenant should receive a custodial sentence.

D, aged 25 and of good character, owned a house which was insanitary and dirty which was let furnished to a tenant who owed £300 in rent. With two others, D went to the house with a monkey wrench where the tenant's relative was harassed, ordered to strip naked, and later ordered to clean the house. Held: It must be made generally known that conduct of this kind would be visited by immediate imprisonment. Nine months imposed by the Crown Court was reduced to six months on appeal (*R. v. Spratt, Wood and Smylie* [1978] Crim.L.R. 102).

D, a landlord of flats above his restaurant, unlawfully evicted a sub-tenant by changing the locks on her flat after the police had advised him that he should obtain a court order before evicting her. Held: A short period of imprisonment to demonstrate the wrongfulness of his behaviour was necessary but a sentence of 14 days' imprisonment (together with prosecution costs) would be substituted for the six month sentence imposed at the Crown Court (*R. v. Alfasatleh* (1989) 11 Cr.App.R.(S.) 24).

4. Corrupt Practice at an Election

23–07   A sentence of imprisonment is correct in principle for offences which interfere with the democratic processes in the kingdom (*R. v. Lucas* [1998] 1 Cr.App.R.(S.) 13).

> D, a woman aged 44 and of good character, pleaded guilty to personating two voters, offences contrary to section 60 of the Representation of the People Act 1983, offences triable either way. She personated an 80-year-old elector who voted by post and a dead elector, by returning herself ballot papers sent to the above-named electors which was fraudulent. Held: Matters of interference with the election process are very grave and serious. It must be in very, very rare circumstances indeed that somebody who deliberately does fraud in order to cast an improper vote should not receive a substantial custodial sentence. A sentence of two months' imprisonment imposed at the Crown Court was upheld, notwithstanding D's record of public voluntary work in the community (*R. v. Phillips* (1984) 6 Cr.App.R.(S.) 293).

5. Bomb Hoax Offences

23–08   Offences involving bomb hoax telephone calls are a public nuisance, causing fear and anxiety, and the public expect that severe sentences will be passed. Substantial terms of immediate imprisonment should be imposed.

> D, aged 24 and of virtually good character, was involved in making a telephone call claiming to be a member of the IRA and saying that a bomb would go off in a large banking building of 49 floors where 2,500 people were employed. Held: An equivalent sentence of 12 months' imprisonment was substituted for one of two years imposed at the Crown Court (*R. v. Browne* (1984) 6 Cr.App.R.(S.) 5).

NOTE: The statute creating this offence has made the maximum sentence one of seven years' imprisonment on indictment, but only six months or a fine not exceeding level 5 if tried summarily (CLA 1977, s.51, as substituted by CJA 1991, s.26(4)). It would seem that on the basis of the above guideline case justices should decline jurisdiction in cases involving bomb hoax telephone calls.

6. Copyright Offences

23–09   Offences in breach of copyright are akin to offences of theft since pirating material, such as video-films, is like stealing the material from the true owner and normally calls for a short custodial sentence.

It has been said that copyright offences cause serious damage to legitimate commercial and propriety interests (*R. v. Duckett* [1998] 2 Cr.App.R.(S.) 59).

> D, aged 24, of previous good character, pleaded guilty to making pirate copies of a quantity of video-cassettes and also to making 15 satellite broadcast decoding cards in breach of copyright, and admitted trading in the items mainly with friends. Held: Owners of copyright are entitled to be protected against unlawful exploitation and to have their commercial reputation protected. In view of D's plea and his previous good character, nine months' imprisonment imposed at the Crown Court reduced to six months' by the Court of Appeal (*R. v. Kemp* (1995) 16 Cr.App.R.(S.) 941).

D, aged 49, with no relevant previous convictions, pleaded guilty to making pirate copies of 219 video-films during an 18-month period, offences which were contrary to the Copyright, Designs and Patents Act 1988. Held: The offences were serious because to make and distribute pirate copies of films is to steal the copyright from the true owner. Nine months' imprisonment suspended for two years imposed at the Crown Court upheld by the Court of Appeal (*R. v. Carter (Carol)* (1992) 13 Cr.App.R.(S.) 576).

NOTE: A suspended sentence may now only be passed if the exercise of the power can be justified by the exceptional circumstances of the case (CJA 1991, s.5). There would appear to be nothing "exceptional" in the facts of this case, although the Court of Appeal has recently shown a willingness to pass suspended sentences in circumstances which Parliament probably did not envisage as exceptional (see paragraph 13–53, above).

7. Obtaining Telecommunication Services with Intent to Avoid Payment

23–10 If there has been a course of conduct over a period of time in which fraud is used in order to obtain free telephone calls, the offence is so serious that a non-custodial sentence cannot be justified.

D1, aged 27, of previous good character, pleaded guilty to using a fraudulent scheme to obtain free telephone calls to Lagos and the United States for a period of six months, incurring a loss to Mercury Communications of between £2,000 and £4,000.

D2, aged 20, with no relevant previous convictions, was convicted of four sample counts in an indictment which involved using three fictitious PIN numbers to obtain free calls abroad and causing substantial loss. Held: In each case the offences were so serious that only a custodial sentence was appropriate. Six months' imprisonment and six months' detention in a Young Offender Institution substituted for 12 months' respectively imposed at two different Crown Courts (in a consolidated appeal) (*R. v. Adewale, R. v. Faradaye* (1994) 15 Cr.App.R.(S.) 790).

Part III

Human Rights

CHAPTER 24

Human Rights

A. INTRODUCTION AND COMMENTARY

1. Background to the Human Rights Act 1998

24–01　The European Convention for the Protection of Human Rights and Fundamental Freedoms is a treaty which was ratified by the United Kingdom in 1951. Since that time the expressions in the Convention have become accepted throughout Europe as defining essential standards of behaviour and decency. While much of English common law could be said to uphold such standards the exclusion of the Convention from domestic law has been an issue of controversy for some time.

A number of distinguished practising lawyers, notably Lord Scarman, argued for a Bill of Rights for Britain as long ago as 1974. Twenty years later, when a Human Rights Bill was proposed in the House of Lords by the peer Lord Lester of Herne Hill Q.C., incorporation enjoyed the support of a number of Law Lords, including the then Lord Chief Justice Lord Taylor of Gosforth. Supporters at that time included also the present Lord Chief Justice and Lord Woolf, Master of the Rolls.

The decision by the present government to introduce a Human Rights Bill may be seen as the culmination of a consensus of opinion which had been building up over years. To a large extent public opinion was prepared for change. The government stated the essential reason for introducing a Human Rights Act in its White Paper *Rights Brought Home* (Cm. 3782). This was to cure the anomaly whereby the United Kingdom was bound by international treaty to observe the Convention yet public authorities in this country were not required as a matter of domestic law to comply with it. This meant that British citizens whose Convention rights had been infringed were forced to go to the European Court in Strasbourg for a remedy. English courts applying domestic common law were not bound to uphold the Convention.

As a matter of law the Human Rights Act 1998 has not "incorporated" the Convention into English law in the sense that Convention rights become directly justiciable and enforceable in domestic courts. The long title states that it is an "Act to give further effect to the rights and freedoms guaranteed under the European Convention . . .". By avoiding the word "incorporation" the supremacy of Parliament is preserved, as is explained more fully in §§24–04 and 24–05, below. The key consequence of the Act is that a remedy may be provided by a domestic court if a Convention right has been denied. In addition, the government has argued that there are further positive reasons for the Act. First, British citizens will be able to have their universal rights as stated in the Convention tested in domestic courts and British judges will be able to make a distinctly British contribution to the development of human rights jurisprudence. Secondly, and more importantly, the concept of rights will feature more prominently in British jurisprudence and universal human rights may thus be woven into our law. Thirdly, the decisions of British judges will provide the European Court with a new and useful source of reasoning and interpretation of Convention points.

2. Convention Rights and Qualifications

24–02   The Convention is set out in a number of Articles each of which is a guarantee of a basic human right. These are right to life (Article 2); prohibition of torture or inhuman or degrading treatment or punishment (Article 3); prohibition of slavery and forced labour (Article 4); right to liberty and security of person (Article 5); right to a fair trial (Article 6); prohibition of retrospective criminal laws (Article 7); respect for private and family life, home and correspondence (Article 8); freedom of thought, conscience and religion (Article 9); freedom of expression (Article 10); freedom of peaceful assembly and freedom of association; (Article 11); the right to marry and found a family (Article 12), and prohibition of discrimination in the enjoyment of these rights and freedoms (Article 14).

These rights are stated in short statements of general principle, but nearly all of them are subject to qualification. Thus, the broad statement in Article 10 that freedom of expression is guaranteed by the Convention is subject to the obvious qualification that "the exercise of these freedoms, since it carries duties and responsibilities, may be subject to such formatilies, conditions, restrictions or penalties as are prescribed by law and are necessary in a democratic society" (Art.10(2)). Such wording appears also in Articles 8,9 and 11.

24–03   The Convention therefore prescribes that any interference of a basic and fundamental human right must be:

(a) prescribed by law, and

(b) be necessary in a democratic society.

Strasbourg case law has given a number of rulings on the meaning of the words "prescribed by law" and this is discussed below in §24–12. The words "necessary in a democratic society" are those which give effect to the concept of proportionality.

The concept of proportionality is central to Convention jurisprudence. It means that even if there is a restriction imposed on the exercise of a fundamental right, and that such restriction is justified (to prevent crime for example) the method used to limit the right must be proportionate in the circumstances. Inherent in the whole of the Convention is a search for the fair balance between the demands of the general interest of the community and the requirements of the protection of the individual's human rights (*Soering v. U.K.* (1989) 11 E.H.R.R. 439).

The combination of general statement with qualification provides something with which, according to the government, people of this country are plainly comfortable (Cm. 3782, para. 1.3). If this is correct then implementation of the Act will not be an epoch-making event and our comfortable sensitivities will be unchanged. Lord Donaldson M.R. thought that it was difficult to detect any difference between English common law and the principles set out in the Convention (*R. v. Secretary of State, ex p. Brind* [1991] 1 A.C. 696). On the other hand, the passing of the Act has been described as "a quantum leap into a new legal culture of fundamental rights and freedoms, something that Britain was once proud to be able to do without, but which has now become indispensible" (Human Rights and the Judiciary, Professor Sir William Wade Q.C., Annual Lecture of the Judicial Studies Board, 1998).

3. Scheme of the Human Rights Act 1998

24–04   The Human Rights Act 1998 received the Royal Assent in November 1998, and will come into force on October 2, 2000. In moving the second reading of the Bill the Lord Chancellor, Lord Irvine of Lairg, said that its purpose was to give greater effect in our domestic law to Convention rights and to enable persons to rely on the Convention in domestic courts (*Hansard,* H.L. November 24, 1997, col. 830). The Act gives further effect to the rights and freedoms guaranteed by the Convention in two essential ways:

  (i) by requiring courts to read and construe primary and subordinate legislation in a way which is compatible with Convention rights so far as it is possible to do so (s.3(1)); and

  (ii) by making it unlawful for a public authority to act in a way which is incompatible with a Convention right (s.6(1)).

A public authority includes a court (s.6(3)(a)), and any person certain of whose functions are functions of a public nature (s.6(3)(b)). Thus, a magistrates' court is not simply the forum or venue for the determination of Convention points; the court itself must act in a manner compatible with the Convention. Similarly, the Crown Prosecution Service, as a public body, must give effect to fundamental rights and freedoms in the decisions it takes with regard to criminal prosecutions.

Although Parliament itself is not a public authority (s.6(3(b)), primary and subordinate legislation must be read and given effect in a way which is compatible with Convention rights *so far as it is possible to do so* (s.3(1)). The explicit wording of section 3 preserves the supremacy of Parliament and prevents courts from striking down primary legislation on the grounds of incompatibility with the Convention. The government was persuaded that the conventions and customs of the United Kingdom were so rooted in the doctrine of parliamentary sovereignty that this should be preserved. It was considered that judges did not seek powers to usurp the will of parliament and to give them such powers would draw them into conflict with the elected legislature.

24–05 The words, *so far as it is possible to do so*, in section 3 will themselves be the subject of judicial interpretation in due course, and an authoritative ruling will be necessary to determine their precise meaning. If the words are given a narrow construction, namely "only so far as is possible under current canons of construction" then the effect of the Human Rights Act 1998 may be limited. The government itself does not envisage such a limited role for incorporation. In the White Paper (Cm. 3782) it is said the words go "far beyond the present rule which enables the courts to take the Convention into account in resolving any ambiguity in a legislative provision. The courts will be required to interpret legislation so as to uphold the Convention right unless the legislation itself is so clearly incompatible with the Convention that it is *impossible* (emphasis added) to do so."

If this view is later upheld by the higher courts as being correct the task of justices will be to strive to reach a conclusion which upholds Convention rights when construing primary or subordinate legislation. Indeed, there is a positive requirement under the Act to do so. If, in such a construction, previous case law on the point is perceived to be incompatible with the Convention then justices are not bound (as they would have been in the past) to apply previous case law.

It is only if it is impossible for a magistrates' court to read a piece of legislation in a way which is compatible with a Convention right that an incompatible reading must be applied to the issue in question (s.4(4)). If the question is further considered by the High Court (on judicial review or case stated) that court may make a declaration of incompatibility (s.4(5)) but such a declaration will not affect the parties to the case (s.4(6)). The effect of a declaration is to confer on the relevant Minister of the Crown power to amend the legislation by remedial order (s.10 and Sched. 2) which may operate retrospectively (Sched 2, para. 1(1)(b)).

Notwithstanding the wording of section 3 any court (including a magistrates' court) must take into account any judgment, decision, declaration or advisory opinion of the European Court of Human Rights (or opinion or decision of the Commission or Committee of Ministers) if in the opinion of the court such decision is relevant to the proceedings (s.2(1)). The wording of section 2(1) requires the court to "take into account" these judgments and decisions but not necessarily to apply them or to feel bound by them. Thus, existing case law on Convention points will be persuasive and no doubt helpful to English courts when considering the proper application and interpretation of the Convention but no more.

In considering the relationship of the Convention to domestic law it is important to remember the distinction between European *law* and the European *Convention*. In respect of European law there is a requirement under the European Communities Act 1972 for Member States to give priority to E.C. law where such law has direct effect on domestic arrangements. There is no such requirement in the Convention and there are differing models of the manner in which the Convention has been adopted in Member States. The manner in which the United Kingdom has given effect to the Convention is by the Human Rights Act 1998.

If a magistrates' court finds that a Convention right has been infringed then it may (within its powers) grant a remedy which it considers to be just and appropriate (s.8(1)).

24–06 The above short summary reveals the following general principles:

(i) the interpretation of the common law must in future accord with an interpretation compatible with the Convention;

(ii) the Convention takes precedence over any rule of common law;

(iii) courts must, of their own motion, act in a manner compatible with the Convention;

(iv) all statutes must be read and given effect in a manner compatible with the Convention so far as it is possible to do so;

(v) courts must grant appropriate remedies if rights guaranteed by the Convention are infringed; and

(vi) judgments the European Court must in future be taken into account by courts in the United Kingdom in giving effect to the Convention.

3. Giving effect to Convention Rights

(i) General principles

24–07 The most basic general principle is that the Convention is, in terms of international law, a treaty and as such should be interpreted in good faith in accordance with the ordinary meaning to be given to its terms and in the context of its object and purpose (Vienna Convention of the Law of Treaties 1969, Article 31). This broad principle of international law has been applied by the European Court of Human Rights in interpreting the Convention.

The practical application of this broad principle is that there has been an autonomous *Convention* meaning given to such word as "criminal charge", "civil rights and obligations", and "witness" in judgments in the European Court. Plainly, this broad approach will be of considerable influence when the Convention is interpreted by English courts.

In addition there is a body of Privy Council law which applied these broad principles. The judicial committee of the Privy Council has, on a number of occasions, had to interpret Constitutional provisions from commonwealth countries. It has been held that constitutional orders which contain declarations of fundamental rights call for a generous interpretation giving to the individual referred to the full measure of the rights referred to, rather than what has been called "the austerity of tabulated legalism"(*Minister of Home Affairs v. Fisher* [1980] A.C. 319, *per* Lord Wilberforce). In a later case it was held that such provisions should be given a broad, purposeful construction (*Att.-Gen. of the Gambia v. Momudu Jobe* [1984] A.C. 689, *per* Lord Diplock).

The reason for giving a generous interpretation to the rights themselves is that the court is concerned principally with the reality of what is involved (*Wiseman v. Borneman* [1971] A.C. 297) and this is the case whether the approach is to the advantage or disadvantage of the accused or appellant (*Huntley v. Att.-Gen. of Jamaica* [1995] 2 A.C. 1).

This general approach has universal application. It has been adopted by the European Court because of the qualifications which attach to some of the rights. The Court has held that because an individual state may interfere with the exercise of basic rights the rights themselves must be broadly and purposefully constructed (*Niemietz v. Germany* (1992)16 E.H.R.R. 97).

24–08 In addition the following general principles have been applied to the broad, purposeful construction of the Convention:

(i) The Convention is an instrument designed to maintain and promote the ideals and values of a democratic society (*Kjeldsen and others v. Denmark* (1976) 1 E.H.R.R. 711), and that particular features of a democratic society are pluralism, tolerance and broad-mindedness (*Handyside v. U.K.* (1976) 1 E.H.R.R. 737).

(ii) The Convention must be interpreted in the light of present day conditions (*Tyrer v. U.K.* (1978) 2 E.H.R.R. 1).

(iii) The Convention is intended to guarantee rights which are practical and effective, not simply theoretical (*Marckx v. Belgium* (1979) 2 E.H.R.R. 330).

It follows that justices are required to consider Convention points in a conceptual jurisprudential fashion, and to make decisions which may conflict with earlier authority. Justices must endeavour to get to the root of a legal issue and to consider the broad substance and purpose of the submission. In the period immediately following implementation there may be little guidance from the higher courts as to how submissions on Convention points should be approached.

(ii) Margin of appreciation

24–09 Margin of appreciation means that, in Strasbourg jurisprudence, an individual state is given respect as to its own culture and traditions when an individual state has a policy which qualifies Convention rights. An example of the application of the doctrine of margin of appreciation by the Strasbourg Court occurred in *Handyside v. UK* (1976) 1 E.H.R.R. 737. In that case the publisher of a book entitled *The Little Red Schoolbook* had been convicted of having in his possession obscene books for publication for gain and had contended before the European Court that his rights under Article 10 (freedom of expression) had been infringed. The Court held that there was no uniform conception of morals throughout Europe and that state authorities were in a better position than international judges to decide what laws were necessary in a democratic society, subject to universal principles of tolerance, pluralism and broadmindedness. Accordingly, the Strasbourg Court would not take away the task of a national court in deciding the limits to be placed on Article 10 by the qualifications set out in Article 10(2).

It has been said (albeit technically *obiter*) that the application of the doctrine would appear to be solely a matter for the Strasbourg Court and that English courts could not apply or have recourse to the doctrine when giving effect to the Human Rights Act 1998 (*R. v. Stratford Justices, ex p. Imbert, The Times,* February 25, 1999). In that case, which turned on the failure of the prosecution to disclose witness statements in summary only proceedings, it was said that English courts must recognise the impact of the margin of appreciation upon the Strasbourg Court's analysis of the meaning and implication of the broad terms of the Convention provisions.

It is submitted that this observation by Buxton L.J. in the Divisional Court is an important pointer to how English courts will in future have regard to Strasbourg judgments. It means that when giving effect to the Human Rights Act 1998 careful consideration will have to be given to Strasbourg judgments if such judgments have refrained from deciding issues of principle because the margin of appreciation has been applied.

(iii) Qualified rights

24–10 Although two Articles, Article 3 (prohibition of torture) and Article 12 (right to marry), are absolute rights in the sense that no limitation or restriction is placed upon them the remaining rights are either limited or qualified in some way. In criminal practice most submissions involving Convention points will involve a challenge to the prosecution case when a limitation or qualification of a particular right is said to be justified or when the procedure surrounding the prosecution is said to be insufficient to give effect to a right.

For this reason it is important to understand how the European Court of Human Rights has interpreted rights which are qualified. In addition to qualified rights the Convention also allows for derogable rights. These are explained in §24–13, below.

There are two Articles which are themselves Articles of limitation or qualification. Article 17 provides that no state, group or person may engage in any activity or perform any act aimed at the destruction of any of the rights and freedoms or at their limitation to a greater extent than is provided for in the Convention. This provides a restriction on government and the state as well as the individual. It is relevant if either the state itself or an individual engages in activity aimed at undermining the rights of others guaranteed by other Articles. In theory, Article 17 is a safeguard against totalitarianism.

Article 18 states that the permitted restrictions shall not be applied for any purpose other than those for which they have been prescribed. Article 18 only becomes relevant in conjunction with the interpretation of another Article. Thus, if the state seeks to rely on one of the limitations in an Article the limitation can only be used for the purpose prescribed. If it is not, and is used for another purpose, Article 18 may be invoked by the individual.

Articles 17 and 18 apply to the interpretation of Convention rights (HRA 1998, s.1(1)).

CONSTRUCTION OF QUALIFICATIONS AND LIMITATIONS

24–11 Those Articles which contain qualifications or limitations on the fundamental right expressed at the outset are not drafted identically and accordingly different canons of construction apply, depending upon the Article under consideration.

Article 5 (right to liberty and security) permits circumstances in which a person may lawfully be deprived of such fundamental right. It provides as follows: "No one shall be deprived of his liberty save in the following cases and in accordance with a procedure prescribed by law" (Art. 5(1)). The cases are then set out in paragraphs (a) to (f) in the Article 5(1). These circumstances provide an *exhaustive* definition of the circumstances whereby the fundamental right to liberty and security may be curtailed, although they are not mutually exclusive (*Winterwerp v. Netherlands* (1979) 2 E.H.R.R. 387). In addition any arrest or detention must be lawful and carried out in accordance with a procedure prescribed by law.

Article 6 (right to a fair trial) sets out a number of *minimum* rights in Article 6(3)(a) to (e). These minimum rights are only specific aspects of the general fundamental right to a fair trial and are therefore *not exhaustive* (*Edwards v. U.K.* (1992) 15 E.H.R.R. 218). There is a *corpus* of Convention law which establishes how such issues should, in principle, be approached.

24–12 Articles 8 to 11 are rights which have qualifications stated therein in almost identical terms. In each case there is a second paragraph qualifying the fundamental right as follows:

(i) no restriction or interference may be placed on the rights there stated unless it is in "accordance with the law" (Article 8) or "prescribed by law" (Articles 9, 10 and 11), and

(ii) the respective limitations must be "necessary in a democratic society".

Judgments of the European Court have established general principles in relation to the qualifications in Articles 8 to 11. They may be summarised as follows:

(i) the right itself must be interpreted in a broad, purposeful fashion (see §24–08, above).

(ii) the prosecution must show that the *restriction* or *qualification* on the exercise of the right is justified in accordance with the particular conditions set down in the qualifying paragraph of the Article in question but that these exceptions must be *narrowly* interpreted (*Sunday Times v. U.K.* (1979) 2 E.H.R.R. 245);

(iii) the words "prescribed by law" mean domestic law, providing such law is stated clearly enough to be forseeable in its consequences (*Sunday Times v. U.K.*, above);

(iv) the words "necessary in a democratic society" mean in pursuit of one of the legitimate aims set out in the Article itself; "necessary" implies some pressing social need for the interference (*Handyside v. U.K.* (1976)1 E.H.R.R. 737);

(v) there must be a reasonable relationship of proportionality between the means employed and the aims pursued (*Handyside v. U.K.*, above).

(iv) Derogable rights

24–13   The Human Rights Act 1998 states specifically that the fundamental rights and freedoms expressed in the Convention are subject to designated derogation or reservation which may be explicitly made known by the United Kingdom (s.1(2)). Article 15 of the Convention requires a Member State to notify the Council of Europe of any matter of domestic law which may be inconsistent with the obligations imposed by the Convention and thereby to derogate from its obligations in time of war or national emergency.

The United Kingdom chose, in 1988, to derogate from the provisions of Article 5(3) (the right of a detained person to be brought promptly before a judge) because of the extensions to pre-trial detention provided for in the Prevention of Terrorism (Temporary Provisions) Act 1984 as replaced by the Prevention of Terrorism (Temporary Provisions) Act 1989. Derogable rights are not directly relevant to magistrates' court practice but reference to them appears in section 14(1) of the Act which incorporates the derogation for the purposes of domestic law and permits further derogations to be made by the Secretary of State (s.14(1) (a) and (b)).

Both the existing derogation and any further derogations may last for a period of no more than five years (s.16(1)(a) and (b)).

5. Remedies

24–14   It is an elementary principle of justice that the existence of remedies is essential to the enforcement of rights. Article 13 of the Convention provides that "[e]veryone whose rights and freedoms set forth in this Convention are violated shall have an effective remedy before a national authority . . .". Article 13 has not been incorporated (HRA 1998, s.1(1)) but specific statutory remedies are provided for in the 1998 Act itself. The Lord Chancellor, Lord Irvine of Lairg, has said that it would cause confusion to have included Article 13 in the Act because the courts might think that further remedies, beyond those set out in the Act, should be fashioned (*Hansard*, H.L., November 18, 1997, col. 475).

The remedies set out in the Act and summarised below are not exhaustive. Section 11 of the Act which preserves existing rights and freedoms explicitly preserves the right of an aggrieved party to criminal proceedings to pursue a remedy not set out in the Act.

(i) Remedies in the proceedings

24–15 Section 7(1)(b) provides that "[a] person who claims that a public authority has acted (or proposes to act) in a way which is made unlawful by section 6(1) (see §24–04, above) may rely on the Convention right or rights concerned in any legal proceedings but only if he is (or would be) a victim of the unlawful act".

Plainly there is no difficulty in interpreting the word victim in the context of magistrates' courts proceedings; it means the accused or proposed accused. Public authority means the prosecution in this context but a public authority may, of course, include the court itself (s.6(3)(a)). For the remedy when the court itself fails to comply with the Convention see §24–17, below.

Section 7 is sufficiently widely drafted to enable a court to stay proceedings on the grounds of abuse of process, to exclude evidence or to allow submissions of no case to answer based on breaches of the Convention. In addition, it would appear that a proposed defendant could rely on the Convention to prevent a prosecution commencing by raising a Convention point to stop a summons being issued.

The essential point is that the Convention is capable of providing new arguments whereby a verdict of not guilty may be achieved or a prosecution stopped.

(ii) Judicial remedies

24–16 A further remedy, called a judicial remedy, is provided by section 8 of the Act which states as follows. "In relation to any act (or proposed act) of a public authority which the court finds is (or would be) unlawful, it may grant such relief or remedy, or make such order, within its powers as it considers just and appropriate" (s.8(1)).

The remaining subsections of section 8 deal with the remedy of damages which is plainly not relevant to proceedings in magistrates' courts, but the broad general remedy set out in section 8(1) overlaps with that in section 7 to a considerable extent for magistrates' courts proceedings.

(iii) Remedy by way of appeal

24–17 If the public authority for the purposes of section 7 is a court of law then the victim of the unlawful act may only bring proceedings to challenge the court's decision by exercising a right of appeal or by applying for judicial review (s.9(1)(a) and (b)). This provision is without prejudice to existing common law rights to seek judicial review of a decision of a magistrates' court (s.9(2)).

The importance of these provisions is that the court itself must comply with the provisions of the Convention, irrespective of the obligations on any other public authorities who are parties in the proceedings to do so also. It is not enough for justices to scrutinise the observance of the Convention by a party to a case if the court itself fails to comply in the regulation of its own proceedings.

B. APPLICATION TO PROCEEDINGS IN MAGISTRATES' COURTS

1. Criminal Procedure

EQUALITY OF ARMS

24–18 Equality of arms means that there must be a fair balance struck in the procedure surrounding a criminal trial so that each party has a reasonable opportunity to present its case (*Dombo Beheer BV v. Netherlands* (1993) 18 E.H.R.R. 213). This decision of the court is only one instance of the doctrine of equality of arms which was first enunciated in *Neumeister v. Austria* (1968) 1 E.H.R.R. 91. The concept extends the broad principles of a right to a fair trial guarantee in Article 6 of the Convention and has particular relevance to issues of disclosure, legal representation and consideration of adjournments.

REASONED DECISIONS

24–19 There is some authority to suggest that the right to a fair trial under Article 6 will involve a reasoned decision (*Hadjianastastassiou v. Greece* (1992) 16 E.H.R.R. 219) if the tribunal is not a jury. There have been no applications to Strasbourg which have challenged the practice of justices to pronounce a decision without supporting reasons and Convention law on this point cannot be stated with certainty. However, if a case involved an alleged breach of a Convention right it would seem incumbent on justices to give reasons because the accused and the public generally have an interest in knowing whether, in the opinion of the court, a Convention right has been infringed or not. It could be argued that, inevitably, such reasons would appear in an affidavit in judicial review proceedings or in the case stated for the opinion of the High Court. However, at present such reasoning is only given *ex post facto* and it could be argued there is an obligation to give reasons whether or not the accused (or the prosecution) choose to appeal.

2. Sentencing

24–20 The Human Rights Act 1998 will have an impact on sentencing in two respects; first in the application of the Articles themselves to the process of sentencing, and secondly in the use of judicial remedies under section 8 of the Act.

The Articles which are especially relevant to sentencing are as follows: Article 3 (the prohibition of inhuman or degrading treatment or punishment); Article 4 (the prohibition of forced or compulsory labour); Article 5(1)(a) (detention only after conviction by a competent court); Article 6 (right to a fair trial); and Article 7(1) (the prohibition of retrospective penalties). The remedy of passing a lenient sentence under section 8 of the Act may become highly relevant if a court finds it impossible to read an enactment prescribing punishment in a way which is compatible with Convention rights. This is discussed further below.

LAWFUL DETENTION

24–21 In the magistrates' court, where custodial sentences are necessarily short and where the particular issues associated with sentencing juveniles or imposing indeterminate or extended terms of imprisonment do not arise, the impact of the Convention is not likely to be enormous. The length of a sentence imposed lawfully under Article 5(1)(a) is not susceptible to challenge under the Convention (*Weeks v. U.K.*

(1987) 10 E.H.R.R. 293). The offender's remedy is to appeal against the severity of the sentence. Further, the conditions for the offender's detention are a matter for the prison authorities and not the magistrates' court.

There are circumstances when detention may be ordered even if there has not been a conviction by a competent court, for example a sentence for contempt in the face of the court. Article 5(1)(b) provides that detention may be lawful if imposed for the non-compliance with the lawful order of a court or in order to secure the fulfilment of any obligation prescribed by law. This provision would appear to permit detention of a person who infringes the right of another to have a fair trial by behaviour which amounts to a contempt (see further §§10–22 and 10–23, above).

Particular issues arise when detention is ordered for those who refuse to be bound over. These issues are discussed separately in §§9–18 and 9–19, above.

FORCED LABOUR

24–22   Article 4(2) provides that no one shall be required to perform forced or compulsory labour, but forced or compulsory labour shall not include any work required to be done in the ordinary course of detention imposed according to the provisions of Article 5 (Art. 4(3((a)). Thus, work which an offender is forced to perform whilst serving a prison sentence is not a breach of the offender's Convention rights. This exception only applies to work required to be done during the course of detention, and would not appear to apply to work done in the context of a non-custodial sentence.

The Crime (Sentences) Act 1997 abolished the requirement to obtain the consent of an offender before the imposition of a Community Service Order and therefore it is arguable that a sentence of Community Service may now breach Article 4. The contrary argument is that the offender cannot be "forced" to undertake community service because there are procedures for the order being revoked in the interests of justice which does not apply for custodial sentences (see §12–27, above). Further, an offender may not be ordered to undertake community service at times which may interfere with religious beliefs or school needs, thus complying with Article 9 (freedoms of conscience, thought and religion) and Article 2 of the First Protocol (right to education).

SENTENCE AS A REMEDY

24–23   The determination of any criminal charge under Article 6 of the Convention includes the whole of the proceedings in question, including sentence (*Eckle v. Germany* (1982) 5 E.H.R.R. 1). Thus, the Human Rights Act 1998 applies to the stage in the proceedings when sentence is passed. This becomes important when the court is considering section 3 of the Act (interpretation of legislation) and section 8 (judicial remedies). If it is impossible for the court to give effect to an accused's Convention rights under section 3, then the court may find itself having to pass sentence in circumstances which appear unjust. In this instance the court may, under section 8 of the Act, reflect the fact that the court cannot give effect to the accused's rights in the sentence imposed. This is especially important because any subsequent appeal by way of judicial review which results in a declaration of incompatibility is not binding on the parties to the proceedings in which it is made (HRA 1998, s.4(6)(b)). If, therefore, the court passed a tariff sentence even though it felt uncomfortable in so doing because the penal legislation could not be read in a way which gave effect to the accused's Convention rights, the sentence would be unaffected by a later declaration of incompatibility. For this reason, it is submitted, it is legitimate for the court to take the Convention into account when passing sentence in certain limited cases.

HUMAN RIGHTS ACT 1998

(1998 c. 42)

24–24 An Act to give further effect to rights and freedoms guaranteed under the European Convention on Human Rights; to make provision with respect to holders of certain judicial offices who become judges of the European Court of Human Rights; and for connected purposes (November 9, 1998).

Be it enacted by the Queen's most Excellent Majesty, by and with the advice and consent of the Lords Spiritual and Temporal, and Commons, in this present Parliament assembled, and by the authority of the same, as follows:

Introduction

The Convention Rights

1.—(1) In this Act, "the Convention rights" means the rights and fundamental freedoms set out in—

   (a) Articles 2 to 12 and 14 of the Convention,

   (b) Articles 1 to 3 of the First Protocol, and

   (c) Articles 1 and 2 of the Sixth Protocol.

as read with Articles 16 to 18 of the Convention.

(2) Those Articles are to have effect for the purposes of this Act subject to any designated derogation or reservation (as to which see sections 14 and 15).

(3) The Articles are set out in Schedule 1.

(4) The Secretary of State may by order make such amendments to this Act as he considers appropriate to reflect the effect, in relation to the United Kingdom, of a protocol.

(5) in subsection (4) "protocol" means a protocol to the Convention—

   (a) which the United Kingdom has ratified; or

   (b) which the United Kingdom has signed with a view to ratification.

(6) No amendment may be made by an order under subsection (4) so as to come into force before the protocol concerned as in force in relation to the United Kingdom.

Interpretation of Convention Rights

2.—(1) A court or tribunal determining a question which has arisen under this Act in connection with a Convention right must take into account any—

   (a) judgment, decision, declaration or advisory opinion of the European Court of Human Rights,

   (b) opinion of the Commission given in a report adopted under Article 31 of the Convention,

   (c) decision of the Commission in connection with Article 26 or 27(2) of the Convention, or

   (d) decision of the Committee of Ministers taken under Article 46 of the Convention, whenever made or given, so far as, in the opinion of the court or tribunal, it is relevant to the proceedings in which that question has arisen.

(2) Evidence of any judgment, decision, declaration or opinion of which account may have to be taken under this section is to be given in proceedings before any court or tribunal in such manner as may be provided by rules.

(3) In this section "rules" means rules of court or, in the case of proceedings before a tribunal, rules for the purposes of this section—

(a) by the Lord Chancellor or the Secretary of State, in relation to any proceedings outside Scotland;

(b) by the Secretary of State, in relation to proceedings in Scotland; or

(c) by a Northern Ireland department, in relation to proceedings before a tribunal in Northern Ireland—

(i) which deals with transferred matters; and
(ii) for which no rules made under paragraph (a) are in force.

Legislation

Interpretation of Legislation

3.—(1) So far as it is possible to do so, primary legislation and subordinate legislation must be read and given effect in a way which is compatible with the Convention rights.

(2) This section—

(a) applies to primary legislation and subordinate legislation whenever enacted;

(b) does not affect the validity, continuing operation or enforcement of any incompatible primary legislation; and

(c) does not affect the validity, continuing operation or enforcement of any incompatible subordinate legislation if (disregarding any possibility of revocation) primary legislation prevents removal of the incompatibility.

Declaration of Incompatibility

4.—(1) Subsection (2) applies in any proceedings in which a court determines whether a provision of primary legislation is compatible with a Convention right.

(2) If the court is satisfied that the provision is incompatible with a Convention right, it may make a declaration of that incompatibility.

(3) Subsection (4) applies in any proceedings in which a court determines whether a provision of subordinate legislation, made in the exercise of a power conferred by primary legislation, is compatible with a Convention right.

(4) If the court is satisfied—

(a) that the provision is incompatible with a Convention right, and

(b) that (disregarding any possibility of revocation) the primary legislation concerned prevents removal of the incompatibility,

it may make a declaration of that incompatibility.

(5) In this section "court" means—

    (a) the House of Lords;

    (b) the Judicial Committee of the Privy Council;

    (c) The Courts-Martial Appeal Court;

    (d) in Scotland, the High Court of Judiciary sitting otherwise than as a trial court or the Court of Session;

    (e) in England and Wales or Northern Ireland, the High Court or the Court of Appeal.

(6) A declaration under this section ("a declaration of incompatibility")—

    (a) does not affect the validity, continuing operation or enforcement of the provision in respect of which it is given; and

    (b) is not binding on the parties to the proceedings in which it is made.

Right of Crown to intervene

5.—(1) Where a court is considering whether to make a declaration of incompatibility, the Crown is entitled to notice in accordance with rules of court.

(2) In any case to which subsection (1) applies—

    (a) a Minister of the Crown (or a person nominated by him);

    (b) a member of the Scottish Executive;

    (c) a Northern Ireland Minister,

    (d) a Northern Ireland department,

is entitled, on giving notice in accordance with rules of court, to be joined as a party to the proceedings.

(3) Notice under subsection (2) may be given at any time during the proceedings.

(4) A person who has been made a party to criminal proceedings (other than in Scotland) as the result of a notice under subsection (2) may, with leave, appeal to the House of Lords against any declaration of incompatibility made in the proceedings.

(5) In subsection (4)—

    "criminal proceedings" includes all proceedings before the Courts-Martial Appeal Court; and

    "leave" means leave granted by the court making the declaration of incompatibility or by the House of Lords.

Public Authorities

Acts of public authorities

6.—(1) It is unlawful for a public authority to act in a way which is incompatible with a convention right.

(2) Subsection (1) does not apply to an act if—

(a) as the result of one or more provisions of primary legislation, the authority could not have acted differently; or

(b) in the case of one or more provisions of, or made under, primary legislation which cannot be read or given effect in a way which is compatible with the Convention rights, the authority was acting so as to gvie effect to or enforce those provisions.

(3) In this section, "public authority" includes—

(a) a court or tribunal, and

(b) any person certain of whose functions are functions of a public nature.

but does not include either House or Parliament or a person exercising functions in connection with proceedings in Parliament.

(4) In subsection (3) "Parliament" does not include the House of Lords in its judicial capacity.

(5) In relation to a particular act, a person is not a public authority by virtue only of subsection (3)(b) if the nature of the act is private.

(6) "An act" includes a failure to act but does not include a failure to—

(a) introduce in, or lay before, Parliament a proposal for legislation; or

(b) make any primary legislation or remedial order.

Proceedings

7.—(1) A person who claims that a public authority has acted (or proposes to act) in a way which is made unlawful by section 6(1) may—

(a) bring proceedings against the authority under this Act in the appropriate court or tribunal, or

(b) rely on the Convention right or rights concerned in any legal proceedings,

but only if he is (or would be) a victim of the unlawful act.

(2) In subsection (1)(a) "appropriate court or tribunal" means such court or tribunal as may be determined in accordance with rules; and proceedings against an authority include a counterclaim or similar proceeding.

(3) If the proceedings are brought on an application for judicial review, the applicant is to be taken to have a sufficient interest in relation to the unlawful act only if he is, or would be, a victim of that act.

(4) If the proceedings are made by way of a petition for judicial review in Scotland, the applicant shall be taken to have title and interest to sue in relation to the unlawful act only if he is, or would be, a victim of that act.

(5) Proceedings under subsection (1)(a) must be brought before the end of—

(a) the period of one year beginning with the date on which the act complained of took place; or

(b) such longer period as the court or tribunal considers equitable having regard to all the circumstances, but that is subject to any rule imposing a stricter time limit in relation to the procedure in question.

(6) In subsection (1)(b) "legal procedings" includes—

(a) proceedings brought by or at the instigation of a public authority; and

(b) an appeal against the decision of a court or tribunal.

(7) For the purposes of this section, a person is a victim of an unlawful act only if he would be a victim for the purposes of Article 34 of the Convention if proceedings were brought in the European Court of Human Rights in respect of that act.

(8) Nothing in this Act creates a criminal offence.

(9) In this section "rules" means—

(a) in relation to proceedings before a court or tribunal outside Scotland, rules made by the Lord Chancellor or the Secretary of State for the purposes of this section or rules of court,

(b) in relation to proceedings before a court or tribunal in Scotland, rules made by the Secretary of State for those purposes,

(c) in relation to proceedings before a tribunal in Northern Ireland—

(i) which deals with transferred matters; and

(ii) for which no rules made under paragraph (a) are in force,

rules made by Northern Ireland department for those purposes, and includes provision made by order under section 1 of the Courts and Legal Services Act 1990.

(10) In making rules regard must be had to section 9.

(11) The Minister who has power to make rules in relation to a particular tribunal may, to the extent he considers it necessary to ensure that the tribunal can provide an appropriate remedy in relation to an act (or proposed act) of a public authority which is (or would be) unlawful as a result of section 6(1), by order add to—

(a) the relief or remedies which the tribunal may grant; or

(b) the grounds on which it may grant any of them.

(12) An order made under subsection (11) may contain such incidental, supplemental, consequential or transitional provision as the Minister making it considers appropriate.

Judicial remedies

8.—(1) In relation to any act (or proposed act) of a public authority which the court finds is (or would be) unlawful, it may grant such relief or remedy, or make such order, within its powers as it considers just and appropriate.

(2) But damages may be awarded only by a court which has power to award damages, or to order the payment of compensation, in civil proceedings.

(3) No award of damages is to be made unless, taking account of all the circumstances of the case, including—

(a) any other relief or remedy granted, or order made, in relation to the act in question (by that or any other court), and

(b) the consequences of any decision (of that or any other court) in respect of that act, the court is satisfied that the award is necessary to afford just satisfaction to the person in whose favour it is made.

(4) In determining—

(a) whether to award damages, or

(b) the amount of an award,

the court must take into account the principles applied by the European Court of Human Rights in relation to the award of compensation under Article 41 of the Convention.

(5) A public authority against which damages are awarded is to be treated—

(a) in Scotland, for the purposes of section 3 of the Law Reform (Miscellaneous Provisions) (Scotland) Act 1940 as if the award were made in an action of damages in which the authority has been found liable in respect of loss or damage to the person to whom the award is made;

(b) for the purposes of the Civil Liability (Contribution) Act 1978 as liable in respect of damage suffered by the person to whom the award is made.

(6) In this section—

"court" includes a tribunal;
"damages" means damages for an unlawful act of a public authority; and
"unlawful" means unlawful under section 6(1).

Judicial acts

9.—(1) Proceedings under section 7(1)(a) in respect of a judicial act may be brought only—

(a) by exercising a right of appeal;

(b) on any application (in Scotland a petition) for judicial review; or

(c) in such other forum as may be prescribed by rules.

(2) That does not affect any rule of law which prevents a court from being the subject of judicial review.

(3) In proceedings under this Act in respect of a judicial act done in good faith, damages may not be awarded otherwise than to compensate a person to the extent required by Article 5(5) of the Convention.

(4) An award of damages permitted by subsection (3) is to be made against the Crown; but no award may be made unless the appropriate person, if not a party to the proceedings, is joined.

(5) In this section—

"appropriate person" means the Minister responsible for the court concerned, or a person or government department nominated by him;
"court" includes a tribunal;
"judge" includes a member of a tribunal, a justice of the peace and a clerk or other officer entitled to exercise the jurisdiction of a court;

"judicial act" means a judicial act of a court and includes an act done on the instructions, or on behalf, of a judge; and

"rules" has the same meaning as in section 7(9).

Remedial Action

Power to take remedial action

10.—(1) This section applies if—

(a) a provision of legislation has been declared under section 4 to be incompatible with a Convention right and, if an appeal lies—

   (i) all persons who may appeal have stated in writing that they do not intend to do so;

   (ii) the time for bringing an appeal has expired and no appeal has been brought within that time; or

   (iii) an appeal brought within that time has been determined or abandoned; or

(b) it appears to a Minister of the Crown or Her Majesty in Council that, having regard to a finding of the European Court of Human Rights made after the coming into force of this section in proceedings against the United Kingdom, a provision of legislation is incompatible with an obligation of the United Kingdom arising from the Convention.

(2) If a Minister of the Crown considers that there are compelling reasons for proceeding under this section, he may by order make such amendments to the legislation as he considers necessary to remove the incompatibility.

(3) If, in the case of subordinate legislation, a Minister of the Crown considers—

(a) that it is necessary to amend the primary legislation under which the subordinate legislation in question was made, in order to enable the incompatibility to be removed; and

(b) that there are compelling reasons for proceeding under this section.

he may by order make such amendments to the primary legislation as he considers necessary.

(4) This section also applies where the provision in question is in subordinate legislation and has been quashed, or declared invalid, by reason of incompatibility with a Convention right and the Minister proposes to proceed under paragraph 2(b) of Schedule 2.

(5) If the legislation is an Order in Council, the power conferred by subsection (2) or (3) is exercisable by Her Majesty in Council.

(6) In this section "legislation" does not include a Measure of the Church Assembly or of the General Synod of the Church of England.

(7) Schedule 2 makes further provision about remedial orders.

Other Rights and Proceedings

Safeguard for existing human rights

11. A person's reliance on a Convention right does not restrict—

(a) any other right or freedom conferred on him by or under any law having effect in any part of the United Kingdom; or

(b) his right to make any claim or bring any proceedings which he could make or bring apart from section 7 to 9.

Freedom of expression

12.—(1) This section applies if a court is considering whether to grant any relief which, if granted might affect the exercise of the Convention right to freedom of expression.

(2) If the person against whom the application for relief is made ("the respondent") is neither present nor represented, no such relief is to be granted unless the court is satisfied—

(a) that the applicant has taken all practicable steps to notify the respondent; or

(b) that there are compelling reasons why the respondent should not be notified.

(3) No such relief is to be granted so as to restrain publication before trial unless the court is satisifed that the applicant is likely to establish that publication should not be allowed.

(4) The court must have particular regard to the importance of the Convention right to freedom of expression and, where the proceedings relate to material which the respondent claims, or which appears to the court, to be journalistic, literary or artistic material (or to conduct connected with such material), to—

(a) the extent to which—

    (i) the material has, or is about to, become available to the public; or
    (ii) it is, or would be, in the public interest for the material to be published;

(b) any relevant privacy code.

(5) In this section—

"court" includes a tribunal; and
"relief" includes any remedy or order (other than in criminal proceedings).

Freedom of thought, conscience and religion

13.—(1) If a court's determination of any question arising under this Act might affect the exercise by a religious organisation (itself or its members collectively) of the Convention right to freedom of thought, conscience and religion, it must have particular regard to the importance of that right.

(2) In this section, "court" includes a tribunal.

Derogations and Reservations

Derogations

14.—(1) In this Act, "designated derogation" means—

(a) the United Kingdom's derogation from Article 5(3) of the Convention; and

(b) any derogation by the United Kingdom from an Article of the Convention, or of any protocol to the Convention, which is designated for the purposes of this Act in an order made by the Secretary of State.

(2) The derogation referred to in subsection (1)(a) is set out in Part I of Schedule 3.

(3) If a designated derogation is amended or replaced it ceases to be a designated derogation.

(4) But subsection (3) does not prevent the Secretary of State from exercising his power under subsection (1)(b) to make a fresh designation order in respect of the Article concerned.

(5) The Secretary of State must by order make such amendments to Schedule 3 as he considers appropriate to reflect—

(a) any designation order; or

(b) the effect of subsection (3).

(6) A designation order may be made in anticipation of the making by the United Kingdom of a proposed derogation.

Reservations

15.—(1) In this Act, "designated reservation" means—

(a) the United Kingdom's reservation to Article 2 of the First Protocol to the Convention; and

(b) any other reservation by the United Kingdom to an Article of the Convention, or of any protocol to the Convention, which is designated for the purposes of this Act in an order made by the Secretary of State.

(2) The text of the reservation referred to in subsection (1)(a) is set out in Part II of Schedule 3.

(3) If a designated reservation is withdrawn wholly or in part it ceases to be a designated reservation.

(4) But subsection (3) does not prevent the Secretary of State from exercising his power under subsection (1)(b) to make a fresh designation order in respect of the Article concerned.

(5) The Secretary of State must by order make such amendments to this Act as he considers appropriate to reflect—

(a) any designation order; or

(b) the effect of subsection (3).

Period for which designated derogations have effect

16.—(1) If it has not already been withdrawn by the United Kingdom, a designated derogation ceases to have effect for the purposes of this Act—

(a) in the case of the derogation referred to in section 14(1)(a), at the end of the period of five years beginning with the date on which section 1(2) came into force;

(b) in the case of any other derogation, at the end of the period of five years beginning with the date on which the order designating it was made.

(2) At any time before the period—

(a) fixed by subsection (1)(a) or (b), or

(b) extended by an order under this subsection,

comes to an end, the Secretary of State may by order extend it by a further period of five
years.

(3) An order under section 14(1)(b) ceases to have effect at the end of the period for
consideration, unless a resolution has been passed by each House approving the order.

(4) Subsection (3) does not affect—

(a) anything done in reliance on the order; or

(b) the power to make a fresh order under section 14(1)(b).

(5) In subsection (3) "period for consideration" means the period of 40 days beginning with the day on which the order was made.

(6) In calculating the period for consideration, no account is to be taken of any time
during which—

(a) Parliament is dissolved or prorogued; or

(b) both Houses are adjourned for more than four days.

(7) If a designated derogation is withdrawn by the United Kingdom, the Secretary of
State must by order make such amendments to this Act as he considers are required to
reflect that withdrawal.

Periodic review of designated reservations

17.—(1) The appropriate Minister must review the designated reservation referred
to in section 15(1)(a)—

(a) before the end of the period of five years beginning with the date on which
section 1(2) came into force; and

(b) if that designation is still in force, before the end of the period of five years
beginning with the date on which the last report relating to it was laid under
subsection (3).

(2) The appropriate Minister must review each of the other designated reservations
(if any)—

(a) before the end of the period of five years beginning with the date on which the
order designating the reservation first came into force; and

(b) if the designation is still in force, before the end of the period of five years
beginning with the date on which the last report relating to it was laid under
subsection (3).

(3) The Minister conducting a review under this section must prepare a report on the result of the review and lay a copy of it before each House of Parliament.

Judges of the European Court of Human Rights

Appointment to European Court of Human Rights

18.—(1) In this section "judicial office" means the office of—

(a) Lord Justice of Appeal, Justice of the High Court or Circuit judge, in England and Wales;

(b) judge of the Court of Session or sheriff, in Scotland;

(c) Lord Justice of Appeal, judge of the High Court or county court judge, in Northern Ireland.

(2) The holder of a judicial office may become a judge of the European Court of Human Rights ("the Court") without being required to relinquish his office.

(3) But he is not required to perform the duties of his judicial office while he is a judge of the Court.

(4) In respect of any period during which he is a judge of the Court—

(a) a Lord Justice of Appeal or Justice of the High Court is not to count as a judge of the relevant court for the purposes of section 2(1) or 4(1) of the Supreme Court Act 1981 (maximum number of judges) nor as a judge of the Supreme Court for the purposes of section 12(1) to (6) of that Act (salaries etc.);

(b) a judge of the Court of Session is not to count as a judge of that court for the purposes of section 1(1) of the Court of Session Act 1988 (maximum number of judges) or of section 9(1)(c) of the Administration of Justice Act 1973 ("the 1973 Act") (salaries etc.);

(c) a Lord Justice of Appeal or judge of the High Court in Northern Ireland is not to count as a judge of the relevant court for the purposes of section 2(1) or 3(1) of the Judicature (Northern Ireland) Act 1978 (maximum number of judges) nor as a judge of the Supreme Court of Northern Ireland for the purposes of section 9(1)(d) of the 1973 Act (salaries etc.);

(d) a Circuit judge is not to count as such for the purposes of section 18 of the Courts Act 1971 (salaries etc.);

(e) a sheriff is not to count as such for the purposes of section 14 of the Sheriff Courts (Scotland) Act 1907 (salaries etc.);

(f) a county court judge of Northern Ireland is not to count as such for the purposes of section 106 of the County Courts Act (Northern Ireland) 1959 (salaries etc.).

(5) If a sheriff principal is appointed a judge of the Court, section 11(1) of the Sheriff Courts (Scotland) Act 1971 (temporary appointment of sheriff principal) applies, while he holds that appointment, as if his office is vacant.

(6) Schedule 4 makes provision about judicial pensions in relation to the holder of a judicial office who serves as a judge of the Court.

(7) The Lord Chancellor or the Secretary of State may by order make such transitional provision (including, in particular, provision for a temporary increase in the maximum number of judges) as he considers appropriate in relation to any holder of a judicial office who has completed his service as a judge of the Court.

Parliamentary Procedure

Statements of compatibility

19.—(1) A Minister of the Crown in charge of a Bill in either House of Parliament must, before Second Reading of the Bill—

(a) make a statement to the effect that in his view the provisions of the Bill are compatible with the Convention rights ("a statement of compatibility"); or

(b) make a statement to the effect that although he is unable to make a statement of compatibility the government nevertheless wishes the House to proceed with the Bill.

(2) The statement must be in writing and be published in such manner as the Minister making it considers appropriate.

Supplemental

Orders, etc. under this Act

20.—(1) Any power of a Minister of the Crown to make an order under this Act is exercisable by statutory instrument.

(2) The power of the Lord Chancellor or the Secretary of State to make rules (other than rules of court) under section 2(3) or 7(9) is exercisable by statutory instrument.

(3) Any statutory instrument made under section 14, 15 or 16(7) must be laid before Parliament.

(4) No order may be made by the Lord Chancellor or the Secretary of State under section 1(4), 7(11) or 16(2) unless a draft of the order has been laid before, and approved by, each House of Parliament.

(5) Any statutory instrument made under section 18(7) or Schedule 4, or to which subsection (2) applies, shall be subject to annulment in pursuance of a resolution of either House of Parliament.

(6) The power of a Northern Ireland department to make—

(a) rules under section 2(3)(c) or 7(9)(c), or

(b) an order under section 7(11),

is exercisable by statutory rule for the purposes of the Statutory Rules (Northern Ireland) Order 1979.

(7) Any rules made under section 2(3)(c) or 7(9)(c), shall be subject to negative resolution; and section 41(6) of the Interpretation Act (Northern Ireland) 1954 (meaning of "subject to negative resolution") shall apply as if the power to make the rules were conferred by an Act of the Northern Ireland Assembly.

(8) No order may be made by a Northern Ireland department under secton 7(11) unless a draft of the order has been laid before, and approved by, the Northern Ireland Assembly.

Interpretation, etc.

21.—(1) In this Act—

"amend" includes repeal and apply (with or without modification);
"the appropriate Minister" means the Minister of the Crown having charge of the appropriate authorised government department (within the meaning of the Crown Proceedings Act 1947);
"the Commission" means the European Commission of Human Rights;
"the Convention" means the Convention for the Protection of Human Rights and Fundamental Freedoms, agreed by the Council of Europe at Rome on November 4, 1950 as it has effect for the time being in relation to the United Kingdom;
"declaration of incompatibility" means a declaration under section 4;
"Minister of the Crown" has the same meaning as in the Ministers of the Crown Act 1975;
"Northern Ireland Minister" includes the First Minister and the deputy First Minister in Northern Ireland;
"primary legislation" means any—

(a) public general Act;
(b) local and personal Act;
(c) private Act;
(d) Measure of the Church Assembly;
(e) Measure of the General Synod of the Church of England;
(f) Order in Council—

(i) made in exercise of Her Majesty's Royal Prerogative;
(ii) made under section 38(1)(a) of the Northern Ireland Constitution Act 1973 of the corresponding provision of the Northern Ireland Act 1998; or
(iii) amending an Act of a kind mentioned in paragraph (a), (b) or (c);

and includes an order or other instrument made under primary legislation (otherwise than by the National Assembly for Wales, a member of the Scottish Executive, a Northern Ireland Minister or a Northern Ireland department) to the extent to which it operates to bring one or more provisions of that legislation into force or amends any primary legislation;

"the First Protocol" means the protocol to the Convention agreed at Paris on March 20, 1952;
"the Sixth Protocol" means the protocol to the Convention agreed at Strasbourg on April 28, 1983;
"11th Protocol" means the protocol to the Convention (restructuring the control machinery established by the Convention) agreed at Strasbourg on May 11, 1994;
"remedial order" means an order under section 10;
"subordinate legislation" means any—

(a) Order in Council other than one—

   (i) made in exercise of Her Majesty's Royal Prerogative;
   (ii) made under section 38(1)(a) of the Northern Ireland Constitution Act 1973 or the corresponding provision of the Northern Ireland Act 1998; or,
   (iii) amending an Act of a kind mentioned in the definition of primary legislation;

(b) Act of the Scottish Parliament;
(c) Act of the Parliament of Northrn Ireland;
(d) Measure of the Assembly established under section 1 of the Northern Ireland Assembly Act 1973;
(e) Act of the Northern Ireland Assembly;
(f) order, rules, regulations, scheme, warrant, byelaw or other instrument made under primary legislation (except to the extent to which it operates to bring one or more provisions of that legislation into force or amends any primary legislation);
(g) order, rules, regulations, scheme, warrant, byelaw or other instrument made under legislation mentioned in §(b), (c), (d) or (e) or made under an Order in Council applying only to Northern Ireland;
(h) order, rules, regulations, scheme, warrant, byelaw or other instrument made by a member of the Scottish Executive, a Northern Ireland Minister or a Northern Ireland department in exercise of prerogative or other executive functions of Her Majesty which are exercisable by such a person on behalf of Her Majesty;

"transferred matters" has the same meaning as in the Northern Ireland Act 1998; and

"tribunal" means any tribunal in which legal proceedings may be brought.

(2) The references in paragraphs (b) and (c) of section 2(1) to Articles are to Articles of the Convention as they had effect immediately before the coming into force of the 11th Protocol.

(3) The reference in paragraph (d) of section 2(1) to Article 46 includes a reference to Artcles 32 and 54 of the Convention as they had effect immediately before the coming into force of the 11th Protocol.

(4) The references in section 2(1) to a report or decision of the Commission or a decision of the Committee of Ministers include references to a report or decision made as provided by paragraphs 3, 4 and 6 of Article 5 of the 11th Protocol (transitional provisions).

(5) Any liability under the Army Act 1955, the Air Force Act 1955 or the Naval Discipline Act 1957 to suffer death for an offence is replaced by a liability to imprisonment for life or any less punishment authorised by those Acts; and those Acts shall accordingly have effect with the necessary modifications.

Short title, commencement, application and extent

22.—(1) This Act may be cited as the Human Rights Act 1998.

(2) Sections 18, 20 and 21(5) and this section come into force on the passing of this Act.

(3) The other provisions of this Act come into force on such day as the Secretary of State may by order appoint; and different days may be appointed for different purposes.

(4) Paragraph (b) of subsection (1) of section 7 applies to proceedings brought by or at the instigation of a public authority whenever the act in question took place; but otherwise that subsection does not apply to an act taking place before the coming into force of that section.

(5) This Act binds the Crown.

(6) This Act extends to Northern Ireland.

(7) Section 21(5), so far as it relates to any provision contained in the Army Act 1955, the Air Force Act 1955 or the Naval Discipline Act 1957, extends to any place to which that provision extends.

SCHEDULE 1

PART I

[Omitted]

The Convention Rights and Freedoms are printed below at §24–25

PART II

THE FIRST PROTOCOL

Article 1

Protection of property

Every natural or legal person is entitled to the peaceful enjoyment of his possessions. No one shall be deprived of his possessions except in the public interest and subject to the conditions provided for by law and by the general principles of international law.

The preceding provisions shall not, however, in any way impair the right of a State to enforce such laws as it deems necessary to control the use of property in accordance with the general interest or to secure the payment of taxes or other contributions or penalties.

Article 2

Right to education

No person shall be denied the right to education. In the exercise of any functions which it assumes in relation to education and to teaching, the State shall respect the right of parents to ensure such education and teaching in conformity with their own religious and philosophical convictions.

Article 3

Right to free elections

The High Contracting Parties undertake to hold free elections at reasonable intervals by secret ballot, under conditions which will ensure the free expression of the opinion of the people in the choice of the legislature.

PART III

THE SIXTH PROTOCOL

Article 1

Abolition of the death penalty

The death penalty shall be abolished. No one shall be condemned to such penalty or executed.

Article 2

Death penalty in time of war

A State may make provision in its law for the death penalty in respect of acts committed in time of war or of imminent threat of war; such penalty shall be applied only in the instances laid down in the law and in accordance with its provisions. The State shall communicate to the Secretary General of the Council of Europe the relevant provisions of that law.

SCHEDULE 2

REMEDIAL ORDERS

Orders

1.—(1) A remedial order may—

(a) contain such incidental, supplemental, consequential or transitional provision as the person making it considers appropriate;

(b) be made so as to have effect from a date earlier than that on which it is made;

(c) make provision for the delegation of specific functions;

(d) make different provision for different cases.

(2) The power conferred by sub-paragraph (1)(a) includes—

(a) power to amend primary legislation (including primary legislation other than that which contains the incompatible provision; and

(b) power to amend or revoke subordinate legislation (including subordinate legislation other than that which contains the incompatible provision).

(3) A remedial order may be made so as to have the same extent as the legislation which it affects.

(4) No person is to be guilty of an offence solely as a result of the retrospective effect of a remedial order.

Procedure

2. No remedial order may be made unless—

(a) a draft of the order has been approved by a resolution of each House of Parliament made after the end of the period of 60 days beginning with the day on which the draft was laid; or

(b) it is declared in the order that it appears to the person making it that, because of the urgency of the matter, it is necessary to make the order without a draft being so approved.

Orders laid in draft

3.—(1) No draft may be laid under paragraph 2(a) unless—

(a) the person proposing to make the order has laid before Parliament a document which contains a draft of the proposed order and the required information; and

(b) the period of 60 days, beginning with the day on which the document required by this sub-paragraph was laid, has ended.

(2) If representations have been made during that period, the draft laid under paragraph 2(a) must be accompanied by a statement containing—

(a) a summary of the representations; and

(b) if, as a result of the representations, the proposed order has been changed, details of the changes.

Urgent cases

4.—(1) If a remedial order ("the original order") is made without being approved in draft, the person making it must lay it before Parliament, accompanied by the required information, after it is made.

(2) If representations have been made during the period of 60 days beginning with the day on which the original order was made, the person making it must (after the end of that period) lay before Parliament a statement containing—

(a) a summary of the representations; and

(b) if, as a result of the representations, he considers it appropriate to make changes to the original order, details of the changes.

(3) If sub-paragraph (2)(b) applies, the person making the statements must—

(a) make a further remedial order replacing the original order; and

(b) lay the replacement order before Parliament.

(4) If, at the end of the period of 120 days beginning with the day on which the original order was made, a resolution has not been passed by each House approving the original or replacement order, the order ceases to have effect (but without that affecting anything previously done under either order or the power to make a fresh remedial order).

Definitions

5. In this Schedule—

"representations" means representations about a remedial order (or proposed remedial order) made to the person making (or proposing to make) it and includes any relevant Parliamentary report or resolution; and
"required information" means—

(a) an explanation of the incompatibility which the order (or proposed order) seeks to remove, including particulars of the relevant declaration, finding or order; and
(b) a statement of the reasons for proceeding under section 10 and for making an order in those terms.

Calculating periods

6. In calculating any period for the purposes of this Schedule, no account is to be taken of any time during which—

(a) Parliament is dissolved or prorogued; or

(b) both Houses are adjourned for more than four days.

SCHEDULE 3

DEROGATION AND RESERVATION

PART I

DEROGATION

The 1988 notification

The United Kingdom Permanent Representative to the Council of Europe presents his compliments to the Secretary General of the Council, and has the honour to convey the following information in order to ensure compliance with the obligations of Her Majesty's Government in the United Kingdom under Article 15(3) of the Convention for the Protection of Human Rights and Fundamental Freedoms signed at Rome on November 4, 1950.

There have been in the United Kingdom in recent years campaigns of organised terrorism connected with the affairs of Northern Ireland which have manifested themselves in activities which have included repeated murder, attempted murder, maiming, intimidation and violent civil disturbance and in bombing and fire raising which have resulted in death, injury and widespread destruction of property. As a result, a public emergency within the meaning of Article 15(1) of the Convention exists in the United Kingdom.

The Government found it necessary in 1974 to introduce and since then, in cases concerning persons reasonably suspected of involvement in terrorism connected with the affairs of Northern Ireland, or of certain offences under the legislation, who have been detained for 48 hours, to exercise powers enabling further detention without charge, for periods of up to five days, on the authority of the Secretary of State. These powers are at present to be found in section 12 of the Prevention of Terrorism (Temporary Provisions) Act 1984, Article 9 of the Prevention of Terrorism (Supplemental Temporary Provisions) Order 1984 and Article 10 of the Prevention of Terrorism (Supplemental Temporary Provisions) (Northern Ireland) Order 1984.

Section 12 of the Prevention of Terrorism (Temporary Provisions) Act 1984 provides for a person whom a constable has arrested on reasonable grounds of suspecting him to be guilty of an offence under sections 1, 9 or 10 of the Act, or to be or to have been involved in terrorism connected with the affairs of Northern Ireland, to be detained in right of the arrest for up to 48 hours and thereafter, where the Secretary of State extends the detention period, for up to a further five days. Section 12 substantially re-enancted section 12 of the Prevention of Terrorism (Temporary Provisions) Act 1976 which, in turn, substantially re-enacted Section 7 of the Prevention of Terrorism (Temporary Provisions) Act 1974.

Article 10 of the Prevention of Terrorism (Supplemental Temporary Provisions) (Northern Ireland) Order (S.I. 1984 No. 417) and Article 9 of the Prevention of Terrorism (Supplemental Temporary Provisions) Order (S.I. 1984 No. 418) were both made under sections 13 and 14 of and Schedule 3 to the 1984 Act and substantially re-enacted powers of detention in Orders made under the 1974 and 1976 Acts. A person who is being examined under Article 4 of either Order on his arrival in, or on seeking to leave, Northern Ireland or Great Britain for the purpose of determining whether he is or has been involved in terrorism connected with the affairs of Northern Ireland, or whether there are grounds for suspecting that he has committed an offence under Section 9 of the 1984 Act, may be detained under Article 9 or 10, as appropriate, pending the conclusion of his examination. The period of this examination may exceed 12 hours if an examining officer has reasonable grounds for suspecting him to be or to have been involved in acts of terrorism connected with the affairs of Northern Ireland.

Where such a person is detained under the said Article 9 or 10 he may be detained for up to 48 hours on the authority of an examining officer and thereafter, where the Secretary of State extends the detention period, for up to a further five days.

In its judgment of November 29, 1988 in the case of *Brogan and Others*, the European Court of Human Rights held that there had been a violation of Article 5(3) in respect of each of the applicants, all of whom had been detained under section 12 of the 1984 Act. The Court held that even the shortest of the four periods of detention concerned, namely four days and six hours, fell outside the constraints as to time permitted by the first part of Article 5(3). In addition, the Court held that there had been a violation of Article 5(5) in the case of each applicant.

Following this judgment the Secretary of State for the Home Department informed Parliament on December 6, 1988 that, against the background of the terrorist campaign, and the overriding need to bring terrorists to justice, the Government did not believe that the maximum period of detention should be reduced. He informed Parliament that the Government were examining the matter with a view to responding to the judgment. On December 22, 1988, the Secretary of State further informed Parliament that it remained the Government's wish, if it could be achieved, to find a judicial process under which extended detention might be reviewed and where appropriate authorised by a judge or other judicial officer. But a further period of reflection and consultation was necessary before the Government could bring forward a firm and final view.

Since the judgment of November 29, 1988 as well as previously, the Government have found it necessary to continue to exercise, in relation to terrorism connected with the affairs of Northern Ireland, the powers described above enabling further detention without charge for periods of up to five days, on the authority of the Secretary of State, to the extent strictly required by the exigencies of the situation to enable necessary enquiries and investigations properly to be completed in order to decide whether criminal proceedings should be instituted. To the extent that the exercise of these powers may be inconsistent with the obligations imposed by the Convention the Government has availed itself of the right of derogation conferred by Article 15(1) of the Convention and will continue to do so until further notice.

Dated December 23, 1988.

The 1989 notification

The United Kingdom Permanent Representative to the Council of Europe presents his compliments to the Secretary General of the Council, and has the honour to convey the following information.

In his communication to the Secretary General of December 23, 1988, reference was made to the introduction and exercise of certain powers under section 12 of the Prevention of Terrorism (Temporary Provisions) Act 1984, Article 9 of the Prevention of Terrorism (Supplemental Temporary Provisions) Order 1984 and Article 10 of the Prevention of Terrorism (Supplemental Temporary Provisions) (Northern Ireland) Order 1984.

These provisions have been replaced by section 14 of and paragraph 6 of Schedule 5 to the Prevention of Terrorism (Temporary Provison) Act 1989, which make comparable provisions. They came into force on March 22, 1989. A copy of these provisions is enclosed.

The United Kingdom Permanent Representative avails himself of this opportunity to renew to the Secretary General the assurance of his highest consideration.

March 23, 1989.

PART II

RESERVATION

At the time of signing the present (First) Protocol, I declare that, in view of certain provisions of the Education Act in the United Kingdom, the principle affirmed in the second sentence of Article 2 is accepted by the United Kingdom only so far as it is compatible with the provision of efficient instruction and training, and the avoidance of unreasonable public expenditure.

Dated March 20, 1952. Made by the United Kingdom Permanent Representative to the Council of Europe.

SCHEDULE 4

JUDICIAL PENSIONS

[Omitted]

THE 1950 EUROPEAN CONVENTION FOR THE PROTECTION OF HUMAN RIGHTS AND FUNDAMENTAL FREEDOMS

24–25 The governments signatory hereto, being Members of the Council of Europe,

Considering the Universal Declaration of Human Rights proclaimed by the General Assembly of the United Nations on December 10, 1948;

Considering that this Declaration aims at securing the universal and effective recognition and observance of the rights therein declared;

Considering that the aim of the Council of Europe is the achievement of greater unity between its members and that one of the methods by which that aim is to be pursued is the maintenance and further realisation of human rights and fundamental freedoms;

Reaffirming their profound belief in those fundamental freedoms which are the foundation of justice and peace in the world and are best maintained on the one hand by an effective political democracy and on the other by a common understanding and observance of the Human Rights upon which they depend;

Being resolved, as the governments of European countries which are like-minded and have a common heritage of political traditions, ideals, freedom and the rule of law, to take the first steps for the collective enforcement of certain of the rights stated in the Universal Declaration;

Have agreed as follows:

SECTION 1

Article 2

Right to life

1. Everyone's right to life shall be protected by law. No one shall be deprived of his life intentionally save in the execution of a sentence of a court following his conviction of a crime for which this penalty is provided by law.

2. Deprivation of life shall not be regarded as inflicted in contravention of this Article when it results from the use of force which is no more than absolutely necessary:

   (a) in defence of any person from unlawful violence;

   (b) in order to effect a lawful arrest or to prevent the escape of a person lawfully detained;

   (c) in action lawfully taken for the purpose of quelling a riot or insurrection.

Article 3

Prohibition of torture

No one shall be subjected to torture or to inhuman or degrading treatment or punishment.

Article 4

Prohibition of slavery and forced labour

1. No one shall be held in slavery or servitude.
2. No one shall be required to perform forced or compulsory labour.
3. For the purpose of this Article the term "forced or compulsory labour" shall not include:

(a) any work required to be done in the ordinary course of detention imposed according to the provisions of Article 5 of this Convention or during conditional release from such detention;

(b) any service of a military character or, in the case of conscientious objectors in countries where they are recognised, service exacted instead of compulsory military service;

(c) any service exacted in case of an emergency or calamity threatening the life or well-being of the community;

(d) any work or service which forms part of normal civic obligations.

Article 5

Right to liberty and security

1. Everyone has the right to liberty and security of person. No one shall be deprived of his liberty save in the following cases and in accordance with a procedure prescribed by law:

(a) the lawful detention of a person after conviction by a competent court;

(b) the lawful arrest or detention of a person for non-compliance with the lawful order of a court or in order to secure the fulfilment of any obligation prescribed by law;

(c) the lawful arrest or detention of a person effected for the purpose of bringing him before the competent legal authority on reasonable suspicion of having committed an offence or when it is reasonably considered necessary to prevent his committing an offence or fleeing after having done so;

(d) the detention of a minor by lawful order for the purpose of educational supervision or his lawful detention for the purpose of bringing him before the competent legal authority;

(e) the lawful detention of persons for the prevention of the spreading of infectious diseases, of persons of unsound mind, alcoholics or drug addicts or vagrants;

(f) the lawful arrest or detention of a person to prevent his effecting an unauthorised entry into the country or of a person against whom action is being taken with a view to deportation or extradition.

2. Everyone who is arrested shall be informed promptly, in a language which he understands, of the reasons for his arrest and of any charge against him.

3. Everyone arrested or detained in accordance with the provisions of paragraph 1(c) of this Article shall be brought promptly before a judge or other officer authorised by law to exercise judicial power and shall be entitled to trial within a reasonable time or to release pending trial. Release may be conditioned by guarantees to appear for trial.

4. Everyone who is deprived of his liberty by arrest or detention shall be entitled to take proceedings by which the lawfulness of his detention shall be decided speedily by a court and his release ordered if the detention is not lawful.

5. Everyone who has been the victim of arrest or detention in contravention of the provisions of this Article shall have an enforceable right to compensation.

Article 6

Right to a fair trial

1. In the determination of his civil rights and obligations or of any criminal charge against him, everyone is entitled to a fair and public hearing within a reasonable time by an independent and impartial tribunal established by law. Judgment shall be pronounced publicly but the press and public may be excluded from all or part of the trial in the interest of morals, public order or national security in a democratic society, where the interests of juveniles or the protection of the private life of the parties so require, or to the extent strictly necessary in the opinion of the court in special circumstances where publicity would prejudice the interest of justice.

2. Everyone charged with a criminal offence shall be presumed innocent until proved guilty according to law.

3. Everyone charged with a criminal offence has the following minimum rights:

(a) to be informed promptly, in a language which he understands and in detail, of the nature and cause of the accusation against him;

(b) to have adequate time and facilities for the preparation of his defence;

(c) to defend himself in person or through legal assistance of his own choosing or, if he has not sufficient means to pay for legal assistance, to be given it free when the interests of justice so require;

(d) to examine or have examined witnesses against him and to obtain the attendance and examination of witnesses on his behalf under the same conditions as witnesses against him;

(e) to have the free assistance of an interpreter if he cannot understand or speak the language used in court.

Article 7

No punishment without law

1. No one shall be held guilty of any criminal offence on account of any act or omission which did not constitute a criminal offence under national or international law at the time when it was committed. Nor shall a heavier penalty be imposed than the one that was applicable at the time the criminal offence was committed.

2. This Article shall not prejudice the trial and punishment or any person for any act or omission which, at the time when it was committed, was criminal according to the general principles of law recognised by civilised nations.

Article 8

Right to respect for private and family life

1. Everyone has the right to respect for his private and family life, his home and his correspondence.

2. There shall be no interference by a public authority with the exercise of this right except such as is in accordance with the law and is necessary in a democratic society in the interests of national security, public safety or the economic well-being of the country, for the prevention of disorder or crime, for the protection of health or morals, or for the protection of the rights and freedoms of others.

Article 9

Freedom of thought, conscience and religion

1. Everyone has the right to freedom of thought, conscience and religion; this right includes freedom to change his religion or belief and freedom, either alone or in community with others and in public or private, to manifest his religion or belief, in worship, teaching, practice and observance.

2. Freedom to manifest one's religion or beliefs shall be subject only to such limitations as are prescribed by law and are necessary in a democratic society in the interests of public safety, for the protection of public order, health or morals, or for the protection of the rights and freedoms of others.

Article 10

Freedom of expression

1. Everyone has the right to freedom of expression. This right shall include freedom to hold opinions and to receive and impart information and ideas without interference by public authority and regardless of frontiers. This Article shall not prevent States from requiring the licensing of broadcasting, television or cinema enterprises.

2. The exercise of these freedoms, since it carries with it duties and responsibilities, may be subject to such formalities, conditions, restrictions or penalties as are prescribed by law and are necessary in a democratic society, in the interests of national security, territorial integrity or public safety, for the prevention of disorder or crime, for the protection of health or morals, for the protection of the reputation or rights of others, for preventing the disclosure of information received in confidence, or for maintaining the authority and impartiality of the judiciary.

Article 11

Freedom of assembly and association

1. Everyone has the right to freedom of peaceful assembly and to freedom of association with others, including the right to form and to join trade unions for the protection of his interests.

2. No restrictions shall be placed on the exercise of these rights other than such as are prescribed by law and are necessary in a democratic society in the interests of national security or public safety, for the prevention of disorder or crime, for the protection of health or morals or for the protection of the rights and freedoms of others. This Article shall not prevent the imposition of lawful restrictions on the exercise of these rights by members of the armed forces, of the police or of the administration of the State.

Article 12

Right to marry

Men and women of marriageable age have the right to marry and to found a family, according to the national laws governing the exercise of this right.

Article 14

Prohibition of discrimination

The enjoyment of the rights and freedoms set forth in this Convention shall be secured without discrimination on any ground such as sex, race, colour, language, religion, political or other opinion, national or social origin, association with a national minority, property, birth or other status.

Appendices

APPENDIX I

National mode of trial guidelines

The purpose of these guidelines is to help magistrates decide whether or not to commit "either way" offences for trial in the Crown Court. Their object is to provide guidance not direction. They are not intended to impinge upon a magistrate's duty to consider each case individually and on its own particular facts.

These guidelines apply to all defendants **aged 18 and above**.

GENERAL CONSIDERATIONS

Section 19 of the Magistrates' Court Act 1980 requires magistrates to have regard to the following matters in deciding whether an offence is more suitable for summary trial or trial on indictment:

(1) The nature of the case. (2) Whether the circumstances make the offence one of a serious character. (3) Whether the punishment which a magistrates' court would have power to inflict for it would be adequate. (4) Any other circumstances which appear to the court to make it more suitable for the offence to be tried in one way rather than the other. (5) Any representations made by the prosecution or the defence.

CERTAIN GENERAL OBSERVATIONS CAN BE MADE:

(a) The court should never make its decision on the grounds of convenience or expedition.

(b) The court should assume for the purpose of deciding mode of trial that the prosecution version of the facts is correct.

(c) The fact that the offences are alleged to be specimens is a relevant consideration; the fact that the defendant will be asking for other offences to be taken into consideration, if convicted, is not.

(d) Where cases involve complex questions of fact or difficult questions of law, including difficult issues of disclosure of sensitive material, the court should consider committal for trial.

(e) Where two or more defendants were jointly charged with an offence each has an individual right to elect his mode of trial. (This follows the decision in *R. v. Brentwood Justices, ex p. Nicholls.*)

(f) **In general, except where otherwise stated, either way offences should be tried summarily unless the court considers that the particular case has one or more of the features set out in the following pages and that its sentencing powers are insufficient.**

(g) The court should also consider its power to commit an offender for sentence, under section 38 of the Magistrates' Courts Act 1980, as amended by Section 25 of the Criminal Justice Act 1991, **if information emerges during the course of the hearing which leads them to conclude that the offence is so serious, or the offender such a risk to the public, that their powers to sentence him are inadequate.** This amendment means that committal for sentence is no longer determined by reference to the character or antecedents of the defendant.

FEATURES RELEVANT TO THE INDIVIDUAL OFFENCES

NOTE: Where reference is made in these guidelines to property or damage of **"high value"** it means a figure equal to at least **twice** the amount of the limit (currently £5,000) imposed by statute on a magistrates' court when making a Compensation Order.

BURGLARY

Cases should be tried summarily unless the court considers that one or more of the following features is present in the case **and** that its sentencing powers are insufficient.

Magistrates should take account of their powers under section 25 of the Criminal Justice Act 1991 to commit for **sentence**.

NOTE: See paragraph (g)

(i) DWELLING-HOUSE

(1) Entry in the daytime when the occupier (or another) is present. (2) Entry at night of a house which is normally occupied, whether or not the occupier (or another) is present. (3) The offence is alleged to be one of a series of similar offences. (4) When soiling, ransacking, damage or vandalism occurs. (5) The offence has professional hallmarks. (6) The unrecovered property is of high value.

NOTE: Attention is drawn to paragraph 28(c) of Schedule 1 of the Magistrates' Courts Act 1980, by which offences of burglary in a dwelling **cannot** be tried summarily if any person in the dwelling was subjected to violence or the threat of violence.

(ii) NON-DWELLINGS

(1) Entry of a pharmacy or doctor's surgery. (2) Fear is caused or violence is done to anyone lawfully on the premises (*e.g.* nightwatchman; security guard). (3) The offence has professional hallmarks. (4) Vandalism on a substantial scale. (5) The unrecovered property is of high value.

THEFT AND FRAUD

(1) Breach of trust by a person in a position of substantial authority, or in whom a high degree of trust is placed. (2) Theft or fraud which has been committed or disguised in a sophisticated manner. (3) Theft or fraud committed by an organised gang. (4) The victim is particularly vulnerable to theft or fraud, *e.g.* the elderly or infirm. (5) The unrecovered property is of high value.

HANDLING

(1) Dishonest handling of stolen property by a receiver who has commissioned the theft. (2) The offence has professional hallmarks. (3) The property is of high value.

SOCIAL SECURITY FRAUDS

(1) Organised fraud on a large scale. (2) The frauds are substantial and carried out over a long period of time.

VIOLENCE (SECTIONS 20 AND 47 OF THE OFFENCES AGAINST THE PERSON ACT 1861)

(1) The use of a weapon of a kind likely to cause serious injury. (2) A weapon is used and serious injury is caused. (3) More than minor injury caused by kicking, head butting or similar forms of assault. (4) Serious violence is caused to those whose work has to be done in contact with the public or who are likely to face violence in the course of their work. (5) Violence to vulnerable people, *e.g.* the elderly and infirm. (6) The offence has clear racial motivation.

NOTE: The same considerations applied to cases **of domestic** violence.

PUBLIC ORDER ACT OFFENCES

(1) Cases of **Violent Disorder** should generally be committed for trial.

(2) **Affray.**

1. Organised violence or use of weapons.
2. Significant injury or substantial damage.
3. The offence has clear racial motivation.
4. An attack upon police officers, prison officers, ambulance men, firemen and the like.

VIOLENCE TO AND NEGLECT OF CHILDREN

(1) Substantial injury. (2) Repeated violence or serious neglect, even if the physical harm is slight. (3) Sadistic violence, *e.g.* deliberate burning or scalding.

INDECENT ASSAULT

(1) Substantial disparity in age between victim and defendant, and the assault is more than trivial. (2) Violence or threats of violence. (3) Relationship of trust or responsibility between defendant and victim. (4) Several similar offences, and the assaults are more than trivial. (5) The victim is particularly vulnerable. (6) Serious nature of the assault.

UNLAWFUL SEXUAL INTERCOURSE

(1) Wide disparity of age. (2) Breach of position of trust. (3) The victim is particularly vulnerable.

NOTE: Unlawful sexual intercourse with a girl **under 13** is triable only on indictment.

DRUGS

(1) **Class A**

(a) Supply: possession with intent to supply. These cases should be committed for trial.

(b) Possession. Should be committed for trial unless the amount is consistent only with personal use.

(2) **Class B**

(a) Supply: possession with intent to supply. Should be committed for trial unless there is only small scale supply for no payment.

(b) Possession. Should be committed for trial when the quantity is substantial and not consistent only with personal use.

DANGEROUS DRIVING

(1) Alcohol or drugs contributing to dangerousness. (2) Grossly excessive speed. (3) Racing. (4) Prolonged course of dangerous driving. (5) Degree of injury or damage sustained. (6) Other related offences.

CRIMINAL DAMAGE

(1) Deliberate fire-raising. (2) Committed by a group. (3) Damage of a high value. (4) The offence has clear racial motivation.

NOTE: Offences set out in Schedule 2 of the Magistrates' Courts Act 1980 (which includes offences of criminal damage which do not amount to arson) **must** be tried summarily if the value of the property damaged or destroyed is £5,000 or less.

Appendix II

Code for Crown Prosecutors

1. Introduction

1.1 The decision to prosecute an individual is a serious step. Fair and effective prosecution is essential to the maintenance of law and order. But even in a small case a prosecution has serious implications for all involved—the victim, a witness and a defendant. The Crown Prosecution Service applies the Code for Crown Prosecutors so that it can make fair and consistent decisions about prosecutions.

1.2 The Code contains information that is important to police officers, to others who work in the criminal justice system and to the general public. It helps the Crown Prosecution Service to play its part in making sure that justice is done.

2. General principles

2.1 Each case is unique and must be considered on its own, but there are general principles that apply in all cases.

2.2 The duty of the Crown Prosecution Service is to make sure that the right person is prosecuted for the right offence and that all relevant facts are given to the court.

2.3 Crown Prosecutors must be fair, independent and objective. They must not let their personal views of the ethnic or national origin, sex, religious beliefs, political views or sexual preference of the offender, victim or witness influence their decisions. They must also not be affected by improper or undue pressure from any source.

3. Review

3.1 Proceedings are usually started by the police. Sometimes they may consult the Crown Prosecution Service before charging a defendant. Each case that the police send to the Crown Prosecution Service is reviewed by a Crown Prosecutor to make sure that it meets the tests set out in this Code. Crown Prosecutors may decide to continue with the original charges, to change the charges or sometimes to stop the proceedings.

3.2 Review, however, is a continuing process so that Crown Prosecutors can take into account any change in circumstances. Wherever possible, they talk to the police first if they are thinking about changing the charges or stopping the proceedings. This gives the police the chance to provide more information that may affect the decision. The Crown Prosecution Service and the police work closely together to reach the right decision, but the final responsibility for the decision rests with the Crown Prosecution Service.

4. The code tests

4.1 There are two stages in the decision to prosecute. The first stage is **the evidential test**. If the case does not pass the evidential test, it must not go ahead, no matter how important or serious it may be. If the case does pass the evidential test, Crown Prosecutors must decide if a prosecution is needed in the public interest.

4.2 This second stage is **the public interest test**. The Crown Prosecution Service will only start or continue a prosecution when the case has passed both tests. The evidential test is explained in section 5 and the public interest test is explained in section 6.

5. The evidential test

5.1 Crown Prosecutors must be satisfied that there is enough evidence to provide a "realistic prospect of conviction" against each defendant on each charge. They must consider what the defence case may be and how that is likely to affect the prosecution case.

5.2. A realistic prospect of conviction is an objective test. It means that a jury or bench of magistrates, properly directed in accordance with the law, is more likely than not to convict the defendant of the charge alleged.

5.3 When deciding whether there is enough evidence to prosecute, Crown Prosecutors must consider whether the evidence can be used and is reliable. There will be many cases in which the evidence does not give any cause for concern. But there will also be cases in which the evidence may not be as strong as it first appears. Crown Prosecutors must ask themselves the following questions:

CAN THE EVIDENCE BE USED IN COURT?

(a) Is it likely that the evidence will be excluded by the court? There are certain legal rules which might mean that evidence which seems relevant cannot be given at a trial. For example, is it likely that the evidence will be excluded because of the way in which it was gathered or because of the rule against using hearsay as evidence? If so, is there enough other evidence for a realistic prospect of conviction?

IS THE EVIDENCE RELIABLE?

(b) Is it likely that a confession is unreliable, for example, because of the defendant's age, intelligence or lack of understanding?

(c) Is the witness's background likely to weaken the prosecution case? For example, does the witness have any dubious motive that may affect his or her attitude to the case or a relevant previous conviction?

(d) If the identity of the defendant is likely to be questioned, is the evidence about this strong enough?

5.4 Crown Prosecutors should not ignore evidence because they are not sure that it can be used or is reliable. But they should look closely at it when deciding if there is a realistic prospect of conviction.

6. The public interest test

6.1 In 1951, Lord Shawcross, who was Attorney-General, made the classic statement on public interest, which has been supported by Attorneys-General ever since: "It has never been the rule in this country—I hope it never will be—that suspected criminal offences must automatically be the subject of prosecution". (House of Commons Debates, volume 483, column 681, January 29, 1951.)

6.2 The public interest must be considered in each case where there is enough evidence to provide a realistic prospect of conviction. In cases of any seriousness, a prosecution will usually take place unless there are public interest factors tending against prosecution which clearly outweigh those tending in favour. Although there may be public interest factors against prosecution in a particular case, often the prosecution should go ahead and those factors should be put to the court for consideration when sentence is being passed.

6.3 Crown Prosecutors must balance factors for and against prosecution carefully and fairly. Public interest factors that can affect the decision to prosecute usually depend on the seriousness of the offence or the circumstances of the offender. Some factors may increase the need to prosecute but others may suggest that another course of action would be better.

The following lists of some common public interest factors, both for and against prosecution, are not exhaustive. The factors that apply will depend on the facts in each case.

SOME COMMON PUBLIC INTEREST FACTORS IN FAVOUR OF PROSECUTION

6.4 The more serious the offence, the more likely it is that a prosecution will be needed in the public interest. A prosecution is likely to be needed if:

(a) a conviction is likely to result in a significant sentence;

(b) a weapon was used or violence was threatened during the commission of the offence;

(c) the offence was committed against a person serving the public (for example, a police or prison officer, or a nurse);

(d) the defendant was in a position of authority or trust;

(e) the evidence shows that the defendant was a ringleader or an organiser of the offence;

(f) there is evidence that the offence was premeditated;

(g) there is evidence that the offence was carried out by a group;

(h) the victim of the offence was vulnerable, has been put in considerable fear, or suffered personal attack, damage or disturbance;

(i) the offence was motivated by any form of discrimination against the victim's ethnic or national origin, sex, religious beliefs, political views or sexual preference;

(j) there is a marked difference between the actual or mental ages of the defendant and the victim, or if there is any element of corruption;

(k) the defendant's previous convictions or cautions are relevant to the present offence;

(l) the defendant is alleged to have committed the offence whilst under an order of the court;

(m) there are grounds for believing that the offence is likely to be continued or repeated, for example, by a history of recurring conduct; or

(n) the offence, although not serious in itself, is widespread in the area where it was committed.

SOME COMMON PUBLIC INTEREST FACTORS AGAINST PROSECUTION

6.5 A prosecution is less likely to be needed if:

(a) the court is likely to impose a very small or nominal penalty;

(b) the offence was committed as a result of a genuine mistake or misunderstanding (these factors must be balanced against the seriousness of the offence);

(c) the loss or harm can be described as minor and was the result of a single incident, particularly if it was caused by a misjudgment;

(d) there has been a long delay between the offence taking place and the date of the trial, unless:

- the offence is serious;
- the delay has been caused in part by the defendant;
- the offence has only recently come to light; or
- the complexity of the offence has meant that there has been a long investigation;

(e) a prosecution is likely to have a very bad effect on the victim's physical or mental health, always bearing in mind the seriousness of the offence;

(f) the defendant is elderly or is, or was at the time of the offence, suffering from significant mental or physical ill health, unless the offence is serious or there is a real possibility that it may be repeated. The Crown Prosecution Service, where necessary, applies Home Office guidelines about how to deal with mentally disordered offenders. Crown Prosecutors must balance the desirability of diverting a defendant who is suffering from significant mental or physical ill health with the need to safeguard the general public;

(g) the defendant has put right the loss or harm that was caused (but defendants must not avoid prosecution simply because they can pay compensation); or

(h) details may be made public that could harm sources of information, international relations or national security.

6.6 Deciding on the public interest is not simply a matter of adding up the number of factors on each side. Crown Prosecutors must decide how important each factor is in the circumstances of each case and go on to make an overall assessment.

The relationship between the victim and the public interest

6.7 The Crown Prosecution Service acts in the public interest, not just in the interests of any one individual. But Crown Prosecutors must always think very carefully about the interests of the victim, which are an important factor, when deciding where the public interest lies.

Youth offenders

6.8 Crown Prosecutors must consider the interests of a youth when deciding whether it is in the public interest to prosecute. The stigma of a conviction can cause very serious harm to the prospects of a youth offender or a young adult. Young offenders can sometimes be dealt with without going to court. But Crown Prosecutors should not avoid prosecuting simply because of the defendant's age. The seriousness of the offence or the offender's past behaviour may make prosecution necessary.

Police cautions

6.9 The police make the decision to caution an offender in accordance with Home Office guidelines. If the defendant admits the offence, cautioning is the most common alternative to a court appearance. Crown Prosecutors, where necessary, apply the same guidelines and should look at the alternatives to prosecution when they consider the public interest. Crown Prosecutors should tell the police if they think that a caution would be more suitable than a prosecution.

7. Charges

7.1 Crown Prosecutors should select charges which:

(a) reflect the seriousness of the offending;

(b) give the court adequate sentencing powers, and

(c) enable the case to be presented in a clear and simple way.

This means that Crown Prosecutors may not always continue with the most serious charge where there is a choice. Further, Crown Prosecutors should not continue with more charges than are necessary.

7.2 Crown Prosecutors should never go ahead with more charges than are necessary just to encourage a defendant to plead guilty to a few. In the same way, they should never go ahead with a more serious charge just to encourage a defendant to plead guilty to a less serious one.

7.3 Crown Prosecutors should not change the charge simply because of the decision made by the court or the defendant about where the case will be heard.

8. Mode of trial

8.1 The Crown Prosecution Service applies the current guidelines for magistrates who have to decide whether cases should be tried in the Crown Court when the offence gives the option. (See the "National Mode of Trial Guidelines" issued by the Lord Chief Justice.) Crown Prosecutors should recommend Crown Court trial when they are satisfied that the guidelines require them to do so.

8.2 Speed must never be the only reason for asking for a case to stay in the magistrates' courts. But Crown Prosecutors should consider the effect of any likely delay if they send a case to the Crown Court, and any possible stress on victims and witnesses if the case is delayed.

9. Accepting guilty pleas

9.1 Defendants may want to plead guilty to some, but not all, of the charges. Or they may want to plead guilty to a different, possibly less serious, charge because they are admitting only part of the crime. Crown Prosecutors should only accept the defendant's plea if they think the court is able to pass a sentence that matches the seriousness of the offending. Crown Prosecutors must never accept a guilty plea just because it is convenient.

10. Re-starting a prosecution

10.1 People should be able to rely on decisions taken by the Crown Prosecution Service. Normally, if the Crown Prosecution Service tells a suspect or defendant that there will not be a prosecution, or that the prosecution has been stopped, that is the end of the matter and the case will not start again. But occasionally there are special reasons why the Crown Prosecution Service will re-start the prosecution, particularly if the case is serious.

10.2 These reasons include:

   (a) rare case where a new look at the original decision shows that it was clearly wrong and should not be allowed to stand;

   (b) cases which are stopped so that more evidence which is likely to become available in the fairly near future can be collected and prepared. In these cases, the Crown Prosecutor will tell the defendant that the prosecution may well start again;

   (c) cases which are stopped because of a lack of evidence but where more significant evidence is discovered later.

11. Conclusion

11.1 The Crown Prosecution Service is a public service headed by the Director of Public Prosecutions. It is answerable to Parliament through the Attorney General. The Code for Crown Prosecutors is issued under section 10 of the Prosecution of Offences Act 1985 and is a public document. This is the third edition and it replaces all earlier versions. Changes to the Code are made from time to time and these are also published.

11.2 The Code is designed to make sure that everyone knows the principles that the Crown Prosecution Service applies when carrying out its work. Police officers should take account of the principles of the Code when they are deciding whether to charge a defendant with an offence. By applying the same principles, everyone involved in the criminal justice system is helping the system to treat victims fairly, and to prosecute defendants fairly but effectively.

APPENDIX III

The Magistrates' Association Sentencing Guidelines

THE MAGISTRATES' ASSOCIATION SENTENCING GUIDELINES

CONTENTS

Page numbers refer to page numbers in The Magistrates' Association's Sentencing Guide.
Page numbers in square brackets refer to the pages where they are reproduced in this Appendix.

INTRODUCTION AND USER GUIDE

1. Introduction

The Magistrates' Association's *Sentencing Guidelines* cover offences with which magistrates deal regularly and frequently in the *adult criminal courts*. They provide a sentencing structure which sets out how to:

- establish the seriousness of each case
- determine the most appropriate way of dealing with it.

The *Sentencing Guidelines* provide a method for considering individual cases and a guideline from which discussion should properly flow; but *they are not a tariff and should never be used as such*.

2. Using the Sentencing Structure

2.1 GENERAL PRINCIPLES

Only magistrates decide sentence.

The sentencing structure used was established by the Criminal Justice Act 1991. This reaffirmed the principle of *just deserts* so that any penalty must reflect the seriousness of the offence for which it is imposed and the personal circumstances of the offender. Magistrates must always start the sentencing process by taking full account of all the circumstances of the offence and making a judicial assessment of the seriousness category into which it falls.

In every case, the Criminal Justice Act 1991 requires you to consider:

- is discharge, compensation or a fine appropriate?
- is the offence serious enough for a community penalty?
- is it so serious that only custody is appropriate?

Only when the first assessment of seriousness has been made should offender-related mitigation be taken into account. This may not be used to raise the first assessment of seriousness to a higher category; but it may lower it. For example, offender mitigation may bring the seriousness level below the custody threshold into the community sentence range.

ESTABLISHING THE SERIOUSNESS OF THE OFFENCE

The guidance for each offence is set for a case of average seriousness and the decision making process involves *establishing the seriousness of the case before the court compared with other offences of the same type*. Users should:

- consider the various seriousness indicators, rmembering that some will carry more weight than others.
- make sure that all aggravating and mitigating factors are considered. The lists in the *Guidelines* are neither exhaustive nor a substitute for the personal judgment of magistrates. Factors which do not appear in the *Guidelines* may be important in individual cases.
- always bear in mind that the commission of an offence on bail aggravates its seriousness.
- take care in using previous convictions or any failure to respond to previous sentences in assessing seriousness. We recommend that courts should identify any convictions relevant for this purpose and then consider to what extent they affect the seriousness of the present offence.
- note that when there are several offences before the court, the totality principle requires a court to consider the total sentence in relation to the totality of the offending and in relation to sentence levels for other crimes.

When you have formed an initial assessment of the seriousness of the offence, consider the offender.

2.3 USING OFFENDER MITIGATION

The guidelines set out some examples of offender mitigation but there are frequently others to be considered in individual cases. Any offender mitigation which the court accepts must lead to some downward revision of the initial assessment of seriousness, although this revision may sometimes be very minor.

A previous criminal record may reduce offender mitigation.

2.4 SENTENCE DISCOUNT

The law requires that the court reduces the sentence for a timely guilty plea but this provision should be used with judicial flexibility. A timely guilty plea may attract a sentencing discount of up to one third but the precise amount of discount will depend on the facts of each case and a last minute plea of guilty may attract only a minimal reduction.

Discount may be given in respect of the fine or periods of community service or custody. Periods of mandatory disqualification or mandatory penalty point cannot be reduced for a guilty plea.

2.5 The available penalties

2.5.1 ABSOLUTE DISCHARGE

This should be used in the most minor of cases. It acknowledges that an offence has been committed but marks the court's intention to take no further action.

2.5.2 CONDITIONAL DISCHARGE

This is a useful disposal in minor cases where the court needs a sanction which directly discourages further offending.

2.5.3 COMPENSATION

Magistrates have the power to award compensation for personal injury, loss or damage up to a total of £5,000 for each offence, including offences taken into consideration; and have a duty always to consider compensation in appropriate cases. When pronouncing sentence you must give an explanation in open court if you decide not to make an award.

Nevertheless, magistrates should not become involved in disputed and complicated cases. Compensation should only be awarded in clear, uncomplicated cases, and the following points need to be borne in mind.

- personal injury need not mean physical injury, *e.g.* an award may be made for terror or distress resulting from an offence.

- compensation may not generally be awarded for injury, loss or damage resulting from a road accident. Consult your clerk for advice in any cases where this point arises.

- where compensation is awarded for damage, the cost of any necessary repairs must be proved to the satisfaction of the court.

In fixing the amount of a compensation order, the defendant's means must be taken into account and the order should normally be payable within 12 months. In exceptional circumstances it may be payable within a period of up to three years; but courts should always consider whether such an extended order is in the interests of the victim.

A table of suggested awards is set out on page 453.

2.5.4 FINES

Fines are appropriate for cases which are neither serious enough to attract a community penalty nor so serious that only custody is appropriate. The level of fine for any offence must be commensurate with the seriousness of the offence and must take the offender's means into account.

The fine must not exceed the upper limit set by statute for the level of the offence, *i.e.*

For a level 1 offence:	£200
For a level 2 offence:	£500
For a level 3 offence:	£1,000
For a level 4 offence:	£2,500
For a level 5 offence:	£5,000

Before fixing the amount of the fine, the court must enquire into the offender's financial circumstances and we recommend the regular use of means forms.

The Guideline fines in this publication are set at three levels:

Low income—about £100 net per week from all sources
Average income—about £250 net per week from all sources
High income—about £600 net per week from all sources

The fines have not been discounted for a guilty plea.

The principle behind determining the amount of a fine should be that of *equally of hardship rather than equality of monetary penalty*. Punishment does not lie in the amount of a fine but in the degree of hardship and inconvenience caused by the need to pay it. The *just deserts* principle means that each offender should experience the loss of spending power which his or her offending behaviour merits, and levels of fine should always be set with this principle in mind.

Fines are due to be paid at the time they are imposed. Where time to pay is allowed it should not exceed 12 months: in these circumstances best practice should be to order an amount to be paid immediately and then to set a realistic weekly amount, and a date for a court hearing for compliance with the order to be reviewed.

2.5.5 COMMUNITY PENALTIES

Where the offence is *serious enough* a community penalty will be used. They are:

- attendance centre orders (12–36 hours)
- probation orders, with or without special requirements (six months to three years)
- community service orders (40–240 hours' upaid work)
- combination orders (1–3 years' probation plus 40–100 hours of community service)

It is good practice always to order a pre-sentence report when a community penalty is under consideration.

The restrictions on liberty imposed by the sentence must be commensurate with the seriousness of the offence and the order must be the one most suitable for the offender. Rehabilitation is a factor to be taken into account in sentencing and a community penalty may be particularly appropriate for this purpose.

2.5.6 CUSTODY

Custody is only appropriate where the offence is so serious that no other form of disposal is justified. It is good practice to order a pre-sentence report before imposing custody.

An offence is so serious that only custody is appropriate when right thinking members of the public, knowing all the facts, would feel that justice had not been done by the passing of any sentence other than a custodial one (*R. v. Cox* [1993] 96 Cr.App.R. 452, 455).

3. The role of the justices' clerk/court clerk in sentencing

Sentencing is a complex field. Although the decision on sentence rests entirely with the bench, the clerk is under a duty to advise on available sentences and on any case law that may apply to particular types of offence. It is especially important to ask for advice when the bench is considering imposing a custoidal sentence.

The clerk's role is described by a Practice Direction issued by the Lord Chief Justice in 1981:

If it appears to him necessary to do so, or he is requested by the justices, the justices' clerk has the responsibility to ... advise the justices generally on the range of penalties which the law allows them to impose and on any guidance relevant to the decisions of the superior courts and other authorities.

COMPENSATION ORDERS

Priorities

Compensation is an order in its own right, and should be treated as such—particularly where the offender has insufficient means to pay a fine as well.

Damages

Where compensation is to be awarded for damage to, for example, a window, the cost must be proved or agreed.

Payment by instalments

An order for compensation should normally be payable within 12 months, but this can be exceeded up to a three year limit where the circumstances justify it.

Giving reasons

Powers of the Criminal Courts Act 1973, s.35 states that:

> "A court shall give reasons on passing sentence if it does not make a (compensation) order in a case where this section empowers it to do so."

Powers and limitations

Magistrates have power to award compensation for personal injury loss or damage up to a total of £5,000 for each offence. The compensation may relate to offences taken into consideration. There are exceptions including injury, loss or damage due to a road accident unless the damage results from an offence under the Theft Act 1968 or the offender is uninsured and the Motor Insurers Bureau will not cover the loss—if in any doubt, seek advice from the clerk.

An order for compensation should be considered whether or not there is an application by or on behalf of the victim. An award in the magistrates' court will not preclude a civil claim. "Personal injury" need not be a physical injury. An award can be made, *e.g.* for terror or distress caused by the offence.

Criminal Injuries Compensation Board

The Criminal Injuries Compensation Scheme is intended to compensate victims of violent crime and particularly those who are seriously injured. The minimum award is currently £1,000. Courts are encouraged to order offenders to compensate the victim whether or not the injury comes within the scope of the Criminal Injuries Compensation Scheme, in order to bring home to offenders the personal consequences of their actions. To prevent double compensation for the same injury the Scheme provides for an award to be reduced by the amount of any compensation previously ordered by a criminal court.

Suggested compensation

Damages are assessed under two main headings—**general damages**, which is compensation for the pain and suffering of the injury itself and for any loss of facility; and **special damages**, which is compensation for financial loss sustained as a result of the injury, *e.g.* loss of earnings, dental expense, etc. The suggestions given in the table on the following page are for general damages.

The following guidelines are taken from the Home Office Circular issued in August 1993.

The figures below are only a very general guide and may be increased or decreased according to the medical evidence, the victim's sex, age and any other factors which appear to the court to be relevant in the particular case. If the court does not have enough information to make a decision, then the matter should be adjourned to obtain more facts.

TYPE OF INJURY		SUGGESTED AWARD
Graze	depending on size	up to £50
Bruise	depending on size	up to £75
Black eye		£100
Cut: no permanent scarring	depending on size and whether stitched	£75–£500
Sprain	depending on loss of mobility	£100–£1,000
Loss of a non-front tooth	depending on cosmetic effect and age of victim	£250–£500
Other minor injury	causing reasonable absence from work (2–3) weeks	£550–£850
Loss of a front tooth		£1,000
Facial scar	however small—resulting in permanent disfigurement	£750+
Jaw	fractured (wired)	£2,750
Nasal	undisplaced fracture of the nasal bone	£750
Nasal	displaced fracture of bone requiring manipulation	£1,000
Nasal	not causing fracture but displaced septum requiring sub-mucous resection	£1,750
Wrist	simple fracture with complete recovery in a few weeks	£1,750–£2,500
Wrist	displaced fracture—limb in plaster for some 6 weeks; full recovery 6–12 months	£2,500+
Finger	fractured little finger; assuming full recovery after a few weeks	£750
Leg or arm	simple fracture of tibia, fibula, ulna or radius with full recovery in three weeks	£2,500
Laparotomy	stomach scar 6–8 inches long (resulting from exploratory operation)	£3,500

Public Order Act 1986, s.3 Triable either way - see Mode of Trial Guidelines Penalty: Level 5 and/or 6 months	**Affray**

CONSIDER THE SERIOUSNESS OF THE OFFENCE
(INCLUDING THE IMPACT ON THE VICTIM)

GUIDELINE: ➤

IS COMPENSATION, DISCHARGE OR FINE APPROPRIATE?
IS IT SERIOUS ENOUGH FOR A COMMUNITY PENALTY?
IS IT SO SERIOUS THAT ONLY CUSTODY IS APPROPRIATE?
ARE MAGISTRATES' COURTS' POWERS APPROPRIATE?

 CONSIDER AGGRAVATING AND MITIGATING FACTORS

for example
  Racial motivation
  Busy public place
  Group action
  People actually put in fear
  Vulnerable victim(s)

  Offence committed on bail
  Previous convictions and failures to respond
  to previous sentences, if relevant
  This list is not exhaustive

for example
  Offender acting alone
  Provocation
  Did not start the trouble
  Stopped as soon as the police arrived
  This list is not exhaustive

CONSIDER OFFENDER MITIGATION

for example
  Age, health (physical or mental)
  Co-operation with the police
  Voluntary compensation
  Remorse

CONSIDER YOUR SENTENCE

Compare it with the suggested guideline level of sentence and reconsider
your reasons carefully if you have chosen a sentence at a different level.
Consider a discount for a timely guilty plea.

DECIDE YOUR SENTENCE

N.B. COMPENSATION - Give reasons if not awarding compensation

Remember: These are GUIDELINES not a tariff

Aggravated Vehicle-taking

Theft Act 1968, s. 12A as inserted by
Aggravated Vehicle-Taking Act 1992
Triable either way - but in certain cases
summarily only - consult clerk.
Penalty: Level 5 and/or 6 months
Must endorse and disqualify at least 12 months:

CONSIDER THE SERIOUSNESS OF THE OFFENCE
(INCLUDING THE IMPACT ON THE VICTIM)

IS COMPENSATION, DISCHARGE OR FINE APPROPRIATE?
IS IT SERIOUS ENOUGH FOR A COMMUNITY PENALTY?
GUIDELINE: ➤   *IS IT SO SERIOUS THAT ONLY CUSTODY IS APPROPRIATE?*
ARE MAGISTRATES' COURTS' POWERS APPROPRIATE?

➕ CONSIDER AGGRAVATING AND MITIGATING FACTORS ➖

for example
Avoiding detection or apprehension
Competitive driving: racing, showing off
Disregard of warnings, *e.g.* from passengers
or others in vicinity
Group action
Pre-meditated
Serious injury/damage
Serious risk

Offence committed on bail
Previous convictions and failures to respond
to previous sentences, if relevant
This list is not exhaustive

for example
Impulsive
No competitiveness/racing
Passenger only
Single incident of bad driving
Speed not excessive
Very minor injury/damage
This list is not exhaustive

CONSIDER OFFENDER MITIGATION

for example
Age, health (physical or mental)
Co-operation with the police
Voluntary compensation
Remorse

CONSIDER YOUR SENTENCE

*Compare it with the suggested guideline level of sentence and reconsider
your reasons carefully if you have chosen a sentence at a different level.
Consider a discount for a timely guilty plea.*

DECIDE YOUR SENTENCE

N.B. COMPENSATION - Give reasons if not awarding compensation

Remember: These are GUIDELINES not a tariff

Offences Against the Person Act 1861, s.47 Triable either way - see Mode of Trial Guidelines Penalty: Level 5 and/or 6 months	Assault — Actual Bodily Harm

CONSIDER THE SERIOUSNESS OF THE OFFENCE
(INCLUDING THE IMPACT ON THE VICTIM)

GUIDELINE: ➤

IS COMPENSATION, DISCHARGE OR FINE APPROPRIATE?

IS IT SERIOUS ENOUGH FOR A COMMUNITY PENALTY?

IS IT SO SERIOUS THAT ONLY CUSTODY IS APPROPRIATE?

ARE MAGISTRATES' COURTS' POWERS APPROPRIATE?

 CONSIDER AGGRAVATING AND MITIGATING FACTORS

for example
- Racial motivation
- Deliberate kicking or biting
- Extensive injuries (may be psychiatric)
- Group action
- Offender in position of authority
- Premeditated
- Victim particularly vulnerable
- Victim serving public
- Weapon

Offence committed on bail
Previous convictions and failures to respond
to previous sentences, if relevant
This list is not exhaustive

for example
- Impulsive
- Minor injury
- Provocation
- Single blow
- *This list is not exhaustive*

CONSIDER OFFENDER MITIGATION

for example
- Age, health (physical or mental)
- Co-operation with the police
- Voluntary compensation
- Remorse

CONSIDER YOUR SENTENCE

Compare it with the suggested guideline level of sentence and reconsider your reasons carefully if you have chosen a sentence at a different level. Consider a discount for a timely guilty plea.

DECIDE YOUR SENTENCE

N.B. COMPENSATION - Give reasons if not awarding compensation

Remember: These are GUIDELINES not a tariff

Assault on a Police Officer

Police Act 1996, s.89
Triable only summarily
Penalty: Level 5 and/or 6 months

CONSIDER THE SERIOUSNESS OF THE OFFENCE
(INCLUDING THE IMPACT ON THE VICTIM)

IS COMPENSATION, DISCHARGE OR FINE APPROPRIATE?

IS IT SERIOUS ENOUGH FOR A COMMUNITY PENALTY?

GUIDELINE: ➤   *IS IT SO SERIOUS THAT ONLY CUSTODY IS APPROPRIATE?*

 CONSIDER AGGRAVATING AND MITIGATING FACTORS

for example
Any injuries caused
Gross disregard for police authority
Group action
Premeditated

Offence committed on bail
Previous convictions and failures to respond
to previous sentences, if relevant
This list is not exhaustive

for example
Impulsive action
Unaware that person was a Police Officer
This list is not exhaustive

CONSIDER OFFENDER MITIGATION

for example
Age, health (physical or mental)
Co-operation with the police
Voluntary compensation
Remorse

CONSIDER YOUR SENTENCE

Compare it with the suggested guideline level of sentence and reconsider
your reasons carefully if you have chosen a sentence at a different level.
Consider a discount for a timely guilty plea.

DECIDE YOUR SENTENCE

N.B. COMPENSATION - Give reasons if not awarding compensation

Remember: These are GUIDELINES not a tariff

Theft Act 1968, s.9 Triable either way - see Mode of Trial Guidelines Penalty: Level 5 and/or 6 months	Burglary (Dwelling)

CONSIDER THE SERIOUSNESS OF THE OFFENCE
(INCLUDING THE IMPACT ON THE VICTIM)

GUIDELINE: ➤   *IS COMPENSATION, DISCHARGE OR FINE APPROPRIATE?*
IS IT SERIOUS ENOUGH FOR A COMMUNITY PENALTY?
IS IT SO SERIOUS THAT ONLY CUSTODY IS APPROPRIATE?
ARE MAGISTRATES' COURTS' POWERS APPROPRIATE?

 ## CONSIDER AGGRAVATING AND MITIGATING FACTORS

for example
    Racial motivation
    Deliberately frightening occupants
    Group offence
    People in house
    Professional operation
    Forcible entry
    Soiling, ransacking, damage

    Offence committed on bail
    Previous convictions and failures to respond
    to previous sentences, if relevant
    This list is not exhaustive

for example
    Low value
    Nobody frightened
    No damage or disturbance
    No forcible entry
    Opportunist
    This list is not exhaustive

CONSIDER OFFENDER MITIGATION

for example
    Age, health (physical or mental)
    Co-operation with the police
    Voluntary compensation
    Remorse

CONSIDER YOUR SENTENCE

*Compare it with the suggested guideline level of sentence and reconsider
your reasons carefully if you have chosen a sentence at a different level.
Consider a discount for a timely guilty plea.*

DECIDE YOUR SENTENCE

N.B. COMPENSATION - Give reasons if not awarding compensation

Remember: These are GUIDELINES not a tariff

Burglary (Non-dwelling)

Theft Act 1968, s.9
Triable either way - see Mode of Trial Guidelines
Penalty: Level 5 and/or 6 months

CONSIDER THE SERIOUSNESS OF THE OFFENCE
(INCLUDING THE IMPACT ON THE VICTIM)

GUIDELINE: ➤

IS COMPENSATION, DISCHARGE OR FINE APPROPRIATE?
IS IT SERIOUS ENOUGH FOR A COMMUNITY PENALTY?
IS IT SO SERIOUS THAT ONLY CUSTODY IS APPROPRIATE?
ARE MAGISTRATES' COURTS' POWERS APPROPRIATE?

 ### CONSIDER AGGRAVATING AND MITIGATING FACTORS

for example
- Racial motivation
- Deliberately frightening occupants
- Group offence
- Night time
- Professional operation
- Forcible entry
- Soiling, ransacking, damage
- Serious harm to business

  Offence committed on bail
  Previous convictions and failures to respond
  to previous sentences, if relevant
  This list is not exhaustive

for example
- Low value
- Nobody frightened
- No damage or disturbance
- No forcible entry
- *This list is not exhaustive*

CONSIDER OFFENDER MITIGATION

for example
- Age, health (physical or mental)
- Co-operation with the police
- Voluntary compensation
- Remorse

CONSIDER YOUR SENTENCE

Compare it with the suggested guideline level of sentence and reconsider
your reasons carefully if you have chosen a sentence at a different level.
Consider a discount for a timely guilty plea.

DECIDE YOUR SENTENCE

N.B. COMPENSATION - Give reasons if not awarding compensation

Remember: These are GUIDELINES not a tariff

Misuse of Drugs Act 1971 Triable either way - see Mode of Trial Guidelines Penalty: Level 5 and/or 6 months	Class A Drugs – Possession

CONSIDER THE SERIOUSNESS OF THE OFFENCE

GUIDELINE: ➤

IS COMPENSATION, DISCHARGE OR FINE APPROPRIATE?
IS IT SERIOUS ENOUGH FOR A COMMUNITY PENALTY?
IS IT SO SERIOUS THAT ONLY CUSTODY IS APPROPRIATE?
ARE MAGISTRATES' COURTS' POWERS APPROPRIATE?

 CONSIDER AGGRAVATING AND MITIGATING FACTORS

for example	**for example**
An amount other than a very small quantity	Very small quantity
	This list is not exhaustive
Offence committed on bail	
Previous convictions and failures to respond	
to previous sentences, if relevant	
This list is not exhaustive	

CONSIDER OFFENDER MITIGATION

for example
Age, health (physical or mental)
Co-operation with the police
Remorse

CONSIDER YOUR SENTENCE

Compare it with the suggested guideline level of sentence and reconsider
your reasons carefully if you have chosen a sentence at a different level.
Consider a discount for a timely guilty plea. Consider forfeiture and destruction.

DECIDE YOUR SENTENCE

Remember: These are GUIDELINES not a tariff

Class A Drugs – Production, Supply	Misuse of Drugs Act 1971 Triable either way - see Mode of Trial Guidelines Penalty: Level 5 and/or 6 months

CONSIDER THE SERIOUSNESS OF THE OFFENCE
(INCLUDING THE IMPACT ON THE VICTIM)

GUIDELINE: ➤

IS COMPENSATION, DISCHARGE OR FINE APPROPRIATE?
IS IT SERIOUS ENOUGH FOR A COMMUNITY PENALTY?
IS IT SO SERIOUS THAT ONLY CUSTODY IS APPROPRIATE?
ARE MAGISTRATES' COURTS' POWERS APPROPRIATE?

 ## CONSIDER AGGRAVATING AND MITIGATING FACTORS

for example
    Commercial production
    Large amount
    Deliberate adulteration
    Venue, eg. prisons, educational
    establishments
    Sophisticated operation

    Offence committed on bail
    Previous convictions and failures to respond
    to previous sentences, if relevant
    This list is not exhaustive

for example
    Small amount
    This list is not exhaustive

CONSIDER OFFENDER MITIGATION

for example
    Age, health (physical or mental)
    Co-operation with the police
    Remorse

CONSIDER YOUR SENTENCE

Compare it with the suggested guideline level of sentence and reconsider
your reasons carefully if you have chosen a sentence at a different level.
Consider a discount for a timely guilty plea. Consider forfeiture and destruction.

DECIDE YOUR SENTENCE

Remember: These are GUIDELINES not a tariff

Misuse of Drugs Acts 1971 Triable either way - see Mode of Trial Guidelines Penalty: Level 4 and/or 3 months	Class B Drugs — Possession

CONSIDER THE SERIOUSNESS OF THE OFFENCE

GUIDELINE: ➤   *IS COMPENSATION, DISCHARGE OR FINE APPROPRIATE?*
                 IS IT SERIOUS ENOUGH FOR A COMMUNITY PENALTY?
                 IS IT SO SERIOUS THAT ONLY CUSTODY IS APPROPRIATE?
                 ARE MAGISTRATES' COURTS' POWERS APPROPRIATE?

 ## CONSIDER AGGRAVATING AND MITIGATING FACTORS

for example
   Large amount

   Offence committed on bail
   Previous convictions and failures to respond
   to previous sentences, if relevant
   This list is not exhaustive

for example
   Small amount
   This list is not exhaustive

CONSIDER OFFENDER MITIGATION

for example
   Age, health (physical or mental)
   Co-operation with the police
   Remorse

CONSIDER YOUR SENTENCE

*Compare it with the suggested guideline level of sentence and reconsider
your reasons carefully if you have chosen a sentence at a different level.
Consider a discount for a timely guilty plea. Consider forfeiture and destruction.*

DECIDE YOUR SENTENCE

GUIDELINE FINES		
LOW INCOME	AVERAGE INCOME	HIGH INCOME
£90	£225	£540

Remember: These are GUIDELINES not a tariff

Class B Drugs — Supply: Possession with intent to supply	Misuse of Drugs Act 1971 Triable either way - see Mode of Trial Guidelines Penalty: Level 5 and/or 6 months

CONSIDER THE SERIOUSNESS OF THE OFFENCE
(INCLUDING THE IMPACT ON THE VICTIM)

GUIDELINE: ➤

IS COMPENSATION, DISCHARGE OR FINE APPROPRIATE?
IS IT SERIOUS ENOUGH FOR A COMMUNITY PENALTY?
IS IT SO SERIOUS THAT ONLY CUSTODY IS APPROPRIATE?
ARE MAGISTRATES' COURTS' POWERS APPROPRIATE?

➕ CONSIDER AGGRAVATING AND MITIGATING FACTORS ➖

for example	for example
Commercial production Large amount Venue, eg. prisons, educational establishments Deliberate adulteration Offence committed on bail Previous convictions and failures to respond to previous sentences, if relevant *This list is not exhaustive*	Not commercial Small amount *This list is not exhaustive*

CONSIDER OFFENDER MITIGATION

for example
Age, health (physical or mental)
Co-operation with the police
Remorse

CONSIDER YOUR SENTENCE

*Compare it with the suggested guideline level of sentence and reconsider
your reasons carefully if you have chosen a sentence at a different level.
Consider a discount for a timely guilty plea. Consider forfeiture and destruction.*

DECIDE YOUR SENTENCE

Remember: These are GUIDELINES not a tariff

Criminal Justice Act 1988, s.39 Triable only summarily Penalty: Level 5 and/or 6 months	**Common Assault**

CONSIDER THE SERIOUSNESS OF THE OFFENCE
(INCLUDING THE IMPACT ON THE VICTIM)

IS COMPENSATION, DISCHARGE OR FINE APPROPRIATE?

GUIDELINE: ➤   *IS IT SERIOUS ENOUGH FOR A COMMUNITY PENALTY?*

IS IT SO SERIOUS THAT ONLY CUSTODY IS APPROPRIATE?

 ## CONSIDER AGGRAVATING AND MITIGATING FACTORS

for example
- Racial motivation
- Group action
- Offender in position of authority
- Premeditated
- Injury
- Weapon
- Victim particularly vulnerable
- Victim public servant

Offence committed on bail
Previous convictions and failures to respond
to previous sentences, if relevant
This list is not exhaustive

for example
- Impulsive
- Minor injury
- Provocation
- Single blow
- *This list is not exhaustive*

CONSIDER OFFENDER MITIGATION

for example
- Age, health (physical or mental)
- Co-operation with the police
- Voluntary compensation
- Remorse

CONSIDER YOUR SENTENCE

*Compare it with the suggested guideline level of sentence and reconsider
your reasons carefully if you have chosen a sentence at a different level.
Consider a discount for a timely guilty plea.*

DECIDE YOUR SENTENCE

N.B. COMPENSATION - Give reasons if not awarding compensation

Remember: These are GUIDELINES not a tariff

Criminal Damage	Criminal Damage Act 1971, s.1 Triable either way or summarily only. Consult Clerk Penalty: Either way - Level 5 and/or 6 months Summarily - Level 4 and/or 3 months

CONSIDER THE SERIOUSNESS OF THE OFFENCE
(INCLUDING THE IMPACT ON THE VICTIM)

GUIDELINE: ➤   *IS COMPENSATION, DISCHARGE OR FINE APPROPRIATE?*

IS IT SERIOUS ENOUGH FOR A COMMUNITY PENALTY?

IS IT SO SERIOUS THAT ONLY CUSTODY IS APPROPRIATE?

ARE MAGISTRATES' COURTS' POWERS APPROPRIATE?

 CONSIDER AGGRAVATING AND MITIGATING FACTORS

for example
- Racial motivation
- Deliberate
- Group offence
- Serious damage

Offence committed on bail
Previous convictions and failures to respond
to previous sentences, if relevant
This list is not exhaustive

for example
- Impulsive action
- Minor damage
- Provocation
- *This list is not exhaustive*

CONSIDER OFFENDER MITIGATION

for example
- Age, health (physical or mental)
- Co-operation with the police
- Voluntary compensation
- Remorse

CONSIDER YOUR SENTENCE

*Compare it with the suggested guideline level of sentence and reconsider
your reasons carefully if you have chosen a sentence at a different level.
Consider a discount for a timely guilty plea.*

DECIDE YOUR SENTENCE

GUIDELINE FINES		
LOW INCOME	**AVERAGE INCOME**	**HIGH INCOME**
£135	£340	£810

N.B. COMPENSATION - Give reasons if not awarding compensation

Remember: These are GUIDELINES not a tariff

Misuse of Drugs Act 1971 Triable either way - see Mode of Trial Guideline Penalty: Level 5 and/or 6 months	**Cultivation of Cannabis**

CONSIDER THE SERIOUSNESS OF THE OFFENCE

GUIDELINE: ➤ *IS COMPENSATION, DISCHARGE OR FINE APPROPRIATE?*
IS IT SERIOUS ENOUGH FOR A COMMUNITY PENALTY?
IS IT SO SERIOUS THAT ONLY CUSTODY IS APPROPRIATE?
ARE MAGISTRATES' COURTS' POWERS APPROPRIATE?

CONSIDER AGGRAVATING AND MITIGATING FACTORS

for example
Commercial cultivation
Large quantity

Offence committed on bail
Previous convictions and failures to respond
to previous sentences, if relevant
This list is not exhaustive

for example
For personal use
Not commercial
Not responsible for planting
Small scale culitvation
This list is not exhaustive

CONSIDER OFFENDER MITIGATION

for example
Age, health (physical or mental)
Co-operation with the police
Remorse

CONSIDER YOUR SENTENCE

*Compare it with the suggested guideline level of sentence and reconsider
your reasons carefully if you have chosen a sentence at a different level.
Consider a discount for a timely guilty plea. Consider forfeiture and destruction.*

DECIDE YOUR SENTENCE

GUIDELINE FINES		
LOW INCOME	AVERAGE INCOME	HIGH INCOME
£90	£225	£540

Remember: These are GUIDELINES not a tariff

Drunk and Disorderly	Criminal Justice Act 1967, s.91 Triable only summarily Penalty: Level 3

CONSIDER THE SERIOUSNESS OF THE OFFENCE

GUIDELINE: ➤ *IS COMPENSATION, DISCHARGE OR FINE APPROPRIATE?*

IS IT SERIOUS ENOUGH FOR A COMMUNITY PENALTY?

(PROBATION IS ONLY AVAILABLE COMMUNITY PENALTY FOR THIS OFFENCE)

 ## CONSIDER AGGRAVATING AND MITIGATING FACTORS

for example	for example
Offensive language or behaviour With group Offence committed on bail Previous convictions and failures to respond to previous sentences, if relevant *This list is not exhaustive*	Induced by others No significant distrubance Not threatening *This list is not exhaustive*

CONSIDER OFFENDER MITIGATION

for example
   Age, health (physical or mental)
   Co-operation with the police
   Remorse

CONSIDER YOUR SENTENCE

*Compare it with the suggested guideline level of sentence and reconsider
your reasons carefully if you have chosen a sentence at a different level.
Consider a discount for a timely guilty plea.*

DECIDE YOUR SENTENCE

GUIDELINE FINES		
LOW INCOME	AVERAGE INCOME	HIGH INCOME
£45	£115	£270

Remember: These are GUIDELINES not a tariff

Bail Act 1976, s.6	**Failure to Surrender to Bail**
Triable only summarily	
Penalty: Level 5 and/or 3 months	

CONSIDER THE SERIOUSNESS OF THE OFFENCE

GUIDELINE: >   *IS COMPENSATION, DISCHARGE OR FINE APPROPRIATE?*

IS IT SERIOUS ENOUGH FOR A COMMUNITY PENALTY?

IS IT SO SERIOUS THAT ONLY CUSTODY IS APPROPRIATE?

 ## CONSIDER AGGRAVATING AND MITIGATING FACTORS

for example
   Leaves jurisdiction
   Wilful evasion
   Appears after arrest

   Offence committed on bail
   Previous convictions and failures to respond
   to previous sentences, if relevant
   This list is not exhaustive

for example
   Appears late on day of hearing
   Genuine misunderstanding
   Voluntary surrender
   This list is not exhaustive

CONSIDER OFFENDER MITIGATION

for example
   Age, health (physical or mental)
   Co-operation with the police
   Remorse

CONSIDER YOUR SENTENCE

Compare it with the suggested guideline level of sentence and reconsider your reasons carefully if you have chosen a sentence at a different level. Consider a discount for a timely guilty plea.

DECIDE YOUR SENTENCE

GUIDELINE FINES		
LOW INCOME	**AVERAGE INCOME**	**HIGH INCOME**
£60	£150	£350

Remember: These are GUIDELINES not a tariff

Going Equipped for Theft etc.

Theft Act 1968, s.25
Triable either way - see Mode of Trial Guidelines
Penalty: Level 5 and/or 6 months
May disqualify where committed with reference to the theft or taking of the vehicle

---

CONSIDER THE SERIOUSNESS OF THE OFFENCE

GUIDELINE: ➤
IS COMPENSATION, DISCHARGE OR FINE APPROPRIATE?
IS IT SERIOUS ENOUGH FOR A COMMUNITY PENALTY?
IS IT SO SERIOUS THAT ONLY CUSTODY IS APPROPRIATE?
ARE MAGISTRATES' COURTS' POWERS APPROPRIATE?

 ## CONSIDER AGGRAVATING AND MITIGATING FACTORS

for example
    Premeditated
    Group action
    Sophisticated
    Specialised equipment
    Number of items
    People put in fear

    Offence committed on bail
    Previous convictions and failures to respond
    to previous sentences, if relevant
    This list is not exhaustive

CONSIDER OFFENDER MITIGATION

for example
    Age, health (physical or mental)
    Co-operation with the police
    Remorse

CONSIDER YOUR SENTENCE

Compare it with the suggested guideline level of sentence and reconsider
your reasons carefully if you have chosen a sentence at a different level.
Consider a discount for a timely guilty plea. Consider forfeiture.

DECIDE YOUR SENTENCE

Remember: These are GUIDELINES not a tariff

Theft Act 1968, s.22 Triable either way - see Mode of Trial Guidelines Penalty: Level 5 and/or 6 months	Handling Stolen Goods

CONSIDER THE SERIOUSNESS OF THE OFFENCE
(INCLUDING THE IMPACT ON THE VICTIM)

GUIDELINE: ➤

IS COMPENSATION, DISCHARGE OR FINE APPROPRIATE?
IS IT SERIOUS ENOUGH FOR A COMMUNITY PENALTY?
IS IT SO SERIOUS THAT ONLY CUSTODY IS APPROPRIATE?
ARE MAGISTRATES' COURTS' POWERS APPROPRIATE?

 ## CONSIDER AGGRAVATING AND MITIGATING FACTORS

for example
    Adult involving children
    High value
    Organiser or distributor

    Offence committed on bail
    Previous convictions and failures to respond
    to previous sentences, if relevant
    This list is not exhaustive

for example
    For personal use
    Impulsive action
    Low value
    No financial gain
    Not part of a sophisticated operation
    Single item
    This list is not exhaustive

CONSIDER OFFENDER MITIGATION

for example
    Age, health (physical or mental)
    Co-operation with the police
    Voluntary compensation
    Remorse

CONSIDER YOUR SENTENCE

Compare it with the suggested guideline level of sentence and reconsider
your reasons carefully if you have chosen a sentence at a different level.
Consider a discount for a timely guilty plea.

DECIDE YOUR SENTENCE

N.B. COMPENSATION - Give reasons if not awarding compensation

Remember: These are GUIDELINES not a tariff

Harassment, Alarm or Distress

Public Order Act 1986, s.5
Triable only summarily
Penalty: Level 3

CONSIDER THE SERIOUSNESS OF THE OFFENCE
(INCLUDING THE IMPACT ON THE VICTIM)

GUIDELINE: ➤   *IS COMPENSATION, DISCHARGE OR FINE APPROPRIATE?*

IS IT SERIOUS ENOUGH FOR A COMMUNITY PENALTY?

(PROBATION IS ONLY AVAILABLE COMMUNITY PENALTY FOR THIS OFFENCE)

 ### CONSIDER AGGRAVATING AND MITIGATING FACTORS

for example
    Racial motivation
    Group action
    Vulnerable victim

    Offence committed on bail
    Previous convictions and failures to respond
    to previous sentences, if relevant
    This list is not exhaustive

for example
    Stopped as soon as police arrived
    Trivial incident
    This list is not exhaustive

CONSIDER OFFENDER MITIGATION

for example
    Age, health (physical or mental)
    Co-operation with the police
    Voluntary compensation
    Remorse

CONSIDER YOUR SENTENCE

*Compare it with the suggested guideline level of sentence and reconsider
your reasons carefully if you have chosen a sentence at a different level.
Consider a discount for a timely guilty plea.*

DECIDE YOUR SENTENCE

GUIDELINE FINES		
LOW INCOME	AVERAGE INCOME	HIGH INCOME
£90	£225	£540

N.B. COMPENSATION - Give reasons if not awarding compensation

Remember: These are GUIDELINES not a tariff

Public Order Act 1986, s.4A Triable only summarily Penalty: Level 5 and/or 6 months	**Harassment, Alarm or Distress with Intent**

CONSIDER THE SERIOUSNESS OF THE OFFENCE
(INCLUDING THE IMPACT ON THE VICTIM)

IS COMPENSATION, DISCHARGE OR FINE APPROPRIATE?

IS IT SERIOUS ENOUGH FOR A COMMUNITY PENALTY?

GUIDELINE: ➤   *IS IT SO SERIOUS THAT ONLY CUSTODY IS APPROPRIATE?*

 ## CONSIDER AGGRAVATING AND MITIGATING FACTORS

for example
    Racial motivation
    Group action
    Victims specifically targetted
    High degree of planning
    Night time offence
    Weapon

    Offence committed on bail
    Previous convictions and failures to respond
    to previous sentences, if relevant
    This list is not exhaustive

for example
    Short duration
    This list is not exhaustive

CONSIDER OFFENDER MITIGATION

for example
    Age, health (physical or mental)
    Co-operation with the police
    Voluntary compensation
    Remorse

CONSIDER YOUR SENTENCE

*Compare it with the suggested guideline level of sentence and reconsider
your reasons carefully if you have chosen a sentence at a different level.
Consider a discount for a timely guilty plea.*

DECIDE YOUR SENTENCE

N.B. COMPENSATION - Give reasons if not awarding compensation

Remember: These are GUIDELINES not a tariff

Indecent Assault

Sexual Offences Act 1956, ss 14&15
Triable either way - see Mode of Trial Guidelines
Penalty: Level 5 and/or 6 months

CONSIDER THE SERIOUSNESS OF THE OFFENCE
(INCLUDING THE IMPACT ON THE VICTIM)

GUIDELINE: ➤
IS COMPENSATION, DISCHARGE OR FINE APPROPRIATE?
IS IT SERIOUS ENOUGH FOR A COMMUNITY PENALTY?
IS IT SO SERIOUS THAT ONLY CUSTODY IS APPROPRIATE?
ARE MAGISTRATES' COURTS' POWERS APPROPRIATE?

➕ CONSIDER AGGRAVATING AND MITIGATING FACTORS ➖

for example
Vulnerable victim
Breach of trust
Age differential
Injury (may be psychiatric)
Very young victim

Offence committed on bail
Previous convictions and failures to respond
to previous sentences, if relevant
This list is not exhaustive

for example
Slight contact
This list is not exhaustive

CONSIDER OFFENDER MITIGATION

for example
Age, health (physical or mental)
Co-operation with the police
Voluntary compensation
Remorse

CONSIDER YOUR SENTENCE

Compare it with the suggested guideline level of sentence and reconsider
your reasons carefully if you have chosen a sentence at a different level.
Consider a discount for a timely guilty plea.

DECIDE YOUR SENTENCE

N.B. COMPENSATION - Give reasons if not awarding compensation

Remember: These are GUIDELINES not a tariff

| Theft Act 1978, s.3
Triable either way - see Mode of Trial Guidelines
Penalty: Level 5 and/or 6 months | **Making off without Payment** |

CONSIDER THE SERIOUSNESS OF THE OFFENCE
(INCLUDING THE IMPACT ON THE VICTIM)

GUIDELINE: ➤   *IS COMPENSATION, DISCHARGE OR FINE APPROPRIATE?*

                 IS IT SERIOUS ENOUGH FOR A COMMUNITY PENALTY?

                 IS IT SO SERIOUS THAT ONLY CUSTODY IS APPROPRIATE?

                 ARE MAGISTRATES' COURTS' POWERS APPROPRIATE?

CONSIDER AGGRAVATING AND MITIGATING FACTORS

for example	**for example**
Deliberate plan High value Two or more involved Victim particularly vulnerable Offence committed on bail Previous convictions and failures to respond to previous sentences, if relevant *This list is not exhaustive*	Impulsive Low value *This list is not exhaustive*

CONSIDER OFFENDER MITIGATION

for example
    Age, health (physical or mental)
    Co-operation with the police
    Voluntary compensation
    Remorse

CONSIDER YOUR SENTENCE

Compare it with the suggested guideline level of sentence and reconsider your reasons carefully if you have chosen a sentence at a different level. Consider a discount for a timely guilty plea.

DECIDE YOUR SENTENCE

GUIDELINE FINES		
LOW INCOME	**AVERAGE INCOME**	**HIGH INCOME**
£90	£225	£540

N.B. COMPENSATION - Give reasons if not awarding compensation

Remember: These are GUIDELINES not a tariff

Obstructing a Police Officer

Police Act 1996, s.89(2)
Triable only summarily
Penalty: Level 3 and/or 1 month

CONSIDER THE SERIOUSNESS OF THE OFFENCE

GUIDELINE: ➤ *IS COMPENSATION, DISCHARGE OR FINE APPROPRIATE?*
IS IT SERIOUS ENOUGH FOR A COMMUNITY PENALTY?
IS IT SO SERIOUS THAT ONLY CUSTODY IS APPROPRIATE?

 ### CONSIDER AGGRAVATING AND MITIGATING FACTORS

for example
Racial motivation
Group action
Premeditated

Offence committed on bail
Previous convictions and failures to respond
to previous sentences, if relevant
This list is not exhaustive

for example
Genuine misjudgement
Impulsive action
Minor obstruction
This list is not exhaustive

CONSIDER OFFENDER MITIGATION

for example
Age, health (physical or mental)
Co-operation with the police
Remorse

CONSIDER YOUR SENTENCE

Compare it with the suggested guideline level of sentence and reconsider
your reasons carefully if you have chosen a sentence at a different level.
Consider a discount for a timely guilty plea.

DECIDE YOUR SENTENCE

GUIDELINE FINES		
LOW INCOME	AVERAGE INCOME	HIGH INCOME
£90	£225	£540

Remember: These are GUIDELINES not a tariff

Theft Act 1968, s. 15	**Obtaining by**
Triable either way - see Mode of Trial Guidelines	**Deception**
Penalty: Level 5 and/or 6 months	

CONSIDER THE SERIOUSNESS OF THE OFFENCE
(INCLUDING THE IMPACT ON THE VICTIM)

GUIDELINE: ➤

IS COMPENSATION, DISCHARGE OR FINE APPROPRIATE?
IS IT SERIOUS ENOUGH FOR A COMMUNITY PENALTY?
IS IT SO SERIOUS THAT ONLY CUSTODY IS APPROPRIATE?
ARE MAGISTRATES' COURTS' POWERS APPROPRIATE?

 CONSIDER AGGRAVATING AND MITIGATING FACTORS

for example
Committed over lengthy period
Large sums or valuable goods
Two or more involved
Victim particularly vulnerable

Offence committed on bail
Previous convictions and failures to respond
to previous sentences, if relevant
This list is not exhaustive

for example
Impulsive action
Short period
Small sum
This list is not exhaustive

CONSIDER OFFENDER MITIGATION

for example
Age, health (physical or mental)
Co-operation with the police
Voluntary compensation
Remorse

CONSIDER YOUR SENTENCE

Compare it with the suggested guideline level of sentence and reconsider
your reasons carefully if you have chosen a sentence at a different level.
Consider a discount for a timely guilty plea.

DECIDE YOUR SENTENCE

N.B. COMPENSATION - Give reasons if not awarding compensation

Remember: These are GUIDELINES not a tariff

Possession of a Bladed Instrument

Criminal Justice Act 1988, s.139
Triable either way - see Mode of Trial Guidelines
Penalty: Level 5 and/or 6 months

CONSIDER THE SERIOUSNESS OF THE OFFENCE
(INCLUDING THE IMPACT ON THE VICTIM)

GUIDELINE: ➤
IS COMPENSATION, DISCHARGE OR FINE APPROPRIATE?
IS IT SERIOUS ENOUGH FOR A COMMUNITY PENALTY?
IS IT SO SERIOUS THAT ONLY CUSTODY IS APPROPRIATE?
ARE MAGISTRATES' COURTS' POWERS APPROPRIATE?

 ## CONSIDER AGGRAVATING AND MITIGATING FACTORS

for example
    Location of offence
    Group action or joint possession
    People put in fear/weapon brandished
    Planned use

    Offence committed on bail
    Previous convictions and failures to respond
    to previous sentences, if relevant
    This list is not exhaustive

for example
    Acting out of genuine fear
    Not premeditated
    This list is not exhaustive

CONSIDER OFFENDER MITIGATION

for example
    Age, health (physical or mental)
    Co-operation with the police
    Voluntary compensation
    Remorse

CONSIDER YOUR SENTENCE

Compare it with the suggested guideline level of sentence and reconsider your reasons carefully if you have chosen a sentence at a different level. Consider a discount for a timely guilty plea. Consider forfeiture

DECIDE YOUR SENTENCE

N.B. COMPENSATION - Give reasons if not awarding compensation

Remember: These are GUIDELINES not a tariff

| Prevention of Crime Act 1953, s.1
Triable either way - see Mode of Trial Guidelines
Penalty: Level 5 and/or 6 months | Possessing an
Offensive Weapon |

CONSIDER THE SERIOUSNESS OF THE OFFENCE
(INCLUDING THE IMPACT ON THE VICTIM)

IS COMPENSATION, DISCHARGE OR FINE APPROPRIATE?

IS IT SERIOUS ENOUGH FOR A COMMUNITY PENALTY?

GUIDELINE: ➢   *IS IT SO SERIOUS THAT ONLY CUSTODY IS APPROPRIATE?*

ARE MAGISTRATES' COURTS' POWERS APPROPRIATE?

 CONSIDER AGGRAVATING AND MITIGATING FACTORS

for example
> Location of offence
> Group action or joint possession
> People put in fear/weapon brandished
> Planned use
>
> Offence committed on bail
> Previous convictions and failures to respond
> to previous sentences, if relevant
> *This list is not exhaustive*

for example
> Acting out of genuine fear
> Not premeditated
> *This list is not exhaustive*

CONSIDER OFFENDER MITIGATION

for example
> Age, health (physical or mental)
> Co-operation with the police
> Voluntary compensation
> Remorse

CONSIDER YOUR SENTENCE

*Compare it with the suggested guideline level of sentence and reconsider
your reasons carefully if you have chosen a sentence at a different level.
Consider a discount for a timely guilty plea. Consider forfeiture*

DECIDE YOUR SENTENCE

N.B. COMPENSATION - Give reasons if not awarding compensation

Remember: These are GUIDELINES not a tariff

Social Security - false representation to obtain benefit	Social Security Administration Act 1992, s.112 Triable only summarily Penalty: Level 5 and/or 3 months

CONSIDER THE SERIOUSNESS OF THE OFFENCE
(INCLUDING THE IMPACT ON THE VICTIM)

GUIDELINE: ➤

IS COMPENSATION, DISCHARGE OR FINE APPROPRIATE?

IS IT SERIOUS ENOUGH FOR A COMMUNITY PENALTY?

IS IT SO SERIOUS THAT ONLY CUSTODY IS APPROPRIATE?

 ## CONSIDER AGGRAVATING AND MITIGATING FACTORS

for example
    Fraudulent claims over a long period
    Large amount
    Organised group offence
    Planned deception

    Offence committed on bail
    Previous convictions and failures to respond
    to previous sentences, if relevant
    This list is not exhaustive

for example
    Misunderstanding of regulations
    Pressurised by others
    Small amount
    This list is not exhaustive

CONSIDER OFFENDER MITIGATION

for example
    Age, health (physical or mental)
    Co-operation with the police
    Voluntary compensation
    Remorse

CONSIDER YOUR SENTENCE

*Compare it with the suggested guideline level of sentence and reconsider
your reasons carefully if you have chosen a sentence at a different level.
Consider a discount for a timely guilty plea.*

DECIDE YOUR SENTENCE

N.B. COMPENSATION - Give reasons if not awarding compensation

Remember: These are GUIDELINES not a tariff

Theft Act 1968, s.12 Triable only summarily Penalty: Level 5 and/or 6 months May disqualify	**Taking Vehicle without Consent**

CONSIDER THE SERIOUSNESS OF THE OFFENCE
(INCLUDING THE IMPACT ON THE VICTIM)

GUIDELINE: ➤

IS COMPENSATION, DISCHARGE OR FINE APPROPRIATE?

IS IT SERIOUS ENOUGH FOR A COMMUNITY PENALTY?

IS IT SO SERIOUS THAT ONLY CUSTODY IS APPROPRIATE?

 CONSIDER AGGRAVATING AND MITIGATING FACTORS

for example

Group action
Premeditated
Related damage
Professional hallmarks
Vulnerable victim

Offence committed on bail
Previous convictions and failures to respond
to previous sentences, if relevant
This list is not exhaustive

for example

Misunderstanding with owner
Soon returned
Vehicle belonged to family or friend
This list is not exhaustive

CONSIDER OFFENDER MITIGATION

for example

Age, health (physical or mental)
Co-operation with the police
Voluntary compensation
Remorse

CONSIDER YOUR SENTENCE

Compare it with the suggested guideline level of sentence and reconsider your reasons carefully if you have chosen a sentence at a different level. Consider a discount for a timely guilty plea.

DECIDE YOUR SENTENCE

N.B. COMPENSATION - Give reasons if not awarding compensation

Remember: These are GUIDELINES not a tariff

Theft	Theft Act 1968, s.1 Triable either way - see Mode of Trial Guidelines Penalty: Level 5 and/or 6 months

CONSIDER THE SERIOUSNESS OF THE OFFENCE
(INCLUDING THE IMPACT ON THE VICTIM)

GUIDELINE: ➤ *IS COMPENSATION, DISCHARGE OR FINE APPROPRIATE?*
IS IT SERIOUS ENOUGH FOR A COMMUNITY PENALTY?
IS IT SO SERIOUS THAT ONLY CUSTODY IS APPROPRIATE?
ARE MAGISTRATES' COURTS' POWERS APPROPRIATE?

 ## CONSIDER AGGRAVATING AND MITIGATING FACTORS

for example
- High value
- Planned
- Sophisticated
- Adult involving children
- Organised team
- Related damage
- Vulnerable victim

Offence committed on bail
Previous convictions and failures to respond
to previous sentences, if relevant
This list is not exhaustive

for example
- Impulsive action
- Low value
- *This list is not exhaustive*

CONSIDER OFFENDER MITIGATION

for example
- Age, health (physical or mental)
- Co-operation with the police
- Voluntary compensation
- Remorse

CONSIDER YOUR SENTENCE

*Compare it with the suggested guideline level of sentence and reconsider
your reasons carefully if you have chosen a sentence at a different level.
Consider a discount for a timely guilty plea.*

DECIDE YOUR SENTENCE

GUIDELINE FINES		
LOW INCOME	**AVERAGE INCOME**	**HIGH INCOME**
£135	£340	£810

N.B. COMPENSATION - Give reasons if not awarding compensation
Remember: These are GUIDELINES not a tariff

| Theft Act 1968, s.1
Triable either way - see Mode of Trial Guidelines
Penalty: Level 5 and/or 6 months | **Theft in Breach
of Trust** |

CONSIDER THE SERIOUSNESS OF THE OFFENCE
(INCLUDING THE IMPACT ON THE VICTIM)

GUIDELINE: ➤

IS COMPENSATION, DISCHARGE OR FINE APPROPRIATE?

IS IT SERIOUS ENOUGH FOR A COMMUNITY PENALTY?

IS IT SO SERIOUS THAT ONLY CUSTODY IS APPROPRIATE?

ARE MAGISTRATES' COURTS' POWERS APPROPRIATE?

 ## CONSIDER AGGRAVATING AND MITIGATING FACTORS

for example

    Casting suspicion on others
    Committed over a period
    High value
    Organised team
    Planned
    Senior empolyee
    Sophisticated
    Vulnerable victim

    Offence committed on bail
    Previous convictions and failures to respond
    to previous sentences, if relevant
    This list is not exhaustive

for example

    Impulsive action
    Low value
    Previous inconsistent attitude by employer
    Single item
    Unsupported junior
    This list is not exhaustive

CONSIDER OFFENDER MITIGATION

for example

    Age, health (physical or mental)
    Co-operation with the police
    Voluntary compensation
    Remorse

CONSIDER YOUR SENTENCE

*Compare it with the suggested guideline level of sentence and reconsider
your reasons carefully if you have chosen a sentence at a different level.
Consider a discount for a timely guilty plea.*

DECIDE YOUR SENTENCE

N.B. COMPENSATION - Give reasons if not awarding compensation

Remember: These are GUIDELINES not a tariff

Threatening Behaviour

Public Order Act 1986, s.4
Triable only summarily
Penalty: Level 5 and/or 6 months

CONSIDER THE SERIOUSNESS OF THE OFFENCE
(INCLUDING THE IMPACT ON THE VICTIM)

IS COMPENSATION, DISCHARGE OR FINE APPROPRIATE?

GUIDELINE: ➤   *IS IT SERIOUS ENOUGH FOR A COMMUNITY PENALTY?*

IS IT SO SERIOUS THAT ONLY CUSTODY IS APPROPRIATE?

 ## CONSIDER AGGRAVATING AND MITIGATING FACTORS

for example
    Group action
    People put in fear
    Vulnerable victims

    Offence committed on bail
    Previous convictions and failures to respond
    to previous sentences, if relevant
    This list is not exhaustive

for example
    Minor matter
    Short duration
    This list is not exhaustive

CONSIDER OFFENDER MITIGATION

for example
    Age, health (physical or mental)
    Co-operation with the police
    Voluntary compensation
    Remorse

CONSIDER YOUR SENTENCE

*Compare it with the suggested guideline level of sentence and reconsider
your reasons carefully if you have chosen a sentence at a different level.
Consider a discount for a timely guilty plea.*

DECIDE YOUR SENTENCE

N.B. COMPENSATION - Give reasons if not awarding compensation

Remember: These are GUIDELINES not a tariff

Wireless Telegraphy Act 1949, s.1 Triable only summarily Penalty: Level 3	**TV Licence Payment Evasion**

CONSIDER THE SERIOUSNESS OF THE OFFENCE
(INCLUDING THE IMPACT ON THE VICTIM)

GUIDELINE: ➤   *IS COMPENSATION, DISCHARGE OR FINE APPROPRIATE?*

IS IT SERIOUS ENOUGH FOR A COMMUNITY PENALTY?

(PROBATION IS ONLY AVAILABLE COMMUNITY PENALITY FOR THIS OFFENCE)

 ## CONSIDER AGGRAVATING AND MITIGATING FACTORS

for example
    Failure to respond to payment opportunities

    Offence committed on bail
    Previous convictions and failures to respond
    to previous sentences, if relevant
    This list is not exhaustive

for example
    Accidental oversight
    Confusion of responsibility
    Licence immediately obtained
    Very short unlicensed use
    This list is not exhaustive

CONSIDER OFFENDER MITIGATION

for example
    Age, health (physical or mental)
    Co-operation with the police
    Voluntary compensation
    Remorse

CONSIDER YOUR SENTENCE

*Compare it with the suggested guideline level of sentence and reconsider
your reasons carefully if you have chosen a sentence at a different level.
Consider a discount for a timely guilty plea.*

DECIDE YOUR SENTENCE

GUIDELINE FINES (mono in brackets)		
LOW INCOME	**AVERAGE INCOME**	**HIGH INCOME**
£90 (£45 MONO)	£225 (£115 MONO)	£540 (£270 MONO)

N.B. COMPENSATION - Give reasons if not awarding compensation
Remember: These are GUIDELINES not a tariff

Vehicle Interference

Criminal Attempts Act 1981, s.9
Triable only summarily
Penalty: Level 4 and/or 3 months

CONSIDER THE SERIOUSNESS OF THE OFFENCE
(INCLUDING THE IMPACT ON THE VICTIM)

GUIDELINE: ➤

IS COMPENSATION, DISCHARGE OR FINE APPROPRIATE?
IS IT SERIOUS ENOUGH FOR A COMMUNITY PENALTY?
IS IT SO SERIOUS THAT ONLY CUSTODY IS APPROPRIATE?

 ### CONSIDER AGGRAVATING AND MITIGATING FACTORS

for example	**for example**
Group action	Impulsive action
Planned	*This list is not exhaustive*
Related damage	
Offence committed on bail	
Previous convictions and failures to respond	
to previous sentences, if relevant	
This list is not exhaustive	

CONSIDER OFFENDER MITIGATION

for example
Age, health (physical or mental)
Co-operation with the police
Voluntary compensation
Remorse

CONSIDER YOUR SENTENCE

Compare it with the suggested guideline level of sentence and reconsider your reasons carefully if you have chosen a sentence at a different level. Consider a discount for a timely guilty plea.

DECIDE YOUR SENTENCE

N.B. COMPENSATION - Give reasons if not awarding compensation

Remember: These are GUIDELINES not a tariff

Public Order Act 1986, s.2
Triable either way - see Mode of Trial Guidelines
Penalty: Level 5 and/or 6 months

Violent Disorder

CONSIDER THE SERIOUSNESS OF THE OFFENCE
(INCLUDING THE IMPACT ON THE VICTIM)

GUIDELINE: ➢
IS COMPENSATION, DISCHARGE OR FINE APPROPRIATE?
IS IT SERIOUS ENOUGH FOR A COMMUNITY PENALTY?
IS IT SO SERIOUS THAT ONLY CUSTODY IS APPROPRIATE?
ARE MAGISTRATES' COURTS' POWERS APPROPRIATE?

➕ CONSIDER AGGRAVATING AND MITIGATING FACTORS

for example
Racial motivation
Busy public place
Fighting between rival groups
Large group
People actually put in fear
Planned
Vulnerable victims
Weapon

Offence committed on bail
Previous convictions and failures to respond
to previous sentences, if relevant
This list is not exhaustive

for example
Impulsive
Nobody actually afraid
Provocation
This list is not exhaustive

CONSIDER OFFENDER MITIGATION

for example
Age, health (physical or mental)
Co-operation with the police
Voluntary compensation
Remorse

CONSIDER YOUR SENTENCE

Compare it with the suggested guideline level of sentence and reconsider
your reasons carefully if you have chosen a sentence at a different level.
Consider a discount for a timely guilty plea.

DECIDE YOUR SENTENCE

N.B. COMPENSATION - Give reasons if not awarding compensation

Remember: These are GUIDELINES not a tariff

Wounding — Grievous Bodily Harm

Offences Against the Person Act 1861, s.20
Triable either way - see Mode of Trial Guidelines
Penalty: Level 5 and/or 6 months

CONSIDER THE SERIOUSNESS OF THE OFFENCE
(INCLUDING THE IMPACT ON THE VICTIM)

GUIDELINE: ➤
IS COMPENSATION, DISCHARGE OR FINE APPROPRIATE?
IS IT SERIOUS ENOUGH FOR A COMMUNITY PENALTY?
IS IT SO SERIOUS THAT ONLY CUSTODY IS APPROPRIATE?
ARE MAGISTRATES' COURTS' POWERS APPROPRIATE?

➕ CONSIDER AGGRAVATING AND MITIGATING FACTORS ➖

for example	for example
Racial motivation	Single blow
Deliberate kicking/biting	Minor wound
Extensive injuries	Impulse
Group action	Provocation
Offender in position of authority	*This list is not exhaustive*
Premeditated	
Victim particularly vulnerable	
Victim serving public	
Weapon	
Offence committed on bail	
Previous convictions and failures to respond	
to previous sentences, if relevant	
This list is not exhaustive	

CONSIDER OFFENDER MITIGATION

for example
Age, health (physical or mental)
Co-operation with the police
Voluntary compensation
Remorse

CONSIDER YOUR SENTENCE

Compare it with the suggested guideline level of sentence and reconsider
your reasons carefully if you have chosen a sentence at a different level.
Consider a discount for a timely guilty plea.

DECIDE YOUR SENTENCE

N.B. COMPENSATION - Give reasons if not awarding compensation

Remember: These are GUIDELINES not a tariff

| Criminal Justice Act 1991, Sched.2
A fine - maximum £1,000
A Community Service Order (up to 60 hours)
In certain circumstances, an Attendance Centre Order
Revocation of Order and re-sentence for original offence
Commit a Crown Court Order to be dealt with at Crown Court | **Breach of
a community order** |

CONSIDER THE SERIOUSNESS OF THE OFFENCE

 ## CONSIDER AGGRAVATING AND MITIGATING FACTORS

for example
   No attempt to start the sentence
   Unco-operative
   Unacceptable behaviour
   This list is not exhaustive

for example
   Completed a significant part of the order
   This list is not exhaustive

CONSIDER OFFENDER MITIGATION
(including timely admission)

DECIDE IF THE ORDER SHOULD CONTINUE

IF THE ORDER SHOULD CONTINUE:

   IS A FINE APPROPRIATE?

   IS A COMMUNITY SERVICE ORDER APPROPRIATE?

   WHERE THE ORDER IS A PROBATION ORDER, IS AN ATTENDANCE CENTRE ORDER APPROPRIATE?

IF THE ORDER SHOULD NOT CONTINUE AND IT IS A MAGISTRATES' COURT ORDER:

   REVOKE ORDER AND RE-SENTENCE FOR ORIGINAL OFFENCE (see relevant guideline)

NB. IF THE ORDER WAS MADE BY THE CROWN COURT MAY FINE AND ALLOW ORDER TO CONTINUE OR COMMIT TO CROWN COURT TO BE DEALT WITH (CONSULT CLERK)

Remember: These are GUIDELINES not a tariff

INDEX